THE BATTLEFRONTS OF
SOUTHERN AFRICA

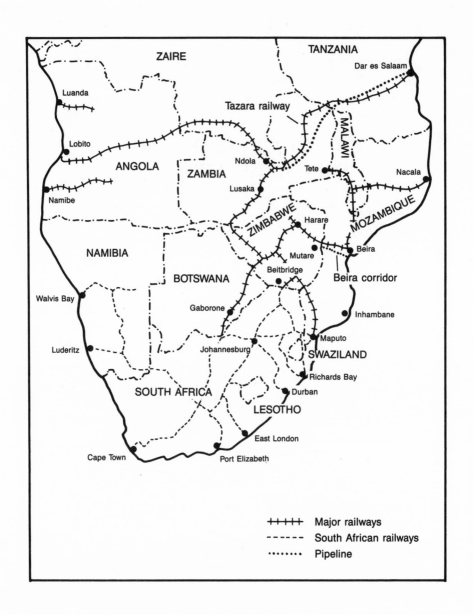

+++++	Major railways
- - - - -	South African railways
········	Pipeline

THE BATTLEFRONTS OF
SOUTHERN AFRICA

COLIN LEGUM

AFRICANA PUBLISHING COMPANY
a division of Holmes & Meier
New York / London

Published in the United States of America 1988 by
Africana Publishing Company, a division of Holmes & Meier Publishers, Inc.
30 Irving Place
New York, NY 10003

Great Britain:
1–3 Winton Close
Letchworth, Hertfordshire SG61 1BA
England

Chapters subsequent to the Introduction have appeared in *Africa
Contemporary Record,* vols. 8–18, © Africa Contemporary Record
1976, 1977, 1979, 1980, 1981, 1984, 1986, 1987, published by
Africana Publishing Company, a division of Holmes & Meier Publishers, Inc.,
New York.

This book has been printed on acid-free paper.

Library of Congress Cataloging-in-Publication Data

Legum, Colin.
  The battlefronts of Southern Africa.

  Includes bibliographies and indexes.
  1. Africa, Southern—Foreign relations—1975–
2. Apartheid—South Africa.   3. Africa, Southern—
Politics and government—1975–   I. Title.
DT746.L425   1988   327.68   87-25481
ISBN 0-8419-1135-5 (alk. paper)
ISBN 0-8419-1144-4 (pbk. : alk. paper)

Manufactured in the United States of America

CONTENTS

1978-1979: THE APPROACHING COLLAPSE OF WHITE RESISTANCE IN RHODESIA

1979-1980: THE ROAD TO AND FROM LANCASTER HOUSE

1980-1981: THE FAILURE OF DIPLOMACY AND WEAPONS

CONTENTS

ix

CONTENTS

INDEXES

ABBREVIATIONS AND ACRONYMS

ANC	African National Congress of SA
ANC(R)	African National Council of Rhodesia
BMATT	British Military Advisory Training Team
CEPG	Commonwealth Eminent Persons Group
CG	Contact Group of Five
CIA	Central Intelligence Agency
CIO	Central Intelligence Organization (Rhodesia/Zimbabwe)
DMZ	Demilitarized Zone (in Angola)
DTA	Democratic Turnhalle Alliance
FLEC	Front for the Liberation of Cabinda
FLP	Front-line Presidents
FLS	Front-line States
FRELIMO	Front for the Liberation of Mozambique
JMC	Joint Military Commission of Angola and SA
MNR (Renamo)	Mozambique National Resistance *(Restancia Nacional Mozambican)*
MPC	Multi-Party Conference of Namibia
MPLA	Movement for the Popular Liberation of Angola
Nibmar	No Independence before Majority Rule
OAU	Organization of African Unity
PAC	Pan-Africanist Congress of SA
PLAN	People's Liberation Army of Namibia
SA	South Africa
SADCC	Southern African Development Cooperation Conference
SADF	South African Defence Forces
SCR 435	UN Security Council Resolution 435
SNASP	Mozambican People's National Security Service
Swapo	South West African People's Organization of Namibia
TGNU	Transition Government of National Unity for South West Africa (Namibia)
Unar	Rombezi African National Union
Unita	Union for the Total National Liberation and Independence of Angola
Untag	United Nations Transitional Advisory Group
Zanla	Zimbabwe African National Liberation Army
Zanu	Zimbabwe African National Union
Zapu	Zimbabwe African People's Union
ZIPA	Zimbabwe People's Army
ZIPRA	Zimbabwe People's Revolutionary Army

INTRODUCTION
1948–1987:
THE MAKING OF A CRISIS

This is a record of a decade of diplomatic initiatives aimed at preventing the Southern African region being turned into a world crisis area and a cockpit of violent racial conflict ending in a radical transformation of political power—but at a heavy cost of human life and suffering, and the possible impoverishment of one of the world's potentially richest and best endowed areas. With only one notable exception—the remarkable denouement of the liberation struggle over the independence of Zimbabwe—it is a dismal record of diplomatic failure, growing violence and paranoiac behaviour, destabilization of a subcontinent, and of increasing international involvement. The situation at the core of the region's conflicts— South Africa's racial system—remains as menacing as when Western governments finally awoke to the dangerous potentialities of the evolving crisis after the collapse of Portuguese colonialism in 1974, which created an opportunity for the Soviet bloc and Cuba to play a role in Southern African developments. Although the Communist nations have failed conspicuously to build on their initial success, the Western powers have suffered both a loss of influence and credibility, both by their failure to take better advantage of the willingness of Africa's most influential leaders to act as their partners in the search for peace, and also because of their reluctance to commit the resources needed to exert a more decisive influence on the course of events. By concentrating primarily on resolving the conflicts around the periphery of South Africa—Rhodesia/Zimbabwe and Namibia—the Western diplomatic initiative was doomed to fail in the region as a whole.

The rationale of Western policies was that eliminating the source of violence on the periphery and containing Soviet influence would ease the difficulties of transforming the racial situation inside South Africa (SA). A fatal flaw in this approach was its failure to take sufficient account of the extent to which the racial conflict inside SA is inextricably linked to the conflicts in the rest of the subcontinent. As the regional power SA is determined to reject and obstruct any terms that might weaken its military domination and undermine its presumptive power to control the pace and direction of change at home. Therefore, an imperative of SA's policy is to seek to prevent threats to its power and security by intervening actively in developments beyond its own borders in order to retain effective control within them. The 'external threat' came to be seen by Pretoria as the precipitant of its internal problems—a psychologically induced political defence against accepting both the responsibility and the guilt for the incontrovertible truth that the increasingly violent situation inside the Republic was caused primarily by the policies of apartheid, while the climate of violence engendered by the externally-based guerilla challenge and by the hostility of the rest of the continent only contributed to the growth of Black militancy inside SA. The links between these two developments are inseparable.

Foreign powers of all descriptions have always encountered difficulties in trying to enforce their writ against strong regional powers—even if the latter are notionally their allies or dependencies—when they see their own wider interests threatened by the obduracy of regional powers pursuing their own interests. This situation is as true of SA as it is of Israel, or of Stalin's calamitous effort to dictate the policies of China which resulted in the historic alienation between the two poles of world communism.

Short of adopting Moscow's policy of using direct military force against recalcitrants like Hungary and Czechoslovakia, the only possible way in which the West might hope to force Pretoria to yield to its wishes is by committing itself to a policy of mandatory and comprehensive sanctions, enforced by a blockade; but for economic as well as political reasons, the major Western powers preferred to take the soft option of seeking to encourage change in SA by concentrating on the periphery conflicts and through persuasion and piecemeal measures—the policy known as 'constructive engagement'. This choice by the Western powers produced precisely the result they sought to avoid: a sharp increase in the momentum of violence and of racial conflict, producing an entirely unpredictable political outcome, possibly favouring the emergence of a post-apartheid government hostile to the West.

However, the present struggle in SA need not necessarily end in violent revolution for, despite their stand, its rulers have not been impervious to the changes at home and in the region, nor to the changing climate of opinion in the Western community. The apartheid Republic of 1987 is a long way from being the apartheid Republic of 1948, or even of 1974 or 1977. The Government's policies have changed, and changed substantially: they have come to accept that the system of apartheid is unworkable, in itself a fundamental change of direction; and they have begun, however haltingly, to accept the need to end exclusive White political rule, although still clinging to the idea of continuing White control within a new system of power-sharing on terms largely dictated by themselves. Instead of being confidently on the offensive—as it was when it first won power in 1948—the Afrikaner Establishment is now heavily on the defensive, and uncertain of how to extricate the country from the mess produced by apartheid, and that, in itself, is a major change brought about by changes in the internal balance of power.

But the discernible shrinking of White power is not yet matched by any measurable increase in effective Black power. In this situation Black militants inevitably tend to overplay their hand, while the troubled White community turns to squabbling among themselves about the right way of protecting their perceived security, cultural and economic interests. These are inevitable consequences of the approaching end of the apartheid phase, but also of the approaching end of a White-dominated, Black-subjugated political system that has endured for over three centuries. The paroxysms of a dying *ancien regime*—particularly one as old as South Africa's—offer either hope of rebirth or the prospects of violent decay. It is impossible, as yet, to predict the final donouement of this struggle.

ORIGINS OF THE CRISIS

Although the situations in SA and Israel are not analogous, there are certain parallels which are useful in tracing the transformation of regional crises into international crises. The apartheid regime and the State of Israel were born at the same time, in May 1948. The Jewish State was founded at a time when Arab nationalism was beginning to stir in the Middle East, and helped to fuel its growth. The Afrikaners' decision to safeguard their future by a system based on racial separation coincided with the beginning of the movement in Africa to shake off the shackles of colonialism, which produced a new sense of Black nationalism and of the oneness of Black people embodied in the ideas of Pan-Africanism—'one for all and all for one'. Kwame Nkrumah captured this mood in his memorable sentence spoken at his country's independence: 'Ghana will not be truly free until the whole of Africa has been liberated.' Thus, South Africa set itself on the road towards entrenching permanent White rule in the southern tip of the continent at the historic moment when Africa was embarking on the task of expelling alien rule. The seeds of the present crises in the Middle East and in Southern Africa were sown in two regions emerging into the post-imperial international political system; both found themselves pitted against pan-nationalist forces.

Both Israel and SA were seen as important outposts of the Western political system. This still holds true of Israel (though less so than before), but it is no longer true of SA. While Israel can still count on the powerful support of the United States, SA no longer enjoys the uncommitted support of any major power; if anything, the Western powers have moved, cautiously as yet, to distance themselves from Pretoria and towards courting its opponents. While Israel can still count on broad Western support and has come to an understanding with its former principal antagonist, Egypt, SA finds itself largely isolated in the continent and increasingly estranged from the Western community.

The Middle East is a major arena of Soviet interest and this, because of proximity and strategic priorities, has made it possible for the USSR both to contribute towards creating strong armies on Israel's borders and to interpose itself as a major actor in the conflict. Because of Western interests and commitments, the Middle East has become an arena of superpower confrontation. By contrast, while international involvement has increased in SA, it is not yet an arena of superpower confrontation. Although the Soviets have an interest in the area—as they have wherever Western influence and interests are strong—Southern Africa does not appear to rank high in Moscow's immediate priorities; besides, it is at a heavy logistical disadvantage because of the region's distance from the USSR. Despite the opportunistic advantage it gained in Angola and Mozambique, Moscow has repeatedly sought to reassure the United States that it has no desire to engage in a superpower confrontation in the region. (The evidence for this will be found in subsequent chapters.) Nevertheless, in keeping with its international role as the champion of anticolonial liberation movements, the Soviet bloc has supported organizations of which it approves—such as the ANC, Swapo and the MPLA. However, as will presently be shown, Moscow does not regard itself as having a major role to play in the present stage of the struggle in SA. Nevertheless, Pretoria remains convinced that the Soviets are its major enemy, blaming all its troubles at home and with its neighbours on communism.

One great advantage Israel possesses over South Africa is that it has only a small minority of Arabs living inside its international borders, whereas the Pretoria regime faces an overwhelming majority of Black Africans inside its own laager.

Of these two international crisis areas, the Middle East lends itself more easily to an early settlement than does Southern Africa. Israel has the chance of safeguarding the future of a Jewish State by agreeing to the creation of a Palestinian State outside its own borders subject to reasonable security safeguards. SA has no such option; peace and racial reconciliation in the Republic are possible only by demolishing completely the White political system, and by accepting (under suitable safeguards) that the White community will be left with only minority rights. Such a transformation is a hard decision for any people or government, used to lording it over the majority, to accept. But, as a state, SA is much more vulnerable than Israel because of the presence of a highly articulate Black majority supported by continental forces, and because of its lack of international support.

Pretoria's rulers are therefore compelled to fight alone in an increasingly hostile international environment. They can be relied upon to fight with all their resources to try and dictate the pace and nature of change until the point is reached where they are forced to accept either a negotiated settlement (as was reached in Zimbabwe, though not by the same process), or are tragically overwhelmed by revolutionary violence which, fortunately for those who value democratic principles, seems unlikely in the immediate future.

THE AFRICAN VIEW OF THE CRISIS

Black South Africans (except for small minority militant groups) have always favoured a negotiated political settlement over a violent struggle. This has been the policy of the oldest nationalist movement, the African Nationalist Congress (ANC), since its formation in 1912, and remains the policy of the present leadership, including the ANC's fighting wing, *Umkhonto we Sizwe*. Their expressed preference is for a fully representative national conference to work out a new democratic constitution which will provide for majority rights and will recognize White South Africans, not as settlers, but as citizens equally entitled with Blacks to regard the country as their home. Although ready to take up arms to fight for their rights, the Black nationalists insist that armed struggle is only an instrument to compel White South Africans to negotiate with them as equals. The abandonment of a policy of violence can therefore be negotiated in exchange for a peacefully negotiated settlement.

This approach has also been the consistent policy of the Organization of African Unity (OAU) which endorsed the Lusaka Manifesto of 1969, lodged as its official policy with the United Nations. (For details see the 1977–78 chapter.) One key passage reads:

> We would prefer to negotiate rather than destroy, to talk rather than kill. We do not advocate violence; we advocate an end to the violence against human dignity which is now being perpetrated by the oppressors of Africa. If peaceful progress to emancipation were possible, or if changed circumstances were to make it possible in the future, we would urge our brothers in the resistance movements to use peaceful methods of struggle even at the cost of some compromise on the timing of change. But while peaceful progress is blocked by actions of those at present in power in the States of Southern Africa, we have no choice but to give to the peoples of those territories all the support of which we are capable in their struggle against their oppressors.

The Lusaka Manifesto was offered to Pretoria eighteen years ago as the basis for peaceful negotiations at a time when there was little or no violence inside the country and when the armed struggle was still only in its infancy. It did not receive even a formal acknowledgment from Pretoria. Nevertheless, the Lusaka Manifesto has remained the guiding principle of the six African leaders of the Frontline States (FLS). The first Western leader to pick up this offer was Dr. Henry Kissinger, and that was only nine years later. Having been proved disastrously wrong by recommending to President Nixon the 'tar baby option' of the National Security Council Memorandum of 1970—which saw the South African, Portuguese and Rhodesian regimes as invincible and called for their support by the US Administration—Kissinger made his own Lusaka Declaration in 1976 in which he affirmed:

> Africa in this decade is a testing ground of the world's conscience and vision. That Blacks and Whites live together in harmony and equality is a moral imperative of our time. Let us prove that these goals can be realized by human choice, that justice can command by the force of rightness instead of by force of arms. These are ideals that bind all the races of mankind.

The Frontline Presidents (FLPs) responded enthusiastically to Kissinger's appeal, forgiving him his past errors. It was Kissinger's initiative that opened the way for a decade of close African-Western diplomatic cooperation in the search for solutions to the problems of Rhodesia, Namibia and SA, and which led to the creation of the Contact Group of the five Western members of the Security Council (US, Britain, France, West Germany and Canada) to try and implement the Council's resolutions on Namibia. The eventual failure of the various Western initiatives (except for that on Zimbabwe) came not as a result of any lack of African support, but because the Western powers' diplomacy failed to sway Pretoria.

The African leaders' decision to cooperate with the West reflected their understanding that only the Western governments had the power and authority to intervene successfully in South Africa and Rhodesia. As Nyerere put it in reply to criticisms by the Soviet bloc and from some leaders of the liberation movements: "We want the two greatest sources of power on our side—God and Kissinger." Throughout a decade of Western-African diplomatic cooperation, the FLPs had frequently to overcome objections from the side of Swapo, the ANC and the Zimbabwe leaders; on each occasion they used their influence (and sometimes indulged in some arm-twisting) to keep the diplomatic initiative alive.

The tragedy of the missed opportunities of a decade of diplomacy is not only that it failed to stem the tide of violence and to produce peaceful settlements (except in the Zimbabwe struggle), but that it proved the Soviet and other critics to be right in counselling that the FLPs were mistaken in trusting the West to deliver on their promises. One outcome of this failure was to erode credibility in Western good intentions when confronted with the choice of either accepting defeat or using the resources available to them.

THE WESTERN VIEW OF THE CRISIS

When General Smuts was defeated in 1948, Western governments were saddened by the loss of a valued old friend and wartime ally but, unlike the defeated warrior who well understood the dangers for the small White community in the policies of apartheid, the coming to power of an Afrikaner Nationalist regime, committed to splitting up the country between Whites and Blacks and intensifying every aspect of traditional segregation policies, was not viewed with serious concern in Britain or other Western capitals. It was not until 1960, with the shootings at Sharpeville, that Western official and public opinion began to express concern and condemnation of the apartheid system. Harold Macmillan's famous "wind of change" speech and the formulation of criteria for membership of the Commonwealth that led to SA's withdrawal marked the beginning of the parting of the ways. But it was to take another 15 years (until the collapse of Portuguese colonialism and the Soviet-Cuban success in Angola) before it came to be felt that Western interests were threatened, and that simply condemning apartheid as 'morally repugnant' was an indequate response to the evolving crisis. It was to take another six years until, in 1985, the Western nations made the Southern African crisis a major priority of their international concerns. Only Sweden and Holland in the European community had taken this view almost two decades earlier.

While the question of human rights was one of the factors that accounted for the shift in Western policy, four other factors played a more important role. The first was the role of the Organization of African Unity which, in 1963, had begun to confront the West with a choice between friendship for Black Africa or continuing friendly relations with the White minority regimes in the continent. Although this challenge of choice only slowly came to play a significant role in Western policy-making, it had the effect of extracting piecemeal concessions—the arms embargo, the sports boycott and other gradual steps along the road to sanctions.

The second factor, closely related to the first, was the role of the Commonwealth of Nations. It was within this community that Britain, Canada, Australia and New Zealand came face to face with African leaders over their policies in the continent. After the first confrontation over SA's continued membership in 1960, the agenda of each succeeding meeting of Commonwealth leaders turned increasingly on the issues of Rhodesia, Namibia and SA. On several occasions the Commonwealth's future was felt to be in some jeopardy; each time this threat was averted by concessions made to African demands. The most important of the concessions forced on Britain was over Rhodesia, when the newly elected Thatcher Government was forced to reverse itself completely over its election manifesto's promise of support for the offer held out by Ian Smith and Bishop Muzorewa, in favour of a formula that led to the Lancaster House conference and the successful independence of Zimbabwe. While the momentum achieved by the Patriotic Front's guerilla challenge was an important element in forcing this change in British policy, it was the determined African stand at the Commonwealth meeting in Lusaka in 1979—strongly reinforced by the role of the Australian Prime Minister, Malcolm Fraser—that forced Thatcher to make her famous U-turn. Again, it was the African stand at the Bermuda conference in early 1985 that pushed the SA issue near to the top of Britain's international agenda.

The third factor was the Black lobby's success in making the SA question an important American domestic political issue, so sensitive that Republicans and Democrats combined to override a veto by President Reagan and committed the United States to enlarging its support for a programme of sanctions.

The fourth factor was the West's fear that unless it acted more decisively in the region to halt the rising tide of violence and to persuade President Botha to move more decisively in dismantling the apparatus of apartheid, the USSR might be able to extend its slender advantage in Angola and Mozambique and win a more important role in shaping developments in SA.

These four factors assumed greater importance when it finally became clear that White South Africa was under siege and that its militant Black challengers could no longer be safely ignored by the West as had been the case in the past. This new situation demanded a complete change of posture by the West. Instead of concentrating on retaining the goodwill of the Pretoria regime while coaxing it to be more accommodating to the demands for majority rule, it called for a more openly critical attitude to the regime; and instead of ignoring the years of pleas by Black Congress leaders, it meant talking to them and seeking their friendship. The dilemma in such a policy is that it does not allow for an even-handed policy towards both sets of antagonists—a dilemma that remains unresolved.

Western economic and strategic interests as well as feelings of kinship with White South Africans have all along been an important consideration in European and American policies. These interests required three conditions: the maintenance of political stability; that violence should not grow to the point where the valuable economic structures of SA came under threat; and that the post-apartheid rulers should not be hostile to perceived Western interests. This concern about not permanently damaging the country's economy has been a major reason for the West's reluctance to impose comprehensive sanctions against SA. But there are also other reasons: doubts about whether the sanctions weapon would, in fact, prove effective in producing a quick transition to a more equitable political system; and the fear that a period of sanctions, however brief, might unleash White and Black forces that would pitchfork the antagonists into a more violent confrontation of a kind that would preclude a sensible negotiated political settlement and, instead, produce a chaotic situation. This remains the Western view—a view that makes it hard to achieve the objective of gaining the goodwill of importance movements like the ANC and PAC.

So long as the White minority appeared to be in full control of the situation, it suited Western interests to do nothing that would weaken its position; but once signs appeared of a possible loss of effective control over developments, a new approach was demanded. The search for a new approach to the crisis in SA has now become a major concern of Western policymakers.

The Western community is not alone in its interest in preventing violent chaos in SA and averting the collapse of its economy; this is of equal interest to both White and Black South Africans. It is not only SA businessmen who, for understandable reasons, want to reduce damage to the economy to a minimum, a fact which explains their breaking ranks with the Botha regime by holding exploratory talks with the ANC. All White South Africans have a stake in preventing economic disaster, while Black South Africans have their own reasons for wishing to inherit an economically prosperous country, for without prosperity they would not be able to undertake the massive task of creating a more equitable society and of repairing the centuries of neglect of their community's education, housing and health needs.

All this adds up to a shared interest between White and Black South Africans as well as of the West—although each has its own ideas about how the wealth of the country should be divided and about the political and economic system most appropriate to reconstructing the country. The crucial test of statesmanship is how to take advantage of this shared interest.

What is the Western interest in South Africa and in the rest of the region? Apart from an obvious economic interest, a major concern is to ensure political stability in an important area of the world—more especially since it also impinges on the stability of much of the rest of the continent and of the Indian Ocean. No less important is an interest in wishing to avert a violent racial conflagration in Southern Africa, both for humanitarian reasons and because a 'White West' would find it hard to make itself credible to both sides. The Soviets are much more likely to appear as uncompromising supporters of the Black side in such a struggle.

Despite these obvious Western interests and the dangers inherent in the situation, there are those in the West who argue that the best policy is either to opt for a low-key role with a minimum of involvement, or to withdraw entirely from what is felt to be an intractable and irreversible racial conflict. These counsels, as yet, carry little weight in policy-making circles; but they are important enough for President Reagan to have addressed himself in 1986 in typically American style to the advocates of complete withdrawal from the region:

> Many Americans, understandably, ask: Given the racial violence, the hatred, why not wash our hands and walk away from the tragic continent and bleeding country? The answer is: we cannot. In South Africa, our national ideals and strategic interests come together. South Africa matters because we believe that all men are created equal, and are endowed by their Creator with unalienable rights. South Africa matters because of who we are. One of eight Americans can trace his ancestry to Africa.

Notwithstanding the disillusioning experience of Africa's leaders over their cooperation with the Contact Group and other Anglo-American initiatives (again, excluding only the resolution of the Rhodesian conflict), no important leader has taken the view that the West has no role to play in Southern Africa; what they complain about is that, too often, Western involvement has been either entirely negative or one-sided. Even after the collapse of the Contact Group's initiative, the FLP's never refused to sit down and talk with Western leaders; and even after the Reagan Administration committed itself to providing armed military support for Savimbi's Unita, the Angolan regime continued to express its interest in negotiating with Washington. Thus, in February 1987, Angola's Foreign Trade Minister, Ismael Markus, declared:

> We are ready to dance. Our young people like American rhythm and we would like to see our countries get together more. But it takes two to dance. If it were our decision alone, then it has already been taken.[1]

The reason for this attitude is plain. African leaders acknowledge that the Western powers are heavily engaged in Southern Africa and that they possess the necessary resources to influence the course of events; therefore it is felt important to engage them in negotiations to try and persuade them to play a helpful role. Offended as most of them are by the policies of Reagan and Thatcher, they recognize that neither is a permanent political fixture nor are they impermeable to domestic and international influences.

No African leaders are entitled to feel more aggrieved by past Western policies than the SA Congress leaders; nevertheless, when first the British Foreign Secretary and then the United States Secretary of State invited the ANC leaders to talks, their response was positive. This is because they know that whatever help they have received from the Soviet bloc and might expect from them in the future, the Soviets are much less influential in the region than the Europeans and Americans. It has not been for want of trying that the ANC has come to have closer relations with Moscow and Havana than with London or Washington, and the PAC with other anti-Western countries. Although there is deep anger against the West among many Black South Africans, these are feelings bred of disappointment and frustration, not of ideology. There is little in the Black experience in SA that endears "Western capitalism" to them; but their politically conscious leaders are sufficiently experienced to know that their best hope of cutting short their struggle and of avoiding a war to the bitter end lies in engagement with the West. What they are still unsure of is whether the West is likely to prove a reliable ally or a stubborn obstacle in the last phase of their struggle.

So, too, with White South Africans; they are thoroughly confused by the anbiguities of Western policies. Having once seen the West as their close ally— especially Reagan's America—they are deeply perplexed to know how much or how little reliance they can place in Western policies. The fear of many Afrikaners, probably rightly so, is that when the chips are finally down the West will pursue its own interests even if it means 'abandoning White South Africans to their fate.'

Although it is convenient to speak of 'Western policies' in discussing broad issues, the use of the collective masks the differences, often sharp ones, between the different entities within the Western community. Thus, although the Western members of the Security Council pursued an agreed policy in establishing the Contact Group to pursue their Namibian initiative, four of its members strongly disagreed with the American policy of linking the implementation of the Security Councils' Resolution 435 (SCR 435), defining the process of bringing Namibia to its independence, with the withdrawal of Cuban troops from Angola. After all the detailed negotiations on SCR 435 were completed, the United States was left on its own to pursue its negotiations with Angola and South Africa over the Cuban issue. (Unlike the United States, all the European countries maintain diplomatic links with Angola.) The West European countries also strongly disapprove of the American decision to give military and other support to Unita which they see as injurious to the efforts to lessen Soviet-bloc and Cuban influence in Angola. The American attitude to the Cuban issue in Angola is dictated both by Washington's perceived hemispheric security concerns and by domestic policies involving both the anti-Castro Cuban lobby and the conservative caucus. None of these factors impinges on West European interests. The Reagan Administration's efforts to compel Chevron-Gulf and other American oil companies to withdraw from Angola are regarded by the Europeans as seriously damaging to wider Western interests since the role of multinationals and the promotion of close economic ties are seen as major instruments in promoting their economic, political and strategic interests. It is in the area of trade, technology and finance that the Western community has a decisive edge over the Soviet bloc in the competition for influence in the Third World. By making an oil multinational a pawn in their diplomacy, the Europeans believe the Americans play into the hands of those who target multinationals as 'imperialist agencies'. Moreover, on a strictly practical level, the withdrawal of Gulf-Chevron would not affect Angola's economy, as a dozen or more European oil companies are in line to take over its valuable holdings.

The ideological stance of a right-wing American Administration on issues such as the role of U.S. multinationals and linkage between Cuban troop withdrawals and Namibian independence finds little response even from similarly right-wing governments in Europe, such as Thatcher's in Britain, Kohl's in Germany, and Chirac's in France. It might be thought that the coincidence of four such conservative governments in the West would have made for a more unified approach to issues raised by the Southern African crisis; but as subsequent chapters show, this is very far from having been the case.

Surprisingly, though, there is a unanimity of Western views on the question of whether the Soviet Union poses a major threat to South Africa, justifying the Pretoria regime's obsessional concerns about a 'total onslaught by the communists'. Irrespective of the political stripe of any Administration in Washington, the Americans have been consistent in their attempts to dissuade Pretoria from blaming South Africa's troubles on Moscow. Spokesmen of the Reagan Administration have been no less outspoken than those of the Carter Administration in counselling Pretoria not to overrate the "Soviet threat" in the present phase of the region's conflicts.

THE SOVIET-BLOC AND CUBAN ROLE

The official Soviet view of the USSR's interests and policies in the region is that, like the United States, it has legitimate interests everywhere in the world, but it questions whether either superpower has vital interests in Southern Africa.[2] However, Moscow makes a distinction between "vital interests" and "international responsibilities." The latter, it claims, include concern about any potential threat to world peace, its duty to honour its treaty obligations with allies, and support for liberation movements struggling for "independence." On the issue of "threats to world peace" Moscow identifies three problems: the racist policies of South Africa, which require positive support for those struggling against apartheid and opposition to foreign powers supportive of the system; Pretoria's policy of destabilizing its neighbours by its trans-border military attacks and support for rebel movements; and the denial of Namibia's right to independence under the terms established by SCR 435.

Moscow's treaty obligations relate to its agreements with Angola and Mozambique which include undertakings to help defend their sovereignty against external attacks. This undertaking justifies its military aid programmes and support for the Cuban troops' presence in Angola. Its "international responsibility" to support liberation movements is the justification for the aid it gives to the ANC and Swapo as well as in the past to Joshua Nkomo's Zapu during the period of armed struggle against the Smith regime. (The USSR has been selective in deciding which of the liberation movements it will support; it refused, for example, to assist Robert Mugabe's Zanu, on the grounds that it had a Chinese orientation; this was also the reason why it withheld support from Samora Machel's Frelimo during its independence struggle. It has also refused to have dealings with the PAC because it regards its approach as "racist" and overtly anticommunist (i.e. opposed to Moscow's policies).

The Soviet Union succeeded in establishing its presence in the region due, primarily, to its support for liberation movements—the MPLA in Angola, Swapo in Namibia and the ANC in SA. Although it had not supported Frelimo, after Mozambique's independence Samora Machel entered into a treaty of friendship with Moscow because he felt the Soviets offered a more credible deterrent against SA attacks than his old ally, Peking. Moscow owes its success in forging its links with the MPLA, Swapo and ANC to the failure of the Western powers to respond to their overtures for active support against the Portuguese colonial power and the SA regime. Soviet success in the region is therefore attributable both to their policy of support for liberation movements engaged in "anti-imperialist" struggles, and to mistaken Western policies in judging the likely outcome of the region's power struggles.

While Moscow sees the ANC as the leading force in the struggle against Pretoria, it does not regard it as the only force. Neither the ANC nor Swapo is viewed by Moscow as a communist organization.

The overall view of the USSR is that they and the United States can and should share a role in managing regional conflicts, whether in the Middle East, Africa or elsewhere, and that such a policy can be helpful in lessening the dangers to world peace. The USSR has repeatedly put forward this idea to the United States. Although their offer has been rejected, the two superpowers have continued to meet at regular intervals to discuss the situation in Southern Africa, and have reached an understanding that conflicts in the region should not be made an excuse for military confrontation between themselves.

Notwithstanding its successful breakthrough as an active participant in the region's affairs, the Soviet bloc has so far failed to capitalize on this success. The reasons for this failure involve its lack of economic resources and of relevant technical assistance to sustain the shattered economies of Angola and Mozambique; its unwillingness to commit more of its resources to the region because—unlike Cuba, Vietnam and Afghanistan—the region does not figure high on its list of short-term strategic interests; and its logistical disadvantage in providing effective military aid sufficient to match the effort of SA, which is acknowledged by Moscow to be the regional power. While the Soviet bloc and Cuba have produced billions of dollars of arms and supplied over 1,000 military assistance personnel, the armies of Angola and Mozambique have remained unequal to the challenge of SA, or to the local opposition forces strongly reinforced by Pretoria.

The USSR does not believe it is possible under present conditions to convert the struggle in SA into a full-blooded revolutionary struggle led by the ANC and its close ally, the SA Communist Party (SACP). Instead, Moscow envisages a two-phase struggle in SA: first a successful national liberation struggle against the apartheid system, and only thereafter the beginning of a national democratic revolution. This realistic assessment of the situation (which is shared by the SACP) has led it to support the need for a negotiated settlement in SA to cut short the first phase of the struggle. This approach was described in a report submitted to the Second Soviet-African Conference of Peace, Cooperation and Social Progress by Gleb Starushenko, a corresponding member of the USSR Academy of Sciences. The report contained five major proposals. First, it endorsed 'the programme of the anti-racist forces' which does not envisage 'a broad nationalization of capitalist property as an indispensable condition,' and supports their 'readiness to give the bourgeosie the necessary guarantees they seek.' Second, it proposed that the ANC 'might work out comprehensive guarantees for the White population which could be implemented after the elimination of the apartheid regime' —such guarantees would suit the liberals and their supporters in the White community as well as neutralize the diehards. The report's third proposal is the most remarkable of all: the idea of a parliament possibly consisting of two chambers—one formed on the basis of proportional representation, and the other possessing the right of veto on the basis of equal representation for all four major racial communities. (This idea of a chamber with veto powers is, in fact, close to a set of proposals suggested by some of President Botha's constitutional advisers.) In support of this particular proposal, Starushenko pointed to Kenya and Zimbabwe as countries where the White minorities have been made to feel safe after independence. While these countries should not be regarded as 'rigid models,' he suggested that they offer examples of what might be achieved in South Africa by offering guarantees to the White and other minorities. Fourth, the report proposed that the post-apartheid state might take the form of a unitary system with 'autonomous components.' The form and substance of such autonomy should be defined with due regard being had to 'the will of the population' revealed, for instance, through referendums, negotiations etc.; concrete issues related to the functioning of such a system might become the subject of a national conference whose components would be the government of the Republic of South Africa and the true representatives of the non-White population. Finally, the report stressed the need for 'a peaceful resolution of the conflict in SA,' and suggested that this might be expedited by resorting to international guarantees, with the different sides each selecting guarantors by agreement from among prestigious international organizations or individual states. Starushenko disagreed with those who think it 'utopian' to imagine the possibility of multiracial societies existing in the modern world without serious discrimination and antagonistic contradictions.

Starushenko emphasized that 'the process of shaping a revolutionary situation which we now witness in SA is far from being completed. Protest demonstrations are largely confined to African townships around the big cities. The broad masses of the Black population, particularly in the Bantustans, often stay aloof. The main participants in the anti-racist action are students and the unemployed. The working class has not yet thrown the full measure of its enormous revolutionary potential into the scale of revolutionary struggle'. He added that if the participation of the proletariat in the liberation struggle were broader, it would afford opportunities for closer cooperation with the Communist Party, 'the recognized and experienced leader of the SA workers and other anti-racist forces.'

Although Cuba's role in Angola has been described as that of a Soviet surrogate, this view is open to question. While it is evident that the Cuban expeditionary force in Angola has well suited the Soviet interest and that the two allies act in concert in helping to defend the MPLA regime, there is substantial evidence to show that Castro was the initiator of the policy of military intervention in Angola and not Moscow's agent. It was the Cubans rather than the Soviets who succeeded in making themselves the close allies of the MPLA during the period of the liberation struggle. Moscow always found the MPLA's historic leader, Dr. Agostinho Neto, to be an awkward customer; their relations were often seriously troubled and, at one time, actually disrupted. The Cubans took the initiative in preparing their expeditionary force before the Soviets became actively engaged. It is arguable that it was Castro who brought Moscow into Angola, rather than the reverse.[3]

Although the Cubans remain committed to keeping their thirty thousand combat troops in Angola for as long as they are needed by the MPLA regime, they are tied by an agreement to evacuate their troops whenever requested to do so by Luanda. There is no evidence to suggest that either the Cubans or the Soviet bloc have been seeking to establish a permanent foothold in Angola. Under the right conditions (e.g. the achievement of Namibian independence and the withdrawal of SA troops from Angola), it is reasonable to believe that the Cuban military presence will be phased out and the Soviet military commitment reduced.

Although the MPLA leaders have every reason to feel grateful to the Soviets and Cubans for their decisive role in ensuring the regime's survival, their experience with their communist allies has not been a satisfactory one. This is notably because of their failure to provide adequate economic support which has forced Angola to make deals with the United States, their failure to fulfil their role as a strategic ally capable of preventing repeated military incursions by the SA army, and their failure to suppress the challenge offered by Unita. To survive as a regime, to establish security and stage an economic recovery, the MPLA needs, above all, a long period of peace. With this as its priority interest, the MPLA Government has shown itself to be less interested in developing the country as a Marxist state and much more concerned with seeking an end to the hostilities that have characterized its entire period of independence since 1975. Towards that end they have leant over backwards in their efforts to encourage Western (and especially American) diplomatic efforts to produce a settlement in Namibia.

THE ROLE OF THE CHINESE PEOPLE'S REPUBLIC

The post-Mao period has seen a considerable lessening of China's active involvement in the region in line with its generally lower profile in the rest of the Third World. Its present leaders are much less adamant than Mao in the belief that ' power comes out of the barrel of the gun. '[4] Their concern over the need for economic reconstruction at home has led the Chinese to scale down their aid programmes in Africa and to dampen their revolutionary fervour against 'Western imperialism.' Until the advent of Gorbachev, China's principal foreign policy interest in Africa was to mobilize support in opposition to 'Soviet hegemonism.' Whether this sharp hostility to the Soviets will continue to diminish depends on the progress made towards a new détente between Peking and Moscow.

I have argued elsewhere[5] that it was the Soviet concern to eliminate Chinese influence in postcolonial Angola that was a major factor in Moscow's decision to join with Cuba in its military intervention on the side of the MPLA against its two challengers, Unita and FNLA, both of which were perceived as being pro-Chinese and pro-American. The defeat of these two liberation movements seriously undermined Peking's ability to engage in an active role in the country without openly siding with Unita—an option that was hardly credible once Savimbi was forced into an alliance with Pretoria.

If the Chinese were the losers in Angola, they emerged as the allies of the two winning sides in Mozambique and Zimbabwe. But just as the Soviets were unable to capitalize on their gains so, too, Peking was unable to produce the kind of military and economic support needed by the Mozambicans and Zimbabweans.

President Machel's decision to enter into a treaty of friendship with Moscow, because of his belief—subsequently shown to have been misplaced—that it offered him a more credible strategic ally, was a blow to the Chinese and led to a temporary estrangement with Maputo. In the case of Zimbabwe, Mugabe refused for several years to forgive Moscow over its support for Nkomo; but faced with SA's destabilization policies and because of his commitment to the struggle against apartheid he found it necessary to establish ties with Moscow and to seek arms from that quarter.

While China has shown some interest in the PAC (as the rival to Moscow's favoured ANC), it never in fact produced much support for the movement. In 1986 the Chinese welcomed an approach from the ANC and took the first steps towards ending its hostility to a movement it had previously condemned for its staunch support of Moscow's 'revisionist' policies. Peking has unwaveringly supported Swapo, but because its guerilla forces are based on Angolan soil (where it receives military support from the Soviet bloc and Cuba), there has been little opportunity for Peking to do much more than give general diplomatic support and limited economic aid to the organization.

Although China now plays a relatively minor role in the region, its standing remains high in the eyes of most African leaders.

THE FUTURE OUTLOOK

The crisis in Southern Africa is still some way from reaching its climax. Since it originates in the South African political system, the future course of events will be determined by developments in the apartheid state. While it may be possible to lessen the severity of the conflicts by settling some of the problems on the periphery—e.g. bringing Namibia to independence, phasing out Cuban troops from Angola, and arranging ceasefire agreements—the dangerous potentialities for much greater violence, a racial conflagration, greater international involvement and economic disaster will remain so long as the White-dominated political system in SA remains in place.

There are two equally possible outcomes: either that agreement will be reached for negotiations to begin about a new post-apartheid constitution, or that the situation will produce a neo-Fascist regime committed to a policy of extreme repression and a drift into revolutionary violence. The situation could be dramatically transformed by an agreement to negotiate a new democratic constitution. To speak of such a possibility is not to speak of a miracle. All of SA's major leaders favour a negotiated settlement, as do Africa's leaders, the Western governments and the Soviet Union. All South Africans have a shared interest in ending the violence and in preventing serious damage to the economy. The question is one of modalities—the terms for round table talks to begin. Although there are major disagreements over terms, these are not irreconcilable. The only serious doubt is whether the present political system in SA is capable of sustaining a government strong enough to withstand the predictable hostility of a fearful White electorate when it comes to the point of seriously negotiating over the abandonment of three centuries of exclusive White rule. On this critical issue there can be no certainty.

A second major point of uncertainty is whether external powers can exert effective pressures to weaken the resistance of the White forces reluctant to take the serious risks involved in the surrender of White power and privilege. There is substantial support for the view that mandatory, comprehensive sanctions can compel White South Africans to sit down and talk with representative Black leaders; but this would require a fundamental change in Western policies. While Western opinion has begun to veer towards the use of sanctions as an effective form of political leverage, there is little evidence to suggest that the Western community is anywhere near ready to making the shift from partial to full-scale sanctions. For this to happen would depend on a dramatic rise in the level of violence in the region and, possibly, a greater role being played by the Soviet bloc. The first possibility seems likelier than the second—although the second development is much more likely to produce a greater commitment by the West. The risks are that if violence were to increase dramatically it could easily become uncontrollable and worsen the climate for negotiations; and that instead of producing a more yielding attitude among White South Africans, it would turn their anxious fears into irrational paranoia. The paranoidal factor in politics (compare Stalin's Russia and Khomeini's Iran) is the biggest of all threats to rational decision-making.

Meanwhile, partial sanctions—unless they are carefully selected and properly targeted—are unlikely to have much effect on the SA economy. The present level of sanctions, or even the possibility of enlarging their present range, could inflict serious damage on the economy, but not sufficient to bring an unwilling Government to the negotiating table. The threat by SA's frontline neigbours to impose sanctions speaks eloquently of their commitment to bringing down the apartheid system but, even if their threat were implemented, it is likely to result in doing more damage to the Frontline States than to SA, whose capability of implementing counter-sanctions is far greater than the capability of their neighbours either to inflict serious harm on SA's economy or to withstand reprisals by Pretoria. This situation is recognized by African leaders who, in the small print of their policy statements on sanctions, have all along made their application of full sanctions conditional on Western participation. Committed Frontline States like Zimbabwe and Zambia are therefore left dangling between their threat to impose sanctions and their reluctance to act on their own—an uncomfortable position that increases their frustration and exposes their vulnerability in a painful way, and which could easily convert into bitter anger against the West. It is a situation that cannot be altogether displeasing to the Soviets and other anti-Western forces. A recent survey of the opinion of Black South African leaders shows that they are already overwhelmingly hostile to the United States—an unhappy portent for their future relations.[6]

While the Western powers might yet succeed in staving off the demands for comprehensive sanctions by progressively adding to those already agreed, they are likely to be faced with a different kind of challenge which they might find it harder to resist. This comes from the commitment by Zimbabwe and Zambia progressively to sever their dependence for communications on SA by developing alternative routes to the sea through the greater use of the Tazara railway line to Dar es Salaam and the Beira Corridor—the 180 mile land strip from Mutare in eastern Zimbabwe to the Mozambican port, across which passes an oil pipeline, a railway line and a road highway. This crucial communications artery crosses territory highly vulnerable to attacks by the MNR. If the Frontline States continue to increase their pressures on SA, Pretoria's obvious counter-pressure would be to obstruct safe passage along the Corridor by increasing its logistical support for the MNR—an eventuality foreseen by the Frontline States, hence their contingency plan to create a Pan-African force, reinforced by carefully selected outside powers, to ensure the Corridor's security. At the time of writing this force is composed only of army units drawn from some of the Frontline States, but with promises of future logistical support coming from India and Nigeria. Other offers of help have come from Iran, Libya, Cuba, Ethiopia and the Soviet bloc. But because of a strong desire to avoid unnecessary external entanglements, none of these offers has so far been seriously considered; however, there is no telling what might happen if the Corridor were seriously threatened. At present, the Western contribution to the Corridor is limited to providing one-third of the £400 million of the cost of improving its infrastructures and the facilities at the Beira port. Britain is also indirectly, though only marginally, involved in providing military training for both the Zimbabwe and Mozambican armies. If the Beira Corridor should become a strategic battleground between the FLS and SA, the Western powers could find it difficult not to respond to appeals for support, especially if the Soviets and Cubans showed their interest in helping to defend it.

International involvement is already an inescapable reality of the situation in Southern Africa; as the crisis widens and deepens, this involvement is bound to increase. However, in the short term, the major impact on developments in SA is more likely to be made by internal rather than by external forces. The growing militant challenge inside the country coming from Black South Africans and the growing disenchantment with the regime felt both by English and Afrikaans-speaking Whites are bound to hasten the disintegration of the political system as well as significantly increase the political consciousness of Whites in understanding the true nature and seriousness of their present situation. This upsurge of internal discontent is more likely to increase than diminish even though the deployment of military and police forces under a state of emergency may restore the semblance of law and order for short periods.

The dynamics of change in SA contain two inter-related elements: internal explosions and external pressures, with the first element acting as the trigger for the second, and the two acting together to force the pace of change in the country—but in which direction it is hard to say.

NOTES

1. *International Herald Tribune*, 19 February 1987.
2. This view has been expressed in talks between Soviet officials and American academics in their periodic exchanges.
3. See Colin Legum and Tony Hodges, *After Angola: The War over Southern Africa* (1976).
4. See Colin Legum, *Third World Reports* (London) No. AM1, 26 November 1982.
5. See Colin Legum and Tony Hodges, *op. cit.*
6. See David Hirschmann, *Changing Attitudes of Black South Africans Towards the United States of America*. Institute of Social and Economic Research and Development Studies, Rhodes University, Grahamstown: South Africa, 1987.

THE BATTLEFRONTS OF SOUTHERN AFRICA

1975–1976

HOW THE SEARCH FOR PEACEFUL CHANGE FAILED

OVERVIEW

During the early part of 1975 a number of the secrets were revealed about the diplomacy to achieve detente in Southern Africa. These new revelations threw fresh light on the secret diplomacy embarked on by the South African Prime Minister, John Vorster, and the role of the leaders of certain African states.[1] In February 1975 Robert Mugabe, former secretary-general of Zanu (Zimbabwe African National Union) and a detainee for 10 years, produced what came to be known as 'the Mugabe Diary'.[2] Its chief interest lies in his version of the December 1974 negotiations for the release of detainees from Rhodesian prisons, the hammering together of the heads of the rival nationalist leaders in State House, Lusaka, and especially Mugabe's early deep suspicions of President Kaunda which have continued to fester.

It was not until 14 May 1975 that SA's Prime Minister, John Vorster, provided details of his visit to the Ivory Coast President, Felix Houphouet-Boigny, the previous September.[3] He confirmed their rendezvous at Houphouet's official residence in Yamoussoukrou on 22-23 September 1974 which, he claimed, originated with an initiative taken by the Ivorian leader. He added that while they had discussed economic and technical aid from SA, their talks had centred on improving relations between African States, 'of which SA is one'. He also confirmed that contacts between Pretoria and Abidjan were continuing.

The situation at the beginning of 1975 was as follows: the Organization of African Unity (OAU) was still uneasily behind the initiative taken in October 1974 by the Presidents of Zambia, Tanzania, Mozambique and Botswana to find a peaceful solution for the problems of southern Africa in terms of the Lusaka Manifesto of 1967 but there were a growing number of African voices opposed to talks with Vorster. The OAU was simultaneously engaged in strengthening the liberation movements' capacity for armed struggle in case peaceful methods failed. The White Rhodesian leader, Ian Smith, was still refusing to accept Vorster's advice to negotiate realistically and was playing for time to allow an extremist White blacklash to develop against Vorster at home. Vorster and Kaunda (working through his envoy, Mark Chona) remained in close touch to keep the bridges open. By March 1975, according to Vorster, there had been15 meetings between Zambia and SA since the first contact was made on 5 October 1974; but he denied that, up to that time, he had ever met Kaunda personally.[4] The divisions in the Black Rhodesian ranks continued to widen despite their agreement to form a single African National Council (ANC).

Black Africa's stand was restated by President Julius Nyerere at the opening of the 24th session of the OAU Liberation Committee in Dar es Salaam on 8 January 1975. Independence for Rhodesia, he said, could be only on the basis of majority rule; but if Smith wished to retreat from UDI to the *status quo ante* of being a British colony he could achieve the transition period to majority rule which he seemed to favour. Nyerere went on to explain: 'We have stated these things over and over again. First, we are determined to achieve independence for Rhodesia on the basis of majority rule. Second, we prefer to achieve this objective around the conference table. Third, if the racists reject the conference table, or if they come to the conference table only to sabotage the achievement of independence on the basis of majority rule, Africa must and will intensify the armed struggle. This intensified war will then be waged either until independence has been achieved on the basis of majority rule, or until Africa's enemies are willing to talk realistically. We want both Africa's friends, and Africa's enemies, to accept that we mean what we say in those three statements. They must believe us. We said similar things in relation to the Portuguese colonies; both our friends and our enemies in Portugal have now accepted that we mean what we say. It would have been infinitely better if they had believed us years ago—much misery would have been avoided. But if the bloodshed and suffering in the Portuguese colonies has convinced the authorities in Southern Africa that we mean what we say in those three statements, everyone concerned could be saved from even more disastrous and terrible wars.'

The OAU Liberation Committee adopted what it called the Dar es Salaam Declaration on 17 January. It called for intensified pressure to ostracize the SA Government and to intensify the armed struggle. OAU funds were in future to be allocated with a special priority for the struggle in Rhodesia and Namibia.

Ian Smith chose this moment to say in a special message to SA that there was no question of handing Rhodesia over to Black majority rule. 'I am not repudiating my own policy.'[5] In a reference to the difficulties of implementing the Lusaka Agreement[6] especially over the interpretation of a ceasefire, he said: 'I am only being realistic when I say that in my opinion our chances of success in this exercise are slim.'

PRETORIA NEGOTIATIONS WITH LIBERIA

February 1975 brought a new breakthrough for Vorster's diplomacy; on 12 February he flew to Monrovia for talks with Liberia's President William Tolbert. But this time, unlike the Ivory Coast visit which had been kept secret for several months, the actual transcript of the discussions between Vorster and Tolbert was leaked to Leonard Buckley of the London *Times* by the President's brother, Stephen, the Minister of Finance. The publication of the secret exchange[7] took Vorster by surprise. While he confirmed in his Parliament that he had visited Monrovia it took him another 10 days before he agreed to answer questions about what had transpired in Monrovia.[8] His main concern was over a statement by Tolbert[9] that Vorster had told him: 'We do not want an inch of South West Africa's territory and I would be only too pleased to get South West Africa off our back.'

The Liberian President had revealed that in preparation for Vorster's visit he had invited Chief Gatsha Buthelezi of KwaZulu and Sam Nujoma, president-general of Swapo, for consultations in Monrovia. Vorster's concern was to make it clear that he had told Tolbert that Nujoma 'was neither the natural nor the elected leader' of the territory, and described him as 'an adventurer'. However, he did not challenge the accuracy of the transcript. At one point, it quoted him directly as saying: 'If there are no preconditions and if violence stops (in Rhodesia) I can guarantee that a solution can be found.' Another important point in the recorded conversation was Vorster's undertaking to withdraw SA forces from Rhodesia as soon as violence had ended.

Reactions to the Monrovia talks were mixed in SA. Chief Lucas Mangope, Chief Minister of BophuthaTswana, commented that Vorster should first tackle more urgent issues concerning Blacks in SA. The Lebowa Homeland leader, Dr Cedric Phatudi, said 'it would be unfortunate if Mr Vorster built up his foreign policy at the cost of his home policy with Blacks of SA, who should come first'. And the Soweto leader, Lennox Mlonzi, blamed Vorster because he 'has not swept his own house. He must start right here—where we are.'[10]

Thus the Bantustan leaders reflected the same attitude to Vorster's diplomacy as the exile political movements, ANC and PAC. But the White South Africans were jubilant at Vorster's success. Typical of their mood was an editorial in a pro-Government newspaper[11] which said the onslaught of the hawks on the doves in Africa was in full swing, with the doves in the front line of the struggle for peace or war on the continent. It added: 'We must give them all the support we can, without seeing our own destiny as being totally dependent on them. In the final analysis they, too, are acting in their own national interest, and their conception of that interest might change under the merciless pressures that have now been directed against them.'

One of the African hawks was Guinea's President Sekou Toure whose reaction to the Monrovia talks was to say that 'to hold a dialogue with the supporters of apartheid is to add to the racists' injury to Africa, an injury inflicted by Africa itself'. He called on all African Governments to 'reject all proposals for dialogue with SA until the day when the indignity which now soils our continent through apartheid completely disappears.'[12] Toure was not alone in condemning the Monrovia talks; demands quickly built up for an emergency meeting of the OAU to thresh out the questions raised by individual African leaders negotiating with Vorster outside the OAU framework.

The Liberians however were not deterred. Acting independently of the Lusaka initiative, Stephen Tolbert established a regular channel of communication with Vorster through Ambassador Pik Botha. In post-Watergate style, these intimate exchanges were also leaked in considerable detail.[13] Stephen Tolbert revealed that Liberia had rejected an offer of financial help from SA. More interesting was Vorster's response to Tolbert's request that he should intervene over the arrest of Ndabaningi Sithole by Smith. 'I can assure you,' Vorster replied, 'that I am doing my utmost to remove barriers to enable the parties in Rhodesia to resume meaningful negotiations and I have conveyed my own views at the highest level to the Rhodesian Government.' In a telephone conversation, Ambassador Botha told Tolbert that 'at the moment the situation between Vorster and Ian Smith is very critical'. Stephen Tolbert also revealed that he had agreed to try and arrange for Vorster to meet with Kenyatta, Mobutu and Gowon; but he had insisted that 'prior to such a meeting I would require his (Vorster's) doing something spectacularly positive and concrete to show that he is exerting every effort within his powers to convince Africa and the world of his sincerity in bringing a change to the unsatisfactory situation which now prevails in southern Africa . . . African leaders realize how intransigent the SA Government has been in the past and accordingly they now view Mr Vorster's action with great scepticism. This is the reason why I continue to insist that some meaningful change be evidenced before I take the next step . . .' These confidential exchanges continued until Stephen Tolbert died in an aircrash on 28 April.

The disclosure of Stephen Tolbert's secret diplomacy by a journalist engaged to write his biography understandably upset the SA Prime Minister; he tried to cover up his embarrassment by the familiar ploy of attacking the ethics of the paper for publishing 'so-called confidential information', adding it was 'beneath his dignity to make any comment, or to point out the obvious inaccuracies in the report.'[14] Much more to the point was Vorster's concern that the report could 'sow suspicion and disturb relations between SA and Rhodesia and other countries which are engaged in a serious effort to find a peaceful solution for delicate problems'. Smith, especially, was always on the look-out for evidence to justify his suspicions that Vorster was undermining his position through his African diplomacy. A second, perhaps even greater, concern was over the *verkramptes* (hardliners) with their suspicions that Vorster was undermining apartheid at home in order to win friends in Black Africa. The Tolbert disclosures gave ammunition to both Smith and the *verkramptes*.

President Tolbert said in an interview[15] in late March that 'it appears SA is trying to buy time through her present initiatives'. While he felt that 'many changes' would occur in SA, he said what mattered was not whether such changes were acceptable to Liberia but to black South Africans. He disagreed with Vorster's judgement of Sam Nujoma: Swapo, he said, 'is the only Namibian liberation movement recognized bv the OAU.'

PRETORIA NEGOTIATIONS WITH CENTRAL AFRICAN REPUBLIC

February 1975 also brought two other successes for Vorster's policy. A delegation of SA officials and businessmen went to Bangui when they convinced President Bokassa of the Central African Republic that they could provide effective economic and technical aid for his benighted, land-locked country. Official SA sources[16] have disclosed that a R 4m (over £2,2m) loan was provided for a tourist hotel complex, a construction company was negotiating a R6 m (over £3.3 m) housing project, and further tourist projects were being considered. Bokassa's emulation of Malawi's example did not, however, affect his close relationship with General Amin who tirelessly insists that Africa's duty is to 'crush' SA militarily. SA's second success was to strengthen its economic ties with Gabon, whose Government bought space in British newspapers to deny that they had any economic involvement with SA. Yet according to an official SA source[17] Gabon negotiated a loan for R170 m (almost £100 m) from an international consortium in which SA is the chief partner to finance the trans-Gabon railway line. Talks have also been held for SA firms to build an ambitious low-cost housing scheme in Libreville.

According to SA's Finance Minister, Senator Horwood, the Republic's programme of financial and technical assistance to African countries, as well as its export trade, has increased significantly. A commentator[18] claimed that in January 1975 alone the increase in normal exports and aid was c. R200 m. During an 18 month period agricultural experts had made 137 visits to African countries, which had received 24.5 m doses of crop vaccines. He also claimed that 30 African 'Heads of State or Ministers' and 150 senior officials had visited SA during that period. As is the case whenever such figures are quoted, no breakdown is given of the countries involved. But it can be taken for granted that the major part of trade and aid goes to SA's neighbours—Botswana, Lesotho, Swaziland, Rhodesia and Mozambique, and to Mauritius and Malawi.

PRETORIA NEGOTIATIONS WITH ZAMBIA

President Kaunda—who continued to be the cog wheel for the African initiative in the negotiations with SA—slightly lifted the veil on his own secret diplomacy in a conversation with Raph Uwechue, the editor of *Africa*.[19] He disclosed how from the beginning of his contacts with Pretoria in October 1974 he was careful to keep his OAU colleagues fully informed. 'Mr Vorster himself has said publicly ever since that we must negotiate because the alternative is "too ghastly to contemplate". Now, he is a man who is well organized military-wise. He has his BOSS security organization and is well-informed about all these things. He can see on the horizon only real dangers existing, especially in so far as the minority groups are concerned. He and his advisers have understood the message conveyed by both the Lusaka Manifesto as well as the Mogadishu Declaration and they know now that Africa means business . . . When the first hopeful sign reached us I contacted our Chairman, that is the current OAU Chairman, General Siyad Barre, who was then officially visiting West African countries. I sent a message to him and said that I was going to send my colleague, the Minister of Foreign Affairs, as soon as he went back home to explain to him what was taking place. This information and top-level discussion exercise was not carried out by Zambia alone. It was conducted jointly and simultaneously with Tanzania and Botswana. Between our three countries we sent our Foreign Ministers to the various African countries to discuss the developments. The first call Mr Vernon Mwaanga made was on our current Chairman, Siyad Barre, in accordance with my promise to him. He briefed him on the situation and, I believe, a representative of the Secretary-General of the OAU was also at that meeting in Mogadishu. From Somalia he went to brief Mzee Kenyatta in Kenya and from there he flew directly to Lagos to brief General Gowon, then to Ghana, Ivory Coast, Liberia, Sierre Leone, Guinea-Bissau, Senegal, Mauritania and the Gambia. Earlier he had briefed President Mobutu Sese Seko of Zaire. So Zambia had done about 14

4

countries and the rest were done by our colleagues. So, really, we have certainly briefed our colleagues to the best of our ability. In terms of actual support, one is very heartened to see that we received many messages from our brother Heads of State and Government to the effect that they prayed for what we were doing, that they supported the move and hoped that something positive will come out of these contacts. The general understanding, in short, is that we are acting with their support and on their behalf.'

Kaunda also gave an interesting glimpse of the way he sees Vorster's problems: '. . . there is no doubt at all that the Southern African minority regimes are really led by Mr Vorster. Now, as to what he has done to translate his speeches into action, this, of course, I must admit is a very hard question to answer at this material time, because in this very delicate situation one must understand that Mr Vorster has got his constituency and it is a big and complex one, where there are both supporters as well as opponents of current developments. Therefore, anything we say at the moment may endanger or complicate his own position and quite honestly we do not like to do that at all. We want to say only in general terms that we know Mr Vorster is playing some important role in so far as the minority regimes are concerned. He is the unquestionable leader, and therefore certainly he is at the heart of all these things insofar as their side is concerned . . . you will excuse me if I appear not to be forthcoming on this issue because I think it is important at this stage that these matters are kept where they belong until the problem is solved. Then historians and you militants in the Press can dig out the facts at the appropriate time. Right now we are more concerned with achieving results that, hopefully, will. bring peace and justice to Southern Africa and effectively put an end to the suffering of our people there.'

Zambia's Foreign Minister, Vernon Mwaanga, outlining his Government's role in negotiating with Pretoria, told his Parliament on 18 March: 'I want to state clearly that we have not been engaged in dialogue with SA. After all, you can dialogue with a friend. The history of our relations with SA does not prove friendship. It proves two countries which have been in conflict and which basically remain in conflict. It is the cause of this conflict which we have been seeking to understand, let alone to resolve. We do not accept SA interference in Rhodesia; we do not accept SA's continued illegal occupation of Namibia and we continue to call upon SA to grant independence to Namibia on the basis of majority rule. We completely reject any and all plans aimed at dividing Namibia into Bantustans or so-called population groups. We remain vehemently opposed to apartheid. So, there can be no question of our commitment to the struggle in Southern Africa. There is no one country in the world which is in Zambia's position in relation to the struggle the people of Southern Africa have waged since the early 1960s. We have not only paid our budget to the OAU and to the Liberation Committee in full; we have never been in arrears. Above all, we have taken on extra burdens without instructions by the OAU or anyone else in order to consolidate the armed struggle in Zimbabwe, Namibia and the former Portuguese colonies. We have paid in financial and material terms and we have also paid in life and property of our people. So if peace is possible, we will work for it. If armed struggle is the only choice left in Zimbabwe and Namibia, we will support it.'

March 1975 proved to be a troubled time for the protagonists of the peaceful approach. While SA was still euphoric about the success of Vorster's diplomacy, the Prime Minister was having a hard time trying to slip the halter around the Smith regime's neck in order to lead it into meaningful talks about a constitutional settlement. Speaking at a Press conference early in March,[20] Vorster looked forward to State visits from a number of African leaders. He was encouraged by a vote of confidence in the Liberian Parliament on 11 March endorsing President Tolbert's approach to SA. Senegal's President Senghor announced on 13 March that he proposed sending a delegation of jurists to test the opinion of all the communities in the country since 'the dialogue which must be engaged to solve the problem of apartheid is not between Mr Vorster and African Heads of State but between the SA Government, its White opposition and the Black majority of the population'.

A Nigerian journalist, Gbolabo Ogunsanwo, arrived in the Republic to report the situation for his influential magazine, *Afriscope*.[21] But the most important development in March was the announcement that SA had taken the first step to withdraw its forces from Rhodesia by recalling them to Salisbury from the front line in the Zambezi valley—a decision welcomed by Kaunda and his negotiating partners, but a source of deep resentment in Salisbury. An SA pro-Government paper[22] revealed that General Walls, Rhodesia's army commander, 'was apparently not at all happy with the political initiatives taken in the recent past'. The trend of his argument, remarked the paper, seemed to be that SA was 'hustling' Rhodesia into doing something; but if the attempt failed, it would be SA's 'moral duty' to restore the Rhodesians to 'their original position'. The paper felt this was 'a remarkable view of the situation', and said it would be interesting to know if General Walls was expressing the views of Ian Smith. This type of not infrequent comment in the SA Press reflected the growing rift between the two recent allies as Vorster's policy concentrated increasingly on winning new friends in Black Africa.

Two factors inside Rhodesia militated against the effective implementation of the Lusaka Agreement—the continuing armed struggle by Zanu guerrillas,[23] and the increasingly bitter rivalries among Black nationalist leaders in defiance of their agreement to bury their differences inside ANC.[24] Smith was quick to seize the opportunity of trying to sink the Pretoria-Lusaka initiative by arresting Ndabaningi Sithole in March on charges that he had actively encouraged recruitment for the guerrillas, and that he had planned to assassinate Nkomo, Bishop Muzorewa and other ANC leaders. The ANC responded in the way Smith had clearly intended—by refusing to have any talks with him until Sithole was released. With detente on the verge of collapse, Smith brought an influential delegation of his Ministers to Cape Town on 19 March for a confrontation with Vorster. His tactics were plain: he was working to strengthen the *verkrampte* forces opposed to Vorster's detente policies to reverse the Prime Minister's policies; but Vorster was more than a match for his stubborn neighbour. Not only did he inform Smith that he intended to withdraw his forces from Rhodesia, but he insisted that Sithole should be released. It took another visit to Salisbury by SA's Foreign Minister, Dr Hilgard Muller, on 6 April to force Smith to give way. But in announcing his decision to free Sithole, Smith confessed: 'In all honesty, I must tell you that it is not a decision to which the Rhodesian Government readily agreed.' He added that his Government had been assured that this action would 'significantly assist the cause of detente'. How little Smith really believed in this cause was soon to emerge.

THE DAR ES SALAAM DECLARATION

By the beginning of April both sides engaged in the talks to save Rhodesia from more devastating violence became seriously concerned about the likely effects of the failure to make progress towards getting constitutional talks under way before the special session of the OAU Council of Ministers which was due to meet on 7 April. The Lusaka quartet was under heavy attack from a growing body of critics inside the OAU and, more worryingly, from all the Southern African liberation movements. Guinea continued to lead the pack of critics; its Ambassador to Western Europe, Seydou Keita, claiming to speak in the name of 'revolutionary Governments', told a Press conference in Geneva[25] that 'the majority of Black African States are against this idea of Mr Vorster's which is an attempt to demobilize the rest of the continent'. Libya, predictably, gave strong support to Guinea's stand. Algeria was not far behind. Even Lesotho, once the pacemaker in the move to get a dialogue started between Black Africa and SA,[26] denounced detente—an attitude that produced an uncharacteristically public rebuke from Zambia, which accused Chief Leabua Jonathan of acting from pique at being left out of the inner core conducting the negotiations with Pretoria.[27]

Kenya—another country which at one time favoured a softer approach to SA—joined the critics. Speaking to his Parliament on 27 March Kenya's Foreign Minister, Dr Waiyaki, rejected detente 'unless and until the SA regime took concrete steps towards dialogue within the African majority in SA'.

Vorster recognized the crucial importance of stopping the OAU[28] from scotching the Lusaka initiative. Speaking to his Parliament on 1 April, Vorster said the OAU would have to decide which road to take—'peace and co-operation, or escalating confrontations'. For his part he felt he had done all he could to prove SA's *bona fides*—'I now leave the decision in the hands of the African leaders.' But there was one thing more he could do—to place the trump card in the hands of the Lusaka quartet by giving them an undertaking that SA would end its military involvement in Rhodesia by a definite date. This promise was given to Kaunda which enabled his Foreign Minister, Vernon Mwaanga, to announce to the Dar es Salaam meeting that 'Prime Minister Vorster has now assured us that SA security forces will be withdrawn by the end of May.' This positive step helped substantially in deflating the critics who had been arguing that Lusaka had nothing to show for its efforts. Mwaanga could claim credit for getting Vorster to withdraw his troops and in securing Sithole's release. But the tide of opinion was turned decisively by Nyerere's contribution to the conference. In typical workman-like manner, he had produced a draft for the conference on *African Strategy in Southern Africa* which won the support of the great majority. It was adopted as the Dar es Salaam Declaration.[29] Its main conclusion reads:

'African objectives in Southern Africa are unchanged. They are: independence for the whole country on the basis of majority rule in both Rhodesia and Namibia; and an end to apartheid and racial discrimination in SA. Africa's strategy should be to separate the two issues as far as practical, and to give priority to ending the colonial situation in Rhodesia and Namibia.

'In both colonial issues Africa needs to be willing to talk with the SA authorities, and with the local subsidiary authorities, about the mechanics of a transfer of power as soon as there is any evidence of a willingness to accept our objectives in principle. The task of free Africa in this matter is to facilitate the work of the nationalist movement of each country, to provide contact, act as messengers if required, but never to make any commitment on behalf of the nationalists except at their request and never in any way to usurp their authority in their own country. But Africa must act as one on this. If necessary we can designate a neighbouring leader and authorize him to act for Africa in relation to both Rhodesia and Namibia, while asking him to keep the rest of Africa in contact with developments as far as possible. But whatever progress may not be made at any one time in talks about the transfer of power in Rhodesia and Namibia, Africa must be preparing itself for an armed struggle if this becomes necessary, and must be clearly seen to be committed to the armed struggle if the peaceful transfer of power is rejected. Thus Africa needs to be prepared to talk and to negotiate with patience and persistence and skill. But it must also be prepared to support an armed struggle whenever the local nationalist leaders can show that peaceful methods will not achieve anything. And, finally, free Africa must do everything possible to help the nationalists of Rhodesia and Namibia achieve and maintain the unity of all nationalist forces. It is not part of free Africa's duty to train and arm the contenders in a future civil war, nor to support one nationalist group in fighting against another. Apart from this one case of exploring the chances of

7

peaceful progress to independence on the basis of majority rule in the remaining colonies of Southern Africa, free Africa must maintain and strengthen its total boycott of SA. Talking with the SA Government on apartheid is worse than irrelevant. We know what Vorster means by it; we know what it means to the African people of SA as well as to the whole concept of human equality and dignity. Vorster knows what Africa thinks of apartheid. There is no need for any discussion. Further, if and when a SA Government decides to change its policies and wants to discuss the new direction with the African people, it has no need to use free Africa. Nelson Mandela, Robert Sobukwe and hundreds of other non-white SA leaders are either rotting away physically on Robben Island or in other prisons and places of restriction. When Vorster decides to release these men and women, to allow peaceful African political activity, and to listen to what they say, we shall know that justice might well triumph in SA without the bloodshed we fear. Until those signs are evident we must treat SA as an outlaw. The boycott against SA and SA goods will not bring justice to SA. It will do no more than show both Whites and Blacks in SA that the free States of this continent refuse to compromise with a denial of human dignity. It will give heart to the non-white peoples to know that their brothers and sisters elsewhere in Africa are conscious of their problem and want to help. Its extension through the world may force the Whites to realize that their behaviour leads to isolation from decent human society. Let us, the free States of Africa, be united in support of our fellow men who are suffering under colonialism and racialism in SA.'

SA took what comfort it could from the Dar es Salaam Declaration. Vorster told his Parliament that the result of the OAU meeting was that 'detente and dialogue' were out, but consultation and contact with SA in certain circumstances were permissible. Referring to the rejection of SA's policy of Separate Development and of independent Homelands, he said this would not deter him from having discussions with those States which desired to hold talks with SA. An even shinier gloss was given to the OAU decision by the State-controlled radio's 'Africa Survey' which reflects official thinking.[30] 'Statesmanship,' it said, 'has prevailed in Africa this past week, and the Dar es Salaam conference could go down as an historic turning point in search for a better future for the continent.' Significantly it referred to 'the active part played in internal and external dialogue by the authentic Black leaders of SA, such as Chief Gatsha Buthelezi, which has been a spur to the promotion of detente. President Tolbert of Liberia, for one, decided to join the dialogue movement after discussions with Chief Buthelezi'. In another passage the commentator referred to Kaunda's role: 'The Zambian Government deserves the highest praise for courageously adopting its new outlook and sticking to it. President Kaunda has obviously been the key figure. But one cannot avoid a congratulatory word for the Zambian Foreign Minister, Mr Mwaanga, for his straight talking and courage at Dar es Salaam last week. The new Zambian approach has been accepted now by the OAU and this is a tremendous advance towards peace in Africa. Of course, on emotional issues which have for so long been a matter of great dispute, one cannot expect overnight solutions. And so a long road has yet to be walked before a lasting peace is achieved in Africa through normalization of inter-State relations.'

Nevertheless, relations between Vorster and Kaunda did not always move smoothly. In speeches made by the Zambian leader in Washington and to the Commonwealth Prime Ministers' meeting in Kingston, Jamaica, at the end of April, he urged the US and other Western countries 'to join hands and bring pressure to bear on SA directly and indirectly to end their support for the rebel regime'. Although he paid tribute to SA for wishing to disengage from Rhodesia, he also accused the Vorster regime of still being politically committed to Smith. Replying to this criticism, Vorster said that SA's major role 'in the search for peace in Southern

Africa' was not because it found itself in a weak position. While he recognized that Kaunda and his colleagues were at present under very great pressure he wished Kaunda would guard against 'over-reaching' himself as this would not promote the interests of peace.

Having surmounted the OAU hurdle at Dar es Salaam, Lusaka and Pretoria again consulted about how to get the process of negotiating a constitutional settlement started. Kaunda and his colleagues were faced with the difficulty of getting the squabbling ANC leaders to agree to sit down with Smith—a task complicated by Sithole's recent experience and by his decision to remain in exile and, especially, by Nkomo's bid for ANC leadership. Vorster's task was to talk sense into Smith. A well-informed commentator's report[31] on the relationship between SA and Rhodesia in April, disclosed: 'The SA Government's exasperation with the Smith Cabinet knows no bounds. I was told that at the recent summit meeting in Cape Town between Mr Vorster and Mr Smith, one Rhodesian Minister told the SA he could not understand why they were so worried, because "we can handle the munts". ('Munt' is a pejorative term for Blacks.) The SA were appalled by the statement and they are still not wholly convinced that all members of Mr Smith's Cabinet will go through with a settlement. The feeling is that Southern Africa has witnessed the taming of "Smithy" and that, barring a last-minute rush of blood to the head, this stricken man will sit down with the African National Council leaders now to accept the settlement envisaged at the time of the Lusaka talks.'

STAND OF THE IVORY COAST

Meanwhile, the stand taken by the Ivory-Coast at the OAU meeting in Dar es Salaam had foreshadowed a strong determination to pursue a policy of detente. The Foreign Minister, Arsene Assouane Usher, said in the course of his address:[32] 'My dear colleagues, the Ivory Coast has come to this special session because she is for dialogue between African States. We have found, not without incurring the displeasure of some of our colleagues, that dialogue which formerly was considered to be "sterile" now flourishes everywhere and has become a full-bodied reality. Certainly, our Organization can still pass anti-dialogue resolutions—and the farce will continue. Heaven forbid that this does not become a tragedy for Africa as has been the case in other parts of the world. Under no circumstances will the Ivory Coast participate in the farce. Clairvoyance, although difficult to explain, is a well-established phenomenon but my country determines its policies by taking account of what we perceive after having taken the trouble to listen to others. At this reunion we are once again running the risk of presenting a bad image to African and international opinion if we do not guard against our usual pitfalls . . . We regard the argument that Vorster is a two-headed monster—one head a saint with whom one can discuss Rhodesia and the other a demon with whom one cannot conduct dialogue on apartheid—as venomous and full of irony. We have even been told that one does not have dialogue with enemies.' The Ivorian Foreign Minister concluded by proposing that the OAU should pursue objectives which show that whatever disagreements exist between the Ivory Coast and the African States over *means*, they do not differ over *ends:*

1. The independence of Zimbabwe through the application of majority rule.
2. The independence of Namibia in its territorial integrity.
3. Abolition of apartheid and of racial discrimination in SA, and
4. Recognition of equal rights for all citizens.
5. Pressure of all kinds on SA to bring about a change in that country.
6. Material, political and diplomatic aid from African countries to the nationalists in their struggle.
7. Lasting unity of the independent States of Africa with the nationalists.

6 May 1975 marked the expiry date of the six months deadline Vorster had set for

major changes to become visible in the Republic's international relations. With this promise in mind and encouraged by the firm Ivory Coast stand at the OAU and the developing contacts with Liberia, Central African Republic, Senegal and Gabon, Vorster confidently predicted 'a period of more open diplomacy instead of SA having to make "contacts under the table".' SA had proved 'beyond a shadow of doubt its integrity in trying to achieve peace in Southern Africa', and while, he warned, it was not possible to expect that things will always be 'dramatic', the graph was on the 'up and up'. He had, he said, worked harder in the past year than at any time in his life; now he foresaw the period before the next election (April 1979) as 'the most crucial in SA's political history'. He went on: 'Either we come to an understanding with Africa or there will be an escalation of confrontation. Either the Rhodesian situation is settled or . . . Either SA's stated policy with regard to South West Africa is accepted in that period or . . .' He did not spell out the alternatives, but he had previously said 'the alternative to peace in Southern Africa is too ghastly to contemplate'.[33]

Kaunda shared Vorster's fears about the prospects for southern Africa if their talks failed to bring peaceful change to majority rule in Rhodesia and Namibia. He set off at the end of April on a 22-day visit to explain his policy to eight nations and to the Commonwealth Prime Ministers' meeting in Jamaica. In Washington he offended President Ford by breaking the convention of avoiding controversial statements at an official White House reception: the offence was not deliberate, but the intention to produce a serious impact was. Kaunda explained on his return home, on 16 May, that he hoped what he had said would make the US 'think' about its policy in Southern Africa.

President Kaunda's personal adviser, Mark Chona, attended a symposium held in Botswana's capital, Gaborone, at the end of May to discuss the problems of Southern Africa. There he affirmed Zambia's continuing commitment to maintaining communication with SA and to acting as a 'catalyst' in promoting peaceful change. He added: 'We want you to believe us that we do not want war. We understand fully the fears of the Whites in Southern Africa and accept that they are here to stay.' The symposium was also attended by Rhodesian ANC representatives, White Rhodesians, SA politicians and businessmen as well as leaders from Botswana itself. Although the symposium was held under the auspices of the SA Institute of International Affairs, it was financed by Harry Oppenheimer's Anglo-American Corporation.[34]

In his chairman's statement to the annual meeting of the Corporation on 15 May, Oppenheimer spoke of the crucial importance of the 'success of the detente policy' for the future of the region. He acknowledged that the success of an 'external policy of detente' would not of itself make SA's internal policies acceptable to the rest of Africa; but what he felt could be reasonably expected was that the normalization of relations between SA and other African States would have its effect upon SA public opinion to assist the Government in carrying through 'its stated policy of gradually eliminating racial discrimination in the national life'.

June 1975 brought official confirmation of the Ivory Coast's decision to send its Minister of Information, Laurent Dona Fologo, on an official visit to SA. Senegal, too, confirmed that it would be sending its mission of jurists. (In fact the mission was never sent.) New ground was also broken during the month when Kaunda had his first official contact with a Minister of the Smith regime. Wickus de Kock, the Minister of Information, paid a secret visit to Lusaka accompanied by five Rhodesian Front MPs. This visit was followed in July by two secret visits to Zambia by Brand Fourie, SA's Secretary of Foreign Affairs, for talks with Kaunda as well as ANC members to try and break the continuing deadlock over getting the constitutional talks started in Rhodesia. These visits were the prelude to the most dramatic event in the negotiations to save Rhodesia from the knife—the Victoria Falls conference.

August opened promisingly with SA withdrawing the last of its 200 troops from Rhodesia in fulfilment of the undertaking given on its behalf by the Zambian Foreign Minister to the OAU. In the first week of the month there was a secret meeting in Pretoria between SA, Rhodesian and Zambian delegations with Mark Chona leading the latter. On 9 August they jointly signed what has come to be known as the Pretoria Agreement. It committed the Smith regime to attending a formal conference 'without any preconditions' with the ANC at the Victoria Falls before 25 August. The full text of the Agreement was never published but it is reproduced in the Documents Section.[35] The Agreement was subsequently formally endorsed by Tanzania, Mozambique and Botswana. Although Vorster and Smith had what they called 'a fruitful discussion' in Pretoria after the signing of the agreement, Kaunda was still worried about the extent to which the SA Prime Minister was able, and willing, to influence Smith. 'The question is whether Mr Vorster will prevail in persuading Mr Smith to accept the importance of continued negotiations. I hope Mr Vorster succeeds. If not we are in for a bad time.'[36]

The real weakness of the Pretoria talks was soon to emerge: the absence of the Black side of the Rhodesian negotiating team—the ANC. Their leaders, not surprisingly, felt they were being committed to accepting agreements to which they were not a direct party, even though they were being closely consulted. They privately objected to two aspects of the Pretoria Agreement: They felt Clause 3 was a mistake since it committed them to negotiating *inside* Rhodesia; and there was no effective guarantee ensuring that the ANC could choose their own negotiators since a number of their leaders were under sentence of death were they to return to Rhodesia to take part in the talks. Smith was adamantly opposed to giving even a temporary immunity to exiled leaders like James Chikerema, George Nyandoro, Jason Moyo, George Silundika and others; but as a result of contacts between Lusaka and Salisbury on 13 August, Smith sent the following message to Kaunda:. 'With reference yesterday's telephone call, the Rhodesian Prime Minister has confirmed that it was agreed in Pretoria on 9 August 1975 that while negotiations are in progress the ANC leaders in Rhodesia will be completely free to consult with their colleagues outside Rhodesia. The Prime Minister is prepared to give this assurance in writing to the ANC. End of the message.' This assurance was publicly accepted by Bishop Muzorewa the same day and he agreed to the ANC meeting with Smith in terms of the Pretoria Agreement.

THE VICTORIA FALLS CONFERENCE

On 26 August, the disused railway bridge across the Victoria Falls' gorge—the symbolic great divide between Black-ruled and White-ruled Africa—was occupied by coaches from SA's ceremonial train—known as the White Train because of the colour of its coaches. Ian Smith and his Rhodesian Front team sat down together for the first time with their Black challengers led by Bishop Muzorewa, Joshua Nkomo and the Reverend Ndabaningi Sithole, who were flanked by men who had been engaged in building up the guerrilla campaign for almost ten years. No less remarkable was the presence of Vorster and Kaunda; they, too, were meeting each other face to face for the first time. But their role was that of umpire rather than as active participants in the negotiations. After formally addressing the two Rhodesian sides, Vorster and Kaunda, with their delegations, withdrew to another coach to talk among themselves. But no sooner had they left than the two Rhodesian sides found themselves engaged in a discussion over the stubborn core of their disagreements: majority rule.

The Bishop announced: 'We publicly state that the only genuine settlement for the majority of the people of our country is the one that shall be based on the transfer of power from the minority to the majority people of the country, that is to say, majority rule now. Therefore our genuine desire is to negotiate to produce a settlement of this nature.' Smith replied that the condition was 'utterly unacceptable to us,' and called it a flagrant violation of the Pretoria Agreement which had precluded conditions being set. The morning session was adjourned well before lunch to allow the 'non-interfering' South Africans and Zambians to try and resolve the disagreement. The ANC returned after lunch without changing its earlier stand. After another break for more consultations, the ANC returned with what Smith described as their 'bombshell': a set of proposals for continuing with the talks. The document read:

(1) The Prime Minister and other Cabinet Ministers of the Rhodesian Government and the President and other representatives of the ANC met at Victoria Falls on 25 August 1975.

(2) Both parties took this opportunity of expressing their genuine desire to negotiate a constitutional settlement.

(3) Both parties publicly expressed their commitment to work out immediately a constitutional settlement which will be acceptable to all the people of our country.

(4) In pursuance of this objective, the secretary to the Cabinet and the secretary-general of the ANC were instructed to arrange, within seven days, a plenary meeting in Salisbury of nominated representatives chosen respectively by the Government of Rhodesia and the ANC. At this meeting detailed discussions of all aspects of the constitutional issue will commence and, where appropriate, sub-committees will be established to consider and report to the plenary meeting on particular aspects.

(5) The ANC representatives presently in exile shall have the following immunities:

Immunity from enforcement in any way or degree in whole or in part of an existing sentence, order or direction.

Immunity from arrest, prosecution, detention or restriction or any other process whatsoever for any act or omission in or outside Rhodesia before commencement of the next meeting or conference.

Any person nominated by the ANC to attend in any capacity whatsoever any meetings in Rhodesia in connection with the conference or any committee or sub-committee thereof shall have full diplomatic immunity as though they were a diplomatic agent, including, without prejudice, to the generality of such immunity, full right of entry to and exit from Rhodesia without travel documents and full freedom of movement in Rhodesia, but so that the Government of Rhodesia shall not declare such person to be a *non persona grata* except after consultation with the Governments of the Republic of SA and Zambia.

Subject to the confidentiality of the discussions as agreed below every such person referred to in Clause 3 above shall have freedom of expression at all meetings, formal or informal, concerning the business of the conference and any committees or sub-committees, including freedom from observation, harassment or recording.

(6) Because of the urgent need to end the present uncertainty it was agreed that every effort should be made to expedite the proceedings. Accordingly, 31 October 1975 was set as the target date for completion of this stage.

(7) When agreement has been reached on the form and content of the constitutional settlement, a final constitutional conference will be arranged at a mutually-agreed venue, which shall be outside Rhodesia. The purpose of this conference will be to ratify formally the terms of the constitutional document giving effect to the agreement reached.

(8) All those present agreed on the importance of preserving the confidentiality of the constitutional discussions and undertook not to reveal any details to the Press and other media.

Signed:

···

The ANC President.
As witness:

···

The Government of the Republic of Zambia.
Signed:

···

The Rhodesian Prime Minister.
As witness.

···

The Government of the Republic of South Africa.

The Victoria Falls conference marked the highest point of optimism reached in the diplomacy to bring peace to southern Africa. Although the efforts were to continue for another six months, they never again looked so promising. Three major factors produced the disastrous failure of this promising enterprise. The most important of these was the inability of Ian Smith and his supporters to be able to change, or adjust, their traditional attitudes which are based on fears about the future risks to their way of life; on prejudice against the qualities of the Black majority; and on a wholly unrealistic assessment of their economic and military power to resist the combination of forces ranged against themselves. The more threatened the White Rhodesian minority felt itself, the more frightened support it gave to an intransigent Smith. The second serious factor was the bitter rivalries in the ranks of the Black nationalist leadership at that critical moment. Their unbridgeable differences made it easier for Smith to refuse to negotiate meaningfully by exploiting the rivalries between the ANC factions. An even more serious consequence of these divisions was that it prevented Vorster from leaning as hard as he otherwise might have done on Smith to give way. Vorster could only have risked putting maximum pressure on Salisbury if he could clearly see a stable alternative emerging to the regime he was extinguishing; from his point of view it was unthinkable that the result of his role in Rhodesia should be a situation of violent disorder as the Black rivals fought for power over the political corpse of White Rhodesia. The third major factor for failure was the timebomb of Angola ticking away towards the civil war and international involvement that was to explode after the Portuguese withdrawal on 11 November.[37] Another factor contributing towards the failure was the unwillingness of the major Western nations, especially Britain and the US, to play a more effective role in support of the Lusaka initiative. Although both London and Washington were strongly behind the moves towards getting a peaceful settlement in Rhodesia, the operative word is 'behind'. They were ready to encourage Vorster to lean harder on Smith, but without themselves doing anything more than maintain sanctions—and even on sanctions the US Presidency was too feeble to get Congress to reverse its decision to allow the import of Rhodesian chrome.

So far from the Victoria Falls conference bridging the gulf between White and Black Rhodesians, it achieved precisely the opposite result. The ANC divisions grew, making it not only difficult but increasingly impossible to restitch its unity; not only did Nkomo decide to make an open bid for the leadership by manipulating his position as the last remaining veteran nationalist politician in Rhodesia,[38] but a dissident section of Sithole's Zanu, led by Robert Mugabe, adopted an openly hostile attitude to Zambia and against the entire initiative of seeking peaceful change in Rhodesia. With a large section of the ANC no longer prepared to consider talks with Smith, and with another large section actively engaged in such talks, the outlook for

13

a negotiated settlement began to look decidedly unpromising. The Lusaka quartet of Presidents no longer found it easy either to pursue their efforts to unify the ANC, or even to assert a positive influence over the quarrelling leadership. A summit meeting of the quartet scheduled for early September was put off indefinitely because they recognized the moment was not propitious for another attempt to unify the ANC.

The feeling was beginning to grow that the old leaders were too hopelessly divided to expect them ever to come together again, and that the future lay in producing a new unified leadership from among the thousands of young Black Rhodesian recruits who had begun to stream into Mozambique, where they were transferred to three new military camps organized largely by the maverick Robert Mugabe. Kaunda however, still continued to hope that Nkomo might yet be able to produce a miracle—provided Vorster intensified his pressures against Smith. Although Nyerere and Machel did nothing to discourage Nkomo's final bid, they were no longer disposed to think that anything could be expected from the talks. However, none of the African Presidents was inclined to blame Vorster for the impasse. Speaking at Manzini (Swaziland) on 31 August, Tanzania's Foreign Minister, John Malecela, confirmed the African impression that the 'SA Prime Minister was serious when he said he wanted a peaceful solution in Rhodesia.'[39] He said it was in the long-term interest of Southern Africa that the Rhodesian issue should be peacefully settled, but failure to move Smith would leave no alternative to armed violence—and the ability of the Zimbabweans to fight 'was growing day by day at a rate faster than anticipated by Black Africa's enemies.' In a joint statement a week later[40] Presidents Nyerere and Machel commented that despite Vorster's 'much vaunted detente policy, the Africans in SA continue to suffer the indignities of racial discrimination and to be denied all opportunities for human development and fulfilment'. Reaffirming their total support for the liberation movements, they warned that 'if the objectives and aspirations of the people cannot be achieved by peaceful means, then the people will carry out the clauses of the Dar es Salaam manifesto on Southern Africa'.

Smith's first encounter with his Black challengers had served only to strengthen his intransigence and his determination to resist Vorster's pressures by encouraging the emergence of a pro-white Rhodesian backlash inside SA. By early September, with the arrival of the first White Angolan refugees in Rhodesia and a growing exodus into Namibia, Smith's hopes for a reversal of SA policy began to rise. Smith encouraged Vorster's opponents to draw comparisons between the rivalries in the Angolan movements with what was happening in Rhodesia. Although the Transvaal National Party Congress at the end of August showed Vorster still in a dominant position within his party, the feeling among the rank-and-file delegates reflected 'a vague uneasiness about the whole detente operation and about the ultra-conservative allegation that SA was "selling Rhodesia down the river" . . . Nationalists recognize that the situation is not an easy one and that their supporters must be delicately handled.'[41] Smith began to speak publicly about his troubled relations with Vorster. In an interview with the SA Broadcasting Corporation on 2 September, Smith said relations between the two countries 'are under some strain'. He criticized the withdrawal of SA troops as 'a wrong decision'.

The ironic situation existing at the beginning of September was that *everybody* was for a peaceful settlement—except for the majority of White and a minority of Black Rhodesians. Nkomo was the last slender straw in the hands of the Lusaka-Pretoria strategists—and they grasped it as firmly as they could.

The Ivory Coast's Information Minister, Laurent Dona Fologo, finally arrived in SA on 10 September, accompanied by his White wife for whom the apartheid laws had to be waived. Repeating that his country had chosen the path of 'dialogue and negotiation against war and violence', he added: 'Whether the real facts be saddening or pleasing, I must take home the most exact witness of life in SA.' Asked about the possibility of diplomatic relations being established between SA and the Ivory Coast he said: 'It is still too soon to say, but everything is possible if we can achieve peace.' Nor did he shirk from making a strong attack against apartheid at an official lunch, saying that 'at least one poison on this African land' was 'South African racism'. He called for a multi-racial society to be set up in SA to make it a place where 'a man can be a man, which is to say, not just able to walk, eat and drink, but also to vote'. Fologo's visit was supported by Liberia's Ambassador-at-large, Adolphus Tolbert, who said his country favoured detente notwithstanding the decision of the OAU.[42] However, there were also strongly critical voices raised against the path chosen by Ivory Coast and Liberia; apart from Guinea's characteristic line (Fologo's visit was 'spectacular and eloquent proof of President Houphouet-Boigny's collusion with the hangmen of Pretoria') there were other sharp warnings from the Congo and Kenya—as well as from the SA exile movements.

These African fears were that, behind the shield provided by the Lusaka talks with Pretoria and authorized by the OAU, some African States (who have long favoured a policy of dialogue)[43] would undertake their own separate initiatives to improve economic and diplomatic relations with SA in ways that bear no relationship to the OAU's Southern African Strategy policy. The critics of the independent role of the Ivory Coast and Liberia (and these included the Lusaka quartet) believe SA is engaged in pursuing two concurrent policies—the peace initiative through Lusaka and an initiative to resurrect the old policy of dialogue which could divide the OAU between the few States favouring rapprochement with SA from the majority who stand for the Republic's diplomatic and economic isolation. That these fears were not without foundation emerged quite clearly from an address given by SA's Foreign Minister, Dr Muller, to the Foreign Affairs Club in London on 22 September 1975: 'Bilateral contacts are contrary to the Lusaka Manifesto, which seeks to bind all African States to contact with South Africa within the OAU framework. But SA has been having contacts on an increasing scale with African countries . . . The militants in the OAU have feared a wide breach in African solidarity, and a new Declaration to salvage and reaffirm the unity of the OAU was deemed necessary at Dar es Salaam. This activity on our part does not represent a new policy departure. We have for years advocated a policy of contact and dialogue, but only a few leaders of African States have felt able to respond publicly. We are grateful to President Banda of Malawi and President Houphouet-Boigny of the Ivory Coast for having very early seen the dangers for Africa of a policy of confrontation with SA and for having the courage, in the face of pressure from OAU militants, to express publicly and consistently their belief in contact and evolutionary change. There are now many signs that others are prepared to follow their example.' Although SA attaches great importance to getting a peaceful settlement in Rhodesia and Namibia, its Prime Minister believes that even if that effort should fail, it would not necessarily be the end of the road towards detente—provided he will have demonstrated his sincerity in his dealings over Rhodesia.

The basis of SA's confidence in its ability to win over the support of what Dr Muller described as 'like-minded moderate States', was outlined in his London speech: 'I have on several occasions in the past said that SA's foreign relations and our internal policies are inter-related. Normalization of our relations with Black Africa will come more easily as our internal policies evolve and as we move away from discriminatory practices which are based on deep-rooted, inherited attitudes . . . The Government is committed to move away from the discrimination based on race or colour. It is encouraging the abolition of unnecessary discriminatory practices in public places, and by its own example as an employer is working towards the elimination of wage discrimination. The implementation of these measures should do much to reduce the kind of incident which attracts so much publicity overseas and is held out in Africa as the typical symbol of South African society. The development of our various Homelands through self-government to independence is proceeding, and the approaching independence of the Transkei is a clear indication to Africa and the world of our good faith, consistency and the seriousness of our purpose. This is a process which started nearly twenty years ago, and over the years we have had to endure a great deal of criticism to the effect that we would not take the policy to its conclusion of full independence for the African Homelands. Now the Transkei will soon prove these critics wrong . . . With the unfolding of our internal policies along the lines I have sketched, I feel that the prospects of reaching a positive *modus vivendi* with Africa will improve. The policies in essence ensure the protection of minorities and this should evoke understanding in Africa. To the Black African States the question of one-man-one-vote should not be such a burning issue as discriminatory measures which degrade the Black man and impair his human dignity. After all, very few African States have a good record of franchise issues and it is commonly recognized that there are more ways than one of ensuring an orderly, democratic society.'

The end of September saw an astonishing shift away from the China People's Republic's earlier opposition to the Lusaka peace initiatives. Speaking at a banquet for a Zambian delegation in Peking, Vice-Premier Li Hsien-nien praised the virtues of 'dual tactics'—a phrase previously used to denounce those ready to parley with the 'SA racist regime'—and especially to flay the Russians who had earlier given their support to the Lusaka initiative. A Chinese specialist[44] commented that 'dual tactics' had won the nod from Peking on three counts: 'it is in the best *t'an-t'an-ta-ta'* (talk and fight) Chinese tradition— there must always be weapons to give weight to words; that any talking is more likely to widen the gap between Vorster and Smith, and thus render both more vulnerable; and that the Chinese are not going to 'drop a stone on their own foot' by quarrelling with their closest African friends'.

October brought grim forebodings of the likely denouement in the Angolan crisis; it also made more explicit the extent of the gulf that had opened up between the two erstwhile allies—Vorster and Smith. In an interview with London Weekend Television in mid-October, Smith commented: 'I'd go so far as to say that I believe that if this new initiative had not been taken by Mr Vorster, I believe we would have had a settlement by now : . .'[45] It was not clear to which 'new' initiative Smith was referring—whether to Vorster's role in bringing about the Victoria Falls Conference, or to his having started the detente exercise in the first place. He later claimed that he had in mind the latter; but whichever it was, his remark produced an angry reaction from SA. The Minister of Indian Affairs, Marais Steyn, was set up to speak in the Prime Minister's own constituency to roast Smith.[46] It was not until Smith had come to deliver a personal apology to Vorster in Cape Town that he was allowed off the hook of Vorster's injured anger. But by then detente was a rapidly fading dream: no meaningful progress had been made in the talks between Smith and Nkomo, and the fall-out from Angola was producing new tensions instead of relaxing them. A week after Angolan independence, on 18 November, the SA Broadcasting Corporation commented that all the promising developments for detente 'are taking a back seat today as the war in Angola, with its Great-Power rivalry and its danger of spilling over the borders, increases in intensity. The rupture is handicapping a Southern Africa which in other ways is showing significant signs of pulling itself together'.

When President Nyerere, on a State visit to Britain, spoke on *Some Aspects of Liberation* at a meeting at Oxford University on 19 November he was clear in his own mind about Rhodesia: 'We are forced back to the alternative strategy outlined in the

Lusaka Declaration of 1969—support for non-peaceful methods of struggle. Unfortunately, but inevitably, the armed struggle in Rhodesia will have to be resumed and intensified until conditions are ripe for realistic negotiation. And the Freedom Fighters of Rhodesia, like those of Mozambique, will demand Africa's support. We very much regret the need for war. It can only bring dreadful suffering to the people of Rhodesia—both Black and White. It will therefore leave a heritage of bitterness which will make the eventual development of a non-racial democratic society in that country very much more difficult. But we can no more refuse support to the Rhodesian Freedom Fighters now than Britain could have refused support to the Resistance Movements of Europe during the 1940s.'

From then on it was downhill all the way. SA's military intervention in Angola[47] did not occur without the quiet support, and even agreement of a number of African Governments, especially in Francophone Africa. But it was not its role in Angola that brought about the failure of Vorster's strategy: it was SA's tough military action against Swapo, and the wrecking of any prospect of an early settlement in Namibia on terms acceptable to the OAU—but, above all, it was caused by the heavy obduracy of Smith and his supporters. Although warned by Vorster and Kaunda, as well as by Western leaders, that Nkomo offered them their very last chance of avoiding violence, White Rhodesia was deaf and blind to these warnings. Smith's own four chiefs of security had warned him[48] that Rhodesia could not for long withstand a massive guerrilla attack without SA's military support; but Smith probably felt he could ignore this warning because he remained convinced that, when the chips were down, SA would be forced to send its troops back—that was his gamble. And so he continued to plod along in his talks with Nkomo as if there were not 12,000 Zimbabwe guerrillas being trained in Mozambique; as if there were no large shipments of Russian and Chinese arms pouring into Mozambique; as if SA, after its experience in Angola, was not even less inclined to become involved in Rhodesia than before; and as if the Western nations were never further from the temptation of rushing in to defend so indefensible a cause as that of White minority rule—a cause which even the White supremacist leaders of SA thought was not worth defending in Rhodesia. And so the men who made their rebellion in 1965 to delay Black majority rule in their own lifetimes hastened its advent and, what was worse from their own point of view, opened the area to deep communist penetration.

Over the weekend of 7-8 February 1976, the quartet of Presidents were, once again, meeting together at Quelimane in Mozambique. They were unanimous: hope for peaceful change in Rhodesia was no longer possible; the time had come to give unqualified support to the guerrilla struggle. By that time, the political climate of Southern Africa had begun to cloud over as a result of the kind of international involvement that had brought military victory to the MPLA in Angola. The Russians were understandably elated with the success of their Angolan gamble; their allies, the Cubans, had sent the largest expeditionary force ever brought to black Africa; the Chinese—whose careful neutrality in the Angolan struggle had allowed their Moscow enemy to score a significant political victory—were in no mood to see this repeated in Rhodesia; and the post-Imperial West was floundering, not knowing which role was likely to be the least damaging to their interests.

As the last curtain was about to fall over the Lusaka-Pretoria initiative to find a peaceful solution of Southern Africa's problems, President Kaunda summed up his feelings and his fears:[49]

'Due to Smith's intransigence, Zambia has reached the end of the road regarding negotiations as an instrument of change. We have discharged our obligations under the OAU manifesto on Southern Africa. The Western countries have refused to extend a hand of friendship to us by responding positively in Rhodesia. The worst they have feared all along—the factor of Communism—must now inevitably be introduced in Zimbabwe because majority rule must now be decided on the battlefield'. He added that all those parties which had favoured negotiations had become irrelevant to the political process in Rhodesia 'as intensified armed struggle must now take hold.' In a warning to the US, Britain and other Europeans countries, he said: 'The Western countries should not blame anybody when the Angolan situation repeats itself in Zimbabwe, as the freedom fighters will turn to the Eastern bloc countries, the only ones willing and prepared to help them achieve their freedom.' Replying to questions about how a violent struggle in Rhodesia would affect relations between Mr Vorster and himself, President Kaunda said: 'Our contact with SA was based on the resolution of political problems in Rhodesia and Namibia on the basis of majority rule, and on the destruction of apartheid. It was never about economic co-operation. SA has not succeeded in her efforts to produce majority rule in Rhodesia. It must be understood that there can be no co-operation with racist regimes without a common political denominator—the full realization of human rights. 'Zambia, by her principled stand and behaviour, invested all her resources, at great expense, into peace programmes. But Zambia's efforts have not been reciprocated by support from those who have important interests in southern Africa. Therefore, the dreadful consequences, which we have tried to avoid in this area, must now come. Zambia should not be blamed. We have discharged our responsibilities to the international community.'

NOTES

1. All references to country surveys and essays in this chapter refer to *Africa Contemporary Record (ACR)*, 1975–76.
2. The document is headed: 'The Catholic Commission for Justice and Peace in Rhodesia'. Report by Robert Mugabe to the Justice and Peace Executive, Tuesday, 17 December 1974. A summary appeared in the *Rhodesia Herald*, 25 February 1975.
3. *The Times*, London, 15 May 1975.
4. *The Star*, Johannesburg, 1 March 1975.
5. *Ibid* 18 January 1975.
6. See *ACR* 1974-5, pp. A13.
7. *The Times*, London, 17 February 1975.
8. *The Star*, Johannesburg, 1 March 1975.
9. *The Times*, London, 19 February 1975.
10. *Ibid* 20 February 1975.
11. *Die Burger*, 27 February 1975.
12. Conakry radio, 22 February 1975.
13. *The Times*, London, 20 May 1975.
14. *Ibid* 21 May 1975.
15. *Rand Daily Mail*, 26 March 1975.
16. *South African Broadcasting Corporation* (SABC), Johannesburg, 16 April 1975.
17. *Ibid*.
18. *Ibid*.
19. *Africa*, No. 42, London, February 1975.
20. *The Star*, Johannesburg, 8 March 1975.
21. As reported in the *Rand Daily Mail*, 6 May 1975.
22. *Die Beeld*, Johannesburg, 13 March 1975
23. See chapter on Rhodesia.
24. See *ACR* 1974-5, p. A13.
25. Reported in *The Star*, Johannesburg, 1 March 1975.
26. See *Dialogue: The Great Debate*, *ACR* 1971-2, pp. A 66ff.
27. *The Star*, Johannesburg, 1 March 1975.
28. See essay on the OAU.
29. An extensive summary appears in the *ACR* Current Affairs paperback on Southern Africa: *The Secret Diplomacy of Detente*, Rex Collings.
30. SABC, Johannesburg, 13 April 1975.
31. Stanley Uys, *The Observer*, London, 13 April 1975.

32. *Fraternité Matin*, Abidjan, 14 April 1975.
33. *Financial Times*, London, 8 May 1975.
34. See *The Star*, Johannesburg, 7 June 1975.
35. See Documents Section, Political Issues, under Southern Africa.
36. *Financial Times*, London, 11 August 1975.
37. See essay on Foreign Intervention in Angola.
38. For details see chapter on Rhodesia.
39. *Rhodesia Herald*, 1 September 1975.
40. *Ibid* 9 September 1975.
41. John D'Oliveira, *Rhodesia Herald*, 1 September 1975.
42. *The Times*, London, 16 September 1975.
43. See *Dialogue: The Great Debate, ACR* 1971-2, pp. A66ff.
44. Dennis Bloodworth, *The Observer* Foreign News Service, 30 September 1975.
45. *Rhodesia Herald*, 16 October 1975.
46. *Ibid.*
47. See essay on *Foreign Intervention in Angola.*
48. My information comes from a confidential African source who had seen a copy of the report which was obtained by BOSS.
49. *The Observer*, February 1976. In the interview with Colin Legum he is referred to only as 'authoriative Zambian spokesman'.

1976-1977

THE YEAR OF THE WHIRLWIND

'The storm has not struck yet. We are only experiencing
the whirlwinds that go before it.'
—J. B. Vorster, Prime Minister of South Africa.
New Year's Day Speech, 1977

Africa in this decade is a testing ground of the world's conscience and vision. That blacks and whites live together in harmony and equality is a moral imperative of our time. Let us prove that these goals can be realized by human choice, that justice can command by the force of its rightness instead of by force of arms. These are ideals that bind all the races of mankind. They are the mandate of decency and progress and peace. This drama will be played out in our own lifetime. Our children will inherit either our success or our failure. The world watches with hope and we approach it with confidence. So let it be said that Black people and White people working together achieved on this continent—which has suffered so much and seen so much injustice—a new era of peace, well-being and human dignity.

Such were the visions and dreams of the great Afro-American educationist James Aggrey in the 1930s; of the Nobel prize winner Chief Albert Lutuli in the 1950s; and of the martyred Martin Luther King in the 1960s; but these words did not come from any of them: they were spoken by the US Secretary of State, Dr Henry Kissinger, in the Zambian capital, Lusaka, on 25 April 1976. He did rather more than paint dreams of the future; he committed America's influence, if not its power, 'to help achieve human equality in southern Africa' but without resorting to war. Kissinger's eloquence—and the momentous implications of this change in US policy—left his host, President Kenneth Kaunda, weeping openly. Less prone to public emotion, Tanzania's President, Julius Nyerere, quipped: 'Whenever I have thought about the future of South Africa I have always prayed to God and to Washington; now Washington has answered my prayers.'

Nobody supposed that Kissinger himself had undergone a Pauline conversion on the road to Lusaka producing the American commitment to the pursuit of majority rule in Rhodesia, Namibia and SA.[1] It was clearly necessary for Metternich's disciple to reverse his 1970 stand favouring the temporary expedient of helping maintain the political balance in southern Africa in favour of the white minority regimes. Obviously he needed to bring the US closer into step with the historical fact that that balance had shifted irreversibly with the collapse of Portuguese colonialism in April 1974.[2] That shift had taken place against the main thrust of Western policies; and Kissinger needed urgently to restore the West-East balance of influence in the area as it existed before the successful intervention of the Russians and Cubans in Angola in 1975.[3] Western policies in southern Africa were in shreds, and Kissinger was there to offer something new. African leaders were far less inclined to question Kissinger's motives than to evaluate the sincerity of his commitment. In the words of Tanzania's President, Julius Nyerere: 'I believe Dr Kissinger is right in saying, if you want to work for American interests—or Western interests in southern Africa—throw your weight on the side of those who are working for majority rule. If you don't and the war goes on, we have said, we can't give these people arms to fight; they will achieve their independence only through the support which they get from the Communist countries, and this is not in the interests of the Western Powers. So I suppose he is right in doing this, but I am saying, so what? I want his pressure. I want American pressure. I want American pressure on the side of majority rule. And I have no intention of quarrelling with the Americans. What I'm interested in is majority rule in southern Africa.'[4]

Kissinger had made his debut on the African stage just a month after the African Front-line Presidents (FLPs)—Julius Nyerere of Tanzania, Kenneth Kaunda of Zambia, Samora Machel of Mozambique and Sir Seretse Khama of Botswana—had apparently given up all hope of a peaceful settlement in Rhodesia, and so committed themselves in public to support for total armed struggle. They had reached their decision only with deep misgivings. So when Kissinger suddenly appeared in his new role, they were willing to receive him—not as a diplomatic wizard, but as a possible *deus ex machina* who, even at this late an hour, might just succeed in helping either to prevent a disastrous war, or at least to limit its scope by discouraging international involvement in the struggle over Rhodesia and Namibia.

Whatever their reservations, the African leaders' policy (as exemplified by that of the FLPs) was a dual one. First, they aimed to end minority rule in Rhodesia and Namibia and subsequently also in SA, and to do it quickly; and if at all possible to achieve the transfer of power with a minimum of violence and economic dislocation, thus avoiding revolution. Second, they were committed to support an armed struggle in the last resort if peaceful methods should prove unavailing; and, even if it came to war, they hoped to resist external military involvement of any kind on African soil. However, this latter objective was modified in one major respect during the Angolan struggles: a majority of African States adopted the position that SA military intervention in a neighbouring country justified an African Government inviting the help of a friendly superpower. This African concensus on the legitimacy of foreign military intervention is specially relevant to possible future developments in Rhodesia, Mozambique and Namibia.

Two parallel developments in southern Africa interacted strongly with each other throughout 1976 and the early part of 1977. One was the steady build-up for war—with the guerrillas emerging as a credible force, and the white minority regimes adding heavily to their defence capacity. The other was energetic diplomacy to avert the war. The African leaders most directly involved in the confrontation, the FLPs, backed both courses of action simultaneously. They wanted diplomacy to succeed, but they feared it would not; they worked for peace, but prepared for war, as many others have done. Their pessimism grew out of their doubts about the willingness of Western leaders to exert irresistible pressures on Smith's government which they believed was the only way of producing a negotiated settlement. These pressures it seemed could be applied quickly and effectively only through SA's commitment to them. But while the Prime Minister, John Vorster, favoured a peaceful settlement in Rhodesia, he seemed unwilling to apply the necessary pressures on the Smith regime. Therefore, the crucial question for the FLPs was whether the British and Americans could or would turn the screws on Vorster. There seemed little doubt that SA could break white Rhodesia's resistance by turning off their arms and fuel supplies. The question was how to induce them to do so. Again, in Nyerere's words: 'SA supports Smith. Without SA, Smith is not likely to last for very long. The Americans have the necessary power to say to the South Africans, "You are the supporters of Smith, stop supporting Smith or else".[5]

Nyerere and his presidential colleagues accept that 'you can believe Vorster—he's quite serious when he says that he wants this war to come to an end as quickly as possible . . . because if the war goes on very long, the government which takes over is going tò be a more radical government and is going to be more committed to continuing the revolution in southern Africa.'[6] But they also believe that Vorster's problems with his own White electorate would make him reluctant to do what was necessary unless forced to do so. Nothing that happened before Kissinger's shuttle had encouraged them to think that the Americans or British were prepared to act decisively, notwithstanding that it was as much a Western as an African interest to avoid a damaging war in southern Africa. There was just a chance, they felt, that if the guerrillas' challenge in Rhodesia were taken sufficiently seriously in London and Washington—and especially if it looked as though the Russians and Cubans might become involved as their principle allies—that this might become the necessary incentive for a tough Western response to force the collapse of the Smith regime. This, then, was another reason for committing themselves finally to the armed struggle in February 1976. Before taking this step the FLPs had done all that seemed possible to achieve the goal of majority rule in southern Africa by diplomatic methods. They had even accepted to work with 'the devil himself'—John Vorster—in negotiations begun in 1974 and pursued throughout 1975[7] in the hope of achieving two results: to get Smith to negotiate with the Zimbabwe leaders to achieve a peaceful settlement in Rhodesia; and to induce the SA Government to negotiate with the South West African People's Organization of Namibia (Swapo). But these negotiations had led nowhere; and after SA's military intervention in Angola it was no longer possible for the FLPs to keep up their direct contacts with Pretoria. A complete gulf had again opened up between White and Black Africa. That gulf, it seemed, might be bridged by Kissinger. Thus his intervention was unhesitatingly accepted when he signalled his readiness to become involved.

THE ROAD TO WAR: JANUARY-APRIL 1976

The sudden end to four centuries of Portuguese colonialism in Africa in April 1974 had opened a remarkable chapter in African history. It began with Vorster's immediate recognition that SA had to adjust to a new balance of power in the sub-continent. It continued with the ready response of the African Front-line Presidents to accept his offer to talk about peaceful ways of settling the crises in Rhodesia and Namibia, as a prelude to tackling the infinitely more difficult problem of apartheid itself.[8] The high point of this initiative to achieve peaceful change was the meeting at the Victoria Falls in August 1975 between the Smith regime and his Black challengers, with Vorster and Kaunda in close attendance.[9] But their attempt to get White and Black Rhodesian leaders to meet around the conference table failed; by the beginning of 1976 only one nationalist leader, Joshua Nkomo, was still trying to negotiate. Most of the other Black Rhodesian leaders were in exile, either voluntarily or to avoid arrest, where they were keeping up a pretence of unity under the umbrella of the African National Council (ANC).[10] Its top leaders at that time, Bishop Muzorewa and Ndabaningi Sithole, were in fact united only in their criticism of Nkomo's attempts to arrange a 'deal' with Smith. Sithole's own position as the leader of the Zimbabwe African National Union (Zanu) was under strong challenge from Robert Mugabe, who had led a move to depose him while they were still in prison together in Salisbury. Mugabe had from the first refused to co-operate with the ANC, or to have anything to do with the FLPs' moves for a peaceful settlement. He believed only in the armed struggle, and he devoted himself to organizing the 20,000 or more young Black Rhodesians who had crossed into Mozambique after the Frelimo Government achieved its independence in July 1975. This spontaneous exodus was to become a crucial turning-point in the Rhodesian struggle. It brought an infusion of new blood into the guerrillas' ranks with demands for younger leaders in place of the old politicians. Only Mugabe found general acceptance among the Zanu cadres. Nkomo, by continuing to negotiate with Smith, was taking considerable risks to outmanoeuvre his rivals for power; but he did not share Kaunda's view that he would become 'irrelevant' if the negotiations ended up in failure.He was too shrewd a politician to leave himself without a strong fall-back position, and he lost no opportunity to make it clear that his stand was 'negotiate or fight'. At that time, Zapu had few battalions of its own in the guerrilla camps—perhaps 800 to 1,000; but still enough to give Nkomo a place in the guerrilla struggle.

Positions within the Black Rhodesians' camp at the beginning of 1976 can be summed up as follows. The ANC had lost most of its coalition character; Bishop Muzorewa was no longer accepted as the unifying chairman, but could still rely on the support of some of Nkomo's former lieutenants, like James Robert Chikerema and George Nyandoro, and on a popular base at home. Ndabaningi Sithole had resuscitated Zanu in exile and while strongly championing the armed struggle, was rapidly losing ground to Mugabe who was quietly beavering away in the Mozambique bush. All these rival elements were suspicious of, and hostile to, Nkomo's continuing efforts to negotiate with Smith. Nkomo ran the risk of isolating himself from the external movement, but not from the FLPs; Kaunda, in particular, encouraged him to persevere for so long as there was any hope of an agreement.

All these old and new divisions in the Zimbabwean ranks seriously weakened, and even discredited, the Black nationalist position. They also weakened the FLPs' attempts to apply pressures on Britain and SA to play a more vigorous role in Rhodesia.

By February 1976, it was clear that the last black pawn in play was held in checkmate by white knight. Nkomo was preparing to change his strategy; he was beginning to sound just like the other Black militants fully committed to the armed struggle. But Nkomo was alone in expressing his views inside Rhodesia. Smith, the grandmaster of defence, had once again succeeded in scuppering the talks into which he had reluctantly been forced by Vorster. Having previously passed up two opportunities for settlement with the British, he was still relying on the strategy that had served him so well in the past: buying time with which to wear down his opposition, and living on the hope that at the end of the day, SA and the US would be driven by their own interests to back him. But in the meantime African patience had begun to run out. The FLPs, at a crucial meeting in Quelimane (Mozambique) from 7-8 February, unanimously decided that nothing more could be expected from their current efforts to achieve change by peaceful methods; they now declared their unqualified support for an armed struggle. To mark this change in their policy they also decided to withdraw their support from all the Zimbabwean political leaders and parties, and to give their backing to the Joint Military Command formed three months earlier in the camps which had been set up to weld the guerrillas into the Zimbabwe Independent People's Army (Zipa).

Kaunda and Nyerere met at Mbale, southern Tanzania, on 21 February to try and reconcile their differences over Angola, and also to discuss how to get Britain and the US to appreciate how serious the position had become in Rhodesia with the impending collapse of the Smith-Nkomo negotiations and with the FLPs' decision to support the militants. Kaunda sent his envoy, Mark Chona[11] to London, Bonn and Washington to impress on the leaders there the full import of the Quelimane decision. At the same time he published a warning intended to achieve two purposes:[12] he wanted the Western community to understand the reasons for the African stand in opting for the armed struggle; and he still hoped to induce Britain and the US to recognize how close the sub-continent was to war, which could only be averted by immediate Western leverage on Smith and Vorster. Kaunda's published warning marked a new phase. He said: 'The Western countries should not blame anybody when the Angolan situation repeats itself in Zimbabwe, as the freedom fighters will turn to the Eastern bloc countries, the only ones willing and prepared to help them achieve their freedom . . . Due to Smith's intransigence, Zambia has reached the end of the road regarding negotiations as an instrument of change. We have discharged our obligations under the OAU manifesto on southern Africa. The Western countries have refused to extend a hand of friendship to us by responding positively in Rhodesia. The worst they have feared all along—the factor of Communism—must now inevitably be introduced in Zimbabwe because majority rule must now be decided on the battlefield.'

Replying to questions about how a violent struggle in Rhodesia would affect relations with SA, Kaunda replied: 'Our contact with SA was based on the resolution of political problems in Rhodesia and Namibia on the basis of majority rule and on the destruction of apartheid. It was never about economic co-operation. SA has not succeeded in her efforts to produce majority rule in Rhodesia. It must be understood that there can be no co-operation with the racist regimes without a common political denominator—the full realization of human rights. Zambia, by her principled stand and behaviour, invested all her resources at great expense, into peace programmes. But Zambia's efforts have not been reciprocated by support from those who have important interests in southern Africa. Therefore, the dreadful consequences which we have tried to avoid in this area must now come. Zambia should not be blamed. We have discharged our responsibilities to the international community.'

The FLPs' Quelimane decision left the British Government troubled but without any ideas about what effective policy to pursue on Rhodesia. It behaved like the captain in charge of a ship whose engines have been stopped by mutineers in heavy seas, and with the prospect of worse storms to come: it could issue urgent warnings about the dangers ahead, but seemed powerless to act. A few days after the Quelimane warning, the then Foreign and Commonwealth Office (FCO) Minister of State for African Affairs, David Ennals, disclaimed any British intention of going to the rescue of White Rhodesians: 'It should not be thought that, somehow or other, we would be committed to rescuing our kith and kin, who have shown such extraordinary neglect of responsibilities in Rhodesia.' This speech outraged many in the Tory Opposition; but on 19 February, Ennals affirmed that he was not just expressing his own views but also those of the then Foreign Secretary, James Callaghan. He then set out current official thinking about Rhodesia: 'The prospect of armed conflict . . . in what seems bound to be an escalating spiral of violence and bloodshed' had achieved a new dimension after Angola. 'It must surely be in the mind of Mr Smith and his colleagues that if the talks were to end and the battle begin in earnest, there could be no guarantee that there would not be significant and dangerous intervention from outside forces . . .'[13]

Britain made two diplomatic moves at the end of February to try and avert the collapse of the Smith-Nkomo talks. The first was to get the European Economic Community to declare itself on the issues of southern Africa: it affirmed 'the right of the Rhodesian and Namibian peoples to self-determination and independence;'

24

and condemned 'the apartheid policy of SA and all external military intervention in Angola or surrounding African countries'.[14] The second step was to send Lord Greenhill, a former head of the FCO, on a fact-finding mission to Salisbury. Greenhill warned White Rhodesians that their only hope lay in negotiating seriously about majority rule; the alternative would be war and, if it came, there could be no hope of any Western nations intervening on their side—even in the event of a Communist-backed invasion of Rhodesia.[15] Speaking for the Smith regime, the Cabinet Secretary Jack Gaylard replied that 'the only guarantee of future stability, prosperity and harmony in Rhodesia is to retain the reins of government in responsible hands. This does not imply there will be no changes, but it does mean that any request for an immediate handover to Black rule is out of the question.'[16]

The ANC leaders in exile—still suspicious that Britain was engaged in a secret deal with Smith and Nkomo—denounced the Greenhill mission in a statement which rejected any further British role in Rhodesia. Their spokesman, James Chikerema, said: 'We have already declared war. We will not accept any settlement between Smith, Nkomo and the British Government.' Callaghan announced the failure of the Greenhill mission in Parliament on 2 March. The time had come, he said, for White Rhodesians to accept the 'inevitability of an early transfer of power to the black majority. Until they do, and until they recognize that this will come, either by negotiation or through guerrilla activity, I do not think we shall be able to proceed to further calculations about the future of Rhodesia.'

On the next day, 3 March, Mozambique closed its borders with Rhodesia. While this tightened the sanctions cordon, it also brought new problems for the Frelimo Government at a time when its own economic circumstances were little short of disastrous, and its capacity to defend its own borders completely inadequate.[17] This bold but risky step had previously been decided on by the FLPs at their meeting in Quelimane. The FLPs' thinking at that time was expressed by Nyerere in an interview with David Martin in early March[18] in which he repeatedly stressed 'the very real danger' of Britain trying to by-pass 'the Third Force'. 'I want the British to do two things,' he said. 'In the first place to do nothing in Rhodesia. And second, to support Mozambique in applying economic sanctions against Rhodesia.' He added that Britain had trusted the FLPs when they had gone to 'almost ridiculous lengths to give the talks a chance; now Britain should trust them with the second alternative (armed struggle). We are not enemies of Britain. We are building the pressure which will deliver Smith to London.' There was, he thought, 'a lot of hysteria in the West about Cuba in relation to Rhodesia'.

Precisely this anxiety was uppermost in Washington's thinking about Africa as it was in the ranks of the British Tories. In a parliamentary debate on 10 March, the Shadow Foreign Secretary, Reginald Maudling, put the blame on the Mozambique Government for 'conniving, if not fomenting, terrorism and bloodshed across the border of Rhodesia'. The Conservatives therefore opposed the British government's proposal to join with the UN in offering aid to Mozambique in compensation for the closing of its border.

The talks between Smith and Nkomo finally collapsed on 19 March. 'We have come to the end of the road,' Nkomo announced. Kaunda added: 'Africa must now help to intensify the armed struggle which is now in full swing'. And Smith, in a typically ambiguous statement, called on Britain to be prepared to 'resume its responsibilities for Rhodesia,' adding that he would be ready to consider a return to legality 'if I am satisfied, and it could be shown that this or any other decision is necessary in the interests of Rhodesia'. On 22 March, Callaghan set out Britain's terms for a settlement of the crisis.[19] He proposed two stages to independence. The first stage required acceptance of majority rule and elections within 18 to 24 months. The second stage would allow for negotiations about the independence constitution itself. There was to be no independence before majority rule. Thus the British Government firmly committed itself to the long-debated demand for a declaration on NIBMAR (No Independence Before Majority Rule) which, when it was first invented by Nyerere in 1966, almost blew the Commonwealth apart. Now, in 1976, with the war clouds rolling up over the Rhodesian veld and bush, Callaghan's reference to NIBMAR passed unnoticed. Once again, Callaghan's 22 March proposals had shown Britain as the captain of a mutinous ship—able to set a course, but with not the slightest idea of how to get the mutiny under control and so to get the ship moving along it. Nevertheless, Callaghan's speech was to have important, if at that time still unforeseen, results. It provided Kissinger with the clue he had been seeking to carry his personal diplomacy to Africa: the 22 March proposals were to become the basis for his Anglo-American initiative. But while he was planning that initiative, the dangers were continuing to mount. Callaghan sent Ennals to explain his proposals to the FLPs at the end of March. On his return to London at the beginning of April Ennals said that the African leaders saw no altern-ative but 'to fight to the finish'.[20] His conclusion was that unless White Rhodesians were willing to accept conditions for a peaceful settlement 'it seemed that a racial war could not be avoided, and although it might drag on for a long time there could be no doubt about its outcome'. The Foreign Office backed up this warning in replies to questions from the editor of the *Sunday Mail* (Salisbury) on 11 April. White Rhodesians were told that if Smith wanted to satisfy the British Government he would have to agree to 'a rapid and orderly transfer of power'; it was no longer enough just to accept the principle of majority rule. This amplification of Callaghan's 22 March proposals showed a new toughness in British thinking. Rhodesians were bluntly warned that the only alternative to a 'peaceful transition to majority rule in the very near future is an all-out war which the White Rhodesians cannot win'. However, the British Government continued to stand firmly by its original position taken at the time of UDI: it would not send troops to Rhodesia for any purpose. Kaunda had again called for British military intervention on 29 March to arrest Smith's rebels and to install a British-led executive committee composed of an equal number of Whites and Blacks to run the country for a year before holding free elections. On 31 March, Ennals told the House of Commons: 'Our position is absolutely clear. We were not prepared in 1965 to intervene militarily at the time of UDI and we would be no more prepared to intervene militarily today, either to take action supporting the minority against the majority or, as President Kaunda suggested, to arrest those now holding power.'

THE RINGMASTERS: THE ROLE OF THE FRONT-LINE PRESIDENTS
The four Front-line Presidents, joined by Angola's President, Agostinho Neto, in September 1976, have come to play a remarkable role in the continent's affairs, acting as a closely-knit caucus within the Organization of African Unity (OAU).[21] Although there is no formal approval for this role, the OAU has in fact endorsed all their major decisions to date. The original quartet emerged as a purely *ad hoc* group of like-minded leaders in response to Vorster's overtures in October 1974.[22] President Julius Nyerere of Tanzania and President Kenneth Kaunda of Zambia have for long been close friends and neighbours, who were linked in what was once known as the Mulungushi club. (Its third member was Milton Obote, President of Uganda until his overthrow in 1971. President Mobutu of Zaire, admitted in 1973, dropped out in 1975.) Nyerere and Kaunda are both on close terms with President Sir Seretse Khama of Botswana, who sees them as his principle allies in an effort to lessen his dependence on SA. Nyerere was especially close to President Samora

Machel of Mozambique, a friendship which grew out of Tanzania's long and courageous role in serving as the base country for Frelimo's struggle. However, there is a basic difference of outlook between them: Machel is primarily concerned that the independence struggle should itself help shape the revolutionary character of the emergent State; while Nyerere's concern during the independence struggle is simply to produce a representative Black majority. A political and economic philosophy will be moulded according to the people's will after independence.

Nyerere's role as chairman of the FLPs was crucial, for although there were no fundamental differences within the group, there were times (as over Angola) when Kaunda and Machel were at odds. Machel is himself under constant pressures from his passionately revolutionary Marxist colleagues to abandon diplomacy, refuse to have any dealings with the 'Western Imperialists' and concentrate exclusively on the 'correctness of the armed struggle'. Only Nyerere had the trust of all the Frelimo leaders needed for the cooler diplomacy of negotiating with Kissinger and Vorster. Kissinger was anathema to the revolutionaries of Maputo—committed allies of MPLA—so it was no easy matter for Nyerere to persuade them to accept the Secretary of State's initial approaches to the FLPs. Nyerere's credentials as a champion of the liberation movements in southern Africa also give him the standing necessary to overcome criticisms about the FLPs 'usurping the functions of the OAU'. Such accusations were levelled over their decision to give exclusive recognition to the Patriotic Front and, even more sensitively, to adopt a strategy of priorities whereby the overthrow of apartheid in SA was to be dealt with only after Rhodesia and Namibia had been successfully tackled—a decision strongly challenged by the SA liberation movements. Nyerere justified this strategy to a critical audience of students at Ibadan University, Nigeria, on 17 November 1976, on these grounds: 'Compromise on the inessentials and a scale of priorities are unavoidable for African Governments and peoples. Our States and organizations have very limited resources; not every injustice or example of exploitation can be fought at once. Attempting to do so can be an invitation to disaster, and to the triumph of reaction.'

The frequent portrayal of Kaunda as a 'moderate' reluctantly being dragged along behind the militants is, as Nyerere has explained,[23] quite inaccurate. And, notwithstanding their different political attitudes, Machel regards Kaunda as 'a hero of the African liberation struggle'.[24] Without him, he said, Frelimo could not have succeeded. Kaunda was certainly reluctant about going to war; but then so were the others. Perhaps because he is by nature a moralist and a pacifist, he agonized more publicly than the others about his dilemma. It is also true that he dared to hope longer than his colleagues that peaceful negotiations might be possible after all; thus he encouraged Nkomo to go on negotiating long after the rest had given up. Moreover, Kaunda had been most closely involved with Vorster in the abortive negotiations of 1974–5, and had stood out to the end against endorsing the Russian-Cuban intervention in Angola. This made him especially vulnerable to accusations that he was engaged in making 'secret deals with the enemy'. These suspicions, voiced by some Swapo leaders and by the ANC of SA, were assiduously fed by the Russians. However, the truth is that Kaunda was fully in step with his colleagues on all the crucial issues touching on Rhodesia and Namibia.

Samora Machel's position was in some ways the most difficult of all. Throughout 1976 and early 1977 he was burdened with the problems of establishing the authority of his young government in a country overwhelmed by economic dislocation and by border and other security threats. Frelimo's leaders are personally divided over their commitment to a revolutionary ideology, as well as over the hard necessity of having to behave pragmatically in their relations with SA.

27

Machel is as divided inside himself as is his government over the contradictory demands of a revolutionary ideology and pragmatic realism, giving the impression that he might refuse to go along with the other FLPs. But whatever the revolutionary utterances of some of his lieutenants, Machel himself has proved a loyal colleague of the other Presidents.

Sir Seretse Khama is another of the misnamed 'moderates'. He surprised even his Presidential colleagues by the vigour of his support for policies likely to prove acutely embarrassing for Botswana's relations with SA—as over his support for armed struggle in both Rhodesia and Namibia. Despite Botswana's economic and military vulnerability, Khama never once dissented from any of the decisions taken by the FLPs. However, when the Front-line States began offering bases to the liberation movements, Botswana was specifically excluded. Otherwise, as Kaunda explained, 'it would be unfair. We want Botswana to consolidate because she is geographically in a very difficult position.'[25]

The latecomer, Angola's President Agostinho Neto, fitted least easily into the group when he joined in September 1976. Kaunda and Khama had both taken a strong stand against the MPLA's bid for power in 1975, and Zambia was among the last of the African States to recognize the MPLA government. But Nyerere and Machel had both supported Neto, and the Mozambique leader is one of the MPLA's closest allies; both believe in Marxist-Leninism. The FLPs needed Neto's close association if they were to play any effective role in Namibia. Neto, however, made no effort to disguise his disapproval of the FLPs' policy of co-operating with the 'imperialist' diplomatic initiative of Dr Kissinger (see below).

The FLPs' arena is southern Africa; their objective is to achieve majority rule, preferably through peaceful negotiations, but in the last resort by armed struggle. Their script is the Lusaka Manifesto of 1969 [26] written by Nyerere and Kaunda. Their authority as decision-makers has often been questioned, but never seriously challenged. Some countries in the area—like Lesotho, Kenya and Uganda —resented their exclusion from the charmed circle; but others with equal claims —like Malawi, Zaire and Swaziland—made no protest. The FLPs have had problems in handling their relations with other OAU members, particularly with regard to the liberation movements, and especially over the rivalries within Zimbabwe. Both the ANC and PAC of South Africa were also hostile to their dealings with Pretoria, particularly because FLP strategy leaves the issue of SA to be dealt with last. Some elements in Swapo's leadership, at their headquarters in Zambia, had their suspicions of a possible secret deal between Kaunda and Vorster as the price for settling Rhodesia; some even falsely suggested that Swapo's guerrillas had actually been denied active duty in 1976. The tensions within Swapo increased when Kaunda refused to give his exclusive backing to the MPLA which had become Swapo's closest ally after their former Angolan supporter, Unita, had accepted help from SA in 1975.

The ringmasters' most difficult act was to present the divided ranks of the Zimbabwean movement as a credible challenge to the Smith regime. They had impatiently tried to compel the leaders of Zanu, Zapu and Frolizi to unite under the chairmanship of Bishop Muzorewa in the ANC in December 1974—a facile unity which alienated Mugabe and offended Nkomo.[27] A year later they tried again. Withdrawing their support from all the rival politicians, they resolved to build up a 'Third Force'—the Joint Military Command of the Zimbabwe Independent People's Army (Zipa). Henceforth only the fighters were to be allowed to dictate the shape of the struggle. But when the scene was being set for negotiations in Geneva, the FLPs advised Britain to invite the groups led by Nkomo, the Bishop and Mugabe as well as the guerrilla leaders. Later they proposed that Sithole, too, should be asked to attend to avoid the impression that they were choosing the leaders for the Zimbabweans. During the first round of talks at Geneva in October, Muzorewa and Sithole both found themselves increasingly isolated by the Patriotic Front, an alliance of convenience newly-formed by the rivals, Nkomo and Mugabe. Muzorewa in particular lost out. Like the former French Prime Minister, Pierre Mendes-France in his political heyday, the Bishop could complain that everybody was against him 'except the people'. But whatever his popularity at home, he could not count on many guns in the camps—and at that late hour the struggle was seen to have shifted from the political arena to the battlefield. Muzorewa was understandably angry. One of his deputies, Dr G. L. Chavunduka, irresponsibly attacked Kaunda in public for 'plotting with Smith and the Western imperialists' to undermine him. The Bishop refused to apologize when asked by Lusaka to do so. Predictably he was disowned first by Kaunda and then by the other FLPs who, in November 1976, abandoned all attempts at neutrality and recognized the Patriotic Front as the political voice of the Third Force (Zipa). Thus the maverick Mugabe and the 'sell-out' Nkomo (the two men most offended by the FLP decision to recognize the ANC in 1974) emerged as the chosen leaders; Muzorena and Sithole, the beneficiaries of that original decision, were left out in the cold. The idea of coming down firmly on one side was Machel's. He had for long argued against allowing divisions within the struggle that could leave two armies fighting each other after independence, as had happened in Angola. What still remained uncertain was the degree to which Zipa itself was united in its support for the Patriotic Front. As late as January 1977, Mozambique's Foreign Minister, Joaquim Chissano, could only express 'hope' that the recognition of the Patriotic Front would strengthen 'unity within Zipa', because the 'lack of co-ordination at the political level had not inspired confidence in the fighters . . . We hope that the Patriotic Front will be recognized as the leaders of the armed struggle led by Zipa. This is a problem which will be discussed . . .'[28]

The FLPs did not always hold identical views about the different Zimbabwe leaders. Kaunda's preference was for Nkomo; he was alienated from Mugabe because of the latter's wild attacks on him. Machel had been the first to befriend Mugabe, at a time when he was completely alienated from Kaunda and Nyerere, because of his effectiveness in helping to organize the Zimbabwe refugees in Mozambique. Mugabe's single-minded commitment to the armed struggle had also won him many friends in Machel's circle. However, Machel came increasingly to support Nkomo, who was also favoured by Neto. Neither Nyerere nor Seretse Khama showed any particular preferences.

THE PERFORMERS: THE FIGHTERS AND POLITICIANS
The success of the FLPs in masterminding the political strategy against Rhodesia and Namibia depended entirely on the performance of Zimbabwe's politicians and fighters. In this they were badly let down. The political leadership's chronic disunity also inevitably hampered the effectiveness of the guerrilla struggle. The Zimbabwean leaders naturally blamed the FLPs for making their internecine quarrels worse; but, not surprisingly, the source of such attacks depended on who was in or out of favour with the Presidents at any particular time. These reversals of policy cannot be put down just to vacillation or lack of judgement; each change reflected shifts in the ranks of the Zimbabweans themselves. Mistakes were undoubtedly made: for example, Kaunda has admitted that in 1974 they had wrongly accepted Sithole's claims to the leadership of Zanu, regarding Mugabe as a usurper.

THE AFRICAN NATIONAL COUNCIL (ANC): THE RISE AND FALL AND RISE OF THE BISHOP

Abel Muzorewa, a 51 year-old Methodist Bishop, was confirmed as chairman of the ANC on 9 December 1974 in recognition of his position as a 'neutral' political figure and so best suited to head an umbrella organization intended to unite the three Zimbabwe nationalist factions. These were:

1. The Zimbabwe African People's Union (Zapu), formed in 1961, with Joshua Nkomo as its leader. The political leader of Zapu's military wing was Jason Moyo, assassinated in Lusaka in January 1977.

2. The Zimbabwe African National Union (Zanu) was formed in 1963 as a breakaway from Zapu. When its two principal leaders, Ndabaningi Sithole and Robert Mugabe, fell out while still in prison, two separate factions developed inside Zanu. Entirely different reasons led to a split in Zanu's military camp where violent rivalries developed between two Shona clans—the Nyika (or Manyika) and the Karanga.

3. The Front for the Liberation of Zimbabwe (Frolizi), formed initially by a group of young militants who had lost faith in both Zanu and Zapu, was subsequently taken over by two of Nkomo's exile leaders, Robert Chikerema (cousin to Mugabe) and George Nyandoro, who had broken with him.

The ANC had its origins in a remarkable movement which grew up rapidly in 1971-2 to fill the vacuum left when the Smith regime proscribed Zanu and Zapu after UDI. The trigger for this movement was the impending arrival of the Pearce Commission to test African opinion on the acceptability of proposals for independence negotiated between Salisbury and London.[29] Bishop Muzorewa, widely regarded at the time as the caretaker for Nkomo, emerged as its natural leader: his neutrality and political respectability guaranteed by his 'gaiters'. Until the ANC's recognition by the FLPs, the Bishop had shown no personal political ambition. Since Mugabe refused to have anything to do with the ANC and Nkomo remained aloof, the ANC-in-exile passed effectively into the hands of the Bishop, Sithole and Chikerema.

In 1975 and 1976 the Zimbabwe leaders had two constituencies—the cadres in the military camps in Tanzania and Zambia, and their electorate at home. Nkomo chose to work at home, leaving Jason Moyo to look after the Zapu camps. Mugabe concentrated all his efforts on the cadres in Mozambique. The Bishop elected to spend most of his time outside Rhodesia and Sithole, who faced prison if he returned, remained in exile.

Despite the FLPs' official endorsement, the ANC leadership failed to take control of the military camps. They blamed their failure on Tanzania and Mozambique for allegedly hindering their access to the camps. The truth is that they were not welcome there for reasons explained below. In fact, the ANC leaders made only two visits to the military camps in Tanzania in 1975, and none at all to those in Mozambique. However, in April they did go to Nachingwea, while it was still being evacuated by Frelimo forces to make way for a new Zimbabwe training camp.[30] In July, they were taken virtually under escort to an ANC camp near Iringa in Tanzania's central highlands. There they were bitterly criticized by the guerrillas for their continual feuding; allegations were also made that they had virtually abandoned the guerrillas in north-eastern Rhodesia, and had failed to organize supplies and equipment for the men in the camps. The ANC's fragile unity cracked in September 1975 when Sithole decided to form the Zimbabwe Liberation Council (ZLC) in an attempt to re-establish his control over Zanu against the increasingly successful challenge from Mugabe. By November 1975, when the FLPs withdrew their recognition from the political leaders, the Bishop had little visible support among the fighting cadres; two of his principal allies in exile were the two Frolizi leaders, Chikerema and Nyandoro. His political fortunes were at a low ebb when he finally decided—with the approach of the Geneva conference—to end his 15 months' self-exile on 3 October 1976. In Salisbury a crowd estimated at 100,000 welcomed 'the return of the messiah'. There could then be little doubt that he remained a popular figure in the home constituency. On the day before his return, Muzorewa had met Nkomo in Gaborone, the capital of Botswana; the general assumption was that they would form a political alliance. Nkomo certainly wanted an agreement with Muzorewa, but the Bishop was cool—possibly too many of his supporters were personally hostile to Nkomo; certainly they would not accept him as the leader in place of Muzorewa, and Nkomo was never disposed to playing second fiddle. But Mugabe chose Nkomo as his partner in the Patriotic Front, leaving the ANC without much military muscle. The Bishop led his own ANC team to the Geneva talks where his main tactical differences with the Patriotic Front led to the re-emergence of two hostile camps in the Zimbabwe liberation movement, but with the ANC having little support among the military leaders.

On his return home from Geneva on 11 December, Muzorewa was met by another massive turn-out of supporters chanting their distinctive catch-phrase 'Hea-vy'. But he suffered a slight setback when 12 leading supporters, including the Revd Canaan Banana and Nolan Makombe, switched their support to Mugabe. The worst blow came in November 1976 with the FLPs' decision to back only the Patriotic Front. The Bishop angrily accused the FLPs of trying to impose their own leadership on the Zimbabweans, and alleged a Zambian 'plot' to impose Nkomo as 'leader of Zimbabwe'; the Front-line States, he said, 'wittingly or unwittingly, were being used as a cover' with Mugabe 'a mere pawn'. He spoke scathingly of President Kaunda's 'unbeatable record of having backed losing horses'. Later, he even accused the FLPs of being in conspiracy with the 'imperialist powers' (including Britain) and the multi-national Lonrho to install Nkomo as Zimbabwe's first Prime Minister. He demanded a national referendum to allow Black Rhodesians to choose their own leaders. As a result of these extraordinary allegations, the Bishop was declared *persona non grata* in Zambia, Tanzania and Mozambique. In January 1977, the OAU Council of Ministers endorsed the FLPs' decision to recognize only the Patriotic Front, robbing Muzorewa of most of his external African support. He still commands considerable support at home—but how much that will be worth if the country's future is to be decided on the battlefield rather than at the polls remains a question mark for the future.

THE ZIMBABWE AFRICAN NATIONAL UNION (ZANU): (1) THE ECLIPSE OF SITHOLE

The loneliest figure at the Geneva conference was Ndabaningi Sithole. Yet, just two years earlier, when he was freed from a Rhodesian prison—where he was serving a six-year sentence for plotting to assassinate Ian Smith—he was widely regarded as *the* leader of Zimbabwe's militants. But his downfall had begun in prison where an important group of Zanu executive members, led by Mugabe, had resolved to depose him because of allegations that he was in secret communication with the Smith regime. Nevertheless his reputation stood so high at the time of his release that the FLPs rejected Mugabe's allegations without even troubling to investigate them. Sithole's misfortunes were not entirely of Mugabe's making. They stemmed mainly from the bloody internecine quarrels in the Zanu camps in 1973 and 1974 which had culminated in the assassination of Herbert Chitepo on 18 March 1975.[31] Sithole (whose father was a Ndau, a small Shona clan in the east, and his mother Ndebeli) gave his own detailed version of what had happened in an Open Letter dated 10 May 1976:[32] 'The main theme of my letter is that Zanu, as we had first formed it, became [so] constantly subjected to a process of tribalization or regionalization that it completely lost the national perspective, with the result that unprecedented kidnappings and killings within Zanu took place and culminated in the assassination of Zimbabwe's greatly esteemed and admired Herbert Chitepo, who was regarded as a man of great national stature by all Zimbabweans who knew him.' He proceeded to show how 'tribalism or regionalism' had become a consuming element in the affairs of DARE (a Shona word), to whom Zanu's Central Committee had delegated its power in c. 1967 to prosecute the armed struggle. At its full strength in April 1969, all of DARE's eight leaders came from three Shona clans: three were Manyika (Easterners), three Zezuru (North-easterners), and two Karanga (South-easterners). There were no Matabele or members from other tribes. By 1975—after a bloody fight in the Nhari military camp in December 1974—DARE's composition was five Karanga and one Manyika. The Zezuru had been eliminated altogether, and the Karanga were dominant. 'For all practical purposes DARE had become nearly tribalized or regionalized,' Sithole commented. 'It therefore had ceased to represent Zanu as we knew it and had come to represent, in effect, Zatu (Zimbabwe African Tribal Union) or Zaru (Zimbabwe African Regional Union).' He claims that the new Military High Command was formed in November 1975 without proper consultation with the ANC, and that it was 'a continuation of the new and foreign thesis that the gun commands the Party . . . National leadership through the barrel of the gun is anathema to the people of Zimbabwe.' The notions of tribalism or regionalism did not originate with the people at home but with those in exile. He warned: 'The problem which we now face as a new nation is essentially a tribal or regional one.'

Sithole's opponents in Zanu offer a different interpretation of the violence in their military ranks.[33] They claim that Zanu's structure allowed for the removal of leaders by the rank and file at their biennial elections; this process was facilitated by Chitepo's 'democratic style of leadership', and in September 1975 had produced a break between the old conservative Zanu leaders and the young radical commanders. It was at this time that Sithole announced the formation of the Zimbabwe Liberation Council (ZLC) which attempted to entrench the Zanu 'rebels' such as Mukono, Mutambenengwe, Masangomai, Parirewa and Santana. These reactionaries were unacceptable to the Zanu rank and file, and to all Zanla (Zimbabwe African National Liberation Army) commanders as they were held responsible for the attempted coup in November 1974 and for the massacre of 59 Zanla guerrillas. The breach was further widened by Sithole's refusal to protest against the Zambian shooting of 11 Zanla guerrillas in a Zambian 'concentration camp' at Mboroma on 11 September 1975. Once the clash between the conservatives and the young radical commanders had occurred, the latter decided to ignore Sithole's orders to rely on negotiations and to refrain from full-scale guerrilla war. The Zanla commanders immediately requested support from the Mozambique and Tanzania governments. By November 1975, they had gained this support and formed the 18-man Military High Command in collaboration with Zapu commanders: the Zimbabwe Independence People's Army (ZIPA).

Sithole's decision to form the ZLC isolated him not only from the ANC but also from the newly-formed High Command. On 6 October 1976[34] he insisted that whatever Mugabe or anybody else had said, 'I am the boss'. But it was a claim he has so far failed to justify. Dogged by ill-health and by his failure to rally the young cadres to his side, by 1977 Sithole appeared to be only a shadow of the once formidable nationalist leader.

THE ZIMBABWE AFRICAN NATIONAL UNION: (2) THE EMERGENCE OF ROBERT MUGABE

Robert Gabriel Mugabe (49) came into international prominence for the first time by his commanding presence at the Geneva conference. However he has in fact been a powerful force in Rhodesian politics since his return from Nkrumah's Ghana in 1960, where he had been a teacher and a keen student of the newly-emerging pattern of African politics. He immediately began to oppose Nkomo's leadership and assisted Sithole to set up Zanu as a rival to Zapu. But by the time he reached Geneva, his alliances were reversed. Mugabe's alliance with Nkomo is tactical. 'It is possible', he explained, 'to enter into an agreement with your political opponents to fight your enemy; but it is never possible to ally yourself with the enemy to fight your political opponents'.[35] The implication is clear: his alliance with Nkomo—his political opponent—is necessary to destroy Smith; but after the enemy's defeat he will feel free to engage in a further struggle for political power.

Mugabe is a survivor. He spent 10 years (1964–74) in Smith's prisons, passing three law exams and spending the rest of his time teaching young prisoners. On his release he refused to join the ANC or to accept any policy other than the supremacy of the armed struggle. He was defiantly rude to Kaunda and openly described him as an 'enemy' of the Zimbabwe struggle. His decision to take to the bush in Mozambique coincided with the mass exodus of volunteers and refugees across the border so that he found himself ideally situated to take the lead in organizing the new camps that had to be hastily built.

If Sithole's explanation of the tribal/regional conflicts within Zanu's military leadership is correct, it is odd that the Karanga-dominated command should have favoured Mugabe, a Zezuru clansman. Over-simplification of clan or tribal rivalries is clearly something to be avoided, more especially when one sees how many Zezuru are prominent in both ANC and Zapu councils, e.g. Chikerema in ANC (Frolizi); the Revd Henry Kachidza and two other members on the ANC Central Committee, and Willie Masuriwa in Zapu. (A breakdown of the ANC Central Committee in 1975 showed that it comprised five Nyikas, including the Bishop, no fewer than 10 Ndebele, three Zezuru, one Shangaan and one Karanga.)

The most likely explanation for Mugabe's support in the ranks of Zipa was that he, more than any of the other known political figures, accurately reflected the mood in the camps in 1975–6. As a militant intellectual with considerable political experience he was able to articulate the new spirit of the younger cadres with their strong desire to turn their backs on the past years of political quarrelling, unproductive negotiations and mass disillusion: for them, as for Mugabe, victory lay clearly and simply in the armed struggle.

Why, then, did Mugabe (with Zipa's support) go to Geneva? It was not because he thought the Geneva talks would succeed, but because they provided an important opportunity to stamp Zipa's (and his own) leadership on the independence movement. Moreover, on this occasion, Mugabe did not wish to antagonize the FLPs—and especially not Machel who was fully behind the Geneva initiative.

Mugabe insists that he is a socialist, not a Marxist: 'What I am saying is that we are socialist and we shall derive from the socialist systems of Tanzania and Mozambique. One cannot get rid of all the aspects of free enterprise. Even Russia and China have their *petits bourgeois,* but in Zimbabwe none of the White exploiters will be allowed to keep an acre of their land. We will keep our relations open with all countries and will certainly not be aligned to either of the two power blocs. But ours will be a socialist system, for the people . . . Not an inch of land would remain in private ownership. All of it would be nationalized and the Black majority will not give a penny in compensation to any of the white landowners.'[36] But in a subsequent

33

statement made only a few months later on BBC television, Mugabe expressed a more moderate view about white ownership of land: 'Fifty per cent of the land in Rhodesia is in the hands of 250,000 Whites. This is unjust and will be corrected. White farmers must be prepared to part with sections of their lands so that it can be fairly divided. They will be free to choose their country of citizenship. But, of course, certain people, including Ian Smith, who constituted the illegal regime, will have to answer for their crimes in open court.'[37]

What of Mugabe's future? This depends in the short term on whether the Patriotic Front will survive and whether it will yet come to be fully accepted as the political wing of Zipa. Given the fissiparous nature of Zimbabwean politics and the purely tactical nature of the Nkomo-Mugabe association, it would be unrealistic to accept the Front's future as being assured; even the FLPs might, yet again, reverse their stand on recognizing it exclusively. What is even trickier is to try and predict the future of Mugabe's relations with Zipa. Is the Karanga-Zezuru quarrel finally buried beneath the heap of Zanu corpses? The only Zezuru in the Joint Command is the top commander, Rex Nhongo (see below). When the new Zanu executive was chosen in late 1976 the top post of president was inexplicably left vacant. Mugabe was appointed as secretary-general. Most of the other top appointments were Karanga—K. Mudzi (assistant secretary-general and foreign representative), Josiah Tongogara (secretary of military affairs), and Henry Hamadziripi (military commissioner). The other two members are R. Gumbo and K. Kangai.

ZIMBABWE AFRICAN PEOPLE'S UNION (ZAPU): JOSHUA NKOMO—AN OLD STAR RISES AGAIN

Joshua Nkomo (now 60) has played many parts in a political career stretching over a quarter of a century, but never more skilfully than in 1976. He finally emerged from his negotiations with Smith not as a badly compromised and irrelevant politician, but as a serious challenger for Zimbabwe leadership; allied to the militant Mugabe, and with the backing of Machel, Neto and the Russians—as well as of some Western governments. Nkomo's long years in detention have not only filled out his massive physique, but also built up in him a confident authority which was previously lacking. He emerged less the 'jovial Josh' and more the militant Joshua: tough-minded, relentlessly ambitious, and less afraid of showing the kind of anger he must often have felt in the past. His natural tribal constituency (the Ndebele or Matabele, and Kalanga) is a small one, making up less than 20% of the population, while the number of Zapu cadres under arms is probably no more than one-tenth of those in the training camps. (Although Nkomo is generally regarded as being Ndebele his mother is Kalanga, a subsidiary group in Matabeleland. The Kalanga are also a Shona clan, deriving from the Karanga who came south in Mzilikasi's time. The Kalanga are predominant in Zapu's leadership and included such figures, apart from Nkomo, as George Silundika, Edward Ndhlovu and the late Jason Moyo.) Because Nkomo has always been a nationalist he can count on the support of at least some of the older generation of politicians in Mashonaland. Nkomo is firmly committed to majority rule, but beyond that is not trammelled in any way by ideologies. He has always been at pains to make clear that his opposition to White rule does not imply hostility to White Rhodesians. 'They look at the future,' he says 'and think the African leaders, particularly those of the liberation movements, would like to see Whites wiped out. This is completely mistaken. No one is fighting against White people as White people. I have struggled almost 30 years to remove an evil, the separation of people by races. I could not at the end of it find myself applying what I was fighting against. We regard people as people, and White people as people like ourselves, with the emphasis on the *people* not on the *white*. Those of our White friends who decided to make our country their home are just as much citizens as anyone else.'[38] Nkomo's general political attitudes suggest that he is more likely to be a Kenyatta than a Nyerere or a Kaunda. His backing by the Soviets simply reflects their interests in opposing Zanu because the latter receive their military support from the Chinese. Despite his Russian patronage, Nkomo is the African leader whom most White Rhodesians and Anglo-American businessmen would like to see win—unless it is Muzorewa. Nkomo's strategy of continuing negotiations with Smith when the others had despaired was something of a gamble: if he could have pulled off a viable agreement he would have put himself in a commanding position to take over the country's leadership. However he also kept open his option to retreat to the military struggle.

Jason Moyo was the crucial figure in this two-prong strategy. Like his leader, this 52-year old former Bulawayo carpenter had shown a remarkable capacity to survive the many crises in Zapu's military camps. He was the principal link between Nkomo and the Russians. His assassination in Lusaka in January 1977 remains an unexplained mystery. Although it was given out at the time that he was killed by a letter-bomb mailed from Botswana, the authorities there have thrown doubt on the accuracy of this account. The nationalists' explanation for the killing is that it was done by 'Smith's agents'. There are better reasons for supposing that the assassins were Zimbabwean exiles, perhaps interested in weakening Nkomo's links with the Patriotic Front or in undermining Nkomo himself.

THE PATRIOTIC FRONT: A MARRIAGE OF CONVENIENCE

Nkomo went straight from the failure of his meeting with Muzorewa in Botswana to talks with Mugabe in Maputo on 5 October 1976. The groundwork for their agreement had already been prepared by Jason Moyo. The birth of the Patriotic Front was announced in Dar es Salaam on 10 October with a flourish of revolutionary slogans but with nothing to suggest an agreed political programme. The first attempt to formulate the Front's policy was made from 14–17 January 1977 when Mugabe and Jason Moyo (acting for Nkomo) agreed in Maputo to establish a co-ordinating committee of ten members comprising Zanu and 'ANC Zimbabweans', i.e. Zapu. They laid down four basic objectives: 'to liquidate imperialism and colonialism and thereby overthrow the racist minority regime; to create a national democratic state of the people of Zimbabwe; to eliminate all forms of capitalist exploitation and thus create conditions for a full-scale social revolution; and to guarantee national peace, security, equal rights and happiness for all in a free Zimbabwe.'

The Front served its purpose admirably at the Geneva conference as a tactical alliance between Zanu and Zapu and, indirectly, with Zipa. If it survives, it could eliminate the danger of a future civil war between two rival liberation armies—a danger mentioned by Nkomo[39] when he gave his reasons for allying himself with Mugabe: 'We took this very difficult move to try to avoid a war which would tear apart what we have been struggling for, for all these years.' He elaborated on this in a later statement: 'We don't want fighting between Zapu and Zanu. We don't want our people to wage a war after finally getting the freedom they have strived to achieve for years.'[40]

Nkomo's attitude to the Front is as coldly realistic as Mugabe's: 'The only forces that matter in the solution to the present conflict are those that command fire-power', he said in Geneva,[41] and added that only the leaders of the three military forces—Zanu, Zapu and Smith—sitting down together, could stop young Rhodesians fighting each other.

THE ZIMBABWE INDEPENDENCE PEOPLE'S ARMY (ZIPA): THE GUERRILLAS' INTERNAL STRUGGLES

Zipa was formally launched in November 1975 in the hope of ending the longstanding, bitter divisions between the Zapu and Zanu guerrilla forces as well as healing the internecine quarrels within Zanu itself. Up to then more guerrillas had died fighting each other than in fighting their enemy. At one point in 1974, as many as 2,000 guerrillas were in detention in Zambia and Tanzania—1,550 were detained for a time after Herbert Chitepo's death in 1974. Virtually the entire Zanu High Command was in prison, facing charges of murdering Chitepo and 59 guerrilla cadres. The pressures to unify the Zimbabweans came principally from the FLPs, and the initiative was taken mainly by Nyerere and Machel working through Col Hashim Mbita, the leader of the OAU Liberation Committee. Having finally given up hope of uniting the political leadership, they feared that as the end of the struggle came closer, the last phase could be a civil war between two Black armies—the fear referred to by Nkomo above. The military cadres were ripe for the FLPs' initiative.

In September 1975 Zanu's cadres in the Mgagao camp (Tanzania) took the initiative in denouncing all the old Zimbabwe leaders, except for Mugabe. Soon afterwards, Jason Moyo got Nkomo's approval to begin unity talks with Mugabe's men. One of the intermediaries, Simon Mzenda (a Zanu commander), made a secret visit to Kabwe (Zambia) in November to consult with the former Zanu commander-in-chief, Josiah Tongogara, who was awaiting trial for Chitepo's murder. Tongogara authorized him to go ahead; they drew up a list of the nine Zanu leaders who with nine Zapu leaders were to form the new Joint High Command. In the latter part of November the two sides conferred for three days in the Mozambique bush in the presence of the OAU Liberation Committee's representatives where they drew up an agreement which was publicly released in Dar es Salaam at the end of November. On 24 January 1976, Tongogara and two of his fellow-detainees in Kabwe, R. Gumbo and K. Kangai, smuggled out a letter to Mugabe calling on him 'formally to take over the Party leadership'. Mugabe did not reply until 4 April when he accepted the offer. This meant he had the approval of the detained Zanu leaders as well as that of the free commanders.

To implement the 1975 agreement, the FLPs decided it was necessary to integrate the Zapu and Zanu cadres by putting them together in the same training camps—Mgagao, Kingolwira and Nachingwea. After training they would proceed to camps in Mozambique close to the fighting zones. All the cadres would be required to abandon their commitment to old political parties and to take an oath of allegiance to Zipa and its Military Command. However, this method of ending friction in the camps failed. In mid-April 1976 there was a serious shooting affray in Kingolwira between Zapu and Zanu cadres which began over a simple dispute about who should stand first in the food queue: those who had just come off duty or those who were about to go on. As a result, the Liberation Committee removed about 800 Zapu cadres to Mgagao. There was another internecine Zanu fight on 5–6 June when the second most senior of the Zezeru leaders, Zadzu, was among those killed, leaving Rex Nhongo as the only senior commander from that clan. After a further fight in Mgagao, this time between Zanu and Zapu, the two groups again had to be put into separate camps. There was one more serious internecine battle in November 1976 when, according to one report,[42] 33 guerrillas were killed and 14 injured.

Despite these setbacks the unified structure of the Military Command remains intact. Its top leader is still Rex Nhongo (Zanu), a 29-year-old veteran of the bush who wears horn-rimmed glasses and looks like an elegant athlete. He rejects communism and every other label: 'We know what we are fighting for—justice and to free our country.'[43] The other major Zanu figures in the Command are Dzinashe

Machingura (Deputy Army Political Commissar), Elias Hondo (Director of Operations), James Nyikadzinashe (Deputy of Security and Intelligence), Webster Gwayuwe and Dr Tadiwira. The two top Zapu members are Alfred Mangena (Chief Army Political Commissar) and Clement Nunyanyi (Chief of Security and Intelligence.)

All the military training in the camps is directed by the Chinese, Tanzanians and Mozambicans. The Chinese have filled this role ever since the first Zanu cadres were formed in the middle 1960s. By contrast, Zapu's first intake of recruits were all trained in Russia; Alfred Mangena, the Chief Army Political Commissar, is one of the survivors.

It is easier to analyse the nature of Zipa's leadership than it is the attitudes of the rank-and-file cadres, either in terms of their ideological commitment or loyalties to particular leaders. Because the Zanu camps are controlled by leaders opposed to Sithole and Muzorewa, it is possible to impose their political discipline over the cadres, and to suppress support for rival leaders on the justifiable ground of unity. Volunteers from Rhodesia not wanted for the guerrilla forces, or for whom no training facilities are immediately available, are put into labour camps. Muzorewa's lieutenants claim that cadres loyal to ANC have been drafted to these labour camps; this has inhibited others in the fighting ranks from openly stating their support for the Bishop. Whatever the truth of these allegations, there can be no doubt about the heavy emphasis on ideology that now forms part of the cadres' training.

Zipa's analysis of the nature of the Zimbabwe struggle was explained by its Deputy Army Political Commissar, Dzinashe Machingura, in an interview with the Mozambican Information Agency in October 1976: 'Our society is essentially a colonial society, and, as such, we have to launch a national democratic revolution to overthrow national oppression. This national democratic revolution will serve to reconcile the principal contradiction in Zimbabwe, which is characterized by the domination and oppression of the vast majority of the Zimbabwean people by a small minority racist reactionary clique of Whites. From this we can say that all those who are opposed to the liberation and the independence of the Zimbabwean people are our enemies. These comprise the Smith racist regime and the imperialist powers that back him, puppet Africans serving the Smith regime and all those who are opposed to the independence of the Zimbabwean people. The target of the freedom fighters' bullets is the system of exploitation and the capitalistic enterprises and armed personnel which serve to perpetuate it.' Zipa's attitude was further elaborated in a statement broadcast in January 1977:[44] 'The racist part of the Rhodesia Front are trying to make the people of Zimbabwe believe that the present armed struggle is being waged in order to remove certain aspects of the oppressive and segregative social political system, while maintaining the overall system intact. They are trying to make the people of Zimbabwe believe that the liberation war is being prosecuted in order to reform the present social political system. This is a terrible misinterpretation of the Zimbabwean national liberation armed struggle . . . We are waging the national liberation armed struggle in Zimbabwe today in order to remove and destroy root, stem and branch—the present racist oppressive and reactionary economic system. In the words of the chairman of the Front-line Heads of State, President Julius Nyerere of Tanzania: "We have reaffirmed our support for the nationalist movements of Zimbabwe in their struggle to free Zimbabwe from colonialism and racist minority rule. The leaders of the Front-line States reiterated their conviction that the armed struggle is a product of colonialism, oppression and racism in Zimbabwe. This is a statement of fact. Therefore, the removal of these evils will create the conditions for peace and justice and inevitably bring to an end the armed struggle." Further, in our own words we are waging the current armed struggle in order: (1) to smash imperialism, colonialism and the racist regime in our country; (2) to eliminate all forms of capitalist exploitation and thus create conditions for a full-scale social revolution; (3) to create a national democratic state of the people of Zimbabwe; and (4) to guarantee national peace, security, equal rights and happiness for all in a free Zimbabwe. Our armed struggle is both a national and an ideological struggle . . . The people of Zimbabwe are demanding the complete, total and unconditional surrender of political and military power by the racists to the people themselves. Anything short of the total and complete removal and destruction of racism, colonialism and oppression will not do.'

THE DEFENDERS (1) THE RHODESIANS: WHO WILL STAY?

The war most White Rhodesians thought would never come finally hit them in 1976.[45] According to official estimates, there were 1,500 'terrorists' operating inside Rhodesia by the end of the year; another 2,000 fully trained cadres in base camps in Mozambique; and a further 2,000 still in training.[46] The African estimate of guerrilla volunteers immediately available is 20,000, with a limitless supply ready to come forward as the fighting develops. The Smith regime could put a total of 50,000 security forces in the field against them, but only by calling up every able-bodied White Rhodesian and using every Black volunteer; this would stretch even further the already heavily strained economy. Of the total number, 6,000 are regulars; roughly half are White. The all-White Territorial Forces number 16,500; National Servicemen 1,200; the older Reservists c. 3,000; the regular Police Force 7,000 (two-thirds Black), and the Police Reserves c. 12,000, mostly White. The Air Force has 12 Hawker Hunter fighters, 11 Canberra bombers, 24 Vampires and 16 Alouette helicopters. Defence spending has shot up from £34.8m in 1971-2 to £122m in 1976-7—a huge 34% increase over the previous year. Call-up was extended from 12 to 18 months. The economy was under siege with virtually no real growth; manufacturing was down by 7.1% in the first nine months of 1976; the value of retail sales dropped by 3.2%, the worst figure since 1965; and tourism had slumped. Defence spending became the second biggest item in the Budget after education. But the critical figure was emigration—the final test of confidence. In 1976, 7,076 White Rhodesians left permanently—1,158 in December alone. A second vital indicator was that between 2,000-3,000 reservists did not report for duty and over 1,000 young men called up for national service were reported missing.[47]

A new phrase came into vogue: 'chicken-run'. It was used to describe the exodus of the Whites. 'The word "chicken" has now become just about the worst epithet that can be applied in Rhodesia'.[48] There were those who felt 'the sooner we see the last of the chickens, the better. Then we'll know that those who remain are the sort of people we want as fellow countrymen.'[49] But others asked: 'Why should I stay on? What sort of future is there for me? I don't want to get killed fighting for principles I'm not sure are correct'.[50] An 18-year old soldier who had escaped from the army simply felt: 'I'm too young to want to die in a war that can't be won, and, anyway, I don't want to live under Black rule'.[51] But a large number, like Kenneth Street aged 65, were unhappy about the future but couldn't decide to leave: 'Kenya had been good to us and Zambia had been good too. But we were just fed up with being kicked around. I don't know what the Africans had against us. Perhaps it was that we were snobs. We were rather enamoured of what Mr Smith was saying and admired his stand. Everything about Rhodesia appealed to us. People coming out from Britain expected a certain kind of life—and Rhodesia seemed to promise it.

Now the whole thing is going to happen here again . . . We've all decided to stay and stick it out.'[52]

Whatever does happen in the end, it certainly will not be the 'way of life' which UDI was supposed to preserve; the only question for most White Rhodesians is whether the future will offer enough to make staying worthwhile. How long will it take to find out? These are the questions in 1976 over which White Rhodesians have begun to agonize seriously for the first time. It is by no means certain how many 'real' White Rhodesians there are. The figure usually quoted is c. 270,000, which is almost certainly too high—even taking into account the 10,000 to 20,000 Portuguese from Mozambique and Angola who were quietly admitted. If one subtracts the number of fairly recent British immigrants, who only went for 'the good life', and the South Africans, who have no final commitment to stay, certainly not under Black rule, it is doubtful whether the permanent White population is as high as 180,000.

The mood of white Rhodesians shifted between hope and despair in 1976–7. The welcome given to Smith's announcement of his settlement terms with Kissinger in September 1976 showed how anxious the great majority was for a quick political settlement—even if it meant Black rule. Only a tiny extremist minority group supported those who had placed a wreath of white carnations on the base of Cecil Rhodes' statue with a card that read: 'In memory of independent White Rhodesia. Born 11 November 1965. Died 24 September 1976. Murdered by abandoned Rhodesian Front principles.' Yet, when Smith turned his back on Geneva and rejected the British proposals in January 1977, there was no significant protest among Whites. Why not? When Smith announced his settlement terms in September 1976 he laid special stress on the provision that defence and security would remain in White Rhodesian hands during the transition; the impression he deliberately created was that negotiations for a Black majority government would be with 'moderate Africans—chaps like Josh Nkomo'—not with the 'Marxist terrorists' like Mugabe. But the evidence of Geneva was that a settlement was possible only with leaders acceptable to the guerrillas; and now Nkomo was among them, along with Mugabe. Moreover, there could be no question of either the Ministries of Law and Order and Defence remaining in the hands of the Smith regime during the transition; the best that might be hoped for was that they would be held by Whitehall—and this was almost as much of an anathema to the Rhodesia Front leaders as are the guerrillas. There were two other developments which helped to shift White Rhodesian thinking after the euphoria of September 1976. One was the ease with which their troops had crossed into Mozambique on three occasions since November and inflicted heavy punishment on the guerrillas; the other was the new divisions between the Patriotic Front and Bishop Muzorewa's ANC, and the evidence of the Bishop's popular support at home. What now began to seem possible was 'a deal' with the 'moderates'—now led by the Bishop instead of Nkomo; and the likelihood of being able to stop the guerrillas. No less important was the growing belief that Smith might be right after all: if only they could hold out long enough, SA and the US would change their position and come to the defence of a new 'majority-ruled' Rhodesia.

THE DEFENDERS (2) WHERE WILL SOUTH AFRICA STAND?

'Thoughtful South Africans have ever since 1965 asked, with mounting urgency, what Salisbury was going to do about it (sharing freedom within a common society); unhappily without getting answers which fitted the times. So the message became more insistent: "You are in a fix, involving us, which is bound to

get worse. You profess to have a policy for, in effect, decolonizing and emancipating your Black peoples. We have little faith in it, either for you or for ourselves, because it may well end up in Black tribal war and domination; but if you do believe in it, surely now is the time to implement it with all deliberate speed." '—Piet Cillie, Editor of Die Burger, *Capetown.*[53]

South Africa's leaders shared many of the fears felt by White Rhodesians, but few of their illusions. Ever since the collapse of the Portuguese in 1974, Prime Minister John Vorster has made no secret of his view that the only policy for his northern neighbour was to accept the inevitability of majority rule and to achieve it quickly through a peaceful settlement since the alternative was 'too ghastly to contemplate'. The spectre that haunted Vorster was of communism advancing down the continent, behind the 'forces of Black violence', right up to SA's borders. If that day ever came the apartheid Republic would be isolated and exposed to two major risks: incipient Black violence exploding inside the Republic, and withdrawal of Western support because of larger national interests. There was no lack of evidence in 1976 to support both these probabilities. The sea-change in American policy announced by Kissinger in Lusaka in April had shown how sensitive the Western nations were to the shifting balance of power in the region; and the urban violence in Soweto and Capetown from September to December demonstrated the dangerous mood of Black South Africans.[54] For Vorster there was thus everything to be gained from an early and peaceful settlement of his 'two border problems'—Rhodesia and Namibia—which could help defuse the growing mood of violence in the sub-continent, reduce the opportunities for Communist involvement, and (so Vorster believed) buy more time to show that his own solvent for the race problems of SA—Separate Development and independent Homelands—could work. 'Buying time' therefore became a vital determinant of SA foreign policy. This made Vorster a willing ally of any party ready to negotiate a settlement in Rhodesia; it was the pursuit of this policy that first brought him into close contact with the FLPs in his search for detente in 1974-5.[55] When those contacts were broken off because of his miscalculated military intervention in Angola in 1975,[56] Vorster responded eagerly to Kissinger's offer to try to bridge the gap between the leaders of Black-ruled and White-ruled Southern Africa. However, Vorster was not entirely free to play his strong hand in Rhodesia both for fear of possible reactions from his own (White) electorate, and because SA cannot co-operate in the application of sanctions to achieve political change.

These factors require elaboration. First, since effective legal political power is exclusive to the White electorate, the ruling party's parliamentary caucus of Afrikaner MPs must reflect their interests, wishes and fears. The most crucial of their interests is to defend White Supremacy; the task of persuading MPs to accept any policy which could possibly be thought to weaken the *status quo* is a formidable one which has already defeated two of the country's most powerful Prime Ministers. Both General J. C. Smuts and Dr H. F. Verwoerd were thwarted in their attempts to make the kind of radical changes each felt to be necessary to secure the 'White man's future' at the southern tip of the continent. Despite Vorster's commanding authority, his position is by no means unassailable. He has failed to carry his White electorate with him on a number of major changes, especially those affecting the Black urban population which the Government itself believes are urgently necessary. Even in the relatively harmless area of sport, Vorster has failed. Despite his own acceptance of the need for integrated club teams in order to end SA's isolation in international sport, he has failed to muster the necessary support in Parliament to change the law.[57] Nevertheless, he did gather sufficient backing for his policy of accepting rapid majority rule in both Rhodesia and Namibia. He could sell these changes to his electorate as the price for bolstering up their own security; moreover, the two populations concerned are outside the Republic. Even so, both these decisions upset influential groups of the so-called *verkramptes* ('inward-looking people') in his caucus, and this makes it important for him to avoid any false step that could strengthen their position and bring him down. It is a moot point whether Vorster could have been more courageous than he was, both over Rhodesia and at home after the warning of Soweto. However, he was inclined to caution, especially after the failure of his military intervention in Angola. He believes, rightly or wrongly, that his White electorate will back his Rhodesian policy only so long as he is not actually seen to be pressuring the White Rhodesians. This means that every time he leans on Smith he disguises it by vigorously repudiating any such intention.

The second constraint on Vorster's Rhodesian policy arises from the need to avoid co-operating in anything smacking of economic sanctions or blockade, since these are the weapons which the international community has been urged over many years to apply against SA itself to make it abandon apartheid. If White Rhodesia were in the end to be brought down by a blockade, assisted by SA, the case for applying this kind of pressure against the Republic would be strengthened. So, while Vorster has impeded the traffic of Rhodesian goods on the SA railways and harbours system (on the justifiable grounds that his railways and ports are overstrained) he is constrained by these longer-term considerations from closing the border with Rhodesia. Thus, while Vorster sees it as vital to SA's national interest to help produce majority rule in Rhodesia by peaceful negotiations, he is inhibited from taking the two simple measures that would make it impossible for the Smith regime to hold out for five minutes: cutting off their fuel supplies which originate entirely in SA; and stopping the supply of weapons from the Republic's factories. The second measure could, in fact, be taken without closing the border; but it could not be done in secret. Smith would announce to the world that Vorster was preventing White Rhodesians from defending their lives against 'murderous terrorists'. The White blacklash in SA is easy to imagine and Mr Smith is adept at using it against Vorster. At the same time, Vorster is also acutely embarrassed by any publicity given to the supply of SA weapons to the Rhodesian army. This was shown in November 1975 when Smith told the US publisher William Randolph Hearst: 'At present we are getting enough arms from SA to keep us going'.[58] Although the interview with Hearst was in the presence of two of his staff, Smith on the very next day publicly denied that he had said anything about arms from SA: the lines from Pretoria had been sizzling overnight.

So, while it is obvious what steps Vorster might himself take to avoid the 'ghastly alternative' he fears, it is politically understandable that he has not so far gone for the 'quick kill'. He is trapped by circumstances. It is a dangerous predicament, and not just confined to Rhodesia: it applies equally to the internal affairs of the Republic. At a time when SA is passing through the most critical period of its modern history, its Prime Minister is paralyzed by indecision; he knows that urgent changes must be made quickly especially to assuage the Black urban discontent; but he is afraid to move because of the risk of losing White electoral support.[59] The dangers on his home front make it all the more important that diplomatic initiatives over Rhodesia and Namibia should succeed. Meanwhile, like the FLPs, he must prepare for the military alternative in case diplomacy should fail in the end.

International involvement in a war in Rhodesia would present SA with the difficult choice of deciding whether to intervene itself, or to keep its troops south of the Limpopo river. Whatever choice SA finally makes, the conflict seems almost certain to open up greater dangers on three other fronts. An upsurge in Black urban violence is an inevitable result at home. The frontier with Mozambique, which abuts on two Homelands (KwaZulu and Kazangulu), offers the best terrain for the Russian-backed guerrilla forces of the African National Congress, whose leaders (together with those of the SA Communist Party), began to shift their operations to Maputo in 1976. But it is the Namibian front which is likely to test SA's defences most directly, since a military challenge there would certainly fully involve the SA army.

THE FOURTH FRONT: ANGOLA'S NEIGHBOUR NAMIBIA

As events unfolded in 1976 and early 1977, Namibia's immediate future became more directly interlinked with the outcome of the Rhodesian negotiations. This was inevitable for several reasons. The FLPs' *Strategy for Southern Africa's Liberation* (adopted by the OAU in 1975)[60] linked the two territories as immediate targets for independence. The outcome of the Angolan struggle in 1975 had left SA more vulnerable to the guerrilla forces of the South West African People's Organization of Namibia (Swapo) from across the Cunene river. Swapo had acquired a militant ally in President Agostinho Neto's MPLA regime—as well as a new, independent base-country from which to operate, instead of having to rely on the more remote and less satisfactory camps in Zambia. No less important to Swapo was the military presence of the Russians and Cubans in Angola; by their very presence they imposed a threat to SA, and so increased the pressures on Vorster to find a settlement for this 30-year old international dispute between the UN and SA over the future of the former mandated territory. At the same time, they offered the hitherto carefully non-aligned Swapo leadership a new option for military support should they need it.[61]

Although Kissinger's diplomatic initiative put the main emphasis on Rhodesia it also included Namibia; and the FLPs gave equal priority to both. The British Government took an independent initiative by sending a Foreign Office envoy, Martin Reith, to Namibia in September 1975 to test the chances of arranging a Geneva-type conference. Kissinger persuaded Vorster to accept the idea for such a conference in their talks at Zurich (see below). The problem was to agree about who would be invited. Swapo insisted that the Black side of the negotiators should be restricted to themselves and their own nominees, with the SA Government forming the other side. Despite its support for the UN stand that SA is in illegal occupation of Namibia—Swapo believes that nothing practical can be achieved except through direct negotiations with the SA Government. Vorster—who describes Swapo as 'a gang of communists', and who has an undisguised loathing for their burly, bearded leader, Sam Nujomo—simply refused to consider any conference which included Swapo at all, let alone as sole representatives of the Blacks. Vorster believed also that there should be no official role for SA at such a conference; he insisted that it was now the affair only of the Namibians. Nevertheless, he undertook not to stand in the way of a meeting between the members of the 'Turnhalle' conference and Swapo. Turnhalle is the old German hall in Windhoek where 135 White and Black Namibians have been engaged since 1975 in working out an independence constitution for the territory[62] in fulfilment of a SA pledge to the UN to arrange for Namibia's freedom before the end of 1978. Swapo boycotted the conference for two main reasons: it was held under South African rather than UN auspices; and its representatives were selected on an ethnic basis which excluded the political movements.

The task of diplomacy was to arrange 'a table' which would overcome (1) SA's objections to sitting down with Swapo and, indeed, to attending a conference at all;

(2) Swapo's objections to sitting down with the Turnhalle members as an independent delegation; and (3) Swapo's insistence on being recognized as the exclusive spokesman for Black Namibians. While Kissinger made some progress in 'arranging the table', the diplomatic initiative faltered after the failure of the Geneva conference on Rhodesia. Vorster urged the Turnhall delegates to speed up their work to produce a constitution. The clear implication was that he was in a hurry to declare the territory independent, just as the independence of the Transkei was presented as a *fait accompli* to the international community.[63] If any attack were then launched against Namibia it would be against an 'independent State' with a majority Black government, which would be free to 'invite in' the SA army to assist them to defend their independence. Another advantage to SA from such an arrangement would be that the anti-Swapo Black Namibians would have a vested interest of their own to defend—so SA would effectively be dividing the Black ranks. Swapo was by no means alone in denouncing Vorster's plan: the UN, the OAU, the Non-Aligned Nations' Summit, the European Economic Community, the Commonwealth and the US all insisted that Swapo's full involvement in the negotiations for independence was an essential pre-requisite to international recognition of a free Namibia.

While Vorster was urging speed on the Turnhalle conference, Swapo was busy regrouping itself in southern Angola, preparatory to launching a major guerrilla campaign inside Namibia. Its leadership was not agreed about taking up the Russian option (which would have involved 'phasing out' the Chinese military instructors from their camps); but they were getting more Russian and Chinese arms. In September 1975 the OAU Liberation Committee also began flying arms into Swapo's camps in Angola from Dar es Salaam. This arms flow, taken on the initiative of the FLPs, could be interpreted as a move to reduce the pressures on Swapo to take up the Russian option. However, as only the Russians and Cubans are in a position to give Swapo the kind of military support they would need if it came to a major conflict with the massive concentration of SA troops that were congregating south of the Cunene River and in the Caprivi Strip, the chances of Swapo invoking the Moscow factor remain high. Yet Vorster, who fears nothing more than an extension of Russian influence along his borders, gave all the appearances of being ready to ignore this risk rather than to negotiate with a movement which, in the past, has looked more to the West than to the East for its political and moral, if not its military support; and to the Chinese rather than the Russians for the arms which no Western country was prepared to provide.

There are three probable reasons for Vorster's contradictory policies on Namibia. The first is that he genuinely believes that if Swapo were to form the government in Namibia it would be tantamount to letting in 'the communists'—so fixed is his idea about Swapo's true nature. The second reason is that he has already gone too far in his commitment to the Black Namibian leaders engaged in the Turnhalle talks, such as Chief Clemens Kapuuo and the Ovambo trial leaders, to risk their future. (Yet this can only be a partial explanation since Kapuuo and all the other Turnhalle delegates, including the Whites, told the British envoy, Martin Reith, that they were willing to sit down with Swapo.) The third reason is that if Rhodesia goes up in flames, Vorster could not afford to withdraw his army from their forward positions in Namibia. By the same token if negotiations over Rhodesia prove successful, he would have less to fear from coming to an arrangement with Swapo. Successful Rhodesian negotiations were therefore also seen as the key to successful negotiations over Namibia.

THE INTERLOCUTOR: DR KISSINGER'S DIPLOMACY

At the beginning of 1976 the US Secretary of State's career had begun to look distinctly frayed. After Watergate and the CIA investigations had come the defeat in Congress of his proposals to counter the Russian/Cuban military intervention in Angola. For Kissinger, Angola was a personal debacle; for southern Africa it had opened up an entirely new scenario with the prospect of escalated guerrilla wars, the rise of more revolutionary-minded movements, heavier pressures on the more 'moderate' African governments, a shortened time-fuse for the survival of the apartheid Republic, and the real possibility of a greater Soviet role in the subcontinent. African leaders and movements who had looked to Washington for support over Angola had been badly let down; they would be less likely to rely on Western sources in future. Among Western leaders—most of whom had 'looked the other way' in order to avoid getting involved in Angola—only Henry Kissinger seemed to have the imagination needed to try to do something to rescue the situation—and, perhaps, to restore some of the dazzle to his reputation.

Kissinger had given very little of his mind to Black Africa until the Angolan affair; his only major decision in this area was to choose the wrong option from a number offered in the National Security Council Memorandum 39 of 1970.[64] The one he chose—to tilt the balance of US policy towards the White regimes of southern Africa—fitted in with Nixon's ideas and with those of his subsequently discredited lobbyists.[65] But it turned out to be disastrously wrong, resting chiefly on the premise that the Black guerrilla movements would fail in the Portuguese colonies. This error weakened American influence in the area at a crucial time, but without strengthening the White Redoubt. Angola became the tombstone on the grave of NSCM 39.

When Kissinger finally turned his mind seriously to the problems of the subcontinent he quickly came to four broad conclusions. First, that the balance had to be tilted the other way—towards support for majority rule. Second, that no initiative on his part could succeed without the co-operation of the FLPs and, especially of its chairman, Nyerere. Third, that the SA Prime Minister was the key factor; and fourth, that close Anglo-American co-operation was important. Having made up his mind about what should be done, Kissinger began to send out signals that if his services were wanted, he was ready to undertake a diplomatic initiative in Africa.

The connection with Nyerere came about almost by accident. One morning, a Tanzanian official listening to the 'Voice of America' was surprised to hear that Kissinger was contemplating a visit to Africa. His inquiry to the US Embassy in Dar es Salaam confirmed its accuracy. When he passed the message on to State House, Nyerere's response was not only positive but enthusiastic. Only President Machel among the FLPs was at first unsure about welcoming an American initiative. Nyerere is said to have given him the reply which he was later to repeat to those who found it hard to understand why he should have been willing to accept Kissinger's intervention: 'We want the two greatest sources of power on our side—God and Kissinger'. Coming from a true Believer, this reply was not just a clever jest: it reflects Nyerere's understanding of power. While he has written of his fear of the abuse of power (even of his own) he has never been afraid to use it positively. Kissinger, he felt, should be given the chance to prove that he seriously meant to help promote majority rule in southern Africa—even if it upset the Russians and Cubans (see below).

Kissinger's African diplomacy was significantly different from the highly personalized style and squirrelish habit of hiding his strategy deep inside his breast pocket which had characterized his Middle East shuttles. On this occasion he assumed the role of the super-salesman with three major clients—Britain, Vorster and the FLPs—each of them suspicious of him and of each other. He was not going to try to supplant the British by taking over their responsibilities for Rhodesia (which, anyway, would not suit the American mood), but to promote the settlement terms offered in Callaghan's 22 March proposals. And if he succeeded, to stand aside and allow the British to carry on, having used to good effect the US 'muscle' which was lacking in the British negotiating position. To the FLPs and Vorster, Kissinger offered himself as an interlocutor. This was his own description of his role: he saw himself as bridging the gap that had opened between Black and White leaders when their contacts were broken off after the Angolan episode. He could discover what each side wanted, how far they were able and prepared to go, and to clarify misunderstandings. This role was quite different from that of a mediator. Kissinger's aides have described how he worked once he became convinced of the importance of Africa.[66] 'He wants to know everything he can and to meet the various leaders and establish as intimate a relationship as possible to convince them of his even-handedness and sympathy. This requires considerable exchanges of messages, confidentiality and constant travel. He then begins what is regarded by his aides as the most difficult stage: analyzing the positions with all sides and persuading each one, even in the first stage of negotiation, to temper its demands and understand the problems of the others. When the initial proposals and counter-proposals are submitted through Kissinger, he passes them on but inevitably comments on them, telling each side that he knows that a particular demand would be completely unacceptable, but suggesting that if it was modified somewhat it might be acceptable. Meanwhile he and his aides draw up a synthesis of the two positions and offer discreet compromise solutions.' Kissinger stuck rigorously to this role of go-between rather than of mediator except on one occasion—when he met Smith in Pretoria; that single deviation fatally flawed his otherwise impeccable diplomacy.

If the Secretary's sophisticated diplomatic operation succeeded, the US would clearly benefit. Not only would the US (and Kissinger personally) retrieve some of the prestige lost over the blunders of Angola, but by preventing the spread of violence they could hope to choke off the risks of the Russians repeating their Angolan victory in a vital area—and, perhaps, even repeat their Middle Eastern success of throwing the Soviets heavily back on the defensive. All this could be achieved without destroying the claim that the US was serving the cause of world peace by, to quote Kissinger, 'heading off a race war in southern Africa'.

Kissinger saw the first crucial hurdle as winning the support and trust of Nyerere, whom he met for the first time in late April 1976. For their first informal get-together, Nyerere invited Kissinger to dinner at his beach house at Masisini, just outside the capital. Kissinger was naturally anxious to make a good impression; he was also tense (according to one of his aides) because of the strangeness of his surroundings. Having no previous experience of African intellectuals on their home ground, he did not know what to expect, and especially not from a host reputed to prefer Chinese to Americans. Nyerere was at his most quixotic: 'Ah, Mr Secretary,' he greeted his guest, 'I have a surprise for you'. At once he disappeared behind a screen in the reception room. Kissinger's entourage say they could feel the Secretary stiffen as Nyerere reappeared—leading a very ancient woman who came up close to him. Nyerere introduced her as his mother, down for a short visit from her native village of Butiama. Kissinger's relief was brief. The old lady delivered a rapid staccato of strange syllables in Ki-Zanakia tongue not understood even by most Tanzanians present. Before he could make any response, another rapid burst of words was directed at him. Nyerere was apparently much amused, Kissinger totally bemused. His mother, Nyerere finally announced, wanted him to translate what she had said. She wished to greet this distinguished visitor who had come half-way round the world to see her son. She had heard that he was famous in his own country—even a famous professor! She hoped he would not hesitate to point out to her son any mistakes he might make! The ice was broken. By the end of the visit both men felt that, whatever their reservations, they could respect each other.

Nyerere set out the minimum demands of the FLPs. Both saw Vorster as the key to the change in Rhodesia and Namibia. Nyerere felt Vorster had the power to do what was needed in Namibia, and could exercise the necessary pressure on Rhodesia; he impressed on Kissinger the importance of concentrating on Namibia, since he felt a quick breakthrough was possible on that front. He pointed out that while the FLPs were in a position to stop foreign intervention in Rhodesia because they controlled all the access routes, the situation was different in Namibia.

It was at his next stop, Lusaka, that Kissinger unfolded the Americans' new 'post-Angola' policy with its commitment to majority rule in SA, as well as in Rhodesia and Namibia.[67] 'What is unique (in SA),' he said, 'is the extent to which racial discrimination has been institutionalized, enshrined in laws and made all-pervasive'. His peroration, quoted earlier, caused Kaunda to embrace him publicly. It was a personal triumph, but this American 'wind of change' speech did nothing to dispel the war clouds. In the middle of May, Kaunda predicted that southern Africa would become the battleground in an ideological and strategic conflict between the superpowers;[68] the countries in the region would become pawns in the power game of nations whose aim is 'world hegemony'—a familiar Chinese phrase which he thrust at the Russians. This dark picture of the future had for long been Kenneth Kaunda's nightmare of what could go wrong. A few days later, President Machel left on a 'friendship visit' to Moscow. On 20 May the British High Commission in Lusaka, responding to a call made by Kaunda, urged all British passport-holders to leave Rhodesia for their own safety. Ten days later, Kaunda told American journalists that as soon as Zipa was ready a new war front would be opened up from Zambia. The only Whites who would have a place in an independent Zimbabwe, he said, would be those who were themselves 'revolutionaries'. 'They are going to lose their farms, their industries. The people will take them over because this is a revolution now. I cannot see anything else than that. It is too late.' In July, when Nyerere spoke at the formal opening of the Tanzara Freedom railway, built by the Chinese, he declared: 'In Rhodesia the die is cast. The armed struggle is on. Only majority rule will bring that armed struggle to an end . . . In Namibia also the armed struggle has begun. It is not yet a full-scale war . . . We are determined that SA shall belong equally to every one of its citizens regardless of race. Do not let us be under any illusion about the implications of such a commitment.'

Against this darkening background of a sub-continent already engulfed in fighting, Kissinger made his first public move to tackle the 'key factor' in the situation. He met SA's Prime Minister in a small Bavarian village at the beginning of July. Almost nothing that passed between them was allowed to leak out, but clearly enough common ground emerged to encourage both to meet again, this time in Zurich for three days of talks from 3-6 September. Before setting out for Zurich, Kissinger went to Philadelphia on 31 August 'to talk about Africa—one of the compelling concerns of our time'. His speech—the first major statement on Africa he had ever made to an American audience—was important for showing how quickly Kissinger had attuned himself to the African wavelength. 'When we read of young African students killed in riots, of guerrilla raids, or refugee camps attacked in reprisal, the reality lies not in the cold statistics that the media report. In Africa, it is the death of men, women and children; it means hopes extinguished and dreams shattered. The grand issues of strategy or the complexity of negotiations are no consolation to innocent brutalized victims. As long as these conflicts fester, Africans of all races will be caught up in a widening and escalating cycle of violence. Until these wars are ended, Africa faces a future of danger, anguish and growing risks of foreign intervention . . . And in SA itself, the recent outbreaks of racial violence have underscored the inevitable instability of a system that institutionalized human inequality in a way repugnant to the world's conscience . . . I restated on African soil America's rejection of the principle and practice of apartheid. I called on SA to demonstrate its commitment to peace and harmony on the continent by facilitating early solutions in Rhodesia and Namibia . . . There is no better guarantee against foreign intervention than the determination of African nations to defend their own independence and unity . . . One fact is clear: a time of change has come again to Africa . . . What Africa needs now is not a return to the exploitive or interventionist practices of decades past. Nor does it need exuberant promises and vapid expressions of goodwill. It requires concrete commitments to progress—political and economic. It requires our readiness to co-operate as sovereign equals on the basis of mutual responsibility and mutual benefit.' Finally, he stated in advance the message he was proposing to take with him to his meeting with Vorster: '. . . the White population of Rhodesia and Namibia must recognize that majority rule is inevitable. The only issue is what form it will take and how it will come about . . .'

The Philadelphia speech had a predictably bad reception in SA, and especially with Vorster. Nevertheless, their Zurich encounter left Kissinger hopeful that enough had been achieved 'both in procedures and in substance' to justify his embarking on a second mission to Africa. Vorster, by contrast, doused all hopes of a settlement in Namibia by saying flatly that no member of his government would ever sit down with Swapo to talk about the territory's future.

THE KISSINGER SHUTTLE: 'GETTING OUT OF A BLOODY MESS'

'Time is running out. If we can't get negotiations started in Rhodesia by the end of the year, it will be a bloody mess. At issue is not only the future of two States in southern Africa, but the potential evolution of all Africa with its profound impact on Europe and on the Middle East.'—Dr Kissinger

The FLPs met in Dar es Salaam from 5-7 September 1976 to decide whether the confidential information brought to them by Kissinger's special envoy, following his meeting with Vorster in Zurich, offered enough to justify continuing support for the American diplomatic initiative. Now, for the first time, Angola's President Agostinho Neto, became a member of the club. Also, all the liberation movements in southern Africa were invited to present their views—another new procedure. The FLPs' final communique pledged them to 'further intensify the armed struggle in Zimbabwe', but it said nothing about Kissinger's future initiative. However, Nyerere was in fact authorized to inform Kissinger that they 'welcomed the idea' of his shuttle. It was not an invitation, just an assenting nod. The distinction is a subtle but important one—especially when the FLPs were carrying Neto along with them.

Kissinger left for Africa on 13 September in an attempt as he described it 'to head off a race war between Blacks and Whites'. For how many years had critics of the African policies of the US and other Western nations warned of just such a danger? No key figure in a position of power had been less willing to listen to the 'Africa bores' than Kissinger—until he came to realize, as he told Washington journalists on 11 September, that 'the risks to world peace are very severe. War has already started in southern Africa, and there is a grave danger of its expansion. Clearly, if outside powers become very active in southern Africa, the danger of that area becoming an arena for superpower conflicts becomes very great.' Having left it all so late, what more could the President of the US say with truth than that the mission had 'no assurance of success, but it is worth the risk in a continent vital to us all'. A striking editorial in the *Washington Post* (9 September 1976) put the risks in some perspective: 'One can fairly criticize the Administration for coming late to southern Africa and for coming there less out of concern for racial and human justice than out of a fear that the Soviet Union would exploit the larger regional turbulence as it did the struggle inside Angola. But the crisis in southern Africa is real and it threatens to rage out of control with almost unimaginable costs and consequences. For the US to play it safe and to do less than it could to avert a holocaust would not only be bad diplomacy, contributing to world disorder, it would be an abdication by the US of moral obligation and responsibility to the world community. During the years of US neglect of Africa, others have had plenty of time and room to defuse the situation, but nothing has been done.'

NOTES FROM KISSINGER'S CONVERSATIONS EN ROUTE TO EUROPE/AFRICA (13 SEPTEMBER)[69]

'Substantially Namibia is the easier problem, but procedurally the more difficult. Rhodesia is the other way round. It is easier to visualize a mechanism for Rhodesia. Vorster would not have gone this far if he did not want to make a major effort. He knows what the US needs in terms of concessions. We have to assume he is doing it in good faith. We have evidence that SA is putting the screws on Rhodesia. For example, the withdrawal of para-military police last year, the withdrawal of helicopter pilots manning the gunships, and the congestion of Rhodesian goods in the SA rail and port systems which appear to be contrived.' Kissinger said that Nyerere had agreed to some of the details of the US/UK perception of how things might work, but that he (Kissinger) was still afraid that if he failed to get a commitment from the Whites the Blacks might raise their demands. Kissinger's minimum hopes were a commitment from SA to work towards majority rule in Rhodesia on the basis of the US/UK plan—'We don't have that yet'—plus a framework whereby a programme on Namibia could be made. He found the African priority on Namibia at this point 'strange'. The Insurance Fund could only be set up following basic minimum negotiating progress on Rhodesia.

ROUND ONE: DAR ES SALAAM, 14-16 SEPTEMBER

Three days before Kissinger's arrival in the Tanzanian capital Nyerere had warned that the US initiative could be counter-productive,[70] since it was already being welcomed by Smith and interpreted by others as a gesture of support for White minority rule. The Americans' harping on their 'desire to stop communism' simply 'strengthens Smith in his determination to prevent majority rule'. Kissinger was met on his arrival by a student demonstration and was shocked to find that the Tanzanian Government had just released a statement urging the Americans to say that 'if peaceful transfer of power is impossible because of the intransigence of racists, then it will be on the side of those who fight for freedom'.[71] Kissinger complained to his aides that this kind of statement could sink his mission before he even got near Vorster or Smith. (On that very day Vorster and Smith were holding a crucial meeting in Pretoria where the SA Prime Minister was to 'soften up' the Rhodesian leader for the Kissinger 'bite' as he had promised in Zurich.) At the end of the first day of talks, Nyerere was not 'overhopeful' about the main issue on which he looked for success—Namibia. But he felt Kissinger had fully grasped the African position. Although Kissinger undertook to convey the FLPs' views to Pretoria on the Namibia issue, he was clearly focussing on Rhodesia. After the second day of talks Nyerere was still unhopeful about what could be achieved; but Kissinger less so.

NOTES FROM AN AUTHORITATIVE SOURCE

Nyerere argued with Kissinger that conditions were not ripe for hasty action in Rhodesia; but they were in Namibia where Vorster had the power to ordain change. So Kissinger should concentrate on Namibia when he got to Pretoria. Why couldn't Kissinger understand this? For his part, Kissinger explained that once Smith went, there should be a caretaker government with a Black majority in Rhodesia, which Nyerere accepted. Then he proposed a Council of State, equivalent to the Governor, which would have a White majority. Nyerere said no; what would be acceptable was a 'Chissano Government'—something similar to the transitional government in Mozambique, where Frelimo named the members and the Portuguese appointed a High Commissioner. Kissinger seems to have accepted this formula, but said that Whitehall apparently preferred a Council to a single person, though he was trying to dissuade them. Such a government would in fact be of a caretaker nature, and would include Whites. It would probably reflect across-the-board interests rather than be strictly of the Chissano type. Before leaving Dar, Kissinger told Nyerere: 'If you hear I have seen Smith it will be because Vorster has assured me that Smith accepts this thing' (i.e. the Anglo-American proposals).

ROUND TWO: LUSAKA, 16-17 SEPTEMBER

A fortnight before Kissinger's arrival in Zambia, Kenneth Kaunda had voiced his suspicions that the US might try and make a deal with Vorster, whereby majority rule in Rhodesia would be traded for acceptance of SA's own ideas about granting independence to Namibia. But he insisted there could be no trade-offs. 'We have made our stand very clear. Namibia must be free. Zimbabwe must be free on the basis of majority rule and apartheid must be cleared off the face of Africa.'[72]

'If you fail,' Kaunda told Kissinger with considerable emotion as they parted, 'we shall have reached the point of no return. God help you. We want to see peace, but peace with honour, peace with justice and freedom and independence. If we fail to get our demands peacefully, we must fight. We have no romantic views about an armed struggle.'

In Salisbury, the ruling Rhodesian Front Congress was giving Smith a noisy, unanimous and full mandate to participate in the US initiative to 'see what is on offer'. Smith had come back from Pretoria persuaded he must talk to Kissinger. 'Are you coming with me or not?' he demanded of his supporters. 'For God's sake be honest.'

NOTES FROM KISSINGER'S CONVERSATIONS EN ROUTE TO PRETORIA FROM LUSAKA (17 SEPTEMBER)

'If I didn't think it was possible that Smith would yield at some relatively early stage, I wouldn't be here. But I never said it was possible on this trip.'

ROUND THREE: PRETORIA, 17-18 SEPTEMBER

Fresh troubles and shootings were going on in Soweto as Kissinger flew in. Smith arrived on the same day—ostensibly to attend the rugby test match between SA and

New Zealand. In private conversation with the in-flight team of journalists, Kissinger said he would not see Smith to negotiate 'unless some clear result is in prospect: since that is not the case today (the 18th), there is nothing I can add.' However, he appeared to be more hopeful about some progress on Namibia by getting Vorster to agree to a round-table conference to which Swapo would be invited.

NOTES FROM KISSINGER'S CONVERSATIONS. PRETORIA (19 SEPTEMBER), EARLY MORNING

'Vorster has gone along on the whole with the basic approach we follow. The likelihood is that Smith is on the brink of making some decision. I expected that the SA riots would reduce Vorster's flexibility, but they haven't. My judgement is that we are on the road to significant progress. But I might have to take hell for a few weeks.' Kissinger added that Vorster had told him somewhat more than he had expected.

ROUND FOUR: PRETORIA, 19–20 SEPTEMBER

Kissinger decided over dinner with Vorster the previous night (Saturday, 18 September) that Smith was ready to make the necessary concessions; the only thing required were 'psychological reassurances' from Kissinger's own mouth about the bargaining that had already essentially been conducted through Vorster. Kissinger's press spokesman announced the meeting at one minute before midnight (Saturday) after flurried messages to the FLPs.

There had been nothing before this dramatic change of position to suggest that Smith was remotely contemplating giving up all he had stood for—and still believed in. He had led his rebellion to ensure the permanence of minority rule or, as he preferred to call it, 'the retention of government in civilized and responsible hands'. He had repeatedly reaffirmed this stand throughout 1976, beginning with his New Year statement in which he assured Rhodesians that he would not be party to any agreement 'that does not retain government in civilized and responsible hands'. In August when the Quenet Commission reported on ways of eliminating discrimination,[73] he scoffed at the idea of a common voters roll[74] and defended the Land Tenure Act, which divides land equally between the White minority and the overwhelming Black majority. Whatever changes in discrimination were envisaged, he told the faithful, they should not be misinterpreted:[75] 'As far as we are concerned there can be no change and, indeed, there will be no fundamental change of the most fundamental of our principles—that of the retention of government in responsible hands.' In the middle of August, speaking on BBC radio, Smith again rejected majority rule: 'It would lead to a tragedy.'[76] This statement was made after Smith had been to see Vorster (2 August) following his return from Zurich. Finally, on the eve of Kissinger's shuttle to Africa, Smith said there was no such thing as 'the end of the road, defeat or surrender; Rhodesia had proved this over the past decade'.[77]

Now, unexpectedly, here was Vorster assuring Kissinger that if he met Smith he would be ready to 'offer the necessary concessions'. Their meeting was set for 10am on Sunday in the US Ambassador's residence.[78] Scheduled to last for an hour, it went on for four. According to senior American officials, Kissinger conducted the meeting by putting three principal questions to Smith: (1) How do you think Rhodesia can be rescued now that you know you have lost the last two friends on whose help White Rhodesians had been counting—South Africa and the United States? (2) If things are going so badly now, where do you think you will be next March, if the fighting is stepped up? (3) And if you think you will make it through next March, what about next year at this time? Kissinger then produced a summary of three sets of US intelligence reports about Rhodesia's military position. The Defence Intelligence Agency (DIA), the Intelligence and Research Bureau of the State Department (INR) and the Central Intelligence Agency (CIA). All three were in broad agreement; the only difference being their estimates of the time before Rhodesia's military and economic position finally collapsed. These US reports were confirmed by the military evaluation of the SA intelligence service, BOSS, which Vorster had previously given Smith. Faced with these bleak reports, Smith asked Kissinger what he expected of him. Kissinger then produced what he described as the 'British-American' plan, an elaboration of the terms laid down by Mr Callaghan in Parliament on 22 March. It was 2.00 pm when Smith said he wanted 'a few hours' to think over his reply.

The crunch meeting started at 5.40 pm. This time Vorster was present, and they met in the Prime Minister's official residence, 'Libertas', on the high hills over-looking Pretoria. Smith arrived looking tense and nervous. Kissinger was, by now, beginning to look tired. His voice was becoming hoarse, and there were uncharacteristic dark rings around his eyes. His fingernails, as always, were bitten to the quick. 'All I have to offer is my own head on a platter,' Smith began. Kissinger later spoke about the scene where the White Rhodesian surrender became final. He was full of admiration for the dignity shown by Smith and his men on what he described as 'the most painful day of their lives'.

The five points of agreement were accurately set out by Smith on 24 September,[79] though he deliberately interpreted them to give maximum reassurance to his White constituency about the way their position would be safeguarded during the transition to independence. The subsequent controversy about the proposals raised questions about whether secret assurances had been given by Kissinger as an inducement to Smith to accept majority rule. These issues are discussed below. The fact is that the two crucial proposals which subsequently wrecked the entire agreement were not discussed with the FLPs before they were conceded to Smith. The first was for a Council of State in the Interim Government to be composed of an equal number of Whites and Blacks with a White chairman. The second was for a Council of Ministers with a Black majority, but with the Ministries of Law and Order (security) and Defence to be kept in White (Rhodesian) hands until independence. A two-thirds vote was required for decisions in both Councils. These two proposals were put forward by Smith as essential conditions for acceptance of the 'package' for majority rule. Kissinger was in a quandary: should he close the deal there and then, or should he postpone the decision until he could consult the FLPs? Callaghan and Wilson had warned him at the beginning of his shuttle not to make the mistake of letting Smith 'off the hook' if he ever had him on it; they reminded him that Smith had twice before gone into reverse after appearing to have agreed—in talks on the 'Tiger' and the 'Fearless'. 'Make him sign on the dotted line before he leaves the room,' was their advice. Thus, when Kissinger had Smith ready to concede the principle of majority rule, which all the African Presidents had said was unthinkable, he took a gamble. This was the only time during the entire diplomatic exercise that Kissinger abandoned the role of interlocutor. That he did so then was understandable. That he accepted those particular terms showed clearly that he had not understood the suspicions between Blacks and Whites in Rhodesia. Even if they were personally to accept the terms of the agreement, the FLPs would not be able to persuade the guerrilla leaders to lay down their arms in order to accept the authority of Smith's nominees for the Defence and Security posts. Perhaps Kissinger did understand this point, but thought Smith would not remain in politics, or could be removed. Vorster and the British, by contrast, took the view that only Smith could sell a rapid transfer to majority rule to White Rhodesians.

NOTES FROM KISSINGER'S CONVERSATIONS, PRETORIA, EN ROUTE TO
LUSAKA (20 SEPTEMBER)
*Responding to a question about Smith having talked of 'responsible' and not
'majority' rule: 'I want to make it quite clear that the US never had any concept in
mind other than one-man-one-vote. The agreement is within the framework of
proposals decided with the African Presidents and within the Anglo-American
parameter. But it must be remembered that a lot of detail came up which had not
been anticipated. (A reference to Smith's two crucial demands.) By the end of this
week I will have a clear statement on the Rhodesian position that should go a very
long way towards making negotiations possible. Assuming the Black leaders stay
within the framework of prior consultation, I believe a basis for consultation can be
found.' Replying to a question whether the plan involved Smith stepping aside: 'I'm
interested in principles. I don't care who carries them out. It would not be costless
for Smith to double-cross me or "con" me in the presence of the SA Prime Minister
who got us to talk in the first place.'*

ROUND FIVE: LUSAKA, 20–21 SEPTEMBER
Kissinger was encouraged by the warmth of Kaunda's first reaction, but he reserved
his final position until he first had a chance of studying the proposals in detail, and
had consultations with the other FLPs as well as the black Rhodesian leaders.
Kissinger had given him only one copy of the agreement, which had been
immediately whisked away by the President's aides to make copies to be sent by a
waiting courier to Machel in Maputo and to the Zimbabwean leaders.

NOTES ON CONVERSATIONS WITH KAUNDA/KISSINGER, LUSAKA EN ROUTE TO
DAR ES SALAAM (21 SEPTEMBER)
*'When Smith offered his head on a platter on Sunday he said that neither the
White conservatives nor the Blacks wanted him. What is happening now is a process
that will continue with or without him. For what must have been the most painful
day of their lives, the Rhodesians have behaved with great dignity . . . The key to
breaking Smith was Vorster.'*

ROUND SIX: DAR ES SALAAM, 21–22 SEPTEMBER
In contrast to the gloom of their last encounter, Nyerere was almost jubilant when
he received Kissinger. He spoke of a 'breakthrough'; the Rhodesian question was
'drawing to an end'. But he was disappointed that there was no encouraging news
about Namibia. Kissinger also had 15 minutes with Nkomo.
Meanwhile, in Salisbury, Smith was conferring with his Cabinet and caucus. He
had received a message sent by Kissinger from Dar suggesting he was hopeful that
the Africans would accept all the Pretoria proposals. It was this message, Smith
later said, which convinced him to go ahead. The actual meaning of the message
subsequently became a source of acute controversy (see Diplomatic Snafu below).

NOTES ON CONVERSATIONS WITH KAUNDA/KISSINGER, LUSAKA EN ROUTE TO
DAR ES SALAAM (21 SEPTEMBER)
*Nyerere's optimistic Press conference may make the decision for Smith more
difficult in Salisbury. Nevertheless it was welcome as it would pre-empt Machel,
Neto and the Black Rhodesian groups.*

ROUND SEVEN: ZAIRE, 22 SEPTEMBER

President Mobutu said Kissinger had 'convinced the Africans of the American solution instead of the African solution—armed struggle'. Kissinger left with the impression that he had 'the strong encouragement of Mobutu'.

THE DIPLOMATIC SNAFU: WHO WAS LYING?

A number of vital questions were in serious contention at the end of Kissinger's diplomatic shuffle. What secret understandings were reached with Vorster as a 'trade-off' for his support? What was the exact nature of the undertakings given to Kissinger by Smith in Pretoria? Was the agreement a 'package deal' which constituted a binding agreement on the US, UK and SA, even if it were later rejected by the Africans? Smith insists it was binding and that its terms were not negotiable. That undertaking, he says, was given to him in Pretoria, subject to the proviso that Kissinger would advise him whether it was acceptable to the FLPs before Smith committed himself in public. Kissinger had sent him a message from Dar es Salaam on 21 September which gave him the green light to go ahead and make his acceptance speech three days later. Three separate issues are involved in this argument: the negotiability of the terms; the binding nature of the agreement on the US *et al*; and whether the FLPs had reneged on Kissinger.

On the issue of whether the terms were negotiable (which became the major stumbling block at the Geneva Conference), Kissinger said right after the end of his shuttle, on 28 September, in an *NBC Today* interview: 'Obviously there will have to be negotiations for the transition . . . the composition of the Government, the allocation of Ministers, none of this has been settled yet. This requires negotiation.' On 8 October, speaking in 'The Week at the UN' programme, he said: 'I gave Ian Smith my best judgement of what would provide a framework and what might be acceptable'. Vorster agreed with Kissinger that the plan accepted by Smith was considered to be 'a basis for settlement discussions'.[80]

Were the terms binding? Did Kissinger give any secret undertakings in Pretoria about US support for Smith if the terms of the agreement were not observed by the Africans? In October 1976 a spokesman of the Smith regime claimed that 'it was made clear' to Smith during his talks with Kissinger that the US would show 'sympathy' towards Rhodesia if it accepted the terms for a settlement.[81] It added that US 'sympathy' was understood by the Smith regime to include support for the lifting of sanctions and 'logistical support' for its army; such support was primarily expected to take the form of helping it to obtain war supplies from other countries like France. This claim was firmly denied by Kissinger, speaking in President Carter's presence.[82] There was 'no possibility', he said, of the US selling arms to the White Rhodesians, even if talks broke down. Under pressure of questioning, Smith produced much vaguer answers about the supposed US undertaking.[83] 'It is a fact that in the talks I had with Dr Kissinger in Pretoria (19 September) at the commencement of this exercise, that he did give me an assurance that if we entered this agreement and it collapsed because of what the Black Rhodesians had done, as opposed to myself and my government, that he was absolutely convinced that we would get a great deal more sympathy from the free world and also tangible assistance. And he believed it would lead to greater material support.' Pressed on whether the 'understanding' might include military supplies, the Rhodesian leader replied, 'Yes'. He added, however: 'I wouldn't say we have been given any hard and fast undertaking'. He added that no details were discussed.

Did Kissinger mislead Smith into believing that he had African support when he did not? According to Smith, the message he had received on 21 September from

Kissinger in Dar said that on the basis of his talks with Kaunda and Nyerere, he believed the provisions for having the Ministries of Law and Order and Defence in White hands 'can be added' to the other points agreed. In Smith's view, either the FLPs had reneged, or Kissinger had misled him. Bernard Gwertzman, the *New York Times* member of Kissinger's team of 'in-flight correspondents', reported that he had seen the actual text of the 21 September communication from Kissinger to Smith.[84] 'It was,' he wrote, 'an ambiguously worded instruction in a longer message and did not specifically say the Black leaders had accepted the proposal; but it did leave that impression in both Pretoria and Salisbury.'

When Kissinger was asked in his *NBC Today* interview whether the African Presidents had rejected anything they told him they would approve, he replied: 'The African Presidents have not indicated a rejection of anything specific. The African Presidents have made a general statement that they will not accept the dictation of Smith with respect to all the details of the Transitional Government. On the other hand, what Smith has put forward was not his idea, but in itself reflected a compromise between many points of view.' Vorster thought Kissinger's reply 'a very remarkable statement'[85] in that it suggested the proposals that Mr Smith had announced were the result of discussions between the US, UK and Black African Presidents *before* Kissinger had met Mr Smith.

On the same day that Kissinger gave his answer in the *NBC Today* interview, US officials acknowledged that 'details' of the settlement proposals were not accepted by the FLPs in advance of their submission to Smith. They admitted that the actual proposals were Kissinger's 'own refinements of terms for a peaceful settlement'.[86] Ted Rowlands, who succeeded David Ennals as the Minister of State for African Affairs, said that in his talks with Smith about settting up the Geneva Conference, he had talked specifically to him about the negotiability of the proposals; Smith had accepted that there would be a wide range of items on the agenda.[87] 'He even said he would have been surprised if I had suggested anything else. Therefore, it was clearly understood that the five-point plan was not, and could not, be the sole framework for a settlement.' The Rhodesian reply to Rowlands was that Smith had twice been promised by the British Government that it would persuade the Africans to accept the original proposals.[88] While it is true that the British thought the framework of the agreement offered a proper basis for a settlement, it never ruled out negotiations on the points in dispute.

What verdict can be made on the basis of this selection of the best evidence so far available? First, Smith admits that he was told in Pretoria that the settlement terms were subject to the Africans' approval. This, he says, was conveyed to him in Kissinger's September message from Dar. It was an ambiguous message undoubtedly drafted to encourage Smith to make his acceptance public; but it expressed only Kissinger's own *belief* (Smith confirmed this) that the terms would be accepted—not that they already had been. This seems very clear. Second, the claim that the terms were 'not negotiable'—the justification for Smith's stand at the Geneva Conference and afterwards—finds no supportive evidence from Kissinger, Vorster or the UK. Third, it is not in dispute that the FLPs had not seen the actual proposals before they were put to Smith; it is true that the initial reaction of Kaunda and Nyerere to Kissinger's news of Smith's acceptance of majority rule was enthusiastic; but both reserved their final decision until after the FLPs' meeting on 26 September. It was Kissinger's own 'best judgement' that they would accept—and this he transmitted to Smith. Whether he really was as hopeful as his message to Smith conveyed, or whether he was only gambling on a favourable outcome in order to push Smith towards publicly committing himself, will probably never be known. Finally, there is not the slightest evidence to suggest the Rhodesian claim of

54

a secret deal between Smith and Kissinger over US arms or other support. Even the Rhodesians go no further than to suggest that the US would show 'sympathy' if they accepted the deal; their spokesman admits that it was the White Rhodesians themselves who interpreted this as meaning military support. And Smith confirms that he had not been given any 'hard and fast undertakings'.

The conclusion must be that Kissinger's subtle diplomacy led (or misled) Smith to believe much more than was actually conveyed in the crucial, but ambiguously-worded, signal sent on 21 September.

There is one last question: did Kissinger make any secret deals with Vorster to win over his support? Kissinger disavows any 'trade-off' of any kind. But there is more than just a suspicion that he assured the SA Prime Minister that the result (reward?) of his co-operating over Rhodesia and Namibia would be a diminishing of pressures on his regime by the US and other Western nations. If true, what might be the practical effects of 'diminished pressures'? Kissinger himself pulled no punches in continuing to attack apartheid and in urging the need for changes towards the goal of majority rule. A more likely 'trade-off' would be a refusal by Western governments to vote for tough resolutions in the Security Council. This, in fact, occurred when the US, UK and France together vetoed a proposal in the Security Council to make the arms embargo against SA compulsory. The private explanation for this action was that they did not wish to upset SA at a time when the negotiations over Namibia were still in the balance. Other possible US concessions to SA could be to restore the Republic to the list of approved countries for the guarantee arrangements provided by the US Export-Import Bank, and to give the green light to US bankers to raise loans for SA. Although Washington cannot dictate to bankers about foreign loans, the Administration's attitude to particular governments is nevertheless an important consideration in the calculations of bankers about the risks involved in making substantial foreign loans. After the Kissinger shuttle a Citibank consortium was engaged in raising a $100m loan for SA; but this proposal was apparently abandoned later. Instead, SA got a much bigger loan from a consortium of French bankers.

CLIMAX AND ANTI-CLIMAX: SMITH SAYS 'YES'; THE AFRICANS GIVE A QUALIFIED 'NO'

On 25 September, Smith broadcast to the nation his acceptance of 'majority rule within two years': the impossible had become possible. He admitted frankly: 'I would be dishonest if I did not state quite clearly that the proposals that were put to us in Pretoria do not represent what in our view would be the best solution for Rhodesia's problems. Regrettably however, we were not able to make our views prevail, although we were able to achieve some modification in the proposals. The American and British Governments, together with the major Western Powers have made up their minds as to the kind of solution they are determined to bring about. The alternative to acceptance of the proposals was explained to us in the clearest of terms which left no room for misunderstanding . . . What I have said this evening will be the cause of deep concern to you all and understandably so, but we live in a world of rapid change, and if we are to survive in such a world we must be prepared to adapt ourselves to change'.[89] Mr Smith closed by quoting Churchill: 'This is not the end. It is not even the beginning of the end, but it is perhaps the end of the beginning.'

On 26 September the five FLPs met in Lusaka. They 'hailed and congratulated' the people and fighters of Zimbabwe who had 'forced the rebel regime and the enemy in general to recognize and accept the inevitability of majority rule . . .' But they declared that to accept the proposals as set forth by Smith would be 'tantamount to legalizing the colonialist and racist structures of power'. Instead, they asked the British Government to convene a conference 'with the authentic and legitimate representatives of the people' to discuss the structure and functions of the transitional government'.[90] Rightly, Kissinger saw this statement as rather more than half a victory. The ball was now back in the British court. The Salisbury regime complained that it had been misinformed or misled by the US. Reactions in most other African capitals were strongly supportive of the FLPs. The Nigerian Government said the settlement proposals had 'failed to satisfy the most basic democratic principles'. The Sudan Government expressed 'complete satisfaction with the intensified and commendable efforts of the five FLPs. The Ghana Supreme Military Council said it opposed any relaxation of the pressures on the Smith regime. Only Angola's President Neto took a position out of line with the other FLPs. On the day after the Lusaka summit he said: 'The initiative for liberation of peoples can never emanate from the US which is an imperialist country . . . it was necessary to reject all North American efforts aimed at taking the initiative on the liberation of Namibia and Zimbabwe. Such initiatives belonged to those peoples or to the African countries . . .'[91] A similar view was expressed by Radio Maputo: 'This so-called Anglo-American plan is intended to sabotage our (Zimbabwe people's) revolution . . . the Zimbabwean people under the vanguard leadership of the revolutionary organization, Zipa, must reject out of hand this present manoeuvre by the Anglo-Americans'.[92] Zipa had already done so five days earlier at a Press Conference in Maputo. 'We are determined,' they said, 'to fight the Kissinger proposals to the bitter end'.[93] Nkomo found 'serious flaws' in the proposals. So did all the other Zimbabwe Nationalists. But none went so far as Amin in suggesting: 'I would have been happier if the visit had been undertaken by countries like the Soviet Union, China, Yugoslavia and Cuba or even some few Western countries who assisted Liberation Movements'.[94]

THE ROAD TO GENEVA: BRITAIN'S RELUCTANT ROLE IN 1976

The British Government—wearied by some 11 years of futile attempts to rid itself as painlessly as possible of the Rhodesian albatross from its post-imperial neck, and overwhelmed at home by economic crisis and the relentless Ulster ulcer—had been delighted by the opportunity of handing over the burden to the Americans. The one thing it did not want to emerge from Kissinger's initiative was a resumption of an active role for Britain in Rhodesia. David Spanier, the Diplomatic Correspondent of *The Times*, closely reflected the official British mind when he wrote on 23 September: 'The Government has decided, whatever the outcome of Dr Kissinger's mission, that there is no question of a British Governor-General or British judges or British civil servants being sent out to Rhodesia to assist in the transitional arrangements, still less British troops'. It is essential to understand this attitude in trying to follow the shifts of British policy up to and through the Geneva talks. Britain wanted to do no more than it decently had to do, but in the end found itself forced to take on much more than it had contemplated before Kissinger's initiative. As late as 2 January 1977, the British Premier had this to say in a BBC radio interview: 'I'm not very anxious to go in at all. Rhodesia has not been a British colony for years and years and years. But if we have got a role to play that does not involve us in stretching ourselves beyond our capacity and our strength, then we have got a responsibility to do it . . . We've got to husband our resources. We've got plenty to do here to get our situation right.'

Convening a constitutional conference for Rhodesia fell easily within the acceptable limits of British responsibility. When, on 26 September, the FLPs pressed for a conference to be called, the late Foreign Secretary, Anthony Crosland, responded on the very next day. And just one day later, Ted Rowlands went to Africa to negotiate the details, accompanied by William Schaufele, the US Assistant Secretary for African Affairs who had played a key role in Kissinger's shuttle. Smith himself took the initiative in proposing that Rowlands should visit Salisbury. Nkomo, Muzorewa, Sithole and Chikerema all welcomed a constitutional conference under British chairmanship. Nobody objected to Smith being invited.

Rowlands had to achieve three results to rescue Kissinger's initiative: get quick agreement to the conference being convened in order to keep up the momentum; ensure that it would be fully representative; and persuade Smith that the whole 'package' was still negotiable. Although Smith accused the British of 'changing the terms', he nevertheless agreed to come. The FLPs skilfully brought the rival black nationalists across the hurdles; even those committed to the sole tactic of 'armed struggle' agreed not only to come, but to sit down with the 'enemy' Smith—no mean feat. At the beginning of October the British Foreign Secretary spoke of the 'awesomely high stakes' if the initiative failed.[95] 'The war,' he said, 'would escalate; Rhodesia would be plunged into economic chaos and so would the surrounding African States; the South Africans would intervene on one side and, possibly, the Cubans on the other'. By 12 October, he was able to declare that the road to Geneva was open, but his subsequent announcement that the conference would be chaired, not by himself, but by the UK Ambassador to the UN, Ivor Richard, almost scuppered the talks: the Africans questioned whether Britain was committed at a high enough level to the success of the conference.

THE GENEVA CONFERENCE—IN WHICH CHAIRMAN MAO IS PROVED RIGHT
'You cannot win at the conference table what you have not won on the battlefield'—Chairman Mao-tse Tung
The Geneva Conference never stood much of a chance of producing a final constitutional settlement, but it was nevertheless essential for three reasons: to keep a diplomatic initiative alive; to prove genuine African interest in a peaceful alternative to guerrilla warfare; and to establish the minimum conditions for an agreement acceptable to Black and White Rhodesians for a transitional government leading to independence. The talks contributed to all three objectives. At the end of the conference, a new diplomatic initiative was still possible; the FLPs and the nationalists had proved their interest in negotiating for a transitional Government. It also revealed that the gulf which separated the two sides could not be bridged by the Kissinger proposals.

Geneva turned out to be another arena for the Rhodesian struggle in which the protagonists sought to demonstrate their respective strengths. Both sides sought to enhance their bargaining positions at the conference table by escalating the fighting on the actual battleground. This showed that the Rhodesian forces were not yet defeated, nor even as weak as Smith's political surrender to Kissinger in Pretoria might have suggested; the Zimbabweans could not force Smith's capitulation when they had not yet finally won victory on the battlefield.

When the conference finally got under way on 28 October, the guerrillas took the initiative in the field by launching heavy new attacks, but by the end of the conference the military initiative had passed back into Smith's hands. October turned out to be the bloodiest month in the fighting so far with the deaths of 15 Rhodesian soldiers and 144 guerrillas, and 84 civilian fatalities. In November, he sharply escalated the fighting by penetrating deep into Mozambique to strike at the guerrilla camps—a tactic repeated twice in quick succession. These attacks achieved three results: they inflicted heavy losses on the guerrillas, but even worse on Zimbabwe and Mozambique civilians;[96] they exposed the weakness in Mozambique's defences which forced Machel to re-examine the need for external military support; and they boosted the flagging morale of White Rhodesians. Suddenly, defeat no longer seemed inevitable. The Rhodesian tactic of hitting the guerrillas at the rear was militarily sound, but the political risks were high. These were that Mozambique would be compelled to call in foreign military aid to speed up the training of its still scratch army, and to strengthen its border defences. The question was whether Machel would seek African military support (he already had help from the Tanzanian army), or turn to the Russians, Cubans or Chinese—thus introducing the very element of international involvement which the Geneva Conference was designed to avoid. It soon became clear that Smith's military and political tactics were closely linked.

SMITH'S NEW STRATEGY

From the day the conference began Smith took the stand that there was nothing to negotiate other than the implementation of his agreement with Kissinger. If the 'terrorists' and 'militant Marxists' were willing to talk on those terms, he was available; otherwise he was 'not interested in their antics'. Britain and the US, he insisted, had made a solemn agreement with him. As 'a man of his word' *he* was prepared to stand by that agreement; but were the others? When both the British and the Americans insisted that the terms of the agreement had to be negotiated, he announced a new policy. He would abandon the Geneva conference, and implement the agreement unilaterally. Once having fulfilled his side of the bargain to bring about majority rule—in co-operation with 'moderate Africans'—he would expect SA, the US and, less hopefully, the British, to honour their side.

There was another and more dangerous element in Smith's tactics which emerged from the briefings provided by himself and his Foreign Minister, Piet van der Byl. In their view, once Communist forces appeared in any numbers in Mozambique, SA would be compelled to enter the fighting on his side—and when that happened, the US would follow. So the success of Smith's strategy depended on Mozambique and Zipa bringing in the Communists—and the best chance of producing that result was for the Rhodesian troops to continue striking deep into Mozambique. In the Walter Mitty world inhabited by White Rhodesians this kind of thinking sounded less strange than elsewhere. There is undoubtedly some reality in the assumption that SA might blunder back into Rhodesia if Communist forces appeared in Mozambique; but who could believe that the US—especially a Carter Administration—would become involved in a second Vietnam? Yet it was Smith who tirelessly accused Mugabe and the others at Geneva of 'living in Cloud Cuckooland'.

WHO SPEAKS FOR THE AFRICANS?

The Africans' position at Geneva was much more complex than Smith's straightforward and monolithic role. First, there were the three rival groups—the Patriotic Front, the Bishop's ANC and Sithole's Zanu rump—each pursuing its own tactics about how to achieve their agreed objective. Although outwardly united, Nkomo and Mugabe were also engaged in a power struggle over who would finally lead the country. Although the spokesman for Zanu/Zipa, Mugabe, was under strong constraints not to go further towards negotiation than his constituency—the military cadres—were prepared for. He still needed to consolidate his political leadership within Zipa.

At the start of the conference Zipa contented itself with an observer's role. A small delegation included the former Zanu commander, Josiah Tongogara, who had been specially released by a Zambian court in the middle of his trial for Chitepo's murder.[97] Two other Zanu leaders released at the same time accompanied him. Zipa's new military commander, Rex Nhongo, also put in a brief appearance. Although they shared Mugabe's suite of rooms in the Intercontinental Hotel, they were not part of the Patriotic Front's delegation. It was not until the beginning of December that Rex Nhongo brought over a Zipa delegation to 'ensure and protect the independence of the people of Zimbabwe from being sabotaged and hijacked by imperialists, their racist allies and the apologists of imperialism, and to ensure the people's independence against the personal political ambitions of the opportunists and apologists of monopoly capitalism.' Zipa's decision to send a delegation was prompted by two reasons: differences had arisen between Mugabe and Nkomo over the question of whether elections should be held before independence (see below); and there were growing suspicions of a possible 'deal' between Muzorewa, Smith and the British.

Except for Angola, all the ringmasters were also present on the sidelines to keep a watchful eye and, when necessary, to nudge the Zimbabweans into making the tactical concessions necessary to prevent the talks from collapsing. Also on the sidelines were the Americans, playing a similar role vis-à-vis the British.

The Salisbury delegation were reluctant participants playing a spoiling role. Smith himself put in only two brief appearances at the beginning and at the end. His men sniped at the British chairman and at the Zimbabweans. 'Marxist terrorist murderers' was the phrase used by van der Byl in referring to Mugabe and his colleagues. Their strategy was to wait for the Black delegations to break ranks and fight each other, which they believed would inevitably happen.[98]

The only real negotiations that took place were between the British and the Zimbabweans. It took them a full month to overcome the first hurdle—a decision on the date for independence. The Patriotic Front had insisted it should be fixed as an *a priori* condition for discussing the form of the Interim Government. In the end, by a complicated formula,[99] agreement was reached fixing the date for independence on 1 March 1978. This agreement came only as a result of quiet but firm pressures by the FLPs on both the Patriotic Front and the British, and after a joint public demand by Tanzania and Nigeria for the date to be fixed.[100]

PROPOSALS FOR A TRANSITIONAL GOVERNMENT

During the long deadlock, which was broken only on 29 November, all the delegations (including Smith's) had circulated their proposals for the composition of the Interim Government. The Patriotic Front proposed that there should be no Council of State (as envisaged in the Kissinger proposals), but only a single Council of Ministers with full legislative and executive powers, the majority of whom (including the PM) would be drawn from the Liberation Movement. They would control, directly or indirectly, all the Ministries concerned with completing the pre-independence process, including Law and Order and Defence. The Bishop's ANC delegation wanted the Interim Government to be formed after the popular election of a PM, who would form a Cabinet composed of the different groups contesting the election. A British Governor would be installed for the transition, and would preside over a National Security Council responsible for producing a national army.

Sithole proposed a single-tier government with a Presidium and Council of Ministers. The Presidium would be composed of all the delegates at Geneva; and each would appoint four members of the Council of Ministers. A separate Defence Council would be made up of leading representatives from the conference. The Salisbury regime presented a detailed 8-stage plan to implement the Kissinger proposals within 23-25 months.[101] The British introduced an 11-stage plan to implement whatever agreement was reached at Geneva.[102] The British proposals were concerned only with the mechanism for the transition to independence; they included no independent views about the shape of the Interim Government itself.

A crucial difference of opinion arose between Mugabe and Nkomo at the end of November over whether general elections should form part of the process of independence; the latter insisted on elections, while the former took the view that power at independence must pass automatically to the Liberation Movement (as had occurred in Mozambique with Frelimo). Mugabe felt he could not accept Nkomo's proposal without returning for consultations with the Zipa leadership in Maputo. It was after his visit that Zipa sent its independent delegation to Geneva to stop the 'imperialist intrigues'. No finality was reached on this issue by the end of the conference, although President Machel later supported Nkomo's stand on elections (see below).

Muzorewa seized on the issue of popular elections in Zimbabwe to decide who should lead the country during the transition period, and this sharply divided the Zimbabwean ranks. It also brought Smith down in favour of an elected Black leader because he expected the Patriotic Front, and especially Mugabe, to come off worst in an election.

WHAT ROLE FOR BRITAIN?

'Whatever is going to happen will be decided by forces over which we have no control and over which we can make no projections'—Enoch Powell, 21 October 1976

The FLPs, meeting in Lusaka on 17 October, called on Britain to assume its obligations as the colonial power in Rhodesia, not only at the Geneva conference but also during the transition period. Nyerere explained that they wanted a British Governor-General, or similar figure, to be the ultimate authority during that period.[103] This African call for Britain to return—for a time—as the colonial ruler gladdened few British hearts. Only the Conservatives supported the idea of a resumption of British imperial responsibility—a demand made on a number of occasions by the Shadow Foreign Secretary, Reginald Maudling.[104] But in his view, the purpose of such a British role would be to assist Smith to implement the Kissinger proposals and to resist the guerrillas. The Tories' lunatic fringe, led by MPs like Ronald Bell and Julian Amery, went much further in calling for a strong British military commitment openly to support the Smith regime; the former even spoke of a British military base in Rhodesia. But such ideas found little response in the British mood of the 1970s. The experience of Ulster had bred a strong resistance to any new British commitment which would put it in a position of having to exercise 'responsibility without power'—and of being shot at by both sides.

Such anxieties were amply confirmed by the British chairman's experience at Geneva. White Rhodesian attitudes were predictably caustic. Nkomo, Mugabe and Muzorewa all, in turn, accused Richard of favouring the other side, and of 'imperialist trickery'. At the end of November, the Patriotic Front issued a formal statement alleging that Anglo-American 'imperialists' wanted to 'replace the Smith regime by a Black regime which will be less exposed to attack, but will serve their interests even more efficiently'. The thought behind this suspicion was that Muzorewa was being favoured to produce a moderate government at independence. Just a month later the Bishop made an attack in almost identical terms—though naturally his suspicion was that Britain and the FLPs were working for a Patriotic Front victory. Yet despite these attacks, all the Black nationalists insisted, along with the FLPs, that the only way to break the deadlock over who would exercise effective authority during the transition period was through a British presence. Because the Africans totally rejected the idea of defence and security being in White Rhodesian hands, and because the Smith regime would not entrust them to Black hands, the obvious compromise was to restore to Britain the authority which it had legally exercised in the colony until UDI. This view was vigorously resisted only by the Rhodesia Front. But other White Rhodesian leaders, like Sir Roy Welensky, felt that a British role was essential. So did Garfield Todd, a former Rhodesian Prime Minister. (Along with Justice Leo Baron and Dr Ruth Palley, he was acting as an advisor to Nkomo's delegation in Geneva. Dr Ahrn Palley, another White Rhodesian exile, was an advisor to Muzorewa's delegation.)

As Geneva moved heavily from one deadlocked position to the next—while Rhodesia moved towards more concentrated fighting—the initial British resistance to any idea of becoming involved during the transition period began to weaken. The US threw its weight behind the FLPs' demands for Britain to accept an active role in the Interim Government. A lively debate in the British Press also began to reflect growing support for Britain to reassume its legal responsibility for the rebel colony. By the end of November, Ivor Richard had decided that progress was impossible without a new British commitment. 'Re-enter the Governor of Rhodesia?' *The Times* asked in a forward-looking editorial on 23 November. Five days later the Conservatives' new Shadow Foreign Secretary, John Davies, gave his party's conditional support to the idea of a British Governor for Rhodesia. On the same day, the influential US Senator, Dick Clark, chairman of the Senate's Africa subcommittee, declared that the UK had to assume 'at least some of the residual powers that they had before'. On 2 December, Crosland informed Parliament of HMG's readiness to play 'a direct role in the transitional government'; but he added that 'the nature of this British presence would, of course, depend on the structure agreed for the Interim Government.' So, less than two months after the frosty reception given to Nyerere's call on behalf of the FLPs, Westminster had reversed itself —pushed by its friends in Africa and by the US, and encouraged by the Zimbabwe nationalists—but, above all, frightened by the consequences of what could happen if Geneva collapsed for want of a new British initiative.

THE END OF GENEVA

By the beginning of December it was clear that nothing more could be expected from the Geneva talks at that stage. Neither Smith nor his opponents were willing to yield an inch on any of the vital points which divided them: the rival proposals for an Interim Government were irreconcilable so long as Smith continued to stand on his 'package'; the anticipated rift in the Black lute had developed between Muzorewa's camp and the Patriotic Front, though the Mugabe–Nkomo alliance had survived intact despite their differences; the British had accepted the new role thrust on them; and the war in Rhodesia was becoming more worrying by the day. Only renewed pressures on the Smith regime—through a combination of diplomacy, the armed struggle and economic blockade—could improve the chances for a negotiated settlement.

Kissinger, on his round of farewells, flew to London on 10 December and said the initiative must remain with Britain. Speaking at a meeting of Nato Defence Ministers on 10 December, Crosland spoke of his preference for a 'moderate' nationalist government to emerge in Zimbabwe rather than 'a Marxist military dictatorship'. The Patriotic Front leaders took this to confirm their suspicions about secret British support for Muzorewa. On the last day of the conference, Mugabe and Nkomo in a joint statement accused Britain and the US of trying to create a puppet regime in Rhodesia. On this sour note Ivor Richard formally adjourned the conference on 14 December until 17 January 1977. On the same day Crosland announced that Richard would leave for Africa immediately after Christmas on a new mission to try and retrieve the Kissinger initiative.

A NEW BRITISH INITIATIVE: THIS TIME SMITH SAYS 'NO', THE AFRICANS SAY 'PERHAPS'

Ivor Richard unfolded the Anglo-American Mark Two proposals for a settlement on 23 December 1976 in Washington, having previously received US backing as well as Kissinger's personal endorsement. The new plan offered Zimbabweans a choice of four options: (1) Direct control by a British representative of the key posts of Defence and Law and Order in the transition Government. (2) A National Security Council with an equal number of White and Black representatives and 'a neutral chairman'. (3) One of the key posts to go to a Black representative and the other to a White representative. (4) One minister to control both portfolios; he would be White, but not a member of the Rhodesian Front. Whichever option was chosen, Whitehall would provide a British Commissioner as the interim Head of State. There would be no British troops under any circumstances, but there would be an administrative back-up for the Commissioner. A Commonwealth force, too, was ruled out. The central issue of how finally to integrate the guerrilla forces and the Rhodesian army could, in Richard's view, be done only by agreement and consensus: with the political leaders on both sides agreeing that the war should stop, the two forces would at least come together and eventually integrate after independence.

In the first round of his visits to the capitals of the FLPs (but not to Luanda) the new proposals got a fair wind, but the Zimbabwean leaders were harder to tie down. Eventually, on 17 January 1977, the Patriotic Front said that they could make a firm decision only after the final British proposal was put on paper 'clearly and precisely'. In other words, they wanted the British to indicate which of the four options was to be implemented. This at least indicated a readiness to negotiate further. Subsequently Britain did provide more detailed proposals (see below).

When Richard had the first of his two meetings with Vorster he found him unwilling to commit himself to the merits of the plan until he had received categorical assurances from the FLPs that the armed struggle would stop once an agreement was reached. Richard's second round of visits produced firm commitments from Nyerere, Kaunda, Machel and Khama. When he left Dar es Salaam he said he had 'run out of adjectives' to describe how good his meeting had been with Nyerere. But it was in Maputo that Richard scored his biggest triumph, when Machel declared: 'The principle of independence is no longer questioned. Now it is a question of finding the modalities to implement this principle. War is fed by blood and it destroys lives. We therefore say welcome to the chairman of the conference, welcome to Great Britain. We hope you will find all the necessary co-operation'.

The story was different in Salisbury. Even in advance of Richard's arrival, the Foreign Affairs Ministry had dealt a rebuff to the British proposals in a 10-page background briefing which rejected any British role in the transition period and which accused the British of being 'patently out of touch with the realities of the situation' in Rhodesia. The first encounter with Smith on 2 January 1977 produced what Richard later described as 'a good verbal punch-up'. A Rhodesian paper described Smith as having adopted a 'snarling' attitude which had led Richard to lose his temper.

In the middle of his second round of talks on 9 January, the FLPs at a meeting in Lusaka announced their exclusive recognition for the Patriotic Front. This decision was intended to strengthen the unity of the Zimbabwean fighting front, but it had two serious results. The first was that it virtually ensured Smith's rejection of the British proposals since the implications of the FLPs' recognition meant that effective power would pass into the hands of Mugabe and Nkomo, with the former possibly in the stronger position. The second result was that, so far from unifying the Zimbabweans, it widened the rift between Muzorewa's supporters and the Patriotic Front. The decision forced Muzorewa to pursue his own independent initiative inside Rhodesia—just as Nkomo had done a year earlier.

Meanwhile, Richard was able to return to SA carrying with him the FLPs' unequivocal assurances that the fighting would stop once a Transition Government was installed. This time he got Vorster's support for the proposals, and found him as determined as ever to avert a full-scale war in Rhodesia. Back in Salisbury, he had a friendlier meeting with Smith. But on 24 January, Smith broadcast his total rejection of the British proposals. 'My military chiefs,' he said, 'were horrified'. His Foreign Minister described the British terms as being 'worse than those for the Nazis. They were so intolerable that you would fight even if there was no hope.' Smith still insisted that a settlement would be reached only by implementing his 'agreement' with Kissinger. The British Foreign Secretary told Parliament that Smith's rejection of the proposals—the only one to do so—represented 'a serious setback to all their hopes for peace'. The Conservative spokesmen, John Davies and Reginald Maudling, put the blame for the setback, not on Smith, but on the British Government.

The militants on both sides were, once again, firmly in control of their forces. Cries of 'good old Smithy' were once again popular in Salisbury.[105] 'It would be better to die to the last man and the last cartridge than to die in front of one of Mugabe's People's Courts,' was the view of a typical Smith hardliner—his Foreign Minister, P. J. van der Byl.[106] But there were also some saner voices in Rhodesia who thought 'Smith must be crazy'.[107] Sir Roy Welensky insisted that there was no alternative to accepting a British presence. The three White Opposition groups—Rhodesia Party, Centre Party and the National Pledge Association—joined forces to form a pressure group to back a negotiated settlement. And a handful of White Rhodesians carried placards in a demonstration calling for a peaceful end to the fighting.

BRITAIN'S PROPOSALS FOR A TRANSITION GOVERNMENT
Ivor Richard handed over the following Note to the Geneva delegations 'for further discussion and negotiation':

'In formulating these ideas the British Government have attempted to meet the general concern that the process of transition to independence should be rapid, guaranteed, and orderly. It is the particular concern of the nationalists that the minority should not be able to exercise such a control over the transitional government as to allow it either to delay independence or so to influence the drawing-up of the independence constitution as to prevent it from giving full effect to genuine majority rule. It is the particular concern of the minority that there will be a genuine transitional period, during which the security situation will be properly controlled, and that there will be a place for them in an independent Zimbabwe.

'In pursuance of these interests, the two sides in the negotiations have hitherto adopted incompatible positions concerning the power-structure during the transitional period: the nationalists have pressed for an immediate transfer of full power to themselves; the minority have insisted on a structure for the transitional government which would have the effect of leaving control over the vital areas in their own hands. In the view of the British Government both of these positions are unrealistic. A negotiated settlement is possible only if both sides agree to a structure for the transitional government which strikes a reasonable balance between them and which gives adequate protection to the legitimate interests of both. This would have to provide for a visible and effective African majority in the government but also for a participation by representatives of the European minority sufficient to ensure that their interests were taken into account. While power in sensitive areas, such as internal security and the drawing-up of the independence constitution, could not be left in minority hands, it should not pass, during the transitional period, wholly into the hands of the nationalists.

'The suggestions in this paper are designed to provide such a structure. They proceed on the basis that where solutions can be found using purely Rhodesian elements, that should be done. But where that is not possible, it is suggested that a British presence could usefully be introduced to assure each side that neither can prevent the achievement of the legitimate aims of the other. There would have to be a number of pre-conditions for the introduction of any British presence into the constitutional arrangements for Rhodesia during the transitional period. Among the most important of these would be that it was clearly accepted by all parties concerned that guerrilla activity would cease as soon as agreement had been reached on the setting up of the transitional government; and British readiness to continue to play a part in the agreed transitional arrangements would be conditional upon all other parties abiding by that agreement.

'In the light of the above considerations, the British Government suggests that the parties should now discuss a structure for the transitional government of Rhodesia on the following lines: the transitional government would be headed by an interim commissioner who would be appointed by the British Government, after due consultations. There would also be a deputy interim commissioner, appointed in the same way, who would act as interim commissioner whenever the former was unable to do so. In addition to the interim commissioner, the transitional government would have three principal organs:

(a) A Council of Ministers.
(b) An Advisory Council of senior Ministers.
(c) A National Security Council.

'The Council of Ministers would contain equal numbers of members from each of the political groups represented by the delegations to the Geneva conference and a further similar number of members appointed by the Interim Commissioner from among members of the European minority. It would thus have a substantial African majority. The leaders of the delegations to the Geneva conference would be members of the council of ministers and would together form an Inner Cabinet (perhaps called the Advisory Council) which would act in a general advisory capacity to the Interim Commissioner and would also have other specified functions.

'The Council of Ministers would have full executive and legislative competence for the Government of Rhodesia, subject only to the Interim Commissioner's reserve powers.

'Except where his reserve powers were involved, the Interim Commissioner would be required to act in accordance with the advice of his Ministers in exercising all his executive functions and in assenting to legislation. If there were agreement on the choice of one of the African members of the Council of Ministers as a First Minister, the meetings of the Council of Ministers would be presided over by the

First Minister who would, as such, also have other specified functions. If not, other arrangements would have to be made: e.g. the chairmanship of meetings of the Council of Ministers might rotate among the members of the Advisory Council. In any event, the person presiding over the Council of Ministers would not have a casting vote.

'The Interim Commissioner would not be a member of the Council of Ministers and would ordinarily not attend its meetings. However, he would be empowered to do so when he considered that matters might be discussed which could affect his residual responsibilities (see paragraph below).

'The Interim Commissioner would have residual responsibility for certain subjects (primarily external affairs, defence, internal security and the implementation of the programme for independence). His powers in the Council of Ministers in relation to these subjects would enable him to ensure, on the one hand, that the minority in the Council of Ministers could not impede the transition to majority rule and independence and, on the other hand, that the Transitional Government did not act in a way which would imperil the orderly nature of that transition or which was incompatible with the exercise of the United Kingdom's constitutional responsibilities.

'The question of voting procedures in the Council of Ministers could be regulated in a number of different ways. In choosing the appropriate voting system, the aim should be to ensure that the will of the substantial majority of the members of the Council of Ministers prevailed in matters of day-to-day government and in maintaining the momentum of the transition to majority rule and independence; but also to ensure that the representatives of the minority community, while not being able to impede that transition, were given an effective voice in all decisions of special concern to their community. Where the Interim Commissioner's residual responsibilities were involved, a special majority would be required and the Interim Commissioner would himself be given a vote which, in certain situations, could operate as a casting vote. Apart perhaps from defence and internal security (see paragraph below) and possibly also external affairs, all departments of government would be in the charge of a Minister. The Council of Ministers would have collective responsibility for governing Rhodesia.

'Defence and internal security would be the responsibility of the National Security Council, though this would not necessarily preclude the allocation of these portfolios to individual ministers if agreement on that matter could be reached. The Council would consist of the Interim Commissioner (and perhaps also the deputy Interim Commissioner); the leading members of the Council of Ministers; and the two chiefs of staff of the armed forces and the Commissioner of Police. These three officers would themselves be appointed and removable by the Interim Commissioner. The Interim Commissioner would preside over meetings of the National Security Council and would be in a position to exercise a casting vote.

'The day-to-day organization and operational control of the armed forces and the police would be the responsibility of the respective chiefs of staff and the Commissioner of Police. But these would be responsible (either directly or, if there were ministers for defence and internal security, through those Ministers) to the National Security Council which would give them general directives of policy with regard to the maintenance of public security and generally with regard to the organization and employment of the forces under their command.

'The National Security Council, with the concurrence of the Interim Commissioner, would have the power to appoint and remove the holders of certain senior offices in the armed forces and the police. The National Security Council would also be responsible for supervising the reorganization of the defence and internal security forces.

'The Council of Ministers would be responsible for the implementation of the programme for independence and in particular for the working out of the independence constitution. For this purpose, it would appoint a constitutional committee which would include representatives of the various political parties and also constitutional and other experts (perhaps from outside Rhodesia). The constitutional committee would formulate recommendations to the Council of Ministers. The Interim Commissioner would himself preside over the constitutional committee (as well, of course as taking part in the consideration of its recommendation in the Council of Ministers).

THE MERCENARY FACTOR IN THE RHODESIAN CONFLICT

'Would you like to work in fun? Then come and join the Rhodesian Army'—Advertisement for foreign volunteers

The SA Prime Minister has refused to commit himself in advance about the role of the Republic's army if the war is not checked in Rhodesia. He insists that the final decision, if one ever has to be taken, will be made by Parliament. But Africa is already concerned with a different aspect of this question: even if SA or the Western nations do not intervene openly, what clandestine role might they play? Their suspicions are reinforced by the influx of 'volunteers' or 'mercenaries'. No matter which description one cares to apply to the foreign recruits in the Rhodesian army, this element is certain to become a crucial factor in relations between Africa and the West. The emotional response from both sides over this question was shown at the time of the trial of 'mercenaries' in Angola in 1976,[108] and in Rhodesia feelings will be much stronger for three reasons. First, SA could exercise the softer 'option' of allowing its soldiers to enlist in Smith's army, rather than fight in their own uniforms. Second, there is already evidence of a considerable 'volunteer force' of Whites going to the defence of White Rhodesia. (The current rate of pay for volunteers is roughly $4,000 a year for privates, $6,400 for sergeants and $7,600 for junior officers.) Third, since the actual number of regular soldiers in the Rhodesian army is very small, it will not take a large influx of volunteers to give it the character of a foreign White army.

Just how many foreigners already form part of the Rhodesian army's 6,000 regulars? According to Hugh Lynn, a British deserter from the Rhodesian army, there were 2,000 Britons in 1976, many of them former paratroopers, and over 100 Americans, mostly Vietnam veterans. In a Botswana radio interview, two other army deserters corroborated the estimate that about a third of the regular forces are already made up of foreign volunteers. Robin Wright, reporting from Salisbury, put the number of foreign recruits at 1,000, with volunteers coming from Germany, Canada, Greece, Holland, Australia, Portugal, France, New Zealand, Britain, Sweden—and even one from Sri Lanka.[109] She put the American contingent at 400. A South African reporter, Paul Smurthwaite, also put the American contingent at 400. He supported the overall figure of 1,000.[110] There are 20 Australians, mostly Vietnam veterans fighting in Rhodesia; an Australian TV unit which filmed them was deported in early 1977.

There are no reliable estimates of the number of recruits from SA, only hints about their existence. A 25-year old soldier sentenced to death in December 1976 for the murder of a black taxi-driver was said in court to have been South African. The Lisbon paper *Diario de Lisboa* (December 1976) reported that recruits for the Rhodesian forces were being trained at Iscar, near Valladolid in Spain. This is the camp of the so-called Guerrillas of Christ the King and the Adolf Hitler Commando who are involved in Portugal's own clandestine counter-revolutionary movement. According to the Lisbon report, some units were also being trained there to go to Rhodesia for operations against Mozambique. A similar military element is being provided by the Mozambique United Front according to the Voice of Free Africa, an anti-Frelimo radio station which broadcasts from Rhodesia. This force is believed to include both White and Black opponents of Machel's regime.[111]

The Tanzanian Government paper, *Daily News,* reported in December 1976 that 1,500 mercenaries had been recruited abroad. It doubted whether such recruitment could have been undertaken without prior knowledge of the governments concerned. For their own reasons, the Russians have made a regular feature in Radio Moscow of reports to Africa about 'Western mercenaries' in Rhodesia.

Major Nick Lamprecht, Rhodesia's chief army recruiting officer, has denied that the foreigners are 'mercenaries'.[112] He explains their motive as 'enthusiasm about fighting communism—they don't want to see a repeat of what happened in Vietnam'.

Major Lamprecht's 22-year old son, Vincent, took a totally opposite view from his father's. After completing his own national service he emigrated to South Africa where he said: 'I think the situation in Rhodesia is getting out of hand.' He cited as indications that Rhodesia is approaching the brink, frequent call-ups, constant shortages, announcements of 'all-out drives to wipe out the terrorist menace'. He added, 'You can't win by trying to fool the people into believing you're going to wipe out the terrorist menace once and for all by calling up reservists. It becomes difficult to fight for something you don't think has a hope of succeeding.'[113]

THE INTERNATIONAL TRUST FUND

President Nyerere was the first to propose a fund to compensate White Rhodesian emigrants. His idea, first mooted in 1975, was that a useful way of undermining Smith would be to assist the departure of Whites who would prefer to leave if it were financially possible for them to do so. Nyerere's idea was directly contrary to British contingency plans designed to encourage Whites to stay in Rhodesia. This is because the British feared a repetition of the experience in Mozambique and Angola whose economies were badly disrupted by the large-scale exodus of Portuguese doctors, technicians, industrialists and skilled workers at independence. British proposals were based on the Kenyan experience where a compensation fund had been set up for farmers on the White Highlands, though there the fund was linked to the Kenyatta Government's own economic planning and formed part of British aid to Kenya.

At the first talks between Vorster and Kissinger in Bavaria in June 1976, the SA Prime Minister came out strongly in favour of a fund to compensate White Rhodesians who wished to leave, or whose land and property might be nationalized. After that meeting Kissinger began to develop the idea of an International Trust Fund, whose resources would be banked outside Rhodesia to provide a greater element of confidence about how they would be used. A committee of US, British and South African representatives was set up to work on the details of the plan. In its final shape the Trust Fund was designed not just to provide funds to compensate Whites, but to act as an international consortium to raise substantial amounts of foreign aid for Zimbabwe's independent government. As in Kenya, the Fund would enable the Zimbabwean government to pay for land or property taken over from Whites, as well as help emigrants get compensation for what they were forced to leave behind. But an incentive to remain would be provided by increasing the rate of compensation for those who stayed on longer.

Kissinger talked optimistically of a fund of two billion dollars; this was later scaled down considerably. The Ford Administration formally approached Western European nations and Japan to become participants. West Germany and France both responded. President Carter endorsed the proposal for the Trust Fund before he took office in December 1976. On the strength of his support, Britain formally invited 25 countries to contribute up to $1.3 billion to the Fund. When Ivor Richard visited Rhodesia in January 1977, he assured a trade union delegation that a Trust Fund would be set up to guarantee the position of White Rhodesians in case of need.

FULL CIRCLE: SMITH'S SECOND UDI

Almost a year after Kissinger had set out in April 1976 to halt a race war and to prevent southern Africa becoming a cockpit for international rivalry, the situation was more ominous than before the start of his mission. No progress at all had been made towards resolving the crisis in Namibia; and Smith had declared his 'second UDI'—this time to implement unilaterally the settlement terms he had negotiated with Kissinger. Even should he succeed in getting enough Blacks inside Rhodesia to co-operate in this effort, Smith would not get either African or international recognition for a 'majority rule' Interim Government masterminded by the Rhodesian Front. Vorster told him so when Smith went to seek his support for the plan on 9 February 1977—and Vorster, after all, is in a good position to offer this kind of advice, since his own plans to produce a similar settlement for Namibia and for the independence of the Transkei had run up against precisely the same problem of non-recognition by the international community. Smith has nevertheless gone on believing that the US would 'honour' the agreement reached with Kissinger. By refusing to negotiate seriously with the Africans at Geneva, Smith destroyed any chance of winning their co-operation; and by rejecting the amended proposals accepted by the UK, US, the FLPs and SA, he made it less likely than ever that he would get the kind of support he would need from abroad if his new plan were to succeed. Smith had in fact led Rhodesia back into the *cul de sac* from which Kissinger had seemed to rescue it. The resignation of the Rhodesian Minister of Defence, Reg Cowper, in February 1977 pointed up the Rhodesians' acute dilemma. The country had by then reached the stage where its economic and manpower resources were so stretched that a choice had to be made between calling up more White Rhodesians to keep the guerrillas at bay, or keeping them at work to prevent the economy from collapsing under the combined pressures of economic sanctions and the growing burden of the defence costs. Cowper insisted that the first priority should be to increase military manpower; Smith took the side of those concerned with defending the economy. The conclusion is inescapable: without a settlement, Rhodesia cannot survive.

SA's dilemma also remains. It desperately needs to stop the war in Rhodesia, but Vorster is unwilling to apply the necessary pressures on the Smith regime, a position he reiterated when speaking in his Parliament on 28 January 1977. Without a settlement in Rhodesia he is not ready to move towards a radical settlement for the Namibian crisis. And without that the fighting will escalate there—with Angola becoming the base country for Swapo, as Mozambique is for Zipa, but with an even greater risk of active foreign involvement on the Namibian front.

After the failure of the Richard initiative, Britain's Foreign Secretary told Parliament (25 January 1977) that the chances of 'armed Marxist' participation in Rhodesia had been greatly increased, bringing with it the danger of Russian and Cuban intervention in the conflict. The urgent need, he argued, was for yet another Anglo-American diplomatic initiative.

The US Administration's position, stated by the Secretary of State, Cyrus Vance, on 10 February 1977, was that 'under no circumstances can the Rhodesian authorities count on any form of American assistance in their effort to prevent majority rule in Rhodesia', or for their efforts to enter into negotiations which 'exclude leaders of the nationalist movements'. He added that Washington still remained committed to finding a peaceful alternative to war in co-operation with

Britain, SA and the African leaders.

The FLPs, while still not closing their minds finally to the need for further diplomatic efforts, have grown even less confident of diplomacy than when they first welcomed the Kissinger and, later, the Ivor Richard initiatives. They saw no way that diplomacy could succeed unless—as Nyerere told the US Ambassador to the UN, Andrew Young, on 6 February 1977—Smith was 'ousted'. He thought this objective could be assisted by further tightening the economic pressures on Rhodesia. While not ruling out the value of further diplomatic efforts, their own priorities were to help intensify the armed struggle of both Zipa and Swapo, and to assist Mozambique in the defence of its borders.

The OAU secretary-general, William Eteki Mboumoua, proposed in January 1977 that a pan-African military force should be stationed in Mozambique, Angola and Zambia. This idea had previously been discussed with Nigeria during state visits made by the Presidents of Tanzania and Zambia. The creation of such an African border force was explored at the meeting of the OAU Liberation Committee in Lusaka at the end of January 1977, making the prospect of African military involvement along the borders of Rhodesia and Angola come into realistic focus for the first time. Such a force is likely to reduce the risks of non-African powers becoming involved, but it would also mark a further notch up the scale of military involvement in the southern African struggle.

The recognition accorded by the FLPs to the Patriotic Front (subsequently endorsed by the OAU) gave them a sharp edge over Muzorewa's ANC, thus sharpening the rivalry between them. The ANC believe that they not only command overwhelming majority support inside the country, but also that they have a considerable following inside Zipa, which (for reasons already explained) remains inarticulate. Their future tactics must be dictated by the immediate advantage they hold inside their constituency at home. They have been left as the only African movement with whom the Smith regime could still negotiate. So, at one level, the ANC was weakened by the FLPs' decision; but at a different level, they were left in a stronger position to initiate any new negotiations that might take place with the Smith regime. The implications of the continuing rivalries among Zimbabweans therefore remain serious for the future.

THE RUSSIANS' RINGSIDE SEAT

'The Soviet Union's stand on the problems of southern Africa is clear and definite: the Soviet Union has no, and cannot have, any "special interests", neither in south nor north, nor in any other part of Africa. The USSR does not look for any benefits for itself there. It only strives for the sacred right of every people to decide its own destiny, for the right to choose its own way of development. This is our unwavering principle, which the Soviet people will never abandon.'—Yuri Kornilov, in *Tass*, 11 October 1976

The Russians' successful military intervention with the Cubans in Angola[114] strengthened their influence in southern Africa, but they failed to follow up their success in the immediate post-Angolan phase. This, possibly short-term, setback can be attributed to five different factors. The most crucial was the FLPs' determination to avoid international military involvement in Rhodesia and Namibia if at all possible. This wish to avoid foreign entanglements does not rule out military support for the liberation movements from any quarter—subject only to all arms being channelled exclusively through the OAU Liberation Committee in Dar es Salaam. In this way the FLPs can hope to control the flow of arms and prevent rival forces being sustained by outside Powers, as happened in Angola. The second factor was the FLPs' strong preference for a peaceful rather than a violent settlement of the crises in Rhodesia and Namibia: this preference led to their decision to co-operate with Kissinger. The third factor was the diplomatic momentum set up by Kissinger, which left the Russians fulminating on the sidelines against what their Foreign Minister, Andrei Gromyko, termed 'political gimmickry'. (This charge of 'mere gimmickry' could equally be applied to the FLPs since their role was essential to Kissinger's diplomacy.) The fourth factor was Zanu's refusal to accept a Russian role in their military camps since this would have meant breaking with the Chinese with whom their military cadres have worked closely for ten years. As Zanu comprises by far the biggest element in Zipa, Moscow's urgings that Cubans be brought in as instructors in the use of Russian weapons could be resisted. Zanu's relations with the Chinese had earlier led the Russians to adopt Nkomo's Zapu as their favourite (see above). However, Zapu's cadres had been mostly trained in Eastern Europe, and there were no Russian surrogates in the Zapu camps in Tanzania. What remains unclear is how Zanu/Zapu co-operation in the Patriotic Front and in Zipa's Joint Command will affect their relations with Peking and Moscow. The Chinese, who speak of the Cubans as 'Russian mercenaries', successfully took a strong stand against any of Castro's military instructors being brought into the same camps as themselves. The final factor was Swapo's strong wish to remain strictly non-aligned. Although the instructors in their own camps are Chinese, their leaders have carefully avoided taking sides in Sino/Soviet disputes. However, Swapo began seriously to re-examine its options in 1976 and appears to have moved closer to taking up the Russian offer for reasons already explained (see The Fourth Front above).

Kissinger's diplomacy produced two quandaries for the Russians. Until the Secretary of State made his Lusaka speech in April 1976 announcing the new US policy towards southern Africa, Moscow could—with considerable justification —hold up the Americans as supporters of the White-ruled regimes, and especially of SA. It became much harder to do this after the US commitment to work for majority rule throughout the region. Moscow's propaganda in Africa therefore concentrated on trying to show that the Americans had not genuinely stopped being 'the patrons of the racialist regimes', but that they had simply changed their tactics to bolster up their 'Nato alliance' and to undermine the increasingly successful liberation movements. If Anglo-Americans were genuine in wishing to overthrow the 'racialist regimes' why, asked Moscow, did they not use their power to remove them? The Soviets' warning to Africa was that the Nato partners remained primarily interested in preserving the position of the 'imperialist monopolies' in Rhodesia and SA; and that this explained their 'slandering policy' against the Soviets—'the African people's most faithful allies'.[115] The answer to these manoeuvres, said Moscow, was to establish 'a united anti-imperialist front of African states'.[116]

It was easier for the Russians to criticize the 'hypocrisy and duplicity of the imperialists' than it was to explain why the FLPs had worked with Kissinger. Why had Nyerere and his colleagues not seen that Kissinger's shuttle diplomacy was, as *Pravda* described it (16 September 1976), 'a dangerous plot between imperialists and racists?' Was it because the 'collusion' was going on behind the Africans' backs, or because of the imperialist 'pressures' on African leaders?[117] In other words were the Russians really saying that Nyerere, Kaunda, Machel and Khama were too stupid to see the 'plot' for themselves, or that they were too weak to resist the 'imperialist pressures'? These were the logical conclusions to be drawn from the Soviet analysis of the implications of Kissinger's diplomacy, but of course they were never openly referred to in Moscow's broadcasts to Africa, which were always careful to avoid the slightest hint of criticism of the FLPs. Nor was there any attempt to report or analyse the African leaders' reasons for working with Kissinger.

It would be a serious mistake, though, to suppose that despite the Soviets' failure to gain any significant advantage from their Angolan achievement, they might not yet succeed in their objectives. Among advances they could claim in 1976 was the consolidation of their relations with Angola through the Friendship Treaty.[118] Machel, an old friend of China, went on a 'friendship visit' to Moscow, and began to show interest in closer Russian military relations if the South Africans should become involved in Rhodesia. Swapo had also moved somewhat closer to accepting the Russian offer of military support. The pro-Moscow groupings in the SA liberation movement became more effective from their new operational headquarters in Mozambique.[119] If the Western diplomatic initiative should fail in the end, the Russians will almost certainly be the foreign power most likely to benefit. The visit of President Podgorny to southern Africa in March 1977 showed that the Russians remain closely interested in the future of the sub-continent.

The Chinese, in sharp contrast to the very active role they played in the Angolan affair,[120] kept an extremely low profile in Mozambique and Rhodesia, while sustaining their customary attacks on the 'modern tsars'. Their present activities have been confined to maintaining their training presence in the guerrilla camps.

The Cuban role in Mozambique and Rhodesia appears to have been greatly exaggerated in 1976. Their numbers in Mozambique were variously estimated at between 500 and 1,000 by the Rhodesians and South Africans. A much likelier estimate is between 100 and 200 Cubans working mainly as technicians, doctors and skilled workers for the Maputo government. They do not seem to be directly involved in the military struggle—not yet—at any rate. However, their interest in the area remains keen, as was shown by Fidel Castro's whirlwind tour of the area in March 1977.[121]

NOTES

All newspaper references are to British papers unless otherwise indicated. References to 'this volume' and 'Documents section' relate to 1976-7 edition of *Africa Contemporary Record*.
1. See *Africa Contemporary Record (ACR)* 1974-5; pp. A3ff, A94ff. Also *ACR* 1975-6, pp. A118ff, C97ff.
2. See *ACR* 1974-5, pp. A69ff, B527ff.
3. See *ACR* 1975-6, 'Foreign intervention in Angola', pp. A3-38.
4. Interview with Julius Nyerere, Thames TV, 23 September 1976.
5. *Ibid.*
6. *Ibid.*
7. See *ACR* 1974-5, 'SA: the Secret Diplomacy of Detente', pp. A8ff; *ACR* 1975-6, pp. A39ff.
8. *Ibid.*
9. *ACR* 1975-6, pp. A49ff.
10. *Ibid*, pp. A47ff.
11. *ACR* 1974-5, pp. A8, A11f. *ACR* 1975-6, pp. A48f, B639, C75.
12. See article by the author 'Rhodesia on Verge of All-Out War' in *The Observer*, 15 February 1976. The 'authoritative Zambian spokesman' quoted was in fact President Kaunda.
13. Speech to the Royal Commonwealth Society, London; 19 February 1976.
14. For statement see Documents Section p. 162.
15. *Financial Times,* 27 February 1976.
16. *Daily Telegraph*, 27 February 1976.
17. See chapter on Mozambique in this volume.
18. *The Observer*, 7 March 1976.
19. For the terms see Documents Section, pp. C161f.
20. *The Times*, 5 April 1976.
21. See essay on 'The OAU in 1976' in this volume.

22. See *ACR* 1974-5, pp. A7ff.
23. In an interview with David Martin, *The Observer,* 7 March 1976.
24. *Zambia Daily Mail*, Lusaka, 29 April 1976.
25. *The Star*, Johannesburg, 24 April 1976.
26. See *ACR*. 1969-70, pp. C41ff.
27. See *ACR,* 1974-5, pp. A12ff.
28. *Radio Maputo*, 28 January 1977.
29. See *ACR,* 1971-2, pp. C144ff; 1972-3, pp. C139ff.
30. See David Martin's account in *The Observer*, 7 March 1976.
31. See *ACR* 1975-6, p. B386.
32. *The Zimbabwe Star*, 12 June 1976.
33. *Chimurenga: Zanu Monthly Newsletter*, 1:6 (31 May 1976).
34. *Daily Telegraph*, 7 October 1976.
35. Interview with the author.
36. *Daily Telegraph,* 19 October 1976.
37. *Rhodesian Herald*, Salisbury, 1 December 1976.
38. *Ibid*, 4 December 1976.
39. *Ibid.*
40. *Ibid*, 6 December 1976.
41. *Ibid.*
42. *The Times,* 27 November 1976.
43. *Ibid*, 10 September 1976.
44. Radio Maputo, 22 January 1977.
45. See chapter on Rhodesia in this volume.
46. E. Sutton-Pryce, Deputy Minister in the Prime Minister's office; *Financial Times*, 26 January 1977.
47. *The Times*, 21 January 1977.
48. Peter Younghusband in the *Daily Mail*, 13 December 1976.
49. *Ibid.*
50. *Ibid.*
51. Interview with the author.
52. John Edwards in the *Daily Mail*, 16 October 1976.
53. *Daily Telegraph*, 4 October 1976.
54. See chapter on South Africa in this volume.
55. See note 7.
56. See 'International Involvement in Angola,' *ACR* 1975-6, pp. A3ff.
57. See under Sport in chapter on SA in this volume.
58. *Rand Daily Mail*, Johannesburg, 15 November 1975.
59. See chapter on SA in this volume.
60. See *ACR* 1975-6, p. C71.
61. See chapter on Namibia in this volume.
62. See *ACR* 1975-6, pp. B556ff.
63. See chapter on Transkei in this volume.
64. See *ACR* 1974-5, pp. A93ff.
65. See *ACR* 1974-5. pp. A87-101; 1975-6, pp. A120ff.
66. See Documents Section, pp. C157.
67. Quoted by Bernard Gwertzman, *New York Times*, 8 September 1976.
68. *The Times*, 18 May 1976.
69. This and subsequent notes from Kissinger's conversations come from a number of sources close to him during his shuttle.
70. Interview with Bridget Bloom, *Financial Times*, 11 September 1976.
71. *The Guardian*, 15 September 1976.
72. Interview with David Martin, *The Observer*, 5 September 1976.
73. See chapter on Rhodesia in this volume.
74. Radio Salisbury, 27 August 1976.
75. *Ibid.*
76. *The Times*, 3 September 1976.
77. *Daily Telegraph*, 16 August 1976.
78. Part of this account appeared previously in *The Observer,* 26 September 1976.
79. For details, see Documents section, p. C157.
80. *The Guardian*, 29 June 1977.
81. *International Herald Tribune*, Paris, 20 November 1976.
82. *Ibid*, 15 October 1976.
83. *Ibid*. 20 November 1976.

84. *New York Times*, 16 November 1976.
85. *The Guardian*, 29 January 1977.
86. Murray Marder, *International Herald Tribune*, Paris, 28 September 1976.
87. *The Guardian*, 28 January 1977.
88. *Ibid*, 29 January 1977.
89. For details of proposal announced by Smith, see Documents Section, p. C157.
90. For full text of FLPs commonuique, see Documents section, p. C158.
91. Radio Havana, 27 September 1976.
92. Radio Maputo, 5 October 1976.
93. Full statement broadcast by Radio Maputo, 30 September 1976.
94. Radio Kampala, 30 August 1976.
95. *The Times*, 1 October 1976.
96. See chapter on Mozambique in this volume.
97. See chapter on Zambia in this volume.
98. Henry Kamm (*International Herald Tribune,* Paris, 14 October 1976) quoting a Government source, reported that Salisbury 'holds it more than likely that the talks will stalemate because of "posturing" and mutual "outbidding" by the Nationalist spokesmen.'
99. The agreed formula was: 'It is the British Government's firm position that all the agreed processes in Rhodesia will be completed in time to enable independence to be granted by 1 March 1978. The British Government therefore fix 1 March 1978 as the latest date by which Rhodesia will become independent and on this basis independence could come even by 1 December 1977. Before the conclusion of the conference and after agreeing on the establishment of the interim Government, the conference will revert to the question of fixing a date for independence so that a firm date can be agreed upon.' *The Observer*, 28 November 1976.
100. *Rhodesia Herald*, 22 November 1976.
101. *Ibid*, 25 November 1976.
102. See Bridget Bloom in *The Financial Times*, 12 November 1976.
103. *The Guardian*, 18 November 1976.
104. e.g. House of Commons debates, 21 October 1976. *The Times,* 18 September 1976.
105. *The Times*, 25 January 1977.
106. *Daily Telegraph*, 26 January 1977.
107. *The Times*, 25 January 1977.
108. See chapter on Angola in this volume.
109. *International Herald Tribune*, Paris, 10 December 1976.
110. *Daily Dispatch,* East London (SA), 22 December 1976.
111. *The Times*, 11 February 1977.
112. *International Herald Tribune*, Paris, 10 December 1976.
113. *The Star*, Johannesburg, 24 July 1976.
114. For relations between Moscow and Havana, see essay on Cuba in Africa in this volume.
115. Vladimir Petrov, Radio Moscow, 30 September 1976.
116. *Ibid*, 7 September 1976.
117. Boris Kalyagin, Radio Moscow, 14 September 1976.
118. See Documents section, pp. C151ff.
119. See chapter on South Africa in this volume.
120. See *ACR* 1975-6, pp. A3ff.
121. See note 114 above.

1977–1978

ANGLO-AMERICAN COOPERATION AND A NEW WESTERN INITIATIVE

That Southern Africa did not become another area of armed international intervention in 1977, or even in early 1978, was due entirely to a remarkable exercise in diplomacy between Africa and the Western community, which kept open the possibility of negotiated settlements in Rhodesia and Namibia. But while this active diplomacy was effective in preventing foreign intervention on the lines of Angola or the Horn of Africa, there is still no certainty that it will succeed in its major purpose of helping to establish majority rule in the three White-ruled territories. The initiator of this new diplomatic approach in 1976 was the US Secretary of State, Dr Henry Kissinger;[1] but his tentative, ambiguous and highly personal diplomacy was given more shape, clarity and consistency early in 1978 after the advent of the new Carter Administration and the arrival at the British Foreign Office of Dr David Owen. Their new joint initiatives also began to find favour among members of the European Community, changes in the West's attitude to the problems of Southern Africa having been induced by the success of Soviet and Cuban intervention in Angola.[2]

The significant element in this new Western approach was a belated response to the offer of an international accord held out by the Organization of African Unity (OAU) on the basis of the Lusaka Manifesto of 1969.[3] That seminal document opened with the warning that: 'When the purposes and the basis of States' international policies are misunderstood, there is introduced into the world a new and unnecessary disharmony. Disagreements, conflicts of interest or different assessments of human priorities already provoke an excess of tension in the world and disastrously divide mankind at a time when united action is necessary to control modern technology and put it to the service of man.' The Lusaka Manifesto was an invitation to the international community to co-operate in achieving peaceful change in order to avoid more violent conflicts and the introduction of big power rivalries into the area. The appeal was addressed especially to the Western powers because of their direct involvement with the *status quo* regimes; it urged them to come out positively in support of the following two basic African aims:

'Our objectives in Southern Africa stem from our commitment to [the] principle of human equality. We are not hostile to the Administrations of these States because they are manned and controlled by White people. We are hostile to them because they are systems of minority control which exist as a result of, and in the pursuance of, doctrines of human inequality. What we are working for is the right of self-determination for the people of those territories. We are working for a rule in those countries which is based on the will of all the people and an acceptance of the equality of every citizen.

'Our stand towards Southern Africa thus involves a rejection of racialism, not a reversal of the existing racial domination. We believe that all the peoples who have made their homes in the countries of Southern Africa are Africans, regardless of the colour of their skins; and we would oppose a racialist majority government which adopted a philosophy of deliberate and permanent discrimination between its citizens on grounds of racial origin. We are not talking racialism when we reject the colonialism and apartheid policies now operating in those areas; we are demanding an opportunity for all the people of these States, working together as equal individual citizens, to work out for themselves the institutions and the

74

system of government under which they will, by general consent, live together and work together to build a harmonious society.'

The Lusaka signatories affirmed that the form of governments to be established in place of the White-ruled systems 'must be a matter exclusively for the peoples of the country concerned working together. No other nation will have a right to interfere in such affairs. All that the rest of the world has a right to demand is just what we are now asserting—that the arrangements within any State which wishes to be accepted into the community of nations must be based on an acceptance of the principles of human dignity and equality.' They also asserted their preference for peaceful change:

'We would prefer to negotiate rather than destroy, to talk rather than kill. We do not advocate violence; we advocate an end to the violence against human dignity which is now being perpetrated by the oppressors of Africa. If peaceful progress to emancipation were possible, or if changed circumstances were to make it possible in the future, we would urge our brothers in the resistance movements to use peaceful methods of struggle even at the cost of some compromise on the timing of change. But while peaceful progress is blocked by actions of those at present in power in the States of Southern Africa, we have no choice but to give to the peoples of those territories all the support of which we are capable in their struggle against their oppressors.'

Acceptance of these proposals by Dr Kissinger in his own Lusaka Declaration of 25 April 1976[4] opened the way for two major Western diplomatic exercises in 1977: the Anglo-American initiative in Rhodesia, and the mediation effort in Namibia by the five Western powers on the Security Council (US, UK, France, West Germany and Canada). There was also a more purposeful, though less actively pursued, diplomatic approach to South Africa's racial problems.

This new Western approach to the problems of the region contained five major elements. First, every stage of planning and implementing the two initiatives involved close consultation with the African States most directly concerned—the five Front-line States (Tanzania, Zambia, Mozambique, Botswana and Angola), as well as Nigeria. Second, in the case of Rhodesia and Namibia, the leading liberation movements (the Patriotic Front and Swapo, respectively) were brought directly into the negotiating process. Third, the stated objective was to achieve majority rule. Fourth, the agreed aim was to defuse the violence: while not condemning the armed struggle, the premise of the diplomatic approach was that armed violence was not necessarily the only road to majority rule. Fifth, explicit opposition to the introduction of big power politics into the region. (The justification for the Anglo-American role was that both countries were already involved in the area and could use their leverage positively. Meanwhile, no new foreign powers should be brought in as this would complicate the negotiating process and impede the achievement of majority rule.)

These five broad objectives were accepted by both the Anglo-Americans and the African leaders involved in this diplomatic exercise. Thus, for the first time, African and Western policies were in harmony in Southern Africa—at least so far as the immediate objectives were concerned; this made diplomatic co-operation possible, although suspicions, misunderstandings and even sharp disagreements were never entirely absent.

Anglo-American/African diplomatic co-operation did not please the Soviet bloc: how could it be otherwise? Yet the Russians and Cubans did not venture to criticize the African leaders openly; their criticisms, though sharp, were implicit and indirect. However, the Africans had no interest in upsetting the Russians and Cubans, which would not only offend their non-aligned aspirations, but also rob them of a vital element of support and leverage against the Western powers. Since the West had begun to change course precisely because of the 'Soviet threat' in the area, the Africans clearly did not wish to lose this source of pressure. Moreover, the Africans could not be sure that the Western powers would consistently and energetically pursue their new Southern African diplomacy or, even if they did, that they would invest sufficient of their resources to ensure final success. The Africans also felt it important to maintain a second string to their bow through the intensification of the armed struggle, both to keep up the pressures against Rhodesia and Namibia and, in the event of the failure of the diplomatic approach, to fight to victory. For this purpose they relied on arms and military training from the Communist world.

This dual strategy of the Africans made it inevitable that if the Western diplomatic effort failed, the Soviet factor would have to be invoked, as in Angola. Thus, while the Western powers held the diplomatic initiative for so long as negotiated settlement seemed possible, the Soviet bloc would be likely to replace them if this failed. The Chinese role in this diplomatic strategy was comparatively minor (see below).

African-Western co-operation was by no means easy. For one thing, many African leaders mistrusted French policy and felt unsure about the future of British policy—especially if there were a change of government. While generally encouraged by the new direction of the Carter Administration, they were uneasy about the possible influence in Washington of Carter's National Security adviser, Zbigniew Brzezinski. They also needed constant reassurance about West Germany's policy. Some of the African leaders (like President Neto of Angola) went along with the Anglo-American initiatives only because they were endorsed by dominant elements within the Front-line States; however, they opposed any major American role on the grounds that it introduced big-power involvement in the region. Somewhat contradictorily, this group favoured a larger Russian/Cuban role.

There were also disagreements among the Front-line Presidents (FLPs) over particularist interests—such as Zambia's favouring Joshua Nkomo's wing of the Patriotic Front.[5] However, President Nyerere's authority as the FLPs' chairman was decisive in maintaining the group's unity, though not without opposition, some of which came at particularly sensitive points in the Rhodesian negotiations. On the other hand, the flow of the Namibian negotiations was not impeded by any serious disagreement between the FLPs and the Western group.

The real difficulties, though, arose from the natural desire of the liberation movements to win the Western powers' unqualified support for their position.

The conflict between the two wings of the Patriotic Front also introduced the Sino-Soviet quarrel into their camp, foreshadowing the possibility of another Angola should the attempts at peaceful negotiations fail. The Russian/Cuban element also came to assume much greater significance in Swapo's strategy, since it relied on the Communists for the training and arming of its guerrillas, as well as a means of applying pressure on the Western powers (and through them on SA) for a settlement on its own terms. While Swapo's annual conference in 1977 went out of its way to praise the Scandinavian countries and Holland for their assistance, it paid special tribute to 'the socialist countries and other progressive forces'.[6]

The links between the African National Congress of SA (ANC) and the Soviet bloc had become so close by early 1977 as to take on the appearance of an open alliance. Although nationalist elements in the ANC-Communist Party front continued to try to assert the movement's non-aligned position, Marxist elements emphasized the 'historic role' which the USSR was playing in the 'liberation struggle in Southern Africa'.

To sum up, the pattern of international involvement in Southern Africa in

1977–78 had the following characteristics:
1. The diplomatic initiative was held by the Western powers in co-operation with the more significant of the African leaders.
2. While these African leaders were willing to support Western initiatives, they remained critical—and always suspicious—of the degree of Western commitment to the need to impose effective pressures before the Rhodesian and South African regimes would make the concessions required to avoid an all-out armed struggle. Meanwhile, they kept the Soviet and Chinese factors in play both to strengthen the liberation movements and as a constant reminder to the West of the presence of possible alternative allies.
3. Although the Soviets, Cubans and Chinese were restricted to the wings, with the West holding the centre of the diplomatic stage, they were significantly increasing their participation in the movements most likely to dominate if Western diplomacy failed.

THE THREE ARENAS OF CONFLICT
1. SOUTH AFRICA
The problems of Rhodesia and Namibia are of course only peripheral to the real crisis area in the region—the Republic of South Africa. Solving the problems of the peripheral areas would actually only clear the decks for what will undoubtedly become the major arena of conflict in the coming decade. However, the way in which Rhodesia and Namibia achieve their independence could decisively determine the shape of the future struggle over SA. There are two likely scenarios. First, that negotiated settlements will be reached in both Rhodesia and Namibia, thus avoiding large-scale violence and the exodus of Whites to the South. Second, that one or other of the two problems will fail to yield to diplomatic pressures and so inevitably result in an all-out armed struggle which will attract greater African, Russian and Cuban military involvement in the region. If attempts to reach a settlement fail in both the peripheral regions, this would further widen the area of territorial involvement.

The first scenario represents the way in which the overwhelming body of African and Western opinion desires to see the future. It would displease only the anti-Western powers and the as yet small revolutionary-minded African movements. The African interest is to see majority rule established under conditions most likely to favour the newly independent regimes in Zimbabwe and Namibia. The Western interest is to offload two of its embarrassments in whatever way is least likely to harm their economic and other interests. If the West had acted much earlier, it would have stood a far better chance of avoiding the second scenario of Namibia and Zimbabwe reaching majority rule as Angola and Mozambique did—through violence, with the new Marxist-type regimes buttressed by the Communist powers and with the exodus of the White communities.

There is the further probability that in Namibia, if not necessarily in Rhodesia, SA will become militarily engaged and that the African liberation movements will in turn be compelled to call on the Soviets and Cubans for massive military intervention. Such a move would be endorsed by many African states for the same reason that they approved of the Communist involvement in Angola *after* SA's military intervention in that country, and would be likely to have at least four major results. First, it would probably weaken the anti-Communist stand of most present-day African governments, since they would have reason to feel (whatever their suspicions or reservations) that the Communist world is a truer ally in a struggle of crucial continental importance. This trend is already noticeable in the changing attitudes of anti-Communist leaders like President Kaunda, who had strongly opposed Russian and Cuban intervention in Angola. Second, it would raise serious problems for the Western powers about their role in a situation of great violence and in all probability of large-scale killing of Whites as well as of Blacks. This could seriously jeopardize detente—in the widest sense of the term—and thus pose a threat to world peace. Third, since there is very little likelihood of any Western military intervention, the outcome of the struggles in Rhodesia and Namibia would be determined by the weight of Soviet military power—thus strengthening Moscow's influence throughout the region. Fourth, Communist involvement would decisively affect the pattern of future political developments in SA.

If, on the other hand, majority rule were to come to Rhodesia and Namibia through negotiation—bringing to power non-Marxist leaders, avoiding economic chaos and offering a future to their White communities—this would in no way reduce the pressures on the SA political system. On the contrary, it would strengthen them. Moreover, a non-disruptive transition in the peripheral states could have a number of positive advantages. It could encourage SA to use the time still available more urgently and more positively to seek new constitutional arrangements acceptable to all South Africans, which would mean involving representative Black leaders in meaningful negotiations. It could also create a less frightened atmosphere in which a purposeful White leadership might hope to convince its electorate of the truth of the warning given by the chairman of the Broederbond, Prof Viljoen, that 'to try and hold on to everything could lead to losing everything'. [7]

But if majority rule were to come to SA's neighbours as a result of a violent struggle backed by the Russians and Cubans, it would be bound to encourage Black South Africans to adopt similar methods and to choose the same allies. The tide of Black violence, the defeat and killing of Whites, and the unwillingness of the Western powers to act decisively would almost certainly strengthen the 'siege mentality' of White South Africans and so toughen their resistance to democratic change. Even if it did not, if the regime did evince a greater readiness for compromise, the possibility of finding representative African leaders willing to negotiate on terms minimally acceptable to the Whites would have been seriously weakened. Black South Africans would undoubtedly be encouraged to believe that power was slipping out of the hands of the White minority and that they could therefore hold out for maximalist terms. One could thus expect a repetition of the familiar historic experience of those with power being prepared to adjust to inevitable change only when it is too late to retain what might be regarded as their proper rights.

For all these reasons, the method of transferring power in Namibia and Rhodesia is likely to be of decisive importance in determining the future course of events in SA. The Vorster regime clearly understands this, but its desire to promote African leaders of its own choice frustrated the Western initiative over Namibia. To some extent, too, it has shown a willingness to co-operate with the Anglo-American settlement efforts in Rhodesia, but with one major proviso: a complete refusal to use its power to compel the Smith regime to accept the Anglo-American proposals. In fact, these represent the only hope of ensuring a quick end to the war in Rhodesia and of establishing a representative Black government not beholden to the Communists. It is entirely within the power of Vorster to force the Smith regime—overnight—to give its support to the Anglo-American plan, either by stopping the flow of oil into Rhodesia and/or halting the supply of arms from SA.

Why, then, did Vorster refuse to act in what would so clearly seem in the interest of White South Africa? There are several possible explanations, including the likelihood that he genuinely misread the chances of the 'internal settlement' working. There is no doubt that he was sceptical about its chances unless Joshua Nkomo could be brought in, and that he tried hard to persuade Smith and others to induce Nkomo to return to Salisbury. More important, perhaps, are the two major constraints on Vorster: his difficulty in getting his White electorate to support a policy of openly pressuring the Smith regime, and his unwillingness to resort to the weapon of sanctions to change the Rhodesian political system since his enemies advocate an economic embargo to end apartheid. The combination of these three factors probably accounts for what could turn out to be a critical mistake in Vorster's calculations of how best to defend his concept of the South African national interest.

The defenders of the *status quo* in SA have three major fears: the growth of urban Black violence in support of a liberation struggle; the advance of Communist powers to positions of influence in countries close to SA's borders; and the abandonment by the West of any support for SA. 1975–76 saw the advance of a Soviet/Cuban military presence up to the border of Namibia—SA's military frontline. 1976 saw the beginning of serious urban Black violence. 1977 brought Soviet President Podgorny and Cuba's Fidel Castro on goodwill visits to SA's bordering states; it also saw the continuation of urban Black violence and, crucially, the beginning of a real threat of Western disengagement from SA.

President Carter's decision to send Vice-President Walter Mondale to Vienna in May 1977 to warn Vorster formally that SA-US relations were 'at a watershed' may in retrospect come to be seen as just such a parting of the ways. Certainly Vorster has interpreted it in that light. The isolation of SA from the West has been traumatic for White South Africans: 'We cannot negotiate on our destruction, either now or tomorrow,' was the biting comment of SA's Foreign Minister after the Vienna meeting.[8] Afraid of the gathering darkness, the Vorster regime has taken to whistling loudly to keep up the courage of White South Africans. A typical reaction was that of the SA Broadcasting Corporation: 'The present campaign against SA being led by President Carter in the US is unifying the people of this country as never before'.[9] Even if this were true of White South Africans, it is almost certainly not true of Blacks. The revolt of the youth in Soweto in 1975 and 1976 marked the opening of a new chapter of Black urban militancy.

2. RHODESIA/ZIMBABWE

The US became directly involved in the Rhodesian situation through Kissinger's diplomacy in 1976, although the Secretary of State was careful to limit Washington's role by insisting on Britain's primary responsibility. Thus, although Kissinger's involvement had been decisive in getting Smith to accept the September 1976 Pretoria agreement (which endorsed the objective of majority rule for Rhodesia),[10] the lameduck Ford Administration acted only as an observer at the abortive Geneva conference which was intended to implement the Smith-Kissinger agreement.[11] After the failure of the Geneva talks, the US left the subsequent initiative to Britain through its UN ambassador, Ivor Richard.

Dr David Owen's approach to the problems of Southern Africa was completely different from that of his predecessor, Tony Crosland, who had opposed the idea of the Foreign Secretary taking personal charge of Southern African problems. Owen decided to make the area one of his priorities. Unusual among British politicians, he also strongly favoured an active UK-US partnership in Southern Africa, accepting the need for American 'muscle' to strengthen Britain's negotiating position with both the Smith and Vorster regimes. He made one further crucial policy departure—reversing a position previously strongly defended by Prime Minister Callaghan—by insisting on the need for Britain to assume direct responsibility during the transition period to Zimbabwe's independence. This change in British policy was in part a reflection of Owen's own personal commitment to majority rule in Southern Africa—a commitment he shares with Carter in the importance of promoting human rights.

Owen's position would have been untenable had his coming to office not coincided with the arrival of the Carter Administration whose position on Southern Africa was almost identical to his own. This opened the way for a new Anglo-American relationship. When the new US ambassador to the UN, Andrew Young, came to London in February 1977, he responded at once to the opportunity for closer collaboration. 'Our countries,' he said, 'ought to be able to move things forward' from where they were left by the Geneva talks and the Richard's mission.[12] He added: 'I would say that President Carter sees there can be no future for Southern Africa unless there is a rationally-negotiated peaceful and meaningful agreement.' Young later explained that the US government would not have become involved in the joint initiative 'if it had not been for the insistence of African States that we had a role to play in the transformation of the entire Southern African continent and the achievement of majority rule . . . . It is the result of our commitment to majority rule throughout Southern Africa that we became involved in the process of listening to the Front-line Presidents, the liberation movements and all of the parties that have been involved in the struggle.'[13]

Thus the groundwork was laid for what was to become a joint Anglo-American initiative on Rhodesia. Encouraged by Carter's decision to move urgently to impose a ban on Rhodesian chrome imports to the US, Owen went to Washington in March 1977 to explore the possibility of a joint effort with the new US Secretary of State, Cyrus Vance. By early April, Owen was ready to embark on his first African mission which he announced had the support of the US.[14] An element new to British policy since the Unilateral Declaration of Independence (UDI) in 1965 was contained in Owen's announcement that it was wrong 'to think that the only person who can deliver a solution in Rhodesia is Ian Smith. He is only one aspect of White Rhodesian opinion.'[15] After Owen's exploratory talks in Dar es Salaam, Pretoria and Salisbury, his first step was to formalize the Anglo-American initiative by getting agreement for a joint team of officials. John Graham, a senior member of the British Foreign Office, and Stephen Low, the US ambassador in Lusaka, were appointed and began their collaboration in May. The next step was to agree on a set of proposals for a Rhodesian settlement which would carry US-UK endorsement and to plan how the new initiative was to be developed under Owen's chairmanship.[16]

The Patriotic Front—which had been recognized by the OAU Heads of State in June as the only representative body of Black Rhodesian opinion[17]—turned down the Anglo-Americans' draft proposals when these were put to them in Lusaka on 7 July by Graham and Low. They argued that it was wrong to begin by seeking agreement about an independence constitution; the first task was to secure Smith's surrender.[18] Smith's response was to declare the Patriotic Front (PF) as 'public enemy No 1'.

This enmity between the Smith regime and the PF was of course nothing new; on the other hand, the OAU's rejection of the claims to recognition by Bishop Muzorewa's United African National Council (UANC) and the Rev Ndabaningi Sithole's Zanu (renamed ANC-S) did create a new situation which was soon to change the course of events. It was only to be expected that once Africa turned its back on them and they were no longer free to operate externally, their only alternative was to consolidate a power base for themselves inside Rhodesia (in rivalry to the PF and the majority of OAU members) in the belief that they could command majority Black support. The effect of the OAU decision was thus to drive Sithole and Muzorewa into the waiting arms of Smith, who lost no time in exploiting this opportunity.

Owen again visited Washington on 23–24 July to get final agreement for a detailed Anglo-American plan to be presented to all the parties in the Rhodesian conflict as well as to the FLPs. Carter demonstrated his close interest in the initiative by participating in these preparatory talks. A second round of talks followed in London between Owen and Vance, who together had a meeting with the SA Foreign Minister, R. F. Botha. Their aim was to engage SA's support for the Anglo-American plan. At the end of August 1977, David Owen and Andy Young embarked on an African mission to discuss their proposals (in advance of publication) with the FLPs, the PF, Sithole and Muzorewa, Smith and Vorster.

The Anglo-American approach was described by ambassador Young as seeking to establish the following five objectives:

First, the initiation of an irreversible process leading to majority rule in an independent Zimbabwe;

Second, the creation of a neutral political process which would allow all political factions in Zimbabwe to compete fairly for political leadership through elections which truly reflect the will of the majority;

Third, an end to hostilities, followed by the maintenance of stability, law and order during the transition period to ensure the fairness of the process and thus its durability;

Fourth, agreement on an independence constitution that provides for a democratically-elected government, the abolition of discrimination and the protection of individual human rights, including the right of members of the minority as well as the majority;

Fifth, having presented a proposal based on these goals to the Security Council, the US together with the UK [would undertake] a series of discussions and negotiations with all of the principal parties concerned. [19]

It was soon evident that there were differences over how the Rhodesian army should be constituted once a ceasefire was arranged and a British Resident-Commissioner installed in Salisbury. The FLPs were categoric in demanding, in the words of President Nyerere, 'the complete dismantling of Smith's army' and the installation, by stages, of the guerrilla forces in their place. London and Washington accepted the idea of running down the Rhodesian forces and of reconstituting a new army by integrating the guerrillas into it, while introducing a UN Peacekeeping Force to hold the ring during the interim period. But this idea was flatly rejected by Vorster when Owen and Young discussed it with him in Pretoria on 29 August. He saw the plan as a recipe for chaos and dismissed the idea of allowing any role to the 'Marxist-Leninist terrorists' of Mugabe and his associates. He also made it clear that he would not apply any pressures on Smith to accept the Anglo-American proposals, promising only to support whatever was acceptable to the White Rhodesian leader. In effect, Vorster was giving Smith the sole right to veto any proposals put before him. Even before Owen and Young arrived in Salisbury, Smith had made it clear that he would not accept any suggestion which affected the composition of his forces and that he would have his own counter-proposals to make. [20]

When the Anglo-American plan was finally published on 1 September, [21] it left open the future of the Rhodesian forces by proposing only that a new Zimbabwe National Army would be 'formed as soon as possible' after a Transitional Administration was established under a British Resident Commissioner. Field Marshall Lord Carver, who was named for this post, would also be the new Commander-in-Chief. Primary responsibility for security during the transition period would be with the police, supported by a UN Zimbabwe Force. Since a ceasefire was to precede the establishment of the Transition Administration, there would be no immediate call for the services of an army.

The Anglo-American plan was rejected by the Smith regime and heavily criticized by the PF: both found some common ground in viewing it as a 'colonialist' concept. However, Muzorewa and Sithole thought the proposals worth considering and a supportive resolution was adopted by the Security Council. Owen took an optimistic line when he talked to the Young Fabians on 2 October 1977, saying that he believed a settlement could bring independence and majority rule to Rhodesia before the end of 1978—'far more quickly than even the most optimistic supporters of the armed struggle think'. [22] Before the end of October, the Security Council gave even more positive support to the Anglo-American plan by agreeing to designate Maj-Gen Prem Chand as the commander of the putative UN Zimbabwe Force. But when Carver and Chand undertook a reconnaissance in early November to determine the chances of getting a ceasefire, they received little encouragement from either the PF or Smith.

The four months between September 1977, when the Anglo-American plan was published, and January 1978 were crucial in that they gave the Smith regime the opportunity to develop its alternative strategy of an 'internal settlement'. Struggling with its own deep internal divisions, [23] the PF failed to set out its own practical alternative proposals to improve the Anglo-American plan, though still criticizing it in general terms for the 'dictatorial' powers envisaged for Lord Carver. They refused to endorse a UN peacekeeping presence, were ambiguous about their acceptance of elections before independence, and insisted on the PF playing the dominant, though not the exclusive, political and military role during the transition period. They also refused to allow Muzorewa, Sithole and Chirau to have any part in negotiating 'the surrender of the Smith regime'.

The FLPs, too, had their internal difficulties during these months (see below), mainly over the question of whether elections should be held before or after Zimbabwe's independence. Both the PF and the FLPs argued that the Western powers had the strength to force Smith's 'abdication' by exerting direct pressures on Vorster to stop the flow of oil and the supply of arms to Rhodesia, which alone made it possible for the regime to hold out. The African argument was that if the Western powers were as committed to achieving the removal of Smith as they claimed to be, they should be ready to use their leverage against SA to force Smith to step down. The Anglo-American reply was that its task of removing Smith would be considerably facilitated if there were agreement with the PF, underwritten by the FLPs, about the way in which the new Zimbabwe was to be created. The US and UK were clearly not willing to implement tougher economic sanctions against SA in an effort to compel it to observe the embargo against Rhodesia. Although disputes over these issues troubled relations between the FLPs and the Anglo-Americans, there was no sign that the African leaders intended to break off or abandon the negotiations. However, the FLPs did support the move to increase the fighting effectiveness of the Zimbabwe guerrilla forces, insisting that this could be achieved only if the two wings of the PF agreed to integrate their 'armies'. But although the FLPs gave high priority to achieving this military unity, their efforts were unsuccessful.

A new situation arose in January 1978 when Smith announced that he was willing to accept majority rule and independence by the end of 1978, having persuaded first Sithole and Chirau, and later Muzorewa, to begin serious negotiations about an 'internal settlement'. This prospect produced a greater sense of urgency in the ranks of the FLPs and the PF to intensify the Anglo-American initiative. In February 1978, the PF leadership travelled to Malta for talks with the US and UK and for the first time produced detailed counter-proposals to the Anglo-American plan.[24] These included a number of important concessions such as acceptance of elections before independence with the right of all White and Black Rhodesians to participate freely in them; a readiness to consider a possible UN role during the transition; and an indication that if a negotiated settlement were possible, they would not insist that the 'armed struggle' offered the only path to independence.

There were concessions, too, from the Anglo-American side. In order to meet the objection to Lord Carver's 'dictatorial powers', it proposed that he be assisted by an advisory Governing Council which would comprise himself, a UN representative, and two members each from the Smith regime, Muzorewa's UANC, Nkomo's Zapu, Mugabe's Zanu and Sithole's ANC-S. The PF objected that the new proposals would leave it in a minority of four against eight—and of four to six against those participating in the 'internal settlement'. They objected even more strongly to the Anglo-American proposals for an interim Security Council (which would exercise control over all the security forces including the guerrillas) since it would be composed in the same way as the Governing Council. The PF argued that the only reason why Smith had reversed his position on the issue of majority rule was because of the pressures of the armed struggle which the PF alone was waging; now claiming the upper hand militarily, it insisted that its dominant position be recognized in the transition institutions. While the Malta talks thus made some gains, the gap between the PF and the Anglo-American positions still remained very wide.

The announcement on 15 February 1978 of the successful conclusion of the 'internal settlement' negotiations in Salisbury marked the opening of a new chapter in the Rhodesian crisis. The PF saw it as an act of betrayal by 'Smith's Black collaborators'; it refused to take seriously Smith's promise to hand over power to the majority and regarded the agreement as simply another of his ploys to 'divide and rule'.

These attitudes were fully endorsed by the FLPs. What the African Presidents expected was unequivocal condemnation of the 'internal settlement', but this was not forthcoming, either from London or Washington. The British Foreign Secretary said in the House of Commons on 16 February 1978: 'It seems there are crucial issues yet to be resolved including the composition of the transitional government and its powers; the composition of the security forces and the extent to which other nationalist parties will be involved in the transition and in fair and free elections on the basis of universal suffrage. We will continue, as we have done from the start of the Anglo-American initiative, to work with all parties, inside and outside the country, to promote an overall settlement compatible with the principles endorsed by this House and to work for the cessation of all violence.'

Although Andy Young was known at first to have favoured outright condemnation of the 'internal settlement', he came round to accepting an agreed position developed within the Administration after consultations with the British. President Carter described the 'settlement' as inadequate. A fuller amplification of the American position was offered by Andy Young in a statement to the Security Council on 15 March:

'I am the first to recognize that anything which Mr Smith has negotiated merits the

BATTLEFRONTS OF SOUTHERN AFRICA

most careful scrutiny. But I am also willing to credit good faith to the participating Nationalist leaders. They, as much as the other Nationalist leaders of Zimbabwe, want freedom and independence for their country and full political equality for all the people of the country. It is fair, then, to ask what they have achieved in Salisbury. Compared with the kinds of settlement proposals which Smith has entertained in the past, the Salisbury Agreement marks some progress. (1) The nationalist leaders have gotten Mr Smith to agree to the principle of universal adult suffrage. (2) Smith's signature has been obtained on a commitment eventually to step down. There is still no ironclad assurance, however, that he will do so. (3) Finally, there is recognition that during the transition period, some sharing of power must take place among the participating groups. . . . We must consider whether the agreement announced in Salisbury takes sufficiently into account the enormous difficulty of managing the transition period. This crucial watershed must be handled in such a way that the violence of the present struggle for liberation can be transformed into an irreversible political process which will result in the approval by all the people of Rhodesia of their own form of government and the selection of their own leaders.'

The Security Council adopted a resolution on 15 March 1978 which described the 'internal settlement' as 'illegal and unacceptable', and condemned 'attempts and manoeuvres' by the White minority to retain power. The five Western members of the Security Council abstained from voting on the resolution. This was after the African group had softened their original proposals, which included the threat of sanctions against SA, because of threats by the US and UK to exercise their veto. Nigeria's ambassador to the UN, Leslie Harriman, had in turn warned that his country would leave the Commonwealth if Britain were to use its veto against the resolution.

The PF was deeply suspicious that Britain in particular might be tempted to move towards endorsement of the internal settlement, to abandon the Anglo-American plan and turn against the Front. Although these suspicions are understandable, there was in fact never any question of either the US or UK governments moving in this direction for reasons of polity as well as principle. The point of principle, repeatedly stated by Dr Owen, was that 'any settlement must be acceptable to the people of Rhodesia as a whole'. The major political reason, he told the Commons, was that 'an internal settlement which excludes one of the leading nationalist groups cannot bring about a ceasefire during the elections or give peace and stability to a newly independent Zimbabwe. Nor would it eliminate the threat to international peace and stability and therefore would be most unlikely to be recognized by the Security Council. . . . It is necessary for the UN to have a crucial role in this settlement, either in a military, peacekeeping or supervisory role in order to ensure fair elections and for any administration by a British Resident-Commissioner to be seen to be fair. . . . We cannot ignore the weight of international opinion, the Security Council, the Commonwealth and the OAU. . . . How can it be seriously argued that Britain, in the midst of a major conflict which clearly demonstrates a divided nation, unilaterally and in direct contravention of the fifth principle, recognize the internal settlement and lift sanctions? It would be utterly wrong to do so. It would leave Britain with barely a friend in the world, discredited and despised, and even more important, it would be a betrayal of the people of Rhodesia as a whole. We owe them a debt of honour, and it is a debt I intend to discharge. Britain had no debts or obligations to individuals or parties in Rhodesia. They had no interest in choosing between the differing Black nationalist leaderships. This was for the people of Rhodesia as a whole'. The plan always envisaged that sanctions would be lifted at the start of the transitional period and in order to achieve international support for lifting sanctions, they had to ensure the irreversibility of the process towards independence. This irreversibility was fundamental if they were to satisfy others that sanctions should be lifted and recognition should be given to any government. Under the internal settlement, there was no such guarantee, no transfer of power and no ceasefire. . . . As to saying that progress can be made only when the PF agrees, it is a fact that while two armies fight each other, we need both sides to agree to a ceasefire. A ceasefire between two armies, neither of which has won or lost, is extremely difficult to achieve. History shows that. One should strive to do this, however.'[25]

Both before and after the 'internal settlement', the aim of Anglo-American policy was to try and secure agreement among all the major Zimbabwe leaders—first because of the need to fulfil the principle of 'acceptability' by the majority of the country's inhabitants; and second, in order to avoid the real risk of a civil war developing among rival Black movements after independence, as occurred in Angola. This latter threat was a major concern of the FLPs. In retrospect, it will be seen that the OAU's exclusive recognition of the PF was a major precipitating factor in deepening divisions among Zimbabweans—a danger fully recognized just before the 'internal settlement' was signed when Nyerere and Machel sent urgent messages to Muzorewa urging him not to enter into any deals with Smith, as this would finally put him 'beyond the pale'. But by then, Muzorewa had come to feel so bitterly towards the FLPs he did not even deign to reply to Nyerere, and responded with an extremely provocative letter to Machel telling him not to interfere in the internal affairs of Zimbabwe.

The thrust of the Anglo-American initiative after February 1978 was to try and bring all the major leaders in both the external movement and the 'internal settlement' to an all-party conference to try to find common ground. In mid-April 1978, the British Foreign Secretary and the US Secretary of State embarked on another trip to Dar es Salaam, Salisbury and Pretoria in an attempt to persuade the PF and the new Rhodesian Transition Administration to agree to all-party talks. Although Nkomo and Mugabe accepted the idea and made further concessions on the Anglo-American plan (such as over the role of a UN force after the achievement of a ceasefire, and for an Executive Council to meet under Carver's chairmanship), the 'internal settlement' signatories replied that they could see no value in trying to hold talks with the PF.

While the Anglo-American initiative remained alive up to July 1978 and still had the support of the FLPs and even of the PF, it appeared to offer little hope of progress. Nothing would be achieved until it became clear that the 'internal settlement' could not meet the three basic requirements to establish peace and an orderly transfer of power to a majority-ruled Zimbabwe: a ceasefire leading to an end of hostilities; the lifting of sanctions, which requires the approval of the Security Council; and free elections to test the opinion of all Zimbabweans—a prerequisite for the introduction of legislation by the British parliament to grant legal independence to the new State.

3. NAMIBIA

'Namibia is a challenge without parallel to the authority of the United Nations.'
—Dr Kurt Waldheim, UN Secretary-General,
20 May 1977

In 1947 a relatively little-known Anglican cleric, the Rev Michael Scott, first appeared in the lobbies of the UN carrying a petition from the then Herero chief, the venerable old Hosea Kutako. It was Scott's intervention which blocked an attempt by the then South African Prime Minister, Gen J. C. Smuts, to have the old League of Nations mandate set aside and incorporate the territory (known as South West Africa) into the Republic. [26] Over the next 30 years the world body tried, though not very hard and without any success, to bring Namibia to independence under conditions that would free it from SA's hegemony. [27] By early 1977, SA stood poised to confer its own approved style of independence on the territory through a constitution prepared by the Turnhalle conference. [28] At this point the Western nations for the first time asserted their authority and influence to stop SA in its tracks.

The nine members of the European Community warned Pretoria on 7 February 1977 that the Turnhalle proposals did not meet with their approval and would certainly not be accepted by the UN, which had international responsibility for the future of the former trust territory. This collective European confrontation with the Vorster regime reflected two major Western concerns. First, by going ahead with its own plan for Namibia's independence, SA would inevitably invite a tough UN reaction along the lines developed by the OAU, including the application of extensive sanctions against SA. While this course of action was not favoured by the Western nations, they felt they would have no choice but to support it because of the need to uphold the authority of the UN and to avert a dangerous rift with the African nations. Second, the West could foresee that the result of unilateral action by SA in Namibia would be international military intervention. The challenging Swapo liberation movement, based largely in neighbouring Angola, would intensify its armed struggle with the full support, not only of the OAU, but also of the Russians and Cubans who were already engaged in training and arming Swapo's People's Liberation Army of Namibia (PLAN).

The Western nations agreed that no acceptable settlement could be achieved for Namibia which did not involve both SA and Swapo. Dr Kissinger's efforts to get Vorster to involve Swapo in the negotiations for Namibia's independence in 1976 had been fruitless. Vorster adamantly insisted that under no circumstances would SA agree to meet with 'a bunch of communist terrorists'. [29]

In February 1977, faced with the imminent prospect of the UN being called upon to react to an 'internal settlement' in Namibia, the five Western members of the Security Council (US, UK, France, West Germany and Canada) met to discuss how to avert this threatening crisis and agreed that Security Council Resolution 385 of 1976 must be upheld. This demanded that SA accept elections under UN supervision and control before independence; release all political prisoners; abolish racial discrimination; permit all exiles to return without fear of arrest or intimidation; and withdraw its illegal administration in favour of a temporary UN presence. The five were also agreed that Swapo must be fully involved in the negotiating process. They then consulted with the Africa Group at the UN, as well as with the UN Secretary-General, both of which accepted the proposed Western initiative to mediate between SA and Swapo.

That was the beginning of what came to be known as the 'Contact Group'—or more derisorily the 'Gang of Five'—under the chairmanship of ambassador Don McHenry, deputy to Andy Young at the UN. McHenry was formerly involved in South African affairs in two ways: as a State Department official, he had strenuously opposed the implementation of the National Security Council Memorandum 39 (NSM 39) endorsed by President Nixon on Kissinger's recommendation; [30] having lost that fight, he resigned and later visited SA to complete a study on the role of US firms in the Republic. [31] At the first meeting of the Contact Group and Vorster in April 1977, the South African Prime Minister—faced with a collective Western stand—adopted a much more compromising position than at any time previously. The explanation Vorster gave for his turnabout was that whereas 'in the past, SA had been ignored, Western countries had now realized that this could no longer be done, and that it was in their interests and in those of SA to sit around a table and discuss problems'[32] (a statement quite at odds with the long efforts made by Western nations to involve SA in negotiations with the UN and Swapo). The Contact Group and SA together established the following basic principles for negotiations: SA recognized the need for an internationally acceptable solution in Namibia; SA recognized the need for elections in Namibia held under universal suffrage without literacy qualifications; SA said that the electorate would initially choose the members of a constituent assembly whose immediate and principal responsibility would be to draft a constitution for an independent Namibia; SA accepted the principle of UN involvement in the elections; all people and parties would be free to participate in the elections; freedom of speech and assembly would be guaranteed; political prisoners and detainees would be released; SA would withdraw from Namibia in stages, 'in consultation with those mainly involved'. In addition, SA planned to establish a central administrative authority to govern the country before independence; it agreed to refrain from seeking parliamentary approval for the Turnhalle constitutional proposals, as part of its general understanding that it will avoid taking steps which might foreclose an internally acceptable solution.

In pursuing its initiative throughout 1977, the Contact Group was faced with two major problems involving both the major antagonists. The first was to decide whether the Vorster regime seriously meant the negotiations to succeed. Was it going through the motions simply to give the West an appearance of reasonableness while believing, or hoping, that Swapo's obduracy would cause the negotiations to break down? Or was it genuinely interested in reaching an internationally acceptable agreement? Don McHenry confessed that he could never quite make up his mind about what he described as Vorster's 'two-track strategy': 'SA would prefer an internationally acceptable solution if the price is right. At some point, if they conclude that the price is too costly, they would go off on their own internal settlement. They are probably trying to do as many of those things that are internationally acceptable as they possibly can as a way of rationalizing the internal settlement. Up to this point, track one and track two have been down the same road. The real question comes what happens when you get to the fork; whether you must turn left to get to track one which is the international settlement, or you must turn right to track two. It . . . is something which we and the South Africans have always taken in account from the very beginning.'[33]

The second problem was the extreme suspiciousness of Swapo and especially of its leader, Sam Nujomo, about the Contact Group's dependability. Nujomo's view was that the West's 'declaration of principles' on Namibia was worthless unless backed up by a Security Council economic and arms embargo against SA. Short of such a Western policy, he remained convinced that Namibia would finally be liberated only through 'a protracted armed struggle'.[34] This led him to concentrate on building up PLAN's military power in co-operation with Cuba and Russia. In March 1977, for instance, he asked President Podgorny during his visit to Zambia for increased arms supplies. McHenry's view was that Swapo, like SA, was also engaged in a two-track strategy: 'they co-operate and engage in negotiation but fear all the time that they may be walking into a trap' and so remain ready to go on fighting if they cannot achieve their goals through negotiations.

By the end of 1977, the Contact Group had established its terms for a negotiated settlement.[35] While the proposals, based on the requirements of Resolution 385 and the maximum concessions it believed could be extracted from both sides, won the broad approval of the FLPs, neither SA nor Swapo was ready to endorse the plan when it was finally presented to them in February 1978. SA's Foreign Minister, R. F. Botha, broke off his talks with the Contact Group in New York, declaring: 'There are aspects of these proposals that would be so totally unacceptable and so dangerous that there is a serious and real danger of the people in the territory being overrun and being governed by a Marxist terrorist organization. I have not said that there is no hope left, but it is a very serious situation.'[36]

Swapo was equally antagonistic to the proposals, mainly over the location of the remaining 1,500 South African troops during the transition; the failure to include Walvis Bay in an independent Namibia; the role of the South African police during the elections; and the failure to provide for the dismantling of the Bantu tribal authorities.

Although these tough reactions seemed to doom the Western mediation effort to failure, a renewed initiative in March and April 1978 in favour of a slightly modified set of proposals brought new hope. The role of the FLPs was decisive in sustaining the talks, which seemed almost certain to collapse after the South African army's massive attack against Swapo civilian and guerrilla camps at Cassinga, deep inside Angola, early in May 1978.[37] This coincided with the last and most critical phase of negotiations. Yet within a few weeks, on 25 May, Vorster announced SA's acceptance of the Western proposals. If he was gambling on Swapo rejecting them and so giving SA a strong diplomatic advantage, he had reckoned without the FLPs (including Neto). They again proved their inestimable value in helping to promote a peaceful settlement by persuading Swapo not to break off negotiations, despite SA's singularly provocative attack.

In mid-1978, the FLPs arranged a meeting in Luanda between the Contact Group and Swapo's leadership; this time a major breakthrough was achieved when Sam Nujomo accepted the Western proposals on 13 July. With both SA and Swapo giving their broad support to the terms for achieving Namibia's independence, the West's new African diplomacy brought hope that, barring accidents, one of the three crisis areas might be rescued from the violence and disruption of an all-out armed struggle.

THE AFRICAN ROLE IN THE DIPLOMATIC PROCESS
THE FRONT-LINE PRESIDENTS

The FLPs' basic approach to the Rhodesian problem has remained unchanged since late 1976. Despite temporary divergences by both Kaunda and Neto, the group maintained its internal unity by accepting majority decisions. The role of Julius Nyerere as chairman was also of decisive importance.[38] The starting point of the FLPs' approach was that Smith was the only obstacle to progress and that he should therefore be 'removed, voluntarily or otherwise'. (No clear indication was ever put forward as to how this should be done if he refused to step down of his own accord: that, they felt, was up to the British and Americans. As Kaunda put it on one occasion: 'If the Western powers could get rid of Hitler, what is so difficult about removing a pigmy like Smith?') The FLPs supported the idea of a two-year transition period leading to independence, during which time a Black majority caretaker government should be formed, but only after a conference, under British auspices, had drawn up an independence constitution. They were insistent that there should be elections before independence—a point on which Kaunda was in a minority (see below).

The explicit assumptions underlying these proposals was that responsibility should rest with Britain until independence; that there should be a carefully planned transition to final independence; that Black unity, especially between the rival guerrilla armies, was essential; and that the principle of NIBMAR (no independence before majority rule) should be upheld.

Despite the failure of the Geneva talks and of the subsequent Richard's mission, Nyerere urged in January and again in February 1977 that 'it would not be wise' for Britain to give up the search for an agreement simply because Smith had rejected the British proposals: the aim should be to get agreement between Britain and the nationalists.[39] However, at the same time, the FLPs were agreed on the importance of maintaining and if possible of increasing their pressures on both Smith and the British through the armed struggle. In April 1977—immediately after President Podgorny's visit to the region (see below)—the FLPs met in Quelimane (Mozambique) to review his offer of military and other support. They also discussed how to strengthen the PF's forces and how to defend Mozambique, Zambia and Botswana against incursions by the Rhodesian army. Although Mozambique signed a 20-year Friendship Treaty with the USSR during Podgorny's visit—which allowed the Frelimo regime to call on Moscow for assistance in situations threatening its peace—President Machel at no time objected to American involvement in the Rhodesian negotiations as Neto originally had done.[40] The Soviets naturally strongly opposed American involvement from the beginning. Even when the Anglo-American's initiative in Rhodesia and the Contact Group's mediation in Namibia were attacked by Robert Mugabe and Sam Nujomo at the UN Conference in Support of the People of Zimbabwe and Namibia, held in Maputo in May 1977,[41] Machel insisted that Britain's new initiative could constitute 'a positive factor'. He stated that the Western negotiations over Namibia 'could contribute to the acceleration of the resolution of the conflict'—so long as the aim was to achieve genuine independence.[42] On the other hand, the Angolan President objected to American involvement, but not so strongly as to dissociate himself from the FLPs' decision to engage in both Western initiatives. Tanzania's Prime Minister, Edward Sokoine, told his National Assembly on 22 June 1977 that 'Africa respects the efforts currently being shown by Western powers in ending racism and bringing about majority rule in Southern Africa'.

At their July 1977 meeting, the FLPs devoted most of their time to discussing the problem of disunity within the PF. Nyerere said after the meeting that it was not the FLPs' intention to 'impose leaders on the people of Zimbabwe—they must elect their own leaders'; but they felt it was necessary to have a single liberation army because of the dangers of several armies and the necessity to sharpen the armed struggle.[43]

During his visit to the US, Canada and Britain in August 1977, Nyerere placed great emphasis on the importance of adhering strictly to the agreement reached at the June Commonwealth Prime Ministers' meeting.[44] This stated that any negotiated settlement for Rhodesia 'must entail not only the removal of the illegal Smith regime, but also the dismantling of its apparatus of repression in order to pave the way for the creation of police and armed forces which would be responsive to the needs of the people of Zimbabwe and assure the orderly and effective transfer of power'. After his London visit, Nyerere said he had come away feeling 'confused' about the British position towards dismantling the Rhodesian forces. He felt that the British 'should show the same sense of urgency' about getting rid of the 'racist regimes' in Southern Africa as he had found in the US where President Carter was 'speaking the same language' as himself. He was not asking the West for arms. 'The Russians are giving us arms. The US should provide us with the rest of the pressures needed against the racist regimes.'[45]

The question of dismantling the Rhodesian army became the central point of disagreement at the summit meeting between the FLPs, the PF, Dr Owen and Andy Young held at Lusaka on 26–27 August 1977. The purpose of that meeting was to convey details of the Anglo-American plan before it was published. Speaking as chairman of the FLPs, Nyerere made it clear that unless the proposals were changed to meet the African demand for dismantling the Rhodesian forces, they would be unacceptable. [46] When the plan was published on 1 September, it did reveal some important changes in this respect (see above), but nevertheless received only a cautious welcome from most African governments and a rather critical reaction from the Angolans. [47] However, when the FLPs met to discuss their reply in Maputo on 23–24 September, they agreed that the proposals 'form a sufficient basis for further negotiations between the parties concerned'. Nyerere qualified his support by saying: 'We find that these proposals still have many negative elements and leave many questions unanswered'. [48]

The FLPs' cautious support for the Anglo-American plan was considerably strengthened over the next three months—partly due to greater clarification of some of the proposals, but principally to changes in Salisbury where negotiations for an 'internal settlement' had begun to prosper. Alarmed by this development, the African leaders began to find the Anglo-American alternative increasingly attractive.

By early 1978, after the signing of the 'internal settlement' agreement, the FLPs' immediate concern was whether the Western powers would allow the Anglo-American plan to wither through inactivity, and whether the US and UK would move towards accepting the Salisbury alternative. From February, they began to insist on the rapid implementation of the Anglo-American plan, and to persuade the PF to modify its objections to facilitate this process. Praise for the plan from individual Presidents was heard rather more often than criticism. For example, on 23 February, the Mozambique Foreign Ministry issued a statement affirming the 'positive points' in the plan which made serious negotiations possible. The statement called for the rapid and positive conclusion of the talks between the PF, the US and UK. Under this kind of pressure from the FLPs, Mugabe and Nkomo agreed to attend the Malta talks in February and to adopt a more constructive attitude to the proposals, though they themselves were by no means yet satisfied with them.

At their meeting in Dar es Salaam on 25–26 March 1978, the FLPs addressed the following statement to Washington and London: 'If they still support these proposals, they should move ahead and convene in the shortest time possible a meeting to follow up what was agreed in Malta. If, on the other hand, they have decided to abandon their commitment to their own proposals for which they had requested and obtained the support of the PF, the Front-line States and the international community, they should so declare unequivocally without any further delay.' A few days before this summit meeting, Nyerere had declared that the Front-line States 'would continue to regard the Anglo-American proposals as the basis for genuine independence for Zimbabwe'. His forthright endorsement was not reflected in the attitudes of the PF, however. Although it began to move forward from the positions adopted in Dar es Salaam on 13 April in their meetings with Cyrus Vance and Dr Owen, the differences between the two sides were still too great to allow new momentum to be built up in favour of the Anglo-American initiative. This had been considerably slowed down both by the prolonged negotiations to win PF acceptance and by the new situation created by the 'internal settlement'. In a communique after their next meeting in Beira on 17–18 April 1978, the FLPs 'reaffirmed their commitment to the principle of negotiating with the colonial power the modalities of the transfer of power to the people of Zimbabwe, underlining the positive aspects of the Anglo-American proposals'. The Presidents also renewed their commitment to the armed struggle and to 'a single leadership structure' for the PF.

While Nyerere was successful in June 1978 in getting Nkomo and Mugabe to agree to attend all-party talks (proposed by the Anglo-Americans in an effort to bring together all the external and internal elements), this further attempt to seize back the initiative from Salisbury failed to materialize.

THE ROLE OF ZAMBIA

Although President Kenneth Kaunda supported the FLPs' overall strategy, he nevertheless embarked on a number of unilateral initiatives which at times separated him from his two closest colleagues, Nyerere and Machel. Mounting internal economic, security and political problems made it less easy for Kaunda than for the other FLPs to wait patiently while the Anglo-American initiative unfolded. He was also more anxious over the PF's failure to establish a truly united movement. Kaunda's policies differed from those of his colleagues—and especially from Nyerere's—over three major issues: his championing of Joshua Nkomo as the major leader within the PF; his doubts about the wisdom of insisting on elections before independence; and his greater readiness to involve the Cubans and Russians in the struggle against Rhodesia.

In February 1977, Kaunda and Nyerere took different positions over Britain's central role in the Rhodesian negotiations. The Tanzanian leader insisted that he did not think it wise for the US to take over Britain's responsibility for Rhodesia; the Zambian leader, on the other hand, told Andy Young that he believed the British lacked 'the will and ability' to fulfil their proper role in Rhodesia and suggested that 'it is now up to the US to decide how to do it'.[49]

During the Angolan civil war in 1975-76, Kaunda and Nyerere had strongly disagreed over the Russian/Cuban intervention: while Nyerere had approved, Kaunda had not only condemned their action but had warned Africa of the threat of 'a tiger and its cubs' to the continent.[50] But in March 1977, on the eve of President Podgorny's visit to Lusaka, Kaunda contrasted the failure of the West to provide a single weapon for the liberation movements with what the Russians and other Communist countries had done. 'We and the Soviet Union are colleagues and comrades in the struggle, and this is going to be the case until the wars of liberation accomplish their objectives.'[51] On 31 March, he declared: 'If the West is afraid that the visits of President Podgorny and Dr Castro are going to end up in Southern Africa being communist-influenced, it is the West that is to be blamed'.[52] He was especially bitter over the failure of the Western nations to ensure that their oil companies did not break the Rhodesian embargo, and began legal action against four oil multinationals whom he accused of keeping Smith's 'war machine' operating.[53] He stated: 'We are at a turning point in the Southern African revolutionary struggle. The pace is intensifying and the Soviet Union is one of the major representatives of the progressive forces in the world fighting for liberation. . . . Anyone who assists the liberation struggle is welcome.'[54] He also indicated that the time might come when, if Rhodesian attacks continued against Zambia, he might find it necessary to invite 'a foreign power' to come to his country's assistance; he did not specify any particular country. In May 1978—on the eve of an important mission to Britain and America—he said that he could foresee the possibility of the PF wishing to invite the Cubans to assist them actively in their struggle against the Smith regime. He indicated that if this were to happen, he would be willing to allow them to use Zambia as a base country.[55]

Kaunda was mainly responsible for persuading the OAU summit in Libreville in June 1977 to give exclusive recognition to the PF. Yet despite his general support for the Front, there was no doubt about his personal commitment to Joshua Nkomo and his Zapu forces who were established on Zambian soil. On 25 September 1977, Kaunda met Ian Smith in Lusaka, where he listened to the Rhodesian leader's proposal that Nkomo be persuaded to join in the move towards an 'internal settlement'. This meeting greatly incensed Mugabe, who accused Kaunda of acting behind his back and of spreading disunity in the ranks of the PF.[56] The Zambian Press in turn ferociously attacked Mugabe, calling him an 'imitation freedom fighter' and even proposing that he be banned from Zambia.[57] Although nothing came from the meeting with Smith, Kaunda defiantly declared that if he thought anything could be achieved, he would be willing to talk to him again. Soon afterwards, however, he finally became convinced that nothing could be hoped for from the Rhodesian leader.[58]

One crucial difference between Kaunda and Nyerere was over the FLPs' stand on elections in Rhodesia before independence. Nyerere remained firmly committed to his longstanding demand of 'no independence before majority rule'—a formula he had been the first to put forward. In late September, Kaunda began to argue that to hold elections in Rhodesia during a six-month transition preceding independence would only exacerbate deep racial, tribal and clan tensions. Instead, he believed Zimbabwe should become independent with a 'Government of National Unity' based on the PF, whose guerrillas would also form the core of the new national army. This serious difference of view between Kaunda (supported only by Neto) and his colleagues persisted until late November 1977 when, at a meeting between Kaunda and Nyerere at Mbale, the Zambian gave way, although still remaining unconvinced about the wisdom of NIBMAR.

In December 1977, Kaunda angrily announced that he was pulling out of the Anglo-American negotiations because of the response of Dr Owen to a Rhodesian attack on camps in Mozambique in which 1,200 Zimbabweans were reported to have been massacred. He said: 'We withdraw from the table. We will no longer sit around a conference table to discuss the proposals.' Dr Owen at once said he regretted that his remarks had given offence to the Zambian leader whom he greatly admired. Anglo-Zambian accord was finally restored when Kaunda visited London in May 1978.

THE ROLE OF OTHER AFRICAN STATES

Although the OAU endorsed the role of the FLPs in masterminding African strategy in Southern Africa on a number of occasions, this endorsement was not without its critics. For example, there was strong opposition to the FLPs' recommendation to the OAU summit in June 1977 that African Heads of State give exclusive recognition to the PF.[59] Several OAU members maintain close relations with Muzorewa's UANC or Sithole's ANC: Libya has trained guerrillas for both groups, and both Presidents Amin and Banda continue to support Sithole. A number of Francophone African states, notably Ivory Coast and Senegal, also look with favour on Muzorewa and Sithole but have not come out in support of the 'internal settlement'.

President Mobutu was an especially sharp critic of the FLPs, for his own particularist reasons. In March 1977, he attacked them for seeking 'to divide Africa. . . . In fact, we are now watching the birth of a restricted club, a club where hypocrisy is the only slogan.'[60] He accused members of trading with Pretoria (meaning Zambia, Mozambique and Botswana) 'and even of receiving loans from SA's economy and therefore [benefiting] from its apartheid policy'. While it is true that the three FLPs do trade with SA, their policy is openly declared and has been accepted by the OAU as necessary to their survival. None of them receives 'loans from SA', whereas Zaire both trades with the apartheid Republic and receives loans from it.[61]

By far the most important supporter of the FLPs is Nigeria, which threw its weight fully behind their efforts in Southern Africa in 1977, having begun to move in that direction in 1976. Nigeria is not only a major force in the OAU system, but has also come to be regarded by both Western and Communist nations as the most important country in Black Africa—a view endorsed by Andy Young when he went to Lagos for talks in February 1977. After his meeting with Gen Obasanjo, the Nigerian leader said: 'Generally, we agreed on what should be done, our courses of action, methods of approach and our tactics'. The US ambassador in Lagos, Don Easum, characterized the meeting as 'the most interesting and perhaps the most important conversation of this nature I've had in 23 years in the Foreign Service'.[62] One result was that Nigeria endorsed an American role in Southern Africa. Obasanjo visited Lusaka in September 1977 where he discussed how his country could participate more effectively in the FLPs' strategy. Despite a willingness to co-operate with the Western initiatives in Rhodesia and Namibia, Nigeria's leaders continued to maintain a suspiciously critical attitude to Western policies. Thus, the Commissioner for External Affairs, Brig Garba, insisted that 'Africa will never trust any foreign powers as mediators in the situation in Zimbabwe until the territory achieves independence'.[63]

The Nigerians have been especially concerned about the failure of the African countries to organize their own defence system to deal with threats to security in the continent. On a number of occasions, their spokesmen referred to the 'shame' of African countries having to rely on foreign forces of intervention. In one such typical comment, radio Lagos said on 28 March 1978: 'One would have thought that by now the OAU would have found an answer to Smith's naked aggression of the Front-line countries'. Referring to a reported decision of Mozambique and Zambia to organize a joint force to defend their borders, radio Lagos called on the OAU to help bring this proposal to reality. 'Apart from serving as a deterrent to Ian Smith, its value is that it can be the beginning of a much-desired African High Command.' There were numerous reports in 1977 that Nigeria was prepared to use its large army to assist the Front-line States or to take over from the Cuban forces in Angola, but this kind of speculation was repeatedly denied by Lagos.

THE ROLE OF THE PATRIOTIC FRONT

The PF's role in Anglo-American-African diplomacy was typical of any liberation movement which believes that victory is within sight—though not yet within im- mediate grasp. While accepting their need for African and foreign support, both Joshua Nkomo and Robert Mugabe fiercely defended their independence and resisted any attempt to shape their tactics or to make them submit to 'unacceptable' conditions. They strongly resented anything that smacked of 'interference', irrespective of whether it came from African Presidents or from Westerners. Both wings of the PF were particularly suspicious of any move which appeared to favour one side over the other—hence the tensions between Zanu and Zambia and to a lesser extent with Tanzania. Mugabe was also resentful of the Western capitals' clear preference for Nkomo.

The principal source of trouble between the PF and the FLPs was over the latter's repeated attempts to unify the two guerrilla armies—Zanla and Zipra. Although both Nkomo and Mugabe recognized the military importance of a single integrated army and of a Joint Command, neither for a moment lost sight of the power struggle between their rival movements which proceeded simultaneously with their liberation war.[64]

The PF leaders felt ambivalent toward the Anglo-American initiative throughout

1977–78, welcoming it only insofar as they believed that London and Washington were committed to 'removing Smith' and preparing the way for a PF victory—not just for majority rule. But for the most part they remained unconvinced of the genuineness of Anglo-American intentions; at no time did they feel that the Western powers would act decisively to topple the Smith regime, for example, by exerting direct pressures on SA to halt the flow of arms and oil into Rhodesia. Nevertheless, under the persuasions of the FLPs, they engaged as reluctant partners in the Anglo-American negotiations, becoming rather less reluctant after the signing of the 'internal settlement' (see above).

This uneasy involvement in Anglo-American diplomacy was only one option in their strategy, however. The second was to pursue the armed struggle with undiminished vigour, in which course they were forced to rely on the anti-Western powers for arms and military training. For this reason the Communist factor gained strength as the Anglo-American negotiations became more prolonged—a prolongation due partly, but only partly, to the PF's insistence that any plan for independence should essentially reflect their own ideas about what was acceptable. This duality in the PF's role—co-operating with the West politically while relying increasingly on the East militarily—guaranteed that if Western diplomacy failed, Communist intervention would almost inevitably follow. Another dimension to the progressive internationalization of the Rhodesian problem was Sino-Soviet rivalry. From the beginning of Zanu's armed struggle in the late 1960s, the movement (then still based almost entirely on Tanzania) relied on the Chinese for military support. This prompted the Russians to back the rival Zapu, despite the fact that Nkomo hardly cuts the figure of a revolutionary Marxist. Pragmatist that he is, Nkomo willingly accepted offers of Russian and Cuban assistance, particularly after he began to build up Zipra's numbers to rival those of Zanla. As Kaunda was unwilling to have Russian and Cuban instructors in Zapu camps in Zambia, Nkomo was obliged to transfer his guerrillas to Angola for training—where the Russians and Cubans were *in situ*.

Typical of situations in which rival liberation movements find themselves supported by Moscow and Peking, Nkomo began to make the kind of speeches which would please Moscow and Havana, while Mugabe came increasingly to move in a Maoist direction, the difference between the two being that, by September 1977, Mugabe was genuine in his commitment, describing himself as a Marxist-Leninist of 'Maoist Thought'.[65] Zanu and Zanla cadres were being schooled, not just in guerrilla tactics, but in Maoism as well. During a visit to Peking in May 1977, Mugabe criticized the Russians in familiar Chinese parlance as 'social imperialists'.[66]

By March 1978, Nkomo no longer denied the support his forces were receiving from the USSR and Cuba. In reply to interviewers who asked whether he thought the Russians and Cubans could become more involved as the fighting increased in Rhodesia, Nkomo said they were already giving him 'all necessary help'.[67] He added that the fighting would be intensified with 'more men, more arms, more war. . . . Things are taking a very dangerous turn. . . . We are reluctant, but we have no alternative.'

THE INTERNATIONAL DIMENSION OF THE SOUTHERN AFRICA CRISIS
AMERICAN POLICY[68]

Testifying before the Africa subcommittee of the House of Representatives' Committee on International Relations, Philip C. Habib, Under-Secretary for Political Affairs, said on 3 March 1977 that 'the whole question of US policy towards Southern Africa is under urgent and comprehensive review within the

Department of State and other concerned executive agencies. I can tell you that the general thrust of our policy review has been to find ways of strengthening the commitment of the US to social justice and racial equality in Southern Africa.' He described US principles and goals in the region as follows: (1) A firm and clear commitment of opposition to racial and social injustice wherever it exists, with a reminder of Carter's personal commitment to human rights. (2) A belief that the people of Africa hold the key to the solution of African problems. While the US would use its political and economic influence and its diplomatic offices to support racial and social progress on the African continent, 'it is not for us, or for any other external power, to attempt to impose its own ideas and solutions'. Another important reason for preferring African solutions is 'to avoid situations which make Africa an arena for great power rivalry, as in Angola'. (3) Prolonged violence in Southern Africa 'could create opportunities for foreign intervention and confrontation'. (4) Recognition that other developed nations also have important interests in Southern Africa, especially Europe and Japan. (5) The US has nothing to fear for its economic and strategic interests from 'the necessary and inevitable achievement of racial equality and social justice in Southern Africa'. (6) The US has a stake in what happens in the region 'because of our belief that political harmony can and must be achieved in diverse societies like our own. . . . Success in achieving orderly transitions to democratic rule in Southern Africa, with protection of human rights for all, will help those everywhere who seek peaceful resolutions to conflict arising from ethnic, racial or religious differences.'

Jimmy Carter's own approach to the problem of Southern Africa was unusual in that he was the first US President who, from his first weeks in office, personally supervised the development of an American policy for Southern Africa—a region that, except for a very brief period in Kennedy's Administration, has hardly figured on the White House agenda. One of Carter's earliest actions was to send his Vice-President, Walter Mondale, to meet with Vorster in Vienna in May 1977 with a clear message that future relations between the two countries would depend on SA moving positively towards democratic rule. [69] Carter's visit to Nigeria and Liberia in 1978 was undertaken primarily to underline US commitment to its African, and especially its Southern African, policy. In Lagos, Carter summed up the aims of this policy as freedom from racism and the denial of human rights, freedom from want and suffering, and freedom from the destruction of war and foreign intervention.

As Vice-President Mondale pointed out in a NBC television programme on 8 November 1977, the key figure in the making of America's African policy was ambassador Andy Young. His approach to the problems of Southern Africa was blurred and often distorted by the American and British Press which focused on his lack of 'diplomacy'. Young's approach to Africa included the following five essentials: (1) By marshalling political and economic forces, it is possible to bring about change without resorting to armed struggle. A combination of pressure and incentive can prove more effective than violence. [70] (2) A peaceful settlement of the problems of Southern Africa is the best way of ensuring that Americans 'who are dependent on the region for 13 natural resources and minerals' will continue to get reasonable access to them. (3) Sanctions are not necessarily the surest way of achieving desired goals, especially if they are not directed at specific targets. (4) The US ought not to have any pre-determined formula for solving SA's problems, but should challenge 'the blanket denials of the rights of the Black majority to participate in the shaping of their destiny'. [71] (5) The US should not seek to force SA into isolation in the world community; the extent to which this was happening was the result of SA's own policies. [72]

Although from early 1978, Young and Brzezinski disagreed about the right way to respond to Soviet and Cuban policies in Africa, the President's National Security Adviser did not challenge the Administration's policies for Southern Africa. Unlike some in the Administration, however, he did not perceive the problems in the region as likely to explode 'in the near future' in a way that would pose a major threat to US policy—an assumption he put forward in a little-criticized 12-page memorandum written to the Black Caucas on 27 December 1977 in response to their 12 recommendations for US policy towards SA. The Brzezinski memorandum begins: 'The discussion which follows must be seen in light of the Administration's general approach to SA. We do not believe that the problem of apartheid and hence the problems in US-SA relations will submit to either an easy or a quick solution. Cataclysmic changes, events or reversals are unlikely. Therefore we see this situation as one whose progress will only be made by determined effort over the long haul. This is the intent behind our actions towards SA. It is also clear that our influence and leverage within SA are limited. We do not have the capacity to greatly influence events from afar according to our will, and therefore our policy must proceed on this basis. As we are operating with limited resources, and as we see this to be a struggle over the long haul, we believe it quite important to husband our limited resources and use them when they promise to do most good.' The 'long haul' view was of course the basic premise of British policy in the 1960s until the changing of the guard in the Foreign Office in late 1976. Like Brzezinski, British policy-makers also argued, and still do, that the UK's leverage and resources are limited.

The Secretary of State, Cyrus Vance, took a position rather closer to Young's than to Brzezinski's. In a number of major speeches, he warned of the need to make quick progress because of the dangers existing in Southern Africa: 'The risk of growing conflict and of increased foreign involvement in the racial disputes in the region 'was real, and violence was growing in SA. . . . A policy of leaving apartheid alone for the moment would be wrong and would not work. . . . The beginning of progress must be made soon in SA if there is to be a possibility of peaceful solutions in the longer run.'

The Administration's African policy was not seriously challenged in Congress—but neither was it significantly supported except by stalwarts on Senator Dick Clark's and Congressman Charles Diggs' sub-committees on Africa. The most professional of the snipers at the Administration's policies was George W. Ball, a former Under-Secretary of State under Kennedy and Johnson, who had won great credit for his steadfast opposition to US policies on Vietnam. On the issues of Southern Africa, he spoke for the great conservative majority of American—and European—public opinion. Only his formidable intellectual approach and polished diplomatic style disguised the placebos he was offering in place of realistic policies. There can be no doubt about Ball's deep loathing of apartheid, but he has chosen to follow other Brahmin diplomats, like the late Dean Acheson and George Kennan, in proposing that neutrality and inactivity are the best ways for the US to influence events in SA: 'No matter how much we abominate the excesses of apartheid, we are not—nor should we become—the ally of any particular South African race, group or faction. . . . Our best chance to discourage any adventures by the Soviets, the Chinese or their surrogates is for us to hold firm to the thesis that this is a South African problem which the people of SA must settle in their own way. . . . No one this side of the Iron Curtain wants a military crisis in SA; that is the last thing we need.'[73] This argument for doing as little as possible, as decently and quietly as possible, while hoping for the maximum benefits, has obvious attractions for those who think that the West should not 'interfere' in SA for fear of upsetting the apple-cart. If Carter's politics fail to yield successes, the Ball thesis is likely to attract influential support, and not just in the US.

BRITISH POLICY[74]

Except for the factor of geographic proximity, Britain is in every sense a Front-line State in Southern Africa: it is internationally responsible for Rhodesia; hundreds of thousands of British subjects or close kinsfolk live in Rhodesia and SA; and its economy is closely interwoven with those of the whole region. In the past these interests have had a severe inhibiting effect on British policy in the region, but concern about them began to take the country in a different direction in 1977. 'We stand to lose more than most if things go wrong', the Foreign Secretary told a Labour Party meeting in Cumbria on 17 March 1978. 'Prudent businessmen and prudent investors, no less than the British Government, should be taking a hard look at their South African connections.' For over 20 years, critics of British policy had been saying just that; it took Angola in 1975 and Soweto in 1976 to make British policy-makers and investors aware that the old order in Southern Africa was in the process of collapsing. Another major new factor contributed to Britain's rethink of its Southern African policy: the changing pattern of British trade between SA and Black Africa, and Nigeria's decision to begin to force Western multinationals to choose between doing business with Nigerians or with the apartheid republic.[75]

Dr Owen signalled a change of course in a major speech he made to Young Fabians in Brighton in October 1977,[76] which received only scant attention in the British Press. Even less notice was taken of a second major statement on the need for policy change (made in a speech in Cumbria in March 1978):

'The very closeness of our economic relationship with SA makes us dangerously vulnerable. Our huge economic involvement in a Republic whose future is uncertain and where the risk of social disruption is high is not only bad politics: it has now become economically risky too. As regards investment, figures are not easily obtainable, but it is generally understood that the total stock of UK investment, including portfolio investment, in SA measured in market values is of the order of £5,000m. This is probably double that of the US or of Germany and greatly exceeds that of France or any other Western country. As far as trade is concerned, our relationship is also closer than that of our partners. British exports to SA in 1976 were worth £653m, somewhat lower than those of the US and Germany, while our imports from SA, at £612m in 1976, were in round figures about double those of Japan, the US and Germany. But another very important consideration is that our exports to Black Africa (£1,329m in 1976) and our imports from Black Africa (£1,058m in 1976) are now almost double the exports to and imports from SA. At the moment we are in the position of depending on SA far more than is healthy if we are to pursue consistent and viable foreign and economic policies. But since we already have economic links with SA, we should use them positively to bring about change. . . . In investment and in trade, this country faces a painful dilemma in its relationship with SA. We must reduce our overdependence on that country economically. We stand to lose more than most if things go wrong.'

Other government spokesmen supported the new line taken by the Foreign Secretary, including the Chancellor of the Exchequer, Denis Healey (see chapter on SA: Relations with Britain).

British policy in Rhodesia and Namibia (as described above) took full account of the risk of the region becoming an outright war zone. Speaking in Dar es Salaam in April 1978, Dr Owen lamented that African leaders appeared to understand far better than some people in Britain the threat of Communist military intervention in Rhodesia and elsewhere if the Western initiatives faltered or made a false step.[77]

EUROPEAN POLICIES

The former West German Chancellor, Willy Brandt, warned in Lusaka early in 1978 of a 'real danger that racial conflict and armed struggle in Southern Africa could plunge the world into a bloody conflict'.[78] A few months later, when Schmidt paid his first visit to Angola and Zambia, he too spoke gloomily about developments in the sub-continent.

The former Swedish Prime Minister, Olof Palme, led a delegation of distinguished social democratic leaders on a fact-finding mission to Southern Africa in June 1977 on behalf of the Socialist International. They subsequently produced a programme of action calling for wide-ranging policy changes by European and other governments.[79] Palme also strongly endorsed the findings of the Stockholm International Peace Research Institute (SIPRI) that Southern Africa may become the next major international battlefield. 'The SIPRI study,' he said, 'also points to the risk of the extensive international investments in SA helping to internationalize the conflict. The country's raw material resources and its strategic position may furnish a pretext for further involvement on behalf of the White dictatorship. At the same time, however, such involvement would encourage the other super-power to become more active in the area. Thus there is a serious risk of Africa becoming a new battlefield between East and West. This is something which is least of all desired by the Africans themselves. In this situation, European social democracy should have the important task of working for peace, liberty and social justice, exactly as we did in Greece and Portugal.'[80]

As discussed above, the European Community began to act in concert on issues affecting Southern Africa in 1977–78, making two démarches to Pretoria over Namibia; endorsing the Anglo-American initiative in Rhodesia; adopting a Code of Conduct for European firms in SA; and sending a collective Note to Pretoria, not just protesting against South African policy, but calling for the revocation of the bannings and the release of prisoners taken during the massive operation to crush the Black Consciousness movement in October 1977.[81] The Note also expressed strong concern about the direction that events were taking in SA and emphasized the need for a peaceful evolution towards the granting of full rights to all of SA's inhabitants.[82] (For further details about the policies of the EEC, see chapter on SA: West European Relations.)

SOVIET UNION'S POLICY

While Moscow's principal African preoccupation during 1977–78 was with the Horn of Africa and in buttressing the MPLA regime in Angola, the Russians were extremely active in Southern Africa. The new emphasis being given to the region was shown by the decision to send President Podgorny on a visit to Mozambique, Zambia, Tanzania, as well as Somalia (before the break with that country).[83] The USSR now has two Treaties of Friendship in the region—with Mozambique and Angola—both of which include Russian commitments to come to the aid of these two Front-line States in case of any military threat to their borders.[84] Moscow's two declared aims in the region are to strengthen the liberation movements and to improve its ties with the Front-line States. Aleksey Nikolayev explained the Soviet's policy of giving 'multilateral aid to freedom fighters' (i.e. through the OAU or African governments): 'A basic characteristic of Soviet help should be underlined. By giving disinterested support to all those fighting against national and social oppression and against capitalist exploitation, the USSR has, contrary to what Rhodesian and South African ministers say, never helped any nationalist movements, that is, any splittist groups. Using the pretext of struggle for national independence, the leaders of those movements are in fact seeking to obtain advantages for themselves and for the imperialist monopolies which are behind them.' He identified the 'splittists' in Angola as Unita, FNLA and FLEC, and added: 'The MPLA alone embodied the interests of the whole nation, and it was this movement which was given the wide support of the socialist countries, above all the Soviet Union and Cuba. In Southern Africa, the USSR supports Swapo in Namibia. In SA, the USSR supports the ANC which operates in alliance with the South African Communist Party. In Zimbabwe, the USSR supports those forces which would not let themselves be influenced by national differences existing between the Shona and the Matebele peoples, and which are now fighting for the liberation of the country from the racist and imperialist rule. This is the core of the Soviet policy towards the national liberation movements. It is totally different from the policy pursued by the imperialist forces which, as Nikolai Podgorny said at a dinner given in honour of the Ethiopian delegation, use a whole series of manoeuvres which are as old as imperialism itself, namely exacerbation of national antagonisms, provocation, blackmail and pitting peoples and countries against one another.'[85]

Nikolayev's explanation raises several interesting issues. The first is the definition of 'splittists' as being all the groups not supported (and therefore mentioned) by the Russians—e.g. Mugabe's Zanu and the PAC of SA, apart from Unita, FNLA, etc. It is also interesting to note that Nikolayev does not identify Nkomo's Zapu as the recipient of Moscow's favours. Did he perhaps forget its name or is there another explanation, perhaps that Moscow supports some elements in Zapu but not the movement as a whole? The emphasis on the alliance between ANC and the South African Communist Party is now standard practice in all Russian broadcasts and is particularly significant in that it is the only case in the history of Moscow's support for liberation movements that a local communist party has been recognized alongside a nationalist movement. This raises important questions about the exact relationship between the ANC and SACP.

As might be expected, Russian commentaries on the Western initiatives over Rhodesia and Namibia all followed the same strongly hostile line: the Anglo-American moves were designed 'to achieve a neo-colonialist settlement',[86] and the Western powers were continuing their 'efforts to impose on the Front-line States their version of a Rhodesian settlement'.[87] The issue never discussed by Russian commentators was why, if Moscow could read Western designs so clearly, the liberation movements like Zapu and Swapo (which have its support) were also not clever enough to see through these 'imperialist' manoeuvres and refuse to join in them? Even more slighting was the suggestion that the Front-line Presidents (who, after all, include some good Soviet friends like Machel and Neto) might somehow be pressured to accept Western settlement conditions. The fact that Machel not only warmly advocated the Anglo-American initiative in Rhodesia, but also commended its plan as offering 'positive elements', might suggest (in Russian eyes) that he had in fact allowed himself to be 'imposed' upon by the 'imperialists'. It is of course possible that the Russians fail to appreciate the insulting nature of this line of propaganda; yet what other line can they take when Marxist and other African Presidents, as well as approved-in-Moscow liberation movements, choose to cooperate with the Western powers in their search for peaceful solutions?

Although the Western initiatives were treated with hostility by the Russians, they might well draw encouragement from the obvious fact that, as yet, the Western powers have no coherent policy to offer for SA, even though they can put together credible solutions for Rhodesia and Namibia.

THE CUBAN POLICY
Fidel Castro's personal entry into the Southern African zone early in 1977 was

undoubtedly a great personal triumph—much more so than that of the elderly and rather less glamorous Russian President whose itinerary was overlapped by Castro's.[88] Soviet-Cuban policies in Southern Africa appear to coincide—as they did in Angola and in the Ogaden campaign, if not in Eritrea. In a joint communiqué issued in Moscow on 23 April after a visit by Cuba's Foreign Minister, Isidoro Malmierca Peoli, the two countries pledged support for Swapo, ANC and the PF. The fact that they did not single out Nkomo's wing of the PF for approval and reject Mugabe's was possibly just a tactical decision. Despite this close co-operation between the Cubans and the Russians, African leaders like Kaunda and Nyerere make a clear distinction between the two. They see Cuba as an independent revolutionary country within the Third World, and Russia as one of the super-powers. The question is whether 'the cub' will ever operate in a crisis area without 'the tiger'.

The Cubans acquired a key role in 1977 in the training of Swapo and Zapu guerrillas in Angola. While there are some Cubans in Mozambique, there is no hard evidence to show that they are involved in training the Zanla forces of Mugabe, whose main instruction is provided by the Chinese.

There was considerable speculation in 1978 about whether the Cubans would be willing to become actively involved as combatants in Rhodesia (as they did in Angola and Ogaden) if invited to do so by the PF. According to one reliable source,[89] Cuban diplomats gave firm assurances to Washington that Cubans would not fight inside Rhodesia, although they would continue training Zimbabwe guerrillas. However, since the PF leaders still insist that they must fight their own war, the question may never arise, at least not unless Zimbabwe's independence were followed by a civil war between rival guerrilla forces.

CHINA'S POLICY

Peking's only direct involvement in Southern Africa was through its close political ties with Mugabe's Zanu and its military training programme for the Zanla forces in Tanzania and Mozambique (see above).

China sees Southern Africa 'as one of the explosive spots' in the continent partly because of the rivalries of the two super-powers, but mainly because of the aims of the 'arrogant new tsars'. The official Peking view of the situation is as follows:

'The Soviet Union covets the rich resources there and has for years attempted to seize control of the supply line to Europe from the Indian Ocean round the Cape of Good Hope. Especially since its setback in Egypt, Moscow has stepped up its drive to dominate Southern Africa as part and parcel of its major strategic plan. This constitutes a grave threat to the Southern African people in their struggle against colonial and racist domination and for national liberation. Since the beginning of 1976, the Soviet Press has time and again stressed that the outcome of the Southern African liberation struggle "depends on external factors," in other words, on Soviet interference. . . . To win victory in their liberation struggle, the people of Southern Africa, while intensifying their armed struggle, have engaged the enemy sharply at the negotiating table. However, Moscow resorted to different tricks of deception out of its need to contend with Washington and control this part of Africa. At one time it prattled about "reconciliation" being the "correct line", and at another, it pledged "support" for the armed struggle there.

'What deserves attention is the Soviet stock trick of division and disintegration, a trick it played in Angola and is playing in Southern Africa. It is sowing dissension among the Front-line countries, infiltrating into the liberation movement to split it by supporting one faction and attacking another, and waiting for an opportunity to stir up another fratricidal war among the Africans. Thanks to the lesson of Angola, the people in Southern Africa are fully aware of the consequences of Soviet interference in their liberation struggle. Therefore, they have time and again reaffirmed that the destiny of Southern Africa must be placed in the hands of the people there. Robert Mugabe, a leader of the Zimbabwe Patriotic Front, said: "We will not call in anyone; we flatly refuse to let those who give us help make themselves our masters." A leader of the Pan-Africanist Congress of Azania said: "The Soviet Union pays lip service to supporting the national liberation movements in Africa. Its real aim is to split them. We will never allow the Angola incident to be repeated in Azania," he declared. In the past year, the Southern African people have closely combined the struggle against racism with that against hegemonism, refusing to be taken in by the Soviet Union in its southward offensive and severely punishing the racist regimes. This is bringing about a new situation both in the armed struggle and in the mass movement.

'Playing with fire in the heartland of Africa, the Soviet Union has wilder ambitions than the old-line colonialists. Its strategic goal is to grab the whole of Africa and threaten Western Europe by cutting the African continent right in the middle to facilitate its southward invasion and to isolate and encircle the independent African countries. . . . The new tsars are more crafty than their old colonialist predecessors. They drove mercenaries to the front as cannon-fodder while they themselves remained behind the scenes. Soviet armed invasion of Zaire through mercenaries aroused the African people to action against their common enemy. To fight against aggression, they formed a joint armed force which, in 80 days of bloody fighting, badly battered the Soviet-armed mercenaries and sent them fleeing helter-skelter. Experience of this war against Soviet mercenary invasion opened a new way for the African people to fight future Soviet aggression. The Soviet-paid mercenaries looked powerful when they temporarily succeeded in their armed intervention in Angola in 1976. But their repression and persecution of the masses incurred bitter hatred, and the Angolan people rose in opposition. Guerrilla activity all over Angola has set the mercenaries on tenterhooks.'[90]

NOTES

References are to chapters or essays in *Africa Contemporary Record (ACR)* Vol 10, 1977-78. Unless otherwise mentioned, all the sources quoted are South African newspapers or journals.

1. See *ACR* 1976-77, pp. A3ff.
2. See *ACR* 1975-76, pp. A3ff.
3. See *ACR* 1969-70, pp. C41-45.
4. For text, see *ACR* 1976-77, pp. C159ff.
5. For a discussion of their role, see *ACR* 1976-77, pp. A10-12.
6. See chapter on Namibia.
7. *Sunday Times*, 6 March 1977.
8. *The Observer*, London; 22 May 1977.
9. Radio Johannesburg, 31 October 1977.
10. See *ACR* 1976-77, pp. C157ff.
11. *Ibid*, pp. A41ff.
12. *Rand Daily Mail (RDM)*, 3 February 1977.
13. Statement by Ambassador Young to Security Council on 28 September 1977.
14. For details of the Anglo-American initiative, see chapter on Rhodesia.
15. *The Guardian*, Manchester; 4 April 1977.
16. *The Times*, London; 6 June 1977.
17. See essay, 'The Disunited OAU', and Documents section, p. C3.
18. *International Herald Tribune (IHT)*, Paris; 8 July 1977.

19. Speech by Ambassador Young to Security Council on 15 March 1978.
20. *Daily Telegraph*, London; 31 August 1977.
21. For details, see Documents section, pp. C59–72. Also see chapter on Rhodesia.
22. *The Times*, 3 October 1977.
23. See chapter on Rhodesia.
24. *Ibid.*
25. Statements to the House of Commons, 26 January, 3 February and 5 May 1978.
26. Michael Scott, *A Time to Speak* (London: Faber, 1958).
27. For brief background see ISIO monograph by Colin Legum, *The UN and South Africa* (University of Sussex, 1970).
28. See *ACR* 1976–77, pp. B769–70; and chapter on Namibia in this volume.
29. See *ACR* 1976–77, pp. A26–27.
30. See *ACR* 1974–75, pp. A93ff; 1975–76, pp. C93ff.
31. Don McHenry, *US Firms in South Africa* (London: Africa Publications Trust, 1976).
32. Radio Johannesburg, 1 May 1977.
33. Interview on Voice of America, 18 November 1977.
34. Agence France Presse (AFP), 11 April 1977.
35. For details see Documents section, pp. C211–15.
36. *The Times*, 13 February 1978.
37. See chapter on Namibia.
38. *The Observer*, 19 September 1976.
39. *The Star*, 12 February 1977.
40. For text of treaty see Documents section, pp. C17–19. For statement by Machel during a visit to Finland, see *Financial Times (FT)*, London; 5 May 1977.
41. For text of conference resolutions see Documents section, C31–38.
42. *The Times*, 17 May 1977.
43. Radio Lusaka, 25 July 1977.
44. For Commonwealth decisions see Documents section, pp. C44–49.
45. *The Guardian*, 16 August 1977.
46. *The Observer*, 28 August 1977.
47. Radio Lusaka, 7 September 1977.
48. *FT*, 24 September 1977.
49. *IHT*, 7 February 1977.
50. See *ACR* 1975–76, pp. A27–29.
51. *Daily Telegraph*, 26 March 1977.
52. *The Times*, 1 April 1977.
53. For details, see chapter on Zambia.
54. *To the Point*, Brussels; 4 April 1977.
55. *The Observer*, 7 May 1978.
56. See chapter on Rhodesia.
57. *The Guardian*, 22 October 1977.
58. For details of the Smith-Kaunda meeting, see *FT*, 26 October 1977.
59. See essay, 'The Disunited OAU'.
60. Radio Kinshasa, 14 March 1977.
61. For details, see chapters on Zaire and South Africa.
62. *IHT*, 11 February 1977.
63. Radio Lagos, 21 January 1978.
64. See chapter on Rhodesia under Patriotic Front.
65. *Ibid*; also see *Zimbabwe News*, Maputo; Vol 9, No 3, 5 June 1977.
66. *Peking Review*, 1 July 1977.
67. Interview with James Pringle in *Newsweek*, Washington; 6 March 1978.
68. See essay on 'The US Year in Africa'.
69. For text of Mondale statement, see Documents section, pp. C27–31.
70. *The Times*, 20 May 1977.
71. Speech to Security Council, 1 November 1977.
72. *Ibid.*
73. *The Atlantic*, New York; June 1977.
74. See essay, 'Britain's Year in Africa'.
75. This is discussed in the chapters on South Africa and Nigeria.
76. For a summary of Dr Owen's speech, see Documents section, pp. C19–21.
77. *Daily Telegraph*, 17 April 1978.
78. *The Star*, 7 January 1977.
79. See *X-Ray on Southern Africa*, January/February 1978 (London: Africa Bureau).
80. *Socialist Affairs*, London; July–October 1977.
81. See chapter on SA: Black Consciousness.

82. *The Times*, 28 October 1977.
83. See essay, 'Soviet and Chinese Policies in Africa'.
84. See chapter on Mozambique.
85. Radio Moscow, 13 May 1977.
86. Tass, 11 July 1977.
87. Radio Moscow, 5 April 1977.
88. See essay, 'Cuba: The New Communist Power in Africa'.
89. Jonathan Steele in *The Guardian*, 15 April 1978.
90. *Peking Review*, 6 January 1978.

1978–1979

THE APPROACHING COLLAPSE OF WHITE RESISTANCE IN RHODESIA

Developments in the Southern African region during 1978 and early 1979 seemed to confirm the predictions (and hopes) of those who believe in the necessity for, and inevitability of, revolutionary struggle; they alone could derive any satisfaction from the gales of violence which swept across the Zambesi and Cunene rivers and over the Inyanga mountains and the Manicaland plains. The Western and African initiatives over Namibia and Rhodesia both faltered;[1] while the situation in Namibia still appeared to be negotiable in mid-1979, the chances of reaching a negotiated settlement in Rhodesia looked almost hopeless—barring the miracle of an agreement being worked out among the Zimbabwe rivals themselves. Despite much talk about 'change' in the Republic of SA, there was still not the slightest evidence that the White minority was even thinking of moving towards power-sharing with the Black majority, let alone of being ready to concede the possibility of majority rule. Meanwhile, a critical point was marked by the decision of many Black youths that the time had come to abandon their efforts to achieve change by peaceful means and to opt for armed struggle instead. Of the 2,000 or so who quit SA, at least half joined the guerrilla training camps in Mozambique, Angola and Tanzania, while many of those who stayed behind demonstrated their readiness to support violence. With the first gunfights between guerrillas and security forces occurring on SA soil in early 1979 and the beginning of what the authorities described as 'urban terrorism,' there was no lack of evidence that White South Africans were acutely aware of and sensitive to the new dangers impinging on their society.[2] In earlier times, the frontiersmen had made a laager by drawing their ox-wagons into a circle and had screened themselves behind a shelter of thorn-tree branches; in the more modern conditions of 1978–79, the Afrikaners built—in the words of their Chief of Police Security, Brig C. F. Zietsman—'a ring of steel' around the threatened Republic's borders.[3] Defence spending for 1979–80 went up by a massive 33% over the previous year to reach over £1 bn (R2,073m).

The SA government had hoped—and worked for—one of two outcomes to the Rhodesian crisis: either an internationally recognized settlement, as proposed in the Anglo-American/Front-line States' initiative; or an African majority government under 'moderate' Black leadership, capable of attracting enough international recognition to end sanctions and enjoying enough military support to defeat the 'Marxist-Leninist terrorists' in the Patriotic Front, especially Robert Mugabe's Zimbabwe African National Liberation Army (Zanla). When the Anglo-American initiative was blunted by the Internal Settlement in March 1978,[4] the Pretoria regime enlarged its involvement in Rhodesia by undertaking to give economic and military support to Bishop Muzorewa's government in the hope (and apparent belief) that it could survive long enough for 'the pusillanimous West' (a phrase reflecting Prime Minister Botha's attitude) to 'come to its senses' and call a halt to 'the advance of Communism' in Africa.

Bishop Muzorewa admitted in June 1979 that his government 'probably would not be able to survive without military aid' from SA.[5] He therefore found himself—or, rather, put himself—in much the same position as Dr Jonas Savimbi, the leader of the National Union for the Total Independence of Angola (Unita), in his civil war struggle with Dr Agostinho Neto's People's Movement for the Liberation of Angola

(MPLA) in 1975[6]—but with this difference: Muzorewa was in formal charge of the government, while Savimbi was not. In the African context, any Black leader in open alliance with Pretoria carries the mark of Cain. If it were not sure before, Muzorewa's candid admission ensured that the Patriotic Front could count on the support of the Organization of African Unity (OAU)—as well as on that of the Soviet bloc, Cuba and China. One predictable result was that the level of international involvement in Rhodesia would rise and inevitably spill over into the rest of the region.

In Namibia, the SA government had been 'smart' (ambassador Andrew Young's word) in running along a two-track policy. On one track it co-operated with the five Western members of the Security Council (US, Britain, France, West Germany and Canada)—the so-called 'Contact Group'—to discover whether it was possible to get an internationally recognized settlement which would not result in handing over power to the South West Africa People's Organization (Swapo). On the other, it moved towards an Internal Settlement with the Turnhalle Alliance which, if the first track failed, could provide the basis for a handover of power to a local majority-style government. While this dual policy occasionally entailed jumping the lines, which produced sharp tensions with the Western powers and the UN, Pretoria nevertheless succeeded—up to the time of writing in mid-1979—in keeping its two-track policy intact. Thus, while avoiding any serious open confrontation with the West, it was able to buy valuable time to build up a base of support for anti-Swapo forces inside Namibia.[7]

These tactics worked in the short term in favour of Pretoria, but the longer-term outlook was much less favourable for a number of reasons. First, the liberation movements of Zimbabwe, Namibia and SA were able to use the prolongation of their armed struggles to build up more effective guerrilla forces, while the climate of intensified violence favoured the policies of those who were genuinely committed to a revolutionary armed struggle. By early 1979, over 80% of Rhodesian territory was under emergency rule; Zanla had between 8,000–10,000 of its cadres on the ground inside the country, and another approximate 5,000 either in training or in base camps in Tanzania and Mozambique; Joshua Nkomo's Zimbabwe Independent People's Revolutionary Army (Zipra) had c. 2,000 guerrillas inside Rhodesia, and another 8,000–10,000 in camps in Angola and Zambia; Swapo (which has suffered the heaviest casualties in proportion to its numbers) had c. 3,500 trained men across the border in Angola; the African National Congress of SA (ANC) had c. 2,000 trained guerrillas in Angola, Mozambique and Tanzania—many of them young militants fresh from Soweto and other urban areas; while the Pan Africanist Congress (PAC), which had been largely moribund, had c. 500 guerrillas in training in Tanzania, Uganda and Libya. One important new feature of this build-up was the guerrillas' greater politicization in Marxist ideas which was undertaken in the training camps by Russian, East German, Cuban or Chinese instructors.

Second, the growing violence in and around Rhodesia, Namibia and SA spilled over the borders into neighbouring countries—Botswana, Angola, Mozambique and Zambia. SA and Rhodesian military attacks across these borders undermined internal security but did not have the result of either seriously weakening the guerrillas or the resolve of the frontier states to go on supporting them—although it did encourage Zambia and Angola especially to support Western initiatives to find political settlements in Rhodesia and Namibia. The pressures on Zambia, Angola and Mozambique—and their vulnerability to Rhodesian and SA attacks—resulted in stronger military ties with the Soviet bloc and were therefore directly counter-productive to the SA (and Western) aim of preventing the spread of Communist influence. Zamiba, which had been in the forefront of the African states which opposed Soviet-Cuban intervention in Angola, increasingly turned to the Soviet bloc and China for military aid. Angola, which had a national interest in reducing its military dependence on the Soviets and Cubans and improving its economic links with the West, found it necessary to maintain its Communist ties. Mozambique, which had been reluctant to become involved in the Sino-Soviet struggle, found it expedient to strengthen its ties with the Russians as 'a strategic ally with superior weapons,' rather than with the Chinese. Thus, the effect of the military tactics of Rhodesia and SA was precisely the opposite of that intended—to prevent the spread of Communist influence.

Third, the Soviet-Cuban influence and presence in Southern Africa grew because the Communist nations proved themselves to be 'reliable friends of the liberation movements' and because they were ready to commit themselves militarily on the side of the frontier states. These developing relations put the Soviet bloc in a stronger position to evolve its own strategy towards Southern Africa (see below).

Fourth, the failure of the Western powers—especially the US and Britain—to bring either of their initiatives in Rhodesia or Namibia to a successful conclusion eroded their influence and caused their friends to look for allies more unambiguous in their commitment. Thus, during 1978 and in the first half of 1979, the capacity of the Western powers to influence the course of events in Southern Africa diminished significantly; this was especially true after the emergence of a lobby in the US Congress strong enough to thwart the policies of the Carter Administration.

Fifth, the role of the Front-line African States and Nigeria in co-operating with the Western powers declined as they began to lose faith in the willingness of the US and Britain to commit enough of their resources to secure the independence of Rhodesia and Namibia on terms acceptable to the OAU and the rest of the international community.

Together, these five developments contributed towards heightening the climate of violence in Southern Africa and of producing greater international involvement in the area through the enlarged role of the Communist states—a role increasingly encouraged and sanctioned by African leaders, even by some who in the past had been regarded as strongly anti-Communist and even pro-Western.

THE THREE ARENAS OF CONFLICT
1. NAMIBIA

The five Western members of the Security Council (the US, Britain, France, West Germany and Canada) first embarked on their initiative in April 1977 to try to find a way of bringing the SA government and Swapo to agree to terms for a settlement based on the principles of Security Council Resolution 385. Known as the 'Contact Group,' they scored a notable success in April 1978 when both parties agreed to a set of proposals which was endorsed by the Security Council.[10] The proposals did not attempt to finalize all the details involved in a settlement, which were left to be negotiated by Martti Ahtisaari, who was named by Dr Kurt Waldheim as the UN Special Representative, between the Administrator-General of Namibia, Mr Justice Steyn, and Swapo. Both SA and Swapo raised strong objections to Ahtisaari's report on how the proposals should be implemented. Swapo proved to be exceptionally difficult in the negotiations following the brutal raid in May 1978 by SA forces against their camps in Cassinga, deep inside Angola.[11] Thanks to the good offices of the Front-line Presidents (FLPs)—and especially of President Agostinho Neto—Swapo's objections were overcome at meetings held with the Contact Group in Luanda in July 1978. One of the contentious issues was over the future of Walvis Bay, on which Swapo gave way. However, when the UN Secretary-General published his plans for implementing the agreement, new and angry controversy erupted—this time, more from SA which raised two fundamental objections: against the proposal that the internationally-supervised elections be postponed until after December 1978 (which Waldheim insisted was necessary to allow the political process seven months to develop from the time when both parties finally signed the agreement); and against the size of the proposed 7,500-man UN Transition Assistance Group (UNTAG). Swapo offered on 10 September to sign a ceasefire agreement with SA and announced its willingness to accept Waldheim's report, but with certain reservations.

Ten days later, on 20 September, simultaneous with his sudden resignation as Prime Minister, John Vorster announced that SA would unilaterally arrange for an election in Namibia. He explained that all 'options would be open' to the new Assembly, which could decide to draw up a new Constitution, proceed to implement the Western proposals as originally agreed, or accept the Waldheim report. Swapo predictably responded by declaring that it was left with no option but to step up the war; its Vice-President, Misheck Muyongo, called for 'all-out military assistance' from Communist countries. The internal Namibian National Front said it would oppose holding the elections in November—'even armed struggle would not be excluded.' Mr Justice Steyn agreed only to postpone the elections to 4 December 1978. On 29 September, the Security Council adopted Resolution 435 which approved Waldheim's recommendations (including the UN Force) to implement the Contact Group's proposals. It also condemned SA's decision to hold elections. Only the USSR and Czechoslovakia abstained; China, as usual, was absent. The Africa Group at the UN had attempted to introduce a resolution calling for comprehensive sanctions against SA if it went ahead with unilateral elections in defiance of the UN, but was dissuaded, with great difficulty, by the Western powers from insisting on bringing its proposal to a vote. In an effort to save the Western initiative and to preclude a call for sanctions if SA moved towards granting Namibia independence in defiance of the UN, the Contact Group's Foreign Ministers went to Pretoria in October 1978 to intervene with Vorster's successor, P. W. Botha. This marked the first time that the Western powers had made a joint démarche against SA at such a high level. A joint statement issued in Pretoria on 19 October gave very little away about what had actually transpired, beyond stating that SA intended to go ahead with the elections, which should be seen as an 'internal process to elect leaders,' and that joint discussions between Ahtisaari and Steyn should be resumed to determine the modalities for a further election under UN supervision.

Although the door was thus at least kept open for a UN-agreed settlement, Swapo rejected restarting negotiations. On 13 November, the Security Council passed Resolution 439 calling for the December elections to be cancelled immediately, and warning that failure to agree to UN-supervised elections would compel it to initiate 'appropriate action' under the Charter, including mandatory sanctions under Chapter 7. The resolution was passed by ten to nil, with all five Western powers abstaining. In a flurry of diplomatic activity, SA's Foreign Minister, Pik Botha, went to New York in late November for urgent talks with Waldheim and the US Secretary of State, who also arranged for him to meet President Carter in order to give further emphasis to America's commitment to upholding the UN's authority. Pik Botha also stopped over in London for talks with the British Foreign Secretary. The positive outcome of this round of diplomacy was that on 3 December—the day before the elections were due to be held in Namibia—Waldheim was able to report to the Security Council that he had been advised by Pretoria that it would 'retain authority in Namibia' pending the implementation of the proposed UN-supervised elections. This met Swapo's point that SA alone should be its negotiating partner in the talks for a settlement on the grounds that the Pretoria regime wielded effective power in Namibia.

Namibia was again debated by the UN General Assembly from 7–12 December 1978. Speaking for the Western powers, the British Foreign Secretary called for a UN presence to be established in Namibia early in 1979 preparatory to internationally-supervised elections, and for swift completion of the negotiations over electoral arrangements. The Namibian Constituent Assembly, formed on 20 December after the elections, passed a resolution three days later accepting UN-supervised elections in 1979—but was persuaded to do so only after the SA Prime Minister personally addressed it in secret session. Ahtisaari returned to Namibia for talks in January 1979; he also visited the Front-line States and had discussions with Swapo. These contacts made it clear that both SA and Swapo were seeking to obtain advantages in the process of implementing the UN decision which they had not achieved in previous rounds of negotiation. SA began to insist that UNTAG should monitor Swapo bases in Angola; Swapo asked that, after the ceasefire came into operation, it should have time to move 2,500 of its armed men into five bases to be established inside Namibia. Swapo's proposal was clearly more of a 'try on' than SA's. Waldheim rejected both and instead presented proposals on 26 February 1979 to resolve the outstanding issues. His report provoked a new crisis which still remained unresolved in June 1979.

Waldheim's report stated that while the settlement proposal made no specific provision for the monitoring by UNTAG of Swapo bases in neighbouring countries, those countries had nevertheless been asked to ensure that the provisions of the transitional arrangements and the outcome of the election would be respected. In addition, Waldheim was seeking the agreement of the Governments of Angola, Botswana and Zambia for UNTAG liaison offices to be established in their countries to facilitate co-operation in implementing the proposal. He also specified arrangements for the handling of Swapo armed personnel, carefully differentiating between those inside Namibia at the time of the ceasefire and those outside. Those inside would be restricted to designated locations; all Swapo forces in neighbouring countries would, on the commencement of the ceasefire, be restricted to bases in those countries.

SA again reacted negatively to the Secretary-General's proposals, in particular to the fact that no provision was made for UNTAG monitoring Swapo bases in Angola and Zambia, and to the handling of Swapo armed personnel inside Namibia at the time of the ceasefire. To avert a breakdown of the initiative over these issues, another round of 'proximity talks' was held at Ministerial level in New York from 19–20 March. Vance and his colleagues presented the Contact Group's view to SA's Foreign Minister that the Secretary-General's report was consistent with the original proposal which SA had accepted. During those talks, the Swapo delegation accepted the restriction of their own forces outside Namibia to bases outside Namibia; accepted the Secretary-General's proposal for designating locations to which any Swapo armed personnel inside Namibia at the start of the ceasefire would be restricted and monitored; accepted the Secretary-General's intention to designate only one or two such locations; and stated that it had no intention of infiltrating any armed personnel into Namibia following the start of the ceasefire and that, in fact, they had no intention of infiltrating any armed personnel during the period between the signing of the ceasefire and its actual commencement.

Swapo thus accepted the implementation plans of the Secretary-General, which the Contact Group also fully supported, and was now prepared to move ahead accordingly. During these 'proximity talks,' the Front-line States reiterated their commitment scrupulously to ensure the observance of the ceasefire agreement.

However, two principal issues still stood in the way of SA's acceptance. First, its demand that UNTAG monitor Swapo bases outside Namibia. SA had been informed prior to its acceptance of the Western proposals in 1978 that such a provision was unacceptable to the neighbouring states, and that this element had been taken into account in determining the size and functions of UNTAG. It was explained that neither the Western powers nor the UN could dictate to sovereign nations which were themselves not party to the settlement.

The second issue, and the one which became SA's primary objection, was the Secretary-General's proposal regarding Swapo armed personnel in Namibia at the start of the ceasefire. He had decided, and the Western powers had supported him, that such Swapo armed personnel, estimated at perhaps several hundred, should be identified and restricted by the UN at designated locations in such a way as to facilitate their monitoring. Ambassador Don McHenry, chairman of the Contact Group, said that although it was possible to engage in a legalistic argument over whether or not the establishment of such Swapo locations was envisaged under the settlement proposal, what mattered was the practical problem which had to be solved. The Secretary-General was sensitive to the need to ensure that the electoral process was not adversely affected by the manner in which this issue was handled. The locations would, as far as practical, be away from population centres.

Several lesser issues which could still be raised to a higher degree of importance include the composition of the military component of UNTAG and the timing of the UN-supervised elections. Neither Swapo nor SA has yet given its formal agreement to the composition proposed by Waldheim, although this should be achieved relatively easily once the major issues are resolved.

The position in June 1979 was that Swapo was prepared to proceed with this settlement; so were the five Western powers, the UN Security Council and the international community generally. But SA had not agreed, insisting that it must consult the Namibian political groups before making its final decision. Summing up the situation before the US Congress subcommittee on Africa, Ambassador McHenry said: 'The Front-line States believe that, since they have brought Swapo to accept the settlement, it is now up to "the Five" to obtain SA's agreement. If SA does not agree, there will be increasingly strong calls at the UN for us to support our own negotiations by exerting real pressure on SA—in other words, some form of economic sanctions. We have continually told the Front-line States and other African nations that negotiation is a real alternative to the armed struggle in Southern Africa. Our inability to obtain SA's acceptance would almost certainly be seen as proof of an ultimate lack of will in the West to press SA to co-operate with a negotiated settlement. It would be seen by Africans as proof of the ineffectiveness of negotiation for peaceful change as a viable alternative to long and bloody military solutions. It would surely adversely affect the prospects for negotiated settlements in the rest of Southern Africa. It would result in an escalation of hostilities and chaos, and open further opportunities for outside forces and alien ideologies. . . . At this stage Namibia is still a relatively small problem in Southern Africa—and the one most susceptible to a negotiated solution. With time, however, it will become increasingly complex and difficult. Bitterness will exceed reason. Today's compromise solution will be overshadowed by non-negotiable demands. . . .'

2. ZIMBABWE-RHODESIA

The Anglo-American initiative to get its proposals[12] discussed at an all-party conference was blunted by the Internal Settlement (IS) in Rhodesia in March 1978 and the formation of a Transition Government including Ian Smith, Bishop Abel

Muzorewa, the Rev Ndabaningi Sithole and Chief Chirau. Although the two special emissaries—Stephen Low, the US ambassador in Lusaka, and John Graham, Deputy Under-Secretary at the Foreign and Commonwealth Office—had literally scores of meetings with all the Zimbabwe-Rhodesian leaders and with the FLPs between March and October 1978, their efforts failed to revive the earlier momentum of the Anglo-American initiative.[13] Another higher-level attempt was made to breathe new life into the endeavour in November 1978 when the British Prime Minister sent a former senior Minister, Cledwyn Hughes MP, on a fact-finding mission to try to discover whether there was any way in which the IS supporters and the Patriotic Front could be brought round the same table. His findings, reported to Callaghan on 20 December, were pessimistic: even if the two sides could be persuaded to attend a conference, there was no reasonable prospect of any agreement being reached. 'Each side in the war,' he reported, 'is convinced that it can reach its goal—or at least not lose—by continuing to follow its own present policies.' He felt that the Salisbury regime was 'under no effective pressure from the SA government to negotiate an alternative arrangement with the Patriotic Front'; nor did he think Pretoria was inclined to support the idea of all-party talks until after elections had been held under the new Constitution. Nevertheless there was only one occasion, on 11 September 1978, when the possibility of all-party talks was considered to be 'dead and buried'—the words used by Nkomo when reacting to Smith's warning to Zambia and Mozambique that Rhodesia could not 'tolerate terrorists operating from their territories.' But Nkomo was careful to add that he was speaking only as Zapu's leader and not for the Patriotic Front. Indeed, on the following day, Zanu's secretary-general, Edgar Tekere, said the Front was still committed to negotiations.

The American side of the partnership began to weaken after mid-1978, not because of any change of attitude by the Carter Administration, but as a result of the emergence of a conservative lobby in the Senate. At about the same time, the hitherto close unity among the Front-line Presidents began to show signs of strain. These changes seriously undermined the already lagging Anglo-American/African initiative. On 26 July, the US Senate voted by 48–42 against an amendment to the Foreign Aid Bill, which demanded the immediate lifting of sanctions against Rhodesia. A similar amendment was defeated in the House of Representatives. In order to deflect this move, liberal Congressmen proposed the expedient of a compromise which in fact resulted in making it more difficult for the White House to pursue its own favoured policies and led to further compromises. The resolution passed by the Senate on 10 August 1978 proposed that sanctions would be lifted after 31 December 1978, subject to a judgement by the President that the Salisbury regime had meanwhile demonstrated its willingness to negotiate in good faith at an all-party conference, and that a government had been installed in Salisbury on the basis of free elections in which all population groups had been allowed to participate. At that stage the elections in Rhodesia had been set for December 1978, a date later changed to May 1979. Despite this weakening resolve by Congress over sanctions, Dr Owen told the House of Commons on 2 August 1978 that Britain would maintain its policy on sanctions while continuing to work for a negotiated settlement.

By August 1978 it had also become increasingly clear that the power of the White Rhodesian minority was slipping rapidly, and that its Black partners in the IS were even more openly disunited than the two wings of the Patriotic Front. Evidence of the decline of the White Rhodesians' position was provided by their increasing exodus from the country; the loss of effective security over at least 80% of the country; the failure of the Transition Government to make much progress towards implementing the IS agreement; the sharply accelerated rate of killing; and the necessity to escalate the war by making more damaging attacks across the borders into Zambia, Mozambique, Botswana and Angola—thus further enlarging the sphere of violence. By this time the Rhodesian security forces had already given up trying to maintain security and effective administrative control over the whole country; but they were still capable of mobilizing all their available resources to strike effectively against any single target or to any specific operation either inside or outside the country. (For details see chapter on Zimbabwe-Rhodesia.)

The escalation in the fighting further increased the economic and military pressures on the over-strained resources of Rhodesia, as well as on those of Zambia. One result was that both Smith and Kenneth Kaunda began to share a mutual interest in finding a solution. As on other occasions, 'Tiny' Rowland, the head of the London-based multinational Lonrho, stepped in as a middleman by helping to arrange a secret meeting between Smith and Nkomo in Lusaka. This mediation effort won the important backing of Nigeria which came to play a crucial role in the negotiations. Details of this secret meeting were supplied on 31 August by a Zanu (Sithole) spokesman and confirmed by a Muzorewa spokesman. They claimed that Smith had offered Nkomo the chairmanship of the Transition Government until elections could be held. Sithole and Muzorewa were both alarmed by this move to negotiate secretly with Nkomo, especially when they learned that Smith had promised to drop them in favour of Nkomo, Mugabe and Chief Chirau if the two Patriotic Front leaders were ready to co-operate. Meanwhile, Nkomo met Mugabe in Lusaka from 18–20 August to discuss Smith's approach. Mugabe declared himself opposed to negotiating with Smith, believing that the Patriotic Front should agree to negotiate only with the British government as the legal power in Rhodesia. Mugabe flew to Lagos for talks with the Nigerian leaders and then returned to Lusaka with Brig Joseph Garba, Nigeria's Commissioner for External Affairs. Although Mugabe was led into a room where Smith was waiting with Nkomo to start the talks, he walked out. Garba went on to Maputo to report on the negotiations to President Samora Machel and to persuade him to influence Mugabe to change his mind. Machel declined to do so. Not only did these efforts at involving the Patriotic Front in talks with the IS parties lead nowhere, but they had two negative results: they deepened the suspicions between Mugabe and Nkomo, and they widened the differences between President Nyerere and Kaunda who, until 1977, had been the closest of political allies and the principal unifying force within the FLPs.[14]

A variety of motives had led the different parties to these secret meetings in Lusaka. Kaunda desperately needed a settlement of the Rhodesian conflict for both nationalist reasons and for reasons of national interest; but he also had a stake in helping Nkomo assume power in Zambia. Mugabe obviously did not share this aim; he also objected in principle to negotiating with Smith—having all along insisted that he would deal only with the British government. The Nigerians, having embarked on a period of activist diplomacy to try to help settle as many African conflicts as possible—ranging from those in Chad and the Horn of Africa to Southern Africa—were keen to help end the war in Rhodesia. The White Rhodesian leader was pursuing two parallel interests: to split and so weaken the Patriotic Front; and to use Nkomo as a lever against Muzorewa who, at that stage, was still proving obdurate in negotiating the implementation of the IS agreement. Smith was also under pressure from Vorster to try to involve Nkomo in the settlement and to make whatever compromises were necessary to get it implemented. Vorster had said as much to Cyrus Vance and David Owen when they visited him in Pretoria, and also in a speech at the end of May 1978.[15] When news of the secret talks became public, White Rhodesian opinion was shocked that Smith should have proposed giving a key position to the 'terrorist' leader; but Sithole and Muzorewa were stunned—sufficiently for the Bishop to become less stubborn in coming to terms with Smith, who thus alone gained from the enterprise.

Another twist was given to the unfolding of events in Rhodesia when the conservative group in the US Senate invited Smith, Muzorewa, Sithole and Chirau to visit America in October 1978. This move forced Carter into making another compromise by agreeing to issue the necessary visas while emphasizing that the visit had no official standing. Making a virtue out of necessity, the State Department explained on 4 October why it had agreed 'on an exceptional basis' to grant the 27 Senators' request. It said it believed the visit could contribute to the process of achieving a settlement and could enhance the American public's 'understanding of this complicated matter.' The statement also made it clear that the US had never favoured one side or the other in the conflict. Once the Rhodesian delegation was in Washington, Cyrus Vance found it expedient to meet its members in an attempt to persuade them to agree to all-party talks before their elections and to put forward new Anglo-American proposals for them to consider.[16]

Although Smith and his colleagues were given enormous exposure by the media and their Senatorial hosts, there was a general consensus that they failed to make a good impression. Even the London *Daily Mail*, which strongly backed the IS, reported the visit under a banner headline *SMITH'S FLOP*.[17] Smith himself admitted that he had got 'not the slightest encouragement or support from the US or the UK.'[18] Britain refused to extend a similar invitation to Smith and his colleagues. Nkomo followed Smith to the US to put forward the Patriotic Front's case; Mugabe's reaction was to tell Washington to 'keep out' of Rhodesia's affairs in the future.[19]

There was considerable misunderstanding about the nature of the new Anglo-American proposals which Vance put to the Rhodesian delegation. These, in fact, presented three options drawn up following the negotiations based on the original Anglo-American proposals. One of the options (to which the US and the UK were not themselves committed) was that, if the parties to the conflict agreed, elections might be postponed until after independence, a course especially favoured by Nkomo and Kaunda. The Zambian leader had unsuccessfully pressed his colleagues in the Front-line States to support this idea.[20]

Meanwhile, because of acute economic and security pressures, Zambia was beginning to take a course more independent of the other Front-line States. Kaunda had for years accused Britain of condoning the evasion of Rhodesian sanctions by its multinational oil companies by 'oil swap' arrangements made through SA. Kaunda's campaign on this issue had the strong backing of 'Tiny' Rowland, whose Lonrho company had suffered heavily when its oil pipeline from Beira to Rhodesia had been shut down under sanctions. Their campaign got unexpected support from Jorge Jardim, a close supporter of the former Portuguese Prime Minister, Dr Salazar. Jardim had amassed considerable documentary evidence about how the 'oil swaps' worked while he was in control of oil shipments through Mozambique. The report of Jonathan Bingham QC, who was appointed by the British government to investigate these allegations, bore out the truth of a number of the charges. Publication of his report raised a political storm in Britain and also added to growing strains between Zambia and the Callaghan government. A hurried meeting was arranged between Callaghan, Owen and Kaunda in Kano (Nigeria) on 22 August 1978. However, instead of a row developing over the disclosures made in the Bingham report, Kaunda used the occasion almost exclusively to catalogue his urgent economic and security problems. He explained that the next maize crop could face disaster unless he succeeded—within a matter of weeks—in importing large quantities of fertilizer held up because of congestion on the available transport routes from the sea. While the British government was unable to do anything to solve this transport problem directly, it indicated understanding for Kaunda's position if he should decide to reopen the border with Rhodesia in order to facilitate the faster movement of goods from the ports of Mozambique and SA. Callaghan also agreed that Britain should do what it could to meet Zambia's defence needs, including the dispatch of a military team to help improve its Rapier missile defence system.

Kaunda came away from Kano feeling that he could not expect Britain and the US to do anything quickly—if at all—to break the Rhodesian deadlock and so rescue his country from the damage it had suffered throughout its long opposition to the Rhodesian rebellion. James McManus wrote this percipient view of Kaunda's position in early September:[21] 'The Zambian leader was left looking at a war relentlessly grinding towards a military solution in Rhodesia and a disastrous internal economic situation which pointed to national collapse.' His response was to reopen the Rhodesian border early in October. While this brought quick relief to Zambia, allowing its imports to move faster, it was deplored by the Patriotic Front and damaged relations with the other FLPs. Nyerere and Machel flew to Lusaka on 7 October in a last-minute effort to get Kaunda to change his mind—but to no avail. According to James McManus, 'Nyerere was left close to tears as his old friend forcefully held his ground and refused to reconsider a decision that has driven a deep wedge between the two leaders and their countries. Reliable sources report that Nyerere argued passionately that the border opening would weaken the liberation struggle in Southern Africa. The counter-argument was simple. Zambia's survival was at stake and past sacrifices could not be continued to the point of national ruin. To avoid collapse, the country needed speedy imports of fertilizer and industrial lubricants and a rapid export of copper to foreign markets.'[22]

By January 1979, with the predictable failure of the Cledwyn Hughes mission (see above), the Anglo-American initiative was overshadowed by two parallel developments inside Rhodesia: the escalating guerrilla war, and the preparations for elections as a prelude to the creation of the new Zimbabwe-Rhodesia state. The elections in May 1979 were unexpectedly favourable to the IS partners; they showed that, while not in complete command of the security situation, the Rhodesian forces could still prevail over the guerrillas, whose campaign to wreck the polling was a palpable failure.

White power in Rhodesia, while not yet ended, was extensively eroded by the new constitutional arrangements. However, the birth of Zimbabwe-Rhodesia on 3 June 1979 did not yet mean that effective majority rule had been established; nor did it bring greater hope that the war would soon be ended. The Patriotic Front and its African supporters (with the backing of the Soviet bloc, China and Cuba) insisted that they had no alternative but to settle the issue on the battlefield: at least that was their publicly stated position (see below).

The advent of Conservatives to power in Britain, coinciding with the election of the new Zimbabwe-Rhodesia government, helped to further strengthen the conservative bloc in the US Congress. Thus, at a critical moment, Western policy was in disarray; spurred on by Mrs Thatcher's Administration, it stood poised to adopt a totally different course from that set and striven for by Prime Minister Callaghan and President Carter. But within four months of taking office, Mrs Thatcher grasped the realities of the situation and the dangers of proceeding along her earlier course. A speech she made in parliament at the end of July led to a new consensus at the Commonwealth conference in Lusaka in early August, bringing an unexpected chance for a possible settlement in Rhodesia.

3. SOUTH AFRICA

The humiliating circumstances surrounding the political downfall of John Vorster and of his right-hand man, Gen Hendrik van den Bergh, the former BOSS chief, graphically symbolized the evolving drama of Southern Africa.[23] Whatever might be said against the policies of these two powerful SA figures, the fact remains that both understood far better than the new Prime Minister, P. W. Botha, the issues involved in the confrontation between their apartheid Republic and the rest of the continent. Vorster had been quick to size up how the balance of power in Southern Africa would be affected by the collapse of Portuguese colonialism in 1974.[24] He had also understood the importance of trying to achieve a new relationship with SA's neighbouring Black states. Failure on this score, he had warned his parliament in October 1974, would be 'too ghastly to contemplate.' At the time of his fall from power, Vorster's attempt at détente had ground to a halt; relations with Black Africa were, if anything, worse than they had been before he embarked on this exercise, while the chances of resuming a dialogue were less promising than they had been in 1974. Vorster's mistake was to think that it was possible to restructure SA's foreign policy in relation to Africa without restructuring the country's internal policies. While reforms in 'petty apartheid' and even more substantial economic concessions to Black workers[25] were sufficient to encourage Western hopes that SA was responding positively to the developing challenges to its system, these cut little ice with Black African states. For them, the test of change was a clear commitment to abandon Separate Development in favour of a new approach to powersharing which would involve negotiations with representative Black leaders. Since neither Botha nor Vorster was willing—seemingly at any price—to embark on the structural changes demanded by the Black SA majority, the apartheid Republic stood in mid-1979 facing the 'too ghastly' future foreseen by John Vorster.

The failure of Vorster's attempt at détente not only left SA isolated in the African continent—an Ishmael with the hands of most of its neighbours turned against it—but also led to its becoming even more removed from the Western Community. Botha's regime responded to these threats by pursuing a foreign policy with two major objectives: first, to create a constellation of friendly African states around SA and, second, to accept the fact of the West's 'abandonment' by adopting a 'neutral' position in world affairs.[26] Both these elements seemed out of touch with the realities of the modern world. The magnet to attract a ring of friendly neighbouring states was to be provided by SA's economic strength and advanced technology and by its powerful military machine. It was hoped that the former would attract Black states to draw closer to SA in order to develop their own economies, while the latter would appeal to those African leaders who shared SA's interest in halting the advance of Russian and Cuban influence in the continent. The economic argument was not new, having been a central feature of the foreign policy devised by one of the earliest architects of apartheid, the late Dr H. F. Verwoerd. The only difference was that he had envisaged a Commonwealth of African states, beginning with the neighbouring territories of Botswana, Lesotho and Swaziland, and including the new Black Republics to be carved out of SA itself. However, in the 30 years since this Verwoerdian dream was first unfolded, the thrust has been in the opposite direction. Lesotho has moved away from its earlier friendly attitude to one of implacable hostility; Botswana, always a critic, has taken positive steps to develop political links with its northern Black neighbours; and Swaziland has continued to maintain its careful, but purposeful, policy of political neutrality. Transkei, the first of the new Black Republics to emerge from the balkanization of SA, broke off its diplomatic links with SA in 1978. The second, Bophuthatswana, has from its inception adopted an attitude of critical hostility to Pretoria's apartheid policies. Mozambique and Angola had, within the last five years, become Marxist states. The future orientation of Rhodesia and Namibia still remains in doubt. The single positive political gain has been Malawi but, after the collapse of Portuguese colonialism, it too has begun to show a less positive desire for too close political ties with Pretoria. During the 30-year period of apartheid, SA's trade links with its neighbours have in fact substantially declined, even though they did begin to pick up again in recent years. Nevertheless—and this is crucial to the SA argument—these signs of improving trade and of other economic ties have not meant any improvement in the African trading nations' political relations with Pretoria. Mozambique is the prime example of an African country which, from force of circumstances, has had to rely heavily on its economic and communications ties with SA, but it has nevertheless remained militantly hostile to Pretoria. The same goes for Zambia, Botswana and Lesotho. In the post-colonial era, the flag does not necessarily follow trade.

Nor is there any evidence to support the belief that anti-Communist African leaders would be prepared to make common cause with SA in resisting the expansion of Soviet influence. Even a rock-fast opponent of Communism like President Kaunda showed when the chips were down that he would prefer to turn to the Soviet bloc and China for military aid. There is nothing to justify the view that the heterogeneous collection of anti-Communist African states—which includes such countries as Ivory Coast, Senegal, Egypt and Somalia—would look to SA for military or other support to resist the Russians and Cubans. On the contrary, all have showed that they pin their hopes on the Western countries for help in resisting such pressures. Unlike SA, these African countries have not altogether lost their faith in the West.[27]

The shallowness of the African dimension of SA's foreign policy was matched by its avowed aim of disengagement from the West in favour of a position of 'neutrality.' This 'sucks to you' psychological response to Western unresponsiveness—'you won't play with me, so I won't play with you'—is easily understood, but it does not really add up to a serious policy.[28] All it does is to adjust to the reality of Western disengagement and to recognize the probability that this trend will increase—whatever temporary respites might be effected by a Thatcher government or a conservative US Senate. France's 1977 decision to distance itself from SA (especially as a military supplier) was only the latest of a series of injustices inflicted on the Republic's national psyche. The essentially *verkrampte* (inward-looking) reaction was to stop giving the appearance of wooing the West, either by making concessions or by continually appealing for sympathy and understanding; instead, Pretoria proposed to go through the motions of disengagement—a policy much more likely to sustain Afrikaner morale.

One obvious question is what 'neutrality' could mean in SA's circumstances. In the peacetime rivalry between the West and the Communist world, there is no way in which a people as obsessed by fears of Communism as White South Africans could remain neutral, and in any likely war SA would be highly vulnerable to threats of attack from anti-Western forces. Moreover, to be neutral a country must be free to exercise its diplomatic options; but for SA there is no such choice: there are no serious options open to it in the Communist world—even though Prime Minister Botha has spoken on a number of occasions about the possibility of establishing links with China! In fact, when the Botha regime speaks of 'neutrality,' it really is talking about old-fashioned 'isolationism' in the Midwest Republican tradition of Col McCormack. By conceding its state of isolation while talking of 'neutrality,' SA was in fact moving towards accepting a 'polecat' status in the world community, first mentioned as a possibility after Sharpeville in 1960 by Paul Sauer, chairman of the committee which drafted the ruling party's apartheid policy.

Thus, at a time of growing internal and external violence, with the Soviet bloc and Cuba becoming ever more closely involved with the challenging Black forces, and with Western influence no longer what it was, the Republic found that it either had to come to terms with its growing isolation or change its internal political structures to meet its foreign policy needs. Vorster misjudged the degree of internal change that would be needed to develop meaningful relations with Africa and so to conciliate the West, passing on to Botha discredited foreign and domestic policies at a time when the 'ghastly' future he forecast did indeed seem to be taking shape.

THE INTERNATIONAL DIMENSIONS OF THE SOUTHERN AFRICAN CRISIS
THE ROLE OF THE WESTERN POWERS

The policies of Western states towards Southern Africa are primarily defensive, the problem being how best to safeguard their economic and strategic interests in a situation which they recognized would inevitably change, but along unpredictable lines. Accepting the inevitability (if not wholeheartedly the desirability) of fundamental shifts in the internal balance of power, Western diplomacy was concerned with helping to ensure that the shift would occur in ways least disruptive to themselves and to SA's advanced industrial society, and most likely to produce successor governments in SA, Rhodesia and Namibia which, at the very least, would not be hostile to the West. Genuinely non-aligned governments—as in Nigeria, Tanzania or Zambia—would be considered the most hopeful outcome in Southern Africa; the worst would be either Black racist or Moscow-orientated regimes dependent for their immediate survival on Soviet bloc military support.

After the dramatic collapse of Portuguese colonialism in 1974 and, with it, the illusions which had helped shape NATO policies, Western diplomacy has been concerned with finding ways of influencing change so as to achieve the objectives just described.[29] These efforts have been hamstrung by two sets of largely incompatible requirements set by the American and major West European governments. First, to maintain their trading and other connections with SA, while at the same time convincing African leaders that they were genuinely working to overthrow apartheid. Second, to keep up pressures on White SA, but without upsetting the economy altogether or pushing Afrikaners 'even deeper into their *laager*.' Western policies, overall, reflected these dilemmas—more in the case of some countries than in others. Furthermore, because of political, economic and military pressures as well as differences of perception about the balance of interest among decision-makers, Western policy did not exactly shine forth with anything like the clarity achieved by the centralized policy-making machinery of the Communist states. The Soviet bloc had the additional positive advantage that, with no economic stake in the subcontinent, it was free of any entanglements with the *ancien* regimes. On the other hand, the Western community has considerably more natural influence throughout Africa than the anti-Western powers, and a majority of the continent's leaders—whatever their doubts or criticisms of Western policies (and, especially, as many saw it, of their ambiguities and hypocrisies)—still preferred King Log to King Stork. This historic, if strongly ambivalent, relationship provided the basis for an alliance of mutual convenience between the Western powers (especially Britain and the US) and the Front-line African States (with the addition of Nigeria in 1978) to launch the two initiatives over Rhodesia and Namibia and, within that framework, to handle the divergent strands of Western policies towards the White minority regimes in the subcontinent.

If those initiatives could have been brought to a successful conclusion, at least three important results would have followed. First, there would have been greater

African confidence in the West, which would have made it somewhat less difficult to develop a joint approach to the crucial problem of SA at the end of the African line. Second, the belief in the central importance of armed conflict as the only means of effective struggle would have been dealt a salutary blow. Third, the opportunities open to the Soviet bloc to take advantage of the violent situation—and of the ambiguities and ineffectiveness of Western policies—would have been substantially reduced.

As it is, the seeming failure of both these initiatives was due very largely to an unwillingness—or inability, because of domestic and other constraints—to commit sufficient Western resources to them. In the case of Rhodesia, Western policy favoured doing everything possible to topple Smith—short of military intervention or of exerting substantial pressures on his only effective ally, SA. In the case of Namibia, Western policy again stopped short of exerting effective pressures on SA which could have been achieved by indicating clearly its readiness to support selective sanctions. The refusal to do so reflected Western reluctance to upset the SA economy or its links with it. There were also other considerations. First, the Western powers were not convinced that sanctions would actually work, even if applied comprehensively, because of SA's powerful and to a considerable extent self-reliant economy; or, second, that they would be successful in persuading Afrikaners to adjust their policies to meet the demands of the world community. The Western view by and large was that sanctions would achieve only the negative result of entrenching even more firmly the White South Africans' *'laager* siege' defence mentality and so make it even less likely that they could be persuaded to accept the radical changes required of them. However, the West's African allies were not at all persuaded by such arguments; in their view, Western reluctance to exert greater pressures on Pretoria was entirely due to economic interests. The argument could be settled only by putting sanctions to the test—either to compel SA to observe the UN's oil embargo on Rhodesia, or to accept the UN Secretary-General's proposals for internationally-supervised elections in Namibia. In the absence of any such test, the arguments over the possible efficacy of sanctions must inevitably remain open-ended and provide a constant source of suspicion in relations between the West and Africa.

Two conflicting tendencies were clearly visible in mid-1979: that Western governments were, by early 1979, probably moving further away from any possibility of implementing sanctions than had seemed likely in 1977 or 1978;[30] and that as more African leaders lost faith in the West's ability to play an effective negotiating role, they were becoming more conditioned to accepting the need for armed struggle—with all the consequences that entailed, including greater Soviet-Cuban involvement in Southern Africa.

The trend of thinking in the Western community was by no means wholly in a more conservative direction. The governments of Sweden and Holland (as well as of Canada, while still led by Trudeau) became the pacesetters in trying to harmonize Western policies with those of the dominant voices in Africa as reflected by the FLPs, as well as to reflect that section of opinion which felt that proper Western interests could only be defended by keeping alive Euro-American and African alliances. Sweden, under a liberal government, was the first to legislate against any new investments in SA; Trudeau's government gave an official tilt towards disengagement, while the Dutch Parliament enacted a number of strong measures to disengage their nationals from involvement in SA. France, rather belatedly, joined in the international arms embargo against SA and showed other signs of changing its stance towards Pretoria, principally in its unwavering support for the work of the Contact Group in Namibia. Britain, on the other hand, substantially changed

117

course with the election in May 1979. For example, whereas Labour had begun to prepare public opinion to accept disengagement from the SA economy, the Thatcher government announced that SA trade and investments were of 'central importance' to the British economy. In Canada, too, a Conservative Administration replaced Trudeau's. These two developments meant that the 'White' membership of the Commonwealth of Nations now comprised a solid conservative bloc, whereas three years earlier it was made up entirely of Labour governments. However, Australia's Prime Minister, Malcolm Fraser, pursued a strong line against apartheid and a policy different from the British Tories towards Rhodesia. While West Germany under Chancellor Schmidt showed a greater readiness to support firmer diplomatic action against SA, it firmly rejected any thought of sanctions for reasons of economic self-interest, reasons set out clearly in a policy document prepared by its Foreign Ministry.[31] The Carter Administration's more radical policies towards Africa also began to lose momentum in late 1978 for a number of reasons: the President's low poll rating; his need to court the Senate to get the SALT II agreement passed; and the growing influence of a conservative bloc in the Senate in favour of ending Rhodesian sanctions and recognizing Bishop Muzorewa's government, and opposed to imposing any pressures on SA.

These changes in the West brought about a sharper polarization between conservatives and radicals, both in government and in public opinion. The consensus of the European and Canadian democratic Left was reflected in a policy document prepared by Sweden's former Prime Minister, Olof Palme, and adopted by the Bureau of the Socialist International in Vancouver in November 1978. Its main proposals were: (1) to stop all arms exports to SA and all military co-operation with its government and to oppose the transfer of nuclear and other strategic technology; (2) to work for a prohibition of new investments and export of capital to SA and Namibia; (3) to increase support to the Front-line States; (4) to give political support and humanitarian aid to ANC (SA), Swapo of Namibia and the Patriotic Front of Zimbabwe; (5) to increase contributions to help the victims of apartheid; (6) to encourage regional co-operation between governments in Southern Africa, aimed at reducing dependence on SA; (7) to stop the flow of mercenaries to the racist regimes; (8) to intensify solidarity work on the national level, start campaigns in order to mobilize public opinion, raise funds and counterbalance racist propaganda in the mass media; and (9) to ask their governments to assist popular movements like trade unions, churches and other bodies working in support of the liberation struggle in Southern Africa.

Despite all that has been said on the subject, however, there is no 'Western policy'—coherent or otherwise—to counter the expansion of Soviet influence in Africa and its adjacent areas. The best broad approach to this issue was offered by Marshall Shulman, the US Secretary of State's Special Consultant on Soviet Affairs, in a speech on 2 December 1978. Referring to the 'advances' made by the Soviet Union in places like Angola and Ethiopia, he said: 'I think it would be a mistake to assume—and I'm sure the Soviet leaders don't make this mistake—that this is a secure base for them. They have in times past had similar advances in other countries—in Egypt, in Nigeria [sic] and in Guinea—which, with passage of time, proved to be unstable. And there is increasingly a limiting factor in Africa, with the growing national self-consciousness of the African leaders, even among those who turn to the Soviet Union for weapons, even among the revolutionary leaders who use the weapons of the Soviet Union to strengthen their position. There has been a caution lest they repeat the experience of other countries that have risked their own independence, their national independence and freedom of movement, with the Soviet Union. . . . [But] we shouldn't project through the present trenchant . . .

advances of the Soviet Union to believe that this is part of an ongoing movement which will result in an extended or permanent position for the Soviet Union in Africa. It is not that we can regard these movements with complacency. We need to deal with them; but we need to deal with them appropriately. And that is primarily by dealing with the forces on the ground. . . . Our primary way of dealing with the prospect of Soviet political advances in this area, the Persian Gulf and elsewhere, is to try to deal effectively with the local political forces, so that there are not created opportunities for exploitation by the Soviet Union. That is the only effective way of dealing with these problems, although it is slow, it is halting, and it does not produce immediate results. . . .'

THE ROLE OF THE COMMUNIST STATES
The Soviet Union considers its expanding influence in Southern Africa as already presenting a direct challenge to Western policies, as was claimed by Prof Anatoliy Gromyko, the director of Moscow's African Institute: 'Now that the forces of the national liberation movement in Africa and the Front-line States have a reliable ally—the land of the Soviets, the world community of socialist countries—and [now] that they are assisted in political and other aspects by the most active African states, the strategy and tactics of the West in Southern Africa must take this into consideration.'[32] At the same time, however, Soviet commentators constantly criticized the way in which they claimed Moscow's policies were falsely represented in the West as harmful to détente. A typical view on this aspect of a growing debate was expressed in an *Izvestiya* article on 31 January 1979 entitled 'The South African Knot': 'The Soviet Union is actively pursuing the line towards strengthening the détente process in every way and spreading it to all areas of the world, including Africa.' Georgiy Tanov insisted that 'the liberation struggle of the people [in Southern Africa] doesn't run counter to a relaxation of international tension. It is fully compatible with the ideas and decisions of the UN and OAU. What is more, only a victory—a complete victory—of the patriotic and anti-fascist forces in the southern part of this continent can turn the region into a zone of permanent and stable peace.'[33]

Soviet-beamed propaganda to Africa concentrated heavily on trying to show that the 'racist regimes' in the region owed their continued existence to the support they got from the NATO powers led by the US, and on insisting that the Western nations had the power to dictate policies to them. Thus, when Vorster resigned as Prime Minister, Moscow's Radio Peace and Progress programme (30 September/1 October 1978) claimed that his state of health was not a determining factor. 'Vorster left his post on the categorical demand of Washington and London.' It went on to explain that, under the growing pressures of the armed struggle, London and Washington 'decided that Vorster should be substituted by a less odious political functionary and, what is more important, by a more flexible [sic] one.' However, it added: 'British-American economic and strategic interests are so significant that they demand the preservation of the White racist regime in the south of Africa at all costs, be it with Vorster or without him.' In somewhat similar vein, Soviet commentators like Arkadiy Butliskiy wrote that military support for Rhodesia is a 'longstanding policy of the US.'[34] Britain and the other NATO powers were accused of providing military support to the Smith regime and of planning to intervene militarily 'under the pretext of saving the White population of Rhodesia.'[35]

Moscow welcomed any sign of a breach developing between the Front-line States and the West, an alliance which they had all along considered incompatible on the part of such 'Marxist' Presidents as Neto and Machel, as well as of Nyerere.

Although always careful not to criticize the role of the FLPs directly,[36] a commentary by Andrew Dolgov on Moscow Radio (28 March 1978) acknowledged that 'the position of the Front-line States is of paramount importance—for being in the forefront of the struggle for liberation in Southern Africa, these states can exert the most immediate effect on the evolution of the situation in Rhodesia.' What most troubled the Soviets was the persistent way in which the FLPs had continued to try to keep alive the two Western initiatives in Rhodesia and Namibia, even beyond the point where constructive negotiations seemed possible.

Soviet bloc and Cuban military and other aid to the parties engaged in the regional conflicts increased substantially during 1978 and especially in 1979. While no reliable figures are available, this conclusion seems clear from the increasing amount of sophisticated weapons used by the three liberation movements supported by Moscow (Swapo, the ANC of SA and Joshua Nkomo's wing of the Patriotic Front), as well as by the Communists' greater role in the training camps of these movements—particularly in Angola where most of the military instruction was given.[37] East Germany elected to play a substantially larger role in fulfilling this Soviet military commitment[38] and looked like becoming the most important element in the Warsaw Pact's involvement in the region—not only in its support of the liberation movements, but in military training programmes for Angola and Mozambique.[39] It also sent two military teams to Zambia to draw up contingency plans if President Kaunda decided to take up the option offered by the Communist countries in the event of an irretrievable breakdown in negotiations over Rhodesia or of a continued escalation of Rhodesian operations across the Zambesi.

The Soviet bloc, however, faced a number of difficult issues over its expanding military role, chief of which was the continued rivalry within the Patriotic Front. Awkward policy issues were raised when Nyerere, as chairman of the FLPs, formally requested the Russians not to take sides within the Patriotic Front by giving military aid only to Nkomo's forces. Although the Russians indicated a willingness to support Robert Mugabe's Zanla, their condition for doing so was that he should stop siding with Peking and give up describing himself as being a 'Marxist-Leninist of Maoist thought.' When an East German delegation, headed by the GDR leader Erich Honecker, visited Mozambique in early 1979, it tried to persuade Mugabe to break with Peking, but without success.[40] Nevertheless, Mugabe's forces did begin to get Soviet supplies through the Ethiopian leader, Col Mengistu Haile Mariam, with whom he had developed particularly close relations during a visit to Addis Ababa in early 1979 (see below). Cuba's links with Zanu appeared to have increased after Zanla cadres were sent to Ethiopia for military training in early 1979. The Cubans insisted on inviting Mugabe to attend the International Youth Festival against Nkomo's vigorous protests.[41]

As at mid-1977, Moscow was still maintaining a strongly hostile attitude towards Mugabe, but was also becoming increasingly anxious about the military advantages his cadres were gaining on the ground in Rhodesia. According to a Soviet informant, a contingency plan had been worked out whereby 5,000 Cuban troops would be involved in helping Nkomo secure a 'liberated zone' from where he would proclaim an independent Zimbabwe government which the USSR, Cuba, Ethiopia and other African countries would recognize. Other contingency plans (not involving Cuban combat troops) have been mentioned by Zapu sources—the likeliest being a possible plan to enable Nkomo to seize Salisbury and Bulawayo, from where he could later expand his power-base to the countryside as the MPLA had been able to do in Angola—though not with complete success. Obviously, though, the Soviet bloc would prefer to support a unified Patriotic Front army.

Another difficult decision facing the Soviets in the region was the extent of their commitment to Swapo. During the negotiations with the Contact Group over Namibia (see above), their principal ally in the region, Angola, demonstrated a strong reluctance to support policies which would produce a major military confrontation between the SA army and Swapo; this would seriously add to the considerable security problems which already exist along Angola's southern border with Namibia. The Russians and Cubans also appeared to be unwilling to take on the kind of military commitment which would be involved in a direct confrontation between Swapo and SA. Soviet strategy appeared to favour completion of the Rhodesian struggle before opening another front in Namibia. An additional element which made the Russians favour postponing a major confrontation over Namibia was that they appeared to be far from satisfied that the politicization within Swapo had gone far enough to produce a sufficient number of Marxist cadres able to dictate policy correctly in the event of Swapo assuming power.

Although Moscow's policy towards Southern Africa can be described as opportunistic—in the sense that it relies on making *ad hoc* decisions in reaction to developing situations—it also showed signs of much longer-range strategic planning about the subcontinent's future. Clear traces of this policy appeared in the remarkable manifesto produced by unnamed Communist and other 'progressive' parties in Tropical and Southern Africa during the latter part of 1978.[42] The manifesto's emphasis on the central role of the Communist vanguard in the developing struggle, its praise for Soviet policies and its strong hostility to China gave it the unmistakable imprimatur of Moscow, where it was first publicized. It has appeared in full only in the *African Communist*, the organ of the strongly Moscow-oriented SA Communist Party. The main strategy outlined in the manifesto calls for the development of a close alliance between 'progressive' forces, including nationalists and others, and Communists. The model for this alliance already exists in the present set-up between the SACP and the ANC, which draws all its foreign support from the Soviet bloc.[43]

Sino-Soviet rivalry has remained a crucial feature of the policies of both the world Communist centres in relation to Southern Africa.[44] Among the numerous allegations levelled by Moscow against Peking were that the Chinese operate in open collusion with the NATO powers against the liberation movements; that they maintain a considerable trade with SA (which allegedly has already reached $12m a year); that they even export handcuffs for use in the apartheid Republic's prisons; that they have sent military instructors to Namibia to support Unita forces in co-operation with the SA army; and that they are co-operating with the US in helping to promote SA's nuclear weapons programme. A staple of Soviet propaganda against China was that Peking's interest as a 'world hegemonist power' was to attain a position where it could use the continent to dump millions of Chinese settlers.[45]

China's counter-propaganda lacked none of the Russians' venom. Addressing the UN, the Chinese Foreign Minister, Huang Hua, called the Russians 'the most dangerous source of a new world war.'[46] While attacking both super-powers for their role in Africa, Radio Peking (13 October 1978) described the Soviet Union as 'the chief culprit guilty of bringing turmoil to the African countries,' and accused Moscow of trying to contend with the US 'to achieve its strategic aim of controlling Africa and encircling Western Europe.' The *Peking Review* (2 June 1978) insisted that the May invasion of the Shaba province of Katanga was started by 'Soviet-Cuban mercenaries,' an action which threw further 'light on the wild ambitions of Soviet social-imperialism to dominate Africa.' An editorial in the *People's Daily* (Peking, 18 September 1978) warned against the intensification of Soviet 'expansionist activities' simultaneously in Africa, the Middle East, the Red Sea and the

Gulf areas, and pointed out that 'Africa, in particular, has become the hot spot in super-power rivalry.'

Chinese policy gave some grounds for the Soviet criticism that Peking was 'colluding' with the NATO powers in Africa. For example, an editorial in the *Peking Review* (16 June 1978) praised the signs that 'the Western countries are beginning to see that it would be fatal to Western Europe if Africa [were] occupied by the Soviet Union.' The same editorial gave strong support to joint Western-African co-operation to resist the Russians: 'There is a growing tendency in West European and African countries to take joint action against Soviet infiltration in Africa. On the question of safeguarding African security and containing Soviet expansionism, there are still complicated contradictions among the African countries, among the Western countries, and between the African and Western countries. To achieve African unity and Afro-Western unity may encounter difficulties and obstructions. But this will not prevent the further growth of the trend for them to get together to cope with aggressive Soviet expansion.'

China's only major direct involvement in any of the liberation movements was with Robert Mugabe's Zanu (see above). It maintained some contacts with Swapo, but these appeared to have grown weaker after the Namibian organization moved all its forces to camps in Angola. Notwithstanding concerted efforts by the PAC (SA) to develop close links with Peking, and despite the hostility of both the Chinese and the PAC to the ANC, China has steadily refused to give its support to the PAC. The reason for this was not clear. During the visit of the Chinese Vice-Premier, Li Hsien-nien, to Mozambique and Zambia in January 1979, he had talks with ANC leaders as well as Swapo and Zanu.

China's closest links among the Front-line States remained with Tanzania and Zambia. While its relations with Mozambique improved somewhat in 1978, those with Angola remained angrily hostile.[47]

Yugoslavia was the only other Communist country to provide the liberation movements with military training and was the only one which succeeded—at least for a time—in training Zipra and Zanla cadres in the same camp. This ended when Nkomo insisted that his supporters should be trained separately. The Yugoslavs apparently refused and now train only Zanla forces. About 350 officers (200 Zanla, 150 Zipra) are believed to have completed the Yugoslav scheme for advanced commander training.

THE ROLE OF THE AFRICAN STATES

The Front-line States (Tanzania, Zambia, Angola, Botswana and Mozambique) have continued to speak and act for the overwhelming majority of the OAU states in masterminding Black Africa's strategy in Southern Africa.[48] Their negotiating strength grew in 1978 when Nigeria became more directly involved in their work. On the other hand, the internal unity of the Front-line Presidents (FLPs) declined during 1978, mainly because of differences between the chairman, President Nyerere, and President Kaunda. These differences were only partly due to conflicting attitudes over the FLPs' policies, but stemmed in the first place from quarrels over the handling of Zambia's goods through the port of Dar es Salaam and over their shared Tazara railway line.[49] However, there were also major disagreements over Zambia's favouring of Nkomo's Zapu against Mugabe's Zanu, and especially over Kaunda's decision to reopen his border with Rhodesia in October 1978. Even though these disputes were serious, they did not disrupt the work of the FLPs and certainly did not threaten to break up the alliance.

The FLPs were completely united in their policies over Namibia, never wavering in their support for the Western initiative and—after consultation and negotiation—accepting the detailed proposals made by the Contact Group and the UN Secretary-General. The only difference between the Western side and the FLPs (and, indeed, with the rest of the OAU) was over the question of using sanctions as a means of inducing Pretoria to implement the UN-endorsed proposals for a settlement. While the FLPs left it to the Western powers to win over SA's support for the initiative, they themselves accepted responsibility for 'delivering' Swapo. This involved some arm-twisting in June 1978 when Sam Nujoma appeared reluctant to continue the search for a negotiated settlement. At the FLPs' meeting in Luanda in mid-June 1978, the Angolan President's pressures on Swapo were particularly crucial in obtaining Nujoma's signature to the agreement (see above).

There was disagreement among the FLPs over the secret meetings arranged in Lusaka between Smith and Nkomo in August 1978, but a meeting in Lusaka in early September again found the FLPs united behind a policy of encouraging talks for a settlement—'even with the devil himself,' in Nyerere's words[50]—provided they involved both wings of the Patriotic Front and were not designed to split the movement. There was also continued support for the idea of all-party talks among those principally involved in the Rhodesian conflict, as well as for the implementation of 'the major provisions of the Anglo-American proposals.'[51] 'We will continue talking—and we will encourage the possibility of the meeting between outsiders and insiders,' Nyerere said in an interview after the Lusaka discussions in September. 'But we want that meeting on the basis of the Anglo-American proposals.'[52]

The most serious crisis affecting the FLPs' unity was the Zambian decision to open its border with Rhodesia on 6 October 1978 (see above). Nyerere and Machel were both equally critical of Kaunda's decision, and had made strong efforts to dissuade him; nevertheless, when the five Presidents met for their next meeting in Dar es Salaam in late October (which was not attended by Machel, but not for any policy reasons), their final communiqué spoke of an 'atmosphere of open cordiality and mutual understanding.' In early April 1979, the FLPs met in Luanda to discuss how to deal with the new situation created by the election pending in Rhodesia in accordance with the new constitution for 'majority rule.' The Nigerians participated in this meeting, and the six unanimously agreed to exert pressure on the OAU and the international community not to recognize the new Zimbabwe-Rhodesian government. They restated their complete support for the Patriotic Front and agreed to meet the new challenge by intensifying the military struggle.

Even though the FLPs increasingly lost faith in the ability of Britain and the US to influence events in Rhodesia and accordingly prepared themselves to support a 'war to the finish,' they nevertheless continued to offer to co-operate in trying to arrange all-party talks. In December 1978, Kaunda announced that the point had been reached where 'it is imperative for Zambia to arm to defend itself';[53] he said he was prepared to turn to the Soviet bloc for arms to fend off the attacks from Rhodesia.[54] Nyerere, though, continued to insist that the situation in Rhodesia was not irretrievable. As late as January 1979 he was still expressing support for British military intervention to avoid the prospect of a civil war breaking out between the rival Black nationalist movements.[55] The British, he said, 'can land a battalion or two, and in a few days it is all over.'[56] He also continued to maintain that the Anglo-American proposals offered the best solution. He told an interviewer early in 1979: 'I am not being diplomatic, I am quite serious and I keep on clinging to this hope. If you do not have a single army [a reference to the two armies of the Patriotic Front], the best thing is to have a negotiated settlement.'[57] For Nyerere, the biggest threat remained the danger of a civil war among Zimbabweans themselves. Even after the election of a British Conservative government, all the FLPs encouraged Mrs

Thatcher's special envoy, Lord Harlech, to work for all-party talks between the Patriotic Front and the Muzorewa government.

The Nigerians adopted a very tough attitude towards the British Tories. On 1 May 1979, the Federal Military Government warned that any breach of UN sanctions or recognition of the new government in Salisbury would be regarded by Nigeria as a deliberate challenge to the OAU 'and the Black race.'[58] Any such moves, it warned, would be met with an appropriate response. The Nigerians were as good as their word; when Mrs Thatcher indicated that she was ready to end sanctions and move to recognition of the Muzorewa government, they announced that, as an interim measure, British firms would not be allowed to tender for contracts in their country.

Apart from Nigeria, the only other African country which played an active role in the region was Ethiopia under its Marxist leader, Col Mengistu Haile Mariam. After talks with Mugabe and Nkomo in Dar es Salaam in February 1979, he agreed to begin a major training programme for their guerrilla cadres in Ethiopia. Nkomo, however, said he would accept this offer only if the two armies could be trained in separate camps—a policy he said he would insist on until the political unification of the two wings of the Patriotic Front could be agreed.[59] Nkomo's attitude upset Mengistu who, in any case, found himself drawn more to Mugabe despite their divergent views on China. Zanla forces began to go to Ethiopia for training following Mugabe's February visit to Addis Ababa—a development which also produced a link between Mugabe and the Cubans (see above).

NOTES

1. See *Africa Contemporary Record (ACR)* 1977–78, pp. A3ff.
2. All references to country surveys and essays are to *ACR* 1978–79.
3. *To the Point*, Brussels, 28 April 1978.
4. See chapter on Zimbabwe-Rhodesia.
5. Quoted in *The Star*, Johannesburg, 5 June 1979.
6. See *ACR* 1975–76, pp. A3ff.
7. See chapter on Namibia.
8. See *ACR* 1975–76, pp. A27–28.
9. See *ACR* 1977–78, pp. A14–17.
10. See chapter on Namibia and *ACR* 1977–78, pp. C211–15 for text of proposals.
11. See *ACR* 1977–78, pp. B845–46.
12. See *ACR* 1977–78, pp. C73–76.
13. See *ACR* 1977–78, pp. A3ff.
14. *Ibid.*
15. *The Times*, London, 29 May 1978.
16. See chapter on Zimbabwe-Rhodesia.
17. See Simon Winchester, *Daily Mail*, London, 13 October 1978.
18. *The Times*, 12 October 1978.
19. *The Guardian*, London, 13 October 1978.
20. *Ibid*, 5 October 1978.
21. *Ibid*, 13 October 1978.
22. *Ibid.*
23. For a description of these events, see chapter on SA.
24. See *ACR* 1974–75, pp. A3ff.
25. See chapter on SA.
26. See chapter on SA, under Foreign Affairs.
27. See essay on 'The OAU in 1978.'
28. See chapter on SA, under Foreign Affairs.
29. See *ACR* 1975–76, pp. A3ff.
30. See *ACR* 1977–78, pp. A82–84 and chapter on SA.
31. See chapter on SA, under Foreign Affairs.
32. *Mezhdunarodna Zhizn*, Moscow, quoted by Tass, 10 February 1979.
33. Radio Moscow, 16 June 1979.
34. Quoted by Moscow Radio, 12 January 1979.
35. Radio Peace and Progress, 14 September 1978.

36. See *ACR* 1977–78, p. A28.
37. For more details, see chapters on Rhodesia, SA and Namibia.
38. See essay in this volume on 'The Two Germanies in Africa.'
39. See chapters on Angola and Mozambique.
40. See Note 38 above.
41. See chapter on Zimbabwe-Rhodesia.
42. For an extensive summary of the manifesto, see Documents section, pp. C61–66.
43. See chapter on SA under Black Political Movements.
44. See *ACR* 1977–78, pp. A29–30.
45. See, for instance, article in *Sovetskaya Rossiya*, quoted by Tass, 26 September 1978; and Radio Peace and Progress, 17 April 1978.
46. *International Herald Tribune (IHT)*, Paris, 31 May 1978.
47. See essay in this volume on Soviet and Chinese Policies in Africa.
48. See *ACR* 1976–77, pp. A10–13 and 1977–78, pp. A17–20.
49. For details, see chapters on Tanzania and Zambia.
50. Radio Dar es Salaam, 4 September 1978.
51. Interview with Nyerere, Radio Dar es Salaam, 3 September 1978.
52. Radio Dar es Salaam, 4 September 1978.
53. *Financial Times*, London, 19 December 1978.
54. *The Guardian*, 18 December 1978.
55. *IHT*, 8 January 1979.
56. *The Weekly Review*, Nairobi, 19 January 1979.
57. Interview with Altaf Gauhar in *The Guardian*, 8 January 1979.
58. Radio Lagos, 2 May 1979.
59. See chapter on Zimbabwe-Rhodesia.

1979–1980
THE ROAD TO AND FROM LANCASTER HOUSE

. . . . In mid-1979, the chances of reaching a negotiated settlement in Rhodesia looked almost hopeless—barring the miracle of an agreement being worked out among the Zimbabwe rivals themselves.

This was our summing up of the Rhodesian situation in the last chapter, on White resistance in Rhodesia.[1] The hoped for, but unexpected 'miracle' occurred almost immediately after the above statement was written. In the five months between August and December 1979, fighting had stopped; the disastrous and illegal regime of Ian Smith's Rhodesia Front had come to an end; a British Governor was once again installed in Government House; and preparations were under way for internationally-supervised free elections. For the first time in history the combatants in a cruel war had agreed to decide who was the stronger by setting aside their guns in favour of the ballot-box. A miracle indeed.

Credit for this astonishing achievement has been claimed by, and given to, a variety of people: the British Prime Minister was acclaimed for her 'statesmanship' in changing her Government's policies by, among others, the Marxist President of Mozambique, Samora Machel; the diplomacy of the British Foreign Secretary, Lord Carrington, was widely praised—even by such an unlikely admirer as US Congressman Stephen Solarz, the radical chairman of the House of Representatives' Africa subcommittee, who proposed him for the award of the Nobel Peace Prize; Lord Soames, in particular, was hailed as the far-sighted proconsul whose wisdom and skill turned the tide from seeming failure to triumphant success—a role he came close to claiming for himself;[2] the Commonwealth as an institution and its Guyanan secretary-general, Shridath (Sonny) Ramphal, were cited by some as having played the key role; yet others stressed the importance of the role played by the five African Front-line Presidents. While there is no doubt an element of truth in each of these claims, the 'miracle' was in fact the result of two factors: the confluence of interests which in the past had been strongly divergent; and the coincidence of a number of leaders holding their particular positions at the point where the armed struggle of the Patriotic Front (PF) had succeeded in weakening the capacity of the defending Rhodesian forces to hold out much longer.

However, even at that crucial turning-point in the lamentable chapter which began with the anti-historical last-ditch stand of the White Rhodesian minority to entrench their supremacy through their Unilateral Declaration of Independence in November 1965[3] there still remained the strong possibility of Britain and the US adopting the wrong policies because of the mistaken assumption that Bishop Abel Muzorewa was capable of carrying the day if he only had the full backing of the major Western Powers and South Africa. It was certainly the case that the Russians, basing their policies on their own erroneous analysis of the nature of Western and African interests (as well as misjudging the actual relative strength of the two wings of the Patriotic Front), misjudged events completely. Their misjudgment was also shared (though obviously for different reasons) by SA; like the Russians, it also believed that the Western powers would resist victory going to the PF; and they also completely misjudged the strength of the Black nationalist forces by making their wish for the Bishop to win the father of their policies.

PRELUDE TO LUSAKA MAY–JULY 1979

Margaret Thatcher had come to office in May 1979 at the head of a Tory Administration committed by its election manifesto to encouraging international recognition of Bishop Muzorewa's regime and ending sanctions.[4] She was also personaly dead set against continuing the former Anglo–American co-operation in seeking a settlement in Rhodesia. President Carter was under severe pressure from Republicans in Congress to recognize Muzorewa and to end sanctions. Under P.W. Botha's regime, SA was more heavily committed than ever to supporting Muzorewa both militarily and economically. Rhodesia, making its last desperate bid to stave off defeat, was widening the war in an effort to weaken the will and capacity of Zambia and Mozambique to continue their support for the PF forces; and its forces were indeed successful in bringing the economies of both countries to the point of collapse, as well as seriously undermining their security. The unity of the Front-line States had begun to fray, and the tensions between the two wings of the PF were such as to make it credible that Joshua Nkomo's Zimbabwe African People's Union (Zapu) might be willing to engage in a separate deal with Muzorewa, thereby not only isolating Robert Mugabe's Zimbabwe African National Union (Zanu), but also splitting Zambia from the rest of the Front-line States.

That was the situation in the months immediately preceding the crucial Commonwealth conference due to meet in Lusaka in August. The conference was to become the decisive turning-point in the Rhodesian conflict.

As late as June 1979, Mrs Thatcher was still repeating in an interview in Canberra that Britain was determined to lift sanctions. She repeatedly affirmed her commitment to recognizing the Muzorewa regime, subject to two provisos—that the 1979 elections were found to have been 'fair and free', and that enough international support could be found for this proposal. She had been left unpersuaded by the efforts of her own Foreign Secretary, Lord Carrington, and the Foreign and Commonwealth Office, as well as by Australia's Prime Minister, Malcolm Fraser.

The Foreign Office, to its credit, had all along taken a much wider view of the consequences of lifting sanctions and recognizing Muzorewa. It feared the effect on Anglo–African relations, and especially of economic retaliation by Nigeria; it was anxious about the consequences for Anglo-American relations as well as for other members of the European Community; and it foresaw the possibility of inviting much greater Soviet and Cuban involvement (with African backing) in the war, which it forecast would not be ended by a Muzorewa government. Lord Carrington was himself easily converted by these arguments, but his Prime Minister was still strongly guided by her own inclinations, which were those of the Right-wingers of the Conservative Party—and they were breathing heavily down her neck to implement party policy.[5] However, not all Conservatives were happy with her stand. Carrington's strongest ally, surprisingly enough, was the Australian Prime Minister.

Although the grim-visaged Malcolm Fraser is a conservative in the Thatcher mould, he had developed a strong antipathy to apartheid while still a student at Oxford University. He showed his stripe at the 1977 Commonwealth conference when he strongly opposed racism in sport and stressed the importance of helping the Third World to get a better deal from the international economic system. Even before the British general election in May 1979 he had spoken to Carrington of his concern about a future Conservative Government making a deal with Muzorewa and Smith. Just one week after the Conservative electoral victory, he sent two of his senior officials on a private visit to London to urge Thatcher not to rush ahead with lifting sanctions or recognizing the Bishop. Since the Canadians (even under a Government not headed by Pierre Trudeau) could be counted on to support Australia's view on Rhodesia, it meant that the 'White' Commonwealth would be divided at Lusaka if Thatcher stuck to her intentions; she could count only on Robert Muldoon, the crusty Conservative Prime Minister of New Zealand and perhaps the most unpopular of all men at Commonwealth gatherings.

Another development, completely unknown at the time, was a small initiative taken by a non-Commonwealth leader, Mozambique's President Samora Machel; it was later to become a crucial factor in helping to get the right decision on Rhodesia. One day in July 1979, Machel surprised his close colleagues when, after listening to a BBC broadcast of a speech by Margaret Thatcher, he exclaimed: 'That lady can help us end the war in Rhodesia.' He did not say why he had leapt to this strange conclusion; instead, he asked his colleagues what they knew about the Commonwealth. It was not much. He at once despatched Fernando Homwano, his very able young special assistant on Front-line affairs, to London to find out all he could about the way the Commonwealth works. Homwano—a product of the élitist Waterford school in Swaziland and a graduate of York University—is fluent in English and in British ways—so much so that, although a convinced Marxist, he can still tease that he is 'a product of the British public school system'. The report Hamwano brought back from London convinced Machel that he was on the right track—even though his approach was diametrically opposed to what his Marxist friends in the Soviet world might have expected from him—and indeed his enemies in the anti-communist world as well. Machel next sent Homwano, this time accompanied by Dr Jose Cabaco (now Minister of Information) to observe the Commonwealth conference in Lusaka. Later on, they were sent as observers to the Lancaster House conference, subsequently as liaison officers in Salisbury during the transition period and, finally, to carry Machel's personal congratulations to the British Prime Minister for her role in Rhodesia! The role of Machel and his two emissaries were crucially important in the dénouement of the Rhodesian story.

On the eve of the Lusaka conference Thatcher completely changed her line on Rhodesia to that which had been urged upon her by her Foreign Secretary. It was a decision as brave as it was unexpected; her Right-wing supporters were shocked. The change of policy was revealed in the House of Commons on 25 July 1979, when she announced that 'we are wholly committed to genuine Black majority rule in Rhodesia', and that while 'the progress Rhodesia has made towards democracy in the past two years cannot be brushed aside; at the same time, because it is in Rhodesia's own interest to be accepted fully into the international community, we must have regard to the views of other Governments.' Thus, for entirely pragmatic reasons, Thatcher announced her readiness to go to Lusaka ready for negotiations rather than stand rigidly by what she had proposed earlier—even though she still referred in her speech to the liberation struggle in Rhodesia as a 'terrorist war'. Only later was she to make a major issue of the undemocratic features of the Internal Settlement Constitution.

The Commonwealth Secretariat had played a notable role in drawing attention to the constitutional defects in a detailed critique it had published—much to the annoyance at the time of the pro-Muzorewa lobby—which was endorsed by all but the British member of the Southern Africa Committee of the Commonwealth Group which meets regularly in London. The Committee is comprised of all the Commonwealth High Commissioners and a representative of the British Foreign Office and acts as an influential pressure group in British and Commonwealth affairs.

THE LUSAKA COMMONWEALTH CONFERENCE, 1–7 AUGUST 1979

Everything still looked rather grim as delegates from 39 Commonwealth countries gathered at Lusaka, with an important section of the British media intent on creating a hostile atmosphere around the meeting with wildly exaggerated reports about the danger to Queen Elizabeth II (who is always present on these occasions as Head of the Commonwealth). Prominence was given to pictures of 'terrorist gunmen' (Nkomo and Mugabe aides sitting close behind Margaret Thatcher). (Mugabe was at the time visiting Bulgaria.) The full import of Thatcher's speech to Parliament a few days earlier had not yet percolated through to the delegates. The sense of crisis was heightened by Nigeria's announcement on the opening day of the conference that it was confiscating the assets of British Petroleum. This was made to look like a Nigerian warning against a possible sell-out over Rhodesia—an impression the Nigerians fostered at the time, although the move was motivated differently.[6]

In his opening speech, President Kaunda declared that the new Rhodesian Constitution and elections had not transferred power to the majority: 'What we have in Salisbury is White power clad in Black habiliments.' He added: 'Africa will win this war.' A more conciliatory note was struck by Australia's Prime Minister. He said the essential cause of the grave situation in Southern Africa was racialism. 'All oppression is repugnant, but there is an obscenity about oppression based on no more than the colour of a person's skin.' But, he went on, the recent Rhodesian election had created conditions for movement. 'In itself, the election settles nothing. It has, however, brought about a different situation. It has created new facts and disturbed a stalemate.' What happened next, he said, was 'not in the lap of the gods. It is, to a very large extent, in our laps.'

On his way to Lusaka, Fraser had paid a State visit to Nigeria where he had put together some ideas on how to achieve a consensus over Rhodesia. His plan, in essence, was to build on what had already been achieved by getting the unacceptable Internal Settlement Constitution amended to satisfy the PF.

In his role as chairman of the Front-line Presidents, President Julius Nyerere was recognized to be the key figure in the Commonwealth meeting. On the day after its opening, Thatcher paid him a 25-minute courtesy visit. Nyerere told her he was willing to accept reserved seats in Parliament for racial minorities in a Zimbabwean constitution. But he was not prepared to see the White minority left in control of the Armed Forces, Civil Service, Judiciary, Police and holding a blocking vote in Parliament to prevent these constitutional clauses ever being changed. As long as such a system remained in force the war would continue. Britain, he said, must resume its colonial responsibility, draft a new constitution and convene a constitutional conference. Then, before independence, there must be internationally supervised elections. At some point in this process he would obtain a ceasefire from the guerrillas. Nyerere emphasized that the principals of the constitutional conference must be Britain and the PF. Although Joshua Nkomo described Muzorewa as a 'traitor' and refused to sit with him, Nyerere accepted that Muzorewa would have to be invited. Later, in his own statement to the conference, Nyerere said that he was 'very encouraged' by Thatcher's statement that Britain was wholly committed to genuine majority rule, and that the aim was to bring Rhodesia to legal independence on a basis acceptable to the international community as a whole. He emphasized that 'free and fair elections' were possible only if there were a ceasefire, and if they were internationally organized and supervised. 'These two conditions—a democratic constitution and internationally-supervised elections—are essential if the war in Rhodesia is to be brought to an end quickly and by means other than military victory.' He said he did not rule out the existence of reserved seats for minorities—'even out of proportion to the numbers involved'. He also revived his earlier idea for a resettlement programme and fund to help those White Rhodesians who did not wish to live and work under an African government.

Thatcher spoke last—no one knew when she stood up whether she was about to slice the Commonwealth in pieces or not. Tension was briefly broken when she said: 'Our predecessors publicly committed the Commonwealth to the ideals of democracy, individual liberty and equality for all under the rule of law.' But the suspense remained as she went on to touch on the impact of world inflation and higher oil prices on Britain's economy (and even more on those of developing countries) and on the Vietnam refugees. Towards the end of her speech she addressed herself to the 'ever more urgent need for a settlement of the Rhodesian problem'. There was complete silence as she promised to 'listen with the greatest attention' to what was said at the conference. Then, in two sentences, she defused the explosive atmosphere. 'The British Government', she said, repeating what she had told the Commons a few days before, 'are wholly committed to genuine Black majority rule in Rhodesia'. And she added—this time going further than the Commons statement—that the aim 'is to bring Rhodesia to legal independence on a basis which the Commonwealth and the international community as a whole will find acceptable.'

In the main debate on Friday, when Thatcher, for the first time, spoke of the defects in the Rhodesian Constitution—especially the provision that 'makes it possible for the White minority to block in the Parliament constitutional changes that would be unwelcome to them'. No such blocking mechanism, she pointed out, appeared in any other independence constitution approved by Westminster. While refusing to allow the words 'Patriotic Front' to cross her lips, she agreed that it was essential in the search for a solution that 'the present external parties' should be involved. And she accepted that it was Britain's responsibility to bring Rhodesia to legal independence on a basis of justice and democracy, 'fully comparable with the arrangements we have made for the independence of other countries'. The main speeches in the debate showed that there was a meeting of minds; what was needed was a formula acceptable to all. The sought-after consensus was worked out by an informal caucus of six members representing a cross-section of the Commonwealth—Kenneth Kaunda, Julius Nyerere, Margaret Thatcher, Nigeria's Commissioner for External Affairs, Maj-Gen Henry Adefope, Jamaica's Prime Minister, Michael Manley, and Australia's Prime Minister Malcolm Fraser.[7] Despite one serious hitch, involving the British and Australian Prime Ministers, the caucus had little difficulty in agreeing on five objectives: genuine majority rule; the involvement of 'all parties to the conflict' in reaching a settlement; the urgency for such a settlement; a democratic Constitution including 'appropriate safeguards for minorities' as a precondition for independence; and 'free and fair elections' supervised under British Government authority, and with Commonwealth observers present to choose the first Government of an independent Zimbabwe.[8]

The jubilant chairman of the conference, Kenneth Kaunda, declared: 'I have no doubt in my mind, having dealt with a number of British Prime Ministers, that I have been meeting with one who is capable of doing something on this issue.' But, he added, 'A meeting cannot be historic unless it leads to historic change.' While the PF was encouraged by the outcome, its spokesmen remained suspicious. Zanu's spokesman, Edgar Tekere, acknowledged that the communiqué encompassed the basic principles for which the PF had fought, 'though we regret the introduction of a racist element in the requirement for special racial privileges'—the very point for which Nyerere had argued.

There was predictable anger in Salisbury, first because the Bishop had not been allowed to come to Lusaka although the PF leaders were present; and second, because Thatcher had moved away from her original commitment.

The next task would be to persuade the Rhodesia–Zimbabwe side to enter into negotiations with the PF at a conference to be convened by Britain.

FROM LUSAKA TO LANCASTER HOUSE, AUGUST 1979
The rival sides in the Rhodesian conflict had not been brought together around the same negotiating table since the abortive Geneva conference in late 1976—when Chairman Mao was proved right in his belief that 'you cannot win at the conference table what you have not won on the battlefield'.[9] At the time, the Rhodesian military forces still comfortably held the upper hand; the PF had only been formed in January 1977,[10] and still had no real sense of unity; Muzorewa's UANC and the Rev Ndabaningi Sithole were then still beginning to develop their internal role, and the former had not yet made any deals with the Smith regime.

Despite Salisbury's initially hostile reaction to what had been agreed in Lusaka, Britain's task in achieving an all-party agreement was much less difficult than had at first appeared likely. While the Bishop characterized the Commonwealth peace proposals as 'totally unfair and, in fact, an insult', Smith broke ranks and was the first to announce his willingness to attend. The ice was broken in a way that could not have been foreseen. On 7 August 1979, Robert Mugabe announced his conditions for attending the talks to include the prior ending of the Salisbury regime, the disbanding of the Rhodesian military forces and acceptance of the PF forces as the national army.[11] Mugabe's tough demands changed Muzorewa's mind. He felt that the PF's obdurate stand would mean that they would not in fact be ready to go to London, and that this would give his side an opportunity of negotiating alone with Britain.[12] In fact, this hope that the PF would prove intractable and that, in the end, Britain would have no option other than to come to terms with Salisbury, was to become a Will-o'-the-wisp pursued by the Bishop throughout the Lancaster House talks. On 15 August the Salisbury regime announced its willingness to accept the British invitation. Meanwhile, the Front-line Presidents set about encouraging Mugabe and Nkomo to follow up the Commonwealth initiative; President Samora Machel was especially influential in persuading Mugabe to retreat from his earlier tough position. Nkomo was much more pliant. On 24 August he said he was optimistic about the chances of getting a settlement and, in characteristic vein, he went out of his way to reassure White Rhodesians of their future in an independent Zimbabwe.[13] However, there was still some doubt about the PF's readiness to agree to sit down around a table with Ian Smith. Typically, the latter spoke out of both sides of his mouth. In the course of one interview[14] he said that he would stay away from the conference if his presence would prove an obstacle to a settlement, and then added that if he went he would be going only to talk to the British Government, not to the PF. 'Their presence is unnecessary; they are merely an appendix invited by the British. A settlement could be achieved without talking to them.' In the end, everybody agreed to attend the talks without preconditions.

THE LANCASTER HOUSE CONFERENCE, 10 SEPTEMBER TO 21 DECEMBER 1979
LORD CARRINGTON'S ROLE
The British Foreign Secretary's diplomatic skills were undoubtedly a major element in the success of the negotiations. On the face of it, his task as the mediator between two sets of irreconcilable views seemed hopeless. However, he could count on one vital asset: the commitment of the Front-line Presidents to the success of the enterprise. At the end of the day he knew he could count on them to keep the PF

talking. Nevertheless, there were times when he overrated their readiness to go along with all his proposals; these were the most dangerous moments in the 14 weeks of the talks.

The PF suspected throughout the long negotiations that the secret British intention was to go through the motions of seeking agreement from both sides but that, in fact, the real aim was to drive the PF into a situation where it would withdraw from the talks and so enable the British Government to achieve a separate agreement with Muzorewa, possibly one that would also detach Nkomo from Mugabe. In view of the well-known British preference for Muzorewa and Nkomo (in their eyes the perfect team to lead Zimbabwe into its independence), these suspicions were perfectly understandable. However, Carrington's approach to the Lancaster House talks was different. He was guided by what he called 'the first prize' and the 'second prize' to be won at Lancaster House. The first prize was an agreement with all parties; he was convinced that this was, in fact, the only way of ending the war and of avoiding damage to Anglo–African relations. Only if that objective proved impossible to obtain would he be ready to settle for the second prize, an agreement without the PF.

How did Carrington see his own role in the Lancaster House talks? Certain things always stood out clearly, in his mind.[15] To try to do everything at once would create difficulties; the negotiating process had to go through a number of stages. The first was to get both parties hooked to negotiations, even though they made their participation conditional. Neither side particularly liked that approach. He had to lift the veil of secrecy on his proposals for a ceasefire before he was ready to do so, only because Kaunda had insisted on knowing what was in his mind. The important thing, he felt, was to keep the proposals simple. The more he looked at the Anglo-American plan,[16] the more difficult it seemed to him to achieve agreement over its proposals. (In fact, as the Lancaster House negotiations proceeded, Carrington was forced to go into even more detail than the Anglo–American plan.) The important thing was to play it by ear, since he did not know from day to day what to expect. The trouble was that neither side trusted each other, nor Britain much, after all their experiences over the previous 14 years. The most remarkable step was to get the Bishop to concede the possibility of relinquishing power after elections. Carrington frankly did not think it was possible to wrest that concession from the Bishop at the start of the negotiations; only because he did was it possible to carry on. The proposals he was forced to accept for the transition period were not ideal, but the best to be had under the circumstances; he saw no alternative to using the existing machinery in the country supervised by Britain. There was never much room for negotiations over the ceasefire. At no stage did Carrington feel he was home and dry. As late as 14 November, he still felt fairly pessimistic. It was a mistake, he insisted, to suppose that he was not genuinely interested in achieving an all-round settlement. However, if the talks were to break down at any stage, there still remained a basis for a settlement—but that meant getting only the second prize. The PF, he thought, had compromised in a very big way. He always felt that Nkomo was more interested in a settlement than Mugabe. Nkomo, he thought, was a true negotiator, with a certain 'touch' in his style. The 'cleverest' man in the talks, he felt, was Mugabe—but not the best negotiator. The Bishop was much tougher than one had supposed.

ROLE OF THE FRONT-LINE PRESIDENTS

Zambia and Mozambique as well as Nigeria sent teams of observers to the Lancaster House talks; Tanzania and Botswana used their High Commissioners. Kaunda's representative was his special envoy in front-line relations, Mark Chona.

Mozambique's team comprised the Minister of Transport, Dr Jose Cabaco and Fernando Homwano (see above). Nigeria was represented by the elder statesman, Maitama Sule, who had been prominent in Nigeria's external affairs in the moves leading up to the establishment of the OAU. While the Front-line observers had no formal role in the talks, they were regularly briefed by the Foreign Office; they saw the PF delegations on an almost daily basis; and they maintained liaison with the Commonwealth Secretariat. There were also regular communications between the Presidents and Carrington through diplomatic channels. Nyerere and Kaunda both visited London during the talks; the latter's personal intervention was crucial at a point in mid-November when the talks were completely deadlocked. In December, at the most critical stage in the talks, the Front-line Presidents met with the PF leaders in Dar es Salaam in what was to be their most decisive intervention. The idea, though, that the FLPs' role was to apply pressures on the PF was wholly erroneous and shows a misunderstanding of the nature of their relationship which is properly characterized as 'influence through consultation'. While the Presidents individually expressed their own strong opinions on issues—especially Samora Machel—there was no occasion on which they tried to dictate to the PF leaders. On the other hand, they did try to use pressure as well as influence on Carrington and Margaret Thatcher directly. The points at which the Presidents played a role in the negotiations are described in the account of the progress of the negotiations given below.

ROLE OF THE COMMONWEALTH

The Commonwealth Secretariat in London chose to play an active role in ensuring that the spirit of the Lusaka agreement was observed in the negotiations, and in helping to overcome difficulties as they arose. The Secretariat also maintained a close liaison with the PF and held regular meetings with all the Commonwealth High Commissioners in London to brief them on what was happening. Its secretary-general, Sonny Ramphal, was regularly briefed by the Foreign Office. To say that his activist role was not always to the liking of Carrington is to understate their deeply uneasy relationship. On at least one critical occasion, Ramphal's role can be seen (at least in retrospect) to have been crucial to saving the talks. Ramphal was determined, above all, to see that the Commonwealth should fulfill its role as observer at the elections in conformity with what he felt was agreed at Lusaka. At the end of the day it would be for the Commonwealth to decide whether the elections had been fair and free.

THE NEGOTIATING PROCESS

The Lancaster House talks came close to failing on a number of occasions. The first crisis came at the beginning over the actual scope of the negotiations, with Muzorewa's side insisting that they had come for the single purpose of discussing a new constitution, and the PF standing firmly by their line that a settlement could only be reached if all the stages to independence were discussed and resolved including arrangements for the transition and the final handing over of power. Carrington sided with the PF on this issue. He chose to ignore the Bishop's threat to leave the conference after the first stage—discussion of the Constitution—was completed.

From the first, it was clear that neither side was in a mood for compromise. The Bishop insisted on referring to the PF as 'cowardly terrorists' and promised that his side was 'determined to reject any wanton robbery of their powers by some wanton dictator in the making'.[17] Nkomo replied in kind by insisting that the Bishop was simply a front for the Salisbury regime which remained 'in the hands of Ian Smith and his White clique'.[18] The PF was determined to treat Muzorewa as an untouchable, even though they mixed socially with Ian Smith, other members of the Rhodesian Front and individual Black members of the Bishop's delegation. During a break on the third day of the conference, there was a remarkable moment when Smith engaged in convivial exchanges with Josiah Tongogara, the commander of Zanla's guerrilla army.[19] In a BBC interview Tongogara said that if there were a settlement he would be prepared to work with the Rhodesian army commander, Gen Peter Walls, 'in any capacity'.

Contrary to what was generally expected, the PF acted as a strongly united force from start to finish, while Muzorewa's team showed early signs of being split. Sithole was the first to break ranks within the first few days of the meeting by giving his support to the idea of a new constitution instead of merely tinkering with the Internal Settlement Constitution, which Muzorewa insisted was all that was necessary. But Smith created more serious problems for the Bishop with his rigid insistence that the White minority should retain their veto right in any new constitution. The Bishop was plainly against such a proposal, and Smith's attempt to get Carrington on his side failed; nor did he succeed in getting more than one supporter in the Bishop's team. The idea, therefore, that Muzorewa was simply Smith's creature was wholly wrong. Smith, in fact, was virtually out on a limb on his own, even though he could still claim to have the support of the RF leadership.[20] However, in the end, Smith accepted that he had lost his last fight to retain an element of White supremacy.[21]

Carrington's method of dealing with one problem at a time left him in some difficulties over the way he overcame the first hurdle. Having accepted the PF's position that they should have a two-point agenda—Constitution and Transition Arrangements —Carrington then went against the PF in favour of Muzorewa by insisting that the Constitution should be discussed first—a decision strongly opposed by the PF. How, they asked, could they discuss a Constitution before they knew that the war was to end and elections were agreed. In truth, they feared that once a draft Constitution had been agreed, the Bishop would then carry out his threat to boycott the rest of the conference, leaving Carrington to impose a Constitution which he could claim had been accepted by the PF. To meet the PF's fears Carrington agreed, as the record shows, 'that agreement on a Constitution was contingent on the conference reaching agreement on suitable independence arrangements'.[22] So both sides stayed to consider the Constitutional proposals, a 34-page document, which was formally tabled on 30 October although it had been privately circulated three weeks earlier. (For full text, as amended, see Documents Section.) Carrington was loathe to allow any major point of his proposed Constitution to be amended because he believed that neither side would compromise and that his proposal represented the solution most likely to secure agreement. While Muzorewa's side had no serious objections to what he proposed, the PF were hostile to much of it e.g., the proposal for a non-executive President; a separate representation for Whites; granting full citizenship to all, including those who had immigrated since UDI; entrenched rights for all senior officials in the public service; and, especially, the provision in the Bill of Rights dealing with land tenure which safeguarded against expropriation of land and property except in cases required for public or defence purposes. The PF felt that this would entrench the *status quo* with Whites holding a predominant share of the land. But Carrington pointed out that the provision allowing for land to be taken over for rural resettlement gave considerable scope for change. When the talks were deadlocked, mainly over the land issue, Carrington introduced his tactic of using an ultimatum to win agreement. On 3 October he gave both sides five days within which to indicate their acceptance, or to risk wrecking the talks. Mugabe's response was to accuse Carrington of making 'a secret deal' with Muzorewa.[23] He said that the Foreign Secretary's behaviour had 'marred the original image which he struck, and on the basis of which we put our confidence in him. At the moment I am afraid I no longer have any confidence in his impartiality'. Muzorewa announced his acceptance of the British proposed constitution, but Smith described it as the 'worst of any since UDI'.[24] On the day the ultimatum expired the PF rejected the plan and tabled a constitution of its own. 'We have not come here', Nkomo said, 'to have a dictated settlement. Land is one of the most vital issues. . . . The war is all about land.'[25] On 9 October Carrington carried his brinkmanship a step further by giving the PF a new deadline, until the next day, to accept his proposals. He said he could entertain no further changes. When the deadlock remained unbroken after a week, Carrington indicated that he was ready to move on to the next stage of negotiating over the transition arrangements with whoever was willing to continue the talks. Gen Peter Walls arrived in London to engage in this stage of the negotiations and Ian Smith returned to Lancaster House as well. It seemed that Carrington was ready to go for 'the second prize', when he continued the talks with the Muzorewa side only.

At this point, too, SA chose to show its hand in a clear effort to encourage Carrington to make a separate deal with Muzorewa. Its Foreign Minister, Pik Botha, brought a message to Thatcher from his own Prime Minister. To Carrington he expressed fears about the security arrangements during the transition period, and urged him not to make any further concessions to the PF.

The Commonwealth secretary-general, Sonny Ramphal, issued a public statement claiming that Carrington's latest stance was not 'within the letter or the spirit of the Lusaka agreement'. He had previously obtained approval for his statement from four of the six countries which had drafted the Lusaka agreement— Tanzania, Nigeria, Jamaica and Zambia; the Australian Prime Minister could not be contacted in time. Carrington's spokesman refuted Ramphal's charges, insisting that the Foreign Secretary was 'scrupulously fulfilling the Lusaka agreement'; however, he went on, the Commonwealth agreement did not entitle any party to obstruct the right of the people of Zimbabwe to elect their own government on the basis of democratic rule.[26] The weekend of 13–14 October was critical.

Meanwhile, the Front-line Presidents met in Dar es Salaam to discuss the deadlock. Before their meeting, Nyerere described the atmosphere of crisis as 'utterly artificial', adding: 'The only real problem is the issue of who provides money for compensation to settle farmers. This is not a constitutional question but simply a policy question, and it could easily be resolved by Britain and her allies.'[27] The US Assistant Secretary of State for African Affairs, Richard Moose, happened to be in Dar es Salaam at the time of the FLPs meeting, and Nyerere sent a message through him to President Carter asking him to intervene to save the talks. The weekend of 20–21 October was also critical. Ramphal contacted the US ambassador in London, Kingman Brewster, to urge him to get a promise from his Government to make a substantial contribution towards a land compensation fund. He stressed the importance of securing an American reply by Monday. Consultations involving President Carter took place in Washington, and by Sunday morning Brewster was in a position to tell Ramphal that the US would be willing to make a substantial contribution, but without mentioning any figure. On Monday Carrington received a memorandum from the US Secretary of State, Cyrus Vance, formally confirming America's willingness to help with land compensation through a multi-donor programme within a wider Southern African concept. Vance also wanted information about Carrington's intentions concerning the transitional arrangements leading to independence. It was agreed that Tony Lake, the chairman of the State

Department's Planning Commission, should be sent to London for a full briefing.

The talks at Lancaster House reached the point of collapse on Monday over Carrington's demand that the PF should accept unconditionally the British Constitutional proposals. Ramphal arranged a secret meeting in London between Mugabe, Nkomo and Gibson Lampher, the US Embassy's desk officer for African affairs. Lampher explained that Washington felt it necessary to be cautious about the phrasing of its response. But the Front leaders recognized the nature of the compromise being offered and had no trouble with the American phraseology. It was sufficient for them to inform Carrington that they had obtained satisfactory assurances that if the conference succeeded, Britain, the US and other countries would provide financial aid for land, agricultural and economic development.

As a result of the stand taken by the Front-line Presidents in encouraging the PF to reach a settlement and the American assurances, the PF withdrew its objections to the constitutional proposals on 19 October, saying it accepted assurances that the US, Britain and other countries would 'assist in land, agricultural and economic development programmes . . . which go a long way in allaying the great concern we have over the whole land question. . . .' Mugabe then gave Carrington the assurance he had asked for: 'We are now able to say that if we are satisfied beyond doubt about the vital issues of the transitional arrangements, there will be no need to revert to discussion on the Constitution, including those issues on which we reserve our position.'[28]

This vital PF concession enabled the talks to move into their seventh week for discussions on arrangements during the transition period. Carrington unfolded his plan for a British Governor to be sent to Rhodesia to re-establish legal rule; this would require of Muzorewa that he should give up power on the arrival of the Governor; a ceasefire would be arranged; and elections would be held within two months under British supervision. Carrington's plan invited a double veto: Muzorewa adamantly rejected any idea that he should surrender office before the elections; and the PF regarded the two months' period to achieve a ceasefire and to complete elections as ridiculous; also, it demanded UN rather than British supervision of the elections. Muzorewa at first held out for sanctions to be lifted immediately as a precondition to his Government's resignation; however, despite strong objections by Smith, Muzorewa surprisingly yielded on this crucial point—something which Carrington had feared would not happen, and which he regarded as the decisive point in making the agreement possible. Smith described Muzorewa as 'wet putty' and a man incapable of dealing with Nkomo and Mugabe who, he said, were more clever than 'our Blacks'.[29]

However, with confrontation between Carrington and the PF at its fiercest at the end of October, Commonwealth leaders began to play an even more active role. Jamaica's Prime Minister, Michael Manley, had talks with the British Prime Minister, urging her to strengthen the proposed role of the Commonwealth monitoring force during the election period, and urging that Nyerere and Kaunda should be invited to London to save the talks. Commonwealth High Commissioners also expressed their concern about aspects of the proposed transition arrangements.

When Kenneth Kaunda arrived in London on 9 November he found the talks on transitional arrangements still completely bogged down on a number of points, including PF objections to the use of the Rhodesian police during the elections; the composition of the 1,500-strong Commonwealth peace force which, while mainly British, would include token forces from Kenya, New Zealand, Fiji and Australia; the proposed two months' period for elections and, especially, the role of the guerrilla forces after the ceasefire. At dinner at No 10, Kaunda clashed sharply with Carrington; the Zambian President said he could now understand why the PF leaders had complained to him about the Foreign Secretary's stubborn tactics. Kaunda's major point was to press that equal status should be given to the PF forces once the Governor became the commander-in-chief of all the armed forces. In an eight-page letter to Thatcher, he wrote: 'in the name of God and in the interests of peace, Margaret, I urge you to consider these proposals. . . . I would like to underline that it is vital to use political solutions to resolve military and security problems facing the conference. One of the areas where this is urgent and necessary is the equality of treatment between the Rhodesian and Patriotic Front Forces. . . . This would have a tremendous and positive impact in the maintenance of peace and stability in the country.' On 15 November Carrington announced in a statement to Mugabe: 'I can confirm that your forces and the Rhodesian security forces will be under the authority of the Governor. The PF forces will be required to comply with the directions of the Governor.' Mugabe replied: 'In the light of the discussions we have had, and as a result of President Kaunda's proposals to the Prime Minister, if you are prepared to include the PF forces in paragraph 13 of the British paper, we are able to agree to the interim proposals, conditional on a successful outcome of the negotiations on the ceasefire.'

The ceasefire proposals, tabled by Carrington on 16 November, became the biggest obstacle of all to reaching agreement—more especially since at a time when these were being negotiated between British military officers, Gen Walls and the PF military commanders, a severely damaging attack was launched by the Rhodesian army into Zambia destroying a number of its vital land communications. Thatcher at once sent her sympathy to Kaunda, while Carrington personally urged Walls to desist from any further attacks at the stage when peace was in sight. On 23 November, Carrington issued two more of his ultimata: he wanted assurances from both sides that cross-border military attacks between Rhodesia and Zambia would cease; and he wanted an answer within three days—on 26 November—saying whether or not 'they can accept our proposals for the implementation of a ceasefire'. His statement, according to Mugabe, 'produced a pandemonium at the end of the conference'. He said that the ultimatum would be ignored, adding that Carrington 'could go to hell'. Carrington's view was that the two parties were so far apart that it was necessary for Britain to present the compromise. But the PF argued that at no time had there been proper discussions about the ceasefire proposals. Mugabe insisted: 'Considering the advances we have made in the war, we cannot see them reversed in London at the stroke of a pen, our victory transposed into defeat, Gen Walls gaining at Lancaster House what he failed to achieve on the battlefield.'

Meanwhile, anti-British rioting broke out in Lusaka over the latest Rhodesian raids. An angry Kaunda, speaking to a crowd of 6,000 demonstrators, denounced the British as 'great apes'; and his Foreign Minister described Britain as 'a spineless hyena'. Zambia asked for the immediate recall of the British High Commissioner. In this crisis atmosphere Nkomo and Mugabe flew to Dar es Salaam for a meeting with the Front-line Presidents. But Margaret Thatcher remained coolly confident. 'We are within an ace of success,' she said on 23 November, 'all the parties have contributed towards these achievements. Everyone has made concessions.' Muzorewa's latest concession was to agree to stop further raids into Zambia.

The PF leaders failed to get much encouragement from their meetings with the Front-line Presidents. Indeed, at one point when Mugabe ended his intervention on a defiant note of 'the struggle continues', Machel remarked coldly that there was no struggle to continue; the PF should go back to the negotiating table to consolidate what they had won. On the day of the expiry of the ultimatum, the Rhodesian delegation leader, Dr Silas Mundawarara, announced that although aspects of the ceasefire proposals were 'extremely unpalatable', his side was ready to accept them in full. But the PF leaders were absent from the session. Although Ian Smith accused the British Government of pandering to the PF, he went on to tell a press conference that if the PF won in free elections 'we will work with them. It is no use living in the past. The past is gone.'[30] Ignoring the expiry of his own ultimatum, Carrington engaged in further talks with Nkomo and Mugabe on 27 November. They produced a ten-page report elaborating their own ceasefire proposals. These repeated their demand for a large-scale Commonwealth peacekeeping force, as distinct from a monitoring force, the dismantling of the units of the Rhodesian army, and a two-month period to make the ceasefire fully operative before elections could be got under way. Nkomo also continued to insist on his demand that integration of the various armed units—PF and Rhodesian—should begin as soon as the ceasefire became operative to ensure that Zimbabwe would have the beginnings of a national army at its independence. A crucial issue still remained—that of the number and distribution of camps into which the guerrillas would move when they left the bush. Mugabe insisted that he was not prepared to allow his men to be herded into 'death camps'—which he feared would be the position if the ceasefire failed to hold and no adequate peacekeeping force was stationed in the country, especially since the Rhodesian forces would be headquartered in their own barracks.

Meanwhile, Sonny Ramphal had been determinedly pursuing his demand for a collective Commonwealth team of ten prominent members to act as election observers. He insisted they should be organized by the Commonwealth Secretariat. But Carrington rejected the idea, preferring that it be left to each Commonwealth country to send its own observers. The difference between the two plans was that Ramphal was after a collective Commonwealth report on the outcome of the elections, while Carrington wanted individual reports, fearing that the dynamics of 'Commonwealth consensus' would result in the militants' view prevailing over the moderates. But Ramphal argued that the Lusaka agreement called for a Commonwealth verdict on the fairness or otherwise of the elections. By then, Carrington was treating the Commonwealth Secretary-General as being essentially sympathetic to the PF and hostile to the Salisbury regime.[31] Ramphal's final move was to call all 42 Commonwealth High Commissioners in London to a meeting where, by consensus, they backed his plan as against Carrington's. The Foreign Secretary felt he had no option but to accept that decision. The conflict between the British Foreign Secretary and the Commonwealth Secretary-General had become very hostile indeed. In retrospect, this controversy might seem to have been something of a side-issue, but only because of the way events finally turned out. The situation could have been very different if the PF had not won the elections so handsomely.

Came December, and failure seemed certain: but, as in chess, end-game moves are always the hardest—except that neither the PF nor Carrington were playing games. Carrington was convinced that any further move he made towards meeting the PF demands would lose him the advantage trick he already held of an agreement with the Salisbury regime, but he also knew from the Front-line Presidents that having seen a settlement within sight, they would be unlikely to see it lost at that late stage of the talks. The PF found themselves in a very genuine dilemma: while they desperately wanted to see the settlement succeed for their own reasons (as well as to meet the wishes of the Front-line Presidents), they strongly suspected they might be walking into a British trap, which could lose them the war they had won. Their fear was that once the guerrillas came out of the bush and were concentrated in their camps, a pretext could be found by the Rhodesians and South Africans (they were also suspicious of possible British collusion) to break the ceasefire, surround the camps and decimate the guerrillas. (That suspicion was to remain with the PF leaders up to the day they finally won the elections; it helps to explain some of the problems that developed after the British Governor had taken over.) But now, in London, with total deadlock, Carrington's next move was to issue yet another of his ultimata. On 3 December he gave the PF leaders five days within which to accept or reject his ceasefire proposals. At the same time he put in hand plans to implement the proposed settlement—with or without PF support. He announced that an Order-in-Council would be presented to Parliament to enable the Governor to take over legal control in Rhodesia.

Nor was this simply a threat; at that point a thoroughly dispirited and somewhat overwrought Carrington was prepared reluctantly to settle for the second prize. Naturally, this possibility aroused fresh optimism in the Muzorewa camp that, even at that late hour, Britain might still be thinking of making a deal with them.[32] On 4 December, the Rhodesian Parliament, with one lonely dissident, voted to accept the proposed new Constitution. But if Carrington was adamant, so was the PF. It asked Carrington for a simple yes or no to their own proposals which, by then, had been narrowed down to four main points: the disposition of the PF and Rhodesian forces in their various gathering points, with the latter returned to barracks before the guerrillas emerged from the bush; the grounding of all Rhodesian military aircraft; the enlargement of the Commonwealth monitoring force; the withdrawal of all South African forces who, the PF alleged, were being poured into Rhodesia. At this point the PF was strengthened in its stand by support from Kaunda and Machel, who had met each other in Maputo.[33] The OAU also took a hand through its chairman, President Tolbert of Liberia; after a meeting with Nyerere and President Shagari of Nigeria, he sent a message to Thatcher urging Britain to be patient and to avoid the impression that it was giving orders instead of negotiating.[34] The three OAU leaders urged particular consideration for the issue of the disposition of the forces.

At this most difficult moment since the start of the talks twelve weeks before, Ramphal, working through the informal Southern African group of Commonwealth High Commissioners in London, provided a key to break the deadlock. He submitted three alternative formulae to Carrington and the PF by which to overcome the main obstacles. One proposal was that further consideration should be given to the suggested 14 assembly places for the guerrillas; a second proposal related to assurances about the removal of SA troops; and a third dealt with the control of the Rhodesian air force. On 5 December, Carrington ('very cheered compared with what I felt two days ago') gave the PF specific assurances that the Rhodesian air force would be kept in check and disarmed; that the Commonwealth monitoring force (with Britain's force increased to 1,200 men) would be large enough to do the job required of it; and that SA would be told not to intervene. But this last point was covered by a formula which promised: 'There will be no external involvement in Rhodesia under the British Governor. The position has been made clear to all the Governments concerned, including SA.' Mugabe accepted these assurances and formally announced PF acceptance of the British proposals. This agreement then still left the details of implementing the ceasefire to be finalized. Discussion of these brought the next, and final, crisis on the very next day when Nkomo told Sir Anthony Duff, acting as chairman of the plenary session: 'Forget the agreement.' The conflict was over the continuing contentious question about the disposition of the rival forces, the timing of their withdrawal to their ceasefire positions, and over the assembly points for the guerrillas, which the PF insisted were insufficient in number. In an effort to break this latest deadlock and compel PF agreement, the British Government began to put into practice the Lusaka House agreement as if it had been approved by all the parties—thus reaching the position which the PF had feared all along might be sprung on them. Lord Soames was named as Governor of Rhodesia with Sir Anthony Duff as his deputy. On 6 December the Zimbabwe Bill was introduced in Parliament, which allowed the country to be brought to independence at an appropriate moment; and sanctions were finally ended—without, incidentally, any reference to the Security Council under whose authority mandatory sanctions had been imposed. (The Security Council itself formally voted to end sanctions on 21 December.)

Even at that late hour the Rhodesian forces (despite their earlier assurance to the contrary) launched major air attacks across the Zambian border to strike at Nkomo's guerrilla camps on 10 December. The reason given for this action was that Nkomo was engaged in infiltrating large numbers of his men across the border in advance of the ceasefire. On 12 December, Lord Soames arrived in Salisbury to haul up the Union Jack and re-establish legal British rule after 14 years.

Meanwhile, back at Lancaster House, the arguments continued. Nkomo was still insisting that 'under no circumstances would the PF agree to put their signatures to what was proposed. We would be signing our own death warrant, and we have not fought a successful war to do that.'[35] Carrington warned the PF on 13 December that if they did not agree to the ceasefire, Britain would go ahead with a settlement without them; but, he added, 'no doors have been finally closed'. He made one final concession, adding one more assembly point for the guerrillas and promising that the Governor would decide if more were needed. Carrington's high-risk diplomatic strategy finally paid off when the PF accepted the terms for the settlement on 17 December. Attributing the success of the conference to the 'sacrifices, sweat and blood of our gallant fighting men', the PF declared that although the agreement had shortcomings it provided 'a sound basis on which to build a truly democratic Zimbabwe free from racism and the exploitation of man by man'. The agreement was formally signed by all the parties on 21 December, with Carrington saying that if the wounds could be healed in Rhodesia, it would give new heart to the search for a peaceful settlement in Namibia and encourage resolution of the issues which divided SA from the rest of the continent.

Why did the PF abandon its opposition to the proposals for implementing the ceasefire? First, because it was faced with a *fait accompli* and it feared that with a British Governor established in Salisbury events could make their position more difficult; having compromised on so many important issues, Mugabe and Nkomo felt it was pointless to hold out any further. But there was a second, more important reason: the PF was supremely confident that in any reasonably free elections they would win easily—and the agreement over a Commonwealth observer team would ensure that no election that was not fairly conducted would win international approval. But because they left Lancaster House having failed to secure what they felt to be proper safeguards for their fighting cadres, they intended to tread warily to the assembly points; by no means all of their trained cadres would leave the bush. It was this failure of the negotiations to satisfy the PF's anxieties over the safety of their men that produced a situation which came so close to wrecking the Lancaster House agreement in the following two months.

THE LEGACY OF LANCASTER HOUSE
Besides keeping old suspicions alive and leaving a number of key questions undecided for the sake of keeping the negotiating process going, the agreement itself created several serious problems for the future. As has already been noted, the arrangements for the transition period depended for their success largely upon fortuitous circumstances. The Governor, though armed with dictatorial powers, had no means of enforcing his authority if the ceasefire broke down; all he could do was to leave the colony, or else call on either the PF forces or the Rhodesian army to

help him enforce his policies, more likely the latter as, in fact, turned out to be the case when minor ceasefire breaches occurred; at no time did he call on the PF to deal with Bishop Muzorewa's Auxiliaries. Members of the small staff taken to Salisbury by Lord Soames were not expected to do any more than act as liaison officers with the army and the new Military Advisory Council. As it turned out, none of the predictable disasters occurred, although there were several shaky moments when the enterprise was seriously threatened. The more serious, long-term problems, though, arose from concessions and guarantees built into the Independence Constitution itself, e.g. the over-representation of the White minority in Parliament with provisions making it difficult to change this entrenched provision by constitutional means for ten years; the security of tenure given to all the incumbent public officials and army officers for seven years (by virtue of the nature of the old regime, virtually all the top and middle-rank positions were held by Whites); the creation of a non-Presidential system of Government, which has failed to work in almost every Third World country, with the outstanding exception of India.

The most serious short-term error, though, was the failure to allow for sufficient time before independence for the two wings of the PF forces and the Rhodesia army to be integrated into a single national army. Although a start was made with integrating the forces during the transition, progress was minimal. Although the crucial land issue was settled in a way that allowed land to be taken over for extensive resettlement, it remained subject to funds being available to pay compensation. Two reasons explain most of the defects of the transition arrangements. The first was the British refusal to accept a Commonwealth peace-keeping force, supposedly because it would be resisted by the Rhodesians—but seeing how far they were forced to retreat on other matters, was it really impossible to get them to swallow this proposal as well? The point is that this proposal was not even entertained by Carrington because he was opposed to allowing any non-British element in the transition arrangements, except for his personally hand-picked Commonwealth Monitoring force—signficantly drawn mainly from the 'White Commonwealth'. The argument that a large peace-keeping force proved not to be necessary is to argue with the experience of hindsight. The second reason was Thatcher's adamant insistence that the British presence should be as brief as possible: her 'quick-in-quick-out' argument arose from the fear that Britain would become bogged down in a morass of conflicting interests if the transition were not rushed through at great speed. The shape of the Constitution was dictated by the familiar British wish to establish a Westminster model of parliamentary democracy—thoroughly worthy, but how practical? But even though Whitehall did not seriously suppose it was practical, they argued that Westminster should not itself be asked to enact a non-Westminster type of Constitution and the White Rhodesians could not be expected to accept a system that was not based on principles of parliamentary democracy, even though the Smith regime had itself paid only lip-service to this ideal.

There is the more substantial, indeed overwhelmingly strong, argument that the compromises, guarantees, etc. were indispensable for getting the two sides to reach the final agreement as well as to persuading the British Cabinet to undertake even a brief period of renewed stewardship in Rhodesia; indeed, one was left with the distinct impression that nobody really believed the Constitution itself would hold up for any lengthy period beyond independence. In other words, the Lancaster House Constitution should be looked at as a means of transferring power, not as a viable system of government for the new Zimbabwe society.

141

BATTLEFRONTS OF SOUTHERN AFRICA

RHODESIA ON THE EVE OF INDEPENDENCE

Some years ago White Rhodesians produced an expensive copper plaque on which was inscribed their commitment to their 'war of independence'. It read:

DIDN'T FIGHT FOR FUN

In World War One, when things were bad, and England needed men—
We rallied to our country's flag, Rhodesians answered then.
And many asked us as we went, 'whose battle do you fight?'
'Our country needs us', we replied, and fought with all our might.
And some came back, but hundreds not, but you must understand,
We didn't fight for fun, my lad, we fought to save our land.

Two decades passed and once again the call to arms went out.
Rhodesians answered as before—was ever there a doubt?
Where did we go? Why, everywhere, on land and air and sea.
We fought in every battle, and we helped to set men free—
And some came back, but thousands not, but you must understand
We didn't fight for fun, my lad, we fought to save our land.

The years rolled by, and once again, the battle cry is made.
This time Rhodesians fight alone, few come to our aid.
Both young and old, both black and white, we'll keep our country free.
And make it safe for everyone—not just for you and me.
Yes, some will live, and some will not, but you must understand
It isn't any fun, my lad, to fight to save our land.

Sydney E. Lassman

It is not difficult to imagine the feelings of these White Rhodesians who had clung so single-mindedly and tenaciously to those ideas on that suitably damp and grey morning of 13 December 1979, when, for the first time in 14 years, 'God Save the Queen' was heard again, marking not just the return of a titular British Governor, but of direct British rule for the first time in 90 years. Paradoxically too, the colonizer was returning to the plaudits of Black Africa, who saw it as a positive act in the final discharge of Britain's colonial responsibilities—a point insisted upon, throughout their long negotiations, by the Front-line Presidents. Few rated Lord Soames' chances of success very high; nobody underrated the very real problems he faced; possibly only his own total lack of African experience shielded him from despair.

Rhodesia's dictator for a few months could rely only on influence, diplomacy and an inborn instinct for muddling through. What could he do when informed that some bungling policemen had arrested the former, respected Prime Minister, Garfield Todd, on serious (but erroneous) charges of assisting guerrillas who had disobeyed the ceasefire instructions? A witness who was present in Government House when the news was brought to Soames saw him fulminate in frustrated rage. Yet this was only one of scores of actions taken without his knowledge, let alone his agreement.

There was the much graver affair when, behind his back, the Rhodesian army commander, Gen Peter Walls, negotiated an agreement with SA to leave a small army unit on the Rhodesian side of the Beitbridge crossing to protect it against possible sabotage, thus ensuring that the quickest escape route to the south would remain open in case things went wrong; of course it could also allow the SADF to intervene if the ceasefire broke down without the risk of being accused of 'invading' Zimbabwe since they would be on its territory by negotiated agreement. Soames at first tried to put a bold face on this arrangement with SA, covering up as best he could for what was a blatant breach of Carrington's undertaking—one of the hard-fought points of compromise at Lancaster House (see above)—that no foreign forces would be allowed to remain in Rhodesia after the Governor's arrival. Naturally, much was made in the cover-up of the Beitbridge affair to publicize the presence of a number of Mozambican soldiers in Zanla's ranks; but, unlike SA, Mozambique showed it was immediately ready to clear all its soldiers out of Rhodesia.

Although Soames was nominally the commander-in-chief of all the forces, he failed from the start to prevent the Rhodesian command from issuing its own daily communiqués, giving its version of the ceasefire operation—which gave the impression that this reflected the C-in-C's views as well. His two immediate problems were over Gen Walls' decision to keep Muzorewa's political army, the Auxiliaries, in the Tribal Trust Lands (TTLs) where they were feared and hated; and the failure of Zanla, especially, to order all its guerrillas to leave the bush, while in fact bringing more men across the border from Mozambique. Even though many more Zanla and Zipra forces had emerged from the bush than Rhodesian or British intelligence had knowledge of, thousands more remained outside the assembly points, while Nkomo kept a substantial part of his forces in Zambia. Their action was predictable in view of the suspicions they had voiced at Lancaster House; but it was not a decision that Soames could accept. He could use the failure of Zanla, in particular, to bring out all its guerrillas as justification for accepting Walls' action over the Auxiliaries. Soames quickly came to share Walls' suspicions about Mugabe's true intentions of possibly wrecking the Agreement. While Soames was supposed to rely on his 1,500-strong Commonwealth Monitoring Force and his small election Commission to act as his eyes, they were thinly spread, especially in the TTLs. It soon transpired that they came to rely for their information mostly on what they were told by the old 'Native Administration' officials (a prejudiced body of men, filled with animus against the PF). These reports came to be accepted as gospel in Government House, because they came from the Monitoring Force and the Election Commission; this resulted in a largely one-sided view about the extent of intimidation in which Zanu and Zanla were supposedly engaged. When specific allegations of intimidation were investigated by the Commonwealth observers and by the scores of other international observers, many were shown to be quite untrue. But because of the official line taken by Government House, the PF, and especially Zanu—came to believe that Soames was biased against them; and there is no doubt that initially he was strongly prejudiced against Mugabe for reasons stated above.

But what was to be expected? There was Soames sitting in Government House largely isolated from personal knowledge of what was actually going on in the country, depending for his information on mostly official channels, which often turned out to be tainted at source. Fearfully suspicious that he might be assassinated (a suspicion that was later to prove to be well-founded on several occasions), Mugabe delayed his return to Rhodesia, and this encouraged some of Soames' advisers to consider excluding him altogether from the elections and to work assiduously for a Muzorewa-Nkomo alliance which, almost to the end, was what the British and many White Rhodesians favoured. In all these circumstances it was hardly surprising that Government House should have remained in such ignorance about the real degree of popular support Mugabe enjoyed in the country. However, this ignorance in Government House was not shared by the Governor's military team, under Maj-Gen Sir John Acland, who played a notably independent role in the Governor's retinue. The soldiers, reporting from the field, showed a different picture about the level and sources of intimidation. Significantly, Acland's men were the only element in the British mission to have predicted Mugabe's landslide victory. Since Soames did not pay heed to what his military team was reporting, it must be assumed that he made the common error of preferring to rely more on what his political advisers were telling him.

The Commonwealth Observer Group's magisterial report on Soames' stewardship is summed up in this key paragraph:

> Peace has been restored to Southern Rhodesia by means of a democratic exercise without historical precedent. Never before have elections been held at a time of tenuous ceasefire, without agreed battle lines, and with rival armies uneasily apart. That this has proved possible redounds to the credit of all those involved.
>
> In the extraordinary circumstances in which the elections were held, we could hardly have expected to find the levels of administrative propriety and public rectitude associated with the concept of free and fair elections at their ideal best, a level not always or everywhere achieved even in stable societies with long experience of democratic institutions. In the event, the degree to which they approached those levels was praiseworthy indeed. . . .
>
> Inevitably there were imperfections. . . . Sometimes they flowed from a less than impartial functioning of the principal agencies of government or an unwillingness to respond to higher authority. . . . That there was a certain degree of violence and fear is incontestable. But the extent of intimidation was often exaggerated either for political purposes or as the result of incorrect or slanted information. Blame was not confined to any one quarter. Nevertheless, we firmly believe that its impact on the voters' freedom of choice was strongly countered, if not frustrated, by the widespread belief in the secrecy of the ballot.[36]

The British Government's suspicions that a 'collective Commonwealth view' would damage its role in the final chapter of decolonization were proved groundless by the warm and unanimous endorsement given by ten respected Commonwealth leaders under the chairmanship of that distinguished Indian public servant, ambassador Rajeshwar Dayal.

Like all great British proconsuls, Soames showed qualities of statesmanship in the way he accepted the victory of the man he had come to mistrust and dislike. While naturally putting the finest possible gloss on his own percipient role, he later came to speak in the highest possible terms of Mugabe.[37]

As it had done during the Lancaster House talks, Mozambique played an independent and significant role in the transition period, again showing Samora Machel's perceptiveness and pragmatism. Having formed the view that the key figure who could decide the failure or success of the transfer of power (now that Smith had become only a shadowy figure) was Gen Peter Walls, he overcame his own feelings towards the soldier who had been Mozambique's most deadly enemy, and through his envoys in Salisbury (Jose Cabaco and Fernando Homwano), invited Walls for talks in Maputo. Although Machel did not personally meet Walls on that occasion, his top military aide did. The overt purpose of the meeting was to get Walls to understand that Mozambique would call in its allies in the event of a South African military threat to Mozambique because of its support for the PF. A second reason was to establish a working relationship with Walls. His surprising visit to Maputo showed that this was possible. On Walls' return to Salisbury, Cabaco and Homwano helped to arrange an historic meeting between Walls and Mugabe in the latter's house. Their meeting began a relationship which gave Mugabe the confidence to appoint Walls as Zimbabwe's first military commander—a decision of crucial importance in helping White Rhodesians to get over the shock of Mugabe's electoral triumph.

THE ROLE OF GENERAL WALLS

The Rhodesian army commander played an extraordinary role in the Lancaster House talks and in the developments that flowed from it. In London he made no attempt to disguise his opposition to his old comrade-in-arms, Ian Smith. His influence on the Bishop was a major determinant in getting him to make the concessions that were essential for the success of the negotiations. From his subsequent actions during the ceasefire period it is clear that Walls believed it was possible to manipulate the military position which then obtained to ensure Muzorewa's victory, possibly in alliance with Nkomo. His primary aim was to ensure Mugabe's defeat. But once it became clear that this was was not possible, he shifted his position again. Walls justified these shifts of position by claiming that he was simply a soldier doing his duty—a claim which is hardly supported by the record. There is only one satisfactory explanation for Walls' role. He did not want to find himself cast in the role of a General who had lost the war. By the time of the Lancaster House meeting he knew the war could no longer be won; the only way of avoiding outright defeat was to negotiate a ceasefire. This would create a new situation with fresh opportunities for military and political manoeuvring in close association with his South African ally. His attempts to frustrate the ceasefire and Soames' mission and to harass the PF fighters clearly demonstrate his tactics of trying to pluck some kind of victory from the military defeat into which he and Smith had led the country. However, in moving against Smith and, especially, by agreeing to command the forces after independence he incurred the hostility of White Rhodesians. When he subsequently tried to regain some creditworthiness among them by his notorious British TV interview, he alienated the new Zimbabwe leadership, while causing the White community to lose all confidence in him. Walls was simply not clever enough to play the role he had cast for himself even though he was able to avoid having to admit defeat on the battlefield.

ZIMBABWE–SOUTH AFRICA RELATIONS

The Pretoria regime had never been well-disposed to Ian Smith from the first days of UDI; but, having failed to persuade him not to make that decision, mistaken in the eyes of both Verwoerd and Vorster, they nevertheless did what they could to prevent the success of sanctions out of concern that this weapon might be turned against SA if it proved successful in Rhodesia; and later, when the armed struggle developed, they gave their military support to the Rhodesian army because of their interest in preventing the success of guerrilla operations. However, throughout the 14 years of UDI, the Pretoria regime always stood ready to support initiatives to achieve a political settlement, which could equally avoid the dangers they foresaw in the Rhodesian situation. In their view the correct Rhodesian policy, as they told Sir Roy Welensky in 1963 and Winston Field in 1965, was to help produce a 'moderate' Black leader (their model was Malawi's President Banda). When Smith finally came round, under growing pressure, to make his internal settlement with Bishop Muzorewa, SA seized the opportunity to try and prove that their idea was feasible. Money was poured in to help build up the Bishop's UANC; substantial transport and other support was given to help him win his April 1979 elections; and SA's military role was substantially increased to the point where it had just under 1,000 identifiable soldiers in Rhodesia at the time of Lord Soames' arrival. Prime Minister Botha pinned his hopes on the Muzorewa regime being able to win international recognition after the election of a Conservative Government in Britain, and was encouraged by the strength of the Republican lobby in the American Congress. The Lusaka Agreement was a setback for these hopes, greeted by Pretoria as 'appeasement'; nevertheless, it still hoped that the Lancaster House negotiations might result in Muzorewa winning the recognition that eluded him because of the expected PF obduracy which would wreck the talks. When Carrington appeared to be appeasing the PF, SA's Foreign Minister, Pik Botha, was sent to London to protest against this sign of British 'weakness' (see above). Having seen their hopes again frustrated at Lancaster House, Pretoria once again provided substantial financial support for Muzorewa to enable him to win the elections. Right up to the announcement of the final poll, Pik Botha was confidently assuring his Cabinet colleagues that Muzorewa would win. Mugabe's overwhelming victory was received with stunned surprise for several reasons. First, it showed the efficiency of the armed struggle ('communist terrorists backed by Moscow'), with its predictable influence on the morale and ideas of Black South Africans already encouraged by the guerrillas' victories in Mozambique and Angola. Second, it bolstered Swapo's confidence in Namibia. Third, it opened up the possibility of Zimbabwe offering bases to the ANC and PAC guerrilla forces. And finally, it destroyed any hope there might ever have been for P. W. Botha's strategy of a 'Constellation of Southern African States'.[38]

Botha's immediate reaction to Mugabe's victory was hostile, warning him of the direst consequences if he allowed Zimbabwe to be used as a base for South African guerrillas. Although Mugabe had announced in one of his earliest public statements that he would not allow Zimbabwe to be used for guerrilla operations, this did not satisfy Botha since he well understood (as Mugabe later confirmed) that the PF Government would provide other forms of assistance for the SA liberation movement. Anxieties about the new threat from the north were exemplified by a warning from SA's Minister of Manpower Development, Fanie Botha, who threatened that SA would 'wipe out' any guerrilla bases found in Zimbabwe.[39] Relations deteriorated further in July 1980 when Mugabe, while attending the OAU summit in Freetown, insisted that SA agents had recruited thousands of soldiers in Zimbabwe. Although he confirmed Zimbabwe's intention of establishing economic relations with SA, he said there could be no question of diplomatic relations, and he closed down the South African diplomatic mission in Salisbury on 4 July.[40] Mugabe committed Zimbabwe to honouring the public debt run up with SA by the formerly illegal regime, but made this conditional on clarification about the nature of the debts incurred. At the time of writing, no progress had been made in normalizing economic relations between the two countries; nor had the Pretoria regime finally made up its mind about its future policy towards the Mugabe regime. One body of Botha's advisers argued in favour of a policy of destabilizing Zimbabwe to keep it weak, while others took the view that SA stood more to gain through helping to produce stability in Zimbabwe. The final outcome of this debate would obviously be crucial to developments in Southern Africa.

NAMIBIA AFTER ZIMBABWE
With the coming of independence to Zimbabwe, the time for decision in Namibia was brought significantly closer. Dr Kurt Waldheim proposed in early April that 15 June 1980 should be fixed as the deadline for implementing the UN's plan for independence; but this deadline still found the negotiations bogged down in arguments with Pretoria over details about the terms of the proposed UN Transitional Administrative Group (Untag) and peacekeeping force.[41]

There are five distinct elements in SA's Namibia strategy. First, it does not wish to be seen to be responsible for breaking off the negotiations with the UN or the 'Contact Group' of the five Western members of the Security Council (US, UK, France, West Germany and Canada).[42] Second, it wishes to keep open the option of an internationally-supervised settlement. Third, it seeks to use the time gained through its delaying tactics to build up the strength of the Internal Settlement regime of the Democratic Turnhalle Alliance (for details, see chapter on Namibia). Fourth, it works to discredit and weaken Swapo by political and military methods. Fifth, it is building up SA's and Namibia's military defence capacity; by mid-1980,

Namibia's internal defence force was approaching 20,000.[43]

The Botha regime, having reassessed its Namibian strategy in the light of the defeat of the 'Internal Settlement model' in Rhodesia, decided nevertheless to continue on the same road but to speed up the timetable for limited self-rule. On 1 May 1980 Botha announced that full internal self-government was to be granted to Namibia in two months' time as a prelude to full independence. A Cabinet was formed under the Prime Ministership of the DTA leader, Dirk Mudge, with a majority of Black Ministers; but Pretoria still retained the right to appoint the Administrator-General with full supervisory powers and the ultimate right of veto. The vital post remained in the hands of Dr Gerrit Viljoen, former chairman of the Broederbond. Although this move failed to unite the rival political parties inside Namibia (despite their enmity to Swapo), Botha insisted: 'They have chosen independence, and they must accept the consequences.' However, he did not rule out the possibility of agreement on an internationally-accepted settlement for independence; 'a political solution', he felt, 'is absolutely essential.'[44]

Dr Viljoen and Pretoria appeared to be speaking with different voices on their future relations with the UN. The former came out as a proponent of a new idea to bypass the UN by entering into direct negotiations with the Angolan and Zambian Governments, and possibly with Swapo. Accusing the UN of following 'a clear pattern of escalating demands', he described Waldheim's proposals as 'notorious', and spoke of their 'glaring partiality' towards Swapo.[45] On the other hand, the Pretoria regime accepted the need for continuing negotiations with the UN when it replied on 11 May 1980 to Waldheim's proposals for a settlement based on the Security Council Resolution 435. On this occasion, Pretoria gave its approval to five points in the latest UN proposal: the port of Walvis Bay, technically South African, could be used for logistic supplies to Untag; the SA Defence Force (SADF) would give maximum logistical support to Untag; Untag's air component could be military; the full Untag complement of 7,500 men could be deployed for peacekeeping purposes; the number of SA military bases in the territory could be reduced by half from 40 during the proposed twelve weeks' transition period. Having made these concessions, Pretoria then went on to seek 'further clarification' from the UN on whether its offer to reduce the number of South African bases in the zone was acceptable and whether the size of the Untag force to be deployed in the zone would be increased.

SA had also asked whether the UN's original proposal for Swapo to be allowed to maintain bases in Namibia would be dropped in favour of a demilitarized zone. This was of particular concern to the South Africans, who initially rejected the UN settlement plan because of its provision for Swapo bases in Namibia during the ceasefire period.

The South Africans also introduced a new element into the already tortuous Namibia settlement talks by reintroducing the Unita factor into the negotiations for a settlement—thus repeating an earlier ploy for delay. In March, Unita sent a telegram saying that it must be consulted about plans to establish a demilitarized zone in Angola. The South Africans stated that the implications of Unita's telegram should 'not be underestimated'.

Western diplomats' initial reaction was that the South African response was more constructive than some had expected.[46]

Notwithstanding confident assertions about Swapo standing no chance of winning power through free elections, Pretoria was clearly uncertain about putting the issue to the test, especially after its predictions had been proved so wrong in Zimbabwe. While official sources in Pretoria had claimed before the Zimbabwe results that Swapo could hope to win only 5% of the vote in Namibia, by April 1980 Dr Viljoen admitted it might be as high as 40%, having himself said before the Zimbabwe elections that it would be no higher than 25%.[47] Prof Gerhard Totemeyer, SA's leading academic specialist on Namibia, said after a fact-finding mission in April 1980 that he had no doubt Swapo would win more than 50% of the vote.[48] An experienced SA reporter in Windhoek, Peter Kenny, wrote: 'Speak to anyone ranging politically from far Right, to centre, to far Left in SWA and they are likely to say that Zimbabwean experience proves for SWA that if a UN-supervised election were held in the territory tomorrow, Swapo would win.'[49]

Swapo's leader, Sam Nujomo, remains Pretoria's *bête noire* bracketed with Mugabe as 'a communist terrorist'; but after the Zimbabwe elections, Dr Viljoen said Nujomo was 'no Mugabe' (adding gratuitously that his lieutenants were 'not very bright either').[50] Although Swapo continued to insist that 'the armed struggle is our only solution for freedom',[51] Nujomo offered on 18 March 1980 to enter into immediate bilateral negotiations with the SA Government subject to the single precondition that the talks should be about 'ending SA's illegal occupation of Namibia. . . . I am ready to begin negotiations anywhere, and at any time— tomorrow if Botha likes.'[52] Nujoma also expressed his readiness to 'participate in genuine, free and democratic elections under the supervision and control of the UN'.[53] He promised that Whites in Namibia 'would not be robbed' when Swapo gained power; its government would not wage war with SA, but would give its support to such organizations as the ANC.

Angola remains a very strong proponent of the initiative to use the UN to negotiate a settlement in Namibia. Like Mozambique and Zambia over Rhodesia (Zimbabwe), Angola has a strong national interest in wanting to see the conflict ended in Namibia and the SA military threat removed from its troubled borders; hence its concession to the UN in agreeing to a demilitarized zone to be established on its territory along the border. The late President Neto was still wary of the UN plan as late as March 1979, when he and Nujomo found themselves in strong disagreement at a meeting of the Front-line Presidents in Luanda with the Presidents of Zambia, Botswana and Mozambique and Vice-President Jumbe of Tanzania. What appears to be an authentic minute of that summit in Luanda was published by Fleur de Villiers in the Johannesburg *Sunday Times* (20 May 1979). Following that meeting, however, Neto showed himself, as did his successor, to be a willing party to the UN initiative on Namibia.

The level of the guerrilla war continued to rise in 1979 and early 1980, but although Swapo was using more sophisticated weapons, its actual combat performance was not significantly greater. Its improved achievement was in hitting at selected targets, e.g. twice plunging Windhoek into darkness in a week in April 1980 by blowing up the pylons carrying electric power from the Ruacana Falls. It also kept up its tactics of killing village headmen loyal to the regime, mine-laying and ambushing SA troops. Casualty figures went up on both sides—SA claimed to have killed 695 guerrillas between April and December 1979, while Swapo claimed to have accounted for over 1,000, but this was an obvious exaggeration. SA admitted 36 of its men had been killed in combat for the first five months of 1980; this compared with totals of 52 for the whole of 1979 and 50 for 1978. The most threatening aspect of the low-intensity guerrilla war was the escalation of the conflict between SA and Angola, the base for Swapo's forces. In October 1979, the SA Air Force attacked deep into Angola, dropping 150 specialists from Puma heli-copters to carry out specific acts of sabotage. (See *ACR* 1979–80 for details of other attacks.) An even more serious attack followed in June 1980 when, according to Angolan claims, 3,000 SADF troops struck across the border and remained on

Angolan soil for several days carrying out operations said to be limited to Swapo military targets. The SA forces met with no serious resistance from the Angolan army or Cuban combatants. During a Security Council meeting called to censure SA, the Angolan ambassador warned that his country would in future call for outside military help if its own forces were unable to repulse the SADF.

Another disturbing element in the Angola–Namibia situation was the undiminished resistance of Dr Jonas Savimbi's Unita forces backed by the SADF. Savimbi clearly still commands considerable support among the Ovimbundu people in the south of the country, and receives substantial financial and arms backing from abroad—notably from a consortium of European business and political interests based in France, China, Saudi Arabia, a number of Arab Gulf States, Morocco, Ivory Coast and Senagal. While Savimbi makes no secret of these sources of support, both he and SA deny that there is military co-operation between them any longer. It is difficult to establish the truth of their denials. Although Zaire is faithfully promoting its détente with Angola under its 1980 agreement, it nevertheless allows regular passage of arms and other supplies for Savimbi through its airports.

While the 34-year-old international conflict over Namibia is plainly approaching its climax, it is still impossible to discern any clear direction in the final stages. SA could decide to try for an 'internal settlement' in defiance of international opinion; or it could risk elections under UN auspices; or it may seek to bypass the UN through negotiations with a number of regional states and Swapo. Trapped in his own political strait-jacket at home, Botha has obviously not yet finally decided how to extricate SA from Namibia (see chapter on South Africa in *ACR* 1979–80.

INTERNATIONAL DIMENSIONS OF THE SOUTHERN AFRICA CRISIS
THE WESTERN ROLE IN SOUTHERN AFRICA
The collective Western view of events in Southern Africa was exemplified by a statement of Robert Keeley, US Deputy Assistant Secretary of State for African Affairs. Addressing the World Affairs Council of Oregon on 12 October 1979, he said: 'The signature of violence is written all over the southern region of Africa. If it remains unchecked it will wreak havoc among lives and societies of that region and imperil our interests.' After saying that 'the spirit of peace and negotiations, based on compromise among Blacks and Whites should prevail over the spiral of violence in Southern Africa', he went on to warn that 'apartheid without tears' will not be enough; in the end what will matter are 'the arrangements under which Blacks gain power.'

The Western powers were in substantial agreement over Britain's handling of the Rhodesian problem after the Lusaka Agreement. Despite Margaret Thatcher's repudiation of the previous Anglo–American initiative, President Carter showed no animus towards her; he fought a tough rearguard action against his Congress not to recognize the Muzorewa regime or to lift economic sanctions against Rhodesia. As already discussed, he played a useful role at a critical point in the Lancaster House talks in helping to avoid a breakdown over the land issue. (But despite Carter's promise of substantial aid to independent Zimbabwe—a promise made earlier, in even larger amounts, by Dr Kissinger when he was Secretary of State—the US ended up giving only a paltry $45m to the new Republic over a period of 17 months, criticized by Mugabe as 'disappointing'.[54] His Finance Minister, Enos Nkala, termed it 'peanuts'.)

With Rhodesia out of the way, Western Governments accepted that unless the impasse could be broken over Namibia, they would be faced with an almost irresistible demand for sanctions against SA at the Security Council. The Thatcher

Administration is instinctively strongly opposed to the idea; but it is also opposed for solid economic reasons. And even if Carter were to survive the Presidential elections, it seems doubtful whether, after his mauling at the hands of Congress over the retention of Rhodesian sanctions, he would be keen to support sanctions against the much tougher proposition in SA. Nor are the West Germans likely to support sanctions although, for their own idiosyncratic reasons, the French might well do so. The need to avoid facing this issue of sanctions acts as a strong spur to the Western Governments to persuade Pretoria to yield to a UN-type settlement. If these moves should succeed, Namibia might well produce a 'second miracle' after Zimbabwe; but if they fail, the West could be brought face to face with the moment it has sought to postpone for so long as possible: a direct confrontation with SA.

Asked what he thought the right Western policy should be towards SA, President Julius Nyerere replied:

> The South Africans will have to be confronted with a tough international community, including the West. The South Africans then decide: 'Do we confront the world because of Namibia . . . or because of South Africa? Namibia is a colony like any other, so let Namibia go . . .' But when the West decide to be nice to the South Africans, they . . . decide to get tough. They are not fools. They have problems of their own. Their real commitment is to SA. There is a limit to which you go out and dig into areas which are not really your priority.[55]

The new phase of East–West confrontation following events in Iran and Afghanistan,[56] sharpened the debate in the West about the extent to which African policy ought to reflect concern over Soviet behaviour. Although the debate was by no means confined to Americans, two of their diplomats most clearly reflected the differences of approach in Western circles. Joseph J. Sisco, former Assistant Secretary of State and now President of the American University in Washington, told a Congressional hearing on 16 October 1979 that while the US should continue to place the emphasis in US–African relations on recognizing African national aspirations and on aiding their economic development, it should not shy away from using the military option in the face of a growing Soviet and Cuban presence in Africa. 'African States seeking military support from one side or the other is not new,' he said. 'What is new is the current asymmetry in the willingness of Western and Communist powers to respond to African requests.' Opposing this view, the US ambassador at the UN, Don McHenry, said in a speech in Detroit on 13 December:

> It would be naïve to imply that the involvement of the Soviet Union and some of its allies as suppliers of arms and troops to selected revolutionary movements and governments has not affected our view of Africa. So has Africa's proximity to the Middle East. In the end, however, America's African policy cannot be based on the fallacy that Africa's importance stems from its position of West–East issues. Neither can it be based on a desire to protect the existence of resources, or to acquire lucrative markets for American goods. Instead, the US should base its relations with Africa on our desire to promote and facilitate the same opportunity for African nations that our country was given two centuries ago—the chance to develop themselves politically, economically and socially, and to do so without outside interference.

Consideration of the Soviet factor in the context of developments over Namibia and SA will undoubtedly be an important determinant in shaping Western policies. In the end it is likely that the differences between the Sisco and the McHenry views are likely not to be as great as their proponents make them out to be.

THE SOVIET AND CUBAN ROLE

In an analysis of likely developments in 1979, the distinguished Soviet Africanist, Prof Anatoly Gromyko, forecast that the West would continue to come forward with numerous initiatives for the 'settlement' of the problems of Southern Africa; but he warned:

This imitation of 'arbitration' must not give rise to feelings of complacency on the part of Africans. Experience over the past few years has graphically shown that the words and deeds of Western politicians too often diverge. Why multiply diplomatic initiatives if the essence of the question is perfectly clear? What Africans are striving for is the eradication of racism. Now that the forces of the national liberation movement in Africa and the Front-line State have dependable allies—the Soviet Union and the world's socialist community as a whole—now that they are aided politically by the most dynamic of African states, the Western strategies and tactics with regard to Southern Africa must take account of this. They become a little more flexible from time to time. But this is a limited 'flexibility', for it is confined within a rigid racist and imperialist strait-jacket. [57]

Not too rigid, though, as it transpired, to prevent agreement at Lancaster House—an agreement made possible only with the help of the Front-line States who, on this occasion, appear to have acted as 'less reliable allies' than the Soviet Union clearly expected of them.

Soviet policies on Rhodesia went completely awry in the final chapter of the independence struggle. The Russians ended up by having backed the wrong horse—Joshua Nkomo's Zapu. They were chagrined—but should they also have been surprised?—to find that the leader and movement backed by China, Robert Mugabe and Zanu, emerge as the decisive victors. But the Russians also completely misread the outcome of the Lancaster House conference. 'The conference,' Valeriy Belyanskiy wrote, 'was doomed even before it began.' [58] This was a constant theme of Soviet comment on the conference—until the day of its success. It seemed difficult for the Russians (and perhaps not only for them) to imagine that the PF could negotiate successfully with the British Government, let alone with the Salisbury regime. Soviet bloc commentators found it no less difficult to believe that the PF would be allowed to participate in free elections, or that they would be allowed to win. When they did, Brezhnev at once cabled his congratulations to Comrades Mugabe and Nkomo. [59] With the 'most dynamic political force in Zimbabwe in control,' Petko Bocharov wrote, 'real preconditions are taking shape for setting up a community of States in the Southern part of the continent (from the Indian Ocean to the Atlantic) which is similar in social structure and political orientation. The presence of such a belt of independent African states (Zimbabwe and Namibia in this number) will be qualitative and quantitative change in the *status quo* south of the Sahara—something which will inevitably force the reactionaries currently ruling in the Republic of South Africa to give up apartheid.' But, he added, such a prospect was not to the liking of SA or to the 'political and military strategists in the Western capitals'; while they would at first seek to embrace Mugabe, it is not a relationship that can be expected to last.

Meanwhile, though, the Soviet Union and East Germany found their energetic efforts to establish diplomatic ties with the new regime before independence day rebuffed by Mugabe. When their diplomats tried to see him during a brief visit to Lusaka, he explained he was too busy. Nor did Samora Machel prove any more willing to assist their efforts when he was approached to persuade Mugabe to relent. Mugabe naturally did relent, but only after the independence celebrations.

Nevertheless, it is possible that Moscow lost only a battle in Zimbabwe but not the war: if Western policies fail to succeed in 'mediating' the problems still remaining in Namibia and SA itself, the setback received by Moscow in Zimbabwe could easily be retrieved.

The Cubans played only a minor role in Southern Africa in 1979 and, indeed appear to have reduced their active military role throughout the continent. They did not play a combatant role in support of the Angolan forces against the SADF incursions; nor did they play a conspicuous fighting role against Unita. However, despite Fidel Castro's problems at home, there are no reasons for supposing that Cuba might be recasting its role in Africa.

CHINA'S ROLE

If Mugabe's victory was disappointing to Moscow, it was hailed as a triumph by the Chinese, who had been Zanu's principal non-African military ally since 1967. Mugabe described himself as 'a Marxist of Maoist thought'. After its recent setbacks in Africa at the expense of the Russians, Beijing saw Zimbabwe as a turning-point. In sharp contrast to Moscow, the Chinese saw the Zimbabwe election success as 'due to the common efforts of the three participants at the London meeting— Britain, Rhodesia and the PF—and the African Front-line countries as well as the Commonwealth supervisory troops'.[60] Characteristically, Beijing declared: 'That Super-power which tried to meddle in the affairs of Zimbabwe is unhappy about the London Agreement and the new Zimbabwe Government . . . That ambitious Super-power has always coveted Zimbabwe and all of Southern Africa which is strategically important and rich in natural resources.'

Although not confirmed by Beijing, Dr Jonas Savimbi claims that he receives Chinese arms for his struggle against the MPLA regime in Luanda. China does not yet appear to have found a suitable ally in SA. Reports that it is helping PAC do not appear to be correct. The ANC, on the other hand, closely hews Moscow's line in its hostile attacks on Beijing.

Moscow kept up a ceaseless campaign suggesting that China not only enjoyed close economic links with SA, but was supplying it with arms and was even establishing diplomatic relations. All these charges were vehemently denied by Beijing. 'It is not China but the Soviet Union that engineered civil wars and splits, and carried out infiltration and expansion in African countries by means of dispatching mercenaries and supplying arms,' Beijing riposted to one *Tass* allegation about its links with Pretoria.[61]

THE FUTURE

Zimbabwe's independence under a PF Government marked the advent of the 'African Revolution' on the banks of the Limpopo, virtually completing the isolation of SA which began with the emergence to independence of Mozambique in 1974 and Angola in 1975. All three of these countries finally achieved their independence through the success of the armed struggle. (Lancaster House had only put the final seal of acceptance to the surrender of the illegal regime in Salisbury.) In Namibia, the armed struggle is already advanced, even if it has not yet got very far. In SA itself, the ANC, especially, has begun to infiltrate armed guerrillas into the thickly populated Black urban areas, and have struck their first symbolic blows at strategic objectives like the Sasol oil-from-coal complex near Vereeniging. Political violence and 'urban terrorism' has become a fact of life for South Africans. That is not to say that the successes achieved by the armed struggle in Angola, Mozambique and Zimbabwe will, or can be, repeated in SA itself. Indeed, the view of President Machel and Prime Minister Mugabe is that the Pretoria regime cannot be brought down through a 'bush war'. Nevertheless, the element of political violence introduced by the armed struggle will undoubtedly have an important impact on developments in SA, as was already foreshadowed by the Soweto youth revolts in 1976 and 1977.

Few still doubt that some form of majority rule is inevitable in Namibia, and at some future date in the apartheid Republic itself. All that still remains in doubt is the course of the final dénouement and the time it will take to complete the transformation of the apartheid system into a fully shared society. To those who are interested in speculating on the 'hows' and 'whens' of this next phase, one question might be put: how many of those close observers of African politics forecast in mid-1979 the possibility of a successful agreement at Lancaster House and the establishment of a Patriotic Front Government in Salisbury in under a year?

NOTES

1. All references to country surveys and essays in this chapter are to the *Africa Contemporary Record, (ACR),* 1979–80.
2. Lord Soames' interview with Kenneth Harris in *The Observer*, London, 6 July 1980.
3. For previous surveys of the Rhodesian situation see *ACR* 1968–69, 1969–70, 1970–71, 1971–72, 1972–73, 1973–74, 1974–75, 1975–76, 1976–77, 1977–78, 1978–79.
4. See *ACR* 1978–79, pp. A116–17.
5. See essay on Britain and Africa.
6. *Ibid.*
7. For an informative account of the crucial role played by the Commonwealth secretary-general, Sonny Ramphal, see David Martin in *The Observer*, 9 December 1979.
8. For full text of Commonwealth Conference communiqué see Documents Section.
9. See *ACR* 1977–78, pp. A3ff.
10. *Ibid*, pp. A22–23.
11. *Financial Times (FT)*, London, 7 August 1977.
12. *Ibid*, 8 August 1979.
13. *Daily Telegraph (DT)*, London, 25 August 1979.
14. *Ibid.*
15. Author's notes of briefings with Lord Carrington.
16. See *ACR* 1977–78, pp. C68ff.
17. *FT*, 10 September 1979.
18. *Ibid.*
19. *The Observer*, 16 September 1979.
20. *FT*, 27 September 1979.
21. See *DT*, 26 September 1979; *FT*, 22 September, *Daily Mail (DM)*, London, 18 September 1979.
22. *The Guardian*, 20 September 1979.
23. *The Observer*, 7 October 1979.
24. *DT*, 8 October 1979.
25. *DM*, 8 October 1979.
26. *The Guardian*, 17 October 1979.
27. *Ibid.*
28. *FT*, 19 October 1979.
29. *The Guardian*, 29 October 1979.
30. *Ibid*, 27 November 1979.
31. *DT*, 23 November 1979.
32. *DT*, 4 December 1979.
33. *Ibid.*
34. *The Guardian*, 5 December 1979.
35. *The Observer*, 9 December 1979.
36. *Southern Rhodesia Elections, February 1980; The report of the Commonwealth Observer Group*, Commonwealth Secretariat, London.
37. Lord Soames' interview with Kenneth Harris, *The Observer*, 6 July 1980.
38. See essay 'Constellation, Association, Liberation: Economic Co-ordination and The Struggle for Southern Africa'; also chapter on South Africa.
39. *The Guardian*, 5 July 1980.
40. *The Observer*, 6 July 1980.
41. For a detailed discussion of this debate see *The Observer*, 20 July 1980.
42. See *ACR* 1977–78, pp. C211–15; 1978–79, pp. A5–8.
43. *Daily Mail*, London, 11 June 1980.
44. *Rand Daily Mail (RDM)*, Johannesburg, 2 May 1980.
45. *Ibid*, 2 April 1980.
46. *The Times*, London, 13 May 1980.
47. *Ibid*, 2 April 1980.
48. *RDM*, 7 May 1980.

49. *Ibid*, 8 April 1980.
50. *The Times*, 2 April 1980.
51. *The Armed Struggle: Our Only Solution for Freedom*, Swapo Publicity and Information Office, undated pamphlet, early 1980.
52. *RDM*, 18 March 1980.
53. Interview with Anne-Marie du Preez of the *Windhoek Advertiser*, quoted in full, *RDM*, 11 April 1980.
54. *The Washington Post*, 2 May 1980.
55. Interview with Jonathan Power, quoted in extenso in *RDM*, 1 and 2 March 1979.
56. See essay on the Horn of Africa.
57. A. Gromyko, Western Diplomacy vs. Southern Africa.
58. Radio Moscow, 17 September 1979.
59. *Ibid*, 5 March 1980.
60. *People's Daily*, Beijing, 6 March 1980.
61. *Ibid*.

1980–1981
THE FAILURE OF DIPLOMACY AND WEAPONS

With Zimbabwe's independence in April 1980, the focus of international attention shifted to Namibia–the last outpost of colonialism in Southern Africa since the Organization of African Unity (OAU) accepts the Republic of South Africa (SA) as being an independent sovereign state.[1] But the chances for an early international settlement in the long-standing dispute over the status of the former mandated territory of South-West-Africa (Namibia) were lost at the UN Conference held in Geneva in January 1981. Instead, the violent conflict between SA and its neighbours–Mozambique, Angola and Zimbabwe–grew sharper, while a greater degree of international involvement was introduced by Mozambique's decision in February 1981 to activate its treaty with the Soviet Union after South African forces had launched an attack on African National Congress (ANC) supporters close to the capital, Maputo. The armed struggle continued in Namibia and spilt over more dangerously into Angola, while the new Republic of Zimbabwe felt itself under threat from the Pretoria régime.

THE DIFFERENT ELEMENTS OF THE SOUTHERN AFRICAN CONFLICT
The situation in Southern Africa is both confused and confusing because of the different levels and dimensions of the conflict, and because it is characterized by both antagonistic and collaborative relationships between the hostile parties.[2] There are at least four important elements in the conflict.
1. *The element of continental and wider international confrontation with the SA regime.* It may seem something of a paradox that while the OAU accepts SA as 'an independent sovereign state', it nevertheless intervenes in its internal affairs by giving its support to the opponenents of apartheid. This approach is, in fact, no different from that of the rest of the world community–except that Sweden is the only Western country which gives direct support to the armed struggle itself. The Lusaka Manifesto clarified this apparent contradiction in international policy:

> On every legal basis its (South Africa's) internal affairs are a matter exclusively for the people of SA. Yet the purpose of law *is* people, and we assert that the actions of the SA Government are such that the rest of the world has a responsibility to take some action in defence of humanity.

2. *The element of conflict between the external SA opposition and the SA political system.* The most important aspect of this element is the armed struggle waged by Swapo's forces against the SA presence in Namibia, and by the African National Congress (ANC), the Pan-Africanist Congress (PAC) and the Black Consciousness African Revolutionary Army against the SA Republic.
3. *The element of conflict between the internal SA opposition and the Pretoria regime.* While common factors link the internal and external conflicts, there are also important differences and, even, conflicting interests among the regime's opponents. For example, prominent leaders of the internal opposition, like Chief Gatsha Buthelezi, do not accept the indispensable need for an armed struggle, either because it is inexpedient to do so, or because of philosophic objections. A

more important difference, though, is the feeling among much of the internal opposition leadership that the main struggle is to be fought on the home front, and that exaggerated importance is attached (especially abroad) to the armed struggle. While they admit to the inextricable links between the internal and external struggles, they are adamant about the central importance of strategies designed to mobilize effective opposition within the country itself. Some of the internal leaders feel that their role is made unnecessarily difficult, and even harmed, by premature, or ill-considered, policies adopted by the external leadership in using the local organizations to enhance the external struggle, instead of using external pressures to strengthen the internal forces. At this stage, there is still a marked lack of coordination of tactics between the internal and external wings of the struggle; this is further complicated by the sharp divisions that exist within each of the wings.

4. *The element of confrontation between SA and its neighbours.* This element has two aspects to it, arising from the roles the neighbours elect, or are forced, to play. One group of neighbours–the so-called BLS 'captive states' (Botswana, Lesotho and Swaziland)–refuse to allow guerrilla forces to operate from, or through, their territories purely for reasons of state-interest involving their economic and security needs; but they readily offer sanctuary for political exiles. However, there are difficulties in controlling all clandestine activities of the external forces, which causes this group of neighbours to exist in a condition of almost permanent tension with SA; this is especially the case with Lesotho and Botswana.

Malawi, on the other hand, refuses to have any truck at all with the external forces, and keeps up its full diplomatic and economic links with SA. It remains the region's maverick.

Zimbabwe resists having guerrilla bases on its territory, but allows them a political presence with a promise of practical support.

Mozambique's stated preference is similar to Zimbabwe's, except that it allows guerrilla cadres to use its space for transit to SA, but not to maintain training or holding camps on its soil. However, after SA's reprisal attacks in February 1981, the Maputo regime indicated a possible modification of its stand to allow greater freedom of action for ANC cadres.

The ANC has its training and base camps in Nachingwea and Morogoro in Tanzania, and a training camp in Angola. Most of its officers and specialists, however, are trained in the Warsaw Pact countries, mainly in East Germany and the USSR, as well as in Ethiopia.

Angola is the base country for Swapo's forces, which lays it open to cross-border attacks by SA's armed forces.

Zambia has ceased to play an active role in the guerrilla struggle since Swapo's forces moved out to Angola in 1976 and Zapu's forces returned home. But the ANC maintains its political headquarters in Lusaka.

Thus, except for Malawi, SA's relations are troubled in varying degrees with all its near neighbours.

CONSTRAINTS ON THE BEHAVIOUR OF SOUTH AFRICA AND ITS NEIGHBOURS
Notwithstanding these troubled relations, important constraints operate to prevent a total break between SA and its neighbours.

The constraints on SA are of two kinds: economic and geopolitical. Trade is important with the Black North; the communication links to Mozambique's ports are valuable, as is the supply of electricity from Cahora Bassa. The need for migrant mine labour, though, has decreased substantially. Pretoria's geopolitical strategy, which seeks to establish an economic association–projected as a 'Constellation of States for Southern Africa'–makes it necessary to maintain existing political links and to extend its economic and communication links. This strategy is seriously harmed by military operations against any of its neighbours. But, since security remains Pretoria's highest priority, military strikes across borders at guerrilla camps, or as a means of discouraging its neighbours from harbouring guerrillas, are regarded as being more important than even the need to create a more peaceful political environment. Therefore, SA's interests and policies are plainly contradictory and appear to be self-defeating. Ultimately, it can hope to establish a friendly community of nations on its borders only if the core problem disturbing their relations are removed: that is, its own racial discriminatory policies. Meanwhile, SA must rely on the economic dependence of its neighbours and on military pressures to persuade them to place their own state-interests above their commitments to assist the liberation movements–at least in respect of the armed struggle.

What are the chances of this happening? The dependence of the BLS group on the SA economic and communications system is inescapable. For the foreseeable future, the economic and communications requirements of Zimbabwe, Mozambique, Zambia and Zaire make collaboration with SA an indispensable element in their national policies; and with the present signs of continuing economic decline in their economic position (except for Zimbabwe), these needs are more likely to increase than to diminish. There appear to be only two ways out of their dilemma: either that fundamental political changes occur within the SA system and so make it possible to lessen their support for the external opposition; or that they can succeed in turning the hopes offered by the Southern African Development Cooperation Conference (SADCC) into practical reality. While neither of these two possibilities can be positively ruled out, the chances of either occurring are, at best, long-term–say, ten years.

But in the crisis situation in Southern Africa, a decade of increasing violence is an alarming prospect. The only glimmer of hope lies in the possibility of achieving an internationally-acceptable settlement in Namibia, which would considerably reduce the tensions between Angola and SA, and so help to reduce the scope of the conflict to the struggle for meaningful change within the Republic itself.

Change is indeed occurring in SA at a rapidly increasing rate; but it is not the kind of change which the Pretoria regime seeks to portray.

THE IMPENDING COLLAPSE OF THE SOUTH AFRICAN POLITICAL SYSTEM
It has taken the ruling power group within Afrikanerdom 33 embittering and frustrating years to learn that their ideology cannot be translated into effective practice. Their dream has faded of creating a multi-national state based on Separate Development, which would offer racial harmony, a secure future for the White minority under Afrikaner dominance, and justice for Blacks. Instead of the promise of greater racial harmony, it is now widely acknowledged that racial bitterness is greater than before; that the threat to White survival has increased; and that Afrikaner survival itself is no longer assured. The Afrikaners' disillusionment with apartheid has been traumatic, threatening to divide them anew and setting old comrades-in-arms at each other's throats.

The apartheid experience has taught the country a number of expensive lessons. The most important of these is that economic integration has gone beyond the possibility of either separating the races physically into viable Black states and a predominantly White state in any part of the country–let alone in the 86% demarcated for exclusive White control; or of creating parallel White and Black economies.

The apartheid era is now approaching its end. In historical terms, apartheid will be seen to have been the watershed between a White-ruled South Africa and a majority-ruled South Africa. The Republic has now entered upon a dangerous period of transition from the old order to the new. The White minority has not yet lost its *will* to rule, but it has begun to lose *confidence* in its ability to retain exclusive political control. Afrikaners, who remain the dominant political element, have no clearly thought-out strategy for what should take the place of the god that failed them: apartheid. They are engaged in a strategy for maintaining control and for White survival, while trying to formulate their ideas about how to achieve the latter objective. The Afrikaner electorate remains the rock core of resistance to meaningful change, and no Afrikaner leader is powerful enough to push through a policy of bold reforms in the teeth of this opposition. Although the present government leadership is potentially capable of influencing White opinion, it remains under severe constraints when it comes to implementing even limited reforms involving the dismantling of the apartheid system.

While the White ruling groups have been pushed on to the defensive, the Black majority now feels confident that the tide has already begun to swing in its favour. Although Black political organizations are far from being united, no disagreement exists over objectives as between moderates, radicals and revolutionaries; only their tactics are different.

The choices facing SA are reform or revolution, with the time factor now crucially important in determining which of the two alternative routes the Republic will take in the post-apartheid era.

One analysis of the present situation rests on the principal assumption that Afrikaners cannot under any circumstances be moved away from their inflexible opposition to fundamental constitutional changes, leads to the conclusion that revolutionary change is unavoidable. A different analysis, taking a more dynamic view of the interaction between growing Black pressures and the limits of White powers of control, as well as of the impact of sharpening internal contradictions, suggests that a constitutional settlement still remains a possibility–even if, as seems likely, the transition period will be marked by increasing repression and considerable violence. The White society does not see repression as either desirable or as an effective way of safeguarding its future; nor do the Black challengers regard violence from their side as desirable but, rather, as a necessary, though minor, element in their struggle. These two trends should be interpreted as inevitable elements in the process of drastic change now occurring in SA.

NAMIBIA: THE ROAD TO, AND FROM, GENEVA
ASPECTS OF COLLABORATIVE BEHAVIOUR

That relations between SA and its neighbours can, on occasion, transcend hostility and, instead, become collaborative is shown by the readiness of Angola's MPLA regime to engage in direct negotiations and, even, to hold face-to-face talks in order to achieve a formula which made it possible for the UN to convene a conference on Namibia in Geneva in January 1981. The Angolan involvement in this diplomatic exercise was very largely a state-interest just as it was in the case of its Marxist ally, Mozambique, which made a crucially important contribution to the success of the Lancaster House conference on Rhodesia as well as to the subsequent peaceful transition to Zimbabwe's independence. Both Angola and Mozambique, while holding to their principled stand of support for the liberation struggles, have at the same time been concerned with their own economic and security needs. For Mozambique, an independent and prospering Zimbabwe offered substantial hope for its own economic development; the removal of an acute security threat; and a lessening of dependence on SA. For Angola, the independence of Namibia would remove SA's military threat; lessen the need for Cuban combat troops on its soil; substantially improve its chances of overcoming the unsettling challenge by Unita; and open up new opportunities for its economic development.

Angola played the leading role among the Front-line African States (the others being Botswana, Mozambique, Tanzania, Zambia and, later, Zimbabwe) in working for a settlement of the Namibia conflict within the UN framework. It showed a readiness to cooperate with the Western 'Contact Group' (UK, US, France, Canada and West Germany), notwithstanding America's refusal to establish diplomatic relations with Luanda. Angola's first major contribution, made while President Agostinho Neto was still alive, was to propose the plan for a Demilitarized Zone (DMZ) to meet SA's security objections.[3] The MPLA regime also used its considerable influence with Swapo to get its reluctant president-general, Sam Nujoma, to accept the UN principles for a settlement; in fact, its strong influence at times amounted to pressure. Finally, when the last obstacle to a UN-sponsored conference was the issue of admitting the Namibian internal parties, an acceptable formula was worked out between Angola and SA. These negotiations began through an exchange of diplomatic notes, transacted through an undisclosed third party, and were completed at several meetings between Angolan and SA officials, held in total secrecy in the Cape Verde islands.[4] Even after the Geneva talks had failed, Angola was opposed to any immediate move to apply sanctions against SA (see below).

THE LAST ROUND OF THE UN NEGOTIATIONS (January-November 1980)

By the beginning of 1980 the differences between Swapo and SA over the details of the UN Plan (which was adopted under Resolution 435 of the Security Council in 1978[5]) had narrowed to the point where it became realistic to think of Namibia's independence by the end of 1981. By then, the controversy over Namibia would have been a regular feature on the UN agenda for 35 years–ever since the Rev Michael Scott, director of the Africa Bureau, first brought the issue to the attention of the world community through a petition from the then Herero Chief, Hosea Kutako, in opposition to Gen J.C. Smuts' proposal to incorporate the territory into the then Union of South Africa.[6]

When UN under-secretary-general Brian Urquhart visited SA, Namibia and the capitals of the Front-line States in March 1980, all that still remained to be settled were some details over the proposed Demilitarized Zone (DMZ) on either side of the border between Angola and Namibia; the size and role of the proposed UN Peacekeeping Force; details about maintaining a ceasefire; and arrangements for the proposed seven-month transition period between the arrival of the UN Transition Assistance Group (UNTAG) and the holding of elections under its supervision. (The elections themselves are to be conducted by the Namibian administration.)

Urquhart's visit helped to clarify these points sufficiently for the Security Council to fix 15 June 1980 as the deadline for SA and Swapo to accept the UN Plan. However, on 12 May, SA's Foreign Minister, 'Pik' Botha, presented a new Note making some concessions and seeking new assurances. He reduced Pretoria's original demand for 40 SA military bases during the transition period to

20–as against the seven proposed by the UN. He asked for a larger number than the 7,500 proposed for the UN Peacekeeping Force. He wanted acceptable arrangements for disarming those Swapo guerrillas inside Namibia, once the ceasefire became effective, and rejected Swapo's demand to have its own bases in the territory during the transition. He also introduced a new issue: the need to get Unita's cooperation in making the DMZ effective since, he argued, their forces were present in the affected area. Finally–and this was to become another major hurdle—he sought guarantees about the neutrality of the UN in view of its recognition of Swapo as 'the sole and authentic representative of the Namibian people', and because the designated leader of UNTAG, Mathi Athisaari, was also the UN Commissioner for the Council of Namibia. The Foreign Minister added that subject to 'positive responses' to these points of 'clarification' he saw no 'insurmountable problems' to implementing the UN Plan.

Swapo predictably rejected all SA's proposals, describing them as 'intrigues to exterminate' their Organization. It continued to stand by the original UN proposals as established by the Security Council's Resolution 435.

Between April and November 1980, SA took a number of decisions which could be interpreted either as preparing for an Internal Settlement in Namibia (rather as Smith had attempted through his unsuccessful deal with Bishop Muzorewa in Rhodesia), or as a way of facilitating Namibia's divorce from SA during the final stages of the negotiations with the UN.[7] In April 1980, the then Administrator-General of Namibia, Dr Gerrit Viljoen, announced that he favoured more direct negotiations with Angola, rather than to continue the talks with the UN.[8] This new tack illustrates the continuing failure of the Pretoria regime to understand the nature of the commitment of the members of the Front-line States to securing agreement on Namibia within the UN framework. The error appears to have arisen from over-optimistic hopes based on their informal diplomatic exchanges with Angola and Zambia. While the leadership of those countries expressed a very strong interest in achieving a Namibia settlement and displayed a willingness to do all they could to help achieve it, they were not–contrary to Dr Viljoen's assumptions–remotely in favour of supplanting the UN's role in Namibia.

In May 1980, SA decided to hand over control of Namibia's security forces to the territory's National Assembly, thus removing Pretoria from direct responsibility for defence–at least notionally. At the same time, SA's Prime Minister announced that 'a body must come into being in SWA which can govern the country, even if it is not independent.'[9] But he added that he still favoured an international settlement if that were possible.

The UN's 15 June deadline passed by without any substantial further progress in the negotiations. Instead, in August, SA's Foreign Minister again wrote to the UN secretary-general, this time announcing that SA's acceptance of the DMZ was based on the assumption that UN conditions applying to bases in the DMZ applied equally to all; that Angola and Zambia accepted responsibility for policing the ceasefire on their sides of the border; that practical arrangements would be made to deploy the UN force and UNTAG throughout the DMZ, i.e. that they would also operate in Angola and Zambia.

Botha's 'assumptions' about the DMZ introduced a new element which had not come up during Urquhart's January visit, and were not raised in his March letter to Waldheim. At the same time, Botha strengthened his challenge to the UN's claims to impartiality, accusing it of being 'the most ardent protagonist of Swapo, which is one of several parties contending for power.'[10]

Pretoria's now familiar technique of discovering new issues as soon as previous ones were met and settled, finally exhausted the patience of the UN, the Western

'Contact Group' and the Front-line States in October 1980. The Security Council committed itself to a meeting in December to reach finalty: either SA accepted the UN Plan, or the Council would decide its future course of action, i.e. to consider imposing sanctions.

Brian Urquhart, accompanied by Athissari, once again returned to SA at the end of October to obtain an unconditional commitment from the Botha regime to agree to implement Resolution 435. By then, SA was already well launched on the programme that had been foreshadowed by the Prime Minister's May speech, with elections under way in Namibia in which each of the ethnic groups were to elect members to the new self-governing National Assembly. Pretoria's hope was that the Democratic Turnhalle Alliance (DTA) would win convincingly, and that Dirk Mudge would win a majority of the White votes. By defeating his *verkrampte* opponents, he could claim the right to speak for all White Namibians and so make it easier for the SA Prime Minister to make any necessary concessions to the UN without serious opposition from his own *verkramptes*.[11] Such a result would, it was thought, help the Botha regime in two ways: it would elevate the DTA into a central role in future negotiations with the UN and the 'Contact Group'; and it would shift responsibility for whatever happened in Namibia off Botha's shoulders to Mudge's. But, as will presently be described, a somewhat different situation was created by these tactics.

The Urquhart–Athisaari talks in Pretoria were tough but, unexpectedly, resulted in substantial agreement being reached. A one-page *aide memoire* was delivered at the end of the visit in which SA reaffirmed its acceptance of Resolution 435, and agreed to a timetable leading to Namibia's independence by the end of 1981. They also accepted the idea of a UN-sponsored Pre-Implementation Conference to settle the details of translating Resolution 435 into practice. The biggest obstacle during this last round of talks was a belated attempt by SA to have the question of Namibia's independence Constitution put on the agenda of the conference–a proposal diametrically contrary to the provisions of Resolution 435, which leave the Constitution to be decided by Namibians after their elections. A compromise was reached that left it open to parties attending the conference to raise any subject they wished, but with no right to insist on decisions being taken outside the framework of Resolution 435.

From October on, the DTA began to play a much more independent role in putting forward its claims to being treated as an equal partner with Swapo by the UN and in other matters. A seven-page memorandum from the DTA to Brian Urquhart on 22 October concluded:

It has now become clear that partiality in favour of Swapo has critically jeopardized the prospect of continuing successfully with the settlement plan on the basis of Resolution 435. . . . Impartiality must be demonstrated before any election process can start because the psychological effect of an arbiter or supervisor which has already recognized Swapo as the 'sole and authentic representative of the people of Namibia' will, without any doubt, influence the outcome of the election.

The DTA added that unless steps were immediately taken to restore confidence, it was willing to 'examine other possibilities in the interests of a peaceful solution'. It concluded: 'Given reasonableness on all sides, independence for Namibia by the end of 1981 should become a feasible proposition.'

Nevertheless, acting on Urquhart's report after his October visit and encouraged by a formula worked out between SA and Angola for the composition of an international conference (see above), Dr Waldheim proposed on 5 November that a date be set for the ceasefire and the implementation of Resolution 435 for early

1981; and that a pre-implementation multi-party conference should be held from 7 to 14 January 1981 under UN auspices, 'in which the parties concerned in the projected UN-supervised elections should be included.'

THE DEMOCRATIC TURNHALLE ALLIANCE BECOMES A NEW FACTOR

Just as Angola had to coax its reluctant protégé, Swapo, to accept its endorsement at various stages in the negotiations over the UN Plan, so SA found itself having to deal with an increasingly awkward protégé. For although the DTA was created as the instrument for Pretoria's initial intention of unilaterally declaring Namibia independent, its apprentice soon acquired its own interests as it grew stronger and grew suspicious of the Pretoria regime's possible willingness to 'sell-out' for the sake of its own state-interest on terms held to be unacceptable to DTA.

It is undoubtedly a mistake to go on treating the DTA as being nothing more than Pretoria's stooge, or to dismiss its claims to having significant Black and White support among Namibians. It is one thing to claim that Swapo enjoys majority support, and quite another to dismiss the DTA as being totally irrelevant. The Black supporters of DTA represent strong minority group interests which, quite genuinely, fear what they regard as 'Ovambo domination', and the 'radicalism' of Swapo. White Namibians, too, have their reasonable interests to protect.

Therefore, UN recognition of Swapo as the 'sole authentic representative of the peoples of Namibia' was bound to become an important issue. Swapo had acquired its special status as part of the international campaign to develop pressures against SA at a time when the Republic was completely opposed to granting any proper role to the UN in deciding Namibia's independence, and when the DTA was still, in every sense, little more than Pretoria's creature. But with the approach of independence a new situation developed. After the November elections to Namibia's National Assembly and the formation of the new Council of Ministers, the DTA began to demand that it should speak in its own right, and that it should no longer be represented by Pretoria.[12] It knew that it did not stand an earthly chance of winning free elections against Swapo so long as it had the Pretoria label hung round its neck.[13] The DTA threatened that it would not attend the Geneva talks unless it could do so independently from SA. Its adamant stand created difficulties for the Pretoria regime, which had already agreed the terms for representation at the Pre-Implementation Conference with Angola. It took considerable persuasion on Prime Minister Botha's part to persuade Mudge to agree to go to Geneva at all.[14] Nor was the DTA in agreement with Pretoria's acceptance of the UN Plan to allow for a seven-month period between a ceasefire and the holding of elections; it felt it needed more time than that to get rid of its image as a proxy for Pretoria.

Thus, the issues that came to dominate and, in the end, to cause the failure of the Geneva talks were the impartiality of the UN, which was linked to its exclusive recognition of Swapo; the DTA's unhappiness at having to take its place under the SA flag; and the period to be allowed for implementing the UN Plan. The actual details of the Plan itself were no longer controversial.

Under the Angolan–SA formula, Namibia's internal parties were to be invited to attend as part of the SA delegation which was to be led, not by the SA Foreign Minister, but by the SA-appointed Administrator-General of Namibia, Danie Hough. (In fact, the Pretoria regime tried to renege on this agreement at Geneva by seeking to have its official delegation take its place among the observers at the conference.)

THE GENEVA CONFERENCE (7–14 January 1981)

The Pre-Implementation Conference was opened by Dr Waldheim but the chair was taken by Brian Urquhart. The actual negotiating partners were Swapo and SA, whose official delegation was led by the Administrator-General, Danie Hough, but also included Foreign Affairs Department senior officials and military leaders, as well as the DTA and a number of smaller parties–the Liberation Front, Namibia Christian Democratic Party, Liberal Party of Namibia, NUDO Progressive Party of Namibia, Namibia People's Liberation Front and Federal Party of Namibia.[15] (Other Namibian internal parties refused to attend because they were unwilling to be seated as part of a SA delegation.) A number of officially-accredited observers were also present: the OAU, the six Front-line States and Nigeria; and the five Western members of the 'Contact Group'. Although Hough played the formal role of leader, the DTA in fact dominated the discussions on the SA side: thus formally establishing the role it had sought for itself as a recognized partner in the negotiating process; but not yet accepted by Swapo or the UN as independent from its SA connection.

Brian Urquhart tried to meet the point of exclusive recognition by saying that once agreement was reached on a ceasefire, 'a number of things will change'; but he made it clear that it was impossible for any UN official to go further at that stage since it was not possible for any official to overturn a UN General Assembly resolution. However, Sam Nujoma said at a press conference that Swapo would surrender its entitlement to exclusive recognition by the UN once agreement was reached on the ceasefire and implementation.[16]

Swapo had an obvious interest in not wanting to lose the advantage of its exclusive recognition and in wishing to portray the DTA as being simply Pretoria's stooge. Nor was it willing to see any extension of the transition period. On this latter point, Swapo had the support of the Front-line States, and especially Angola, which had a strong interest in achieving a settlement as quickly as possible.

Although the Geneva conference failed in the end to achieve a settlement, it nevertheless made progress in a number of ways. First, it showed that none of the parties to the conflict any longer quarrelled seriously over the final details of the UN Plan. Second, it achieved a breakthrough by getting the DTA recognized as a negotiating party in its own right, notwithstanding Swapo's continued repudiation of any such role being granted to it. Third, it produced a formula (accepted by Swapo, though not by DTA) whereby Swapo would lose its exclusive UN recognition at the moment UNTAG was established. (The DTA insisted on the removal of exclusive recognition as a precondition for signing the agreement; but this can be viewed as a tactical position.)

Swapo emerged from the Geneva talks with an enhanced reputation because of its apparent confidence; by its firm stand on Resolution 435; by only protesting and not walking out over the seating of the DTA; and by cooperating so fully with its African patrons. Thus, Swapo's leaders impressed everybody (and possibly upset SA) by their conciliatory role. The decision of the OAU to include the SA delegation (as well as the DTA members) in a reception (paid for by Nigeria) showed both maturity and generosity: it was the first time that SA was not ostracized by the OAU.

On the other hand, the DTA at last opened the door to winning international recognition, even though still forced to sail under SA colours; but few could any longer doubt that, whatever SA might decide in the future, the DTA could no longer be ignored as a serious factor in the negotiating process.

Angola's Foreign Minister, Paolo Jorge, said he did not consider the collapse of the Geneva talks as 'a final breakdown', and proposed new steps to renew the dialogue between Swapo and SA within the UN framework.[17]

All in all, therefore, the search for a final settlement was moved to higher ground by the Geneva talks. Nonetheless, neither the OAU nor Swapo–or even the Western powers–were in the least inclined to reduce the pressure on SA to complete the final act. The British Government said that it regretted the setback[18] and took a new initiative with the incoming Reagan Administration to ensure continuity of the 'Contact Group's' solidarity.

Four hurdles still remain to be crossed in the next lap of the Namibian marathon. First, the likely role of the Reagan Administration, which remains unclear at the time of writing in March 1981 (see below). Second, the future role of the DTA. After the Geneva talks, Dirk Mudge suggested that a time-span of one or two years would be needed between the ceasefire and genuinely free elections, rather than the seven months previously agreed with Pretoria.[19] He also wrote directly to President Reagan asking for a personal interview to explain his objections to the UN Plan. Third, the domestic political situation in SA, with the Botha regime still under constraint from its own Right-wing and from the DTA. Finally, the future relations between Luanda and Pretoria which, having developed promisingly, have become soured by heavier SA military attacks across the border.

At the opening of the General Assembly in March 1981, the OAU secured a 112 to 22 majority (with six abstentions) to exclude the SA delegation from the UN General Assembly. While this step was deplored by the Western nations and angered Pretoria, it served the OAU's purpose of maintaining pressure on SA. This pressure was extended when, on 6 March, the Assembly voted by 125 in favour to none against, with 13 abstentions, for a resolution proposing that the Security Council should adopt comprehensive sanctions against SA to compel it to end its illegal occupation of Namibia. It decided that if the Council were unable to adopt concrete measures, the Assembly itself would consider follow-up action. In a further resolution approved by a vote of 114 in favour to none against, with 22 abstentions, the Assembly condemned SA for manoeuvres aimed at transferring power to 'illegitimate groups subservient to its interest', and supported the Namibian people's armed struggle for freedom under the leadership of Swapo as their 'sole and authentic representative'.

The abstaining votes were cast mainly by Western States–among them Canada, France, West Germany, UK and US. Speaking on behalf of 'the Five', Jeanne Kirkpatrick (US) said that their collective abstention did not reflect any judgement on the merits of the drafts; that the Five remained committed to securing a peaceful, internationally recognized settlement in Namibia; but that few of the resolutions contributed to that. In a resolution on Namibian uranium, approved by a vote of 108 in favour to none against, with 26 abstentions, the Assembly strongly condemned France, West Germany, Israel and the US for 'collusion with SA in the nuclear field.'

In a letter to the secretary-general, SA's Foreign Minister said that the imposition of sanctions against his country would be 'an unmitigated disaster' for Southern Africa as a whole. Because the economies of a number of African countries were closely interlinked with SA, it was they who would be the foremost to suffer. He also said it was not possible to obtain the desired solution for Namibia if the internal parties were excluded from the decision-making process, and if the UN continued to favour one political movement.

SOUTH AFRICA'S STAND ON NAMIBIA

There remains still the vital question of whether SA seriously intends to reach a settlement in Namibia so long as it fears that an internationally-supervised election could result in a Swapo victory. Pretoria is much less sure than it used to be about the extent of Swapo's popular support. If Prime Minister Botha could be confident about a DTA victory, there is little doubt that he would not hesitate for a moment in putting his signature to a UN agreement. Apart from his own conceived ideas about 'a communist takeover' if Swapo should win, his more realistic concern must be over the danger of a Right-wing backlash among his own supporters should Swapo take over Namibia; thus domestic political constraints must weigh heavily on Botha. There is also the further constraint coming from DTA: it can rely on Botha's opponents for support in resisting any moves which might be necessary for SA's state-interest, but which would be felt to be harmful to the interests of the groups it represents. This DTA constraint on the Botha regime should not be underestimated.

It is unwise for anybody to pretend to know what the outcome of free elections would be after seven months of campaigning. On the face of it, Swapo begins with a built-in advantage as the leader of the liberation forces. But there are questions which cannot be answered; for example, will Swapo's unity (maintained only with difficulty under the advantageous conditions of the active struggle) hold up at the hustings? Would the Ovambo traditionalist leadership prove incapable of holding their support without SA's military protection? (Elsewhere in Africa the traditionalist leaders have invariably lost their dominant position once the colonial presence has been removed.) Can the DTA stitch together sufficient support among the minority groups and dissident Ovambos to win a majority? There is no possible psephological guide to the outcome of elections in Namibia; this perhaps is a positive feature of the situation since both sides must believe they are in a position to win if they are to accept the UN Plan.

Finally, there is the crucial SA military factor. How do its army chiefs feel about abandoning their front-line with Angola on the Cunene river? The military hierarchy is divided between those who feel that the 'defence in depth' offered by Namibia is strategically valuable, and those who believe it is more advantageous to shorten the military lines by concentrating defence on SA's Orange river border. It is hardly a secret that the present SA Chief of Staff and former military commander in Namibia, Gen Geldenhuys, favours the second approach.

THE INTERESTS OF OUTSIDE POWERS

The Western Powers and the Front-line States share an interest in wanting to see an internationally-acceptable settlement in Namibia. The African interest has already been described. The Western interest is dictated by a number of factors: they would like to see the Cuban combat forces leave Angola, which is likely to occur only after a Namibian settlement; as a corollary they wish to remove any opportunity for the Soviet bloc to exploit the growth of violence and instability in the region; they want to see a de-escalation of the violent challenge to SA in order, as they believe, to create a better environment to produce change in the Republic; they want to remove the risk of having to impose sanctions against SA or, alternatively, to incur African (especially Nigerian) reprisals if they don't; and they have an economic interest in Namibia's mineral resources, especially uranium. Finally, more benignly, they are concerned with helping to promote stability in Africa.

The Soviet bloc interest in Namibia does not appear to be great. They don't seem to have much of an appetite for becoming too deeply involved in a serious military confrontation with SA; but, in any case, their role is heavily constrained by the wishes of their Angolan ally: like it or not, they must go along with what the

MPLA regime proposes. Soviet media criticism of the Geneva conference was muted, concentrating mainly on warning Africans of the 'imperialist manoeuvres' of the West.

THE ANGOLA–SOUTH AFRICAN BORDER

As we have seen, so long as the MPLA regime was able to take a hopeful view about the chances of achieving a Namibian settlement, it showed itself ready to play a role as mediator between SA and Swapo; but if the prospects of a negotiated settlement were to recede, Luanda can be expected to revert to its earlier hardline stand–more especially if the suspicion grew that the US and SA were cooperating in supporting Savimbi's Unita forces. Then, instead of seeking to diminish its dependence on Cuban and Soviet bloc military support, Luanda can reasonably be expected to invite even greater support from their strategic allies.

The Pretoria regime takes the view that it is precisely because of its military pressures on Angola that the MPLA was persuaded to adopt a more conciliatory attitude; but in this, they could be just as mistaken as they have consistently shown themselves to be in interpreting African opinion, e.g. the exaggerated hopes they placed in staging a dialogue with Black Africa[20]; their hopes to dislodge President Kaunda of Zambia from his alliance with the Front-line States; their belief that Bishop Muzorewa could become a viable alternative to the Patriotic Front in Zimbabwe; and their confidence that Mozambique's economic dependence on SA would lead President Machel to abandon his support for the ANC.

While it is unquestionably true that the heavy military pressures on Angola's southern border and the continuing state of insecurity caused by Unita's activities were two important reasons for Luanda's willingness to cooperate with Pretoria in finding an acceptable settlement in Namibia, it would be a mistake to equate that limited flexibility in the MPLA's position with a capitulation policy involving abandonment of support for Resolution 435.

MILITARY OPERATIONS IN ANGOLA

A Defence Ministry report to the MPLA's congress in December 1980 claimed that 'SA aggression' over the previous three years had resulted in 1,800 fatal casualties and 3,000 wounded, and had caused $7m worth of damage.[21] During 1978–80, 1,800 reconnaissance flights by SA air force planes had been carried out over Angola, 11 fighter-bombers and 12 helicopters were shot down. 'Great but undetermined' casualties were claimed to have been inflicted on SA attacking forces.

According to Luanda, SA forces violated the Angolan frontier 529 times in the first six months of 1980. Of these violations, 476 were said to be reconnaissance flights, 27 aerial bombardments, seven strafing attacks, four raids by paratroopers, and two artillery bombardments.[22] In the third quarter of 1980, SA allegedly carried out a further 175 reconnaissance flights, five minelaying operations on roads, 22 aerial bombardments, seven artillery bombardments, 23 helicopter-borne assaults and four kidnappings.

In February 1980, SA troops were reported to have penetrated up to 25 km into Cunene province and to have bombarded Dirico and Cuangar in Cuando-Cubango. From 1 to 6 March SA troops penetrated up to 20 km into Cunene again, mining roads between Naulila, Roçadas and Kuamato.[23] There were then two important SA raids in May–an attack by helicopter-borne troops on 12 May against the village of Chiede, 25 km from the Namibian border, in which, according to the Angolan authorities, 60 civilians were killed; and on 21 May an attack on Savate, in which the Angolan Government said that over 200 Angolan civilians and soldiers were killed.

The largest series of raids conducted by the SA army since its withdrawal from Angola at the end of the 1975–76 civil war began on 8 June. Over the following three and a half weeks c. 2,000 SA troops invaded the provinces of Cunene and Cuando-Cubango. The invasion was foreshadowed on 7 June by an air strike against the main Namibian camp near Lubango during which, according to the Luanda authorities, three SA Mirage jets were shot down.[24] On 8 June, five SA battalions reportedly moved into Cunene. Five days later, the SA Prime Minister announced that 16 SA soldiers had been killed (the highest number of SA casualties ever admitted by Pretoria during the border war). Botha claimed that the raid was on a Swapo base and that more than 100 tons of military equipment had been seized; but the Angolan Ministry of Defence insisted that towns and villages had been attacked. Moreover, instead of withdrawing their forces, the South Africans sent even more troops into Angola later in the month, this time into Cuando-Cubango as well. The Angolan Defence Ministry reported that SA sent an additional infantry brigade, a tank battalion and two long-range artillery groups into the province on 24 June. On 25 June, it claimed that SA forces had massacred the population of the village of Catomba. The same day, Luanda claimed that SA troops, backed by AML-90 armoured cars, massed to the north of Kuamato and Naulila, both in Cunene. However, the FAPLA claimed to have recaptured Mongua, another small town in Cunene which had been seized by the South Africans on 28 June. Four Mirage jets were said to have strafed and bombed FAPLA reinforcements moving towards Mongua on 29 June, when 19 FAPLA soldiers were killed in the town itself fending off a SA attempt to recapture it. The same day, SA troops were also reported to have advanced to within 22 km of Ngiva, the capital of Cunene, while in Cuando-Cubango nine Angolan militiamen from Organization of Popular Defence (ODP) were said to have been killed when SA forces attacked the small town of M'Pupa. By the end of the month, it was estimated that there were still c. 2,000 SA troops in the country, backed up by three squadrons of Mirages, 20 Puma helicopters and, for parachute assaults, C-130 Hercules transports. The SA forces were thought to have c. 40 AML-90 armoured cars and 32 field guns. The attack finally ended in the first week of July, when Angolan troops claimed to have reoccupied several villages and small towns which had been seized by the South Africans, including Evale, Chiede, Kuamato and Mulamba. All told, 600 had died, most of them civilians, according to Luanda. The commander of the 50,000 SA troops in Namibia, said that 360 Swapo guerrillas had been killed.

The Security Council censured SA on 29 June and ordered the immediate evacuation of its troops. SA replied that it was not engaged in aggression, but was concerned with border problems created by Swapo.[25] However, on 1 July Pretoria announced that all its forces had been withdrawn; this was disputed by Luanda. Its UN ambassador, Elisio de Figueirido, warned that Angola would call for outside military assistance if they were needed to repulse the SA forces.[26] To prove that there were no more troops in Angola, the SA Defence Force (SADF) flew Western military attachés to the border area where they were briefed on 'Operation Smokeshell', claimed to have been a two-phase attack on Swapo base camps.[27] The SA Commanding officer, Gen Geldenhuys, claimed that the pre-emptive strike had forestalled a major Swapo attack on Namibia.[28]

However, within a fortnight of the SA troops' withdrawal, they were again on the attack. On 15 July, the Angolan Defence Ministry announced that five SA soldiers had been killed in an abortive assault on the village of Calai, in

Cuando-Cubango. On 30 July, 80 helicopter-borne SA troops occupied the village of Chitado, near the Cunene River, killing 27 Swapo and FAPLA troops, according to Pretoria.[29] There were further attacks in August when 11 civilians were said by Luanda, to have been killed during an air force bombardment of Castilho on 19 August, when SA planes also hit the residential area of Libongue in the municipality of Chicomba, killing eight members of the ODP. On 25 August, Puma helicopters, covered by Impala jets, landed a force of SA troops south of Xangongo to attack a Swapo base, according to the Angolan authorities, who also claimed that 15 civilians were killed during an attack on villages in the Xiede area on 26 August. On 28 August, Luanda claimed that a battalion of SA troops was engaged in massacres of civilians in the Xiede area; on the next day SA troops were said to be moving through the areas of Mulemba and Monte Negro. On 12 September, Luanda claimed that a SA Impala MK-2 was shot down. On 18 October, there was another SA raid–in which 28 Swapo and FAPLA soldiers were killed, according to Pretoria's version of the incident, or 26 Angolan civilians and ODP militiamen, if Luanda's account is to be believed. According to Luanda, the SA targets were the villages of Donguena, in Cunene, and Iona, in Mocamedes. In mid-November, SWAPO announced that SA troops had attacked Namacunde, just north of the Namibian border, in Cunene. Then, on 5 December, Luanda claimed that two Impala MK-2 jets had strafed a bus on a road near Mongua, in Cunene, and that 16 SA tanks shelled an Angolan border post at Santa Clara on 17 December.[30] The raids continued into 1981, despite the Geneva talks. Just two days before the Geneva conference opened, Pretoria announced that it had killed 81 Swapo members in a large-scale offensive in southern Angola over the previous two weeks.[31] There were more raids after the conference: Luanda reported heavy fighting at Kuamato, in Cunene, which began on 15 January when SA ground forces attacked the small town, supported by six Puma helicopters and a squadron of Mirage jets.[32]

In February 1981, the new SA military commander in Namibia, Maj-Gen Charles Lloyd, warned that he would step up his attacks into Angola, even if it meant engaging Angolans, unless Swapo stopped its violence.[33] One of his senior officers confirmed that SA had a battalion of Black Namibians, organized in 32 Battalion (also known as the Buffalo Battalion), who specialized in cross-border raids. A month later, on 18 March, SA forces again flew almost 200 miles to attack a Swapo camp near its main base at Lubango. Jonathan Steele of The Guardian, who visited southern Angola in January 1981, reported that SA's military operations in the area had grown to such an extent that it was 'waging a full-scale war far from its own borders.'[34] He also claimed that the attacks were often against Angolan targets, not just Swapo bases. A British mercenary deserter, Trevor Edwardes, gave his own version of the operations of 32 Battalion (Buffalo Battalion) whose methods, he said, were so disgusting that he couldn't stand it any longer.[35] The SADF's answer to these allegations was that 'a self-confessed deserter. . . . is trying to commercialize a fabricated story.'[36] They accused The Guardian of not taking into account the fact that a civil war was going on Angola.

HOW FAR WILL SA GO IN ANGOLA?

Four important questions are raised by the confrontational collaborative relationship between SA and Angola on the question of Namibia. How much further is SA prepared to go in bombing Angola into more 'collaborative behaviour' if the Namibia talks were to become bogged down? If the talks were to break down altogether and sanctions were to be imposed, how hard would SA be able and willing to strike at Angola? What would be the response and likely commitment of Angola's strategic allies, the Warsaw Pact Powers and Cuba, as well as African countries who possess effective armies? What role could Dr Jonas Savimbi's Unita play in this kind of conflict?

First, SA seems clearly determined to escalate its military assaults on Angola, which, even if they aimed only at Swapo bases, inextricably involve encounters with Angolan troops, killing civilians and destroying the country's infrastructure. Plans to step up such attacks exist. According to Quentin Peel, the *Financial Times* SA correspondent:

A large map of neighbouring south-eastern Angola, liberally decorated with red stickers, is prominently displayed in the officers mess at Rundu, the SA Military Headquarters for the Kavango region in northern Namibia. Under the stickers there are figures to show the estimated troop strengths of forces belonging to the Government of Angola–and of those belonging to the Unita guerrillas whose struggle against the Angolan Government relies on SA support. The map aroused considerable interest in a party of foreign journalists who visited the SA 'operational area' on the Namibia–Angola border last week. But it was airily dismissed by the Colonel in charge. 'That's nothing to do with me,' he said. 'It's an air force map.'[37]

Therefore, the answer to the first question seems clear: failing an agreement over Namibia, SA has no alternative but to fight Swapo, which means fighting in–and therefore against–Angola. This leads to the next question about the likely response of Angola's allies. It is entirely unrealistic to suppose that the Warsaw Pact powers would not increase their present high level of arms supplies and their military training and technical presence if asked to do so at a time of escalating SA attacks, which would create a sympathetic African climate for Soviet intervention. Sophisticated missiles already enable the Angolan army to shoot down SA helicopters and even, on occasion, low-flying bombers. After the failure of the Geneva talks, East Germany at once flew out 'solidarity consignments' of supplies for MPLA and Swapo. The GDR plays a leading role as Angola's military aid partner.

Although there are still between 11,000 and 19,000 Cuban combat troops in Angola, they were not actively engaged against SA troops during any of the fighting in 1980 and early 1981–a fact corroborated by SA army sources. But they would be available if there was an all-out challenge to cripple Angola's resolve to help Swapo.

In such an eventuality it would be in SA's interest to use Savimbi's Unita forces more fully to destabilize MPLA. Although both SA and Savimbi deny any continuing collaboration, the odds are against this seem improbably high. According to Quentin Peel:

Whatever the denials, there is no question about SA's growing military involvement in Angola, not only supporting the Unita guerrillas there, but also intervening directly to gain the upper hand in a long-drawn war of SA's own against the guerrillas of Swapo.[38]

Quentin Peel reports that the military task facing the SADF is already considerable:

The border between Namibia and Angola stretches almost 1,000 miles from the Atlantic coast to the Zambezi, though virtually all guerrilla activity occurs across the 285-mile 'cut line' which marks the border of Ovamboland, between the Cunene and Kavango rivers. The South Africans believe Swapo has its military headquarters near Lubango, 150km from the southern port of Mocamedes. Although Namibia as a whole is very sparsely populated–barely 1m people in more than 320,000 sq miles–c. 60% of the population live within 30 miles of the northern border. More than half the battle, therefore, is not for military advantage, but for the loyalty of the local people.

'We can win this war,' said Col Leon Martins, commander of the Kavango section of the border. 'But if you allow the terrorists to come into your area, it would take 30 to 80 years. If you knock him out where he is, that is Angola–it will take ten to 15 years.'

The crucially unknown important factor is what role the Reagan Administration would play in the event of escalating warfare between SA and Angola—especially once the MPLA attracted massive additional support from the Warsaw Powers and Cuba, as they had done in 1974–75. (See below.)

How strong is Unita? According to a pro-Savimbi writer, Patrick Cosgrave[39], Savimbi has 15,000 armed men and even without an air force or adequate weapons now manages to control two-thirds of Angola. On the other hand, a pro-MPLA writer wrote that such statements 'belong in the realms of fantasy.'[40] His travels throughout southern Angola failed to show any trace of Unita's presence anywhere, let alone in two-thirds of the country. The more probable position is that Unita does not have effective control over any part of Angola, but it has sufficient strength and support to keep sections of the country in a state of insecurity. Given strong SA and, possibly, American support, Unita could become more than a thorn in the flesh of MPLA. But any overt SA/American move to bolster Unita would undoubtedly unite the whole of Africa against the Americans and any other of its Nato allies who might choose to support such a move. At that point, the confrontation in Southern Africa could assume the proportions of a major international crisis with the Americans arrayed on the side of SA against the whole of Africa, the Soviet bloc, Cuba and, possibly, also against the majority of the Nato nations. It seems inconceivable that the Western Powers would allow themselves to be led by the Dr Strangeloves of the US into such a potentially disastrous situation; but until Reagan's Washington renounces any intention of playing 'the Unita card', the risk of some awful blunder remains.

THE MOZAMBIQUE–SOUTH AFRICA BORDER

The fundamental differences in the positions and commitments of SA and its neighbours would suggest that an increasing level of military conflict and of growing international involvement is inevitable in Southern Africa. The root of these differences lies, on the one hand, in the determination of Angola and Mozambique to allow SA guerrillas of the liberation movements to make some use of their territory and, on the other hand, on SA's equally strong determination to pursue and destroy guerrillas in their neighbouring territories. In the words of Gen Constant Viljoen, Chief of the SADF:

It is the task of the SADF to destroy the enemy *wherever he might be found* before the people of SA have to suffer under their deeds of terror. This we will do fearlessly.[41]

A reasonable conclusion from these two opposite commitments is that unless the situation changes in Namibia and inside SA itself, confrontation and conflict will continue to escalate. The international involvement factor arises from the fact that both Mozambique and Angola have treaties with Moscow guaranteeing military support in the event of aggression against their territory, while Mozambique and Zimbabwe have a mutual defence treaty. Another factor might be American involvement. The Cubans are already *in situ*.

The mutual defence element in the Mozambique–USSR Treaty of 1977[42] was activated for the first time in February 1981 after the SADF attack on ANC quarters at Matolo, just outside Maputo. Within a few days of the attack, the

16,000-ton cruiser *Alexander Suvorov*, and another warship of the Soviet Indian Ocean patrol arrived in Beira and Maputo, and the Soviet ambassador, Valentin Vdovin, announced that more warships were on their way. He declared: 'We are not threatening anyone, but if anyone attacks us or our friends we will give an appropriate response.'[43]

Ambassador Vdovin added that the Friendship Treaty included cooperation in military matters. Although Prime Minister Botha reacted by saying that Soviet guns would not deter the SADF from doing what was necessary, his Defence Minister, Gen Magnus Malan, accused the USSR of planning to open 'a second front against SA'–the first being on the Angola–Namibia border.[44] He claimed that Mozambique already had 250 Soviet tanks, 400 armoured cars, an unspecified number of MiG-21 fighters and a sophisticated system of anti-aircraft missiles.

Thus one consequence of SA's policy of fighting guerrillas, wherever they might be, had the result, by 1981, of increasing both the level of fighting in Angola and Soviet involvement in Mozambique.

Meanwhile, Moscow's military presence in Mozambique is legitimized by a treaty, and is widely accepted in Africa as a positive contribution towards defending an independent State against the continent's common enemy, the Pretoria regime.

Two other developments which flowed from the Matolo attack point to the risk of the military situation in the area escalating very rapidly and, equally rapidly, of rotting relations between Africans and members of Nato. Mozambique's response to the Matolo attack–which had showed up inefficiency and even treachery within its army[45]–was to create a sense of war crisis among its people. The official daily, *Noticias* (27 February 1981), carried a front-page article headed: 'Let us Prepare For War'. The Government set about mobilizing the people to be ready to resist a large-scale SADF onslaught: schoolchildren were taught what to do in case of air raids; air shelters were constructed in strategic areas; young people were recruited for paramilitary training; and People's Militia groups, used in the liberation struggle, were reactivated. The second development was the swift deterioration of relations with Washington after Maputo had ordered the expulsion of four US envoys accused of being CIA agents. The US responded by cutting off its aid to Mozambique, but without severing diplomatic relations. The Americans, routinely denying any CIA role, pinned the blame for the treatment of its embassy staff on Cuban intervention, linking it to the coincidental arrival of a high-level intelligence team from Havana in Maputo. The Mozambican Government then produced three Mozambicans who confessed to having worked with the CIA, two of them covertly, the third as an undercover agent for Mozambique's intelligence service (SNAP).[46] Another ominous turn in this conflict with the US was Maputo's belief that the CIA is working hand-in-glove with SA intelligence–a belief that would be strengthened by any overt shift in the Reagan Administration's policies towards support for SA's right to fight 'terrorism' wherever it exists.

THE ZIMBABWE–SOUTH AFRICA BORDER

Although Prime Minister Robert Mugabe announced after Zimbabwe's independence that SA guerrillas would not be permitted to establish bases in his country[47], he promised to give practical as well as moral and political support to the SA liberation movement.[48] His stand is thus similar to that taken by Mozambique.

Quite apart from the conflict over the question of support for liberation movements, relations between Salisbury and Pretoria have been troubled because of Mugabe's claim that SA had recruited and trained several thousand White and

Black ex-Rhodesian troops. Mugabe said he did not know SA's reasons for recruiting these men–perhaps it was to fight in Namibia and Angola; but he charged the Pretoria regime with helping the anti-Frelimo rebel forces and of engaging in a 'destabilizing process' in order to carry out its aim of dominating Southern Africa.

Although Pretoria has repeatedly denied that it is engaged in recruiting Zimbabweans, Western military intelligence has established the presence of about 700 Shona-speaking soldiers, formerly members of Bishop Muzorewa's auxiliaries, in a camp near Phalaborwa in northern Transvaal. Nor is there any secret about the recruitment of former Selous Scouts and other White Rhodesian soldiers for the SADF. The Scouts have been incorporated into 32 Battalion (see above).

Despite these angry suspicions on the part of the Zimbabwe regime, trade and communications between the two countries have continued to flow freely since the country's independence. This is a common interest which, perhaps, places a greater constraint at this stage on Salisbury's policies than on Pretoria's.

Zimbabwe's shared interest with other countries bordering on SA in diminishing their economic and communications' dependence has led it to take a leading role in promoting the Southern African Development Coordination Conference. (See essay on the SADCC in this volume.)

WAITING FOR GODOT, OR THE $64,000 QUESTION

It can safely be predicted that the White–Black power struggle inside SA and between the Republic and Black Africa will be largely decided in the decade of the 1980s. The level of international involvement in the *dénouement* of that struggle will be determined mainly by the policy decisions of the US rather than of the Soviet bloc, whose ability to influence the affairs of Southern Africa as an active participant depends much less on its own actions than on the opportunities created for the Communist world by the policies of the Western community–and especially those of the US.

At the beginning of this decade it still remains unclear which of the alternative strategies urged on President Reagan by his rival Republican lobbies will be adopted. The hawkish Republicans want an easing up of pressure on SA; support for Savimbi's Unita; encouragement of policies to fight 'terrorism' (including the violence inherent in a liberation struggle); closer military cooperation with SA in the defence of the Atlantic sea route; and a bellicose attitude towards Soviet–Cuban involvement in Africa. Those less hawkish in their views are almost as alarmed by such ideas as are the doves in the Democratic cotes. Having fought his election campaign on the slogan of the hawks, President Reagan was faced with world realities rather different from those of his domestic hustings. But the conservative Senator Jesse Helms from North Carolina proposed an amendment to the Foreign Aid bill for fiscal 1981 which would have repealed the Clark Amendment (the legislation drafted by Senator Dick Clark in the closing stages of the Angolan civil war, which required public debate and approval by Congress for any military or paramilitary US involvement in Angola). Though partially toned down by Senator Paul Tsongas, Helms' amendment ended up by stating that no military assistance could be given to any Angolan group unless the President 'determines that such assistance should be furnished in the national security interests of the US'; and he reports, in classified form, the reasons for, and nature of, the aid to the House of Representatives and Senate Foreign Relations Committees. The amendment was passed in the Senate but was blocked in the House of Representatives Subcommittee on Africa, whose chairman, Stephen

Solarz, successfully persuaded a Senate–House conference on the Foreign Aid bill, on 20 November, to retain the essence of the Clark Amendment, namely, the requirement that any proposal by the White House to provide support for military or paramilitary operations in Angola be submitted to Congress and be approved by a joint resolution of both Houses.[49] During his campaign for the Presidency, Reagan said in an interview with the *Wall Street Journal:*

> Well, frankly, I would provide them (Unita) with weapons. It doesn't take American manpower. Savimbi, the leader, controls more than half of Angola. I don't see anything wrong with someone who wants to free themselves from the rule of an outside power, which is Cubans and East Germans. I don't see why we shouldn't provide them with weapons to do it.[50]

The new US Secretary of State, Gen Haig, seemed to take a similar line to Reagan's when he appeared before the Senate Foreign Relations Committee for his confirmation hearings. On 10 January 1981, he told the committee that the Clark Amendment was a 'self-defeating and unneccessary restriction' on the Executive in a situation that is 'highly dynamic'. He said that Unita was 'still virulent and strong, and functioning.' He later stated that he would not recommend diplomatic relations with Angola so long as there were '18,000 to 20,000 Cuban mercenaries there.'[51] These attitudes held by Reagan, Haig and Helms naturally alarmed the MPLA Government. President dos Santos said that remarks made during the US elections demonstrated a 'new desire to interfere in the internal affairs of the People's Republic of Angola.'[52] Commenting on moves to help Unita, Zimbabwe's Prime Minister, Robert Mugabe said:

> That would be a most hostile act; not only to Angola but certainly to the African States in this region. Africa would obviously condemn it. But I don't want to imagine that the Reagan regime would be that evil.[53]

The hawks fought a prolonged struggle to get one of their own stripe to fill the important post of Under-Secretary of State for Africa; but in the end they lost–at least the first round.[54] The new incumbent, Chester A. Crocker, director of African Studies at Georgetown University, is a hard-line realist whose differences with the Carter Administration would appear to be much more in the emphasis he gives to the kind of tactics to be used in dealing with SA and Black Africa rather than about fundamentals of policy. He has written extensively on how he would like to see US policy develop.[55] The following key passages in his own writing would indicate the kind of policies he would like the Reagan Administration to adopt:

> The many changes occurring today in SA are inherently ambiguous. Nonetheless, it should be possible at least to agree that Black politics are characterized by an increasingly confident experimentation with various strategies for challenging White control, while White politics are demonstrating a degree of fluidity and pragmatism that is without precedent in the past generation. The combination does not make meaningful evolutionary change certain, but it does make it possible for the first time in decades.
>
> In deciding the course of American policy, we need to have some consensus not only about what is going on in SA but also about basic US objectives, the American interests at stake, and the broad principles of policy effectiveness. Clearly, the fundamental goal is the emergence in SA of a society with which the US can pursue its varied interests in a full and friendly relationship, without constraint, embarrassment or political damage. The nature of the SA political system prevents us from having such a relationship now. That goal will remain elusive in the absence of purposeful, evolutionary change toward a non-racial system. Consequently, a basic US objective should be to foster and support

such change, recognizing the need to minimize the damage to our interests in the process, but also recognizing that American interests will suffer inevitably if such change fails to occur.

This statement of the problem rests on a number of straightforward premises. As a multiracial democracy, the US cannot endorse a system that is racist in purpose or effect. By its nature and history, SA is a part of the Western experience, and an integral part of the Western economic system. In addition, the exigencies of US domestic politics virtually rule out disengagement. The task, then, is to steer between the twin dangers of abetting violence in the Republic and aligning ourselves with the cause of White rule.

What part can the US play in the achievement of change? The evolution the US wants to see is unlikely to occur all by itself; external events and policies have always played a role in SA history, and are more likely to as internal power relationships become more equalized. Pressure for change should be a central ingredient in American policy, and that pressure must be credibly maintained if we are not to send misleading signals to South Africans. But pressure is not enough. Also required is a clear Western readiness to recognize and support positive movement, and to engage credibly in addressing a complex agenda of change.

Clearly, US interests lie in strongly encouraging South Africans to get on with deciding their future. How can we do so? . . . . There are many things the West could do to SA in the interests of 'bringing about change,' but would such actions in fact produce the intended result? We might reduce its growth rate by curtailing trade or investment. Comprehensive sanctions backed by naval power could wreak major damage on its economy (and on US and allied economic interests there). They might even spark a sustained uprising, a drastic decline in White living standards, and an outflow of emigrants. But this, presumably, is not the goal. SA capacity to cope with destructive actions is finite, but their ability to pervert our purposes and produce unintended and unforeseen consequences is not. . . .

Americans have no historical mandate to be a policeman in Africa, but neither does anybody else. Since the US and Africa exist in a competitive world, and since some of our regional interests are becoming important, it is clearly unwise to rule out the military instruments of foreign policy. Whether the goal is to promote human rights or to counter Soviet-Cuban destabilization efforts. American restraint and the denial of support to friends will only bolster the local parties that are best organized and armed.

Yet, relatively few situations lend themselves to direct, physical action. An effective response to Soviet-Cuban behaviour in Africa will include many elements and be aimed at demonstrating that Washington knows what its interests are and how to back them in relevant ways. In practice, this means devoting significant resources to the objectives of development; greater stability; and an expanded capacity on the part of Africans to govern and administer. Economic assistance, manpower development, arms sales and military training are important programmes, but they are not enough. African policy must also draw from the state of the global political balance and from US ability to devise worldwide energy and minerals policies.

While it is possible to predict a period of ambiguity in the Reagan Administration's initial policies towards Africa, what remains much less certain is whether Chester Crocker's views rather than those of the Republican hawks will triumph in the medium term.

Meanwhile, on 24 March 1981, 51 African nations at the UN unanimously denounced the US Government for its 'open support of SA', which, they said, could encourage 'state terrorism' by the Pretoria regime and harm America's relations with Africa. This strong stand came after the new US ambassador to the UN, Jeane Kirkpatrick, had received five SA senior military intelligence officers–even though their presence in the country had been criticized by the State Department which had ordered them to leave.

NOTES

1. The Lusaka Manifesto was signed by 13 African countries in 1969, and subsequently endorsed by the OAU.
2. For references to country surveys or essays in this chapter see *Africa Contemporary Record (ACR)* 1980–81, unless otherwise stated.
3. For details see *New African*, London, January 1980.
4. *Die Beeld*, Johannesburg, 5 January 1981; and *Rand Daily Mail (RDM)*, Johannesburg, 6 January 1981.
5. For Resolution 435, see *ACR* 1978–79, pp C73–4.
6. Michael Scott, *A Time to Speak*, London, 1958.
7. See chapter on Namibia.
8. *RDM*, 1 April 1980.
9. *Ibid*, 2 May 1980.
10. *Ibid*, 1 September 1980.
11. For details of elections, see chapter on Namibia.
12. *Die Burger*, Capetown, 30 December 1980.
13. This view was expressed by Dirk Mudge in a conversation with Colin Legum in January 1981.
14. *Die Burger*, 31 December 1980.
15. The six latter parties issued a statement making it clear 'that we do not consider ourselves in any way to be members of the SA Government negotiating team. We have all at various times and, to a greater and lesser extent, been rightly critical of the SA Government's handling of the Namibian situation, and the policies applied by it in our country. We have all publicly pledged ourselves to the implementation of Resolution 435.'
16. *The Guardian*, 13 January 1981.
17. Interview with Jonathan Steele, *The Guardian*, 19 January 1981.
18. Statement by Britain's Under-Secretary for Foreign Affairs, Richard Luce, in House of Commons, 31 January 1981.
19. Namibia Information Service, London, 14 January 1981.
20. See *ACR* 1973–74, pp A3ff.
21. Radio Maputo, 19 December 1980.
22. *The Times*, 1 August 1980.
23. *Marchès Tropicaux et Mediterraneen (MTM)*, Paris, 28 March 1980.
24. *Ibid*, 20 June 1980.
25. *International Herald Tribune (IHT)*, Paris, 29 June 1980.
26. *The Times*, 28 June 1980.
27. *Ibid*, 3 July 1980.
28. *Daily Telegraph*, 3 July 1980.
29. *Financial Times*, 31 July 1980.
30. Radio Luanda, 19 December 1980.
31. *Daily Telegraph*, 17 January 1981.
32. Radio Luanda, 18 January 1981.
33. *Financial Times*, 7 February 1981.
34. *The Guardian*, 29 January 1981.
35. *Ibid*.
36. *Ibid*, 30 January 1981.
37. *Financial Times*, 12 February 1981.
38. *Ibid*.
39. *The Times*, 4 February 1981.
40. *Ibid*, 26 September 1980.
41. *Daily Mail*, London, 31 January 1981.
42. For text see *ACR* 1977–78, pp C19ff.
43. *The Times*, 23 February 1981.
44. *Ibid*.
45. See chapter on Mozambique.
46. *AIM*, Mozambique's official newsagency, 14 March 1981.
47. *The Times*, 7 July 1980; *The Guardian*, 5 July 1980.
48. *Financial Times*, 2 February 1981.
49. *IHT*, 23 April 1980; *Washington Notes on Africa*, Summer 1980.
50. Quoted in *Africa Report*, NY, July/August 1980.
51. *Washington Post*, 11, 15 January 1981.
52. Radio Luanda, 11 November 1980.
53. *IHT*, 2 January 1981.
54. See essay on the US and Africa.
55. *Foreign Affairs*, NY, January/February 1981. *Washington Quarterly*, Summer 1980; *Africa Report*, NY, January/February 1981.

1981–1982
DARKNESS AT THE END OF THE TUNNEL

After Zimbabwe's independence in April 1980, the focus of international attention in Southern Africa shifted more sharply to Namibia, the last colonial territory in the region.[1] (The Organization of African Unity accepts that the Republic of South Africa (SA) is an independent sovereign state.[2]) The future of this former German territory, known as South West Africa under UN mandate to SA, became an issue of contention in 1946 when SA resisted the UN's decision to bring it into the new system of Trust Territories. In that year, too, the people of the territory had formally asked for the ending of SA rule through a petition brought to the UN by the Rev Michael Scott from the Herero Chief Hosea Kutako. In 1966 the UN declared SA to be in illegal occupation of the territory, which was renamed Namibia. When the Pretoria regime refused to accept the UN decision, an armed struggle was launched by the South West African People's Organization of Namibia (Swapo).

With the independence of Angola from Portuguese colonial rule in 1975, Swapo was able to develop a sharper military challenge to SA. The Western initiative to secure an internationally acceptable independence of Namibia, begun in 1977, seemed finally to have foundered at the UN–convened meeting of the parties to the conflict in Geneva in January 1981.[3] However, the three years of negotiations had not been entirely fruitless: they had stalled efforts by Pretoria to make Namibia independent through an internal settlement which ignored the UN's wishes; and they had won acceptance by both SA and Swapo, in principle, of Security Council Resolution 435 (SCR 435) as the basis for securing an internationally acceptable settlement of the conflict. What still remained was to get agreement to the implementation of SCR 435.

Meanwhile, though, the situation in Southern Africa had deteriorated through an alarming growth of violence as SA intensified its cross-border military attacks and engaged in an active policy of destabilizing its neighbours in an effort to stem the growing challenge coming from the liberation guerrilla movements—principally Swapo, based in Angola and Zambia, and the ANC, based in Mozambique and Tanzania. This alarming rise in the level of violence was made more ominous by two other developments: the military presence of the Soviet Union and East Germany and of a sizeable Cuban combat force in Angola, all of whom were in a position to give assistance in arms and training to Swapo; and, even more significantly, the deepening internal political crisis in SA caused by the failure of the policy of apartheid. Thus, at a time when SA was faced with a complete breakdown of its political system, it was also confronted by a growing military challenge by armed insurgents operating from the soil of neighbouring countries. This situation threatened not only to plunge the whole region into violence, but to internationalize the conflicts in the region even further.

Solving the dispute over Namibia would remove one of the major elements of conflict; but it would still leave unresolved the future of SA itself. By mid-1982 there was some light at the end of the tunnel for a resolution of the Namibian

176

conflict, but none at all for the much larger, and much, much more dangerous, conflict over a new dispensation in the Republic of South Africa itself.

THE AREAS OF ARMED CONFLICT
1. THE ANGOLA-NAMIBIA FRONT

The guerrilla phase of Swapo's struggle for the independence of Namibia began in 1966; but it was not until 1971 that SA felt the threat to be so serious as to warrant the introduction of its army into the territory. During the bitter civil war of 1975–76, which had preceded Angola's independence from Portuguese rule, SA sent an expeditionary force of c. 2,000 men deep into Angola in support of Dr Jonas Savimbi's Union for the Total National Independence of Angola (Unita) to try and influence the outcome of the struggle. At the same time, the Soviet bloc intervened militarily on the side of the Movement for the Popular Liberation of Angola (MPLA), whose victory was finally assured by the arrival of c. 20,000 Cuban combat troops.[4]

Angola's new MPLA regime gave its full support to Swapo, allowing it to establish military bases in the country, facilitating the training of Swapo forces by Cuban and Soviet military instructors, and allowing the steady supply of Soviet weapons. With Unita allied to SA, and Swapo to the MPLA, the area of conflict over Namibia extended into Angola as well.

The guerrilla war has remained chiefly concentrated in Ovamboland, an area of 20,540 sq miles criss-crossed by river beds, dotted by salt pans and covered mainly by scrub and stunted mopani trees.[5] Over 60% of the approximate half million Ovambos—comprising nearly half of Namibia's population—live in the central part of Ovamboland, within a radius of 30 miles from the Angola border. Another half million, or so, Ovambos live on the Angolan side of the border. Since Swapo derives a considerable measure of its support from the Ovambos, the area can be correctly described as meeting the classic Maoist definition of the ideal guerrilla environment, providing the sea within which the fish can swim.[6]

Swapo's military strength was estimated at 7,500 before the SA Defence Force launched Operation Protea in August 1981 (see below). But official SA estimates put the number at nearer 6,000. The SA Defence Force (SADF) claims to have killed 4,500 Swapo guerrillas in the past three years, including 1,000 during Operation Protea.

SA maintains a military presence of c.30,000 men in Namibia, a large proportion of them young White conscripts. Conscription was introduced for all Namibians in 1981 as part of the establishment of a Territorial Force which operates under SADF command.[7] The cost to SA of waging the war in this sector has risen sharply over the last five years, amounting to an officially-admitted £230m annually; but the actual cost is undoubtedly higher—sufficiently so for it to have come into SA's calculations of the value to it of Namibia.

SA's Defence Minister, Gen Magnus Malan, believes the war against Swapo is 'winnable'. He told the US Assistant Secretary for African Affairs, Chester Crocker: 'We will reach a stage where the internal forces in Namibia can militarily defeat Swapo.'[8] However, despite repeated claims by SA military spokesman to have crippled Swapo, the guerrillas have shown that they can continue, and even increase, their operations inside Namibia (see below). A significant feature of this developing military situation is the increasing amount of Soviet-supplied sophisticated weapons, closely parallelling the pattern of arms supplies to the PLO in the Lebanon. While Swapo is clearly not in a position to defeat the SADF militarily, it enjoys the advantage of all guerrilla armies in that success does not ultimately depend on gaining military ascendancy but in their ability to maintain a general state of insecurity, to increase their political pressures, and to make the conflict financially costly.

In the last few years, as the Angolan army has become better organized and more professional, the SADF has found it increasingly difficult to maintain a policy of 'hot pursuit' without also engaging the Angolan army, thus extending the dimension of the conflict.

Cuban combat troops have not been engaged in fighting the South Africans because of a deliberate policy of the Angolan regime based on two considerations. The first is that it does not wish to internationalize the conflict with SA more than is strictly necessary, for fear of upsetting its African friends; and, second, because of a risk that this might result in strengthening Western support for SA if its war could be credibly presented as a struggle to prevent growing communist intervention in the region. It is also probable that Havana is reluctant to accept the high casualty rates that would result from their direct military confrontation with the powerful SADF.

A sharp paradox in Pretoria's policy towards Angola is that while its haunting fear is of greater Soviet military involvement in the conflicts of Southern Africa, its steadily mounting military attacks into Angola have directly contributed to the MPLA regime becoming more heavily dependent on their communist allies, and to increasing the input of more dangerously sophisticated weapons into the region. When SA's Foreign Minister, Pik Botha, describes the Soviet involvement in Angola as approaching a position 'not much different from that in Afghanistan,'[9] he is not just trying to impress the Americans and other NATO countries with the dangers of expanding Soviet influence but, much more worrying, he and many other South Africans actually believe this to be true. And because they have succeeded in convincing themselves that this is so, they feel it necessary to continue expanding their arms spending to increase their military preparedness, and to accept the need for escalating the fighting from their side.

SIMILARITIES OF REGIONAL CONFLICTS IN THE MIDDLE EAST AND SOUTHERN AFRICA

By mid-1981, the military and political developments along the Namibian–Angolan borders showed a number of striking similarities to the situation along the Israeli–Lebanese border prior to Israel's decision in June 1982 to invade its neighbour and to lay siege to Beirut in order to force the PLO out of Lebanon, as well as to help change the political system inside Lebanon itself. Substitute Swapo for PLO, the MPLA for the uncertain government in Beirut, Unita for the Falangists and the similarities between the two situations are remarkable—even though there is no ideological or strategic analogy to be drawn between the positions of Israel and SA. The principal elements in the regional conflicts that grew out of the 'border' fighting in the Lebanon and Angola/Namibia are:

1. A guerrilla movement which is offered sanctuary in a sovereign state bordering on the contested territory.
2. The willingness of a major foreign power to provide increasingly sophisticated weapons to the guerrillas, after each hard attack against their positions.
3. The deep security fears felt by the country under military challenge.

What happened in the Lebanon could also happen in Angola (unless the Namibian conflict is successfully ended) and also, in the longer run, in Mozambique and Zimbabwe if the situation in SA were to remain unresolved. The similarities between the situation in the Middle East and in Southern Africa illustrate the risks of wider regional conflicts growing out of low-intensity conflicts if they are allowed to drag on for years with no prospect of relief for either side, and in which one or both the Super-powers are engaged in supporting at least one of the parties to the conflict. The similarities between the Israel/Lebanon and SA/Angola situations are:

1. Israel's justification for its attacks across Lebanon's border was that the PLO's military attacks were posing a security threat to civilian lives in the Galil. Pretoria has advanced precisely the same argument for its incursions into Angola to seek out and destroy Swapo bases, from where civilian lives were said to be threatened, mainly in Ovamboland.

2. Israel's interests coincide with those of the Lebanese Christians, a minority which feels itself so threatened that, purely for their own interests, they were keen to collaborate with the Israelis. Jonas Savimbi's Unita, based on Ovimbundu support, has similarly found it necessary and useful to cooperate with the South Africans to keep up the struggle it lost during the 1974–75 civil war in Angola.

3. The precariously balanced Lebanese Government was unable to assert its authority against the Syrian military presence, the growing PLO takeover of areas of their country, and the Christian Falangists. The MPLA Government—though not faced with any challenge to its authority by Swapo, nor subject to a dominant external power—is nevertheless dependent for its security on foreign allies, especially on the Cuban combat troops.

4. Both the Lebanese and Angolan Governments share the same interest in wishing to see a settlement that would make it decently possible to rid their countries of the guerrilla armies and of foreign troops. It was not politically or physically possible for the Lebanese Government to order the withdrawal of the Syrian army or to expel the PLO, thus removing any justification for Israel's intervention in its country. While it was always physically possibly for the Angolan regime to curb Swapo, this was not politically feasible because of the MPLA's deep commitment to the cause of Southern African liberation. Both countries therefore shared an overriding national interest in wishing to see an end to the trans-border attacks by finding ways of decently ending the use of their soil by the guerrilla movements.

5. Lebanon looked to foreign powers—the Arab world and the USSR, as well as to the Western community—to curb the Israelis; Angola looked to the rest of Africa (but without too much confidence), to the Soviet bloc and Cuba (as deterrent factors) and, especially, to the Western community—to restrain Pretoria. In neither situation were the foreign powers able, or willing, to prevent the trans-border attacks from becoming increasingly heavier. Meantime, the PLO and Swapo, both drawing their military support from the Soviet bloc, have been helped to develop the effectiveness of their striking power through a steady supply of increasingly more sophisticated weapons.

6. The situation in the Lebanon had deteriorated in mid-1982 to the point when Israel felt it necessary to embark on a full-scale invasion of the country, threatening to capture the capital itself. This situation could very possibly be repeated by SA in Angola if a final breakdown were to occur in the negotiations for Namibia's independence. It is certainly well within SA's military capacity to emulate the Israeli example.

7. The demilitarization of the conflicts in Angola and the Lebanon required political negotiations with Swapo and the PLO over their claims to independent statehood; but because both organizations are seen as 'terrorists' and 'communist-controlled' by Pretoria and Jerusalem, respectively, this has ruled out any such negotiations. However, the five Western nations of the CG succeeded in acting as interlocutors between Swapo and SA—a mechanism that was absent in the conflict between Israel and the PLO.

OPERATION PROTEA: A NOTCH CLOSER TO CONVENTIONAL WAR
The level of warfare in Angola rose seriously in August 1981 with the launching of
Operation Protea[10] when the policy of 'hot pursuit' was abandoned in favour of
direct ground and air attacks by between 6,000–11,000 SA soldiers deep into
Angola, and with a preparedness to take on not only Swapo's forces but, if
necessary, also the Angolan army, the Cuban combat troops and military elements of the Soviet bloc countries.

The operation was preceded by a series of warnings from SA's military leaders,
which bear an uncanny resemblance to the warnings given by the Israelis before
they launched their earlier offensive into the Lebanon, following the emplacement
of Soviet anti-aircraft missiles by the Syrians in the Bekaa valley in 1981.

SA's readiness to expand the scale of the military conflict because of perceived
new threats from more sophisticated Soviet weapons was revealed on 10 August
1981 by Maj-Gen Charles Lloyd, commander of the SWA Territory Force. Warning of preparations for an intensification of war along Namibia's northern border,
he announced that he was preparing 'to meet stronger forces than those of Swapo'
(i.e. the Angolan army, Cubans etc). He spoke of the erection of early warning
radar and anti-aircraft missile systems in southern Angola, which were making it
more difficult for the SA air force to operate freely in providing air support to
ground units.[11] Gen Lloyd claimed that Swapo was now using the Angolan army's
air defence umbrella and warned that, while his forces did not want 'to make
contact' with the Angolan army or its civilian population, if that army protected
Swapo, then his forces 'would inevitably have to cross swords with the Angolans.' He accepted the possibility of a conventional war developing, and said that
preparations were in hand for such a contingency. The General went on to say:
'As long as Swapo forces were the only ones on the battlefield, the chances of this
(a conventional war) were slim; but if the Angolan army and the Cubans joined the
battle it would intensify.' Everything depended on whether the Angolans and the
Cubans 'interfered' with the SADF's military operations. While the SA Defence
Minister, Gen Malan, explained that no 'special significance' should be read into
Gen Lloyd's statement since it was routine precaution for any army to be prepared for potential dangers, he added that it was 'well-known that Swapo was
getting increased support from the Angolan army, and that Cubans were instruct-
ing Swapo fighters.'[12] SA defence sources told journalists that Cuban and East
German experts were helping the Angolans to set up new missile and radar installations, and that 'a large force of Cubans' was building a well-equipped armoured
base near Lubango in south-west Angola.

Thus the scene was set for Operation Protea, which was launched on 23 August
and lasted for over a fortnight. The SA forces occupied virtually the whole of
Angola's Kunene province, and thrust to a depth of over 100 miles from the
Namibian border. SA claimed the operation had been successful in killing c. 1;000
Swapo guerrillas and Angolan troops, and in capturing 4,000t of military equipment and weapons valued at £120m.[13] Most of the war booty was of Soviet
manufacture, and included 13 tanks, 60 military vehicles and multiple rocket-
launchers. In an official account of the operation, Lt-Gen Jannie Geldenhuys,
Chief of the SA Army, said it was 'a little more dramatic and spectacular' because
security forces had used a conventional force against the towns of Xangongo and
Ngiva 'where Swapo was fully integrated with Angolan regular troops.'

No evidence was produced at the time of either Cuban or Soviet military
involvement in resisting the SA troops, although much was later made of the
capture of a Soviet army officer and the killing of three Soviet citizens (including
two wives). According to Gen Geldenhuys' version of the incident in which the

Soviet citizens were involved, it occurred during the heavy fighting at Ngiva when a convoy of 25 military vehicles attempted to break out, but were cut off south of Anhaca. He said the fleeing convoy, which was carrying 'Soviet advisers' as well as senior Angolan and Swapo officers, ignored attempts to negotiate a surrender and were then attacked.

SA's military offensive brought down on Pretoria's head severe international condemnation. Only an American veto—cast in opposition to the position taken up by other Western nations—prevented universal censure of SA's actions. (For the US explanation of its policy, see Namibia Negotiations, below.)

Pretoria jubilantly proclaimed that Operation Protea had accomplished its purpose of destroying the ability of Swapo to continue to harass Namibians. This claim was questioned at the time by many commentators, including the London *Times,* which, in an editorial on 31 August 1981, wrote:

> The attack was not only dangerous and illegal but also valueless in contributing to a solution of the problems of the area. Military measures against Swapo are almost certainly doomed to failure in the long run. They have been tried repeatedly since 1975 and have neither discouraged Swapo nor brought a settlement nearer. On the contrary, they have tended to exacerbate tension and confirm Angola in the belief that it still needs Cuban troops and Soviet weapons for its protection. This latest attack by South Africa will have the same effect, and is unlikely to be regarded by Swapo as causing them anything more than a temporary setback.

This view was soon to be proved correct. Only a month after the ending of Operation Protea, SA forces found it necessary to embark on yet another invasion of Angola. Operation Daisy in October was aimed at Swapo's 'main command post' south of Cassinga. This was followed in March 1982 by Operation Super, after the discovery of a large force of Swapo guerrillas in a largely unpopulated areas only 15 miles north of the Namibian border. The SA army claimed to have killed 201 guerrillas and captured tons of military supplies in Operation Super. But, though crippled, Swapo was still a long way from being ineffective. In April 1982 it launched its biggest attack inside Namibia itself when a group of guerrillas attacked the mining town of Tsumeb, causing widespread alarm. It also carried out operations in the so-called 'Death Triangle'—the area bounded at three points by Grootfontein, Otavi and Tsumeb. Several White farmers were killed or wounded, and six members of the security forces were officially admitted to have died when their convoy was hit by rocket-propelled grenades in an ambush in the Etosha area. Although this Swapo operation was not sustained for long, it gave rise to the comment in Windhoek: 'We keep being told that Swapo's *kaput* militarily; but every year they come back with the rains.'[14] The security situation was summed up by Johannes Smit, editor of the outspoken *Windhoek Observer:*

> This country is bleeding heavily, I tell you. Trapped in the hellish world of the curfew! You want to know about mortalities! There are 80,000 machine-guns in our part of the world. All talk of 'our best interests' is pious. . .

2. THE EASTERN, NORTHERN AND WESTERN FRONT

SA's Defence Minister warned of the possible opening of what he called 'a Second Front' against SA, referring to development particularly along its borders with Mozambique. (The First Front is that along the Namibia–Angola border, and there is also a Third Front, that within SA itself, which is discussed below.)

The conflict between SA and its neighbours along its eastern borders (Mozambique and Swaziland), its northern border (Zimbabwe), north-western border

(Botswana), and the interior border with Lesotho, has not yet begun to approximate the open war situation on the Namibia–Angola front. But the same elements that led to the rapid escalation of fighting along that front are also present in the other border areas: regimes hostile to Pretoria, and committed to helping the SA liberation movement; and, in Mozambique's case, a similar readiness to that of Angola to provide facilities (though not actual operational bases) to enable guerrilla cadres to infiltrate into SA. (The ANC and PAC military bases are still confined to Tanzania.) It was Mozambique's willingness to allow ANC guerrillas transit facilities that led to the lightning strike by the SADF against Matolo on the outskirts of Maputo, on 30 January 1981.[15] That operation had two specific objectives: to try and capture prominent leaders of the ANC and the SA Communist Party; and to serve notice on the Frelimo Government that its policy of allowing its soil to be used as a 'launching-pad' for attacks against SA would not escape unpunished. Although there has been no repetition of the direct military offensive into Mozambique since 1981, the risk of this happening in the future remains, and will predictably increase if the ANC's armed incursions into SA become more effective.

The potential for military confrontation between SA and Mozambique is in some ways even greater than that with Angola because it abuts directly on SA territory, whereas Angola's border is only with Namibia—a territory remote from SA's heartland and which, in the last resort, is expendable. No such possibility exists in the case of Mozambique. As the level of guerrilla operations continues to grow—as seems most likely—the need for SA to confront Mozambique directly will inevitably become greater. The forces operating out of Mozambique, unlike Swapo's, are directly and inextricably tied up with the forces of resistance inside SA. Moreover, given Pretoria's paranoia over the 'threat of communism', the ANC's alliance with the clandestine SA Communist Party (SACP), and the latter's intimate ties with Moscow give an even greater urgency to SA's defence along its eastern border.

No similar threat is yet posed by Zimbabwe, whose Government has declared that, unlike Mozambique, it will not allow ANC or PAC guerrillas on its territory. Prime Minister Mugabe has agreed only to allow the ANC and PAC to establish a political presence in Harare; he will not even countenance the use of his territory as transit routes for guerrillas passing on their way to SA. However, Mugabe has said on a number of occasions that if Pretoria were to continue its present attempts to destabilize Zimbabwe (see below), his present attitude to the guerrillas might change. Meanwhile, despite Zimbabwe's limitations on the ANC's operations, there is some evidence to suggest that their cadres do occasionally make their way along a corridor from the Tete province of Mozambique through the south-eastern corner of Matabeleland into SA. The surreptitious use of this route has been made possible by the nature of the terrain, and because of Zimbabwe's pressing security problems which have not made it possible to deploy more troops to police this thinly-inhabited part of the country.

Botswana and Swaziland rigorously enforce their policies of refusing to allow any facilities to armed guerrillas, or for the passage of weapons. Nevertheless, their willingness to admit political exiles from SA to take sanctuary in their countries makes clandestine activities possible—especially in providing regular communications with the resistance movement inside SA. Whenever such activities are discovered, they are rigorously suppressed in both Botswana and Swaziland.

Lesotho adopts a similar policy to that of Botswana and Swaziland. However, there has in recent years been evidence of closer relations between Chief Leabua Jonathan's Government and the ANC. This has contributed to seriously growing tensions between Maseru and Pretoria, which reached the point in 1982 where SA was countenancing the use of its territory by the Lesotho Liberation Army (LLA), which seeks to overthrow Jonathan's regime by violent methods (see below).

Pretoria's response to the developing threats to its security along its borders has been to pursue two courses of action. On the one hand, it seeks to diminish its neighbours' hostility by offers of economic and other forms of cooperation; on the other hand, it seeks to destabilize their regimes to keep them weak through economic and military pressures. (SA's policy of destabilizing its neighbours is discussed below.)

One outstanding example of SA's policy of seeking to strengthen its own security by offering some advantage to its neighbours is its proposed land deal with Swaziland.[16] The transfer of parts of the KwaZulu Homeland and the entire Kangwane Homeland would fulfill two of Swaziland's objectives: to 'unify' the Swazis, a dream of the aged King Sobhuza; and, more important, to provide his landlocked kingdom with an outlet to the sea. The advantages to SA are to develop an even more cooperative relationship with Swaziland, and to create a buffer between Natal and Mozambique which would be policed by an independent African country. The *cordon sanitaire* idea dies hard.

3. THE INTERNAL FRONT

SA's growing security problems along its borders are directly linked to the growth of political violence inside the Republic itself since this relies for its momentum on weapons and trained military cadres provided by the exile movements. The growing capacity of the Black opposition to upset internal security by striking at strategic targets is the most serious single threat perceived by the Pretoria regime—rightly so, since 'urban terrorism', once it takes root, would be devastating.

The rise of political violence has already reached the stage where the SA authorities no longer regard it as reversible in the foreseeable future. Acknowledging this, the Defence Minister said that while most of the 'terrorists' who had succeeded in penetrating the country had been caught, 'well-planned attacks against strategic installations' would continue as 'an eventual on-going exercise.'[17] This view was also endorsed by the SA Police, who in their evidence to the Rabie Commission[18] concluded that the campaign of violence by the ANC 'would increase and intensify.' The Chief of Security Police, Lt-Gen Johan Coetzee, described the 'terrorist groups' as being smaller 'but better-organized than the clumsy groups of 1960: they are thoroughly indoctrinated and much more determined to achieve their objectives.' The Army Chief, Gen Constand Viljoen, spoke of the success of the ANC in politicizing Black South Africans, but he felt they had not 'gone far enough to support revolutionary action.'

The serious view taken of this new internal dimension of political violence is shown by the decision taken in 1981 to prepare for 'area defence' (i.e. internal defence) to complement the extensive precautions already taken to guard the country's borders. This official recognition of the need for internal defence has also led to important changes in the Republic's military organization.[19]

The growth of internal political violence is directly linked to, but not yet controlled by, the external liberation forces.

SA'S POLICY OF DESTABILIZING ITS NEIGHBOURS

The Pretoria regime's response to the growing violence inside the Republic and along its borders has been to pursue three lines of policy simultaneously. First, to try and win over Black support at home by engaging in a policy of—so far still limited—economic, social and political reforms; this policy has contributed only to intensifying the already severe internal contradictions. Second, to expand and modernize its military forces to increase their capacity to engage in both conventional warfare and to deal with internal insurrection. Third, to seek to weaken the sources of the external threat, i.e. those of SA's neighbours who support the military activities of liberation movements. The third policy is carried on through a carrot-and-stick approach to its neighbours—just as the Reagan Administration proposes for its own dealings with Pretoria.

The 'carrot' is dangled in the form of offers of friendship and cooperation, embodied in such nebulous concepts as a 'Constellation of Southern African States' and, more practically, by maintaining economic links and providing economic, technical and other forms of assistance—e.g. by using Mozambique's underutilized railways and ports; by loaning to Zimbabwe locomotives for its railways, engaging in trade and providing outlets to the sea for its exports; by maintaining a Customs Union with Lesotho, Botswana and Swaziland, and by allowing them use of SA's extensive communications network. The overall objective, and effect, of these policies is to keep its neighbours dependent on SA, and to keep them weak.

As the 'carrot' approach has yielded decreasingly fewer dividends in terms of reducing the level of support for the armed opponents of apartheid (Pretoria's key priority), the SA regime has been forced to rely more on 'the stick', which is applied in three different ways: withholding its services (as it did, for example, in withdrawing its loaned locomotives to Zimbabwe at the height of its maize harvesting season, and in refusing, at first, to renew the Preferential Trade Agreement between Pretoria and Harare); by direct military attacks on its neighbours (as in the case of Angola and, on one occasion, against Mozambique); and by engaging in direct subversive activities. It is this last aspect of SA's policy towards its neighbours which has begun to cause them the greatest concern. Thus, SA is engaged in operating precisely the same kind of subversive tactics against its neighbours which it accuses them of using against itself. The only difference is that SA is in a much stronger position to go in for subversion because of its greater economic and military strength, and because its intelligence agencies are much more highly developed.

For understandable reasons, Pretoria vigorously denies in public any involvement in the continuous attempts to harass neighbouring countries. But the facts to the contrary are hard to dispute.

In Angola's case Pretoria has continued to support Unita ever since it intervened on its side in the 1975–76 conflict. While Unita undoubtedly enjoys a large measure of support among the Ovimbundu and is able to keep itself supplied with weapons captured from the Angolan army and the Cubans, the strength of its operations depends to a large measure on the support it gets from SA, e.g. its soldiers are trained in Namibia, where it maintains military 'bases'; Soviet weapons captured by the SADF in their frequent attacks on Angola are handed over to Unita; SA's contingency plans to establish a buffer state along Namibia's borders depend for their implementation on Unita's cooperation; and Unita's main lines of external communications go through SA (though it also uses Zaire for this purpose). By helping to keep Unita in the field as an active military force, as well as through its direct military incursions into Angola, SA has directly contributed to destabilizing the MPLA regime. (Also see Unita's Role, below.)

In Mozambique's case, SA helps the opposition *Resistencia Nacional Moçam- bicana* with arms and the back-up support of its own defence (MNR) forces; it maintains an MNR headquarters base in the Northern Transvaal; its intelligence services cooperate closely with MNR agents; and it maintains a clandestine MNR 'freedom' radio on SA territory. (For details, see chapter on South Africa in *ACR* 1981–82). The MNR's growingly subversive activities inside Mozambique—e.g. cutting communications lines, blowing up the oil pipeline to Zimbabwe, and even cutting the electricity lines from Cabora Bassa—have become a cause for serious concern to the Frelimo authorities, as well as to Zimbabwe because of the periodic disruption of its communications to Beira, and over the delays in renovating and maintaining its vital oil pipeline to the sea.[20]

In Zimbabwe's case, SA maintains a training camp in the Northern Transvaal of former supporters of Bishop Muzorewa and members of Rhodesia's notorious Selous Scouts. (The latter are also deployed in operations against Angola and Mozambique.) Zimbabwe's Prime Minister, Robert Mugabe, has on a number of occasions drawn attention to the unexplained presence of these former Rhodesians in SA, whom he estimates at 5,000 to 6,000. His suspicion is that they might, one day, be used to intervene in Zimbabwe if either its relations with SA decline to a state of direct confrontation, or in the event of a serious security breakdown as seemed to have threatened before the discovery of the large cache of arms in Matabeleland. (See the Role of Zimbabwe, below.) In an interview with the Johannesburg *Financial Mail* (30 October 1981), a prominent White Zimbabwean, Eddie Cross, general manager of his country's Dairy Marketing Board and president of the Institute for International Affairs, said:

> I believe that SA has consciously decided that it would not be in its long-term interests to have stable, prosperous neighbours. In my discussions with senior officials of the SA Department of Foreign Affairs, my view was virtually confirmed.

A striking example of SA's efforts at destabilizing an unpopular neighbouring regime is provided by its open support of Chief Leabua Jonathan's armed opposition, the Lesotho Liberation Army (LLA) led by Ntsu Mokhehle. The only access to Lesotho lies through SA territory; and the fact that the LLA has been able, over four years, to mount an increasing campaign of violence inside Lesotho points inevitably to Mokhehle's men passing through the Republic. Since SA security is justly famed for its tightness and efficiency, there seems to be no possible way in which the LLA can operate through the tiny Homeland of Qwa-Qwa without the knowledge of the SA authorities—a charge repeatedly levelled by Chief Jonathan. Compelling evidence in support of this allegation was provided by a commentary broadcast over the State-controlled SA Broadcasting Corporation which gave an uncritical account of the activities of the LLA, describing it not in the familiar SA terminology of 'terrorists'—but as a 'liberation army'.[21] It is remarkable that, in this particular case, Pretoria should not attempt to disguise approval for a movement seeking to overthrow a neighbouring government by terrorist methods, and that it should present it in such a friendly light.

Finally, there is the still unexplained relationship between the Pretoria regime and the *coup* attempt to overthrow the most distant government of President Albert René in the Seychelles. The admitted involvement of members of the SA's Defence Intelligence Agency in the attempt, and Pretoria's initial reluctance to prosecute the mercenaries led by Col Mike Hoare after they had landed their hijacked Air India plane in SA—a decision changed only under direct pressure from Washington—leaves no room for doubt about SA's complicity in this affair; all that remains unclear is the actual level of Pretoria's involvement. Evidence was produced in the SA Courts of signed receipts issued for arms delivered by an

SA army officer to the mercenaries. In a country as security-conscious as SA, this type of operation can hardly be planned or carried out without senior officials being privy to it.

In the light of all the available evidence there is no reason to doubt the extent to which the Pretoria regime actively pursues a policy of destabilizing its neighbours; such a policy is, in fact, indispensible to its regional strategy.

(The issues discussed in this section are further elaborated in the chapter on The Republic of South Africa, in *ACR* 1981–82.)

THE COURSE OF THE NEGOTIATIONS FOR A NAMIBIAN SETTLEMENT

The negotiations within the framework of the UN to end the 35-year-old international conflict over the future of Namibia seemed finally to have stalled with the failure of the Pre-Implementation Meeting (PIM) in Geneva in January 1981.[22] The Western initiative—begun in 1977 by the five Western members of the Security Council at that time (the US, Britain, Canada, France and West Germany)[23]—had temporarily run out of steam, its energy expended in trying to find a formula for Namibia's independence acceptable to both the SA regime and Swapo. Between 1977 and the end of 1980, Pretoria had shown that it was prepared to negotiate a settlement only on condition that Swapo would not be left in a position to win power against a government well-disposed to itself, viz. The Democratic Turnhalle Alliance (DTA); that this was Pretoria's basic negotiating position was admitted in April 1982 by its Defence Minister, Gen Magnus Malan (see below).

By stubborn, skilful diplomacy, Pretoria had always succeeded in leaving open the possibility of a negotiated settlement—thereby avoiding an open breach with the Western powers and the possibility of international sanctions—two major concerns of Pretoria's foreign policy.

On the other side, Swapo never doubted the true intentions of Pretoria; while always keeping open the option of a negotiated settlement, within the UN framework, it continued to rely on its armed struggle as the instrument to compel SA's withdrawal from Namibia.

Despite the firm positions and suspicious hostility of the antagonists, the Western initiative had succeeded in, at least, establishing the basis for a settlement, embodied in SCR 435[24] and accepted in principle by both SA and Swapo. But further progress was baulked by disagreements about how it should be implemented. This had brought about the failure of the Geneva meeting in early 1981. Over the next twelve months the negotiations were repeatedly sidetracked.

The role of the five Western nations, acting within the framework of the UN, is clearly expressed by the term used to describe them—the Contact Group (CG)—i.e. contact between SA, the Namibian internal parties, Swapo and the African Front-line States.

REAGAN JOINS THE NEGOTIATIONS, JANUARY–APRIL 1981.

President Carter's defeat in November 1980, shortly before the abortive PIM in Geneva, brought a new element of uncertainty into the Namibian negotiations since Ronald Reagan was committed to a very different approach from Carter's: a more conciliatory approach to the Pretoria regime; support for Unita; withdrawal of the Cuban troops from Angola; support for the DTA against the 'terrorist organization', Swapo. This was hardly likely to instill confidence in the chances of securing a negotiated settlement. Indeed, it raised questions about the possibilities of keeping the Western initiative alive at all.

On 20 January 1981—the day Reagan took office—and despite the serious qualms felt by African leaders, a meeting of Front-line Presidents in Dar es Salaam (which was also attended by Nigeria, Kenya and Swapo) agreed, in principle to accept the CG's latest (i.e. pre-Reagan) proposals for settlement. A Tanzanian spokesman announced that 'there was a lot of give and take but, in the end, everyone, including Swapo, agreed.'[25] A Western official summed up the position: 'What the Front-liners and Swapo are saying to the CG is: You have our support, now go and convince SA.' A few days later, speaking in Lusaka, Swapo's leader, Sam Nujoma, confirmed his acceptance of the proposals; but added that his willingness to continue negotiating should not be taken as a sign of weakness, and warned that the guerrilla struggle would be intensified if no settlement seemed likely. He also promised that the rights of the 100,000 Whites in Namibia would be safeguarded.[26] At the UN, the new American ambassador, Jeane Kirkpatrick, disclosed her opening hand in a privately circulated document entitled: *Proposed Declaration of Intent*. Its opening paragraph read:

> We do not wish to usurp the prerogative of the envisaged Constituent Assembly to draw up a Constitution for an independent and sovereign Namibia, but consider that an attempt should be made to reach agreement on broad guidelines for the constitutional future of the Territory. Any agreement so reached could be incorporated in a joint declaration of intent subscribed to by all parties participating in the talks, and would assist in instilling some measure of mutual confidence and trust between the parties.

This document went on to propose that the basic provisions of the Constitution of Independence should include a Bill of Rights; a Constitutional Court to supervise it with power to enforce its judgments; the principle of no nationalization or expropriation without reasonable compensation; the establishment and maintenance of an independent Judiciary; and the maintenance of a multi-party democracy. Finally, it proposed that the interim Constituent Assembly should be required to pass by a two-thirds majority any substantial constitutional changes.

The basic shift of policy envisioned in this initial American move was that important elements of the Constitution should be decided by negotiation *before* independence and before national elections: this was in direct conflict with the provisions of SCR 435.

During the opening months of 1981, the Reagan Administration was preoccupied with clarifying its own foreign policies over a wide range of issues, including Namibia—a process marked by a strenuous tug-of-war between the Right-wing of the Administration and its supporters in Congress on the one side, and the State Department on the other. The principal target of this Right-wing opposition was the new Assistant Secretary of State for Foreign Affairs, Dr Chester Crocker.[27]

It was not until March 1981 that Reagan gave some indication of this attitude towards Namibia. In an interview with the *Washington Post,* after a visit to the State Department by Nigeria's Foreign Minister, Prof Ishaya Audu, Reagan emphasized that he desired 'continued friendship with SA', despite its 'repugnant' policy of apartheid; and that 'we want to see a peaceful solution to the Namibian situation.' He then confirmed the approach set out in ambassador Kirkpatrick's declaration, saying that the proposed election in Namibia 'should follow the adoption of a Constitution that guarantees equal right to all people in that country—property rights, minority rights.'[28] At the same time, the Administration decided to put off, for the second time, Savimbi's proposed visit to Washington.

By early April, relations within the CG had become seriously strained because of the announced US intention of seeking changes in SCR 435 on constitutional issues. Britain, Canada, West Germany and France collectively insisted that it would be fatal to try and tamper with the Resolution. These differences with the US were sharpened when Crocker, on the eve of his first visit to Africa, spoke of his wish to see the 'Zimbabwe Model' accepted for the Namibian negotiations— i.e. that the Constitution of Independence should be settled in advance.[29] Crocker's ten-nation visit, which began in Nairobi on 9 April, was intended to reassure African leaders that the US was not proposing to embrace SA, or to abandon the quest for an acceptable settlement in Namibia. In Salisbury he told Zimbabweans that 'there is no question of a tilt towards, or endorsement of, apartheid.'[30] However, he was in obvious difficulties over America's future policy towards Angola and Unita, and could only say that no decision had yet been taken about providing assistance to Savimbi.[31]

Crocker's real passage of arms came, surprisingly, with the Pretoria regime, especially over his attitude to Swapo. In answer to a newspaperman's question in Salisbury, before his arrival in Pretoria, he said:

> There is no question that Swapo is supported by the Soviets and their friends at present, but I think it would be an over-simplification to think that that by itself accounts for what Swapo does, or what Swapo would do if it were to win the election.[32]

Crocker's view was strenuously contested during five-and-a-half hours of conversations between himself and SA's Ministers of Foreign Affairs and Defence, with the latter insisting that Swapo was a 'communist terrorist organization' and that, if its flag were ever raised over Windhoek, it would be equivalent to hoisting the Soviet flag. (Also see the Role of SA, below.) But when Crocker left Pretoria he made it clear that his view of Swapo remained unchanged.[33]

Pretoria's hopes had been raised by Reagan's election statements that his Administration would treat Swapo as an unacceptable terrorist organization; it therefore came as an early shock to the Botha regime to discover that on this crucial question Reagan's African spokesman was proposing to continue Carter's policy. Despite this initial setback, Pretoria was still entitled to expect from Reagan's first statement on Namibia since he took office that he would not accept SCR 435 as it stood. It also looked to the Americans to support Unita, and to link the presence of Cuban combat troops in Angola to a Namibian settlement.

None of these positions was acceptable to America's four CG partners. They viewed with considerable concern the possibility of a split in the Western alliance over Namibia, as was made very clear to the new US Secretary of State, Al Haig, at his first meeting with Britain's Foreign Secretary, Lord Carrington, in April 1981.

The first CG meeting since Reagan's victory was convened in London for 22–23 April to receive Crocker's report on his exploratory visit to Africa. But even before this meeting, the Five moved to reassure the Frontline Presidents who were due to meet in Luanda on 15 April that all the CG members remained committed to an internationally-accepted settlement for Namibia and were continuing their common effort towards this goal.[34] At their Luanda meeting, the Front-line leaders flatly turned down the idea floated by the US for a 'Zimbabwe model' approach to Namibia, and reaffirmed their stand on SCR 435. Neither of these issues turned out to be contentious at the CG meeting in London. The 'Zimbabwe model' idea was dropped and, more importantly, the Reagan Administration promised continued American support of SCR 435. The CG's communiqué described SCR 435 as providing 'a solid basis for transition to independence in Namibia.' But it went on to speak of 'the possibilities for strengthening the existing plan.'[35] (This was clearly a reference to the proposed new constitutional safeguards.)

Notwithstanding the CG pledge, strong doubts remained among Africans about Western—and especially American—willingness to use their influence to pressurize SA to implement SCR 435. These doubts led to more intensive efforts in the international arena to win support for the idea of sanctions against SA. The Bureau of Non-aligned Nations, attended by 34 Foreign Ministers, decided on 19 April to call for an emergency meeting of the UN General Assembly to review the question of Namibia and to take appropriate measures under the Charter, unless the Security Council agreed to apply sanctions against SA.[36] When the Security Council met in the last week of April, four resolutions calling for sanctions and condemning SA's attacks on Angola were defeated by a veto cast by the US, Britain and France, with the other 15 members either voting for them, or abstaining. The US ambassador to the UN, Jeane Kirkpatrick, attempted to assuage the rage of Africans over the veto by saying that the decision 'in no way affects the determination of the US . . . to find a way to achieve early, internationally-acceptable independence for Namibia.' African anger over this veto was revealed in a statement by Peter Museshihange, Swapo's spokesman for foreign affairs, who accused the Western powers of being 'in cahoots with SA', and of using 'the arrogance of power by a minority to undermine the actions of the majority.'[37]

INTRODUCTION OF LINKAGE BETWEEN A SETTLEMENT AND CUBAN TROOP WITHDRAWALS (APRIL–MAY 1981)

At this stage, in the Spring of 1981, the Americans' intention of establishing some kind of linkage between the Namibian negotiations and the issue of Cuban troops in Angola began to figure more prominently in the negotiations: it was to become a major factor in the subsequent course of the negotiations. During his African visit in April, Crocker had only tentatively raised this issue while in Luanda, but had met with a firm rebuff. Nevertheless, while the MPLA regime refused to consider any form of linkage, it did not resist the idea of the withdrawal of Cuban troops— but on its own terms, and only when it felt that Angola's security was no longer externally threatened. While in New York, attending the UN session on sanctions in April, Angola's Foreign Minister, Paulo Jorge, said for the first time in public in an interview with Jim Hoagland, what his regime had been saying for some time in private: 'When Namibia will be independent, and the aggression against Angola from SA finished, then we will say to the Cuban comrades: Thank you very much, you can go home now.'[38]

This statement did not satisfy Washington, which was after more specific assurances that Cuban troops would begin to leave Angola at the same time as SA troops withdrew from Namibia. Angola's justification for its insistence that the two issues could not be linked was that it would derogate from their sovereignty.

In his interview with Hoagland, Paulo Jorge had also ventured the opinion that the early signals from the Reagan Administration had dimmed hopes for a peaceful settlement, and warned that any resumption of US aid to Unita would start not only a diplomatic confrontation between Black Africa and Washington, but would imperil the economic interests of American firms who already had a $200m investment in Angola and were planning to invest a further $500m in the near future.

A few days after the end of the Security Council debate, the five Foreign Ministers of the CG met in Rome on the eve of a NATO meeting. At the same time as reaffirming their determination 'to take vigorous steps to find a settlement', they unanimously agreed to accept the American position that, while SCR 435 provided a solid basis for agreement, it had not proved sufficient to produce agreement; what was therefore needed were further measures 'to establish understanding among all the parties about the shape of the future independent Namibia'. They set themselves two major objectives: to introduce safeguards which would give losing parties in the elections, whether White or Black, an assurance that they would not be deprived of their political rights; and to demonstrate the impartiality of the UN.

The Americans continued to pursue their own objective—getting the Cuban troops out of Angola; but the other CG members insisted that this should be regarded as a general aim of foreign policy and not specifically tied to Namibia.[39] So, this substantial difference of opinion still remained between the US and its allies.

Haig clarified two aspects of US policy in a speech at St Louis (Mo.) on 29 May, when he announced that he intended to elaborate certain constitutional guarantees within the framework of SCR 435:

> Those guarantees would provide for the rights of minorities. They would provide for the recurrent vote by the population—not one man, one vote, one time; and they would provide for . . . true non-alignment and non-foreign presence in Namibia.
> There is an empirical relationship between the ultimate independence of Namibia and the continuing Soviet and Cuban presence in Angola. Although we intend to proceed unilaterally (sic) along the line for Namibia independence, we cannot ignore this empirical relationship.

THE CLARK MISSION (JUNE 1981)

The US Administration was seriously embarrassed in early June by the leaking of confidential State Department papers about the negotiations between Crocker and the South Africans. (See The Role of SA, below.) The authenticity of these papers was not questioned, but Washington was concerned to discover the source of the leak and to put the events described in their proper time perspective. The papers relate to conversations between Crocker and the SA Defence and Foreign Ministers in January 1981.[40] A State Department spokesman explained that 'a lot of papers get written at the start of an Administration, and a lot of conceptions of how to approach a problem get changed by the realities.'

American decision-making on Namibia moved closer to the White House itself in June 1981, when President Reagan sent his personal friend, William P Clark—then Assistant Secretary of State and later chairman of the National Security Council—on a fact-finding mission to Southern Africa, accompanied by Chester Crocker. Although Clark is renowned for his ignorance of foreign affairs, he also has the reputation of being a good lawyer, being able to learn the essentials of any particular brief quickly. He has the additional advantage that his views carry weight with Reagan. For all these reasons the Clark mission was of considerable importance. Clark appears to have concluded that a settlement of Namibia was not simply a matter of general interest, but was also a particular American interest since a successful outcome would help Reagan fulfill his promise to 'get the Cubans out of Angola', to undercut the 'spreading Russian influence', and to remove a major obstacle to better relations with Pretoria. When Clark later moved over to the National Security Council, it meant that Crocker's views would find a direct channel to the President.

During his visit, Clark met the SA leaders, the internal leaders and Swapo's representatives in Namibia, and had talks in Salisbury with Zimbabwe's Prime Minister, Robert Mugabe. All he ever said in public after his visit was in the course of a speech on East–West Relations delivered to a conference in Alpbach,

Austria, on 21 June: 'While I make no claim that we have found a magic formula, I do promise that we are involved and dedicated to achieving a fair and peaceful settlement—and soon.'

Reporting to a Congressional panel on 17 June on the Namibian negotiations over the previous six months, Crocker claimed that from the time of the Reagan Administration taking office on 20 January it had recognized the importance of finding a settlement for Namibia: in fact, it had become the single subject on which he and his Department had been engaged ever since. He summed up the guidelines of American policy as recognition that:

- The people of Namibia have the right to self-determination.
- The search for the fulfillment of this principle involved a complicated negotiating process 'symbolized' in SCR 435: 'We have no intention of usurping the UN's role or departing from the UN context; however, we cannot be constrained by a rigid adherence to the letter of SCR 435 if, by doing so, an internationally acceptable settlement in Namibia is impeded rather than aided.'
- Continuation of the conflict in Namibia complicates our relations with Black Africa at a time when there appears to be more and more common ground between it and the West. . . . We attach major importance to US interests in Africa as a whole . . .
- America's allies in the CG have significant interests at stake in Africa, based upon their involvement in the Namibia negotiations. The solidarity of the CG allies remains a basic ingredient in the elaboration of a settlement.
- The inescapable fact that Pretoria holds the main key to a settlement, and, therefore, must have a minimum of confidence in any settlement if it is to be implemented.

President Reagan sent a message to the out-going OAU Chairman, President Siaka Stevens, on the eve of the summit meeting of Heads of State in Nairobi in June, reaffirming America's commitment to 'a just settlement in Namibia' and 'opposition to apartheid.' This attempt to reassure African opinion did not save the US from being the main target for attack in OAU resolutions.[41]

Disappointed at the CG's efforts to bring the Namibian question any closer to resolution, and so to put an end to the SA military attacks, Angola proposed a different approach at the OAU Summit in June: another Geneva-type conference, under UN auspices, to discuss how to implement SCR 435.[42] At a meeting with French, West German and British diplomats in Luanda on 19 June, Angola's Deputy Foreign Minister, Venancio de Moura, criticized the attitude of the US. He complained that although it was co-author of the so-called Anglo–American plan, which had resulted in SCR 435, the US 'was now siding with SA with a view to invalidating that same resolution.' He urged the diplomats to persuade their partners—the US and Canada—to honour their undertakings to refrain from interfering in the international affairs of Angola.[43] Why he coupled Canada with the US was not explained.

By mid-1981, the Front-line States and Swapo saw the main obstacles in their negotiations with the CG as being the two new issues introduced by the Reagan Administration: the Cuban linkage and the attempt to prescribe provisions in the Constitution before independence. At that point the question of Unita was not so sharply focused.

At a meeting with Lord Carrington in London of 19 June, Sam Nujoma said of the Constitutional issue: 'We object and abhor that foreigners should dictate our Constitution.'[44] However, Swapo let it be known privately that it had no objection to accepting a Bill of Rights for minorities etc; but this was of its own choice.

191

STALEMATE AND COMPROMISE (JULY 1981)
With the negotiations virtually stalemated in July, a fresh attempt was made to revive the initiative on the sidelines of an Economic Summit of Western Foreign Ministers held in Ottawa over 10–21 July. The push for this initiative came largely from Bonn's Foreign Minister, Willie Genscher, reflecting the FRG's particular concern because of historic and ethnic links with Namibia's German community, many of whom have retained their German citizenship. The new Mitterrand Government also tried to infuse a sense of greater urgency into the negotiations, while Lord Carrington continued to give a high priority to finding a way through the Namibian thickets. However, America's European allies tempered their impatience because of their understanding of the State Department's difficulties in overcoming the unreconstructed Reaganites in the Congress, the White House and the Pentagon; besides, they knew that only Reagan could 'deliver' Pretoria. Hence the need felt for some compromise within the CG; this was reflected in the communiqué of the Ottawa meeting on 22 July. While reporting agreement 'to bring about the independence of Namibia in accordance with SCR 435 in a manner that will command international approval,' it added that the Foreign Ministers had considered measures 'which would complement and strengthen the existing UN plan and provide the confidence necessary for all parties to proceed.' Two follow-up meetings were projected: one at a senior officials level in Paris before the end of July, and one at Foreign Ministers' level during the General Assembly of the UN in September.

Before proceeding to the Paris meeting, Crocker had a meeting with Swapo's representative at the UN, Theo Ben Gurirab, in Washington on 24 July. *Mirabile dictu,* this was the first official contact between a representative of the Reagan Administration with a senior Swapo official, although Crocker had by then been engaged in the Namibia negotiations for seven months. US officials described the meeting as 'a normal part of consultations and dialogue among the various parties in the negotiations'. The session itself was described as 'a good working meeting'.

SA ESCALATES THE WAR AND RENEWED PRESSURES FOR SANCTIONS (AUGUST–SEPTEMBER 1981)
The political climate for a settlement deteriorated badly in August when SA launched its biggest military attack into Angola since independence. This time, the pretext was that Angola had begun deploying SAM-3 and SAM-6 missiles to protect Swapo and was introducing other sophisticated weapons into the area. The Commander of the SA forces in Namibia, Maj-Gen Charles Lloyd, declared that the war was unlikely to expand unless the Angolans and Cubans became involved, when 'we will unavoidably have to cross swords.'[45] (For details, see The Areas of Conflict, above.)

The Autumn attack—Operation Protea—brought universal condemnation of SA's actions, except from the US, which explained that its veto of a resolution condemning SA was because it was 'too one-sided' (see above). In a major policy statement, Washington announced that while it had no desire to act as Africa's 'policeman', it would not hesitate to help friends, or resist others. Washington's position on the invasion of Angola reflected a wish not to lose the confidence of Pretoria, nor that of the President's Right-wing supporters; but it contrasted sharply with the attitudes of its Western allies.[46] The French ambassador to the UN, Jacques Leprette, declared SA's conduct as 'inadmissible', adding that it was 'mendacious' to blame Swapo since the root cause of the problem was not Swapo, but SA's policies. West Germany and Canada both described SA's military attack as 'totally unacceptable'. Britain took the exceptional step of conveying a sharp warning through the SA ambassador in London.[47] America's refusal to condemn the SA raid outright provided the Soviet ambassador to the UN, Richard Ovinnikov, with an easy target—repeatedly challenging the US representative to state openly whether or not he supported Pretoria. In the face of this near-unanimous condemnation, the Botha regime took what comfort it could from America's 'support' and its insistence that SA attacks had to be seen in the context of Swapo's attacks across the border.[48] The state-controlled SA Broadcasting Corporation also stressed the passage in the CG's Ottawa communiqué that 'amendments to SCR 435 were needed in what were termed the new realities. . . .' (See above.)

At the height of this flare-up over SA's invasion of Angola, the OAU sent a delegation to visit all five capitals of the CG members to urge greater Western pressures against Pretoria in order to influence it to implement SCR 435. After meeting Haig in Washington, the delegation's leader—Kenya's Foreign Minister, Robert Ouko—said that, despite all that had happened, Africa's leaders were still prepared to give the West more time to find a peaceful solution: 'We will pursue all the options to ensure the freedom of Namibia, but given the chance we would prefer to choose the peaceful option.'

One of the options was to renew pressures for sanctions against SA, but this time avoiding a Security Council veto by getting a two-thirds majority decision in the UN General Assembly under the 'Uniting for Peace' procedures, which were legitimized by the US and its allies during the Korean war at the time when the USSR was boycotting the Security Council. This idea was floated at the beginning of September at a special session of the General Assembly held to consider the Namibia issue. The session began with a flurry when a member of the American delegation at the UN, Steven Munson, suggested that the US would boycott the special session. Although this was quickly ruled out by Washington,[49] these contradictory statements were seen as further evidence of a two-track policy being followed by Reagan's Administration which kept America's allies guessing and the Africans worried and undecided. This lack of a clear direction in American policy was felt particularly over the issue of linkage between the Cuban troops in Angola and a Namibian settlement. While Chester Crocker argued that it was a 'problematical assumption' that Cuban troops would automatically leave after a Namibian settlement, all the other CG members remained united in their refusal to endorse the idea of linkage.[50]

The special session of the General Assembly voted in September overwhelmingly in favour of a recommendatory resolution calling on all UN members to stop all dealings with SA. Sweden's ambassador, Anders Thunborg, proposed an urgent meeting of the Security Council to consider again the question of making sanctions against SA mandatory.[51] All five CG members abstained from the final Assembly resolution on the ground that, so far from contributing to a peaceful international settlement, it would only complicate their initiative at a time when negotiations had reached 'a crucial stage'. Speaking for the CG, Canada's representative, John Reid Morden, explained that their collective abstention neither reflected nor implied any judgment on the merits of the recommendations contained in the resolution. He read an agreed ten-point declaration by the CG which, *inter alia*, promised that the modalities for implementing SCR 435 would be announced 'in the near future'. He added:

> These proposals, and I should like to emphasize this point, will fully respect SCR 435. Our proposals will concern the implementation of the UN Plan, and will provide

193

the added assurances we believe essential in order to gain the confidence of all parties concerned, and to obtain their agreement.

HOPES RISE FOR AGREEMENT (SEPTEMBER–OCTOBER 1981)

During the Assembly debate on Namibia, parallel talks were taking place in Washington between Haig and SA's Foreign Minister. On 6 September, Haig spoke optimistically of a possible breakthrough. 'We're not where we want to be yet, but we are farther ahead on where we want to be,' he told the *New York Times* on 3 September. He claimed that SA had 'softened' its attitude. This decidedly upswing view of the situation also surfaced at a meeting of EEC Foreign Ministers on 6 September.[52] Official sources suggested that SA had indicated its willingness to resume negotiations on the basis of SCR 435, and that the next phase of the Western initiative would be primarily concerned with constitutional guarantees to safeguard the position of minorities and measures designed to ensure acceptance of the impartiality of the UN in supervising the transition process.

Meanwhile, speaking on behalf of the EEC in the General Assembly debate, Britain's representative, Sir Anthony Parsons, criticized recent measures taken in Namibia as being divisive; he referred especially to the extension of conscription, the enlargement of powers of the Council of Ministers, and the introduction of second-tier elections for the various ethnic groups.[53] Parsons said the EEC viewed these measures as likely to 'exacerbate tensions inside the territory,' and as not being 'consonant with an internationally acceptable solution.'[54]

The Washington talks between Haig and Pik Botha were quickly followed up by a meeting in Zurich between Botha and Chester Crocker. Before going to this meeting, Crocker briefed a Congressional panel on 16 September on 'the substantial elements of progress' that had been made in pursuing the Namibian initiative.[55] He claimed that there was 'a substantial gap' between the perceptions of what was happening and the reality:

> The fact of the matter is that we are hearing from African leaders . . . that they know that only we can do what we're seeking to do. They want us to do it, and they're expecting great things from us. We don't see anybody else volunteering to stand up and go deliver the South Africans on Namibia. We don't see anybody in Southern Africa proposing that we actually apply economic sanctions against SA. None of these things is put forward to us in diplomatic channels, and we know why.

Crocker's statement to the Congress committee met with considerable criticism. In reply to one critical question from a Congressman as to whether the SA Government could be considered to have demonstrated a consistent pattern of gross violations of human rights, Crocker replied: 'I believe that definition of SA certainly applies to many aspects of what happens there—yes indeed.'

A few days after Crocker's appearance before the Congressional panel, there was another apparent lurch in US policy over the Cuban linkage proposal. A State Department spokesman, commenting on a recent Crocker statement that there was 'an intimate relationship' between the conflicts in Namibia and Angola and that a satisfactory outcome could be based only on a parallel movement, declared:

> We are not creating any formal linkage between these two situations. There is no way the Angola situation can be incorporated into SCR 435. However, we do believe we could move this thing forward really quite rapidly if we are able to achieve some form of undertaking or commitment from the Angolan side about a Cuban withdrawal which would obviously have to be related in some general sense to the implementa-

tion of a Namibia settlement. *But we are not talking about a precondition.*[56] (Italics added.)

After talking to the State Department spokesman who had made this statement, Nicholas Ashford of the London *Times* wrote:

> The American plan also indirectly involves the Unita organization of Dr. Jonas Savimbi. . . . The Americans hope that a Namibian settlement linked to a Cuban withdrawal from Angola would persuade the Angolan Government to come to terms with Unita, which at present is clandestinely backed by SA.[57]

A few days later there was an inspired Press leak by diplomatic sources in Dar es Salaam which suggested that all the US was now seeking was 'a gentleman's agreement' from African States that a withdrawal of Cuban troops would accompany a Namibian settlement.[58] As a *quid pro quo*, the US would agree to halt international military backing for Unita. According to this anonymous diplomatic source, the US was not asking the Angolan Government to 'commit suicide' by requiring a total Cuban withdrawal simultaneously with a Namibian settlement. He suggested one possible solution would be for 'the first Cuban' to leave on the same day as 'the last SA soldier' left Namibia. The report quoted Nyerere as having stated publicly that a Cuban military withdrawal would be logical, once Namibian independence had been achieved.

Before leaving for the Zurich talks with Crocker, Pik Botha told his Parliament that the presence of thousands of Cuban troops in Angola made it much more difficult to go ahead with independence talks for Namibia. He added: 'But nothing has happened which makes it impossible to resolve the outstanding problems.'[59]

The Zurich talks, which lasted for only one day on 21 September, were conducted in complete secrecy. However, at the conclusion of the talks, one commentator[60] said that even the most sceptical of the diplomats, wearied by years of fruitless talks, were expressing 'quiet optimism'. On the day of the talks, Dirk Mudge, the DTA leader, declared: 'I think we must take the American initiative very seriously. I do not think that independence can be postponed indefinitely, and the Americans will not allow themselves to be kicked around.'[61] His was possibly the first open recognition that the US was prepared to use some of its diplomatic muscle on Pretoria.

When Chester Crocker reported on the Zurich meeting to the CG Foreign Ministers in New York on 24 September, they agreed that the results gave sufficient encouragement to resume negotiations with the objective of implementing SCR 435 during 1982. They also announced that they had completed their consideration of possible constitutional principles for the Constituent Assembly, and expressed their belief that these proposals would be likely to secure the confidence of all concerned. They decided to restart the negotiations by, once again, sending their senior officials to the capitals of the Front-line States to test the acceptability of their proposals.

On the day preceding the New York meeting, Lord Carrington made an unusually sharp attack on SA in the General Assembly debate.[62] After expressing concern on behalf of the ten EEC countries (of whom he was current chairman) that SA had continued to deny the right of self-determination to Namibians, he went on to say:

> Within SA itself . . . virtually none of the expectations of worthwhile change in recent years have been fulfilled.
> Reforms promised by the SA Government, mostly still not implemented, do not

deal with the fundamental problem of meeting the political, as well as the social and economic, aspirations of Black, Coloured and Asian South Africans.

Without an early move towards government by consent and the abandonment of the system of apartheid, which we all abhor, the trend in SA can only be one of accelerating conflict and violence.

Two days later, Carrington said of the Namibian negotiations: 'We are now back on the rails, but there is still a considerable journey ahead.'[63]

Kenya's President Daniel arap Moi, current chairman of the OAU, also expressed confidence that a settlement now seemed possible in Namibia.[64] Speaking on 25 September, after a meeting with President Reagan, Moi said that a greater understanding had been reached between them on what he called a 'matter of great concern'. He added: 'The US, being a great nation, cherishing those ideals of human dignity and human rights . . . I feel that a solution now may be found in that part of Africa.'

However, Swapo's leaders still remained sceptical. Nujoma described SA's apparent readiness to negotiate as being:

> Just manoeuvres to maintain Namibia under its grip. They are going ahead with their internal settlement. We are prepared to fight a protracted armed struggle.
>
> The war in Namibia has reached a very critical stage. Up to now we have been fighting a basic guerrilla war. Now we need more sophisticated weapons to be able to bring down enemy jet fighters.[65]

He said Swapo would accept weapons from any source.

Something of a sea-change appears to have occurred in Pretoria's thinking in the three weeks between its Foreign Minister's meeting with the US Secretary of State in Washington and the Zurich meeting on 21 September. Any idea of SA having suddenly undergone a Pauline conversion can be ruled out; nor had there been any traumatic event, such as a Western tilt towards sanctions: so, what explains the change? It is unlikely that the actual reasons for this change will become known for some time yet; meanwhile, one plausible explanation was offered by the courageously maverick editor of *The Windhoek Advertiser,* Hannes Smit, on 1 October 1981. He wrote that a confidential Press briefing had been given to the top executives of selected SA media by the Prime Minister, his Foreign and Defence Ministers, and Dr Brand Fourie, the Director-General of Foreign Affairs. After outlining the Western proposals (which later became public, see below), they disclosed that the US was ready to give SA specific guarantees in exchange for accepting the proposals. These included: support for SA's right to prevent the ANC from erecting military bases in an independent Namibia; securing Angola's border with Namibia, with the support of Front-line States and, in extreme cases, SA to have the opportunity of erecting a sea and land blockade around Namibia to prevent the import of Soviet weaponry and military personnel; and far-reaching military and security cooperation between SA and US.

This presentation of the secret terms supposedly offered by the US seems crude, and even unlikely; on the other hand, if the thrust of these intentions are translated into more subtle diplomatic language indicating US support along the specific lines mentioned, it could be credible. However, another major element in the secret understanding reached between Haig and Botha is almost certainly a firm assurance that Cuban troops will be required to leave Angola once agreement has been finalized over Namibia's future: this would satisfy not only an important American objective, but would also serve a direct SA security interest. Moreover, it could provide the SA Prime Minister with a trump card to play against Right-wing accusations of 'selling-out' to Swapo.

COLLAPSE OF THE NEW INITIATIVE (OCTOBER-DECEMBER 1981)
The CG officials relaunched their initiative by arranging for talks in nine African capitals, beginning in Lagos, on 26 October. The leader of this delegation was, again, Chester Crocker, with the British representative, Sir Leonard Allinson acting as spokesman. Their negotiations were based on a document entitled *Principles Concerning the Constituent Assembly and the Constitution for an Independent Namibia.* The text is produced as Appendix 1 at the end of this chapter.
The initial response from most of the Front-line leaders was encouraging. Swapo was positive, but reserved (See Appendix 2). SA was strongly supportive, while the Namibian internal parties (other than the White *ultras*[66]) were receptive. Angola's President, Jose Eduardo dos Santos, said after receiving the CG delegation that all the parties involved in the dispute now had an opportunity to hammer out a just solution.

> It has not been easy to convince the parties involved in the Namibian conflict to find the understanding needed to sign a ceasefire agreement and start the transition process to independence. There is now an opportunity for all of us, the Front-line States, the Five and the parties engaged in the hostilities, to find common ground so that trust can be restored and a just solution found once and for all.[67]

After his talks with the delegation in Luanda, Sam Nujoma reiterated his willingness to sign a ceasefire and to accept a UN peace-keeping force under SCR 435.[68] But he reserved his final answer to the proposals until he had an opportunity of discussing them with his Central Committee. However, he criticized the delegation for proposing to meet the internal parties in Namibia, saying this was tantamount to giving them official recognition.
The delegation found a generally sympathetic response in Lagos, Salisbury, Gaborone, Maputo, Lusaka, Nairobi and Dar es Salaam. After visiting Windhoek, Crocker said that the delegation was 'leaving with a sense of having achieved what we set out to do.'[69]
SA's Prime Minister made his first public reference to the new proposals in a speech on 12 October. While he sharply criticized Lord Carrington and the Australian Prime Minister for their statements at the Commonwealth conference (see below), he said cautiously that there appeared to be 'greater prospects that the central issues will be identified and approached on a more realistic basis.'[70] A week later he went to Windhoek for consultations with the internal parties about their approach to the forthcoming talks with the CG delegation. One political figure who attended the talks said: 'SA seems very serious about getting out of Namibia.'[71] From the subsequent positive response of the DTA and other smaller parties, it seems clear that they were now riding in tandem with Pretoria. Pik Botha described the CG visit to Windhoek as 'a remarkable achievement and a breakthrough'[72]—in the sense that they consulted with Namibian parties other than Swapo—the point earlier criticized by Nujomo. Botha expressed his view that there was a real chance of maintaining the momentum, and he urged the internal parties to prepare themselves for elections to fight Swapo.
The considered replies from the parties consulted by the CG delegation were received in December 1981 after a meeting of the Front-line States, Kenya, Nigeria and Swapo, held in Dar es Salaam on 18 November.[73] The Frontliners' communiqué issued after this meeting was limited to a declaration that Namibia

should become independent in 1982; that Namibians should have the right to work out their own Constitution and elect a government of their own choice; and that SCR 435 was the only basis for resolving the conflict. The African leaders also expressed grave concern over SA's continued military incursions into Angola, and called for international aid to help in its reconstruction work. However, in their confidential reply to the CG, the Front-line States, Nigeria Kenya and Swapo set out their own constitutional proposals which were described as closely following those made by the Western group.[74] They accepted that the Constitution should be adopted by a two-thirds majority; endorsed the Bill of Rights; and accepted the need for an independent Judiciary. (For full reply see Appendix 3.)

A spokesman for the State Department briefed correspondents on 25 November on the replies:

> In general, we feel that we have a basis to proceed, and are cautiously optimistic on that basis. I would also underscore the point that the subsequent phases will be addressing other issues which are, at least, as difficult. We're not saying that we have done more than effectively launch a process, but I think it's a very important step that has been taken.

Crocker described the replies as constructive, including Swapo's. He said the parties had made suggestions and comments, 'but no-one is rejecting anything'. Only Pretoria had not yet replied formally.

The delay in Pretoria's response was almost certainly because it had expected a firmer commitment on the question of Cuban troop withdrawals. This view is supported by the fact that after a SA delegation, led by Brand Fourie, was received at the State Department on 23 and 24 November, one of their senior officials told the SA Broadcasting Corporation representative that 'the withdrawal of Cuban troops from Angola had not been laid down (by the CG) as a condition for independence.'[75]

Another significant development at this time—providing yet another twist to the vagaries of Washington's policies over the Cuban linkage issue—was a statement made by a State Department spokesman in 'clarification or elucidation, of what we're doing in Africa.'[76] He said:

> We have, as you know, said from the outset that we believe there is a very close relationship between events in Namibia and events in Angola; that the conflicts there are inextricably linked, as a matter of reality on the ground. And that there is, therefore, a relationship between progress on the one issue and progress on the other.
>
> In one situation, we have a struggle for the independence of Namibia; in the other we have an internationalized civil war in Angola. The violence spills across boundaries.
>
> So what we have said is the issue of Cuban withdrawal from Angola, while in no way part of a Namibia settlement package, and I would underscore that, it is nonetheless, the kind of thing which, if there is progress, could make a decisive contribution to the effort in Namibia. While at the same time, progress on Namibia, which enables all parties to see that, indeed, independence is coming and that the draw-down of SA forces is underway, will make possible progress on the Angolan issue which, otherwise, might not be possible.
>
> Now I only mention this in order to remove any shadow of doubt that there have been dramatic changes in American policy over the course of the past eight or nine months. When American officials travel in Africa in different capitals, they get very strange questions sometimes—such as: 'When did you drop Angola as part of your concerns in Southern Africa?' We haven't dropped Angola as part of our concerns in Southern Africa. Another question they often get—'When did the Western Five stop

recognizing Swapo as a sole legitimate representative of the Namibian people?' A very simple point. We never did recognize Swapo as a sole representative. So there's a problem of literacy that we often run into in dealing with the Press . . . around Africa, which causes us some concern. We have been consistent on those two points, as we have also been consistent on the issue that independence for Namibia must be negotiated on the basis of SCR 435. It's been consistent since February of 1981.

The CG officials again met in New York and Ottawa in the first half of December to draft their replies to proposals that had come in from the parties engaged in the conflict, and to consider the steps to be taken for Phase 2, which would involve such issues as the organization of the UN Transition Advisory Group (UNTAG), composition of the UN Peacekeeping Force, and ensuring the impartiality of the UN in the eyes of Swapo, the internal parties and SA. Their report was considered on 10 December by the CG Foreign Ministers at a meeting in Brussels. They then announced that the ground was being prepared for achieving 'final agreement on constitutional principles without delay.'[77] On 17 December the revised CG proposals were sent out—and the fat was in the fire.

While SA had by then informed the CG of its formal acceptance of Phase 1 of their proposed plan for bringing Namibia to independence,[78] Swapo now turned angrily against it because of a new detailed proposal about how elections should be arranged for the Constituent Assembly. Based on the West German method of elections, the system would allow for half the seats to be filled by proportional representation and the other half to be elected on the basis of single-member constituencies, with each voter casting two votes—one under each of the two methods of representation.

NEGOTIATIONS AGAIN BREAK DOWN: THE ISSUE OF ELECTIONS (DECEMBER 1981–MARCH 1982)
Sam Nujoma said in an interview with the Yugoslav news agency, *Tanjug*, on 30 December 1981 that he absolutely rejected proposals for a double-vote system as being non-democratic. Later, in a speech in Salisbury (Harare), he described the dual voting system as part of a device to enable 'the Boers to impose a neo-colonialist solution' on Namibia.[79] The fifth annual meeting of Swapo's Central Committee (see below) denounced this proposal as 'the latest imperialist manoeuvre to dilute and amend SCR 435 and to introduce a unique and undemocratic electoral system of one man, two votes.'

The CG members were taken completely by surprise by Swapo's angry rejection of the election procedures. Of all the obstacles they had foreseen in the Phase 1 negotiations, the one proposal they had believed would be uncontroversial was the method of electing the Constituent Assembly. This was seen simply as a version of proportional representation—a method which Nujoma had himself previously suggested as being acceptable. The unusual form of proportional voting was proposed by the Germans, based on their own experience, in order to ensure that the minorities in Namibia would not feel themselves totally excluded from any form of representation in the important Constituent Assembly, while yet allowing a majority party to gain a clear-cut victory. This idea had been enthusiastically received in Pretoria and by the Namibian internal parties—a response which undoubtedly helped to strengthen Swapo's suspicions that the voting method was a trap.

With Swapo now pushed into a corner as the party responsible for obstructing agreement, and with SA in the unusual position of having accepted the Western proposals, a new situation arose in the negotiation process.

At the same time as these new difficulties sprang up with Swapo, another new development—a much more hopeful one—began with moves to achieve an improved relationship between Washington and Luanda. The honest broker in this rapprochement was the French President, who had established closer relations with the Angolans. President dos Santos had declared in a speech on 10 December 1981 that when his Foreign Minister, Paulo Jorge, visited Paris in January, he would be willing to have formal talks with the Americans to discuss the possibility of establishing diplomatic relation. (For details, see Angola's Role below.) Chester Crocker arrived in Paris on 15 January 1982 for three days of talks with Angola's Foreign Minister. Although Paulo Jorge had previously met with Haig, on 25 September, their discussions had been principally over Namibia and not over bilateral relations. The Paris talks ended with an agreement to keep the door open for further discussions. Although there was no prospect of formal diplomatic links so long as the Cuban troops remained in Angola and so, by extension, before there was agreement over Namibia, the Americans and Angolans continued to foster closer economic and trade relations. For example, the State Department had taken the initiative to get the Washington Centre for Strategic and International Studies to arrange a conference in Washington in October 1981 between top Angolan officials and several scores of leading American businessmen.

Crocker was reported to have told Jorge in Paris that Namibia would be on its way to independence within a month, that SA troops would be withdrawing, and that relations between Washington and Luanda would be normal if only Angola asked Cuban troops to leave its territory.[80] He is supposed to have warned that SA would not leave Namibia without a corresponding withdrawal of Cubans from Angola, and to have blamed Angola for helping to contribute to the destabilization of the region by the support it gave to forces like ANC, Swapo and others.

In the meantime, though, the Namibian negotiations remained stalled over the electoral issue. CG officials met in Bonn over 25–26 January 1982 to discuss the latest hitch and to plan for Phase 2. According to some sources,[81] the Five had a stormy passage when Crocker insisted that there could be no question of reopening Phase 1 by renegotiating the proposed electoral procedures. The French and West German delegates were reported to have left one session in 'a very bad mood', and the West German Foreign Minister was said to have had to intervene to prevent the meeting breaking up in disagreement.

There was also a new development in Namibia in February 1982 which upset SA's calculations: the break-up of the DTA with the withdrawal from the alliance of its strongest African partner, the Ovambo-centred National Democratic Party.[82] Speaking in a no-confidence debate in the SA Parliament, the Prime Minister declared on 2 February that 'South West Africa was the mightiest problem of all', and warned that the territory would suffer immensely if there was estrangement with SA—a reference to the Right-wing backlash among Whites in Namibia. He said that SA had worked in close consultation with the internal parties and the US to try and find a solution, but the 'visible partiality of the UN had made progress difficult.[83]

Efforts were made throughout March 1982 to try and convince Swapo and the Front-line States about the advantages of the proposed electoral system. The attitude of the Front-liners was that it was up to Swapo to decide for itself on this particular issue. On 19 March, Swapo categorically refused to accept the double-voting system—a method, it said, which had never before been used in the process of decolonization.[84] Swapo argued that it would 'not be easy to explain the method to the Namibian people whose education level system was very low.' Moreover, it smacked to them of ethnic representation—the method favoured by apartheid. To break the impasse, Swapo proposed direct talks between themselves and SA. The CG turned down this idea as they could not see how it would help to resolve the conflict between the antagonists. Swapo then fell back to its usual position of placing its faith in intensifying the armed struggle. Its Secretary for Foreign Affairs, Peter Museshihange, declared that the 'Gang of Five' were incapable of producing independence for Namibia 'because they consider their economic interests in Namibia as being more important than the Namibian people. . . .'[85]

A fresh effort to break the deadlock in the negotiations was made at the beginning of April when the CG suggested that the electoral procedure for the Constituent Assembly should be based on a single-member constituency, but with each vote counting twice—one, under proportional representation rules, for the party of the voter's choice; the second for a member to represent a particular constituency.

This latest proposal was conveyed to Swapo and the Front-line States in Luanda by Crocker and the French member of the CG negotiating team, Jean Aussell. The British member, Sir Leonard Allinson, took the proposal to Pretoria.

At this stage, Sam Nujoma began to distance himself from the negotiations as a mark of Swapo's disappointment with the CG initiative, leaving Hidipo Hamutenya, a member of the Central Committee, to conduct the talks. On 3 April Hamutenya declared that Swapo was totally opposed to the revised electoral proposals. In its detailed reply to the CG, Swapo noted that what was now being proposed was 'one man, one vote, one vote, two counts' in the place of the earlier proposal of 'one man, two votes'.

While Swapo thought single-member constituencies desirable, such a system would create its own problems. Thus, while it was possible to conduct elections without a previous census, the creation of single-member constituencies would require a complete census under UN supervision, a lengthy process of demarcating constituency boundaries, and compiling a proper register of voters. How, asked Swapo, was it possible to carry out all this work in the seven-month period proposed for the transition period up to the time of elections? Swapo's memorandum charged that the CG had 'dismally failed' to give convincing reasons for the proposed electoral procedures, which were 'based on double standards'. It added: 'We are therefore left to conclude that there exist motives of a political nature, and it is not difficult for us to tell whence their source.' Swapo's memorandum went on to question, for the first time, the CG strategy of a three-phased approach to Namibia's independence—the first being negotiations to get agreement on broad constitutional principles and electoral procedures; the second, to get agreement on the UN role during the transition period after a ceasefire; and the third, the final implementation of the agreed plan. It said that while the phased approach gave 'an illusion of momentum, nothing is actually achieved.' The experience of the past six months had shown that, step by step, Swapo was expected to make concessions—sometimes irreversible ones, while SA yielded practically nothing, not even a binding commitment to independence. It poured scorn on the emphasis placed on the need for the UN to establish its impartiality when the administration of the elections—as already accepted—would be conducted, under UN supervision, by the SA administration itself, with all its well-known hostility to Swapo. The onus, therefore, was on SA rather than the UN to demonstrate *its* impartiality. The memorandum said that Swapo had now fully exhausted the limit of the concessions it was prepared to make, and concluded:

> Our readiness for a negotiated settlement of the Namibian problem should not be misinterpreted. We are fully aware of the nature and strength of the forces opposing

the liberation of Namibia and we are not inclined to under-estimate them. But Swapo's ability to continue its just struggle should not be under-estimated either, all the more so as this struggle enjoys active solidarity and support of African and many other countries. In any case, Swapo is quite capable of ensuring that the expenses of the occupation of Namibia would far surpass its benefits. The situation is already developing in this direction. We believe, however, that it is not in the interest of the West to give solace to Pretoria in its prevarications and obstructionist actions. In our opinion the most correct way of speeding up the negotiations is to consider seriously the constructive proposal of Swapo on convening, under UN auspices, a new Geneva type conference in the course of which suggestions of all parties that are involved in the whole complex of the Namibian settlement could be examined. It is in the light of the foregoing that we once again appeal to the Five to seriously consider, as a matter of urgency, our proposal for the holding of a Geneva-type conference to discuss and resolve all the outstanding issues, that is, all issues involved in the three phases.

Swapo won general support for its stand from a meeting of Foreign Ministers of the Front-line States, Kenya and Nigeria, held in Dar es Salaam on 4 May. Their final communiqué included the following statement:

The Ministers agreed with Swapo's position that this latest proposal has not changed the substance of the Western Five's earlier proposal on the Combination System. The Ministers noted Swapo's continued preparedness to reach a negotiated agreement. They observed, in particular, that Swapo remains ready to abide by its earlier decision to accept two of the three possible electoral methods suggested by the Western Five in their original proposal. By preferring proportional representation while being equally ready to accept a single member constituency system, Swapo had indeed accepted the electoral systems universally practised. The Foreign Ministers commended Swapo for its continued flexibility and goodwill in the negotiations and rejected claims portraying Swapo and the Front-line States as the stumbling block to a negotiated settlement of the Namibia issue.

But given the Western Five's apparent reluctance to impress upon SA to go along with either of these two systems, and considering the Five's insistence on the Combination System, which has resulted in the present impasse in the negotiations, the Ministers noted and shared Swapo's deep disenchantment with the current protracted and sterile phased approach to a negotiated solution of the Namibia question as proposed by the CG.

The Ministers accordingly supported Swapo's proposal that a viable alternative way out of the present stalemate is to set aside the present phase-to-phase approach in the negotiations. The Ministers supported Swapo's proposal conveyed to the Western Five that all outstanding issues should be discussed together in a comprehensive manner in order to resolve them as a package. Such negotiations should ideally take place in a Geneva-type conference under the auspices of the UN. But other means of achieving that objective are not excluded.

BREAKING THE DEADLOCK (JANUARY–JUNE 1982)

This rejection by Swapo and the Front-line States of the CG's electoral proposals put the Western Five in a new dilemma. Having got SA's agreement to the proposals, they would now have to return to Pretoria to try and persuade them to accept one of the two alternatives suggested by Swapo—either proportional representation or direct elections on a national, not a constituency, basis. SA's reply to such an approach would predictably be that this was yet another example of Western unreliability and of 'caving in to African demands.' From their private soundings in Pretoria, the CG felt there was little prospect of SA yielding on the proposed electoral method, which it had used to sell the CG plan to Namibia's internal parties.

In a new effort to break this latest deadlock, Chester Crocker held a secret meeting in Geneva on 10 May with the SA Director-General of Foreign Affairs, Brand Fourie, and the Administrator-General of Namibia, Danie Hough. From Geneva he went to Paris for two days of discussions among CG officials. What emerged from their talks was surprisingly close to what Swapo had proposed in its 1 April memorandum—except for the idea of an actual Geneva-type conference. The suggestion now was to telescope Phase 1 and Phase 2, instead of seeking to complete the one stage before moving on to the next. This meant that the dispute over the electoral method could be set on one side, for the time being, while discussions went on about the even more difficult issues involved in arranging a ceasefire and agreeing on the modalities of the UN peacekeeping force and UNTAG. The CG view was that once everything else was agreed, it would be unthinkable that the whole plan would be wrecked in the end by a failure to reach agreement over the technicalities of election procedures—especially since it stood to reason that any form of election had to be acceptable to all the parties involved.

SA and Swapo had no difficulty about accepting this new approach. Speaking on an official visit to Nigeria, Sam Nujoma said that while Swapo was counting on the intensification of the armed struggle as the only sure way of success, it was nevertheless leaving the door open for further negotiations.[86] Pretoria's reaction was even more welcoming: not only was it willing to endorse Phase 1 (with the original electoral proposals), but it expressed itself as being in broad agreement with the rest of the settlement proposals for Phase 11. (These had originally been put before the Pre-Implementation Meeting in Geneva, where they were strongly resisted at the time by SA.) Whatever else it had up its sleeve, Pretoria was showing an unusual warmth towards the Western initiative and, more remarkably, towards accepting the proposed UN-supervised settlement.

By May, however, the CG's original objective of getting Phase 3 into operation by early 1982 was already off target. It seemed unlikely that, at best, the UN could begin its operations before early 1983. Nevertheless, a meeting of CG Foreign Ministers in Luxembourg on 17 May instructed their officials to accelerate the resolution of outstanding issues 'with a view to maintaining their target of beginning implementation of SCR 435 during 1982.'

The momentum of the negotiations was given a substantial new heave forward at the start of June 1982 by the Americans—now fully in charge of the CG initiative. Acting on the advice of the new chairman of the National Security Council (NSC), William Clark, President Reagan brought in two more of his trusties to support (or guide?) Chester Crocker: Gen Vernon A. Walters and Frank Wiesner. The latter is a former ambassador to Zambia, a Republican Right-winger to his finger-tips, and the African specialist on the NSC. Walters was something else again: a soldier who had worked his way up from the ranks to become a three-star general; a former head of the CIA; an oil consultant and arms dealer, with links in the Third World and a confidante of Morocco's King Hassan.[87] In March 1982 he had spent four hours in conversation with Fidel Castro about a possible resumption of Havana–Washington relations—linked, once again, to the withdrawal of Cuban troops from Angola. The thrust of Walters' initiative was therefore obvious; but whether it would be helpful or harmful to the more professional diplomacy of the State Department remained moot. According to Francis X. Clines:

> Though most of the ambassador's (Walters) travels go unannounced, there are a few Walters-watchers who squint suspiciously at the occasional mentions of his coming or going on foreign news despatches. They recall his missions in the Nixon Administration when he would drop from sight and deal secretly with China and North Vietnam on sensitive matters.[88]

At any rate, June 1982 opened promisingly enough with a meeting in Bonn between Crocker and Nujoma arranged by the West German Foreign Minister. For perhaps the first time since the beginning of the marathon negotiations almost five years earlier, the Swapo leader came away from this meeting sounding optimistic. 'There seems to be a definite degree of seriousness in the so-called CG's approach to the negotiations,' he told the Tanzania newsagency, *Shihata,* on 7 June. A communiqué issued by the State Department after the Bonn meeting contained a significant reference—or was it a slip-up?—to the talks between Crocker and 'President Sam Nujoma'.[89]

The Bonn talks were followed by a new round of visits by CG officials to the Front-line capitals, and with Walters and Wiesner going for separate talks with the Presidents of Tanzania, Zambia and Angola. This time the objective was to get general agreement on the details of Phase 2, prior to a gathering of all the leading actors in the Namibian conflict in Washington in July. The State Department announced on 9 June that the CG's aim remained 'to launch Namibia on the road to independence by the end of the year'.

The unusual wave of optimism which broke over the negotiations in June appeared, at first, to be justified—with Zimbabwe's Prime Minister, Robert Mugabe, declaring that he was now hopeful that the Namibian question was at last going to be settled.[90] He added: 'It is believed that SA is going to be responsible this time, and that it will not stand in the way of the exercise to give Namibia its independence.'

But, once again, the Cuban linkage issue reared its menacing head. On 17 June, in a speech at the Oshivello military base in Namibia, Prime Minister Botha made his first explicit statement affirming that SA's acceptance of the Western plan was contingent on the Cuban troops leaving Angola at the same time as the SA troops moved into their confined bases in Namibia, as required under the proposed ceasefire agreement.[91] 'We make it very clear,' he declared, 'that we cannot complete these three phases unless the Cubans leave. . . . The Cubans must withdraw and the (strength of) SA troops will be gradually reduced.'

A few weeks before Botha's speech, a senior US official said at a press briefing that the two questions of Namibia and Angola had to be resolved 'in tandem', but now he also gave a new emphasis to Unita's role:

> This (Cuban withdrawal) is not an American precondition. This is a fact of life. It reflects the reality on the ground. It reflects the close geographic relationship of the Angolan conflict and the Namibian conflict, and the close political inter-relationship as well.
>
> To assure success on Namibia, we need a commitment from the Angolan Government that Cuban combat forces will depart from Angola in a way coordinated with the departure of SA forces from Namibia as foreseen in SCR 435. Without that, I cannot say that this negotiation will succeed. . . .
>
> We have made clear, and it continues to be our view, that it's difficult to envisage an overall regional solution that does not take into account the interests of the major parties. Clearly, Unita and the people it represents are major parties. Having said that, we have no blueprint or any model for national reconciliation in Angola. We do not believe it is for us to mediate or negotiate, and we have made that clear as well to all the parties. But we find it difficult to envisage the possibility of a regional solution that did not include some discussion leading eventually to some understanding between the key parties in Angola.

The State Department spokesman also confirmed that Gen Walters had recently met with the Angolan President 'to discuss the full range of issues that I am describing here, as well as bilateral questions. It would suffice for me to say that we are seeking to play the role of catalyst in a very complex negotiation.'

Angola's response to this American approach was given by its Planning Minister, Lopo de Nascimento, on 27 June:

> As far as the People's Republic of Angola is concerned, we reject all those who give themselves the right to determine the type of support given to Swapo, just as we reject those who give themselves the right to determine when and how the Cuban troops should withdraw. Those are issues that fall within Angola's national sovereignty.[92]

A week before Nascimento's statement, an editorial in the official Angolan News agency, ANGOP, said the presence of Cuban troops 'has no relation' to the Namibian settlement. The Cubans were in the country at the request of the Angolan Government 'to cooperate in the defence of the country's territorial integrity . . . constantly threatened and attacked by the racist South Africans and their mercenaries and puppets.'[93]

SA's Foreign Minister termed the exposition of this official Angolan view as 'serious', and repeated that no settlement plan in Namibia could be implemented unless all Cuban troops were removed from Angola.[94] On 30 June, a SA delegation—which had arrived in Washington for the proposed meetings—insisted that the withdrawal of Cuban troops was the 'key issue' in agreeing on a settlement for Namibia.[95]

The issue of Cuban linkage surfaced for the first time in an official CG document circulated in June 1982 to all the parties engaged in the negotiations, under the heading 'Other Regional Issues':

> These issues do not fall under SCR 435, nor are they part of the mandate of the Five. But the Governments of the Five individually share the view that action on these problems could do much to advance and facilitate a settlement of Namibia within the time frame we envisage, and would be worth while in itself in bringing peace and contributing to economic development in the area.
>
> A valuable opportunity now exists to achieve a settlement which could resolve other longstanding problems of the region at present hindering the development of the climate of security and mutual confidence necessary for a Namibia settlement.

Commenting on this part of the document, Swapo's spokesman, Hidipo Hamutenya, said:

> Talking to diplomats from certain Contact Group countries, one gets the impression that the onus is now on Angola to accept linkage . . . a very unfair proposition.
>
> Unless one is able to see how linkage can be overcome, one cannot make reasonable predictions about what happens next. As long as there is no answer to our questions about the paragraphs, there is no point in proximity talks.[96]

A NEW CLIMAX: THE NEW YORK TALKS (JULY 1982)
The Namibian negotiations moved towards their second climax in July 1982—the first having ended in failure at Geneva 18 months earlier. This time the negotiating parties met separately in New York for less than a week, from 6 July. A month earlier the CG had handed them a three-page document, *Summary of Points,*[97] which was to be the basis for the crucial New York meeting. Its main points were:

> *Constitutional Principles:* These could be considered as settled, except for the electoral system which should be settled in accordance with the provisions of SCR 435.

The UN Transitional Assistance Group (UNTAG): The UN plan remains intact, including the authorized upper limit of 7,500 for the peacekeeping force. If UNTAG supervised the restrictions imposed on the SADF in their designated bases, and provided Swapo's guerrillas could be supervised in their camps in Angola and Zambia, the need for a Demilitarized Military Zone (DMZ) would be eliminated.

Impartiality of the UN: Instead of asking the UN General Assembly to take a resolution on this issue, the Security Council should be asked to reaffirm the UN's impartiality; this would be based on an understanding between the CG, the Front-line States, Swapo and SA that UN activities which run contrary to SCR 435 should be discontinued.

In this document, the CG did not refer directly to the question of Cuban troop withdrawal, but only mentioned 'other long-standing problems at present hindering the development of the climate of security and mutual confidence necessary for a Namibia settlement.' (See extract, above.)

This 'Other Regional Issues' paragraph disguised an agreed decision among the Five not to try and link the Cuban issue directly with Namibian settlement since this lay outside the providence of SCR 435; instead, there should be parallel talks between the Five with Angola, on one side, and with SA on the other, to reach agreement over the timing of the withdrawal of Cuban troops from Angola and SA troops from Namibia.

For the US this represented not so much a change of policy as a change of approach about how to achieve its particular objective of getting the Cubans out of Angola. Light was shed on this new American approach by Chester Crocker on 2 July[98] when he described the relationship between a Namibian settlement and the Cuban troops' withdrawal as a 'fact of history'. He went on to say:

It's also a fact that no party can lay down prior conditions or preconditions to any other party. That's not going to produce progress. The South Africans cannot be threatened into leaving Namibia, excepting on terms which are in some minimal sense acceptable to them. The same applies the other way. And given the history and the lack of confidence that exists on both sides of that border, we believe that it's unrealistic for any side to say to the other: You go first. What we're seeking is parallel movement on the two questions.

Crocker also disclosed that the US was pursuing the Cuban withdrawal question in bilateral discussions with the Angolan Government.

It is not part of the UN mandate for the Western Contact Group on Namibia. In those discussions with the Angolan Government, the US was saying: 'As a matter of your own national interest, as a sovereign government, here is a possibility for a brighter future for all your people and for the region. If you're prepared to go ahead, we have a chance for an overall regional solution, which is in everyone's interest.' No one is dictating, and there are no preconditions.

Crocker explained that, although the US had discussed with the Angolan Government (only in a general way), the matter of the civil war waged by the Unita forces, a Namibia settlement would create 'an ideal circumstance' for settling that issue as well. National reconciliation within Angola, he added, 'is a very important question that cannot be forever postponed.' He stressed, however, that this was an internal Angolan matter.

The question-mark over the New York talks was whether Angola and SA would be prepared to accept the idea of replacing the former proposal to link the withdrawal of Cuban troops and a Namibian settlement by the new idea of pursuing this aim through parallel talks. It seemed unlikely that the Five would have proposed this new formula so late in the negotiating process without previously having tested its acceptability in both Luanda and Pretoria. The Angolans at first stayed silent on this new development; not so SA's loquacious Foreign Minister. In characteristic style he declared:

> It is of importance that the Cubans and all other foreign forces (*a new point this!* — C.L.) must withdraw from the region and from Angola altogether to create what we would wish to see—an atmosphere free of intimidation . . . so that we can have free and fair elections . . . One thing I insist on—that Phase three (the implementation stage), which ends with an election in the territory, cannot be completed until there is a total Cuban withdrawal.[99]

Even without waiting for progress in the parallel talks, the Western Five reported to the UN Secretary-General on 13 July 'the successful conclusion' of the first phase of the negotiations to bring Namibia to its independence in accordance with SCR 435, and that the way was clear for a start to early implementation. They announced that all the parties to the negotiations 'now accept the principles concerning the Constituent Assembly and the Constitution for an independent Namibia which the Five put forward at the end of last year.'

Their statement was vague about the method for overcoming the obstacle to previous agreement on the First Phase: the methods of elections to the Constituent Assembly. They simply affirmed the principle that it should conform with SCR 435. Finally, the Five said they were still in consultation with 'all concerned' to resolve any other outstanding issues 'to allow us to move ahead to the implementation of the settlement plan in the very near future.'

THE ROLE OF THE LOCAL ACTORS IN THE CONFLICT
ANGOLA: THE PIVOTAL PARTNER IN THE NEGOTIATIONS

As the country most directly affected by the conflict over Namibia, Angola was allowed by the other Front-line States to play the leading role in the negotiations with the CG. The MPLA regime's crucial interest in wishing to help negotiate an end to the conflict was dictated by the country's harrowing economic condition, the devastation caused by repeated SA military attacks, and concern over the security threat posed by Unita, which has received strong SA backing. Notwithstanding its great need for peace, the MPLA has consistently refused to lower its commitment to Swapo's cause.

Although Washington has persisted in its policy of not recognizing the MPLA Government so long as there were Cuban troops on its soil, the MPLA refused to allow this diplomatic nicety to stand in the way of conducting talks with the Americans; instead it has shown a strong wish to develop friendly relations—a development it regards as important to Angola's national interest in establishing unimpeded trade relations with the US and other Western countries. The MPLA's cordial working relations with the American multinational Gulf Oil (which generates 95% of Angola's foreign exchange earnings) had shown that it was possible to engage in commerce with the capitalist world without having to give up any of its own Marxist beliefs. Besides, the Angolans had discovered for themselves that, however important the Soviet bloc was as a strategic military ally, it was not able to provide the kind of economic and technical assistance needed to reconstruct the country's economy which had continued to decline ever since independence, except in the single area of oil production and development. Therefore, while the MPLA showed no intention of abandoning its attachment to Marxist ideas, it pragmatically accepted the need to lessen its heavy dependence on the Soviet bloc. Moreover, the MPLA was itself not wedded to the idea of retaining Cuban troops on its soil; not only were they a burden on the domestic economy, but the behaviour of some Cuban soldiers had upset the peasant population.[100] Thus there was no reason for prolonging the Cuban military presence beyond the time set by Angola's security needs.

Relations between Washington and Luanda had begun to improve under the Carter Administration, with only the Cuban factor remaining as an obstacle to normal diplomatic relations. Luanda therefore viewed with strong concern the election of the Reagan Administration, committed as it was to support for Unita, to a hard line over 'getting the Cubans out of Africa', and to a 'softer attitude' towards SA. These apprehensions seemed to be fully justified by the initial policy positions adopted by the new Administration.

Just two months after Reagan was sworn into office, on 20 March 1981, MPLA's worst fears seemed to be confirmed when James Buckley, the new Under-Secretary for Security Assistance, formally informed Congress that the Administration wanted the Clark Amendment repealed, and announced that Jonas Savimbi would be invited to visit the US. (The Clark Amendment forbids the President from authorizing funds for clandestine military purposes, such as support for Unita.) A month later, Savimbi had a meeting with an Assistant Secretary of State, Lannon Walker, in Morocco. Although the Savimbi visit to the US was twice put off, and while Chester Crocker sought to allay Angolan fears on his first visit to Luanda in April 1981, MPLA suspicions about Washington's dealings with Pretoria remained strong and were kept alive by periodic American actions, such as the decision to veto a Security Council resolution condemning Operation Protea on 31 August. The State Department had earlier warmed hearts in Pretoria by stating that Operation Protea had to be seen in 'its full context', namely, one that took into account the use of Angolan territory by Swapo, the flow of Soviet arms to Swapo, and the Cuban military presence there. The effect was to qualify US opposition to the SA attack, in contrast to the unqualified condemnation of the attack by the Western Europeans.

Paulo Jorge reacted to the US veto in the Security Council by expressing alarm on 18 September at 'the reinforcement of the relations between the US and SA, which could have the objective of destabilizing Angola'.[101] He warned that Angola could brandish 'the oil weapon' if 'Washington threatened Angola's territorial integrity.' Earlier, on 4 September, the Angolan ambassador to France, Luis de Almeida, accused Washington of having 'chosen to side with Pretoria in the name of a crude and unintelligent anti-communism.' He said that 'the Angolan dead in the provinces of Cunene and Kuando-Kubango and Huila perished as victims of racist barbarism with the complicity of the greatest Western power, which proclaims itself a champion of freedom and human rights.'

Chester Crocker seemed at first to be determined to insist on the MPLA regime agreeing to negotiate with Savimbi and to secure the withdrawal of Cuban troops as integral components of the Namibian settlement plans. 'We believe that movement on Namibia can reinforce movement toward Cuban troop withdrawal and *vice-versa,*' he said on 29 August. 'Furthermore, we are convinced that a satisfactory outcome can only be based on parallel movement in both arenas.' He also argued that 'Unita represents a significant and legitimate factor in Angolan politics.'[102] However, during his first brief visit to Luanda in April 1981 Crocker had been left in no doubt that the Angolans would not negotiate on such matters and would oppose any linkage between Cuban withdrawal and the Namibian peace plan.

Although the Reagan Administration consistently denied that it planned to revive US military aid for Unita, it did not rule this out as a possible option—even though US weapons could reach Angola only through Namibia, which would have been seen throughout Africa as complicity in SA's campaign to destabilize an independent African government, with obvious diplomatic consequences. Moreover, it would doubtless have obliged Luanda to reinforce rather than lessen, its ties with the Soviet bloc and its dependence on Cuban troops. It would have emboldened SA to maintain its occupation of Namibia, effectively scuttling the laborious attempts of the CG; and it would certainly have aroused strong opposition from Western European governments.

In fact, the Reagan Administration seemed to want the Clark Amendment's repeal only in order to remove an encumbrance on Presidential power. 'There are no plans to provide assistance to any of the forces inside Angola,' a State Department spokesman, Dean Fischer, explained on 18 December. 'Nonetheless, the restrictions on the President's power in foreign affairs imposed by the Clark Amendment remain unacceptable to this Administration. The President's authority to conduct foreign affairs is a matter of principle upon which we will not compromise.'

Despite the assurances that no aid was planned for Unita, the Reagan Administration's overall policy towards Angola was widely criticized—by African leaders, Congressional liberals, Western European allies and US businesses with interests in Angola's oil-based economy. The Senate Foreign Relations Committee voted in favour of repeal of the Clark Amendment on 13 May 1981, and the full Senate followed suit on 30 September. However, liberal Democrats remained dominant on the African Sub-committee of the House of Representatives' Foreign Affairs Committee. Its chairman, Howard Wolpe, strongly opposed repeal. The Sub-committee voted 7-0, with two Republicans voting against the Administration, to retain the Clark Amendment on 27 April, and the full Foreign Affairs Committee went on to vote likewise on 12 May. On 1 December the House of Representatives decided to leave the amendment on the statute book. A House–Senate conference failed to resolve the issue and the Administration reserved the right to move again for repeal during the next session of Congress.

Towards the end of 1981, President dos Santos appealed to the US for better relations. 'We are ready at any time to discuss with the Government of the US all problems of common interest that fall into a bilateral framework and which could lead to the normalization of relations between the two countries,' he said during a visit to Cabinda[103] A State Department spokesman described his appeal as 'an important and very positive statement to which we have responded in a similarly positive manner through diplomatic channels.' Crocker then held almost 15 hours of talks with Paulo Jorge in Paris over 15–16 January, but he apparently intended to continue withholding diplomatic recognition until the closing stages of a Namibian settlement. According to Simon Malley, the editor of *Afrique-Asie* (1 February 1982), Crocker promised excellent bilateral relations and said the US would sponsor an international conference of Western nations to channel aid to Angola on condition that the MPLA agreed to have the Cubans withdrawn and to talk to Unita. Jorge is said to have repeated his Government's viewpoint that there could not be talks with Unita under any circumstances; that an explicit link between the settlement of the Namibian problem and the withdrawal of Cuban troops from Angola was unacceptable interference in Angola's internal affairs; that relations between Angola and Cuba would remain a matter for these two countries alone to determine; and that, once Namibia had achieved majority rule and SA attacks had stopped, then Angola would begin discussions with Cuba on a timetable for the withdrawal of its troops.

It is not without some significance that the Angolan Government refrained from using any of the options open to it, other than to engage actively in the Western initiative to find a negotiated settlement of the Namibia conflict. For example, under its Treaty of Friendship and Cooperation with the USSR, it had the right to call for Soviet aid to protect the country's border from external attack—and with the presence of a large Cuban combat force this course of action could not be entirely ruled out. However, for the reasons already described, the MPLA refrained from taking a step which would have sharply raised the level of international involvement in the conflict. Nor did Angola pursue another line of action (although it was envisioned in a decision taken by its Council of Ministers on 2 September 1981) to invoke Article 51 of the UN Charter which allows member-states under attack the right to take 'individual or collective self-defence' until such time as the Security Council itself decides to take appropriate measures to maintain international peace. By invoking Article 51, Angola would have been justified in calling on external powers, including the USSR, to come to its military assistance.

Angola's determination, and its ability, to pursue an independent foreign policy, not dictated by the USSR, was clearly demonstrated by President dos Santos' avowal of interest in pursuing his peace efforts through the Western Five and, in particular, with the US.

UNITA: WAITING IN THE WINGS

Jonas Savimbi's twice-postponed visit to the US finally came off in December 1981. Although described as 'a private visit', he was received by the Secretary of State, Al Haig, Walter Stoessel, the Deputy Secretary for Political Affairs, and Chester Crocker. He also had talks with the CIA. Fred Wittering, the former CIA station chief in Mozambique and now director of the Southern African desk in the National Security Council, was closely concerned in making arrangements for Savimbi's visit which was sponsored by a private human rights group, the Heritage Foundation.[104] He was also reported to have had three meetings with President Mobutu and the FNLA leader, Holden Roberto, during his stay in Washington.[105]

A State Department spokesman, Alan Romberg, explained that the Administration was 'open to talk with all the parties to the conflict in Southern Africa, and this obviously includes Unita, which we regard as a legitimate political force in Angola and which must be taken into account if peace is to return to the region . . . Savimbi reiterated his commitment to a political solution to the civil war in Angola.'[106] Replying to suspicions about a possible secret US deal with Savimbi against the MPLA, Romberg pointed out that such a conclusion was 'simply illogical': 'Since it would run counter to the US goals of achieving a peaceful solution in the area. . . there is no way we could pursue those goals and, at the same time, try to get Savimbi to take over Luanda . . . Seen in this context, the Savimbi visit is not sinister, but important.'[107]

The SA Government's attitude to, and relations with, Unita were explicitly stated in the leaked State Department document recording the 'Memorandum of Conversation' which took place in Pretoria on 15/16 April between Chester Crocker, SA's Foreign Minister and the Defence Minister. According to the Memorandum:

> SAG (SA Government) sees Savimbi in Angola as a buffer for Namibia. SAG believes Savimbi wants Southern Angola. Having supported him thus far, it would damage SAG honour if Savimbi is harmed.

There were a number of reports[108] from different sources in September 1981, after Operation Protea, speculating that the SA army was militarily reinforcing Unita. One such report from Luanda quoted Eastern European diplomats there as the source for a statement that a SA motorized column was heading in the direction of the Cuando Cubango province, which is dotted with Unita hideouts. Western diplomatic sources in Luanda confirmed this report, and added that fresh arms supplied were being provided to Unita. Pretoria dismissed these reports as 'ridiculous propaganda.'[109] There was also considerable speculation by well-informed British correspondents in SA that one of Operation Protea's objectives was to establish a buffer in southern Angola by clearing the area of Swapo guerrilla camps and Angolan army units and so making it possible for Unita to police the zone.[110]

Jonas Savimbi described his own relations with SA in these terms in an interview with *Newsweek:*

> We are not cooperating militarily with SA. However, as long as the South Africans are in Namibia we have no choice but to have relations with them. Our own fight in our own country is against the Cubans and the MPLA. But we cannot fight enemies on two fronts. We get our diesel oil and some food from Namibia, but we pay cash for them. It is not something that we need to apologize for. Black men with flat noses can hardly agree with apartheid, but governments throughout this region have contact with SA—even the current government in Angola itself.[111]

In the same interview, Savimbi said that Unita 'strongly supported the independence of Namibia.' Speaking of Swapo, he said:

> We have been the closest of comrades in the past, although international geopolitics have driven us apart against our wills. The Namibian people have the right to freedom, and we believe that Swapo has the support of the people.

Defining Unita's political aims, Savimbi said:

> I still believe that elections are needed. In 1975 it was said that Unita would command 45% of the vote. Now we would get more than 60% because people are so disappointed with the state of the country. I don't understand the logic of those countries that have preached the need for elections and majority rule in Zimbabwe, Namibia and SA but not Angola. No-one has the courage to say we need majority rule and elections in Angola, too.
>
> There is no military victory to be won here. We believe the MPLA will eventually enter into negotiations with us. It is a question of forcing their hand—though it will take a lot of fighting.

Speaking of the aid he had received from other sources, Savimbi declared:

> In 1979 we received 550t of arms from the Chinese. A number of Arab countries, for example, Morocco, and a number of Black African States, such as Senegal and the Ivory Coast, give us small quantities of weapons. We also sent 500 officers for training in Morocco in 1973. Most of our other arms, including our SA-7 missiles, have been captured from the enemy. . . .
>
> We have reason to believe that at least 18 African countries wuld like to see the Americans involved militarily or diplomatically in getting the Cubans out of Angola.

Savimbi described his military position:

> We have four different types of operational zones. Here, we have total control. We have eleven infantry battalions totalling more than 8,000 men, and by the end of the

211

year we will have 15 battalions. To the north, on the central plateau and beyond the Benguela railway, we have c. 20,000 guerrillas and village militiamen operating in areas nominally under MPLA administration. We control the country-side by night because we have the support of the people. Farther north we have teams of unarmed guerrillas working to win acceptance of UNITA's objectives. And in the capital of Luanda and other major towns we have clandestine cells collecting intelligence and committing sabotage. Nearly 50 of our people have been caught and executed by the MPLA in the last two years, but still our operations in the towns continue to expand. . . .

We are ready for the possibility that the Cubans will use armour and air power against us. But air power without infantry is just a waste of time. They will have to involve their troops again in a big way. Although it will be difficult for us militarily, it will be good for us politically because we are going to capture a lot of Cubans.

Savimbi was persistent in his demand that Unita should not be left entirely out of the negotiations over Namibia. He claimed it would not be possible to implement SCR 435 effectively since Unita 'controlled' some of the area to be demarcated as the Demilitarized Military Zone and which was to be policed by the UN peacekeeping force. Without his involvement, he warned, the DMZ could not be guaranteed effective policing—a threat which seemed to imply that he might not recognize the UN's authority in the DMZ unless he were involved in its arrangements. The subsequent decision to drop the DMZ proposal eliminated any such risk.

ZAMBIA—PRESIDENT KAUNDA'S APPROACH TO PRETORIA

President Kenneth Kaunda decided in March 1982 to engage in a personal initiative by offering to have talks with SA's Prime Minister. His decision was critically received by other members of the Front-line States but not, apparently, by Angola. In an interview with the Johannesburg Star (8 March 1982), the Zambian leader had signalled his readiness to meet Botha to discuss the 'potentially explosive' developments in Southern Africa.

The two leaders met in a mobile trailer on the Botswana–SA border on 30 April, after the Botswana Government had initially declared itself opposed to such a meeting taking place on its soil. Botswana also refused to attend the talks in an observer's role. Complete secrecy was maintained about the nature of the talks— beyond a statement at their conclusion that they had been 'frank and useful' in discussing ways to defuse conflict in Southern Africa and, in particular, to end the fighting in Namibia. A week after this meeting, Kaunda went to Luanda to report on his talks to President dos Santòs. A communiqué at the end of their meeting indicated a spirit of complete rapport between the two leaders, strengthening the view that Kaunda's initiative had been taken in consultation with Luanda.

ZIMBABWE AND MOZAMBIQUE: A TIGHT ALLIANCE

Faced with a serious internal political crisis in 1982, brought on by the open conflict between the two Patriotic Front leaders, Robert Mugabe and Joshua Nkomo, the Zimbabwe Government was deeply concerned with the widening conflict in the region as it impinged directly on its own security.[112] Since Robert Mugabe is strongly committed to support for the liberation struggle in Southern Africa— though not to the extent of being ready to invite an open conflict with Pretoria by offering any form of military support to the ANC or PAC (see above)—he found himself trapped in a situation of deep antagonism to the Pretoria regime while, at the same time, being crucially dependent on it for cooperation in trade and for communications to the sea. While these sharply contradictory interests inevitably imposed some constraints on Zimbabwe's freedom of action, Mugabe showed no sign of being willing to lessen his hostile stance towards Pretoria.

Though himself not yet subject to direct military pressures—as in the case of Angola and, to a lesser extent, Mozambique—Mugabe accepted the eventual possibility of his country sharing their fate at the hands of SA. Hence his strong interest in promoting the Southern African Development Coordination Conference, (SADCC)[113] and especially its objective of improving transport routes through Mozambique. It remains doubtful, though, whether even this limited objective can be reached before the developing crisis in the region pushes Zimbabwe and SA into an even more damaging confrontation.

Mugabe takes the view that SA is already deeply engaged in subversive activities in his country as an element in its politics towards the region as a whole. He told a visiting EEC–ACP mission in February 1982 that Pretoria was 'working systematically' with opposition movements in Angola, Zambia, Mozambique and Zimbabwe—as well as in the Seychelles—'creating instability from the Indian Ocean to the Atlantic.'[114] He declared that SA was involved in attempts to bring about the secession of Zimbabwe's southern province, Matabeleland; that it was engaged in training 'a secret army of 5,000–6,000', many of them former members of the Selous Scouts and supporters of Bishop Muzorewa (see above); and that it was involved in specific instances of sabotage attacks inside Zimbabwe itself.

Zimbabwe spokesmen—like its Foreign Minister, Dr Witness Mangwende[115]—expressed his Government's concern about the 'apparent collusion' between some Western countries and SA in the Namibian negotiations. Mugabe, though, remained strongly supportive of the Western initiative. President Reagan spoke with unusual warmth of the Zimbabwe Government in his message to Congress urging economic aid for it; while in his testimony to a Congress committee on 17 July 1981, Chester Crocker declared:

> As a key Southern African State, whose successful development receives strong support from Washington, Zimbabwe is clearly one of our strong interlocutors on the Namibian issue.

Zimbabwe and Mozambique are closely allied with each other in terms of a common political outlook, personal friendship between Mugabe and President Samora Machel (deriving from the latter's support from the triumphant Zanu wing of the Patriotic Front), and because of common security and economic interests. Mozambique is Zimbabwe's only alternative to SA for access to the sea; in time, it will become the major outlet for Zimbabwe's traffic. In the meantime, the state of insecurity in Mozambique is not only a matter of concern for the Frelimo regime, but is also seriously disruptive of its neighbours' communications system. Clearly, any serious destabilization of the Frelimo regime would have a strongly adverse effect on economic and political conditions in Zimbabwe as well. Seen in this light, SA's policy of promoting instability in Mozambique is also a means of applying direct pressures on Zimbabwe.

In July 1981, at a time when the SA-supported dissident Mozambique Resistance Movement (MNR) was successfully expanding its sabotage activities, Mugabe and Machel met to discuss a joint military exercise against the rebels. As a result, Zimbabwe strengthened its military forces along its border, especially in the south–eastern area which the MNR is known to have used for its forays into Mozambique.[116]

Mozambique has continued to rely on the Soviet Union as its principal foreign strategic ally—a relationship acknowledged in the Treaty of Friendship and Cooperation signed in 1977. The treaty includes a mutual defence clause, which President Machel threatened to invoke after SA's military attack on Matola on 31 January 1981. (Mozambique's relations with SA are discussed under Areas of Conflict, above.) Although a few ships of the Soviet navy showed up off Maputo in the weeks following that attack, there has been a conspicuous absence of any Soviet military presence in the country, apart from its shipments of arms. A defence and military agreement was also signed with East Germany in 1979, while relations with Cuba have developed steadily. These relations, however, are mainly confined to economic and technical cooperation which, though not large, is nevertheless important. Cuba is involved in strengthening Mozambique's intelligence service. Frelimo is one of the few African regimes that has consistently voted for resolutions at the UN supportive of Moscow, e.g. its refusal to support the motion condemning Soviet aggression against Afghanistan.

Despite the contretemps with the US following the expulsion in 1980 of four CIA agents, alleged to have worked closely with SA intelligence services, Mozambique has favoured developing economic relations with America. Machel has also cooperated actively with the US and the other CG members in the Namibia negotiations. In this aspect of his policy, he has shown the same scant regard for the Soviet bloc's sharp hostility to the Western initiative as he did over Moscow's strong opposition to the Lancaster House talks which ended the war in Rhodesia.

THE FRONT-LINE STATES: CHAMPIONS OF PEACEFUL NEGOTIATIONS
The role of the six Front-line States[117] has been that of interlocutor between the CG and Swapo. Although the Front-line Presidents did not always see eye-to-eye with Swapo—and, on occasion, even disapproved of its stand on particular issues—they never actively sought to apply pressures on the Namibian leadership, although they did try to influence them when, in their view, Swapo was being unnecessarily obdurate. This was especially true in the case of Angola which, as already described, was allowed to play a leading part in shaping Front-line policies and attitudes. Angola's strong national interest in wishing to see the Namibian conflict brought to an end sometimes led to a feeling among Swapo's leaders that their own interests might be subsumed by those of Angola; yet, because of their total dependence on Angolan goodwill and support, such differences as sprang up from time to time were overcome, without sharp animosity, because of their overriding common interests.

As chairman of the Front-line States—a position he has held since its inception—President Julius Nyerere continues to remain a key figure. Although he personally strongly disapproved of President Kaunda's initiative in engaging independently in talks with SA, Nyerere did not allow this difference to disturb relations between the Front-line Presidents. Despite such occasional departures from the rule of consensus observed by the group, their internal cohesion over issues affecting Southern Africa has remained surprisingly strong.

The pattern followed in the negotiations with the CG was for each of the Presidents to meet separately with the missions sent out by the Western Five, and then to meet at summit meetings on an *ad hoc* basis whenever major issues had to be confronted, or when a collective reply was called for in respect to specific proposals.

Although not a formal member of the grouping, Nigeria became involved in all its activities as an *ex officio* member—a position reflecting the importance attached by the Front-line Presidents to the diplomatic muscle of Black Africa's largest and economically strongest country and, especially, because of its influence with the Western nations.

Another change in the practice of the Front-line States introduced in 1981 was to invite the current chairman of the OAU—in this case President Moi of Kenya—to their regular meetings, thus institutionalizing the relationship between this grouping and the OAU.

A major incongruity in the Front-line group is that although Botswana is a member, the other two border states with SA—Lesotho and Swaziland—are not. Lesotho has on several occasions complained about being left out, but without success. One possible reason for this is the desire to keep the grouping as small as possible for the sake of convenience; another possibility is that, if Lesotho were admitted, it would be difficult to keep out Swaziland whose policies towards SA are less consistently in harmony with those of the other Front-line States.

Although the Front-line Presidents do not act as a caucus in promoting the objectives of the Southern African Development Coordination Conference, all are members of this association. There is an obvious overlay of interest between the objectives of the SADCC and the political objectives of the Front-line States.

SOUTH WEST AFRICAN PEOPLE'S ORGANIZATION OF NAMIBIA (SWAPO): PRETORIA'S PRINCIPAL ANTAGONIST

Swapo has become the principal challenging force to South Africa's rule in the Namibia conflict not primarily because of its military prowess as a guerrilla movement, but because of its unshakable popular support—not just, as is frequently asserted, among the Ovambos but in all the urban communities, and particularly among the youth. Its charismatic leader, Herman Toivo ja Toivo, has been a prisoner on Robben Island since the early 1960s. By the beginning of 1980, few doubted that Swapo would win a convincing majority in any genuinely free election. This was the fear that has dictated Pretoria's policy in Namibia in recent years. In its eyes, Swapo is an out-and-out communist organization, closely allied to Moscow (see below). Such a view derives not from Swapo's policy declarations but because almost all of its military aid, and much of its diplomatic support, comes from the Soviet bloc and Cuba; and because the base country for its guerrilla forces is Marxist Angola.

Swapo began its extra-continental political life in the West, mainly in Britain, where it found considerable sympathy for its aims, but absolutely no support from Western Governments. It was this experience, not ideology, that led Swapo to seek its support from the communist world—a policy that was fortified when the Soviet bloc and Cuba became the armourers of Angola and its principal military allies.

Swapo's political programmes are, in fact, non-communist and essentially socialist, in the Western sense. Only if Swapo's policy statements are dismissed as camouflage (as Pretoria does) is it possible to conclude that Swapo is a Soviet-controlled, communist organization—which is not to say that there are no communist cadres within Swapo: there certainly are. But, as yet, they form a small minority whose size has grown as the struggle for independence has lengthened and deepened.

Swapo's president-general, San Nujoma, is not himself a Marxist ideologue. He might well see the growth of a sizeable communist group within Swapo as a threat to his own leadership. Although the Marxist cadres have become a pressure group within Swapo and are represented on its Central Committee, none of their number is to be found among the organization's top leadership.

215

A problem in evaluating Swapo's policies are the discrepancies between the statements by its leaders at various times (especially between what is said in private and in public), as well as between its congress resolutions and other declared policy objectives. These contradictions are particularly marked between what is said by its publicists—more particularly on Radio Free Namibia, which broadcasts from Addis Ababa—and by its leaders in negotiations with the CG and the Front-line Presidents.

These conflicting positions are however, explicable in terms of Swapo's very deep suspicions about the West's dealings with SA. At times when Swapo has reason to feel the Western initiative seems to offer a way of shortening their armed struggle, its attitude is completely different from that when the CG seems to be asking the Organization to make concessions to Pretoria. Throughout the long negotiations, Swapo has remained unsure about the sincerity of the CG initiative because of the Western nations' failure to use its full potential to persuade the Pretoria regime to move ahead in implementing SCR 435, which Swapo has accepted from the time it was passed, despite its having originated from an Anglo–American initiative. This strongly suspicious aspect of Swapo's ambivalent feelings about the motives of the Western initiative was thoroughly aroused when President Reagan was elected; here, after all, was a man who used the same language as Pretoria in talking of Swapo as 'a terrorist organization.' It took Crocker almost six months to allay, even minimally, the hostility of Swapo to the Reagan Administration—but the suspicions continued to lie buried not very far below the surface. It did not take much to change Swapo's stance from being a constructive partner in the CG negotiations to denouncing the whole operation as a 'sinister mechanism, conspiracy and collusion of imperialism and racist SA.'[118]

The other side of Swapo's suspicions of 'imperialist conspiracy' has been the consistent way in which Sam Nujoma has worked to strengthen friendship with Western nations—spending as much time, or even more, in Western capitals than in those of the Soviet bloc. There is also the significantly different approach of Nujoma and his lieutenants in their private talks with the CG negotiators from their public utterances. Yet, none of this is really surprising since the sharp changes from positive to negative attitudes is inherent in the paranoid experience of all liberation movements.

Nevertheless, the contradictory statements emanating from Swapo makes it possible to select only those statements useful to advancing whatever particular point of view interested parties wish to promote. The clearest and most reliable description of the policies a Swapo government is likely to pursue was outlined by its influential secretary-general, Moses Garoeb, in an interview he gave in Zimbabwe in November 1981.[119] Speaking of Swapo's commitment to racial reconciliation, the rule of law, political stability and a pragmatic economic policy, he said a future Swapo Government would be prepared to work with the DTA leader, Dirk Mudge; but that it would not allow the existence of 'racist parties'. Swapo, he said, would not allow the ANC to establish military bases in Namibia, and it would seek 'correct and cordial relations with SA'.[120] Praising Mugabe's example of seeking racial reconciliation, he said that Swapo's aim would be 'a conscious policy of deracialization.' Garoeb gave the following outline of Swapo's approach to other key issues:

'A peaceful transition is our very serious commitment. It is not a propaganda stance.'
But mineral and other contracts previously agreed between the SA Government and multinational corporations would have to be renegotiated. 'We are definitely not

216

going to allow a situation by which there is unchecked exploitation of our resources where there is no reinvestment in Namibia.'

Mineral and other resources would be regarded as national assets and the conditions under which they were exploited would depend on an independent Namibia's national interest. 'We must stress that we want the economic transition to be peaceful and to provide continuity. Like Mr Mugabe in Zimbabwe, we want a radical economic transformation without disrupting production.'

'A Swapo government will want to ensure there is no violence after independence. We foresee a period of gradual catching up for the Blacks in line with what we want— an egalitarian society. In the first few years of independence, our people may not necessarily get the fruits of independence, but years later we may begin to realise our objective.

Swapo would not impose a one-party state. A decision on such a system would be made by the people.

Trade and other relations with SA would depend on whether it was in Namibia's interest to have them, and they would have to be conducted on the basis of 'respect for each other's sovereignty'. A Swapo-ruled Namibia would, however, try to reduce its economic dependence on SA through membership of the SADCC. Its foreign policy would be non-aligned.

Swapo's role in the negotiations with the CG were usually described by Western sources as 'obdurate'; but this was not the view taken by the Front-line Presidents who, even while not always agreeing with Swapo's negotiating positions, found Nujoma helpful and constructive despite his fundamentally suspicious approach to the negotiations. Nujoma was certainly 'obdurate' in the manner in which he rejected unacceptable proposals—such as that over the proposed voting system for the Constituent Assembly; but he also showed himself receptive to many, indeed most, of the proposals emanating from the CG. (For details, see 'The course of the Negotiations', above).

Nujoma's Western critics sometimes refer to him as 'stupid'—'not clever like Mugabe' is a remark attributed to Lord Carrington. But those who know Nujoma well, speak only of his slowness in making up his mind; of the plodding, but consummate, political skill he has shown in remaining the undisputed leader in exile of the heterogenous groups within Swapo; of his unwavering courage in confronting a redoubtable foe like Pretoria, and in his dealings with uncertain friends in the West; of his genuine lack of any racist or tribal feeling; of his widespread personal support among Namibians, not just among his own Ovambo people. Such a leader cannot simply be written off as being 'stupid'.

REPUBLIC OF SOUTH AFRICA: A REGIONAL POWER IN NEED OF FRIENDS

Pretoria's policies towards its neighbours have already been described and are further elaborated in the subsequent chapters on South Africa's role. In its regional setting, SA sees itself as being at the end of the line of the 'African Revolution' which has swept down from the Mediterranean, carrying all before it, but now held back by the White barrier along the Cunene and Limpopo rivers. It sees this tidal sweep forward of African nationalism as a mortal threat to the established SA political system, and an incitement to the Republic's own Black population to rise up and join with the rest of the continent in putting an end to White minority rule. In this over-dramatized but essentially correct picture of its own situation, Pretoria sees the communist nations as being not only the allies of the 'African Revolution', but also as its propelling force; hence all those who militantly advance its cause must necessarily be the 'lackeys' or 'agents' or 'dupes' of Moscow. Pretoria's view of the Western democracies is that they are primarily responsible— through their 'pusillanimous policies'—of allowing Africa to become a continent of 'chaos, corruption and economic bankruptcy', and of opening it to 'Russian penetration.' Its mistrust of Western policies is constantly fed by the sense that White South Africans have been abandoned by the Europeans and North Americans, and left to stand alone.

Given this *weltanschaung*, it isn't difficult to understand the fears, attitudes, misconceptions, as well as correct conceptions, that have gone into developing the total strategy policy which the Pretoria regime offers to the embattled White South African community as its way to survive.

Two hopeful elements in Pretoria's otherwise gloomy policy assumptions are that the whole of the West need not be written off as irrecoverably lost, since those who see 'the Russian danger' in the same light as itself—such as President Reagan and Franz-Josef Strauss of West Germany—are still to be won over if only SA remains resolute, while the nature of the 'communist menace' in Africa becomes better understood; and that not all Africans are necessarily opposed to White South Africa's interests—sharing, for example, a common concern about 'the threat of communism'. To win over these African 'moderates', Pretoria's foreign policy interests calls for a policy of reforms within the Republic itself.

Stated in its simplest form, SA's foreign policy is based on the need to prepare for the worst, but at the same time to believe that the worst is not inevitable. Preparing for the worst calls for a steel defence barrier and a powerful striking force capable of delivering crippling blows against any of its neighbours harbouring guerrillas; building on the belief that the worst can be avoided calls for a sustained effort to try and win friends and influence people in the West and in Africa.

SA's policies in the Namibia/Angola conflict offer a clear illustration of the way in which these policies are applied; on the one hand, there is a strong military commitment to defending the Namibian laager by all means possible, including hitting as hard as is necessary across the border into Angola; and, on the other hand, there is a readiness to engage in negotiations with the West—especially with the Reagan Administration—to try and retain its friendship, thereby hoping to get the best possible terms from any likely settlement over Namibia.

The duality in SA's regional policies has already been discussed in the review of its efforts at destabilizing its neighbours. The positive element in this policy calls for the pursuit of friends by diminishing active hostility through offers of economic cooperation. Its negative element lies in its readiness to engage in punitive measures to discourage its neighbours from lending support to cadres of the armed struggle. These two lines of action are held to be not alternatives, but as parallel—with only the emphasis changing in response to particular developments. While Pretoria's obvious preference is for promoting the positive element in its policy, its overriding concern is with its own security interests—as explained by its Army Chief, Gen Constand Viljoen:

> Some of SA's neighbours have been warned at top level that SA security might, in due course, outweigh cooperation with them. If they allow terrorists to use their countries as springboards for terrorist attacks on SA, this country will have no other choice but to put its security interests above its humanitarian and economic ideals for a stable sub-continent.[121]

Yet another example of the thinking behind this punitive policy comes from a statement made by SA's Foreign Minister, Pik Botha, as recorded in the leaked State Department Memorandum already referred to. The memorandum minuted that:

Botha argued the central issue in Southern Africa is subversion. *Noting that what ANC does, SA can do better,* Botha stressed the need for agreement on non-use of force. If the region starts to collapse, fire will spread; there will be no winners. This is not meant as a threat, but simply stating facts. (Italics added.)

Pretoria's view of Moscow as the major threat in the sub-continent and the puppet-master of those working to overthrow the regime was also strikingly brought out in the recorded conversation with Crocker.

Botha noted that SAG (SA Government) thought it important for US to stop Soviet gains. But if you say Swapo not Marxist, you move in same direction as previous Administration. Swapo's people are indoctrinated in Marxism every day. Savimbi considers Swapo universally Marxist. SAG's bottom line is no Moscow flag in Windhoek. If US disagrees, let sanctions go on, and get out of the situation. SA can survive sanctions. Eventually, SA can get support of moderate Black African States . . . At moment, US doesn't believe SAG view of Swapo; you're soft on Swapo. . . . Without Soviet support, others won't accept Nujoma's rule. . . . Botha concluded by saying that SAG doesn't want Namibia to go the wrong way; that's why SA is willing to pay the price of the war. We pray and hope for a government favourably disposed to us. The internal parties don't want us to let go until they have sufficient power to control the situation. We want an anti-Soviet Black government . . .

Malan (the Defense Minister) declared that Angola/Namibia situation is number one problem in Southern Africa. Angola is one place where US can roll back Soviet / Cuban presence in Africa. Need to get rid of Cubans, and support Unita. Unita is going from strength to strength, while Swapo grows militarily weaker.

The way in which Pretoria's view of the Soviet's role in the region translates into policy is revealingly shown in this commentary by the State-controlled radio on a statement made by the Foreign Minister on 1 March 1982.

Mr. R. F. Botha, has forecast that if Swapo wins the forthcoming election in SWA/Namibia, then Russia will be sitting pretty in Windhoek. And SWA will go the way of Zimbabwe and many other African states where economies have crumbled and all vestiges of freedom have disappeared. This could be regarded as a sweeping statement, but unfortunately the supporting evidence is far too telling to ignore. The ties between Swapo and the Soviet Union are extremely strong. It's noteworthy that frequently Swapo leader Sam Nujoma found himself in Moscow prior to important decisions on SWA. and, of course, South African raids into Angola proved conclusively that the SWAPO fight is fought with Soviet weapons. *It does not take much imagination to conclude, therefore, that the Soviet Union and her surrogates would move into SWA should Swapo come into power.* The reason would simply be the same as that fabricated by Angola, namely that the Communist forces are necessary in order to keep South African forces out of an independent SWA. SA would be projected as a country threatening Namibia. However, the factual situation would be far different. The Cubans, East Germans and Russians would be necessary in Namibia not to keep SA out, but rather to keep Swapo in power indefinitely. This is what is happening in Angola, where Cubans are seldom used in clashes with SA forces, but are there exclusively to protect the MPLA Government from the forces of UNITA and the FNLA.[122] (Italics added.)

It is precisely because the SA authorities are themselves deeply persuaded of the nature of Soviet policy and its 'hold' over the liberation movements that their reactive policies need to be taken seriously. They do not simply use the 'communist bogey' to drum up support for their policies. Because they are themselves so thoroughly alarmed by the threat the Soviets hold for them, they are willing to go to any lengths to oppose those they identify as communists. They have little

difficulty in turning up evidence which justifies their fears. After Operation Protea, Pik Botha claimed that captured arms, documents and 'indoctrination material clearly showed that the Russians were building up to a major offensive.'
(None of the incriminating documents was produced.) It was on this occasion that
he dramatized the situation by suggesting that Soviet involvement was 'approaching a situation not much different from that in Afghanistan', adding that 'the
Soviet Union *might have been preparing* to back guerrillas of Swapo, or *possibly*
preparing for a full-scale invasion of the whole territory (Namibia).'[123] (Italics
added.)
    Referring to the same 'evidence', Gen Malan said he

> Trusts that the Western world has taken note that apart from Cubans, Russian
> officers were also found at the Angolan and Swapo headquarters in southern Angola.
> Clear evidence was found of their plans for Southern Africa, and it does not augur
> well for freedom and the free world. . . . The time has come for the West and Africa to
> open their eyes and take note of what was happening in Southern Africa. It has
> nothing to do with so-called liberation, but it was all about Soviet penetration.[124]

    That the Soviet Union is closely interested in deriving what advantages it can
from the deteriorating situation in Southern Africa hardly needs arguing; but what
is more seriously open to question is Pretoria's view of Moscow as the puppet-
master in the region. In fact, the challengers to Pretoria's rule are the products,
not of Moscow's fertile inventiveness, but of SA's own policies. In their struggle
against a powerful antagonist like the SA regime, they need all the help they can
get, including that of the Soviets. Yet none of the successful liberation movements
in the region has shown any real inclination to become Soviet satellites once they
have gained power. So far from becoming a Soviet ally after its successful liberation struggle, Robert Mugabe's Government refused for almost a year even to
establish diplomatic relations with the USSR.[125] When Mozambique's President
Machel risked upsetting his closest ally, China, by signing a Treaty of Friendship
with the USSR, it was because of concern over a possible military threat from SA;
and despite these ties with Moscow, Machel took no notice of the Soviets' active
hostility to the Anglo–American initiative to end the Rhodesian conflict but, following his own interest, he became a key figure in promoting the success of the
Lancaster House negotiations.[126] And, even though Angola remains militarily
dependent on the Soviet bloc and Cubans, it has keenly pursued Western, including American, friendship; and it continued to play the leading African role in the
negotiations with the CG in spite of Moscow's relentless attempts to show up the
Western initiative as an 'imperialist trap'. (See Soviet Union, below.)
    Yet, despite all this evidence on its own doorstep, Pretoria continues to view
the Soviet role in terms of its own preconceptions. For example, the SADF White
Paper on Defence and Arms Procurement, published in April 1982, lumped Zambia and Mozambique with Zimbabwe and Angola as 'Marxist satellite States': this
was just one month after the SA Prime Minister held his talks with Zambia's
President, Dr. Kaunda.
    Embattled against real and imaginary enemies, how does Pretoria see its future
in the region? SA's Foreign Minister told his Parliament on 17 September 1981:

> What is required is a realistic appraisal of the dilemma in which we find ourselves.
> If we fail to do this, the drift towards confrontation and conflagration in Southern
> Africa will become inevitable . . . and no winner will emerge from such a conflict
> situation . . . I believe the Angolans, the Zambians, the people of Zimbabwe and the
> people of Mozambique are tired of the turbulence of our region. If that is the case

then I believe there rests an historical responsibility on all the leaders of Southern Africa to get together, somehow, and objectively and constructively to review the whole situation in Southern Africa. I believe the time for this is ripe . . . This Government is prepared to do so and act in that spirit.

THE ROLE OF THE MAJOR FOREIGN ACTORS
THE UNITED STATES: LEARNING TO WORK WITH ITS ALLIES
Few had really expected when she was elected that it would be the ultra-Tory, Margaret Thatcher, who would play the leading role in ending the long anguish of Rhodesia; it was even less predictable that a Reagan Administration would become a major factor contributing to a Namibian settlement. If, in the end, settlement is successfully implemented, it will be very largely because a moderate American policy was pursued by a conservative Republican like Ronald Reagan. Without a man of his stripe in the White House, it is unlikely that the Botha regime could have been won over to the extent of accepting the proposals for a settlement reached in July 1982. But nor was this measure of success attainable without Reagan moving away from his original positions in several major respects.

Reagan's election had, for very good reasons, been enthusiastically received in Pretoria; not only did it spell the end of the reviled Jimmy Carter, Andy Young and Don McHenry; but the new President had brought to the White House a bundle of commitments on Southern Africa. For the very reasons that these commitments had brought joy to Pretoria, they cast a deep gloom over the rest of the continent.

Before his election, Reagan had promised to adopt a non-confrontational attitude to SA, with a strong preference for 'constructive engagement' as opposed to the OAU's attempts to isolate Pretoria. He had pledged support for Unita in its effort to overthrow the 'illegitimate' MPLA regime. Like Pretoria, he had described Swapo as a 'terrorist organization'. He had committed himself to 'halting the Soviet advance' in Africa and, specifically, to getting the Cubans out of Angola. Much of this brought concern, not just to Black Africa, but also to America's Western allies. It took the Reagan Administration less than six months to rediscover the constraints of American power as the leader of the Western alliance and to digest the realities of the situation in Southern Africa, which were very different from the way they looked on the election trail from Santa Barbara across the Republican belt of the United States. In the end, Reagan's policies turned out to be not very different from those of the traduced Carter Administration, except in two major respects: a softer attitude towards the Pretoria regime; and a tenacious determination to link the withdrawal of Cuban combat troops from Angola with a settlement in Namibia.[127] And in one important respect Reagan went even farther than Carter: actively promoting closer American economic ties with Angola, despite the absence of diplomatic links.

This transformation of American policy quite understandably upset Pretoria, which, once again, felt itself 'let down by the West'. Nevertheless, because Reagan was such a hard-nosed conservative, and not just a 'limp liberal', and because he was seen as a 'friend' of SA, Pretoria could not afford to ignore his wishes once they were convinced that proposals advanced during the negotiations were not just those of Haig and Crocker, but had the personal backing of the President. And whatever, still secret, inducements may have been given to Pretoria, Washington's success was in persuading the Botha regime to make the kind of concessions they had previously refused even to consider. Once the Front-line Presidents saw that Reagan's policies were not as inflexible as he had made them appear, they were only too glad to resume their role as interlocutors with Swapo.

221

Describing the results of the re-evaluation of American policy after the new Administration had taken over, Chester Crocker listed two major conclusions:

First, we determined that we were going to have an active African policy. It was not going to be an arena that we were going to downplay or to give the backburner treatment to in any sense. And, secondly, we were determined that it was important in terms of both Western and, specifically, American interests that we engage constructively in Southern Africa.

It is sometimes thought, I believe, that constructive engagement apples only to SA. It applies to the whole region. We're seeking to engage constructively throughout Southern Africa, which means that no-one is going to tell us that we must choose between Black Africa and South Africa. We are in a unique position to communicate across that barrier, or that fence, if you will. We are determined to do so, because it is in our interests to do so, and we also believe it's in the interests of Africans that we do so.

To get more specific, we looked at the Namibia problem; we are absolutely convinced that it was important to move it forward, to get a negotiated settlement that would be internationally acceptable, on the basis of SCR 435, and the sooner the better. The continuation of the Namibia problem could only undermine our African position, undermine the Western position, and play into the hands of our global adversary.[128]

A chronic suspicion about the conduct of the negotiations with Pretoria was that Washington was considering making new defence and other commitments as a means of influencing the Botha regime—a suspicion that became particularly strong in June 1981 when Pretoria suddenly seemed to have changed its negotiating position, but no obvious reason for doing so. (See the Course of the Namibian Negotiations, above.) On 18 June 1981, the State Department found it necessary to deny categorically that the US was preparing to enter into a military alliance with SA, or that it was contemplating the arms embargo—suggestions described as having 'absolutely no foundation'. These denials followed a hearing by the Congress Sub-Committee on Africa during which its chairman Howard Wolpe, had asked Crocker whether the US contemplated the training of the South African Coast Guard, and whether there were 'any other ideas that have been considered by our Government (that) would be helpful in achieving a settlement of the conflict in Namibia?' Crocker said there were 'several areas,' such as the case you referred to, which are under review, and in which negotiation and discussion is currently under way between the US and the SA Government.' But, he added, 'I'm not in a position to make announcements at this point as to whether that will come about.' Crocker denied that these discussions were tied to negotiations on Namibia's independence.

Speaking on a different occasion[129] about the Reagan Administration's view of the Soviet role in 'the volatile region of Southern Africa,' Crocker told a Senate sub-committee:

We proceed on the basis that the Soviet Union does not have a grand design for Southern Africa, that it is, in fact, taking advantage of targets of opportunity that present themselves to act counter to Western interests. The Soviet Union, alone, has a vested interest in keeping the region in turmoil. It is to no-one else's advantage—neither to that of the South Africans, the other Southern Africans, nor certainly to the US and the West.

On this occasion, too, Crocker comprehensively reviewed the Administration's outlook on Southern Africa and its interests in the region:

It is an indisputable fact, faced squarely in policy terms by President Reagan's Administration, beginning in January 1981, in consultation with our Western allies, that a wide range of vital Western interests, and US interests in particular, are engaged in the Southern African region.

The ten nations of Southern Africa comprise an area of great mineral wealth, including resources critical to Western strategic interests. Angola, SA, Mozambique and the territory of Namibia are all littoral states on the strategic Cape sea route, a lifeline of Western commerce. America's two-way trade with the countries of Southern Africa amounted in 1980 to $7,200m and US direct investment in the region is estimated at $2,300m.

All of these factors obviously make Southern Africa an area of great interest also to the Soviet Union and to its surrogates. In recent years we have remarked a substantial increase in Soviet interest and involvement in the area. In Angola and Mozambique the number and range of activities of Soviet, Cuban and other foreign communist advisers and technicians, in the civilian and military domains, has increased implying concomitant political and economic influence. The Soviet Union has concluded arms agreements with Zambia and Botswana, complementing those countries' previous arms supply relationships with Western nations. Zimbabwe recently requested North Korea to train and equip a brigade, although that country continues to work closely with Great Britain as its primary foreign source of military equipment and training. Other countries of the region, and of Africa in general, have remarked with concern the increase in Soviet activity in the region, noting particularly that the Soviet Union has concentrated its efforts there on military assistance, showing little interest at all in contributing to the economic development of the region.

It is also clear that the Soviet Union has continued to play a very active role in Southern African political/military organizations such as Swapo and the ANC. Swapo's military elements are based primarily in Angola and other neighbouring countries, and carry out some actions within Namibia itself. We estimate that Swapo receives some 90% of its military support from communist sources. It also receives direct assistance from African States, Western States other than the US, and some UN bodies.

The ANC, which seeks to replace the present Government in power in SA by violent as well as other means, receives comparable percentages of its military and other support from communist and other sources. It is basically an African nationalist organization with a long history, founded in 1912, five years before the 1917 revolution in Russia. A main thread in the history of the ANC over the years is the unvarying degrees of internal and external communist influence that have characterized what is basically an African organization. These conflicts within the organization have often been very bitter and have resulted in various segments and individuals breaking with the ANC at different points in time.

We categorically condemn all terrorist and other violent acts that either of these organizations take to try to bring about change in Namibia and SA. Our policy in relationship to both seeks to channel the impetus toward change into peaceful channels. We seek in general in pursuing our objectives in Southern Africa to strengthen and make more viable the possibilities of peaceful change. As we have repeatedly stated in the Namibia/Angola context, we believe the spiral of violence is a two-way street, and we deplore it. In so doing, we seek to obviate the necessity for terrorism that some parties involved in the region choose to believe.

In SA we are pursuing a careful policy of constructive engagement, encouraging the Government of Prime Minister P.W. Botha and other elements in SA society to move away from apartheid toward a SA changed, modern and strong, with bright prospects for stability and development rooted in justice, free of the problems that now stand in the way of closer US/SA relations. We believe that a process of peaceful, evolutionary change promises a much better immediate and long-term future for all South Africans than the protracted bloody terror and violence that is the alternative for that nation.

Washington was not much impressed by the efforts of Pretoria, after Operation

Protea (see above), to convince the Western nations that the Soviet Union was escalating its military role in Angola, and that Swapo should be seen as a Soviet proxy. Responding to SA's attempts to arouse the West to the danger of 'an Afghanistan', the State Department spokesman, Dean A. Fischer, said on 2 September 1981:

> We have been aware for some time that there are approximately 1,000 Soviet personnel and an additional 400, or so, East German and other Eastern European personnel in Angola. We know that the Soviets and the East Europeans serve as military advisers and technicians with the Angolan armed forces, and that they work in some Government Ministries. . . .
> While we have repeatedly noted that the Soviets are assisting Swapo with arms and supplies, we have no information which would either confirm or refute the (SA) statement that there were Soviet advisers with Swapo units.

WESTERN EUROPE AND CANADA: AMERICA'S TROUBLED ALLIES

At the beginning of 1981 it seemed for a time as if the Western initiative over Namibia would finally have to be abandoned because of the differences between the New Guard in Washington and its NATO allies. In recent years West European and Canadian attitudes had become sharper towards SA—both over its internal policies and over Namibia—in strong contrast to Reagan's proposed new tilt in America's policy.

Britain's Foreign Secretary, Lord Carrington, had shown a greater impatience with Pretoria since the settlement in Zimbabwe, which had been a tonic for his Conservative Government. Carrington was anxious to see Namibia disposed of in a similar fashion through the rapid implementation of SCR 435. In this he was supported by the Bonn Government which, because of its own historic ties with Namibia, wished to see the conflict ended. A new spirit of activism had also been breathed into the NATO alliance by the advent of President Mitterrand's Socialist Government in France. Canada, under Pierre Trudeau, could always be relied upon to support the most radical of the positions taken by the Europeans.

Reagan's initial stand—e.g. casting doubt on the value of SCR 435—made the US the odd man out within the alliance at a time when other aspects of his Administration's policies were producing strains within NATO.[130] While Reagan was still busy wrestling with his ultra-conservative supporters (and his own conservative instincts) over, for instance, the endorsement of Chester Crocker as his point man on Africa, his tentative ideas about Namibia and Angola were being strongly resisted by members of the CG. It was their pressure, perhaps more than anything else, that, finally enabled the State Department to win its fight against the President's advisers in the White House.

Although the Europeans and Canada were relieved at getting the US back on the rails over SCR 435, they never reconciled themselves to the Americans' efforts to link the Cuban troops' withdrawal from Angola with a Namibian settlement—no matter how much Washington phrased and rephrased the nature of the 'linkage'. In the end, they succeeded in persuading Washington to accept the idea of dealing with the Cuban issue through parallel talks and not linked directly to Namibia. However, they always recognized the value of having the US at the spearhead of the Namibian initiative—and more so, now, because of Reagan's potential influence in Pretoria.

Almost as much negotiating went on among the CG members themselves as between them and the other parties to the conflict. The differences of attitude occasionally showed themselves in public, as over the differing responses to

Pretoria's attacks against Angola—especially over Operation Protea in August 1981. As David Watt, the influential director of Chatham House, wrote:

> The contrast between Lord Carrington's harsh denunciation of the latest SA incursion and the State Department's far more guarded deprecation is the outward and visible sign of a difference which months of argument between Washington and most of the other Western capitals have failed to resolve.[131]

In the sharp reprimand to Pretoria delivered to the UN General Asembly (see above), Lord Carrington spoke for all ten members of the European Community. By casting its solitary veto on that occasion, the US completely isolated itself from its Western partners.

Britain was also closely tuned into the opinion of its African Commonwealth partners.[132] The firm resolution on Namibia taken at the Commonwealth meeting of Government leaders in Melbourne in October 1981[133] met with the warm approval of Swapo, through a statement issued on its behalf by Peter Katjivivi, the Organization's observer at the Commonwealth talks. And although Britain and other Commonwealth members refused to consider the application of sanctions against SA, the communiqué declaration on SA apartheid was unusually forthright.

SA reacted with predictable scorn to the Commonwealth and European stand—thereby further emphasizing its isolation from the EEC members and its greater dependence on a friendly Washington.

If the Front-line Presidents played the role of interlocutors between the CG and Swapo, the West Europeans and Canada filled a similar role between the African leaders and Washington, e.g. the French were responsible for arranging the direct talks between the US and Angola's Foreign Minister (see above); the West Germans were involved in arranging the meeting between the Americans and Sam Nujoma (see above).

But while the West Europeans presented a united front on the Namibian issue, their basic policies towards SA itself changed but little. They not only firmly resisted any idea of imposing sanctions, but were rather guarded in their criticisms about the pace and direction of change in the apartheid Republic. Their view of SA is based on the belief that SA's only chance of long-term survival lies in the interconnected policies of instituting real internal reform, of allowing Namibia to go its own way, and of reaching reconciliation with its Black neighbours. But the Whites still remained loathe to risk the benefits deriving from their economic ties with SA, or to commit any part of their resources to pressurizing the Pretoria regime to move more purposefully towards achieving any one of the above requirements to more violent changes in Southern Africa.

Unexpectedly, the most outspoken voice in the Western Establishment on the issues of Southern Africa was that of the former Conservative Prime Minister, Edward Heath. His own reluctance while in office to fully support an arms embargo against SA had alienated African leaders in the early 1970s; but in 1982 he emerged as a strong challenger to traditional British and Western attitudes towards SA—not only in the trenchant speech he made in Johannesburg in October, but by his stern warnings over Namibia and his criticism of American policy in pursuing the idea of a Cuban linkage with a Namibian settlement. Writing in *The Times* (5 November 1981), after a visit to SA and Namibia, he said:

> If Namibia is not soon brought to independence and if brutal SA attacks on Angola persist, there is the danger that these very Cuban troops may be drawn increasingly

into the conflict. This is a 'link' which Western policy must certainly try to avert—for the Soviet Union is the only country which would really stand to gain from it.

Heath described an internationally-recognized settlement to the Namibian problem as being 'in its own right of vital interest to the West. To make it conditional on anything else would be to create an unnecessary and potentially dangerous hostage to fortune.' He also warned that the longer a settlement was delayed, the greater the danger that Swapo would be pushed into the hands of the Soviet Union. It would suit Soviet purposes very well, Heath added, 'to see the West alienated more and more from Black Africa and increasingly incapable of achieving the diplomatic aims it has set itself.'

THE SOVIET BLOC: A WORLD POWER UNABLE TO HELP ITS FRIENDS AFTER INDEPENDENCE
The most striking feature of Soviet policy in Southern Africa in recent years has been its failure to follow up the initial advantages gained through its support of the liberation movements (although it did happen to back the wrong horse in Zimbabwe).

The Soviet bloc appears to be either unwilling or incapable, of supplying even Marxist-oriented countries, like Angola and Mozambique, with the kind of aid they need to develop their economies and so to stabilize their regimes, even though it has measured up very well to the demands made for purely military requirements. However, once the liberation struggle has been won—apart from the need to consolidate the security of the new State—the importance of military aid declines while that for trade, loans, foreign investment, technical aid and expertise increases. In these non-military fields the Soviet bloc's aid has been felt to be seriously inadequate by those African leaders who had looked to them, in the first instance, for economic backing. They were therefore forced to turn increasingly to the West and, markedly, to the US, for economic ties—a development not at all consonant with the Soviet's declared objective of helping to free African economies from 'American imperialism'. So far from establishing itself as a challenging presence, the USSR's actual image in Southern Africa is that of a world power helpless to assist those wishing to take the road of non-capitalist development, and unable to persuade 'clients' not to fall for the 'imperialist manoeuvres' of the Western initiative over Namibia. Time and time again, as the CG struggled to keep up the momentum of its quest for peace, the Soviet leaders sought to expose the 'sinister plotting' by the West in order to alert the Front-line leaders about the dangers of falling into their trap.

When Crocker returned from his first African mission in April 1981, Geliy Skobolev described it as 'a failure' which had served only to confirm 'the invariability of the imperialist neo-colonialist course of the US ruling circles.'[134]

Later in a commentary broadcast by Moscow (12 July 1981), Nikolay Gavrilov declared that while the Western countries favoured a settlement in Namibia, their aim—especially that of the US—is 'to turn Namibia into a sort of barrier between independent Africa and its allies in racist SA, and thus to make a strategic stronghold out of SA.' He added that the transfer of power to Swapo would put an end to the Western powers 'predatory and uncontrolled activity of foreign monopolies in their country.' In October, Aleksandr Lebedev warned that 'actually the US wants to perpetuate the domination in Namibia of a handful of White planters, and is trying to make representatives of the other Western powers of the CG to take an active part in that.'[135] A week later, Vladimir Korochantsev warned that the US was canvassing a proposal that would place 'the Swapo military bases and detachments under control, in others words, to help the occupiers to make short work of the patriots . . . the West and the racists seek to attain through diplomatic means those aims which they failed to attain on the battlefield.'[136] Broadcasting in Zulu, Radio Moscow (29 October) said: 'The only answer to these unacceptable propositions is to take up arms as Swapo has said and done.'

The Soviet media attempt to undermine the Western initiative was complemented by efforts through normal diplomatic channels. African leaders, however, needed no instruction about the conflicting interests of the global powers, nor were they flattered by the suggestion that they could not always be trusted to decide for themselves how, and with whom, to negotiate to advance their own interests.

Soviet concern over its failure to persuade a country like Angola not to continue to negotiate with the Americans was shown, for example, by a speech of Premier Nikolai A. Tikhonov at a Kremlin lunch for a visiting MPLA delegation in which he warned his guests of 'an American plot to return the African nation to the American sphere of influence.'[137]

But if at the end of the day the Namibian negotiations should fail, it will be because of the failure of Western diplomacy and not due to any successes achieved by Soviet diplomacy.

The USSR reaction to the killing of some Soviet citizens and the arrest by the SADF of a Soviet officer in Angola showed no eagerness to use these incidents as a pretext for expanding its military role in the area. It preferred to work quietly for the release of the detained officer through diplomatic channels.

Although the USSR constantly accused Western capitalism of exploiting Namibia's natural resources, it was not itself above engaging in this trade. Martin Bailey revealed in an article in the London *Observer* (25 October 1981) that Britain was sending uranium from Namibia to be enriched at a Soviet plant. The British Central Electricity Generating Board confirmed that it was due to receive 70,000 lb of this enriched uranium from the USSR, and admitted that the source of the uranium was Namibia. Although Britain has never accepted the UN Decree forbidding trade in the territory's natural resources, the USSR has. There was no subsequent announcement of a Soviet decision to refuse to use Namibian-supplied uranium.

CUBA: ANGOLA'S FIGHTING ALLY

Although the Cuban military presence in Angola was turned into one of the key issues in the Namibian negotiations by both the Americans and South Africans, this in no way affected the close ties between Hanava and Luanda. Nothing said by either side gave any reason to suppose that Fidel Castro has any interest in keeping his combat troops in Angola for a day longer than is necessary: on the contrary, all the signs point to his wishing to withdraw them—both because of their cost to Cuba (even though most of it is indirectly borne by the USSR), and the increasing unpopularity among Cuban soldiers of serving in Angola. Although their military casualties are slight, the Cubans have suffered quite badly from tropical and other diseases; nor is life in the bush or in rural villages much to their taste.

In fact, a steady rundown of the number of Cuban troops has continued quietly, dropping from the estimated 20,000 who had arrived in 1975, to 11,000–13,000, possibly even less. An estimated 3,000 were withdrawn during 1981; but the pull-out was halted when SA stepped up its military attacks in August.

At no time did the MPLA ask the Cubans to become more directly involved in resisting the SA military attacks. On 25 August 1981, when President dos Santos sent a cable to Castro informing him of the latest severe SA attack, he asked him only to use his office as chairman of the Non-aligned Movement to launch an international campaign to apply pressures on Pretoria to stop its aggression.[138] In his reply Castro promised:

> The Government and people of Cuba will not hesitate to join the heroic people of Angola, as they have done in the past, to repel the racist and fascist aggression and to defend their independence and national integrity.[139]

Angolan–Cuban relations were reviewed at a meeting of their Foreign Ministers in Luanda in February 1982. One of the declared purposes of the meeting was 'to make it perfectly clear to the international public opinion why Cuban forces remain in Angola.' In a long statement issued after the meeting, the two Foreign Ministers said they wished to 'remind international public opinion' that the forces came 'at the request of President Agostinho Neto and have remained at the Angolan Government's invitation to help train the People's Armed Forces for the Liberation of Angola,' and to help them defend the 'territorial integrity and sovereignty' of Angola, which are 'threatened and attacked by the SA racists, imperialism, its mercenaries and puppets.' The key paragraph in the ten-point statement[140] reads:

> Thus, when the Governments of Angola and Cuba deem it appropriate, the withdrawal of Cuban forces stationed in Angola will take place as a result of the sovereign decision of the Government of the People's Republic of Angola, once there is no longer the possibility of attack or armed invasion. The Cuban Government reiterates that it will unhesitatingly abide by any decision made by the sovereign government of the People's Republic of Angola as to the withdrawal of those forces.

THE PEOPLE'S REPUBLIC OF CHINA: MAINTAINING A LOW PROFILE
The position China took during the Angolan conflict in 1974/75 was that the government of independence should be composed of all three liberation movements—MPLA, Unita and FNLA. This position was in line with the policy taken at that time by the OAU. Earlier, during the liberation struggle against Portuguese colonialism, China's main support had gone to FNLA although, later, some military supplies went to Unita. China strongly condemned the Soviet/Cuban military intervention which made the MPLA's victory possible.[141] It was therefore natural that relations between the MPLA and Beijing would be strained after independence. However, in mid-1982, talks were begun to establish normal diplomatic relations.

China has continued to view the conflicts in Southern Africa as being in large part due to the rivalry between the two Super-powers; but it reserves its most severe criticism for the 'hegemonistic ambitions' of the Soviets. China's view of events in Southern Africa is typically expressed by Wu Yixin, the NCNA correspondent in Gaborone:

> It is noteworthy that in the past year (1981), the Soviet Union has expanded its influence in Southern Africa by continuing the delivery of arms and the dispatch of military personnel to some Southern African countries. SA newspapers reported that it is easier for SA to buy arms made in Soviet bloc countries then to buy them from Western countries.[142]

THE UNITED NATIONS: THE SOURCE OF LEGITIMACY
The UN has played a crucially important role as the central focus of diplomatic activity over all the conflicts in Southern Africa. It has remained the main forum for the African States to secure an international hearing for their views, and to

apply pressures both against SA and the Western nations to gain support for their policies, e.g. in their continuous efforts to extend the arms and sports embargo against SA into all-embracing sanctions. It is to the UN that Angola, Mozambique, Zambia and other member-states have come to lodge their complaints against SA aggression, and to mobilize international support. The UN Anti-Apartheid Unit is a major agency for promoting the cause of the liberation movements. Above all, it was the UN which, since 1946, has kept alive the issue of Namibia's independence.

For all these reasons the UN is understandably regarded by Pretoria as being both hostile and biased—more especially since the General Assembly has excluded the Republic from its sessions. Although some of the Western nations, and especially the US, regard the UN as being too strongly dominated by the Third World, on balance they regard it as a valuable forum for the discussion (if not necessarily the conduct) of international affairs.

The central importance of the UN in the negotiations was its role in providing Namibian legitimacy for the Western initiative. Although the five Western nations have pursued their negotiations with the Front-line States, SA and Swapo as an independent group, they have been constrained by the need to remain within the framework of the UN and of SCR 435 which established the guidelines for an internationally acceptable settlement of Namibia's independence. Ultimately, it is generally accepted (though with extreme reluctance by SA) that the UN will be responsible for supervising the transition to independence, as well as providing the peacekeeping force to ensure that the ceasefire is observed once it has been agreed.

Without the UN, therefore, it would not have been possible to conduct the search for a final peaceful settlement of the conflict within an internationally acceptable framework, which has been the indispensable factor in the progress of the negotiations. However, because of the overtly hostile attitude of the great majority of the UN members to SA and the UN's earlier endorsement of Swapo as the 'only legitimate representative of the people of Namibia', it will be just as necessary, at the end of the day, to persuade SA and the Namibian internal parties that the UNTAG and the UN Peacekeeping Force will be impartial in supervising the difficult and dangerous transition to independence, as it will be to persuade Swapo that the SA Administration and police will not be partisan during the election campaign preceding independence.

APPENDIX 1
Full text of Western constitutional proposals
Principles concerning the Constituent Assembly and the constitution for an independent Namibia (October 1981)

A. *Constituent Assembly*

1. The Constituent Assembly should be elected so as to ensure a fair representation in that body to different political groups representing the people of Namibia.

2. The Constituent Assembly will formulate the Constitution for an independent Namibia in accordance with the principles in part B below and will adopt the Constitution as a whole by a two-thirds majority of all its members.

B. *Principles for a constitution for an independent Namibia*

1. Namibia will be a unitary, sovereign and democratic state.

2. The Constitution will be the supreme law of the state. It may be amended only by a designated process of either the legislature or the votes cast in a popular referendum.

3. The Constitution will provide for a system of government with three branches: an elected

executive branch which will be responsible to the legislative branch; a legislative branch to be elected by universal and equal suffrage which will be responsible for the passage of all laws; and an independent judicial branch which will be responsible for the interpretation of the Constitution and for ensuring its supremacy and the authority of the law.

The executive and legislative branches will be constituted by periodic and genuine elections which will be held by secret vote.

4. The electoral system will ensure fair representation in the legislature to different political groups representing the people of Namibia—for example by proportional representation or by appropriate determination of constituencies or by a combination of both.

5. There will be a declaration of fundamental rights, which will include the rights to life, personal liberty and freedom of movement; to freedom of conscience; to freedom of expression, including freedom of speech and a free press; to freedom of assembly and association, including political parties and trade unions; to due process and equality before the law; to protection from arbitrary deprivation of private property or deprivation of private property without prompt and just compensation; and to freedom from racial, ethnic, religious or sexual discrimination. The declaration of rights will be consistent with the provisions of the Universal Declaration of Human Rights. The declaration of rights will be enforceable by the courts, at the instance of an aggrieved individual.

6. It will be forbidden to create criminal offences with retrospective effect or to provide for increased penalties with retrospective effect.

7. Provision will be made to secure equal access by all to recruitment to the public service, the police service and the defence services. The fair administration of personnel policy in relation to these services will be assured by appropriate independent bodies.

8. Private cultural, social, health, and educational institutions will be open to all without discrimination.

9. Provision will be made for the establishment of elected councils for local and regional administrative and fiscal purpose.

Additional Document from Five (26 October 1981)

If international recognition of the following principles were desired they could be embodied in reciprocal undertakings among the parties concerned. These principles could be formalized later in a form to be determined, possibly in the context of an endorsement by the Security Council.

1. All States will respect the independence, the sovereignty, the territorial integrity and the policy of Non-Alignment of Namibia, in particular by refraining from the unlawful threat or use of force, or from any other act inconsistent with the purposes of the United Nations. All states are urged to manifest their will to respect these principles.

2. The State of Namibia will live in peace and develop friendly relations with other states in accordance with international law. It will therefore not permit organised activities within its territory directed towards the commission of any act of aggression or any other act which involves an unlawful threat or use of force against any other state. The neighbouring states will follow the same principle regarding their relations with Namibia.

3. The state of Namibia will not permit within its territory the installation of foreign military bases or the presence of foreign military units except by virtue of or in accordance with the exercise of its right of self-defence, if an armed attack occurs against it, as provided for in the Charter of the United Nations.

APPENDIX 2

Swapo's response to the proposal of the "Contact Group" on a one vote-two count system presented to Swapo on 1 April 1982

We have carefully studied the document submitted to us on April 1st 1982 by the Contact Group. In this connection, we have the following to say:

First,

We have noted that the Five are now proposing 'one man one vote, one vote, two counts', in the place of 'one man two votes'. In this connection we see that the Five are unbendingly insisting upon double standards regarding the choice of electoral system. The 'Contact Group', however, dismally failed to give convincing reasons or justifications for their insistence on the choice of electoral method based on double standards. We still do not see juridical or practical reasons why the Five should so unyieldingly be insisting on such an extraordinary electoral system. We are therefore left to conclude that there exist motives of political nature and it is not difficult for us to tell whence their source.

Pretoria no doubt understands that SWAPO will win if free fair and honest elections are held in Namibia. Therefore the apartheid regime is trying its best to prevent a SWAPO electoral victory. We are convinced that the idea of 'one man two vote one vote two counts' or 'one man two votes', as it were, is contrived in order to create special circumstances under which SWAPO could be deprived of the chance of gaining two thirds majority of the seats in the Constituent Assembly required to adopt Namibia's independence constitution. With SWAPO deprived of such two thirds majority through specially contrived and indeed dishonest electoral method Pretoria would have opportunity to use its political puppets to start an endless debate on the constitution and ultimately to delay the granting of independence to Namibia.

This is why the South African rulers felt the need to resort to complicated and totally unjustifiable electoral procedure. This procedure is clearly designed to ensure on the one hand guaranteed representation for the white minorities in the Constituent Assembly. This becomes clear when we consider the low 2 percent (instead of the standard 5 percent) sealing or cut off point which the Five have proposed. On the other hand the choice of such an electoral double standard is aimed at giving Pretoria an opportunity to use and accentuate tribal or ethnic factors against SWAPO.

We believe that simplifying the voting procedure does not necessarily by itself eliminate all the complications which the application of electoral double standards will cause. It is clear for example that the more rounds of counting there are the greater the room for fraud.

Therefore SWAPO deems it necessary to re-emphasise its unequivocal stand that elections in Namibia must be held with strict observance of the one man one vote principle.

This principle is ascertained by the whole practical history of decolonization of Africa. Its sense is clear to everyone. Moreover it fully corresponds to the traditional African notion of free-will exercise. It is appropriate to recall that quite recently official representatives of Western powers not only recognised the said principle but also considered it a key to the solution of the political problems of Southern Africa as a whole. In our view there is no solid reason to make an exception from the principle in Namibia's case. We believe that any honest and fair proposal on such an important issue as organising elections should not deviate from the life-tested one man, one vote principle.

Second:
The Five have now put forth in the latest proposal single member constituency as the preferred voting procedure. SWAPO has consistently pointed out that desirable as it may be the procedure of single member constituencies would create its own problems. It is for instance clear that while it is possible to conduct elections without census being taken under proportional representation, single member constituency procedure will require complete census under U.N. supervision of the population, demarcation of the country into constituencies and finally registration of voters. Could it be possible to agree beforehand as to how many people would be required, how and whether all that most important work can be fulfilled within the seven months stipulated in the U.N. plan for UNTAG operations? No responsible political organization, not SWAPO in any case, can give such a consent in advance. Yet the discussions of the composition, size and deployment of UNTAG is postponed to 'Phase two'!

Third:
After serious consideration of the developments since last October, when the 'Contact Group' adopted a phased approach to the negotiations, we have come to the conclusion that apart from an illusion of momentum, nothing is actually being achieved.

Six months have now elapsed during which the negotiations have been confined to exchange of notes about 'Phase one' of the proposed 'Three phases'. We are convinced that this phased approach will not assist the early implementation of Resolution 435.

231

The experience of the last six months has shown that the phased approach to the negotiations is being used to force SWAPO, step by step, to make concessions, sometimes irreversible ones, while South Africa is yielding practically nothing. Pretoria has as yet made no binding commitment to grant independence to Namibia.

Moreover, those who keep on harping on about impartiality are insulting the intelligence of those U.N. member states who have voted for General Assembly Resolution 3111 of December 1973. They are also glossing over the fact that the real problem about lack of impartiality is South Africa which has more than 40,000 civil servants and police force in Namibia and has unilaterally turned Walvis Bay into a huge military garrison. These South African civil servants and police are well known for their open hostility towards SWAPO. Yet they will have an important role to play in the administration of elections. Therefore the fact is that the onus is actually more on South Africa than the U.N. to demonstrate impartiality. Here too the issue of so-called confidence building cannot be meaningfully dealt with in isolation from the adoption of electoral procedure, agreement on the size, composition, deployment of UNTAG personnel as well as agreement on the dates of the ceasefire and arrival of UNTAG in Namibia.

We would like to clarify two important aspects of our stand regarding the negotiations:
1. SWAPO has fully exhausted its limit of concessions. We have come to the conclusion that any further concession if it were not recompensed by a manifestation of goodwill from the other side, would be a concession made at the expense of principles and of the fundamental objectives of the struggle. Being a liberation organisation responsible to the Namibian people, SWAPO cannot make concessions of this sort.

Our readiness for a negotiated settlement of the Namibian problem should not be misinterpreted. We are fully aware of the nature and strength of the forces opposing the liberation of Namibia and we are not inclined to underestimate them. But SWAPO's ability to continue its just struggle should not be underestimated either, all the more so as this struggle enjoys active solidarity and support of African and many other countries. In any case SWAPO is quite capable of ensuring that the expenses of the occupation of Namibia would far surpass its benefits. The situation is already developing in this direction. We believe however that it is not in the interest of the West to give solace to Pretoria in its prevarications and obstructionist actions.

In our opinion the most correct way of speeding up the negotiations is to consider seriously the constructive proposal of SWAPO on convening, under U.N. auspices, a new Geneva type conference in the course of which suggestions of all parties that are involved in the whole complex of the Namibian settlement could be examined. It is in the light of the foregoing that we once again appeal to the Five to seriously consider as a matter of urgency our proposal for the holding of a Geneva-type conference to discuss and resolve all outstanding issues, that is, all issues involved in the three phases.

In suggesting this we proceed from the assumption that the Five are correct in what they told us that unlike in January 1981 South Africa is now ready to proceed with the implementation of the U.N. plan for the independence of Namibia.

Thus in short we are appealing that the Western Five show their goodwill and give their necessary support to this constructive proposal of SWAPO.

On our part we are ready to formulate our detailed proposals towards the achievement in the immediate future of a negotiated settlement to the Namibia problem, a settlement based on the provisions of U.N. Security Council Resolution 435 (1978), as well as on other important U.N. decisions on Namibia.

SWAPO would like to know the Five's point of view on the essence of this proposal.

APPENDIX 3
The position of the Front-line States, Nigeria, Kenya and Swapo (November 1981) on principles concerning the Constituent Assembly and the Constitution for an independent Namibia

A. *Constituent Assembly*

1. Elections will be held to select a Constituent Assembly which will adopt a constitution for an independent Namibia. The Constitution will determine the organisation and powers of all

levels of Government. Every adult Namibian will be eligible, without discrimination or fear of intimidation from any source, to vote, campaign and stand for election to the Constituent Assembly. Voting will be by secret ballot, with provisions made for those who cannot read or write. The date for the beginning of the electoral campaign, the date of the elections, the electoral system, the preparation of voters rolls and other aspects of electoral procedures will be promptly decided upon so as to give all political parties and interested persons, without regard to their political views, a full and fair opportunity to organise and participate in the electoral process. Full freedom of speech, assembly, movement and press shall be guaranteed.

2. The Constituent Assembly will formulate the constitution for an independent Namibia in accordance with the principles in Part B below and will adopt the Constitution as a whole by a two-thirds majority of its total membership.

B. *Principles for a Constitution for an independent Namibia.*

1. Namibia will be a unitary, sovereign and democratic state.

2. The Constitution will be the supreme law of the state. It may be amended only be a designated process of either the legislature or the votes cast in a popular referendum.

3. The Constitution will determine the organisation and powers of all levels of government. However, we note that most governments are structured on the basis of an elected executive, a legislature elected by universal and equal suffrage which is responsible for the passage of all laws, an independent judiciary which is responsible for the interpretation of the Constitution and for ensuring its supremacy and the authority of the law, and that the executive and legislative branches are constituted by periodic and genuine elections which are held by secret vote.

4. The electoral system will be consistent with A(1) above.

5. There will be a declaration of fundamental rights, which will include the rights to life, personal liberty and freedom of movement, to freedom of conscience, to freedom of expression, including freedom of speech and a free press, to freedom of assembly and association, including political parties and trade unions, to due process and equality before the law, to protection from arbitrary deprivation of private property without just compensation, and to freedom from racial, ethnic, religious or sexual discrimination. The declaration of rights will be consistent with the provisions of the universal declaration of human rights. The declaration of rights will be enforceable by the courts, at the instance of an aggrieved individual after proven breach of these rights.

6. It will be forbidden to create criminal offences with retrospective effect or to provide for increased penalties with retrospective effect.

7. Provision will be made to secure, equal access by all to recruitment to, and balanced restructuring of, the public service, the police service and the defence services. The fair administration of personnel policy in relation to these services will be assured by appropriate independent bodies.

8. Private cultural, social health and educational institutions will be open to all without discrimination.

9. Provision will be made for the establishment, by an act of parliament, of elected councils for local administration.

NOTES

1. All references to country chapters and essays refer to *Africa Contemporary Record (ACR)*, 1981-82.
2. This was affirmed in the Lusaka Manifesto of 1969 signed by 13 African countries and subsequently ratified by the OAU.
3. See *ACR* 1980-81, pp A10-13.
4. For a survey of these developments, see *ACR* 1974-75, 1975-76 and 1976-77.
5. See Michael Hornsby in *The Times*, London, 24 March 1982.
6. *Ibid.*
7. For details, see chapter on Namibia.
8. *The Observer*, 30 August 1981.

9. *The Times,* 4 September 1981.
10. For details of Operation Protea, see chapter on Angola in *ACR* 1981–82.
11. SABC, Johannesburg, 10 August 1981.
12. *Ibid,* 11 August 1981.
13. *Daily Telegraph (DT),* London, 16 September 1981.
14. *Financial Mail (FM),* Johannesburg, 23 April 1982.
15. See *ACR* 1980–81, pp B705–706.
16. For details, see chapter on Swaziland in *ACR* 1980–81.
17. For details, see sections on Security and The Armed Forces in the chapter on South Africa.
18. *Ibid.*
19. For details, see chapter on South Africa; as well as chapter on Mozambique in *ACR* 1980–81 and 1981–82. 1981–82.
20. For details, see chapters on Mozambique in *ACR* 1981–82.
21. SABC, Johannesburg, 17 June 1982.
22. See *ACR* 1980–81, ppA10–12.
23. See *ACR* 1977–78, ppA3ff.
24. For text of resolution, see *ACR* 1978–79, ppC73ff.
25. *The Guardian,* Manchester, 21 January 1981.
26. *Ibid.*
27. See essay in *ACR* 1981–82 on The US and Africa.
28. Quoted in *International Herald Tribune (IHT),* Paris, 30 March 1981.
29. *IHT,* 2 April 1981; *Guardian,* 2 April 1981.
30. *Financial Times (FT),* London, 10 April 1981.
31. *Ibid,* 13 April 1981.
32. *The Star,* Johannesburg, 14 April 1981.
33. Ibid, 16 April 1981.
34. *DT,* 15 April 1981.
35. *Guardian* and *FT,* 24 April 1981.
36. *Ibid,* 20 April 1981; Radio Algiers, 19 April 1981.
37. *The Times,* 2 May 1981.
38. *Washington Post,* 25 April 1981.
39. *The Times,* 4 May 1981.
40. *Guardian,* 2 June 1981.
41. For the text of OAU resolutions, see Documents Section.
42. *Guardian,* 25 June 1981.
43. Angola Press Agency (ANGOP) 20 June 1981.
44. *Guardian* 20 June 1981.
45. *FT,* 11 August 1981.
46. *Rand Daily Mail (RDM),* Johannesburg, 31 August 1981.
47. For details, see essay on Britain's Year in Africa in *ACR* 1981–82.
48. SABC, 27 August 1981.
49. *DT,* 3 September 1981.
50. *Ibid.*
51. *IHT,* 11 September 1981.
52. *The Times,* 7 September 1981.
53. For details, see chapter on Namibia.
54. *The Times,* 9 September 1981.
55. International Communications Agency (ICA) press release, Paris, AF-403, 17 September 1981.
56. *The Times,* 19 September 1981.
57. *Ibid.*
58. Martha Honey in the *Guardian,* 22 September 1981.
59. *Guardian,* 18 September 1981.
60. Christopher Munnion, *DT,* 21 September 1981.
61. *The Times,* 22 September 1981.
62. *DT,* 23 September 1981.
63. *Ibid,* 25 September 1981.
64. *ICA,* AF-502, 25 September 1981.
65. *DT,* 17 September 1981.
66. See chapter on Namibia.
67. *ANGOP,* 27 October 1981.
68. Radio Luanda, 27 October 1981.
69. See *The Times,* 29, 30 and 31 October 1981.
70. *Ibid.* 14 October 1981.
71. *DT,* 20 October 1981.
72. *The Times,* 4 November 1981.
73. Radio Dar es Salaam, 18 November 1981.
74. *The Times,* 20 November 1981.
75. SABC, Johannesburg, 26 November 1981.
76. ICA, AF-508, 26 November 1981.
77. *Guardian,* 11 December 1981.
78. *Star,* 27 January 1982.
79. *The Times.*
80. *The Star,* 2 February 1982, quoting the Paris magazine *Afrique-Asie.*
81. See *RDM,* 27 January 1982.
82. For details, see chapter on Namibia.
83. *The Citizen,* Johannesburg, 3 February 1982.
84. Radio Luanda, 20 March 1982; *ANGOP,* 26 March 1982.
85. Radio Freedom, Addis Ababa, 3 March 1982.
86. Nigerian News Agency (NAN), Lagos, 17 May 1982.
87. *The Times,* 22 May 1982; also see essay on US Year in Africa in *ACR* 1981–82.
88. *IHT,* 5/6 June 1982.
89. ICA, AF-302, 6 February 1982.

90. *The Times*, 8 June 1982.
91. *Ibid*, 18 June 1982.
92. *ICA*, AF-102, 14 June 1982.
93. *IHT*, 28 June 1982.
94. *The Times*, 21 June 1982.
95. *IHT*, 1 July 1982.
96. *FT*, 1 July 1982.
97. For text, see *FM*, 7 July 1982.
98. ICA, AF-502, 2 July 1982.
99. SABC, Johannesburg, 13 July 1982.
100. *Guardian*, 2 September 1981.
101. *Marches Tropicaux et Mediterraneans (MTM)*, Paris, 20 October 1981.
102. *Africa Report*, Durham, November/ December 1981.
103. *Foreign Report*, Washington, 25 December 1981.
104. *Africa Confidential*, London, 11 December 1981.
105. *Afrique-Asie*, 1 February 1982; *Guardian*, 11 December 1981.
106. *ICA*, AF-310, 9 December 1981.
107. *Ibid*, AF-402, 10 December 1981.
108. *The Times* and *FT*, 5 September 1981.
109. *IHT*, 5-6 September 1981.
110. See Michael Hornsby in *The Times*, 13 September 1981; and Christopher Munnion in *DT*, 12 September 1981.
111. *Newsweek*, Washington, 7 September 1981.
112. For details see chapter on Zimbabwe in *ACR* 1981-82.
113. See essays on SADCC in *ACR* 1979-80 and 1981-82.
114. *The Herald*, Harare, 3 February 1982.
115. *Ibid*.
116. *Guardian*, 14 July 1981.
117. For the history and role of the Frontline States, see *ACR* 1976–77, 1977–78, 1978–79, 1979–80, 1980-81.
118. Statement by Swapo Central Committee; Addis Ababa Voice of Namibia, 15 January 1982.
119. *The Herald*, 10 November 1981.
120. The only part of Garoeb's statement which was later denied was his reference to not allowing the ANC to have bases in Namibia. Radio Dar es Salaam, 14 November 1981.
121. SABC, Johannesburg, 22 August 1981.
122. *Ibid*, 1 March 1982.
123. *DT*, 5 September 1981.
124. SABC, Johannesburg, 31 August 1981.
125. For details of Zimbabwe/Soviet relations, see chapter on Zimbabwe in *ACR* 1981–82.
126. For President Machel's role in the Lancaster House talks, see *ACR* 1979–80.
127. See essay on America's Year in Africa in *ACR* 1981–82.
128. *ICA*, Af-202, 23 February 1982.
129. ICA, Af-102, 22 March 1982.
130. See, for example, David Watt, 'Angola—Another Strain on the Western Alliance,' *The Times*, 28 August 1981.
131. *Ibid*.
132. Also see essay on Britain's Year in Africa in *ACR* 1981–82.
133. For Text, see Documents Section, *ACR* 1981–82.
134. *Tass*, 22 April 1981.
135. Radio Moscow, 20 October 1981.
136. *Selskaya Zhizn*, as reported by Tass, 3 November 1981.
137. *IHT*, 23–24 January 1982.
138. *Granma*, Havana, 4 September 1981.
139. *Ibid*.
140. For full text see *ACR* 1981–82.
141. See Colin Legum and Tony Hodges, *International Intervention in Angola*, Holmes & Meier, N.Y.
142. NCNA, Peking, 22 December 1981.

1982–1983
THE DYNAMICS OF VIOLENCE

Even with Namibia out of the way, the source of the growing violence and deepening instability in the region would remain: it is the political system in South Africa itself which is in the process of change and decay. The dynamics of the political process in Southern Africa can be reduced to a simple formula: the greater the threat (violent and non-violent) coming from the challengers to the apartheid system, the greater and more widespread the violence and repression coming from its defenders.[1]

Since the challengers to apartheid are hardly likely to give up their struggle, or to be cleanly defeated, and since the defenders of 'White South Africa' are similarly unlikely to abandon their position, this leaves only one set of alternatives: violence will either increase on both sides, spreading across the entire region and bringing with it even greater internationalization of the conflict; or the trauma of violence will produce the kind of political change inside SA which is not yet seriously contemplated even by the reformist regime of Prime Minister P. W. Botha.

The events of 1982 up to mid-1983 (the period surveyed here) suggest that the combination of greater violence and timorous reforms (timorous in terms of Black aspirations, but fairly bold in terms of what the White society, so far, feels it necessary, or safe, to make) are more likely to strengthen the hands of the White *ultras*—the *verkramptes*—than of the more enlightened *(verligte)* supporters of the present regime.[2] If this reading of the situation is the correct one, then hopes of averting even greater violence and much more serious destabilization of the region seem slender. However, an apocalyptic view of the situation would ignore the complexities of the continent's most sophisticated and economically developed multiracial society—complexities and plural interests which allow for a variety of political options that would remain available once enough South Africans of all races come to see the collapse of the present system as being inevitable.[3]

The immediate importance of settling the problem of Namibia is that it would remove a flash-point which, at any moment, could dangerously escalate the military conflict in Southern Africa, probably draw the Soviet bloc and its allies more deeply into the region on the side of a widely popular African cause, push the Western Powers into an awkward defensive position, and further internationalize the conflict—not just politically, but also militarily. If there are some who see value in further internationalizing the conflict in Southern Africa, these do not include the majority of African leaders, and least of all those whose countries border on South Africa. Nevertheless, if the pressures on their own regimes continue to increase, as they did in 1982 and 1983, even the otherwise reluctant leaders of the Front-line States (Tanzania, Angola, Mozambique, Botswana, Zimbabwe and Zambia) would, as they have already indicated, rather take the risk of invoking the Soviet factor than of submitting to Pretoria's superior economic and military forces.

A settlement in Namibia would gain more time for the political process in SA to develop beyond the level of reforms which are now proposed; however, gaining more time is not of itself a guarantee that it will be used gainfully. It is this lack of response to the developing situation that led Dr Henry Kissinger to comment in Johannesburg in September 1982:[4]

> History is kind to political leaders who use a margin of choice while it is still available; those who wait on events are usually overwhelmed by them.

But even that incorrigible optimist and universal provider of formulae for conflict resolution had to admit that he did not have an answer to SA's problems which 'the centuries have spawned, and the decades made intractable.' However, Kissinger made some shrewd observations:

> South Africans should not deceive themselves with comforting thoughts about strategic geography and resources into believing that severe moral and political differences would not over-ride them. Well-wishers would not help South Africa so long as institutionalized racial discrimination persisted.
>   Present SA policy would NOT provide the ultimate solution to the problem of power-sharing. (What would?) A system which respects human dignity, extends due process, provides for equal individual rights and protects the principle of citizenship.

By mid-1983 the SA regime and its internal and external challengers had reached a historical crossroads. The spreading urban guerrilla violence had reached a new stage with the damage caused by a car bomb planted outside the headquarters of the South African Air Force in Pretoria, following on a number of sophisticated attacks on strategic targets—such as the nuclear installations at Koeberg; the Waterkloof air force base outside of Pretoria; and the Sasol coal-to-oil complex near Vereeniging. But these were only the dramatic high points of the creeping violence of urban guerrilla tactics; scores of other lesser incidents occurred up and down the country.[5]

However, like the PLO, the SA guerrillas—especially the ANC—while capable of striking wounding blows, were not making any real impact on the Republic's defence system, except to cause more money to be spent on strengthening it. Also like the Palestinians, they had increasingly involved the border-states in their struggle. As a result, South Africa, like Israel, became increasingly concerned with the situation beyond its borders, as well as inside the Republic itself. A crucial difference with Israel is that SA has reason to be even more concerned with its internal situation than with the situation along its borders. But, like the Israelis, the South Africans are able to hurl their military forces into any area of perceived threat with the certainty of achieving a limited objective. As a result, the highly vulnerable border states have begun to show a serious interest in finding a willing and credible 'strategic ally'—just as Egypt did under Nasser. Since none of the Western Powers was clearly a candidate for such a role, and as China has neither the military delivery capacity nor the desire to take on a major military role in the African sub-continent,[6] this has left only the USSR as a potential 'strategic ally'.

By mid-1983, too, there was the first real evidence of serious consideration being given by members of the Front-line States (FLS) to invoking the Soviet military factor—something more than just buying Soviet weapons or relying on friendship treaties of the kind already signed by Mozambique and Angola. After returning from a visit to Hungary, Czechoslovakia and East Germany in May 1983, Zimbabwe's Prime Minister, Dr Mugabe, announced that he would shortly visit Moscow and hinted at a possible interest in signing a security treaty with the

237

Soviet bloc.[7] Earlier, in October 1982, he had spoken of the need to create a unified army command for Southern Africa, saying:

> It is high time that Africa was united against the racist apartheid regime in SA. It is also high time Africa unites its forces and teaches the regime and its forces a lesson.[8]

Few African leaders have been more deeply hostile to Moscow in the past than the Zimbabwe leader, who defied the USSR during the liberation struggle in Rhodesia by insisting on describing himself as 'a Marxist of Maoist thought'. His antipathy to Moscow was mainly due to Soviet support for Joshua Nkomo's wing of the Patriotic Front, and on its insistence that he should abandon his friendship with China as a condition for receiving Soviet military supplies. Therefore, for Mugabe to have reached the point of considering inviting the USSR to become a 'strategic ally', marked yet another major change in the region's deteriorating security situation.

PARALLELS WITH THE MIDDLE EAST

Allowing for the pitfalls of relying too literally on historical analogies, it is nevertheless useful to draw on the experiences of the Middle East since the end of the 1940s to illustrate the situation that has developed in Southern Africa over precisely the same period. Two particular developments that had produced fundamental changes in the relations among the local and foreign powers in the Middle East are especially relevant to the situation which now exists in Southern Africa. The first of these developments came in the late 1950s when, after Egypt's inadequately trained and armed forces had been twice worsted by the burgeoning Israeli Defence Force, Col Abdul Gamel Nasser introduced the Soviet Union as the Arabs' 'strategic ally' into the region. The second development was the Yom Kippur/Ramadan War of October 1973, which began a period that, on the one hand, brought peace with Egypt and, on the other, brought war with the PLO, leading to the Israeli invasion of Lebanon. These two developments in the Middle East have occurred on a different time-scale in Southern Africa.

The Middle East, on the eve of the war in October 1973, was a seriously destabilized region because Israel's neighbours had refused to accept the reality of the Jewish State or, at least, to recognize its borders. Israel had become a fortress state primed to respond with superior military force whenever it felt itself threatened from across its borders; the Western Powers pursued ambiguous policies, seeking to reassure Israel while, at the same time, striving to keep on reasonable terms with its Arab neighbours; the Soviet Union was firmly on the side of the Arabs as the champion of the Palestinians, striving to establish a wider regional role for itself; and the PLO was then still ineffectually struggling to establish itself as a serious military force by acquiring more sophisticated Soviet weapons (especially missiles), and training professional fighting cadres.

The October 1973 War became a watershed in the Middle East. It showed that while Israel still held military superiority in the region, this was no longer as overwhelmingly great as it once was; and that future battles could be won only with heavy losses of life and at a risk of greater involvement of the Super-Powers; it restored Egyptian morale sufficiently to enable the late President Anwar Sadat to make its peace with Israel—an act which polarized the Arab world and which sharpened the challenge of the PLO guerrillas, heavily esconced in the destabilized border-state of Lebanon. Instead of relying on short, sharp military thrusts across its borders to hit at its enemies, the Begin government felt itself driven to the necessity of making a full-scale assault on Lebanon to destroy the PLO 'once and for all'. Its action failed to do so, but one result was to impose serious strains on its relations with its Western allies and, especially, with its strongest backer, the United States. It also had the result of forcing Syria into a closer military alliance with the USSR. Today, the future of the Middle East remains as uncertain and worrying as at any time since the founding of the State of Israel 35 years ago.

Although there is no valid or just comparison between the parliamentary democratic system of Israel and the racist system of SA, their similarities as unpopular regional powers are unmistakable; but the South Africans are still in the position held by Israel at the time of the Six-Day War in 1967. While there is no potential military equivalent to Egypt among SA's neighbours, the Pretoria regime is at two crucial disadvantages compared to Israel. First, as already mentioned, its home front is overwhelmingly opposed to the *status quo*, which constitutes an important different dimension compared to the Middle East. Second, Israel has a powerful ally in the US, while SA has no allies at all. Yet, the essential similarities remain: both countries ultimately rely for the preservation of their systems on their military superiority; and both deeply mistrust their friends in the West, though desperately dependent on them: two circumstances that contribute to their similarly paranoid reactions to foreign intervention in their respective regions.

The most crucial difference between the two embattled states is that while Israel's internal political situation is essentially stable, South Africa's is not. It is this instability inside the apartheid republic that principally determines it relations with its neighbours. After 35 years of practice of apartheid (interestingly enough, the apartheid regime came to power in the same month as the state of Israel was born) this experiment to solve SA's manifold racial problems has patently failed.

The politically dominant White South African minority is no longer able to maintain a system of government resting on White supremacy, and it is anxiously undecided about how to engineer a different form of government which will not 'submerge' them under Black majority rule; on the other side, the Black majority appears confident that they will rule in the long run but they remain uncertain about the best ways of producing this change without destroying the country's valuable economy and without engaging in an all-out struggle of racial violence.

ANATOMY OF VIOLENCE

The growth of political violence has come at a time when a formerly strong and confident regime has been pushed into seeking to maintain its power through government by manipulation—tinkering with the system of apartheid at its rougher edges; making concessions to Black demands wherever it is thought necessary to ease dangerous tensions; and, all the time, concerned to avoid a White backlash from an Afrikaner electorate which still believes that firmness and the rule of the gun remain their best defence for the future.

Violence in SA takes different forms. There is the violence of the state in pushing through those elements of apartheid which are considered essential to 'White survival', e.g. the forcible removal of millions of Black people to give some semblance of meaning to Black homelands and a 'White South Africa'; police repression, often accompanied by extreme brutality, against militant political opponents; and military trans-border attacks to strike at the exile forces of liberation which have opted for armed struggle. Increasingly, too, Black South Africans (especially among the younger generation) have come to accept that 'the barrel of the gun' is the best means of producing change. A stage has already been reached where the Chief of Military Intelligence has admitted that the country must learn to live with a situation of on-going violence.

More than anything else, the Pretoria regime rightly fears the destabilizing effects of oppositional violence which it wrongly sees as being encouraged primarily by the externally-based liberation forces—the African National Congress (ANC), the South-West African People's Organization of Namibia (Swapo), the Pan-Africanist Congress (PAC), and the still evolving Black Consciousness Movement (BCM). For the present, its principal concern is with Swapo and the ANC, both of which—like the PLO—have turned to the Soviet bloc for military support.

These exile liberation movements enjoy the full support of the rest of the continent through the OAU. They also have the backing of the communist world and of considerable bodies of liberal opinion in the Western community. In these respects their situation is little different from that of the PLO, with its endorsement coming from the Arab League. Thus, in the same way as Israel feels itself to be at war with the Arab world (minus Egypt), so White South Africa feels itself threatened by most of Africa. *Both countries see themselves largely isolated within their own continental environment.*

The OAU has placed a duty on all its member-states to give whatever support lies within their power to the SA liberation movements—a responsibility which falls particularly heavily on the Front-line States lying closest to SA's borders. They interpret their responsibilities for the struggle against apartheid in different ways; thus, while all are equally opposed to apartheid, not all of them are equally willing to put the security of their own countries at risk; nor are they equally convinced of the desirability of an armed struggle.

The OAU has designated a number of its member-states to carry special responsibility for handling the affairs of Southern Africa. Formally known as the Front-line African States, they are composed of Tanzania (as chairman), Angola, Botswana, Mozambique, Zambia and Zimbabwe. Although Lesotho, a tiny island in the heart of SA, is closely associated with the grouping, it is not formally a member of it; while Nigeria, though far away, is regarded as an *ad hoc* member because of its size and influence.

While all of SA border states accept political refugees and allow them reasonable freedom of movement, only Angola, Mozambique, Zambia, Zimbabwe and Tanzania allow the liberation movements to maintain either a political or a military presence on their territory. Zimbabwe is particularly concerned about not allowing guerrillas to operate from its territory, or even to enjoy the right to transit into SA. Mozambique does not allow guerrillas to train inside its territory, but it does allow them the right of transit on their way to their target areas; it also allows both the ANC and SA Communist Party leaders to maintain offices close to the capital, Maputo. Angola is the main military training area for Swapo and an important one for the ANC; it also allows Swapo to maintain military bases from which to attack Namibia. Tanzania permits military training camps for both the ANC and PAC. (Since the PAC does not enjoy transit facilities across Mozambique or Zimbabwe, and has no political presence in Angola, it experiences difficulty in getting its trained cadres into SA.)

None of the other border-states—Lesotho, Botswana and Swaziland—allows any overt guerrilla presence on its soil. However, where there are political refugees, there is bound to be a network of contacts for the liberation movements. Pretoria's official stand is that it will not accept that any of its border-states should provide facilities *of any kind* for 'the terrorists'. All facilities—even those granted to political refugees suspected of being in contact with the guerrilla movements—

are described as 'terrorist bases'. Prime Minister Botha has stated on many occasions that his government feels itself free to take any military action it regards as being necessary to strike at guerrilla 'bases', wherever they exist, and regardless of any considerations of the 'sanctity' of borders. *This policy amounts to an 'open border' for military operations throughout Southern Africa.*

The South African Defence Force (SADF) has operated, both openly and clandestinely, in neighbouring countries since the 1970s, when it supported the regime of Ian Smith in Rhodesia and collaborated with the Portuguese colonial authorities in Mozambique and Angola. In 1975 it openly intervened on the side of Jonas Savimbi's National Union for the Total Independence of Angola (Unita) against the Movement for Popular Liberation of Angola (MPLA) and its Cuban combat allies. Since that time, in pursuit of its campaign against Swapo, the SADF has continued its support of Unita and has repeatedly made deep military thrusts into Angola—where it has now established effective military control over a sizeable area in the south of the country. The SADF has also made incursions into Zambia and, in 1980, made a direct attack against the alleged ANC headquarters at Matolo, a suburb of Mozambique's capital. In December 1982 it sent an airborne commando group to kill ANC supporters in Maseru, the capital of Lesotho.

The Pretoria regime is frankly unapologetic about these military operations, which it insists are carried out for the sole purpose of defending SA's security by striking at its enemies before they are able to undertake military incursions into the republic. The Defence Minister, Gen Magnus Malan, has said that the only mistake made by Israel was that it allowed the PLO to build up a formidable force in Lebanon before it was forced to invade that country; no such opportunities, he indicated, would be given to Swapo, the ANC or any other guerrilla force.

But Pretoria remains secretive about the clandestine support it gives to movements opposed to regimes considered to be hostile to SA by virtue of their support for guerrilla movements. Although Pretoria admits having given military support to Unita in the past, it insists that it no longer does so; but this disclaimer is open to serious doubt. It firmly denies that it is behind the Mozambique National Resistance (MNR)—the armed resistance movement to President Samora Machel's government in Mozambique, which has succeeded in spreading its forces across one-third of Mozambican territory. Here, again, the evidence to the contrary is overwhelmingly strong. (For details, see below.)

Lesotho's Prime Minister, Chief Leabua Jonathan, has accused Pretoria of giving its support to the Lesotho Liberation Army (LLA), led by Ntsu Mokhehle and seeking to destroy his regime by force. Since the only entry to Lesotho is through SA, and since Pretoria's military intelligence is superb, it is highly unlikely that the LLA could conceivably carry out its military operations without the knowledge and agreement of the Botha government. (For details, see below.)

What is much less clear, though, is whether Pretoria is actively involved in supporting the dissident forces of Joshua Nkomo's former guerrilla army who have plunged the Matabele area in the south of Zimbabwe into a state of extreme insecurity. Prime Minister Mugabe has repeatedly accused his neighbour of training thousands of dissident Zimbabweans at its military camps in the northern Transvaal. So far, however, the SA involvement in Zimbabwe's troubles has been minor; but its potential is certainly great if this option were ever to be taken up by Pretoria. (For details, see below.)

Another serious aspect of these trans-border military and political activities are the pressures which SA is able to apply indirectly on its neighbours in an effort to compel them to desist from continuing their support for the liberation movements.

241

Zimbabwe's road and rail communications to their nearest ports in Mozambique have been repeatedly cut; the oil pipeline from Beira to Mutare has been sabotaged; oil installation tanks in Beira were blown up, virtually depriving Zimbabwe of fuel for more than a month in early 1983. Mozambique's own internal communications system has been seriously disrupted. While most of these operations were carried out by the MNR, its known links with Pretoria suggest that its pressures on, especially, Zimbabwe at a time when Pretoria was engaged in 'teaching Mugabe a lesson,' is hardly coincidental.

Because of these military and economic pressures, SA stands accused of pursuing a policy of destabilizing neighbouring regimes with the deliberate aim of keeping them weak, if not of seeking to topple them altogether. As already mentioned, Pretoria's answer to these charges is that it has no wish to promote a policy of destabilization in the region. It insists that its sole aim is to prevent the destabilization of SA itself, which results from its neighbours' policies of supporting the 'terrorists', as well as to discourage the introduction of Soviet and Cuban military forces into Southern Africa. 'If we really want to destabilize the region, we could bring the whole works to a standstill overnight,' SA's Prime Minister has boasted.⁹ Western governments (including the US) are foremost in pointing out to Pretoria that the chances of greater Soviet and Cuban intervention in the region are enhanced by SA's military operations against its weaker neighbours; this is precisely what happened in the Middle East.

The conclusion to be drawn from this survey is that a process of destabilization is occurring in Southern Africa at an accelerating pace. The explanation for this is twofold. First, because Black South Africans and their continental and other supporters are determinedly engaged in seeking to destroy the system of apartheid. And, second, because the embattled Pretoria regime is engaged in seeking to prevent internal instability by carrying the war across its borders. Therefore, the root of instability lies within South Africa itself. There is no good reason to suppose that this process of destabilization will be arrested until there is a new, and more acceptable, political dispensation inside SA itself.

Meanwhile, the immediate outlook remains threatening. A great deal depends on the success of the American-led initiative to bring Namibia to its independence. If this effort should finally fail, there is little question but that SA will step up its support for Unita and effectively maintain its own military control over southern Angola. This would unquestionably lead to greater Soviet and Cuban military support for the MPLA regime. Next, if it were felt to be in Pretoria's perceived interests, it could take up the military option open to it in Zimbabwe by giving its full support to the Ndebele secessionist forces there, and so produce a situation in the south of Zimbabwe similar to that which now threatens in Angola. At the same time, Pretoria could further increase its support for the MNR, and so spread further chaos in Mozambique.

This scenario is not entirely fanciful—as developments in the Middle East have shown. With a regime in Pretoria dedicated to the protection of SA's security through military force, and with little hope of producing thorough-going political changes in the Republic in a short period, the only reasonable prognostication must be less than optimistic—unless, and this is always to be hoped for, a *deus ex machina* appears out of the region's enveloping darkness. It is notionally possible that a changed sense of realism will occur among the leaders of the region, actively promoted by the Western Powers, which might yet prevent the emergence of a Middle Eastern crisis area in the African sub-continent. But much as this is to be desired, it would be unwise to count on it happening.

THE DESTABILIZATION OF SOUTHERN AFRICA: AREAS OF CONFLICT

The SA Government denies all responsibility for the growing destabilization of Southern Africa.[10] Its Defence Minister, Gen Magnus Malan, ascribed it to two causes: the supply of communist arms to Southern Africa which, he claimed, exceeded SA's armaments purchases and production; and the inability of African leaders to extricate their countries from their economic difficulties.[11] His breathtaking claim that more Soviet weapons have been supplied to the countries bordering on South Africa than the Republic has spent on its total arms manufacture and procurement—something of the order of £8bn since 1977—is patently absurd.

SA's neighbours, on the other hand, put the entire blame for the region's growing insecurity on Pretoria's policies, as exemplified by this statement of Botswana's Vice-President, Peter Mmusi[12]:

> SA has acted to undermine the development of regionally coordinated action and the building of prosperous, forward-looking economies in our countries. Its actions are a direct threat and hindrance to the implementation of technical and economic cooperation within the SADCC.[13]

As already argued, although each side believes the other to be responsible for the economic disruption and growing violence in the region, destabilization is not the result of any single factor; it is part of the process of a changing order.

SA's own economic and security interests are not in fact served by having unstable, economically weak and hostile neighbours on its borders. It needs a growing market in its hinterland; and it needs governments strong enough to maintain a firm control over law and order. It needs, if not friendly, then at least cooperative governments on its borders. Its preference is for Malawis rather than Mozambiques, and for Swazilands rather than Lesothos or Botswanas. However, this preference is clearly overridden whenever Pretoria see its security interests to be involved.

SA does not need to subvert its neighbours to make, or keep, them weak: they already are that. None of them is in any position to threaten SA, either economically or militarily. But, to the extent that they are willing and able to give direct or indirect support to those forces engaged in undermining SA's *status quo,* they are understandably seen by Pretoria as a threat. And so long as the SA regime remains determined to maintain the essential fabric of the country's traditional political system and continues to see itself as the victim of a 'total onslaught',[14] led by the Soviet Union, its natural stance will be to hit as hard as it can, or as it dares, at those it identifies as allies of its enemies.

The qualification of hitting as hard 'as it dares' suggests that, as yet, important constraints exist on the way SA uses its superior force. Otherwise, as Prime Minister Botha told his Parliament: 'If we had really wanted to destabilize, we could bring the whole works to a standstill overnight.'[15] Or, as the Defence Minister said in a debate on the same occasion: 'If the government had wished to take over, or overthrow the Seychelles Government, it could have used the best defence force in Africa and disposed of this small task in a jiffy.' Only the Western Powers, but mainly the US, act in any way as a constraint on Pretoria's transborder military operations. While Pretoria can hope to get away with defying the Western Powers, it cannot risk alienating them altogether (see, for example, Kissinger's statement quoted earlier). In this respect, SA's position again resembles that of Israel—but with the important qualification that Israel is an ally of the US, whereas Pretoria is an embarrassment to the West and has no committed allies there.

When the SA government says it wants good neighbours, i.e. friendly ones, it does really mean it; but the 'good neighbour' is one who will cooperate with Pretoria by ensuring that the externally-based guerrillas are denied all facilities or opportunities for transiting into SA. This remains a fundamental determinant of the Pretoria regime's policies towards it neighbours, as explicitly set out in statements such as the following:

> South Africa's aim must be to drive all terrorists out of all countries with whom we share common borders, and this must be done by military and economic force if needs be. The stronger the terrorists' presence is allowed to get in countries on our borders, the closer South Africa gets to an Israeli situation. Does your reporter wish to see us forced to fight a conventional war against the ANC before we act at all?[16]

The Botha regime has shown itself to be ready to use the same kind of subversive methods that it alleges against its opponents: *using subversion to fight subversion is now a feature of the process of destabilization in the region.*

Prime Minister Botha has declared his readiness to consider giving aid to 'anti-communist guerrillas in Southern Africa if they ask for it because communism is bad for Africa.'[17] Guerrilla movements which profess their anti-communism include Unita, the MNR and the LLA. SA's Defence Minister went even further than his Prime Minister when he told Parliament that, if necessary, he would allow movements like Unita and the MNR to operate from bases in SA itself.[18] In other words, he would be ready to follow the very policy which he accuses SA's neighbours of practising, and which provide the pretext for military attacks against them. In fact, of course, Unita, the MNR and other armed opposition groups have already been trained for some years in SA or Namibia, and have operated from the Republic's soil. (See below.) Presumably, what Gen Malan wished to indicate was that the government would be willing to bring its clandestine operations into the open, and to expand them. His policy was strongly attacked in a five-day debate on a no-confidence motion in the SA Parliament by the leader of the Opposition, Dr F. van Zyl Slabbert, who warned that it would push Southern Africa 'into a process of war.'[19]

The logical outcome of the kind of policies foreshadowed by Botha and Malan is a military struggle which SA would fight through proxies against hostile neighbours who, predictably, would summon the help of their 'strategic allies'. However, SA would start such a military confrontation from a very strong position. It possesses the strongest army in the region, which is backed by the most advanced industrial base in the continent. It already has in the field the nucleii of rebel armies in Angola, Mozambique and Zimbabwe and a close working relationship with the Lesotho Liberation Army. The SADF now occupies a sizeable part of Angola (the Cunene Province), while Unita and MNR are spread over one-third of Angola and Mozambique, respectively. And although SA has not yet disclosed its full hand in Zimbabwe, it already has thousands of exile Zimbabweans in training in its military camps, and in Matabeleland it has a troubled area which it could exploit in a manner similar to south Angola.

The most worrying scenario for Southern Africa is undoubtedly that Pretoria will one day decide that its best interests lie in encouraging separatist movements in south Angola, south Zimbabwe and south-west Mozambique to set up their own states. Nor is such a development altogether fanciful when one considers the kind of contingency plans proposed by security agencies in Pretoria.

ANGOLA: THE 'TWO KOREAS' PLAN

A plan to create a new state of Ovimbundu has been on the drawing-board of SA strategists since 1981 when it seemed that the UN Security Council Resolution 435 might be implemented and that there was no sure way of beating Swapo in internationally-supervised elections. The core of this plan is that the northern areas of Namibia—Ovambo, Kavango and Caprivi—would be attached to southern Angola. It would be called Ovimbundu, after the dominant ethnic group in the area—to which Jonas Savimbi belongs. One well-placed source for the leak about such a plan is *Die Republikein*, the mouthpiece of the Democratic Turnhalle Alliance (DTA), formerly led by Dirk Mudge, who himself thought it necessary to probe into this idea by asking at a public meeting whether it was 'in anybody's mind to divide Namibia and Angola in this way'. US diplomatic sources are reported to have described the architect of the plan as 'an idiot'.

Reporting these rumours, *Die Republikein* said that the speculations had 'assumed such proportions' that they can no longer be ignored.[20] It called for a government statement to clarify the position. None was forthcoming. According to the paper, the plan was discussed on two or, possibly, three occasions (the first time in Gaborone in 1981) at a meeting attended by the Unita leader, Jonas Savimbi; Peter Kalangula the Ovambo leader who broke away from the DTA; and Mishake Munyongo, a former Swapo leader who formed the Caprivi National Union (Canu) after his expulsion from the movement.

While it seems almost certain that such a plan was discussed in some SA security quarters, it is difficult to treat it as seriously as another plan to establish a Unita government in a separatist Ovimbundu Republic covering only the southern part of Angola. Such a state could, it is thought, give Savimbi a better platform from which to push his claims of leadership over the whole country.

If such ideas seem to lack credibility at present, they are not likely to look so impractical if the Namibian negotiations should fail in the end. The MPLA and its African allies would, then, probably find themselves with little alternative other than to accept a much greater degree of Cuban and Soviet military involvement; this would present a much more difficult problem for SA's defence lines in South Angola, as well as for Unita. Savimbi's policies and Pretoria's relations with him are discussed under the Namibia section, below.

MOZAMBIQUE: THE NATIONAL RESISTANCE MOVEMENT

Pretoria's denials that it has any involvement with the Mozambique National Resistance (MNR)[21] are not to be taken seriously. Even Pretoria found it difficult to keep up its pretence after the US State Department confirmed in 1982 that the MNR 'received the bulk of its support from SA.'[22] The origins, growth and present role of the MNR offers an interesting case-study of how SA conducts its clandestine operations and how it is able to exploit the dissatisfactions of Africans with their own governments.

By early 1983, the MNR was reckoned to have 5,000-6,000 armed men inside Mozambique and to have succeeded in establishing a network of several hundred camps across the country—from the western borders of Zimbabwe and Malawi, the southern borders of SA and Swaziland, right across one-third of the country to below the three northern provinces of Cabo Delgado, Nampula and Niassa, south of the Makonde territory which abuts on Tanzania. But it had nowhere succeeded in establishing 'liberated areas' as Frelimo did in its successful struggle against Portuguese colonialism.

Thus, the real nature of the MNR threat is not the chances of its overthrowing the Frelimo government, but its capability of disrupting the country's vital communications, and of promoting a widespread sense of insecurity. This is particularly worrying to the authorities at a time of serious economic hardship, worsened by a severe drought in much of the country. Moreover, the success of the MNR in establishing a 'no-go' area in the dissident Inhambane province is unquestionably a serious blow to Frelimo's authority. President Machel identified two main factors to explain this remarkable change in the fortunes of the Frelimo regime since its triumphant victory over the Portuguese just eight years before. First, the efforts of SA in seeking to destabilize Mozambique; and, second, the failures and mistakes of his own ruling party, especially in the rural areas. If it were not for rural discontent with local Frelimo leaders and policies, the MNR would not have found a welcome among a sufficient number of dissidents to enable its cadres to survive hundreds of miles from their orginal base in the Sitatonga Mountains on the Zimbabwe border.

Writing in AIM, the official Mozambique news agency, Paul Fauvet and Alves Gomes give a forthright answer to the question: Does the MNR enjoy local support?

> The answer must be a qualified yes. Those who lost their old privileges when Frelimo came to power were quite prepared to throw in their lot with the MNR. Apart from the *fetishists* (i.e. witchdoctors) and regulos (tribal chiefs), there are those who failed to succeed in the Frelimo elections for the People's Assemblies, etc; and those who failed to get Frelimo party membership after liberation, especially in Inhambane province.

There are also those who fell out with Frelimo's leaders after independence, especially in the army—some for ideological reasons and others because of their abuse of power. It is this group that has, in the main, provided the militant leadership of the MNR; while the dissident middle class and intellectual elements (Black Mozambicans and Portuguese settlers) have supplied the personnel for the MNR's extensive propaganda machine.

President Machel himself laid particular blame on the arrogance, insensitivity, corruption and inefficiency of prominent party leaders in the provinces, whom he publicly disciplined. Complaints by peasants of the behaviour of some leading party cadres—arrogance, corruption, indolence and abuse of power—were seriously addressed at the Frelimo conference in March 1983. It was followed by a shake-up of the party's rural leadership. Winning back the confidence of the peasants—the backbone of Frelimo's successful liberation struggle—is therefore a top priority.

There is also the problem of training the national army in counter-insurgency operations. After independence, Frelimo's own insurgency forces were either disbanded or integrated into a more disciplined, modern army, trained to use tanks, heavy artillery, sophisticated missiles and to fly modern warplanes. The task of training such an army was initially entrusted to the Soviet Union, which has a large team of military instructors at the main training camp at Nampula. While these modern weapons and conventional battle tactics might be useful if it were ever to come to confronting a direct attack by the SA army, they are of little use in fighting a bush war against guerrillas. But Frelimo needs to relearn the lessons it taught the Portuguese when its own forces were fighting a bush war—the first of which is that the peasants should see the army and the authorities as their friends and protectors.

Guerrilla tactics are not exactly the strongest point in Russian military expertise—as has been shown by the difficulties in Afghanistan, and the repeated failures of the Warsaw-Pact generals who have been advising the Ethiopians in their struggle against Eritrean guerrillas. The Frelimo government began to develop military ties with nations other than those of the Soviet bloc. It entered into a military training agreement with its former colonial rulers, the Portuguese, and it enlisted the help of the North Koreans for special army training.

Military assistance was also provided by its neighbours. Zimbabwe took over responsibility for patrolling two-thirds of the 500-mile oil pipeline, and there were unconfirmed reports of the presence of small military units from Tanzania and Zambia.

THE ORIGINS AND AIMS OF THE MNR

The MNR claims to be the true heirs of the martyred creator of Frelimo, Eduardo Mondlane, who was killed by a parcel bomb in Tanzania in 1969. Borrowing Frelimo's slogan, *A Luta Continua* (The Struggle Continues), it identifies the new struggle as being against communism. This makes it an ideal ally of SA, providing a coincidence of interests between dissident Mozambicans opposed to their own Marxist regime, and a Pretoria regime concerned about a communist (Soviet) inspired external threat to its security.

The MNR was set up in 1976 by the Rhodesian Central Intelligence Organization of Ian Smith's regime. Its two original purposes were to utilize Portuguese-speaking Mozambicans (Black and White) to gather intelligence about Robert Mugabe's Zimbabwe African National Liberation Army (Zanla); and to harass the newly-established Frelimo government which was backing Mugabe's guerrillas. Although the initiative for establishing the MNR came from the Rhodesians, the SA military showed a close interest in its activities from the start. A great deal is now known about the beginnings of the MNR from four reliable sources:

1. A book about the controversial Selous Scouts recently published in SA by its former commander, Col Ron Reid Daly, who writes with pride about their role in training the MNR.

2. Documents captured by the Mozambique army when they overran an MNR base at Garagua in December 1981.

3. Volunteered information by Ken Flower, former chief of the Rhodesian Central Intelligence Organization (CIO).

4. Reports by former members of the CIO who now work for Zimbabwe intelligence.

The MNR first announced itself in June 1976 through *Voz da Africa Libra* (Voice of Free Africa), which began to broadcast from three stations at Gwelo (Gweru), Umtali (Mutare) and Fort Victoria. The broadcasts declared war against Frelimo's 'communism', and praised the Smith regime. One of its themes was: 'Rhodesia stands for tranquility and respect among all its citizens.' The first MNR recruits included Portuguese unwilling to stay on in Mozambique after independence, and Black Mozambicans, who included former soldiers in the Portuguese colonial army; dissidents from Frelimo; middle-class businessmen; some intellectuals; and *regulos* (colonial-appointed chiefs). Their first commander was Andre Matade Matzangaiza, a former Frelimo fighter and Quartermaster in the new Mozambique army.

According to Ken Flower, Smith's former top security official, the first MNR training group was set up at Bindura in Rhodesia in September 1976. Another training camp was established later at Mutare. One of Flower's main collaborators was Orlando Cristina, a private secretary to Jorge Jardim, the controversial Portuguese millionaire who acted as Dr Salazar's personal representative in Mozambique. (Jardim had also served as honorary Portuguese consul in Malawi, and had frequent access to President Banda.)

Orlando Cristina was an officer in the Portuguese intelligence service (PIDE). Both were involved with the Portuguese army and PIDE in promoting and recruiting three separate units for the army—the Special Groups (GEs); the Very Special Groups (GMEs), who were used for special assignments in Tanzania and Zambia; and the Special Paratroops Groups (GEPs)—as well as the *flechas* (arrows), who came directly under PIDE. The *flechas* were especially brutal (they were responsible, for example, for the 1973 massacre at Inhaminga). Much of the early recruitment for the MNR came from the *flechas*.

MNR groups began to make some tentative military attacks in late 1976/early 1977 against targets along the border zones of Manica and Tete and, to a lesser extent, Gaza. They attacked villages, abducted peasants and burnt shops. Their activities were primarily disruptive, and they did not seek to engage the Mozambican army. Their main value to the Rhodesian forces lay in their intelligence-gathering and in accompanying the Selous Scouts and others to attack Zanla camps, acting as guides and interpreters. The MNR was used as a proper attacking force for the first time in 1979. The Selous Scouts helped to establish the first MNR base inside Mozambique high up on the Sitatonga mountains. After coming under heavy attack by the Mozambican army in June 1980, they moved their base 300 km to the south at Garagua, near the Save river, the border between the Manica and Gaza provinces.

The MNR's first commander-in-chief, Andre Matade Matzangaiza, was a Frelimo officer who, at independence, was promoted to the rank of Quartermaster in the new Mozambican army. But he was soon charged and convicted of stealing army funds and was sent to a Re-education Centre, from which he managed to escape in 1976. He was a dynamic leader, but was killed when he walked into an ambush at Gorongoza. After his death a violent power struggle broke out when Afonso Dhlakama (Jacomo) attempted to take over the leadership. Dhlakama, a former officer in the Portuguese army, had opted to join the new Mozambican army of Frelimo in 1974. But, like Andre, he too was convicted of theft, cashiered from the army and succeeded in escaping to Rhodesia.

While Orlando Cristina backed Dhlakama, the Rhodesians backed the man who had been Andre Matzangaiza's deputy, Lucas M'lhangu. The power struggle was settled in a gunbattle at Chisumbanji (in the south of Zimbabwe) when M'lhangu was killed and Dhlakama became the new undisputed commander-in-chief. M'lhangu's supporters fled back into Mozambique and handed themselves over to the army. At the same time, the MNR's Political Commissar, Henrique Sitoe, fled with the others. By November 1980, as Dhlakama later admitted, the outlook for the MNR was bleak. But with Mugabe's victory and the defeat of Smith's Rhodesia, a new chapter opened up for the MNR, with the South African army replacing the defeated Rhodesians.

THE SOUTH AFRICAN CONNECTION WITH THE MNR

SA military personnel were present at the MNR camp in Gorongoza, Mozambique from 1979, according to reports by former Rhodesian CIO officers. When the MNR base at Gorongoza was destroyed by the Mozambican army in November 1979, they moved their forward headquarters to Garagua in Mozambique, where at least one SA military liaison officer served in the camp. Documents captured when Garagua was over-run on 7 December 1981 refer to him as 'Colonel Charlie'; but, on one occasion, he is identified as Col van Niekerk.

After Mugabe's election victory, and a few days before Zimbabwe's independence in April 1980, two SA army Dakotas flew the MNR headquarters' staff from their camp at Bindura, while the *Voice of Free Africa* radio equipment and staff were picked up by a SA C-130 transport plane at Mutare. Both these operations were witnessed and reported at the time by the British military team, under Lt-Gen Sir John Acland, who were supervising Rhodesia's transition to independence. American military intelligence sources later confirmed that the MNR headquarters was established at Phalaborwa in northern Transvaal, near the Mozambique border. It was later moved to a nearby camp at Zoabastad. The MNR commander, Afonso Dhlakama, has boasted to a Portuguese radio interviewer that when he was made a Colonel in 1981, Gen Magnus Malan, now SA's Defence Minister, said: 'Your army is part of the South African Defence Force.'

In early 1981, the MNR's fighters were transported into Mozambique in what Zimbabwe military observers describe as 'an armada' of SA army helicopters, which overflew Zimbabwe airspace. This infringement was officially protested at the time by Mugabe's government. The base camp at Garagua, near the Save river—the boundary between the Manica and Gaza provinces—was two kilometres in diameter and had a helicopter strip. By the time it was finally overrun by the Mozambican army in December 1981, the MNR had succeeded in establishing itself in camps over a large part of the country. Until its fall, the Garagua base was supplied by regular air drops by the SA Air Force. Reports that there are up to 20 SA military instructors in the main MNR camp have not been substantiated, other than the definite identification of Col van Niekerk. No South Africans were found in the Garagua camp when it was captured.

The SA navy is also reported to have dropped off MNR men and supplies through sea-landings at camps in the Inhambane area between Maputo and Beira. This was obviously an easier way of establishing them along the coast than crossing the entire breadth of the country.

Daily contact is maintained between the MNR base camps in Mozambique and their headquarters in SA through two mobile radio stations. Messages are uncoded and can be picked up fairly easily by interceptors. Messages are exchanged at almost hourly intervals throughout daylight hours. There were over 370 such messages in December 1982. They contain news of the day's activities and requests for medical and military supplies.

REASONS FOR THE SUCCESSES OF THE MOZAMBICAN REBELS

The relative ease with which the MNR had spread across the country during 1981 was, according to one Mozambican official, due to 'our army having gone to sleep' after Zimbabwe's independence. When they woke up to what was happening, they tried to rely on conventional arms and tactics, including the use of tanks. These methods, reflecting the training of the new army by the Russians, were useless against cadres trained to fight as guerrillas. MNR tactics changed flexibly during 1981, reflecting not only the need to apply pressures on Mozambique but, increasingly, on Zimbabwe as well and, for a time, on Malawi. The disruption of the latter's rail and road communications to the sea—which at one point led to a critical shortage of petrol—came at a time when President Banda was engaged in establishing friendlier relations with President Machel's government to which he had previously been opposed. The MNR concentrated on three target areas in 1981:

- The railway lines from Maputo and Beira to Zimbabwe.
- The strategic oil pipeline from Beira to Mutare in Zimbabwe.
- The main paved roads in the centre of the country and along the coastal route.

Significantly, the easiest target of all—the Cahora-Bassa power-line—was cut in November 1980 and twice in 1981; but not since then. The line supplies SA with 7% of its electric power. It is believed that the single attack was meant to disguise MNR's connections with SA. The power line is at least as vulnerable as the frequently disrupted oil pipeline to Zimbabwe. It is also notable that there has been no disruption of the railway line which carries SA goods for export through Maputo.

The MNR has run up a creditable tally of successes in the past 18 months—successes which have seriously harmed the economies of Mozambique and Zimbabwe and, to a lesser extent, those of Zambia and Malawi. How much of the credit belongs to the MNR and how much to clandestine SA military forces is a moot point; but some of the operations are clearly so sophisticated as to be beyond the capacity of the MNR. For example, a high degree of expertise in the use of explosives was needed to blow up the strategic bridge across the Pungue river which, for a time, cut off road communications to Beira. A month later, in November 1981, the marker buoys at the entrance of the Beira harbour were destroyed. This sophisticated sea operation was obviously well beyond the capacities of the MNR. Moreover, it is known that the idea of taking out the buoys was seriously considered by Smith's security forces and was repeatedly advanced by a Rhodesian officer, who later went to SA. He argued that destroying the markers would crippled sea traffic into the harbour for a long time. In fact, this proved not to be the case.

There is also direct evidence of an officer in the SA Army having been involved in sabotaging the Beira–Mutare railway on 14 October 1981. He was killed when the detonator set to blow up the line exploded prematurely; all that was recovered were his ear and some hair and, in his knapsack, the manuscript of a novel about fighting in Northern Ireland. These remnants were sufficient to identify the saboteur as Alan Gingles, a former officer in the hardline Ulster Defence Regiment, later recruit to the Selous Scouts and, after Zimbabwe's independence, the SADF. Shortly after this sabotage attempt, the SADF announced that Gingles had been killed 'in action against terrorists' in an operational area.[23]

The major blow struck at the oil tank installations in Beira in December 1982—at the precise hour when the SA army was engaged in carrying out its heavy punitive attack against suspected ANC guerrillas in Lesotho—resulted in the imprisonment of four Portuguese and one South African-educated British citizen, all residents of Beira. They were accused not of the act of sabotage but of failing to report to the authorities their foreknowledge that it was to take place. What was not cleared up at their trial was who the accused were working for. The saboteurs showed great skill in blowing up 14 tanks and placing their explosives in such a way as not to cause maximum damage—which they could have done by destroying the pumping station as well. On this occasion, too, the Mozambican army guards had 'gone to sleep'.

On the other hand, the MNR has shown itself capable of the easier job of planting land mines to impede and make travel unsafe along main roads; sabotaging the oil pipeline; and ambushing trucks and even trains. But the MNR engages only in hit-and-run attacks and in laying ambushes: typical guerrilla tactics.

Like Unita, the MNR has also engaged in kidnapping foreigners as hostages in order to gain international attention and to seek rewards for their release. They captured British headlines by taking as hostage a British ecologist, John Burlison, and demanding as a condition for his release that he should publish a letter sympathetic to the MNR cause in the British press. They later captured six Bulgarians working on a technical project, and have killed at least six Portuguese technicians.

The MNR make use of all the familiar bush methods in forcing the cooperation of peasants in those areas where they are least welcome. They employ witchcraft and practice considerable brutality, mutilating lips, ears, arms and breasts. Supporters of Frelimo, after having had their lips sliced off, have been sent away with the admonition: 'Now you can go and smile at Samora' (i.e. President Machel). Reports of this kind of brutality are consistent from many of the areas in which the MNR operate. Apart from press-ganging young peasants into anti-government actions and so making it necessary for them to stay with the rebels, the MNR have also been able to recruit supporters from among people disgruntled with Frelimo's rule and by making an ethnic appeal. Both Afonso Dhlakama and the man he replaced, Andre Matzangaiza, came from the Manica province, where they seem to have had some success in recruiting on an ethnic appeal.

THE LEADERSHIP OF THE MOZAMBICAN REBELS
No dissident movement can become a serious threat to an established government, even if it has powerful foreign backing, unless it has an element of popular support. This thesis has been proved over and over again—not least by the attempts to overthrow governments in Latin America and South-East Asia. While the MNR can count on the support of the Pretoria regime, of important Right-wing forces in Portugal and White Rhodesians who supported the Smith regime, it has succeeded in becoming formidable enemy to President Machel's regime only because it enjoys a measure of support inside the country. It is impossible to know just how extensive that support is, although its failure to establish any 'liberated zones' would point to its having only limited support in any single province, and not much in two-thirds of the country.

There is hard evidence of only one Portuguese citizen actually fighting with the MNR in Mozambique—the Chief of Operations, Commandant Marquez. However, there are a number of Portuguese in its leadership and more engaged in its international relations operations. The known leadership of the MNR is as follows:

Afonso Dhlakama (known as Jacomo): Commander-in-Chief of MNR. Fought in the Portuguese army until the collapse in 1974; made Quartermaster in 1975. Convicted of theft and discharged. Went to Rhodesia, and took over when the first military commander, Andre Matade Matzangaiza, was killed in a power struggle in October 1979.

Orlando Cristina: Secretary-general. Former officer in Portuguese intelligence (PIDE). Helped establish MNR with the millionaire Portuguese businessman, Jorge Jardim. Moving spirit behind the *Voice of Free Africa*, and chief propagandist in South Africa and Portugal. He was assassinated by an unknown assailant in Pretoria in early 1983.

Samuel Guideon Mahluza: Chief of Department of Politics and Foreign Relations. Former deputy president of UDENAMO, one of the groups that merged to form Frelimo during the liberation struggle. But he broke with Frelimo in 1962.

Adriana Bomba: Head of Information and in charge of *Juventude Mocambicana* (JUNO), the MNR youth wing. Former Mozambican air force pilot who defected in a MiG-21 to South Africa in 1982. Employed for a time by SA army intelligence and translation work.

Raul Domingos: Chief of Defence and Security. Also Dhlakama's chief secretary, and in charge of finance.
Commandant Antonio Juliane: Chief of Education and Social Affairs.
Commandant Marquez: Chief of the Department of Operations.
Commandant Zeco: Chief of Security.
Vincente Zacharias Ululu: Adjutant to the Chief of the Department of Politics, responsible for International Political Affairs.
Armande Khemba dos Santos: Adjutant for External Relations.
B. Bema: Commissioner for National Politics.

Among other Portuguese playing an active role in the work of the MNR are:
Casimir Moteiro: who was tried and sentenced to 18 years in prison *in absentia* for his part in assassinating Salazar's chief rival, Gen Delgado, in 1965. He is also suspected of having been involved in the assassination of Eduardo Mondlane, Frelimo's founder. He is believed to be living and working in Johannesburg.
Dr Evo Fernandes: Editor of the MNR publication *A Luta Continua* (Lisbon) Former PIDE agent. Coordinator of the Department of Politics and External Relations. Worked for Jorge Jardim; acted as his business manager for *Noticias da Beira.* Describes himself as European representative of MNR. Lives in Cascais, Portugal.
Joao Maria Tudela and Antonio Pires de Carvalho: both at one time worked for *Voice of Free Africa.* The latter was involved in the abortive counter-coup in Mozambique in September 1974, when he helped to take over Lourenco Marques' radio station.

ZIMBABWE: A SECOND UNITA IN THE MAKING?

Relations between Pretoria and Harare declined swiftly in 1982 and early 1983; however, despite some tough economic measures and 'a serious warning' to the Mugabe government in June 1983 not to allow ANC 'terrorists' to pass across Zimbabwean territory, Pretoria has so far been careful to avoid playing an overt military role across the Limpopo river. Constraints operating on SA's role in Zimbabwe include the interests of 200,000 Whites still living in the country, many of whose future could be jeopardized by any serious military conflict with SA; the very close British connections with Zimbabwe, where it still maintains a military training team; and SA's own trade and investment interests in the country. Because of Zimbabwe's economic vulnerability and dependence for its access to the sea through Mozambique or SA, it is a relatively easy matter for Pretoria to exert strong non-military pressures—as happened in December 1982/January 1983 when the oil supplies from Beira were disrupted, plunging Zimbabwe into a desperate transport situation for over six weeks. Earlier, SA had severely handicapped Zimbabwe by recalling locomotives at the height of the maize crop season; and there has been continuous disruption of its communications and of the oil pipeline from Beira (see above).

The Zimbabwe authorities view SA's clandestine security role with considerable alarm and do not accept that it is as innocent of involvement in the dissident groups as Pretoria would have it believed. There is, for example, the question of why a large number of Bishop Muzorewa's military auxiliaries were taken to a military training camp near Phalaborwa in the northern Transvaal in the few months after independence. (Mugabe has put the number at between 5,000-6,000, but Western intelligence sources estimate c. 1,500.) SA has always denied this accusation, though admitting that they have recruited many former White Rhodesian soldiers, including members of the notorious Selous Scouts.

One border incident in August 1982 raised a number of unanswered questions.

252

A party of 17 SADF soldiers were ambushed in Southern Zimbabwe; the three White members of the party were all killed; the 14 Black soldiers made their escape back to SA. Mugabe described the attack as one of continuing 'acts of destabilization inside Zimbabwe'.[24] Gen Constand Viljoen, Chief of the SADF, apologized for the incident and explained that the three White soldiers were former Rhodesians who had joined the SA army. They were on 'an unauthorized mission' to free political detainees (Whites). He promised that 'personal emotions would have to be taken into consideration in future before a soldier was posted to any particular area.' He said nothing about why 14 Black Rhodesian soldiers were in the party, or what they were doing serving in the SADF.[25]

The Zimbabwe security services remain convinced that there was close collaboration between some of Joshua Nkomo's lieutenants from his Zipra command and SA special services before and during the troubles in Matabeleland in late 1982 and early 1983.[26] They blamed the sabotage of 14 Hunter strike planes at their air base on agents collaborating with SA. They also submitted evidence during a number of political trials of former White Rhodesians who pleaded guilty to having been in contact with SA agents.

For the present, though, it is the smoke rather than the fire that troubles the Zimbabweans: their fear is that, as the security situation continues to deteriorate in the region, Pretoria will seek to develop an armed political opposition force to the Mugabe government along similar lines to those of the MNR and Unita. It is this concern that has led Prime Minister Mugabe to speak of the need for a possible security agreement with the Soviet bloc (see above).

LESOTHO: SA'S MOST VULNERABLE NEIGHBOUR

Pretoria's support of Ntsu Mokhehle's Lesotho Liberation Army (LLA) is a mirror image of what it describes as unacceptable behaviour by some of the border states. The LLA is engaged in armed violence in an effort to overthrow a legally-recognized government; it engages in terrorism and political assassination. All this precisely fits Pretoria's description of a terrorist organization; yet the LLA's armed cadres are allowed to make their incursions into Lesotho from 'bases' in SA. Given the high state of watchfulness and efficiency of the Republic's intelligence network, such operations over a long period can occur only with the knowledge and consent of Pretoria. Moreover, the State-controlled SA Broadcasting Corporation described the LLA in a commentary on 17 July 1982 as 'a liberation army'.

In October 1982, during one of the regular meetings between the two neighbouring governments (see below), SA's Foreign Minister surprised his opposite number by proposing to exchange the LLA leader for a wanted ANC refugee. According to Chief Jonathan:

> Our Foreign Minister was told: 'You can go and tell your Prime Minister that if we can come to a deal with him over handing over Tembi Hani (an ANC refugee suspected by Pretoria of being a highly-trained 'terrorist'), we are prepared to hand over Ntsu Mokhehle to you. How could they hand over Mokhehle if he wasn't working with them in South Africa? Naturally, I turned down their proposed deal. I advised Hani to leave since he appeared to be a marked man.[27]

There is other irrefutable evidence of collusion between the LLA and Pretoria. A reporter of the Bloemfontein newspaper, *The Friend,* reported in November, 1982, that three Free State farmers with land bordering on Lesotho—Mrs. D Whitson of Omega, Mrs Johanna Coleman of Beginsel and Mr Danie Joubert of Tuinplaas—said they believe that LLA cadres cross their lands at night to make their strikes against Lesotho. The Whitsons say that they saw suspected LLA vehicles leaving their farm on the night of 28 July after having fired mortars at the country residence of Prime Minister Jonathan, which lies close to the border. They reported the matter to the police but no further action was subsequently reported, even though it was the home of a neighbouring Prime Minister that was attacked from South African soil.

A fortnight earlier, a home-made bomb blew up in the house of Pheta Matlanyane, a prominent member of Mokhehle's party, the BCP. No police action followed. A few months earlier, five LLA members were convicted in a Bophuthatswana court at Thaba Nchu (c. 40 km from the Lesotho border) of being in illegal possession of arms. They were given a suspended sentence. When their leader, Tsiliso Rapitsi, walked out of Court a free man, he declared: 'We will resume the struggle.'

Other Free State farmers have publicly complained about the unhindered movement of LLA cadres across their land. Yet no official action has ever been taken by the South African authorities—even though some of the LLA attacks have included the murder of Lesotho's Minister of Works, and of W. Chakela, a former prominent leader of the BCP who had broken with Mokhehle.

The SADF made a helicopter-borne commando raid on 9 December 1982, on the homes of ANC refugees living in Maseru, killing 37 men, women and children, seven of whom were, in fact, Basotho. Gen Viljoen justified the attack on the grounds that the ANC had been planning a Christmas campaign of terror inside SA and the Bantu Homelands. He claimed that 'well-trained terrorists' had recently moved to Lesotho to carry out this plan, and added: 'The SA government repeatedly warned governments of all neighbouring States not to allow terrorists to use their territory and facilities as a springboard against SA.'

One unusual feature of this trans-border attack is that no complaint of the kind mentioned by Gen Viljoen had been previously conveyed to the Lesotho authorities. Chief Jonathan insisted in an interview:

> I want to make it perfectly clear that nobody from Pretoria told me or my Ministers before the attack on 9 December that they suspected the ANC of planning attacks on the Republic. This is a very strange way of behaving. I was very disappointed that they felt they had to take this line when, at the same time, they are misleading the world by saying that they want to live in peace with us.
>
> We have a Consultative Committee which goes into all matters of mutual concern between our two countries, such as economic and labour questions, and even mutual security problems. To my surprise, the issues relating to the ANC were never raised in the Consultative Committeee, although it had met only a month or so before the attack.[28]

In reply to questions about SA's relations with its neighbours, the Lesotho Prime Minister said:

> It is a deliberate policy of Pretoria to destabilize all the independent countries bordering on SA for the simple reason that they want to have puppet governments. This is their whole policy. You will recall that when Lesotho got its independence from the United Kingdom, we had working relations with SA—so much so that many of my colleagues in Africa even suspected me of being a puppet of Pretoria. But they didn't understand me—nor did Pretoria. My stand on independence is much better understood now. At that time I was the first nationalist leader to break the ice by meeting with the SA Prime Minister, Dr Verwoerd, because I believe in détente; after

all, you can change your friends but not your neighbours. Well, the South Africans didn't understand me. They thought I was going to be their puppet, whereas my independence is not for sale. I think Pretoria understands me better now. However, what I still have in mind is to find some way of solving our problems, peacefully and together; but this cannot be on the basis of the present *status quo* in SA.

Lesotho was subjected to different kinds of pressures after a bomb exploded in Bloemfontein, 80 miles from Maseru, on 18 May 1983. The SA authorities slowed down all traffic across the main border post on the Caledon river to search every vehicle. A Pretoria source confirmed that the slowdown was designed to remind Lesotho of SA's unhappiness over the continued presence of ANC members in Maseru.[29] The security checks went on for a fortnight, severely disrupting Lesotho's commercial life and, as admitted by SA's Foreign Minister, bringing relations between the two countries to 'the lowest point in our history'.[30] The crisis was finally relieved at a meeting between the two Foreign Ministers on 3 June 1983 when, according to Pik Botha: 'We agreed it was of decisive importance than no element of subversion should be used against each other.'

This was taken to mean that SA would, in future, curb Mokhehle's LLA. But Chief Jonathan was quick to point out that his government had not agreed to act against genuine ANC refugees.

BOTSWANA: A GATHERING PLACE OF REFUGEES

Botswana, as the border country which gives sanctuary to more SA refugees than any other African country, plays a particularly sensitive role in the region. Its government applies a strict policy of refusing to allow armed guerrillas to transit the territory, or to indulge in open political activities. Its policy of seeking to restrict all unemployed refugees in a camp some distance from the capital makes for difficulties between them and the authorities. So, President Quett Masire's government attracts animosity from all sides. But its most difficult problems come from the activities of a large network of SA spies and informers, who occasionally kidnap or even kill activists wanted in SA.[31]

Pretoria's more recent concern has been over Botswana's decision to buy selected weapons from the Soviet Union, even though this deal has not been accompanied by any sign of change in Botswana's foreign policy orientation or traditionally moderate attitudes.[32] Reports in June 1983 that Bostwana had signed an agreement with SA not to allow subversion directed from their countries against each other, were officially denied in Gaborone.[33] The Masire government declared that it had no knowledge of any such agreements, nor did it see the need for them since it was a longstanding policy of his country not to allow its territory to be used for launching attacks against its neighbours.[34]

ZAMBIA: A PRESIDENT'S FEARS

Although President Kaunda declared himself ready in August 1982 to have a follow-up meeting to the one held in April with Prime Minister Botha,[35] the SA leader indicated that there was no purpose in repeating that performance. His reaction was perhaps understandable since Pretoria now has its own direct line of contact with Luanda and, more especially, since Kaunda had indicated that one of his reasons for wanting another meeting was to use it as an opportunity to make SA's political leaders aware that time was running out to find a solution for the problems of their country.[36] He warned that unless a peaceful solution was found soon there would be a bloody explosion in the region—a message he also delivered during his state visit to Britain in March 1983. Speaking in London, he claimed that apartheid was strengthened by Western investment, and added that unless changes came in SA within three to four years, there would be 'a major explosion'.

THE SEYCHELLES: THE SMOKING GUN

Notwithstanding a full-scale debate in the South African Parliament, considerable doubts continue to persist about the actual role played by Pretoria in the badly bungled coup by Col Mike Hoare's mercenaries against President René's regime in the Seychelles on 26 November 1981.[37] The authorities admitted that Martin Dolinchek, one of the leaders of the coup (who was caught and later convicted in the Seychelles) was employed by SA's National Intelligence Service (NIS— formerly known as BOSS).[38] His service with the NIS was terminated only on 31 July 1982, eight months after the coup, on the grounds of his being absent without permission! The Prime Minister admitted that Dolinchek had informed the NIS on 21 July 1981 of a plan to stage a coup by the former Seychelles President, James Mancham; but he claimed that Dolinchek was told by the NIS Director that the service should not become involved. The coup plan had then been monitored by the NIS until it was satisfied that it had been called off. If this official version is accepted, it reflects very seriously on the efficiency of the NIS, which apparently did not know that one of its agents was involved in the on-going plot; that over 50 mercenaries, including a number of members of the SADF, were being recruited and trained on SA soil; and that army officers were providing a substantial quantity of arms required for the coup. Details of the findings of an internal board of inquiry were kept secret, though the Defence Minister said the papers had been sent to the Attorney-General to take any action he thought necessary. The Prime Minister added that disciplinary action had been taken against some people, but he declined to disclose this information except to the Leader of the Opposition on the basis of confidentiality—an offer that was rejected. Dr van Zyl Slabbert had asked 23 questions in Parliament in an attempt to pin down responsibility for the Seychelles affair.[39] Both the Progressive Federal Party and the Conservative Party, led by Andries Treurnicht, called for the resignation of the Defence Minister, Gen Magnus Malan. A former Minister in the Cabinet at the time of the Seychelles coup, Dr Ferdi Hartzenberg, said he knew from personal experience that not all members of the Cabinet would necessarily be aware of the plot.[40] He threw out a challenge across the floor of the House to the Defence Minister asking whether he had previous knowledge of it. Gen Malan answered no.

There was no dispute that SA was the base from which the coup was staged against the Seychelles (which suggests something about the role of influential individuals and agencies in the country); that SA agents and soldiers were associated with the plot; and that a substantial quantity of weapons were provided from the SADF armoury. What is difficult to understand is how the ubiquitous network of NIS agents failed to discover that this elaborate operation had not been abandoned as they were told by Dolinchek.

The leader of the bungled coup, Mike Hoare, was convicted with 41 other plotters on three charges involving the hijacking of an Air India plane—but not of engaging in terrorism or of attacking a foreign government. Martin Dolinchek escaped the death sentence in a court in the Seychelles when he made a grovelling confession of his crimes and inveighed against the 'evils of apartheid.' He explained how he had been drawn in this 'misguided and shameful' operation, and how he had been misled about the true nature of the Seychelles government, to whom he held out a hand in 'brotherhood' to atone for his crime.[41]

NEGOTIATIONS FOR A NAMIBIAN SETTLEMENT
THE COURSE OF EVENTS—AUGUST 1982-JUNE 1983

The negotiations over Namibia's independence reached a third climax in August 1982—the first having ended in failure at the Pre-independence Implementation Meeting (PIM) in Geneva in January 1981[42] and the second in New York in July 1982, where an important breakthrough occurred in getting agreement to most of the conditions for implementing the Security Council's Resolution 435 (SC 435).[43] This left as the last stumbling-block the US and SA requirement that Cuban combat troops should withdraw from Angola as a precondition for the implementation of the decolonization process set out under SC 435. Angola's Foreign Minister insisted on 8 July that the Cuban military presence in his country was 'a bilateral question', and that his government would reject any attempt to make Cuban withdrawal a precondition for a Namibian settlement. Nine days later, President dos Santos told his National Assembly that as neither the Angolan armed forces (FAPLA) nor Cuban forces had ever entered Namibia, it was his country which needed guarantees against attacks, not SA.

The Contact Group (CG) of five Western nations (the US, UK, France, West Germany and Canada) overcame many internal differences in the course of their negotiations which had started in 1977; but on the issue of Cuban linkage, the US got no backing from its four allies. They insisted that the CG's mandate was restricted to negotiating an agreement within the framework of the terms set by SC 435; any negotiations on issues—such as the Cuban withdrawal—had to be carried out in parallel talks between the US, SA and Angola. All the Front-line States (FLS) opposed any idea of linking the Cuban issue to Namibia's independence; they insisted that it was for Angola, alone, to decide whether the Cubans should stay or go: a position similar to that adopted by the CG members other than the US.

Despite Angola's resolute refusal to contemplate linkage, the MPLA regime continued to negotiate with the Americans, as well as with Pretoria because of its desperate need for security and economic reconstruction (see Angola's role, below). The two-way diplomatic traffic between Washington and Luanda almost never stopped. Gen Vernon Walters, the US special envoy and troubleshooter,[44] and ambassador Frank Wisner, the US Assistant Secretary of State for African Affairs, held talks in Lisbon over 20-22 July with Portugal's Foreign Minister, Vasco Pereira, who had just returned from Luanda. According to the official Angolan News Agency (ANGOP, 24 July) Walters and Wisner were told that Luanda would not agree to simultaneous withdrawal of Cuban and SA forces from Angola and Namibia—the latest American ploy to meet the Angolans' security needs. While the Lisbon talks were still proceeding, Pretoria sent a Note to the UN accusing Angola of planning to escalate armed activities through Swapo and warning that the SA Defence Force (SADF) would strike back. They did so—on the very same day—making air attacks on Cahama and Chihemba.

Fidel Castro declared on 26 July that Luanda and Havana had agreed that there would be 'a gradual withdrawal' of Cuban troops from Angola once SADF units had withdrawn from Namibia; when there was no further threat of foreign invasion of Angola; and when all 'imperialist aid' had ceased to Unita (the National Union for the Total Independence of Angola), Comira (the Military Committee for Angolan Resistance) and FLEC (Front for the Liberation of the Cabinda Enclave). This was the first time Castro had mentioned the withdrawal of Cuban troops in the context of developments in Namibia; it also introduced the wider requirement that such withdrawal should depend, not just on SADF's withdrawal, but also on the much harder to prove ending of all aid to the Angolan opposition forces (see Cuba, below).

At the end of July, SA's Foreign Minister, Pik Botha, announced in Windhoek that it was possible for a ceasefire to come into operation on 15 August. He envisaged a trial period of a month to test Swapo's sincerity, and if this worked, suggested that the truce would be extended for a further period of seven months to allow the implementation of SC435 to be completed. Representatives of the CG—who had visited Windhoek over 30–31 July—said that 15 August was an unlikely, if feasible, date for the commencement of the ceasefire. Swapo reacted by describing Botha's ceasefire proposal as 'a manoeuvre' to distract attention; nevertheless, they made it clear that they favoured a ceasefire. This was emphasized by one of Swapo's senior spokesmen, Hidipo Hautenya, speaking in London on 3 August. At the same time, he accused the CG of 'trying to create a false sense of momentum.' However, so far from any end to the hostilities, Angola's Foreign Minister told the abortive OAU summit in Tripoli on 6 August that the SADF was engaged in a 'large-scale offensive' which it had begun on 21 July. His claim was at once denied by an SADF spokesman, but within days there was official confirmation from Pretoria of a renewed operation. An SABC commentary on 11 August 1982 declared:

> There is every justification for SA forces to be in Angola right now, hitting the Swapo terrorist bases—that's because of the evidence of build-up of Swapo forces in Angola, who strike from there at mainly civilian targets. During the latest action against Swapo bases in southern Angola, SA forces uncovered documents which proved that Swapo was involved in a build-up of its forces, prior to a settlement being achieved in the territory. The documents contained orders by Swapo leader, Sam Nujoma, that arms caches be hidden in Namibia prior to a ceasefire and that Swapo supporters launch attacks and raids during the ceasefire. At the same time, they called for the assassination of political leaders inside (Namibia), and even named some of the leaders, such as Ovambo leader, Mr Peter Kalangula.
>
> The large number of Swapo operating from southern Angola is shown by Swapo casualty figures during SA operations against their bases. During August last year, more than 1,000 Swapo terrorists were killed during Operation Protea. In November, during a similar operation, at least 71 terrorists died, and in March this year, Operation Super was launched in which 202 Swapo were killed. So far, during the present operation, more than 200 terrorists have been killed by SA security forces.
>
> The SA government makes no excuses for its attacks on Swapo bases inside Angola, except to point out that it avoids troops of the MPLA as much as possible, because it is not at war with Angola. This is an approach which is a great deal more lenient than that adopted by the Israelis, confronted with a similar situation.

Throughout 1982, heavy doses of optimism were injected into officially-inspired reports from the CG (particularly by the US and West Germans), punctuated by warnings from Swapo that there was no justification for this optimism. On 2 August, the West German leader of a CG delegation visiting Namibia forecast that 'final agreement on an internationally acceptable settlement' could be expected within the next few weeks.[45] At that point, the only outstanding issues affecting the implementation of SC 435 included the one that had helped to wreck the Geneva talks in January 1981—the question of UN impartiality; the electoral procedures; and the composition and functions of the UN peacekeeping force. This optimistic forecast was given more substance when a Front-line leader, Tanzania's Foreign Minister, Salim Salim, spoke on 7 August of the 'good prospects' for the negotiations—provided only that the issue of Cuban troops was not raised. But the issue was again raised during three days of talks in Lisbon over 19–22 August between ambassador Wisner and an Angolan delegation. Washington claimed that 'progress had been made' at the talks—apparently because of an agreement, in principle, to a Demilitarized Zone before Cuban troops were finally withdrawn, and of a ceasefire. The thinking behind this approach was that if the ceasefire held up, it would be easier to convince both sides to agree to move foreign troops—Cuban and South African—out of Angola.

President dos Santos repeated in Tripoli on 9 August that Cuban troops would leave 'once the destabilization factors disappear. . . .' But August came and went and, so far from it having brought a ceasefire, the month had seen a sharp increase in fighting, with both sides denouncing the aggressive intentions of each other. The South Africans lost 15 men when one of their helicopters was shot down over South Angola in an operation in which they claimed to have killed 201 guerrillas. Swapo claimed to have killed 30 SADF personnel and to have attacked the SADF military base at Omahenene; both these claims were dismissed by SADF. On 15 August Major-Gen Lloyd, the Commander of the South-West African Territorial Force (SWATF), announced the completion of operations against Swapo in Angola. He claimed that 345 Swapo guerrillas had been killed. Luanda claimed that the SADF had penetrated over 200 miles into Angola.[46] Notwithstanding this fighting, the CG, FLS and Swapo continued their negotiations in New York on 15 August. On Namibia Day (25 August) the OAU reiterated that linkage between Namibian independence and Cuban troop withdrawals was unacceptable. This stand was repeated on 4 September at a meeting between the FLS and Swapo in Lusaka. Notwithstanding growing misgiving among some FLS members about the way things were going, the MPLA Politburo issued a declaration on 2 September reaffirming Angola's 'entire commitment' to diplomatic efforts through the FLS and CG to achieve Namibia's independence in terms of SC 435. SA's Prime Minister, P. W. Botha, affirmed on 13 September that he was conscious of 'the need to settle the future of Namibia'; but he made final acceptance of the SC 435 terms conditional on Cuban troop withdrawals. On the following day, President dos Santos declared that only Namibia's independence could guarantee Angola's southern frontier and allow for the withdrawal of Cuban troops. On the same day, Moscow put in its own oar by addressing a letter to the UN Secretary-General demanding an end to attempts to block the removal of SA forces from Namibia until the Cubans had left Angola.

New initiatives were taken in September to try and break the deadlock over the Cuban linkage issue. Jean Ausseil, the head of the French Foreign Ministry's African Department, went to Havana on 19 September for consultations. On the next day, Dr Chester Crocker, the US Assistant Secretary for African Affairs, had a meeting with the Soviet Deputy Foreign Minister, Leonid F. Ilichev, in Geneva. This was the first of several attempts to involve the USSR in helping to settle the impasse over the Cubans. But there was still no sign of the Angolans weakening on the issue of linkage. Their stand got the support of the leaders of the five Portuguese-speaking African states when they met in Cape Verde on 22 September. Two days later, the UN Secretary-General conferred with the CG, the FLS, Swapo and Nigeria; and, on the same day, Sam Nujoma held talks in Paris with senior French officials and leaders of the Socialist Party. None of these various moves produced any further progress in the negotiations; but on the war-front the SADF made a new bombing attack on 25 September on Cahama, the only part of the Cunene province in south Angola still in the hands of the Angolan army—the rest was held by the SADF. On 27 September, Frank Wisner was again back in

Luanda for another two days of talks; while Sam Nujoma was in London for talks with the UK's Foreign and Commonwealth Minister of State, Cranley Onslow.

After the euphoria of August and the wide-ranging activities of September, October turned out to be a month of gloom. The CG Foreign Ministers met in New York on 1 October, but could agree only on their commitment to the 'early implementation' of SC 435. On the same day, in London, Sam Nujoma complained that President Reagan was holding Namibians to ransom in order to keep the Cuban troops out of Angola; and the Angolan Foreign Minister, addressing the UN General Assembly on 4 October, criticized the 'paranoia of the US Administration' over the 'permanence of Cuban internationalist forces in Angola.' On the following day, he met the US Secretary of State in New York. On 8 October, Sam Nujoma sent a memorandum to the Franco–African Summit in Kinshasa, claiming that the process 'to lead Namibia to independence through a negotiated solution is now at a standstill.' This was also the view expressed by France's Foreign Minister, Claude Cheysson, who said in Dar es Salaam on 11 October that the CG had 'finished its work,' and that the present 'stagnation' on the Cuban issue lay outside its competence. On the following day, in Nairobi, he denied earlier reports that France had offered to send troops to Angola to replace the Cubans when they withdrew. Cuba's Foreign Minister assured the UN General Assembly on 8 October that Cuba would respect any request by Angola to withdraw its troops.

There was just a brief sign of shift in the Angolan position in a statement by its ambassador to Paris on 14 October when he announced that, 'as a goodwill gesture', his country was prepared to advance the progressive withdrawal of Cuban troops in accordance with the 4 February 1982 Angolan–Cuban joint statement[47] provided all threats and acts of aggression against Angola ceased; that SA withdraw all its troops from Angolan territory and withdrew its support from Unita and other 'counter-revolutionary organizations'; and that SA took concrete steps to implement SC 435, including signing a ceasefire. The British Foreign Secretary, Francis Pym, said on 20 October that the prospects for a settlement were hopeful; but three days later President Shagari and Prime Minister Mugabe issued a joint statement in Lagos accusing the US of blocking a political settlement by insisting on Cuban withdrawal. Two days later, President Julius Nyerere, the FLS chairman, made a similar statement; and Sam Nujoma said the time had come for the UN to review the role of the CG. The US State Department dismissed reports that the CG's negotiations had reached a dead-end as 'grossly inaccurate'.

SA's Foreign Minister said on 26 October that his country's 'only concern' was to see a 'free and fair election' in Namibia, and that if this produced a victory for Swapo there was 'very little SA could do about it.' This was the first time any SA leader had either spoken of a possible Swapo victory, or indicated that it would be prepared to live with such a result. Speaking on the same day, SA's Defence Minister, reported that the SADF 'could not withdraw from SWA until the Cubans had left Angola.'

With signs of a further worsening in the warlike situation in Angola and on the Namibian border, and in anticipation of a special session of the UN on Namibia scheduled for mid-December, Washington intensified its diplomatic efforts during November 1982. The Vice-President, George Bush, announced on 10 November at the start of an African visit of seven countries (Cape Verde, Senegal, Nigeria, Zimbabwe, Zambia, Kenya and Zaire), that the question of Namibia would be the 'paramount issue' in his talks. On the opening day of his travels, the SA navy sent a marine force to attack the southern port of Namibe from the sea. At the same time, they made further air attacks on Cahama. Two days later, at low-key celebrations of Angola's seventh independence anniversary, President dos Santos reiterated his firm rejection of linkage. Although Bush did not visit South Africa, Chester Crocker went to Pretoria on 17 November for talks with the SA Foreign Minister. Two days later, speaking in Nairobi, George Bush insisted that 'the withdrawal of Cuban forces from Angola in a parallel framework with SA's departure from Namibia is the key to the settlement we all desire.' (Note the use of 'parallel framework' as a means of getting away from the term 'linkage'.)[48] On 26 November, after talks in Washington with Secretary of State George Shultz, SA's Foreign Minister felt sufficiently confident to announce that there was 'a 50%-plus' chance of an agreement on the withdrawal of Cuban troops. But on 27 November, 31 African leaders who had assembled in Tripoli for the second abortive attempt to stage the OAU summit, issued the 'Tripoli Declaration on Namibia'[49] in which they expressed total support for the armed struggle led by Swapo, and criticized efforts at linkage.

December 1982 was a month of mixed fortunes and confusing signals. On the 7th, President dos Santos went to Lusaka for a meeting with President Kaunda. The two had come to work closely together in their approach to Pretoria over the past two years. Kaunda had, in fact, held his controversial meeting with SA's Prime Minister in April 1982 with the knowledge and approval of the Angolans.[50] On the day after the dos Santos meeting with Kaunda, the Angolan and SA governments sent delegations to Cape Verde for their first face-to-face talks. The SA team was led by its Foreign Minister, and the Angolans' by the Interior Minister, Lt-Col Alexandre Rodrigues Kito. (For the talks, see below.) On the next day, the 9th, the CIA leaked a report to American papers claiming that 10,000 more Cuban troops had recently arrived in Angola, almost doubling their number there. President Castro refused to be drawn on this CIA report, and playfully remarked that 'if we did send 10,000 more troops, we were simply doing our duty in the face of imperialist threats.'

A significant statement came from President dos Santos on 10 December (the anniversary of the founding of MPLA), when he said that he did not wish to see repeated in Angola what had recently happened in 'another African country' (presumably Chad), where the government had fallen after the withdrawal of troops of a neighbouring State (Libya), which had guaranteed internal stability and territorial integrity. Leaving aside the fact that the Libyan military presence had guaranteed neither of these results—any more than the Cubans have succeeded in doing in Angola—the importance of dos Santos' remark is that it was the first public hint about what MPLA negotiators had been saying in their secret talks: concern that the withdrawal of the Cubans would enable Unita (with SA's secret backing) to further strengthen its challenge to the MPLA's authority. Implicit in this fear was the palpable failure of FAPLA, on its own, to check Jonas Savimbi's forces. (See below.) Angola's internal situation was so parlous in December that, on the 8th, the MPLA Central Committee granted dos Santos special emergency powers.[51]

One new development in December was Chester Crocker's mission to Moscow for talks on Namibia, following on a number of lower-level contacts with Soviet diplomats in Washington. Crocker's visit was officially confirmed by the State Department on the 13th—the same day as the UN General Assembly began its debate on Namibia. During the debate the CG representatives met in New York and SADF launched yet another air attack on targets in the Namibe province. On 20 December the British Foreign Secretary told the House of Commons that he still believed persuasion was the best way of winning SA's support for a Namibian settlement. On the same day the UN General Assembly adopted five tough resolutions criticizing SA and supporting Swapo; but to avoid certain US and British vetoes in the Security Council, the Africans did not insist on a resolution calling for mandatory sanctions against SA.

The year ended with President Kaunda reversing his usual stand, calling on Cuba to increase its support for liberation wars in Southern Africa (22 December); the SA Foreign Minister expressed his belief that the negotiations on Namibia were on the verge of 'an important breakthrough' if Cuban troop withdrawal could be effected; and the US State Department reaffirmed that only a withdrawal of Cuban troops could lead to a rapid resolution of the Namibian conflict. On this single issue Pretoria and Washington were now speaking with a single voice.

WAR ON THE GROUND: TALK ON THE SIDELINES (JANUARY-JULY 1983)
By the beginning of 1983 the position that had been reached in the two sets of parallel negotiations was as follows:

> All the three parties had accepted the political conditions for implementing SC 435, except for the electoral method to be used in choosing the Constituent Assembly.[52]
>
> Agreement in principle, on the role of the UN Transitional Assistance Group (UNTAG) and a UN Peacekeeping force with an upper limit of 7,500 men; but details about the force's composition and UNTAG's mandate remained to be finalized.
>
> All parties accepted the need for a ceasefire and agreed, in principle, on a retreat by the Angolan (including Cuban) forces to a distance of 297 km from the Namibian border, and a simultaneous withdrawal of SA's troops from the whole of southern Angola. This would be a first step towards creating the Demilitarized Zone (DMZ) proposed in the plan.

The key element in the parallel talks was this proposal for FAPLA to withdraw almost 300 km in exchange for the SADF leaving Angola entirely. According to a statement made by the Angolan leader on 9 August 1982, the SADF had 5,500 personnel in southern Angola, and had been occupying territory there since August 1981. This *quid pro quo* arrangement—a prelude to the formal ceasefire— served the immediate interests of both Angola and SA: the former would have got the SADF off their soil; and the latter would have a buffer between the Namibian border and Swapo's bases.

The only party which would suffer at least temporarily from such an arrangement was Swapo, since it would have more difficulty in making armed incursions into Namibia and in supplying its forces there. Swapo also feared that once military pressure was relaxed on Pretoria it would find it easier to pursue what Swapo believed to be SA's real objective—to drag out the negotiations but with no serious intention of ever implementing SC 435. In order to ensure that it would not be placed at too serious a disadvantage if a pullback of forces was agreed, Swapo pushed several hundred more cadres across the border into Namibia in July; this sharply increased the level of fighting in Namibia and gave Pretoria the pretext for starting a new offensive in Angola and for accusing Swapo of sabotaging the negotiations—a charge repeatedly made by Pretoria's spokesmen from December 1982; they also accused Angola of defaulting on a promise to restrain Swapo. To this charge the Angolans retorted (in private) that since the SADF was in military control of the southern part of Angola, any blame for allowing fresh Swapo cadres to enter Namibia should be placed at SA's door, not at theirs.

Once again, the intensification of the fighting in both Angola and Namibia did not halt the negotiations in the early part of 1983; but the level of the fighting strengthened doubts about Pretoria's real intentions. In April, the new UN Commissioner for Namibia, Brajesh Mishra, an Indian diplomat, said that Namibian independence was 'nowhere near'.[53] He had taken over this job from Martti Athisaari, the Finnish diplomat, who retained his post as the designated head of UNTAG. The divorce of the two positions was agreed as a means of establishing UN impartiality—one of the points of earlier contention with Pretoria.

The differences among the CG members was brought into public view at an International Conference on Namibia, sponsored by the UN, in Paris, in April. The keynote speaker, France's Foreign Minister, declared that the CG had 'ended its labours'.[54]

> The three-phase plan drawn up in September 1981 with a view to restoring trust between the parties to the conflict has been accepted by the latter after long negotiations during which the Front-line countries and, above all, Swapo, were primarily involved, demonstrated a spirit of compromise and openness that I, echoing others, want to emphasize here. So everything is ready to implement SC 435 and the settlement plan.
>
> So things had, it was thought, got to the point when Namibia would soon accede to independence, following free elections, under international supervision. Yet, that is not all the case, since other problems, other requirements, other pretexts have been put forward. This is something France cannot accept. It is something which I do not suppose anyone in this room will accept.
>
> This peremptory assertion—which will doubtless be criticized—does not mean my country is unaware of the difficulties and problems that will arise following Namibia's independence, or that it views them with indifferences. But it means that accession to independence, the implementation of the Security Council's resolutions, must on no account be hampered by other considerations. As the UN High Commissioner for Refugees for Namibia said, according to the press, a short while ago, it is not right that the Namibian people should 'serve as a hostage' to force neighbouring countries to deal with other matters, however important the latter may be.
>
> France does not underestimate the legitimate concern of every Southern African country with ensuring its security. We are surprised to see, however, that in some quarters the subject is considered only from the point of view of the security of the strongest, richest and best-armed state in the region; for it rather seems to us that the threat is, above all, serious for the weakest, the poorest, the least well-armed. We also find it surprising that, in the same circles, practically all the talk in this security contest is about the presence of foreign armed forces in Angola, in a country hundreds of kilometres away. It shocks us that, on this basis, some people should be asking for an undertaking that these foreign forces will be withdrawn as a precondition for Namibia's independence; it is doubly anomalous—forgive my understatement—to make the Namibian people's fate dependent on a decision affecting another country, Angola, and to seek to get a decision that is strictly within the field of Angolan sovereignty, taken or recorded at the international level. I want to make a point of recalling that the Contact Group, like France and some of its other members, has never voiced such a demand.

Commenting on Claude Cheysson's sharp statement, a State Department official said that the CG's work 'is substantially complete.'[55] All that still remained was final agreement on the electoral procedures and on the composition of UNTAG. He added that the US was 'working very hard to achieve success in our separate discussions with Angola, and we have had the full support of all our CG partners to that end.' This latter part of the statement contradicted what the French Foreign Minister had stated.

In a further sophistication of the attempt not to link Cuban withdrawal to a Namibia settlement, American spokesmen now came increasingly to refer to the need to get the Cubans out as an important move in opening the way 'to a stable and peaceful regional context, in which Namibia can achieve its independence under the free and fair process envisaged in the UN plan.'[56]

At the Paris meeting, where Cheysson had spoken, Sam Nujoma announced that Swapo's Central Committee had concluded that the CG had 'lost its own contacts with the spirit and letter of SC 435, and that its activity had been transformed into protecting the racist occupants of Namibia.'[57] Nujoma next carried his attack on the CG into the Security Council, which met late in May for the specific purpose of discussing Namibia. He accused the CG of having ceased to be 'honest brokers in the dispute', and asked the Council to find new ways of putting an end to 'their sinister attempts to hijack and misuse the Namibian negotiating process for their own economic and strategic interests.'[58] Speaking later, the UN Secretary-General, Javier Peréz de Cuéllar, warned that delays by SA in granting independence to Namibia was 'a threat to all of Southern Africa.' Speaking for the Non-aligned Movement of 101 nations, India's ambassador, P. V. Narasimha Rao, called for a deadline to be set for Namibia's independence which, if it were not met, would be automatically followed by a trade embargo against SA. The US ambassador to the UN, Jeane Kirkpatrick, acknowledged the frustration over the failure to achieve independence because of factors 'relating to the regional situation in Southern Africa outside the scope of the mandate of the CG.' Here, again, one notes the new codeword used for linkage: placing Cuban withdrawal in the context of regional security. Outlining the current US position on the situation in Southern Africa, she said:

- The US deplores violent cross-border activities in Southern Africa in whatever direction and for whatever stated goal;
- The CG feels that only through a settlement under the aegis of the UN and SC 435 can Namibia have a peaceful transition to independence; and
- The US neither desires nor seeks any special advantage or position for itself in the negotiations.

The Security Council unanimously adopted a resolution on 31 May calling on SA to comply with the UN plan for Namibia's independence and giving the UN Secretary-General a mandate to take an active part in the process. But it did not include a call for sanctions because, once again, the Third World countries felt it was more important to get a unanimous decision than to push for the adoption of a controversial resolution which would be met with a Western veto. Nor was there any proposal to limit the role of the CG, although conferring a more active role on Peréz de Cuéllar might be interpreted as a move in that direction. After the debate, a member of the US delegation to the UN, ambassador Charles Liechtenstein, welcomed the Security Council resolution as making a 'positive contribution'.[59]

During the debate the US Secretary of State held separate meetings with FLS Foreign Ministers and Sam Nujoma, in which he emphasized that a great deal of progress had already been made and felt that what remained was 'resolvable if the surrounding environment in the region is made secure.' Commenting on Peréz de Cuellar's new mandate, the official SA Broadcasting Corporation said on 2 July 1983 that he must take cognizance of 'the most fundamental obstacle to such a settlement—the presence of 30,000 troops in Angola—and the fact that, 'in their bid for power, Swapo and its Soviet backers vastly prefer the prospect of eroding opposition through a sustained campaign of terrorism to the uncertainties of free and fair elections.'

THE ROLE OF THE LOCAL ACTORS IN THE CONFLICT
ANGOLA: THIRSTING FOR PEACE

The MPLA Government went as far as any government—let alone an assertively Marxist one—could reasonably be expected to go to achieve a peaceful settlement in Namibia. Throughout the endless, tantalizing negotiations, Luanda insisted on only two requirements: that its role in supporting Swapo should be respected as an indispensable contribution to the liberation movement which is part of the history of the MPLA; and that its sovereign right to make diplomatic and military agreements with any country of its choice should be recognized. Otherwise, the MPLA leaders were willing to sup with the devil himself for the sake of peace and for the benefits that would bring to their country. The devil was South Africa which had militarily occupied a large part of south Angola since August 1981, and which had kept Unita supplied so that it continued as a major threat to the country's internal security. Even though the Americans withheld diplomatic recognition from Luanda (because of the Cuban issue), the MPLA showed itself ready to enter freely into diplomatic negotiations and commerce with the US. And despite the Soviet bloc's solid military support, the Angolans chose to ignore their hostility to the Western Contact Group's initiative. In this and in other ways the Angolans showed they were their own masters, pursuing their own state interests— primarily the achievement of a measure of security and freedom from external attacks by the SADF, and economic reconstruction. They saw their economic recovery being helped through normal relations with the Western community; but they had no wish to lessen their links with the Soviet bloc.[60]

Angola held the first of its secret meetings with the SA government on Sal, one of the Cape Verde Islands, on 8 December 1982. Its delegation was led by the Interior Minister, Lt-Col Alexandre Rodrigues Kito, and included the Transport Minister, Faustino Muteka. The SA delegation was led by the Foreign Minister, Pik Botha, and the Defence Minister, Gen Magnus Malan. After the meeting, the Angolan Foreign Minister commented acidly: 'SA spoke of the need to establish a climate of confidence, but did not propose a ceasefire.' He added that the Angolan delegation had restricted itself at that first meeting to taking note of what the South Africans had to say, promising to reply at a future meeting.[61]

The second meeting was arranged for February 1983, again at Sal. In the meantime, there had been an increase in the scale of Swapo fighting which had led Pik Botha to say that the chance of getting agreement had receded. To mark its displeasure with this development, Pretoria decided, without previous advice to Luanda, to reduce the status of its delegation by leaving out all Ministers. It was led by the Director-General of Foreign Affairs, Hans van Dalsen. The Angolan delegation was again led by the Interior Minister. Before the meeting, Kito declared that 'Angola is not begging for peace, nor will it give up its stand of saying no to any linkage. . . . The withdrawal of Cuban troops is an internal problem that concerns only Angola.'[62] At the same time, the SA Foreign Minister repeated that 'SA will not budge on the issue of Cuban withdrawal from Angola prior to a settlement being reached on SWA/Namibia.'[63] (Unlike the Americans, he made no attempt to camouflage 'linkage' by discussing Cuban withdrawal in terms of the need for 'regional security'.)

Angola's Foreign Minister paid an official visit to London in February 1983 where he confessed his inability to understand the 'obsession' of the American government with 'linkage'. He reiterated that once a ceasefire was in place and there was a reduction in the 'illegal presence of SA troops' presently in Cunene province, Luanda would 'seriously study the gradual withdrawal of the Cubans.[64]

SWAPO: FEARING A SELL-OUT

Although Swapo was reported by the SADF to have lost 1,268 of their men, as against 77 South Africans, in 1982, there was no sign of the guerrilla campaign flagging. In August 1982 there was, as the SADF itself claimed, a significant new offensive by Swapo, with reports of fighting continuing thereafter. The scale of the killings was much greater than the SADF figures suggest and much lower than the casualties claimed to have been inflicted by Swapo; the greatest number of casualties were those suffered by civilians on both sides of the border—but either nobody counts their numbers, or it is difficult to do so; possibly both.

Like all guerrilla movements dependent for bases and supplies on the goodwill of other governments, Swapo remained highly suspicious of the negotiating process followed by the CG and the FLS—but it naturally voiced its suspicions only about the former (see above). Swapo became particularly concerned about Angola's readiness to enter into talks with SA about a possible pull-back of forces (see above), and a demilitarized zone even before a ceasefire was achieved. These suspicions were understandable since Swapo was in a good position to appreciate Angola's desperate need for peace, and because its own ability to carry on the struggle depended on Angola not agreeing to any arrangements which would inhibit Swapo's freedom of action before the terms of SC 435 were implemented.

While Swapo's president-general, Sam Nujoma, was bitingly critical of the CG and, especially, of the American role in it, his private behaviour at meetings with George Shultz, Chester Crocker and other Western negotiators was remarkably different from his public *persona*. Because of this contradictoriness in Nujoma's behaviour, the CG members dismissed his tirades against them; but it also lowered his standing in their own eyes.

However, Sam Nujoma remained the unchallenged leader of Swapo—a position confirmed by his re-election as president-general at a Central Committee meeting in April 1983.[65]

Swapo's main military support had continued to come from the Soviet bloc ever since 1975 after their successful military intervention with the Cubans in Angola. But even though the Organization now depends heavily on Soviet aid and goodwill, Nujoma has always tried to pursue a non-aligned position *vis a vis* Moscow and Peking. He again proved this in January 1983 when, to the strong displeasure of the Soviets, he paid an official visit to China where he received a pledge of arms. Ignoring possible Soviet sensibilities, Nujoma praised China's 'positive role' as a member of the UN Council for Namibia, its support for Swapo, and its defence of Namibian interests at an international level.[66]

THE FRONT-LINE STATES: TAKING THEIR LEAD FROM ANGOLA

The leaders of the Front-line States (FLS)[67] allowed Angola to take the lead in the negotiations with the CG over Namibia because it stood most to lose, or gain, from the way things turned out. Although there had been criticism of President Kaunda when he agreed to meet SA's Prime Minister in April 1982, none sought to question Angola's decision to hold formal and informal meetings with delegations from Pretoria. President dos Santos' own closest personal ties were with President Samora Machel of Mozambique and President Kaunda.

The FLS leaders continued to meet at frequent, but irregular, intervals whenever they felt the need to exchange views or to coordinate their activities as, for example, before the Non-aligned summit in New Delhi in early 1983 when they assembled at Harare. They met again, this time in Dar es Salaam, in May 1983 to discuss the fast deteriorating security situation in Southern Africa. Throughout all their meetings, the FLS unitedly and resolutely opposed any attempt to link the Cuban troop withdrawals to a settlement in Namibia. At a meeting of the group in Tripoli on 7 August 1982, a communiqué said that implementation of SC 435 was attainable provided 'side-issues are not insisted upon.' At their meeting at Harare in February 1983, they rejected as 'blackmail' attempts by Washington and Pretoria to link the Cuban and Namibian issues.

The increasing frustrations felt by the FLS leaders were compounded by their own impotence to do anything to break the deadlock over the Cuban linkage issue, and because of their feelings that this—to them—extraneous issue was all that still stood in the way of Namibia's independence. Nevertheless, they did not give themselves over to the kind of denunciatory rhetoric against the Reagan Administration that had been heard from them in their denunciations of earlier American and British governments; nor did they insist on a confrontational position with the US (see above). They preferred to trim their demands at the UN to achieve a consensus (as over the Namibia resolution adopted at the end of May 1983) rather than to push the Western Powers into casting a veto. Their doors remained open at all time to visits from the CG. A typical example of this readiness to talk was President Samora Machel's reception of Chester Crocker in January 1983 when he passed through Maputo on his way from Madagascar to Zimbabwe. The visit came at a particularly difficult stage in the negotiations, and in Mozambique's relations with SA; there was a growing feeling in African circles that the time had come to repudiate Washington's role in the Namibia negotiations—the line taken by Nujoma, and one which had won a lot of applause when he personally confronted Crocker in a public session at a meeting of the Afro-American Institute at Harare in January 1983. Yet, President Machel not only agreed to receive this relatively junior American official, but he spent nearly four hours discussing with Crocker the problems of the region. It is small wonder, then, that Crocker and other Western negotiators make such a clear distinction between the public rhetoric of their African critics and the reasonable line most of them (including Sam Nujoma) take in their private talks.

For the FLS leaders, 1982-83 was not a year for them to pick unnecessary quarrels. Most of their countries were undergoing one of the worst droughts in 20 years; their economies were mostly on the floor because of the drought and the state of the world economy; most faced internal troubles due, in large part, to economic frustrations; and the majority of SA's border states were suffering badly from Pretoria's economic and/or military pressures. It was a time when most of the region's leaders were more concerned with survival than with supporting wars of liberation: the remarkable thing is that, hard hit as they were, they did not yield on their commitments to the fight against apartheid.

UNITA: SAVIMBI'S GROWING SHADOW OVER ANGOLA
Seven years after its defeat in the 1975-76 civil war in Angola, Unita under its leader, Dr Jonas Malheiro Savimbi, had not only survived but had made itself an increasingly serious challenger to the MPLA government and a significant factor in the negotiations over Namibia.[68] The principal reason for the MPLA regime's wish to keep Cuban combat troops in Angola was not because of their role in either deterring or engaging the SADF (whom they always carefully avoided on instructions dictated by Luanda for reasons of prudence), but because of their value in bolstering Fapla's operations against Unita. Another reason for Unita's significance in the Namibia context is its role in helping the SADF to establish and maintain its military control in southern Angola. Although Savimbi is not a natural

ally of apartheid, there is a coincidence of interests between Unita and Pretoria. However, a successful outcome to the Namibian negotiations would lose Unita the direct military support of the SADF and access to Namibia in the likely event of a Swapo victory. Savimbi claimed that Unita was now in a strong enough position to carry on without SA's help but, as he admitted in an interview with the BBC in its Panorama programme:[69] 'The only door that we have to get that (foreign) support into Angola is through Namibia. If that border is closed, it will give us some headaches, but we will have to find an alternative.'

If Pretoria were to cut off its support for Unita, this would facilitate the Angolans' decision to send the Cubans back home; but the South Africans insist that they have a moral obligation to Unita—reminiscent of Begin's insistence on guarantees for Major Haddad in Lebanon. But there is also another reason for SA's determined support of Savimbi: he would become indispensable to their strategy if the Nambia talks were to end in failure. (Pretoria's contingency plan for such an eventuality is discussed under Destabilization, above.) In the meantime, both Washington and Pretoria continued, separately, to urge the need for a coalition government between MPLA and Unita—an aim also consistent with Savimbi's own policies. Their interest in such a coalition is that it would dilute the Marxist element in Luanda's government, create the best hope for the country's stability, and so reduce Angola's dependence on Soviet military support.

Pretoria's view of Unita's strength, and of its future, is reflected in a commentary on the state-controlled SA Broadcasting Corporation (Johannesburg, 3 May 1983) which, after asserting that Unita controlled one-third of Angola's territory, said that Unita's greatest military success had begun six months earlier when it defeated Fapla's elite 16th Brigade:

> Now, Unita is aiming at the heart of Angola's diamond and coffee producing areas which together with Cabinda's oil wealth, are responsible for most of the MPLA government's revenue. It would thus be in the interests of the MPLA to opt for a government of national unity in which the role of Unita is recognized as the only other major political force in Angola.

THE REPUBLIC OF SOUTH AFRICA: PRETORIA HAS EVERYBODY GUESSING
Doubts have existed from the very start of the prolonged negotiations over Namibia as to whether Pretoria ever seriously intended to accept an international settlement, or whether it merely found it tactically expedient to drag out the negotiations in order to buy time to strengthen the political forces opposed to Swapo, and to defeat the guerrillas militarily, which Gen Magnus Malan insisted all along it was possible to do. It was likely that Pretoria hoped to wear down the West in the belief that it would finally accept an internal settlement as a *fait accompli* once it had completed the negotiating process and found Swapo an obstacle to agreement.

It is as easy to argue the case in favour of the proposition that Pretoria has been seriously engaged in negotiating away Namibia's independence, as it is the opposite case. Since Pretoria equates a Swapo victory with a Moscow victory,[70] and since the Soviet Union is seen as the major threat to SA's future, it would seem logical to conclude that Swapo's defeat would be a pre-condition for Pretoria's final signature to implementing the agreement on SC 435. The opposite view is that Pretoria does not hold all the cards necessary to play out a winning hand in Namibia. At one stage, when the DTA under Dirk Mudge looked like possibly becoming a serious challenger to Swapo (at least in Pretoria's eyes, which is what matters here), it seemed likely that the SA government might have been ready to risk an internal settlement (believing it could ride out any international storm which that would bring), or that it could contemplate an electoral contest between the DTA and Swapo with some confidence; but once the DTA began to disintegrate in 1981 and with its final collapse after Dirk Mudge was forced out of poliltics in 1982,[71] Pretoria was left with no credible local political ally in Namibia, and it was forced to take over the government of the territory itself. This is a politically untenable position, which no SA government can hope to maintain for long.

SA has been able to contain Swapo militarily, but only by occupying a large part of Angola; raising the level of conventional warfare; accepting higher casualties among its own forces which, though small, have had a seriously demoralizing impact among White South Africans; and by vastly increasing its spending in Namibia and on the war itself.

Economically, Namibia had become a serious drain on SA resources—severe enough to cause concern even to so rich a country. By late 1982 it was conservatively estimated that the cost of administering Namibia and of defending it was running at between £500m-£650m a year, with costs rising rapidly.[72] There comes a time in the course of every war when the financial burden becomes a determinant of national policy. Spending something like £1.5m a day on Namibia is obviously not something that can be left out of the calculations of Pretoria's decision-makers.

Diplomatically, SA would stand to lose a great deal if it persisted in its refusal to agree to a settlement and, conversely, it could gain a great deal by its agreement. The Reagan Administration has made a Namibian settlement a major plank in its foreign policy—primarily because of its own interest in 'getting the Cubans out of Africa': but also because of a more serious understanding in Washington of the explosive dangers of the situation in Southern Africa, with predictable repercussions not only on the local populations but also on Western interests and, especially, the opportunities which might be opened up for the Soviets. A positive gain for Pretoria from a settlement would be the carrot on offer from the Reagan Administration, which is reported to include a number of important financial and paramilitary concessions.

Domestically, however, the Botha government stands to lose ground to its conservative opponents, who have now latched on to Namibia as a cause of their own. Coming at a time when Botha's political fortunes have begun to wane, any serious miscalculation on Namibia could be politically damaging for the future of his regime. On the other hand, if an agreement were to result in the withdrawal of Cuban troops, this could be presented by Botha as a significant victory in his aim of 'driving the communists away from the borders of SA.'

The arguments are therefore well-balanced. Under the right conditions (e.g. Cuban withdrawal), it is by no means uncertain that Pretoria would not agree in the end. But would the withdrawal of the Cubans suffice if, as seems most likely, Pretoria would have to accept a Swapo victory? SA's Foreign Minister, Pik Botha, has said that the country could live with such a result (see above). Others think not.

THE ROLE OF THE MAJOR FOREIGN ACTORS
THE WESTERN CONTACT GROUP: FRIENDS BUT NO LONGER PARTNERS
American perceptions of Western interests in Southern Africa came to differ sharply from other members of the CG once the terms for implementing SC 435

were virtually completed in August 1982. While Britain, Canada, France and West Germany all wish to see the withdrawal of the Cuban troops from Angola, they believe it both wrong and unnecessary to link the issue—however it is dressed up—to a Namibian settlement. They believe that the MPLA government would stick to its promise to begin sending the Cubans home once a settlement had been reached, since it is so clearly in Angola's interest to do so. America's partners in the CG see the Cuban issue as representing a particularist Reagan Administration concern rather than one touching on either a general Western interest, or as one essential to reaching a final agreement on Namibia.

It was over this latter point that the US Administration took particular issue with its partners. It argued that were it not for the promise made to Pretoria by Washington that the Cubans would leave at the same time as the SADF began its withdrawal, they would not have agreed to the August terms for implementing SC 435. The European and Canadian reply to this point is that since SA was informed by the MPLA that a start would be made to withdraw the Cubans once SC 435 was implemented, the quicker this was done, the sooner they would see the back of the Cubans. Since the introduction of the Cuban issue was the only delaying factor, it was plainly a mistake to have done so in the first place. However, neither side succeeded in convincing the other, so the US was left to conduct the 'parallel talks' with the Angolans on its own in an attempt to find a formula that would not formally link Cuban troop withdrawals to a Namibian settlement. As the endless negotiations proceeded, the Americans developed the idea of arguing the case for the Cubans' withdrawal within the framework of Southern Africa's regional security needs *after* Namibia's independence.

This separate US initiative aroused strong suspicion in the minds of Swapo, as well as of some other African leaders that Reagan was collaborating with Pretoria in seeking to wreck the chances of a settlement once its terms had been virtually agreed. Since Pretoria shares Washington's views about the Cubans' withdrawal, while America's partners in the CG do not, it is easy to see why suspicions should have arisen about a possible Washington–Pretoria axis. However, while the interests of Reagan and Botha coincide over 'driving back the communists', there is no objective evidence to suggest that the Americans remain any less determined than the other members of the CG, or the FLS, to wind up the Namibian affair successfully. In fact, the strongly committed interest of the Americans in pursuing this issue (with Chester Crocker spending the bulk of his time on Namibia) suggests a genuine determination to reach agreement.

It is difficult to determine whether the US negotiators are right in suggesting that the only hope of getting Pretoria's signature to a settlement was a prior agreement over the Cubans. It was Reagan, after all, and not Botha who was the first to make an issue of the withdrawal of the Cubans. Although the SA negotiators repeatedly put forward new conditions for accepting SC 435, the issue of Cuban troops surfaced only very late in the day—long after Reagan's negotiators had decided to make an issue of it. But once it was made into an issue, it became a sticking point for both the South Africans and the Angolans. At that stage there could be no retreat by either side; it then became necessary to discover some formula that would satisfy both sides. It was the search for such a formula— into which American policy had led the negotiators—that has held up final agreement and threatened to jeopardize the entire initiative after it had come so close to success.

By far the sharpest critics of the US stand on the Cuban issue were the French, after President Mitterrand had come to office. The new French government position is exemplified by the speech made by its Foreign Minister, Claude Cheysson, to the International Conference on Namibia in Paris on 28 April 1983 (see above). Cheysson's views were shared by the British, Canadians and West Germans (i.e. until the election of the new Kohl Government in Bonn, whose position was not as clear-cut as that of its predecessor). The only difference between the Europeans is a matter of style, with the French Socialists preferring to state their differences with Washington in rather militant terms.

THE SOVIET BLOC: A LEADING ACTOR IN A MINOR ROLE
Strongly opposed to the West's initiative from the start, the Soviet bloc found (as it had done over the Zimbabwe settlement reached at Lancaster House) that its wishes were politely but firmly ignored by all the local actors, irrespective of whether they depended on its military aid or not. The Soviet bloc therefore found itself caught up in a contradictory position: it was increasingly being called upon to provide greater military aid by some of the Front-line States who, nevertheless, continued to pin their hopes for Namibia's independence on the Western initiative, and who preferred a negotiated settlement to an intensification of the military confrontation with SA. However, although the FLS leaders saw the CG initiative as the 'best hope', they were never entirely convinced that it would succeed—so they were careful to prepare for the less attractive alternative of (quite literally) biting the bullet by supporting an intensified armed struggle. If this were to prove necessary, the African focus would change radically from the West to the East.

Unlike their stand in the Middle East, the Americans sought the cooperation of the Soviets in arranging for the withdrawal of the Cubans (see above). But while the Soviets were ready to talk, they, not surprisingly, showed no interest at all in playing a mediator's role on the Cuban issue. However, drawing its own analogy with the Middle East, *Izvestia* alleged on 13 November 1982 that: 'The US is secretly discussing with SA the possibilities of concluding a strategic agreement similar to the one it has with Israel.' No evidence of any kind was offered for this allegation.

The Soviet bloc's military support for Angola seems to have increased in the last part of 1982 and early 1983—a period during which there were a number of exchanges of military visits between Warsaw Pact and Angolan leaders. In October 1982, Gen Lajos Czinege, the Defence Minister of Hungary, inspected 'various military units' and the naval base at Luanda.[73] Shortly afterwards, Angola's Defence Minister, Col Pedro Maria Tonha, led a military delegation to East Germany, where he had talks, *inter alia,* with the GDR Defence Minister, Gen Heinz Hoffmann.[74] In May 1983 President dos Santos went to Moscow. A new trade and technical cooperation agreement was signed between the USSR and Angola, covering the period up to 1990. Moscow announced in March 1982 that it had 250 Soviet specialists helping to train technical personnel in Angola, and that Soviet exports—particularly civil aircraft (AN 26 and Yak-40), tractors and other agricultural machinery—were expanding steadily. The USSR imported Angola's coffee, sisal, quartz and other commodities in small quantities.[75] Nothing was said of Soviet military supplies or training teams. However, there is no secret of the extent of military training given by Soviet, East German and Cuban military instructors to Swapo and ANC cadres in Angola.

CUBA: ONLY TOO GLAD TO RETURN HOME
In private conversations, Angolans make no secret of their wish to see the Cuban

271

combat troops (though not their technicians, doctors and builders) return home; they are no more popular in the countryside than any other foreign combat troops in similar situations. Besides, their heavy local costs must be paid for.[76] Cuban soldiers are equally candid about their own wish to return home. So, only a Namibian settlement and Unita's threat prevent both sides from fulfilling their dearest wishes.

In July 1982, Angola's Foreign Minister and Fidel Castro both reiterated their stand on the question of the Cuban military presence in Angola. Paulo Jorge reaffirmed[77] the importance of a paragraph in the Joint Angolan–Cuban statement of 4 February, which he translated as follows:

> As and when the Angolan and Cuban governments may so intend, the withdrawal of Cuban forces stationed in Angola would be carried out by sovereign decision of the government of Angola, once each and every eventuality of acts of aggression of armed invasion cease to exist.
> The government of Cuba therefore reiterated that it shall implement without hesitation any decision adopted by the sovereign government of Angola on the withdrawal of these same forces.[78]

Speaking at Bayamo, Cuba, on 26 July 1982, Castro declared:

> We Angolans and Cubans have made agreements gradually to withdraw the Cuban troops from Angola within a period of time agreed upon by the two governments when all the South African troops have withdrawn from Namibia to the other side of the Orange river, when there is no threat of foreign invasion to Angola, when there is an end to all imperialist aid to the puppet organizations. . . . Therefore we are going to withdraw gradually, within the time-frame upon which the two governments agree.

Castro then went on to say:

> A reasonable and just solution must be found. Our country has a constructive position, and does not reject a reasonable or just solution. But it has to be based on the 4 February 1982 statement by the Cuban and Angolan governments.

CHINA PEOPLE'S REPUBLIC: BACK IN THE RING
China and Angola agreed to establish diplomatic relations in March 1983. Although Peking had sent its official congratulations to President Neto when the MPLA formed its government in April 1976, relations had remained strained because of the Angolans' allegation that the Chinese were continuing to help Unita. The Chinese firmly denied this, saying they had ended contacts with all three of the Angolan liberation groups in late 1974. However, they were unwilling to meet the MPLA's request to formally announce that their aid to Unita had stopped.[79] In the end, a suitable formula was found and the CPR established an embassy in Luanda for the first time since Angola's independence.

Sam Nujoma paid an official visit to Peking in January 1983 and announced that China had agreed to provide arms, ammunition and humanitarian aid.[80] He praised China's 'positive role' as a member of the UN Council for Namibia and its support for Swapo. On the question of arms supplies, he added: 'We are indeed grateful for this because we recognize that Namibia's liberation ought to be worked out by the Namibians themselves.' This apparent *non sequitur* can be understood as referring to Swapo's right to decide for itself from whom to seek aid—a possible reference to the upset his visit to Peking is believed to have caused in Moscow. (Also see Swapo, above.)

NOTES

Unless otherwise stated, all newspapers and publications cited are South African.

1. All references to country surveys and essays are to *Africa Contemporary Record (ACR)* 1982–83, unless otherwise indicated.
2. For details, see *ACR* 1981-82, pB684ff; and chapter on South Africa in *ACR* 1982-83.
3. For an analysis of this process, see *ACR* 1981-82, pB684ff.
4. *The Star*, 11 September 1982.
5. For details, see chapter on South Africa in *ACR* 1982-83.
6. See Colin Legum's interview with China's Deputy Foreign Minister, Gong Dafei in *Africa Report*, Washington, March/April 1983.
7. *Daily Telegraph (DT)*, London, 30 May 1983.
8. *Rand Daily Mail (RDM)*, 14 October 1982.
9. *Financial Mail (FM)*, 25 May 1983.
10. For an earlier review of SA's policies of destabilization, see *ACR* 1981-82, pA10-12.
11. Statement in the SA House of Assembly, reported in *RDM*, 29 March 1983.
12. *RDM*, 28 January 1983.
13. See R. H. Green, 'SADCC & SA in Confrontation', in this volume; and *ACR* 1981-82, pB684ff.
14. See *ACR* 1980-81.
15. *RDM*, 18 March 1983.
16. P. C. Asmussen, treasurer of the Security Forces Support Committee, Johannesburg, quoted in *New African*, London, March 1983.
17. Interview with J. Lelyveld in *New York Times*, 17 February 1983.
18. *RDM*, 5 February 1983.
19. *Ibid.*
20. Quoted in *RDM*, 22 February 1983.
21. *The Resistançia Naçional Mocambicana* was identified by the acronym RNM in *ACR* 1981-82, Vol 12; but it is now much more generally referred to as the MNR. It has also been referred to as the MRM.
22. This statement was read out in the SA Parliament by the Leader of the Opposition, F. van Zyl Slabbert. See *RDM*, 5 February 1983.
23. See *New African*, April 1983.
24. Radio Harare, 21 August 1982.
25. *The Citizen*, 20 August 1982.
26. For details, see chapter on Zimbabwe.
27. See *New African*, March 1983; and interview with Prime Minister Jonathan.
28. Colin Legum in *New African*, April 1983.
29. *IHT*, 30 May 1983.
30. *The Times*, 4 June 1983.
31. See *ACR* 1981-82, pB605, 607, 610.
32. See chapter on Botswana.
33. *RDM*, 6 June 1983.
34. Radio Gaborone, 7 June 1983.
35. See *ACR* 1981-82, pA39.
36. SABC, 23 August 1982.
37. See *ACR* 1981-82, pB247ff, B775.
38. *Star*, 12 February 1983.
39. *RDM*, 1 February 1983.
40. *RDM*, 5 February 1983.
41. *RDM*, 2 July 1982.
42. See *ACR* 1980-81, pA10-12.
43. *Ibid.*
44. See *ACR* 1981-82, pA30-31; 1979-80, pA163.
45. *The Times*, 21 August 1982.
46. *Angola Press Service (ANGOP)*, 13 August 1982.
47. See *ACR* 1981-82, pA55.
48. For survey of the US attempts to 'delink' the Cuban issue from a Namibian settlement, see *ACR* 1981-82, pA16ff.
49. For text, see Documents Section.
50. See *ACR* 1981-82, pA39.
51. For details, see chapter on Angola.
52. For details, see *ACR* 1981-82, pA56-60.
53. *RDM*, 12 April 1983.
54. *Note d'Actualités*, French Information Service, London, CTL/DISCOM/65/83, 26 March 1983.
55. *ICA*, Paris, AF-205; 26 April 1983.
56. *Ibid.*
57. *ANGOP*, 26 April 1983.
58. *The Times*, 25 May 1983.
59. *ICA*, AF 203, 31 May 1983.
60. For details of its security and economic problems, see chapter on Angola.
61. *RDM*, 23 February 1983.
62. Radio Luanda, 10 and 11 May 1983.
63. SABC, Johannesburg, 10 May 1983.
64. *West Africa*, London, 21 February 1983.
65. For details, see chapter on Namibia.
66. *RDM*, 28 January 1983.

67. Zambia, Zimbabwe, Tanzania, Mozambique, Angola, Botswana.
68. See John Marcum, 'The Politics of Survival: Unita in Angola', *Africa Notes*, No. 8; CSIS, Washington, 18 February 1983. Also see chapter on Angola in *ACR* 1981-82, 1982-83.
69. See *Star*, 16 April 1983.
70. See *ACR* 1981-82, pA46.
71. See chapter on Namibia in *ACR* 1982–83. Mudge only withdrew temporarily.
72. For an expert analysis of Namibia's economy and the cost of the war to SA, see *ACR* 1981-82, pB674ff.

73. Radio Luanda, 26 October 1982.
74. *West Africa*, London, 15 November 1982.
75. *Tass*, 11 March 1983.
76. See chapter on Angola in *ACR* 1979-80, 1980-81, 1981-82.
77. *Financial Times*, London, 9 July 1982.
78. Radio Harare, 26 July 1982; *International Herald Tribune (IHT)* Paris, 28 July 1982.
79. See interview with Gong Dafei, *Africa Report*, Washington, March/April 1983.
80. *RDM*, 28 January 1983.

1983–1984

PAX PRAETORIANA OR PAX AFRICANA?

Pax Praetoriana suggests a security system in Southern Africa imposed and supervised by the regional power, and maintained primarily to defend and promote Pretoria's interests, with the border States playing the role of dependent and, essentially, reluctant partners. *Pax Africana,* on the other hand, suggests a security system based on an alliance of equals, freely entered into, and dedicated to promoting the interests of all its members. The debate that followed the signing of three separate security agreements by South Africa (SA) with Angola, Mozambique and Swaziland centered on whether they were harbingers of a genuine regional security system capable of developing into a durable arrangement for the purpose of promoting peaceful political and economic cooperation in Southern Africa; or whether they were only temporary arrangements forced on SA's neighbours by superior military and economic power.

By Mid-1983 it had become evident that the violent and economic confrontation in Southern Africa had reached such a pitch of intensity that it could not be kept at existing levels: confrontation had either to be lifted to a new plane of fighting, or scaled down to a less dangerous and costly level to provide at least a breathing-space for all the states engaged in the conflict; the guerrilla movements had no interest in scaling down the fighting.

Certain parallels between developments in Southern Africa and the Middle East had become even more striking than in the previous year.[1] President Quett Masire of Botswana drew an analogy between his country's situation and Lebanon (see Northern Front, below). Lawrence S. Eagleberger, the US Under-Secretary of State for Political Affairs, told a conference of US newspaper editorial writers on 23 June 1983 that the tragedies of the Middle East could be repeated in Southern Africa and the interests of the region and the West would be severely damaged unless the cycle of violence was reversed. He blamed outside interests for seeking to turn the southern part of the African continent into an enlarged version of Lebanon, with the sovereignty, independence and economic viability of the States in the region subordinated to a battle between SA and its neighbours. In reality, though, the threat came not from 'outside interests' but from the regional power, SA, in widening the area of conflict to defend its perceived security interests.

While it was possible to envisage temporary military stand-off arrangements between Pretoria and its neighbours, and while there were grounds for hope about achieving a settlement over Namibia's independence, it was harder to detect any evidence of a possible basis for a negotiated settlement of the core issue of conflict: apartheid in SA. However, agreement over Namibia could contribute, at least, to lessening tensions along what SA's military leaders describe as its Western Front (Angola and Namibia). But the situation along the Northern Front (Mozambique, Zimbabwe, Swaziland and Botswana) could be achieved, in the short term, only if those neighbours agreed to deny all military facilities to the liberation movements as the price for Pretoria reducing its military pressures against them. The durability of any stand-off agreements on both those Fronts would ultimately depend on how their State interests were affected by developments on the Home Front, in SA itself, where the confrontation between the Pretoria regime and its opponents seem ulikely to be fundamentally affected by such deals in the long run.

The situation in mid-1983 demanded a choice by SA's neighbours between their State interests and their ideological commitments. Angola could continue to allow the guerrilla forces of the South-West African People's Organization of Namibia (Swapo) to operate freely from its territory, and Mozambique could continue to permit the African National Congress (ANC) armed cadres to transit its territory only by accepting further damage to their security and economies by actions taken by Pretoria. The choice for these two countries was made even harder than for the other border states because both are ruled by movements which won power through a liberation struggle during which they had relied heavily on *their* border states. The MPLA and Frelimo leaderships might have made a different choice if it were not for the terrible economic plight of their people and the fact that the survival of both regimes was in some jeopardy. The alternative to a stand-off agreement was to face the risk of destruction on a scale previously accepted only by North Vietnam in supporting the Vietcong; but there were two crucial differences between their situations: first, Hanoi was fighting for the unification of its own country; and second, it could count on effective military and economic backing from both the Soviet bloc and China. Mozambique and Angola could not count on total support from any major power; the Cubans in Angola were no adequate substitute for Soviet power—even if they had been fully engaged in fighting the South African Defence Force (SADF), which they were not. The test was whether Moscow was willing and able to give its two Marxist allies the kind of support they had produced for Hanoi—or at the level sustained for Cuba, Syria and even Ethiopia. Once the Angolan and Mozambican regimes had understood that Moscow was unwilling to make this kind of commitment, their only available options were either to face a period of virtual dictation by Pretoria, or to negotiate stand-off agreements which would enable them to buy time to rebuild their economic and political bases. The only real surprise was that Mozambique decided to go as far as it did in signing a mutual security and economic pact with Pretoria, unlike Angola which went for a much more limited, tentative agreement.

Angola and Mozambique were both in an extremely parlous condition in mid-1983. The Botha regime was determinedly asserting SA's role as a regional power, deploying the SADF across its border to any point required by its perceived security interests in keeping Swapo and the ANC insurgents at bay. For several years past, the SADF had occupied ever larger areas of Southern Angola and given increasing arms and logistic support to Dr Jonas Savimbi's Union for the Total National Independence of Angola (Unita), whose range of military operations was growing almost by the month despite the efforts of the Angolan national army (Fapla) and the estimated 20,000-25,000 Cuban combat troops. The ruling MPLA—Labour Party was in a state of internal disarray, its regime having lost much of its popular base because of relentless economic hardship and conditions of insecurity; the country's economy was in ruins, and deteriorating even further; its system of internal communications was disrupted; and, despite its oil revenues (due to be doubled in 1984-85), it was unable to utilize its financial resources effectively to rebuild the internal economy. The situation in Mozambique was no less bleak. The SA-supported Mozambique National Resistance (MNR) was spreading havoc in the rural areas, and steadily expanding its field of operations.[2] Frelimo (though still in much better shape than the MPLA) had lost some credibility and a good deal of its popularity because of the security situation and desperate economic hardships suffered by most of the population. Their hardships were bitterly intensified by the worst drought of the century which had forced over 100,000 peasants to trek to Zimbabwe in search of food, and left an estimated 300,000 people either dying from starvation, or suffering acutely from dietary deficiencies; 3m more were affected, though less acutely than those in the worst-hit areas.

It was against this sombre background that the Angolan and Mozambican leaders—by then convinced that they could expect little effective support from the Soviet bloc—turned more urgently to the West. They sought economic, if not military, support and pressed them to take a tougher line over Pretoria's policies of destabilizing its neighbours, and to compel the Botha regime to implement the Security Council's Resolution 435 on Namibian independence. Apart from offers to consider increasing their aid and expanding trade, the advice they received from the Western capitals was that they should enter into negotiations with SA to lower tensions in the region. Typical of such advice was that offered by Frank Wisner, the US Deputy Secretary of State for African Affairs, in December 1983:

> Our point of view remains that the situation in Angola can be solved only through political negotiations. There is no military solution for Angola, nor for the conflict between SA and Angola, nor for the conflict between Unita and Luanda Government. Since there is no military solution, the priority then is to find a political solution.[3]

The advice proffered to the Mozambicans ran along similar lines. Denied effective Soviet help, counselled by the West to seek negotiated settlements, and faced with calamitous situations at home, both Presidents dos Santos and Samora Machel decided to explore ways of achieving stand-off security agreements on respectable terms which they could defend to themselves and to their people, as well as to the rest of Africa. They well understood that their greatest difficulty would be in persuading Swapo, the ANC and the opponents of apartheid inside SA to accept that they were not being betrayed.

Would a triumphant Pretoria regime, claiming success for its tough policies, be willing to concede reasonable terms to its battered neighbours? In fact, not all the cards were held by Pretoria. Its regime, too, needed a breathing-spell; it had become increasingly concerned about the ultimate limits of its own military power; it could not afford to ignore the Western Powers, especially Reagan's Washington; and it was beginning to experience the impact on its own economy of having to fight along three fronts. The cost of holding on to Namibia, though not crippling, had nevertheless become a telling factor in Pretoria's calculations, running at well over £1m a day. Concern over the steady rise of 'terrorist' activities inside the Republic could not be disguised.

A report released by a research institute in Cape Town[4] stated that the number of people killed in political violence and sabotage in SA in 1983 had been six times greater than in 1980; the number of cases of violence had also increased about sixfold. In 1983, 214 people had been killed in 395 cases of political violence and sabotage compared with 39 deaths in 59 cases in 1980. The growing number of White casualties in Angola was producing a reaction against the distant border warfare. Furthermore, Namibia's internal political situation no longer offered the same hopes as before of being capable of producing a credible alternative to Swapo; the territory was being run like a colony, with the Administrator-General (AG) playing the role of a Governor, and without any longer even the pretence of a parliament. With all the details involved in implementing the Security Council's Resolution 435 to achieve Namibia's independence finally agreed, the room for further procrastination was restricted to the single issue of the withdrawal of Cuban troops from Angola.

From mid-1983 two attitudes were emerging more clearly within the SA Government. On the one side, was the use of more conciliatory language than in the past about both the necessity and the possibility of reaching agreements on what were termed 'non-aggression pacts'. On the other side, there was the unconciliatory language of violence. The Foreign Minister, Roelof ('Pik') Botha was threatening that SA was determined to take action against 'terrorists' in border countries even if it meant SA clashing 'with the rest of the world.'[5] The Defence Minister, Gen Magnus Malan, while declaring SA's desire for peace with its neighbours, at the same time warned that the SADF had not yet used its 'iron fist' against those threatening it. He said he hoped it would never be necessary for SA to 'show its true military might', but he warned that its people were getting tired of being 'exposed to and threatened by sabotage and terror for which the ANC claims responsibility.'[6]

Two principal factors combined to crystallize into a fresh approach by Pretoria; the lessons of its major offensive against Angola at the end of 1983; and its re-evaluation of the limits of relying on Unita. Although the SADF offensive in November and December had penetrated more deeply than before into Angola and had swept everything before it, casualties were considerably higher than before, including 21 Whites killed. For the first time, the SADF had encountered SAM-8 missiles, which destroyed at least two of their helicopters; hitherto helicopters had been a vital operational element in bush warfare tactics. The introduction of SAM-8s and other sophisticated weapons reduced the effectiveness of helicopters, and meant that future military operations would become increasingly more hazardous, with higher risks of casualties. For the first time, too, the USSR had sent a message to Pretoria warning it of the consequences of continued attacks on Angola (see the Soviet role, below).

The second factor was the realization that SA's plans to change the situation inside Angola would not work. The idea had been that Unita should be strengthened to the point when it was able either to attack Luanda itself, take over the regime and expel the Soviets and Cubans or, alternatively, to strengthen its challenge to the extent that the MPLA would be compelled to accept Savimbi's terms for a coalition government.

Savimbi had always told his supporters that, while he believed he could force the MPLA to accept his terms for a coalition, he saw no chance of ever capturing Luanda because of the armour and anti-aircraft defences encircling the capital. A CIA evaluation had come to the same conclusion in 1983. But SA Military intelligence had disagreed with the CIA conclusions- until the experience of the November/December 1983 campaigns. The Pretoria regime had, nevertheless, kept up a sustained lobby operation in Washington with Right-wing Reaganites to urge on the President that, instead of leaning on SA to implement Resolution 435, the Administration should actively support the SADF's programme of support for Savimbi. This, they argued, would be the best way not only of forcing the withdrawal of the Cubans, but also of ending the Soviet bloc presence in Angola. Despite the CIA's evaluation report, the State Department had come under considerable pressure to back Pretoria's secret plan 'to defeat the Marxist regime and its communist allies'. Ironically, the pro-Savimbi lobby privately urged on Reagan that he should not continue to press for Cuban withdrawal on the argument that they were 'trapped' in Angola where they could be 'cut up' by Unita, and the Russians 'given a bloody nose'; but, if they were withdrawn, it would mean that 20,000 to 30,000 Cuban troops would be freed to be redeployed in Central America and so cause even more trouble nearer home. However, once SA Military Intelligence came round to sharing the earlier CIA conclusions, Pretoria's hopes that Savimbi could capture Luanda collapsed; more realistically, they kept up the pressure to urge that the MPLA should agree to share power with Unita. But this also meant that Unita should continue to be supported, militarily.

From late 1983, Prime Minister Botha and his colleagues began to talk in a different vein to Western diplomats: now they were saying that SA really had nothing to fear from the 'broken-back' Marxist regimes on its borders:

> Look at the mess they've made of their countries; the Russians were providing them only with arms which they couldn't use properly, but not with economic support. Now they have come crawling to us begging for terms. If that is true of Angola and Mozambique, how much truer would it be of Namibia after its independence because it would be even more dependent economically on us than either Angola and Mozambique. So, we really have little to fear from a Marxist regime in Windhoek. We are willing to accept even Sam Nujoma if he can succeed in winning the elections.

It was at this time that Pretoria first began to talk of releasing Herman Toivo ja Toivo, the hero-martyr figure of Swapo whose prestige had steadily grown during the almost 20 years he had spent in Robben Island.

THE COURSE OF EVENTS (JUNE-DECEMBER 1983)
THE WESTERN FRONT-ANGOLA AND NAMIBIA
The period from June to December 1983 was a time of secret negotiations between SA and its neighbours, and of considerable diplomatic activities by the Americans, Portuguese, the UN Secretary-General and Zambia's President Kenneth Kaunda.

SA's Foreign Minister told his Parliament on 15 June 1983 that it was time all the countries in Southern Africa began to 'reassess their priorities and to agree on the basic principles of healthy inter-State relations.' He revealed that talks were going on not only with Angola, Botswana, Lesotho and Swaziland, but also with Mozambique; however, he complained that in some cases there had been a lack of progress due to 'mistrust'. SA was involved in the following meetings in 1983 and the early part of 1984:

* With Lesotho in Pretoria on 20 April, and again in Johannesburg on 3 June 1983.
* With Swaziland in Pretoria on 9 April, and again in Johannesburg on 3 June 1983.
* With Botswana in Johannesburg on 21 April 1983.
* With Mozambique at Komatipoort (Nkomati) on 5 May 1983 (an earlier meeting had been held at the same venue on 7/8 December 1982).
* With Angola and the US in Cape Verde 19-23 January and 23 February 1983.
* With Angola, the US and Zambia in Lusaka on 16 February 1984.

The UN Secretary-General, Javier Perez de Cuéllar visited SA, Namibia and Angola in August 1983, in pursuance of a Security Council Resolution of May 1983 which had requested that he should visit the area to report back by the end of August on steps for implementing Resolution 435 on Namibia's independence. His visit took place in a pessimistic environment. Pretoria listed three stumbling blocks to the implementation of Resolution 435: the Cuban presence in Angola; the refusal to include Unita in the negotiations for a settlement; and UN partiality for Swapo. His visit to Namibia was boycotted by the Swapo-Democrats (Andreas Shipanga), Swanu and the two all White parties, the HNP and the Namibian Independence Party. In Luanda, the Angolans were sceptical about any progress so long as the SADF occupied part of their country. Nevertheless, by the end of his visit, de Cuéllar was able to claim 'substantial progress' over the details of Resolution 435. He insisted that the question of Cuban withdrawal lay outside his terms of reference. It later transpired that he had won Angola's support for a 30-day trial ceasefire period; this was confirmed in a letter sent by Luanda to the Secretary-General in late December, subject to the withdrawal of all SADF forces from Angola and to agreement from Swapo. Pretoria revealed that it had previously proposed such a truce on 15 December, which it hoped would begin on 31 January 1984. The US quickly welcomed this offer.

However, at this seemingly promising moment, the SADF embarked on its major new offensive into Angola which was to last until early January 1984. Pik Botha also chose this moment to say that while Pretoria was ready for negotiations, he believed that 'the conflict in Southern Africa would become more serious before a solution was found to the problems of the region.'[8]

Earlier, on 1 December, the Assistant Secretary of State for African Affairs, Chester Crocker, had told the Overseas Writers' Club in Washington that 'there never has been a time at which the Namibian aspects of these negotiations have been as completely resolved as they are to-day.[9] But he cautioned that this did not mean it would be easy to implement the plan; Cuban withdrawal remained a problem.

Secret talks took place in January 1984 in the Cape Verde Isles between SA and Angolan delegates, and separate talks between SA and the Americans. The understanding reached was sufficiently encouraging for the US to begin a fresh initiative at the start of 1984 to achieve the proposed ceasefire agreement. After talks in Cape Town on 27 January, Crocker went on to Zambia, Malawi and Tanzania for talks with Frontline leaders. Although Sam Nujoma described Crocker's visit as an attempt to 'hoodwink' people, he nevertheless said he would be prepared to observe a ceasefire on condition that Pretoria agreed to have direct talks with Swapo. Pik Botha's unexpected response was to say that there would be no objections to such talks between Swapo and Namibia's Administrator-General, Dr Willie van Niekerk; but the latter made such a meeting conditional on Swapo first renouncing its 'pointless acts of violence and terrorism.'[10] SA's ambassador at the UN, Kurt von Schirnding, added as another precondition, that the talks should also involve the internal parties of Namibia. Later, on 31 January, Prime Minister Botha told his Parliament that SA would not stand in the way of talks with Swapo, provided other Namibian parties were also involved since he did not recognize Swapo as being the 'sole representative' of the Namibians.[11] This acceptance of Swapo as a negotiating partner—however hemmed in by conditions—reflected the new thinking in Pretoria referred to earlier.

The MPLA Government announced its terms for a ceasefire for a trial period of 30 days on 18 January, 'considering our concern in setting up a climate of peace in Southern Africa'. But it made this offer conditional on the total withdrawal of SA troops; a promise to begin implementing Resolution 435; and agreement by Swapo to any terms negotiated. It added that Angola remained faithful to its accord with Cuba. Pik Botha's response was to reject all the preconditions and to say that the Angolans' terms showed they were 'not really interested in peace' because they expected SA to abandon its long-standing insistence on the need for Cuban troops to be withdrawn before proceeding wtih Namibia's independence.

Even while these exchanges were taking place, the Angolans, South Africans and Americans were holding a series of bilateral meetings in Mindelo on the Cape

Verde Islands. The SA delegation was led by a senior Foreign Ministry official, David Steward, and Angola's by the Deputy Minister of Foreign Affairs, Venacio de Moura. In parallel talks, Frank Wisner met Angola's Interior Minister, Alexandre Rodrigues (Kito). This series of secret talks, held over 19-23 January, was followed by President dos Santos' statement on 25 January, to his National Assembly in which he announced that Angola had been 'complementing its efforts in the defence of the country and the revolution with intense diplomatic activity.' He also disclosed that the Angolan delegation had held bilateral talks with the US on 'matters of common interest, including Southern Africa'; but he denied that the Angolan delegation had had any contact with the SA delegation in Cape Verde. He described what had appeared in the international media on this question as 'nothing but mere speculation.'

Prime Minister Botha also announced on 31 January that SA would immediately begin to disengage its forces from Angola to pave the way for a cease-fire agreement, having accepted an assurance from the US that Swapo would not try to take advantage of the withdrawal of the SADF. He declared that the sub-continent was 'today standing at the cross-roads between confrontation and peace.' While conceding that escalating conflict would damage SA, he warned that the consequences for its neighbours would be 'catastrophic'. Botha's announcement that the SADF had begun its withdrawal from Angola came in the course of a bluntly-worded speech in which he declared that SA was no longer prepared to 'carry the financial and military burdens and international opprobrium attached to its 'stewardship' of Namibia. He put the cost of the 'tremendous financial burden' at £800m annually. (This figure seems exaggerated; it probably includes the whole cost of maintaining a large part of the SADF in Namibia although, if it were not deployed there, its basic cost would still remain. (An estimate of £450-600m would probably be closer to the mark.) Botha claimed that SA's total assistance for a population of just over 1m 'must surely be one of the most generous foreign aid programmes anywhere in the world today.' It would not, of course, appear so generous if the cost of the military effort were deducted, or if the figures were broken down to show the ratio of expenditure between the White and Black sectors of the economy. Addressing himself to the quarrelling and proliferating parties in Namibia (some 42 parties), Botha threatened that SA was not prepared to continue to 'bear this heavy burden if our forces do not enjoy the wholehearted support of the people of South-West Africa. We will not protect others who do not desire our protection.'

In the next stage of the negotiations that had begun in Cape Verde, the Angolans felt that they could not accept the US as playing the key role of mediator; that role was taken over by President Kenneth Kaunda of Zambia, the Frontline leader who stands particularly close to President dos Santos and who has always been ready in the past to have direct talks with SA leaders to test out the genuineness of their offers to negotiate. Talks began in Lusaka on 16 February under Kaunda's chairmanship, with delegations from Angola, SA and the US. The SA Foreign Minister, who led the SA delegation and was accompanied by Defence Minister Gen Magnus Malan said that the talks would focus in the first instance on cessation of hostilities and on steps to restrain future hostilities. The Angolan delegation was led by Lt Col Alexandre Rodrigues, a Politburo member of the MPLA—Labour Party and Minister of the Interior. The US delegation was led by Chester Crocker.

Agreement was quickly reached. A communiqué issued at the end of the first day announced that, responding to President Kaunda's assessment that a historic opportunity now exists to make progress, the tripartite conference agreed to the:

- Creation of a joint SA–Angolan Joint Military Commission (JMC) to monitor the disengagement process in southern Angola and to detect, investigate and report any alleged violations of the commitments of the parties. . . .
- Participation of a small number of American representatives in the activities of the JMC at the request of the parties.

The communiqué described the meeting as 'an important step towards a peaceful resolution of the problem of the region, including the implementation of UN Security Council Resolution 435. SA undertook to complete the withdrawal of the troops by 31 March 1984. However, an Angolan spokesman described the discussions on the issue of Namibia as 'currently at an impasse'. He repeated President Santos' four conditions for a settlement in SA: withdrawal of all its troops from Angolan territory; implementation of Resolution 435 within 15 days of the ceasefire agreement coming into operation; cessation by SA of support for Unita counter-revolutionary activities; and Swapo's final assent to any agreement that might be reached. On the question of the American role in the ceasefire, Luanda stressed that it would not accept the presence of US observers on its soil to supervise the ceasefire; the US would be required to perform 'a neutral role'. They were to be based on the Namibian side of the border. The Angolan statement recalled that the US had given its support to forces hostile to MPLA and that these had retarded national liberation. The US, it added, had not yet recognized the legitimate government of the Peoples' Repulic of Angola, and had continued to support forces intending to 'smother the Angolan revolution.'[12]

Following the Lusaka meeting, SA's Foreign Minister explained that after the SADF withdrawal, the Angolan Government would reassert its sovereignty in the areas vacated and that no members of Swapo or the Cubans would be allowed into those areas. He described the talks as 'a successful and positive event in the history of Southern Africa,' and added that it 'was not only SA that wanted peace' (sic), but also Angola and the other Frontline States. 'The mechanism for peace,' he added, 'had been created in Lusaka. It is now necessary to build confidence and eradicate suspicion.' He said that President Kaunda had 'played a significant role in bringing all the leaders together.' SA would still keep 10,000 troops on the Namibia border after the withdrawal from Angola; this was made clear by the Defence Minister, who told Parliament that the ultimate hope was for peace on the Angolan border but that, in the meantime, the SADF could not afford to reduce its strength there.[13]

The ceasefire arrangements soon ran into trouble. SA military intelligence reported that 800 guerrillas were trying to get across the border—a claim hotly denied by Swapo. An emergency meeting of the JMC met on 26 February and reached some agreement, the nature of which was not stated. Three days earlier, on 23 February, Sam Nujoma told Crocker in Washington that Swapo had committed itself to observe the disengagement of forces in south Angola. He added that this was only a first step to the implementation of Resolution 435.[14]

Official SA commentaries on the allegations that Swapo had broken the ceasefire agreement were typically hostile; whatever else may have changed in the region, the hostility to Nujoma and the allegations of his subservience to the Russians still remained. According to a SABC commentator:

> Swapo is not to be trusted. Sam Nujoma has shown by his recent contradictory attitudes that he is bowing only under pressure to the demands of the ceasefire terms. His public assurance after seeing Dr Chester Crocker last week—that Swapo would abide by the terms of the agreement—was a blatant lie, uttered as it was in the knowledge that at that moment a new terrorist offensive was underway, with some 200 members of the band already having crossed the border.

Swapo has not changed, and both the South Africans and the Angolans, who are sincere about the peace initiative, will have to accept that it is almost certainly not going to change. It owes whatever credibility it has as a pretender to power in South West Africa to the terrorist campaign against the people of the territory. That campaign could never have been sustained for so long, had it not been for the military assistance of the Soviet Union and Cuban troops in Angola—and the last thing the Soviet Union wants is a peaceful settlement in which South West Africans would choose their own government and constitution, free from coercion. Moreover, Swapo itself has no inclination for the democratic test it would have to face up to in such a settlement. Nujoma has stated openly that his movement is not fighting for a democratic independence, but for power.[15]

A second meeting took place in Lusaka on 25 February to discuss the implementation of the ceasefire agreement. Afterwards, the State Department issued a statement saying that Washington had emphasized to all the parties, including Unita, that the US regarded the disengagement as 'an important step along the road to a settlement' in Southern Africa, and that the US expects all parties to respect it. He added:

> It is our understanding that Unita has not taken any actions in the area of disengagement which would jeopardize the disengagement, and we trust that Unita will continue to maintain this posture. At the same time, no ceasefire has been agreed relating to the rest of Angola. Fighting is apparently continuing, with operations undertaken by both sides.
> It has long been our view that there are no military solutions to the problems facing Southern Africa, including Angola. Such problems can only be resolved through negotiations. We have made clear to all parties that we seek no role in Angola's internal affairs, but we are prepared to be helpful if asked.

The first meeting of the JMC was held on 1 March at Cuvelai—the scene of former battles—where plans were agreed for each side to provide 300 soldiers to form a mixed team to monitor the SADF withdrawal with Lt-Col Roberto Montero leading the Fapla contingent, and Lt-Col Jan Geldenhuys leading the SADF contingent. The SA delegation immediately expressed concern about attempts by several hundred Swapo guerrillas to infiltrate into Namibia, while the Angolans spoke of their concern about Unita troop movements into the areas already vacated by the SADF.[16] At the time of the JMC meeting, Swapo, intent on proving that it would be capable of operating inside Namibia despite the ceasefire, mortarbombed Opuwa, a village 35 km south of the Angolan border. SADF reported that Swapo had increased its strength in the area since mid-February from 80 to 800.

In mid-March, Pretoria began to develop a new tactical approach to the talks on Namibia's independence which was to ripen into the Lusaka talks two months later, minus only one of its objectives—the inclusion of Unita.[17] Pik Botha said the time had come for Southern Africa's leaders to resolve the differences among themselves, and announced his Government's willingness to enter into talks with all the parties involved in the present conflict; these he identified as the SA and Angolan Governments, Unita, the Multi-Party Conference of Namibia and Swapo. Such a meeting, he said, could be held without any preconditions.

Pretoria's wildly unrealistic hopes that Angola's agreement to a ceasefire would lead to a lessening of the MPLA's criticism of apartheid were quickly dissipated when President dos Santos, on a visit to Havana in March 1984, signed a joint communiqué with Castro criticizing the 'disgraceful apartheid regime';[18] this caused Pik Botha to question whether the ceasefire agreement made sense any longer. Washington expressed the view that this was an over-reaction and sought, but failed, to get him to moderate his response. In almost the next breath and in total contrast with his previous statement, Pik Botha went on to express SA's satisfaction with the 'co-operative relationship' that was developing within the JMC. The Havana communiqué had also set the conditions for the withdrawal of Cuban troops—the total withdrawal of the SADF from Angola as well as from Namibia; Pretoria guarantees over Namibia's independence; ending of SA and Western aid to Unita.

In the last week of March, Angolan units of the JMC were reported to have tried to stop Swapo insurgents on their way to the border, resulting in eight guerrillas and two members of the JMC being killed in three separate incidents.[19] This was the only reported incident between Swapo and the Angolans.

The 31 March deadline for the withdrawal of SADF passed, with several of its battalions still encamped in Angola. Pretoria claimed this was due to 'procedural difficulties'. To resolve these problems a secret meeting was held at Ministerial level in Lusaka on 25 April attended by SA's Foreign and Defence Ministers, the A-G of Namibia, and Angola's Interior Minister. Kaunda presided.[20] The 'procedural difficulties' were said to have been ironed out amicably; an exchange of prisoners was agreed; and there were tentative talks on the SA proposal for an all-party conference in Namibia.

In early May, the MPLA complained in an official statement about the continued delay in the SADF withdrawal; it warned that there could be no peace so long as Pretoria continued to support Unita and refused to begin implementing Resolution 435. At the same time, on 4 May, the Officer Commanding the SWA Territorial Force, Maj-Gen George Meiring, assured businessmen in Windhoek that the Angolan Government would no longer give its support to Swapo and forecast that the Organization would soon be without refuge anywhere—yet another instance of SA's lack of political realism in its relations with its neighbours.

THE LUSAKA TALKS ON NAMIBIA, 10-12 MAY 1984
President Kaunda took the initiative of following up the SA proposal to hold all-party talks to finalize agreement on implementing Resolution 435. Acting independently of the other Frontline leaders (some of whom claim they were not even kept informed) but in close step with the Angolans, Kaunda persuaded Pretoria to drop its insistence on Unita's participation and influenced Swapo to agree to accept the presence of the Namibian internal parties who, notionally, would be treated as part of the SA delegation. Prime Minister Botha promised to delegate full powers to Namibia's A-G, Dr van Niekerk, empowering him to accept any agreement that might be reached among all the Namibian parties. Van Niekerk was to act as co-chairman with Kaunda. Botha also assured Kaunda that he would be willing to place no obstacles in the way of independence if the Namibian parties could agree among themselves—an assurance he subsequently made public in a statement to his own Parliament.

For the first time, an official South African representative, Dr van Niekerk, shook hands with Swapo's leader and with other members of his delegation. They included the veteran Nambian leader, Herman Toivo ja Toivo, who had spent over 16 years as a prisoner on Robben Island; and Eliazer Tuhudaleni, who was temporarily released from 17½ years under house arrest in Namibia to enable him to attend the talks. The group picture of smiling delegations encouraged the view that, at long last, the nightmare years of conflict in the disputed territory was about to be lifted. At the very least, the ice was broken.

Eleven of Namibia's score or more of internal parties presented a united front through their Multi-Party Conference (MPC). They included the Afrikaner-led Nationalist Party, which was formerly linked to SA's ruling party; and the South-West African National Union (Swanu), a party which had been among the initiators of the demand for the country's independence. Three of the internal parties—mainly representing elements in the influential German community and Christian groups—elected to sit with the Swapo delegation. On the eve of the conference a split occurred in Swanu, with all but one of the top leaders defecting to Swapo's side. This development produced the first rift in the talks, with the MPC refusing to go ahead with the talks if the defectors were allowed to remain as part of the Swapo delegation. After strenuous and angry protests, Swapo agreed to make another concession to save the talks by agreeing to drop the defectors from their delegation. In his opening address, Kaunda spoke of the need to break 'the cycle of violence' in the region, and added:

It is by your own free choice that you have come here for the historic meeting and may I add that this meeting is an act of God. We have gladly accepted to play host to your meeting because we are convinced that this is an important and courageous step forward to the last kilometre on the road to independence of Namibia. You are meeting at a time when there have been significant developments in our part of the world. These developments have attracted world-wide attention and interest. Our region is clearly in the sharp focus of the international community. The situation in Namibia is certainly one of the major causes of the conflict in Southern Africa. The freedom and independence of Namibia, as the elimination of apartheid in S.A. would, without doubt, create the right and realistic climate for regional stability, peace and security. This happy turn of events would also herald a new era of co-operative relationships among the countries of Southern Africa and see accelerated economic and social development for the benefit of all our peoples.

The independence of Namibia is the litmus test as to the genuineness of all protestations in favour of regional stability, peace and security and resolve to break the so-called cycle of violence. The suspended birth of Namibia as a nation is the single most concrete cause of insecurity in Southern Africa originating from outside the national boundaries of all the individual independent States in the region.

I am aware of the differences between Swapo and some of the Internal Parties in Namibia, particularly those represented in the Multi-Party Conference. These differences have led to a climate of mutual suspicion and resentment. But I am also equally aware that the Namibian people are united on the objective of independence for their country. Certainly, I do not know of any Namibian around this table who has openly opposed the independence of his country and advocate its perpetual occupation by SA. This is an extremely important common ground. It would be naive to expect total unity among the Namibian people or to make this a precondition for the independence of their country. On the other hand, devisions among Namibians should not be permitted to be a pretext for continued occupation of their country.

Is the question of the withdrawal of Cuban troops from Angola really relevant to the independence of Namibia? Do you all really feel threatened by Cuban forces who are not fighting you, the Namibian people? I call upon both SA and the US to reconsider their position on this issue as the question of the presence of the Cuban military forces in Angola is totally extraneous and irrelevant to Namibia's independence. I hope that during this meeting, all Namibian patriots will make it abundantly clear that they disapprove of the position of SA and the US on this issue and want their country to be independent irrespective of what happens to the Cubans in Angola. S.A. must listen to the Namibians on this matter. It must not ignore their position and continue to insist on the so-called linkage between Namibia's independence and the withdrawal of the Cuban military forces from Angola. There simply is no linkage between the two. Neither Angola nor Cuba has any intention whatsoever to export those Cubans in Angola to Namibia now or after Namibia's independence. For SA to continue insisting on the so-called linkage and at the same time purport willingness to withdraw from Namibia on the basis of Resolution 435 would be grossly unfair to the Namibians and is punishing Namibians for the sins they have not committed. SA must therefore demonstrate its sincerity on the question of Namibia's independence now, and stop putting spanners in the way to Namibia's independence.

In the course of his conciliatory opening speech, Sam Nujoma declared:

Today, we all are presented with a unique opportunity to rise to the occasion and to seriously discuss the problems facing Namibia and its people and to put an end to the bloodshed, death and destruction which is currently ravaging our country and its people, as well as to racial prejudices and intolerance which divide and keep us apart. I sincerely believe that no Namibian, whatever his or her political persuasion, would be so callous as to wish the present ugly state of affairs to continue indefinitely in our country. I also firmly believe that the Namibian people are capable of rising above their differences, no matter how difficult this might be, to reach an understanding among themselves in order to resolve the problems facing their country. We have an historic duty and responsibility to overcome individual, tribal, racial and sectional self-interest in order to arrive at a common national interest. We owe it to ourselves and to all future generations of Namibians to arrive at a common national interest. It is in that spirit, that I issue, once again, a clarion call to all the Namibian patriots and fellow compatriots to search deep in their hearts and to examine their commitment to the cause of Namibia's independence and, having done so, to rededicate ourselves, individually and collectively, to work even harder to bring an end to the painful agony and misery of our country and its people. It is for this reason that I solemnly urge this important meeting to spare no efforts in ensuring that we lay the foundations of a new nation that must inevitably be born out of the supreme sacrifices and suffering endured by our people over many years of struggle in their search for peace, justice and freedom.

At this juncture, I would specifically like to address myself to the leader of the SA delegation to this meeting who is the Administrator-General of the occupying colonial power in Namibia. Mr Administrator-General, I take special pleasure in welcoming you and your delegation to this important meeting. In doing so, I would like to believe that you have come to this meeting with full authority and a clear mandate from your Government to find an amicable solution to the long-standing independence problem of our country. You have a unique opportunity to go down in history as a man who, at last, contributed through firm and decisive leadership, at this meeting, to the independence of Namibia. On the other hand, history might cast you as the man who, through lack of firm and decisive leadership, contributed to the continued bloodshed, death, destruction and racial hatred in our country. The choice is yours and that of your Government.

I would be failing in my duty if I did not address myself to the Namibian nation, especially the White community. By circumstances of history and colonial legacy, the White section of our nation has found itself in a state of conflict which has created hatred and animosity between it and those of us who are Black. Because of the racist policy of apartheid we, the Blacks, have found ourselves oppressed, exploited and victimized by racial intolerance in all spheres of life at the hands of the Whites. We have fought each other and continue to fight until now. Swapo and its allies wish to state categorically that our fight has always been against the colonial system and apartheid policies in Namibia and not against the White community as such although, unfortunately, in reality this appears to be the case. Swapo wishes, once again, to reassure the Whites that there is room for all Namibians, both Black and White, in an independent Namibia, a country which will be theirs as much as it will be ours.

I now wish to inform the Administrator-General and through him, his government, that I have been fully mandated by the Central Committee of Swapo to sign a cease fire with S.A. right at this meeting and to proceed with the overall implementation of Resolution 435 in order to bring about the independence of Namibia.

Speaking for the Namibian Internal Parties, the leader of the Multi-Party Conference (MPC), Moses K. Katjiongua, declared:

We have come to Lusaka with an open mind and a spirit of national reconciliation and a firm determination to make a constructive contribution to the speeding up of a process of Namibian independence. We have no intention to be inflexible or unrealistic. We have not come here to score petty politics.

We have stated, time and again, that the MPC accepts Resolution 435 as the only concrete plan for Namibian independence in existence. There is no doubt or ambiguity about that. Our problem, today, is the non-implementation of Resolution 435 six years after its adoption and the continued condition of no-peace and no-settlement and the *status quo* of SA rule. Today, SA rule is symbolized by 'one-man-rule' of the AG. We are not happy with that. We want to govern ourselves. . . .

We believe that, while the demand by the US and SA—not by the people of Namibia—to link Namibia independence to the presence of the Cuban forces in Angola, and the debatable position of the UN towards the various political parties are obvious obstacles surrounding the implementation of Resolution 435; the lack of dialogue and reconciliation among Namibians is a factor which extremely complicates these factors.

A few words to the Administrator-General: Sir, for a long time now your Government has *not* been helpful to bringing about Namibian nationhood and independence. Half-baked and bogus solutions like Bantustans, based on the division of our people on tribal and racial lines and the incarceration of people because of their political convictions have been major obstacles to Namibian national unity, freedom and independence. Our brother, President Kaunda, is now on record saying that he believes that SA and its Prime Minister are serious about Namibian independence. We sincerely hope that you will not embarrass this great son of Africa.

Within half an hour of the formal opening of the talks everybody agreed to accept Resolution 435 as the framework for negotiations. But this consensus was quickly eroded when the delegates got down to discussing the implementation of Resolution 435. The first stumbling block was over the question of linking Cuban troop withdrawals to further progress. The SA delegation, backed by the MPC, argued that it was unrealistic to suppose that the US would be willing to support any agreement that was not linked to Cuban withdrawal. This argument was strongly refuted by Swapo, as well as by Kaunda, firmly supported by the Angolans, who had been invited to send observers to the talks. No official American observer was present; but soundings from a State Department source showed that, however much the Reagan Administration might dislike any agreement that excluded the issue of the Cubans, there was no possible way in which the US could refuse to accept any agreement that might be reached among the parties directly involved in the conflict.

The issue on which the talks finally foundered was over the insistence by the MPC that before any progress was made towards implementing Resolution 435, the UN should first drop its recognition of Swapo as the exclusive representative of the Namibians, and that the internal parties should be recognised on an equal basis with Swapo. The MPC's argument was that since the UN peacekeeping force and supervisory team are slated to play the key role in the transition period to independence, their partiality remained strongly suspect so long as the UN refused to have any dealings with the internal parties. This issue was also a major factor in the breakdown of the previous talks on Namibia's independence held in Geneva in 1981.[21]

At that meeting, spokesman for the UN representative had stated that once agreement was reached over implementing Resolution 435, exclusive recognition of Swapo would fall away. This position was acceptable to Swapo. But at Lusaka the MPC insisted that this step should be taken as a precondition for any decision to implement Resolution 435. Swapo's fear is that if this concession were made in advance of the final agreement, the internal parties might renege on their undertaking and insist on more time to enable them to catch up on Swapo's international recognition. Swapo strongly suspected all along that the Lusaka meeting was simply a Pretoria ploy to give respectability to its 'stooges', and did not represent a genuine attempt at negotiating independence. The toughness with which the MPC defended their demand helped to strengthen Swapo's suspicions. In effect, the internal parties were able to exercise a veto over any agreement since SA's only condition for sanctioning independence was that there would be agreement between the MPC and Swapo. Try as he would, Kaunda could find no way out of this dilemma. It has remained a seemingly insurmountable obstacle. The MPC's determination to gain international respectability and recognition is shown by its decision taken in advance of the Lusaka talks, that a delegation of the internal parties should go straight from the conference on a diplomatic mission to a number of African countries and to the US. They claimed to have obtained invitations to visit Gabon, Senegal, Ivory Coast and Morocco. In Washington they were received by the Secretary of State.

Thus, in addition to the Cuban linkage issue, a further precondition has been introduced: UN recognition of the internal parties.

Another point of conflict at the Lusaka talks was over the issue of a ceasefire. Sam Nujoma's announcement that he was empowered to sign an immediate ceasefire agreement was not taken up. SA's position is that signing a ceasefire agreement with Swapo would not only give formal recognition to the 'terrorist' organization, but also accept that it has been engaged in a war with a guerrilla liberation movement instead, as it insists, fighting to defend Namibians from 'terrorism'. Pretoria has all along argued that if Swapo were to stop attacking Namibian civilians, there would be no need for military action; all that was called for was for Swapo to suspend hostilities unilaterally. It has also insisted that the JMC provides all the machinery required to oversee the ending of hostilities.

Although the Lusaka talks ended with no progress made towards achieving Namibia's independence, Kaunda refused to be discouraged. He believed the talks were useful in two respects. First, it established direct contacts between the SA Government, Namibia's internal parties and Swapo; and second, it identified the areas of agreement between the two sides.

Kaunda formed an extremely high opinion of Botha's personal representative, Dr van Niekerk, whom he regarded as being both sincere and influential. He became convinced that it was possible to develop this relationship to influence Botha—whom van Niekerk referred to at the Lusaka talks as Kaunda's 'Fellow-in-Christ'. Swapo's fear was that Kaunda's patent sincerity would be exploited by the South Africans; it would be harder to get them to come to a second meeting at Lusaka without precise assurances that Pretoria would change its attitude on the three issues that caused the collapse of the Lusaka talks.

THE SLOW PULL OUT FROM ANGOLA, MAY-JULY 1984

Ten days after the Lusaka talks, Angolan and SA delegations were back in the Zambian capital, this time for talks described simply as 'regional security'. Lt-Gen Alexandre Rodrigues again led the MPLA team, while SA's team was led by its Foreign and Defence Ministers. Pik Botha said after the meeting on 22 May that the disengagement of the SADF had reached an 'advanced stage' and that the final withdrawal would be a 'matter of weeks, rather than months.'[22]

Towards the end of May, Chester Crocker was back on the African trail for talks with Pretoria and Lusaka. The SA Government told him that it wished to see an end to the civil war in Angola and expressed concern about ANC guerrillas being trained in camps in Angola; these were said to be at Quibaze, Pango, Malange, Vienna and Caxito. It was the first time that this issue surfaced in public.

A Pretoria source said that while SA recognized that the Angolan conflict was a domestic issue, it believed that neither side could win an outright military victory; its advice was that it should be resolved 'through a political accommodation since the escalating conflict creates opportunities for foreign intervention and is of concern to all parties in the region.'[23]

This acknowledgement that neither Unita nor MPLA could win an outright military victory reflects the re-evaluation of MPLA's strength by the SA Military Intelligence (see above). (SA's critics could put forward precisely the same arguments to press the need to resolve the conflict over apartheid by seeking a political accommodation.)

At the end of May, Prime Minister Botha said on his arrival in Lisbon that SA was ready to sign a non-aggression pact with Angola on the same basis as the Nkomati Accord with Mozambique. He claimed that SA had never fought Angola, only Swapo, and promised that the SADF forces would be withdrawn to the border 'in a few weeks'.[24] (A 'few weeks' had already passed since the other Botha had made a similar statement in Lusaka.) A few days after P. W. Botha's statement in Lisbon, the Angolan Government complained that the SADF engagement was proceeding very slowly. On 14 June, SA's Deputy Foreign Minister, Louis Nel, said the reason for the delay in SADF's disengagement was because of Swapo activities in the border area.[25] A military source claimed that of Swapo's estimated 6,500 trained guerrillas, half had been redeployed in the north of Angola in support of Fapla and Cuban combat troops to fight Unita.[26] Swapo repudiated such reports. On 26 June, President dos Santos was again in Lusaka to discuss with Kaunda SA's failure to withdraw all its forces ten weeks after the agreed date. On the same day, Radio Luanda reported that Angola felt Pretoria 'lacked sincerity' over disengagement. Responding to such criticism, an SA spokesman reported extremely distrubing 'information' provided by Jonas Savimbi about Swapo's forces becoming increasingly active in the Cunene province. He added that if this were true, 'it would be impossible for SA to keep to its side of the bargain.'

Meanwhile, the MPLA-Labour Party Central Committee at its session over 20-23 June expressed 'apprehension at the non-fulfillment by the SA racists of the undertakings entered into at Lusaka, and at the Reagan Administration's increased support for SA in sabotaging the implementation of Resolution 435.'[27] The Committee also noted that 'owing especially to the war imposed on us, together with the current unfavourable situation both at home and abroad, the economic and social situation in the country is continuing to deteriorate.'

Lt-Col Rodrigues had a further meeting with Pik Botha in Lusaka on 3 July to discuss the future of the JMC once all the SADF units were out of Angola and the Commission had moved its headquarters to the border. According to an official statement, Angola proposed to delay extending the functions of the JMC pending a guarantee from SA that Angola's borders would not again be violated and provided, at the conclusion of that term, Resolution 435 would be implemented.[28] The same source denied rumours that there were divisions within the Angolan forces in the JMC over the implementation of the Lusaka Agreement.

THE ROAD TO NKOMATI

In October 1983, President Samora Machel embarked on a European tour which took him to Belgium, the Netherlands, Portugal, Yugoslavia, France and Britain. On the eve of his departure the SADF had launched another raid against his capital to attack an alleged ANC 'planning centre' located in an apartment close to the Presidency. While the ANC insisted that the apartment was used as a normal residence for its members, Pretoria was equally adamant in claiming that it 'served as a coordinating headquarters for ANC attacks on SA.'[29] It claimed that the 'terrorists' were divided into specialized groups under the leadership of the Communist exile, Joe Slovo. It also alleged that the ANC had its headquarters in Maputo from which raids were planned against various regions in SA, and that its last raid had found a rocket-launcher, grenades, devices for exploding limpet mines, Soviet sub-machine guns and false-bottomed suitcases. Pretoria reiterated that it would 'hit back whenever necessary. The legal position is very clear. Insofar as international law is concerned and the UN Charter, SA has every right to strike into those countries that harbour terrorists.'

In February 1984 Mozambique's Council of Ministers released a document calculating the losses caused by Pretoria's policy of direct and indirect economic sanctions, at over \$2.6bn.[30] Among the items listed were a drop of one-sixth of the pre-independence revenue from SA traffic chartered through Mozambique ports—a loss of \$248m; a two-third drop in the number of Mozambican workers on SA goldmines—a loss of \$568m in remittances; a concomitant increase of 70,000 unemployed in Southern Mozambique; the loss from scrapping the system under colonialism whereby SA paid one-half of miners' wages in gold at the official price—no estimate given of the loss from this source. In addition, there was the cost of actual physical damage done by MNR—\$333m; this included destruction of 900 rural shops, affecting the facilities of 4.5m people as well as of c. 500 primary schools and 86 secondary schools; 130 communal villages were broken up in 1982, alone, resulting in 100,000 peasants losing their property. In total, the Council of Ministers estimated that SA's policies of destabilization had cost the country over \$4bn—more than three times Mozambique's debt to the West.

Evidence of SA's increasing involvement with the MNR opposition was produced by Lt-Gen Sebastiao Mabote, Chief of the General Staff of the Mozambican army.[31] He said there was evidence of a group of specialized SADF personnel being involved in, for example, logistical support from the air:

> In general, the aircraft fly at night to supply the gangs. We know it very well. Sometimes they begin at 22.00 and last until dawn, depending on the drops they have to make. Sometimes when they miss the trail they go back. There are times when they start from midnight and go on until 0400. They rarely fly during daylight. The only daylight violations that have taken place have been over the capital. Aircraft fly from Ponta do Ouro, Moamba or Pafuri. These violations are almost continuous. When we shot the spy plane down, it had two jet planes behind it. They were reconnaissance aircraft. We shot the spy plane down and the others hastily retreated to SA. These are facts showing that SA directly supports, prepares, arms, equips and supplies the armed bandits.

Gen Mabote's report shows that, despite Mozambique's military alliance with Moscow, its army was in no position to stop the SADF from carrying out its threats to attack the country whenever it chose to do so. Pretoria's support for the MNR continued on an undiminished scale.[32] The rebel force was increasingly successful in destabilizing the country's transport and rural economy. The drought brought misery and the threat of starvation to five million Mozambicans. Machel was in urgent need of vastly more economic and military aid than he was getting from the Soviet bloc and other friendly countries. He was particularly keen to carry forward the rapprochement with Portugal and to explore the kind of aid Mozambique could expect if it abandoned its quest for associate membership of Comecon and became, instead, a signatory ot the Lomé Treaty 3 being negotiated with the EEC. Mozambique's Foreign Minister, Joaquim Chissano, announced on the arrival of his delegation in Brussels that his country needed 'massive and immediate Western investment and aid,' and he spoke of the devastation caused by the drought.[33]

During Machel's visits to the various European capitals, it became clear that he was contemplating a security agreement with SA—even though, while in Lisbon, he likened the SA regime to Nazi Germany, saying it used the same methods of aggression, intimidation, blackmail and propaganda; and he blamed 'the racist regime of SA' for the 'insecurity, the climate of instability and the threat of a generalized war in our region.'[34] A few months earlier, in June, he had called on Mozambicans to 'organize for war', saying that SA could attack by land, sea or air. He described the MNR as SA's 'advance guard', and claimed that the Pretoria regime was out to 'destroy Mozambique because it was a non-racial country.'[35] He told his army: 'The best defence against aggression is to organize for a war.' But the intervening months had caused a change of mind: instead of talking about war, he began to think in terms of peaceful coexistence.

Two months after his visit to Lisbon, Portugal took the initiative in arranging a meeting between Mozambican and SA leaders. The Portuguese Foreign Minister, Jaime Gama, revealed on 9 December that his country was playing a mediator's role 'in its own interests and to promote stability in Southern Africa.'[36] Portugal's interests were concerned chiefly with the heavy cost of keeping up payments on the international loan connected with the Cahora Bassa hydroelectric installations and loss of income from electricity supplies to SA. SA's Foreign Minister visited Lisbon on 8 December and eleven days later Machel disclosed that since returning from his European visit he had received envoys from Portugal and other Western countries, as well as a message from the US, urging the need for talks between Maputo and SA. He added that these countries well understood that Mozambique would not give up its fight against apartheid or abandon its support for the ANC.[37] On 20 December talks opened in Swaziland between a Mozambican delegation— which included Jacinto Veloso, Minister in the Presidency for Economic Affairs, and Oscar Monteiro, Minister of Justice—and a SA delegation, which comprised its Foreign, Defence and Law and Order Ministers. On the same day, Machel was out of his capital attending a summit meeting of Lusophone countries in Guinea-Bissau, where he announced:

> These talks are essential to find a *modus vivendi* with SA. One does not choose one's neighbours. They are uncomfortable for us; we are uncomfortable for them. . . . The principal objective is that no country attacks another.[38]

Pretoria called Machel's statement 'the most positive in years on relations between the two countries.'[39] It added that 'the economic interdependence of these two countries, with their fundamentally opposed political philosophies, is exceptionally close and highly visible'. It blamed Maputo for having broken the ground-rules of cooperation, since it had become

> a main base for the Soviet-supported terrorist offensive against SA. ANC terrorism provoked retaliatory and pre-emptive strikes against the organization's bases, and the ideological preoccupation that led Frelimo to support the ANC was responsible, internally, for a degree of authoritarianism, social dislocation and economic disintegration, that resulted in the popular disillusionment from which Renamo [National Resistance Movement] was born.
>
> President Machel indicates that his Government, under increasing internal pressure, wishes to return to the principles of peaceful co-operation and negotiation over differences. If so, he will find the SA policy unchanged.

Sufficient common ground was found at the exploratory meeting to encourage both sides to move forward towards exploring the details of a comprehensive security and economic agreement. Four committees were established on Security, Cahora-Bassa, tourism and economic relations. These four committees met separately on 16 January 1984—the first in Pretoria, and the other three in Maputo. Opening the talks in Maputo, Jacinto Veloso addressed the SA delegates: 'We interpret your presence here as proof of the intention of the SA Government to carry out actions to end the violence and the escalating war.' He added that the aim of the talks was to 'benefit the whole of Southern Africa,' and expressed his country's wish 'to progress on the basis of previous economic cooperation with SA.'

Among the questions discussed by the committees were the future of the estimated 60,000 Mozambican workers still in SA; the resumption of power supplies to SA to achieve the agreed 1,400 MW which would earn Mozambique $45m a year; and the resumption of tourism and normal trade, including the transport of SA goods through Mozambique's ports. It was estimated that tourism could quickly rise to earn Mozambique $100m a year. At the security talks held in Pretoria there was quick agreement on the principle that neither State should serve as a springboard for violence against the other; the problems would be over monitoring such an agreement.

During the skirmishing in these opening rounds, both sides were concerned with justifying to their own audiences the reasons for the negotiations and to show that there was no abandonment of earlier fundamental policy positions. An editorial in the Frelimo organ, *Noticias,* on 19 January stressed that the adoption by both sides of the rules of international law, respect for territorial integrity, the inviolability of borders, non-interference in each other's domestic affairs and the guarantee that neither of the States, would serve as a base for acts of violence against the other.

The editorial went on to stress that:

> The application of those principles reflected our socialist policy of peace as defined by the fourth Frelimo Party congress. In holding talks with SA, we were fulfilling a basic principle of our foreign policy and contributing to the elimination of a focus of tension in the region and the world. However, we must realize that peace was not a reality that had been achieved; it was a path to be built. Our vigilance must not relax even after we had achieved an atmosphere of peaceful coexistence with SA. United and organized, we will have to apply ourselves in an even more determined manner to the total liquidation of the armed bandits and the development of our economy— guidelines that we would transform into reality in 1984.

The SA perspective[40] was that the moves towards rapprochement 'reflect a coming to terms with Southern African realities' and the economic interdependence of the countries in the region:

> In that sense, it could signal the start of an historic shift from the confrontation attitudes that were sown by political escapism and have produced only grim harvests of self-destruction. But if that breakthrough does materialize it will not be solely the result of the changing attitudes locally; it will be due as much to a coming to terms of reality in the West, and especially in the U.S.
>
> To define the conflict situation in Southern Africa purely in terms of regional differences is to ignore one of the most powerful forces influencing it. The nature of the situation was fundamentally altered when the Soviet Union dispatched Cuban surrogate forces to Angola in 1975 and began involving itself more actively in the affairs of the region as a whole. That action—motivated as it was not by Southern

Africa's interests but by the Kremlin's international strategic aims—introduced an altogether new dimension into the situation. Henceforth, initiatives designed to reduce tensions and resolve disputes through negotiation could not appeal only to the needs and interests of the region's governments. If they were to succeed they would also have to address the global aspect represented by Soviet involvement.

Southern Africa had become an arena of the Super-power struggle. The clear implication, though it was not accepted until Mr Ronald Reagan came to power in the US five years after the Cuban occupation of Angola, was that the West would itself have to become more actively involved in Southern Africa in a role supportive of the moderates. That implication gave birth to the policy of constructive engagement. . .

In Southern Africa today the wherewithal to escape the Soviet embrace in the form of economic aid and effective countervailing power are as necessary to end the confrontation as is the will of the regions governments.

The talks taking place in Maputo and Pretoria are the product of that doctrine applied in support of the efforts of SA and its eastern neighbour. It is a comprehensive approach that is designed to take account of the total multifaceted Southern African situation. It cannot guarantee success in resolving every dispute, but it is the only approach through which success can be achieved.

At a meeting in Maputo on 20 February the two sides agreed to enter into a formal security agreement. Nothing was said to recollect the Treaty of Friendship and Cooperation entered into with the USSR in 1977; which has a clause about assistance in the event of external aggression against Mozambique.[41] The final communiqué said that the region had been 'plagued by conflict for too long,' which had 'retarded progress in the resolution of the common problems of our region.' It quoted President Machel as reaffirming 'the principles of peace, stability, progress and good neighbourliness which underline the current discussions.' Pik Botha explained that the agreement meant that 'the two governments will not allow any form of subversion against each other.'[42] During this meeting Machel had his first personal encounter with his military adversary, Gen Magnus Malan. Someone privy to this encounter reported with wry amusement how Machel appeared to have twitted the SA Defence Minister by putting questions directly to him; each time Gen Malan responded, he rose in his place and stood at respectful attention to deliver his reply.

The few remaining details, mainly over the monitoring of the agreement, were resolved at a meeting in Cape Town on 2 March—the last lap on the road to Nkomati.

Mozambique's major concern throughout the negotiations was to disclaim any weakening of its stand against apartheid, or abandonment of its support for the ANC; but, above all, Machel was determined that, when he finally went to Nkomati for the signing of the agreement, he would not be going to Canossa; he insisted that the agreement was brought about because both sides needed it. Machel's analysis and thinking were reflected in a report by the Mozambique journalist, Carlos Cardoso. The starting-point was that, after nine years of failure, Botha had returned to the position adopted by his predecessor John Vorster on the morrow after the collapse of Portuguese colonialism:

> During last night's press conference at the end of the meeting between the delegations from Mozambique and SA, I asked the S.A. Foreign Minister, Roelof Botha: Now that the agreement is about to be concluded, does it not remind you of John Vorster and his policy? Roelof Botha did not give an immediate answer. For about five seconds he had a vacant look, perhaps recalling old memories, and he ended up diplomatically answering what had been implied in the question. What we are doing, he said, is the continuation of the policy for peace of the successive South African Prime Ministers.

The truth, however, was and is a different matter.

During the eight years of armed regional destabilization, the Botha-Malan military option did not strengthen the regime as a whole, but weakened it internally and externally. The country's economy reached a crisis due to a drop in exports. The war effort . . . seriously aggravated the crisis. Moreover, until 1983 the SA military strategy in Angola was aimed at forcing a compromise between the MPLA and Unita. On the eastern front it was aimed at either causing a structural change in Mozambique, a coup or a compromise between banditry and Frelimo. Through its military option, SA has failed to impose structural changes either on the western or eastern fronts. In other words, the strategic objective of the military option has failed. It was therefore necessary to follow a different policy, that is, an attempt at a policy of coexistence. It is at this point that the more enlightened people here in SA recall the attempt made by Vorster in the 1974-75 period.

There is another element which is extremely important to the current analyses. Here in SA, people are asking—what happened in southern Angola during the last two months of 1983? People ask why SA, which is used to putting out propaganda which spoke of victory after victory, suddenly proposed a withdrawal from southern Angola? The reality is that in Angola the People's Armed Forces for the Liberation of Angola, aided by the Cuban troops, were then much stronger than before. The Soviet military equipment, which finally arrived in Luanda by about September, strengthened Fapla's firepower. It is obvious that the Angolans, while realizing that in view of the war they could not embark in a process of economic development—which they tried throughout the years—had to go for total war. This implied the development of all their firepower—now much stronger than before—in the Cunene territory which was occupied by the SA troops. For Pieter Botha this is an extremely violent move to make. He could lose between 3,000 and 4,000 White South African soldiers that could result in the end of his own regime.

Therefore, the talks with Mozambique and Angola are like going back eight years in history when John Vorster was Prime Minister at a time when he only had party power and not the military power, and was unable to push forward a policy of detente. Moreover, the military option did not stop history, nor did it make history repeat itself. It failed to push Frelimo and the MPLA backward. It ended up strengthening both countries to the east and the west. . . . Therefore, the overall conclusion to make is that within the regime its representatives and leaders are now certainly looking at the mirror of history with a certain degree of self-criticism because, as stated by a SA analyst here, White S.A. seems to have lost eight years of its life rather than follow the former policy which could lead the regime to certain credibility. They opted for a military option which hurt the regime's credibility, which is already extremely weak due to the apartheid policy in the country.[43]

Mozambique unanimously approved the terms of the proposed security agreement at a meeting on 6 March of the Council of Ministers, the National Security Council, senior leaders of the defence and security forces, the Central Committee and Politburo of Frelimo, and the Permanent Commission of the People's Assembly.[44] The unanimity of the vote dispelled rumours that hardliners were opposed to Machel's *detentism* and confirmed both his total political ascendancy in the country and the widespread popular desire for a breathing-period to recover from the years of economic hardship and conditions of insecurity. The Central Committee of Frelimo reflected these feelings when it 'unanimously praised this great victory for peace, stability, good neighbourliness and progress.'

THE NKOMATI ACCORD, 16 MARCH 1984

The Nkomati river marks the border between SA and Mozambique. Komatipoort itself is a small border town in a humid, fever-stricken area. On a site near the banks of the turgid river a white pavilion was erected with an encampment of military tents. Prime Minister Botha, dressed in a formal suit, accompanied by his wife in a decorous party dress, and all his senior Ministers, top army brass, as well as Opposition leaders, who included Andries Treurnicht of the *verkrampte* Conservative Party. President Machel, dressed in his British-style field-marshal's uniform, was similarly flanked by all his top political and military leaders. However, not a single one of the other five Frontline leaders accepted his invitation to be present on this occasion; nor did they send their representatives. Only Swaziland's Prime Minister was present.

Why did Machel choose to make such a show of the occasion? Because he wanted to stand before the world, not as the humbled leader of a defeated country, but proudly and defiantly as an equal of his powerful neighbour.

Extracts of Machel's and Botha's speeches at the signing ceremony are reproduced in Appendix 2 to this chapter. The full text of the Nkomati Accord is reproduced in Appendix 1. Its main provisions bind the two governments to:

- Forbid and prevent the organization of irregular forces or armed bands, including mercenaries by each other's enemies.
- Eliminate bases, training centres, places of shelter, accommodation and transit for use by the enemies.
- Eliminate armaments bases, command posts, communications facilities, and broadcasting stations, and to prohibit recruitment, abduction, and acts of propaganda that incite a war of aggression or acts of terrorism.

A Joint Security Commission was to be set up to supervise and monitor the agreement.

AFRICAN REACTIONS TO THE NKOMATI ACCORD
The African National Congress (ANC)

At the core of the conflict between Mozambique and SA were the two issues of the ANC and the MNR; it was therefore natural that the Nkomati Accord should focus on the elimination of what both sides believed to be threats to their security coming from across their borders. While Mozambique always denied that the ANC enjoyed any military facilities in the country other than the right to rapid transit, the understanding reached was that activities should be closely circumscribed by removing their political presence from Maputo to a place much further north; and by denying ANC cadres and their arms any transit facilities *en route* to the SA border.

Although the ANC maintained a strong political cadre in Maputo (including their alliance-partner, Joe Slovo of the SA Communist Party—a prime target of Pretoria's hostility), they have never in fact had military training camps in Mozambique; these are located in Tanzania and Angola. However, Machel admitted that trained guerrillas and their arms were allowed to transit rapidly through Mozambique, not to remain for any lengthy period in the country. Similar constraints are placed on the ANC in other border countries—Zimbabwe, Botswana and Swaziland. But, until March 1984, the Mozambique–Swazi route was the only direct access the ANC insurgents had to the SA border, except for the direct crossing from Mozambique into northern Natal and Zululand. Once Swaziland was shut off (see below) and Mozambique became closed to them, the ANC was clearly hard hit. The Nkomati Accord virtually blocked their way to getting trained insurgents and arms into the country. Thus the State interests of Mozambique and the interests of the SA liberation movement had come into direct conflict. This was very painful to Machel. According to Jonathan Steele, Machel called Oliver Tambo to a meeting with him one evening in January 1984 at his beach house to the north of Maputo, where he normally went to relax:

All day long the President of Mozambique had been telling his visitor, Oliver Tambo, about his country's dire predicament. Machel described how one calamity had struck after another—three years of drought, a sudden devastating flood, an armed insurgency, organized and financed by SA in nine of Mozambique's ten provinces, and all coming on top of a colonial legacy of neglect and last-minute destruction when the Portuguese withdrew in 1975.

For the last eight years Tambo's ANC had had special facilities in Maputo. The organization's headquarters is in Lusaka, but in the Mozambican capital it had a listening post and a planning centre right on SA's doorstep, less than 300 miles from the industrial heartland of the Transvaal.

Through Maputo came scores of refugees from Soweto and other SA cities, young men ready to join ANC's armed struggle against apartheid. From here many of them went back as saboteurs and organizers, usually after training in Angola, and then passing through Mozambique into Swaziland and SA. Free Maputo, run by a victorious Marxist liberation movement, had for long been an important symbolic and logistic bastion in the ANC's fight against apartheid.

Tambo knew that evening that Machel was engaged in talks with SA for an arrangement to halt the MNR, the rebel insurgency. But Machel mentioned no details. When Tambo finally left, the Mozambican President could contain himself no longer. According to highly-placed Mozambican sources, he broke down for a moment and cried. He had not had the heart to tell Tambo what the looming pact with Pretoria was to mean for the ANC.

It was left to another Minister to give the stunning news—no more transit facilities for ANC fighters to pass through Mozambique, and a drastic reduction of their permanent presence, down to only 10 people in future; a non-aggression treaty with Pretoria; an open door to SA capital, and abandonment of Africa's policy of trying to isolate the apartheid regime.[45]

Nevertheless, Machel insisted:

We deplore the apartheid system as a crime against humanity, and we give political, diplomatic and moral support to the ANC. But Mozambique also considers that SA is a State, and this consideration reflects the fact that SA is a member of the UN. Mozambique, like the rest of the world, has to deal with SA as a State.[46]

On other occasions he compared SA to Nazi Germany (see above) and described the apartheid system as 'an aberration' that will one day 'cease to exist.'[47] Two months after signing the Nkomati Accord, his Foreign Minister said that Mozambique would continue to provide political and diplomatic support to the ANC, as well as providing it 'with any material support, not military in nature.'[48] He added that 'with the balance of power and other strategic realities in the region, Mozambique could not provide military support to the liberation movement.'

In a public demonstration to show that Mozambique had not stopped its political and moral support for the ANC, Machel invited its President-General, Oliver Tambo, to be his guest at the 22nd anniversary celebrations of the founding of Frelimo on 26 June 1984.

Four aspects of the Nkomati Accord negotiations were particularly galling to the ANC according to its officials:[49]

1. At no stage, it seems, was the ANC consulted by the Mozambicans. The news was broken only after the deal had been agreed;
2. The terms of the pact go well beyond what, in the opinion of the ANC, Mozambique requires to ensure its security;
3. ANC officials suspect that senior members of the Mozambique Government are attempting to redefine the ANC's role in SA by talking of a campaign for 'civil

rights' rather than a "liberation war", and stressing SA's status as a sovereign power, distinct from the colonial nature for former White-ruled States in Africa. Such an interpretation could, ANC officials fear, undermine its guerrilla campaign; and

4. By turning what the ANC believes should have been a low-key occasion at Foreign Minister level into a day of pomp and ceremony conducted by the two State leaders, the Mozambicans have made contact with SA more respectable, eroding the ANC campaigns to isolate the Republic, economically and diplomatically.

The ANC was trapped between its obvious total rejection of the Nkomati Accord and the need not to appear in any way to offend Mozambique or the other Frontline States. Its National Executive Committee issued a carefully drafted declaration of its stand on 'the so-called non-aggression pact':

Further accords, concluded as they are with the regime—which has no moral or legal right to govern our country—cannot but help to perpetuate the illegitimate rule of the SA White settler minority. It is exactly for this reason that this minority has over the years sought to bind independent Africa to such agreements.

The ANC is profoundly conscious of the enormous political, economic and security problems that confront many of the peoples of our region, but blame for many of these problems must be laid squarely on the Pretoria regime, which has sought to define the limit of independence on the countries of our region through a policy of aggression and destabilization. We are convinced that this regime, which is dripping from head to foot with the blood of the thousands of people it has murdered throughout Southern Africa, cannot be an architect of justice and peace in our region. Neither can the ally of this regime, the Reagan Administration of the USA, with its so-called pro-apartheid policy of constructive engagement, be an architect of justice and peace in this region, while at the same time it is an angel of war, reaction and repression in other regions of the world, including the USA itself.

A just and lasting peace in our region is not possible while the fountain-head of war and instability in this area—the apartheid regime and the oppressive system it maintains in SA and Namibia—continues to exist. The Botha regime knows that no peace has broken out; rather it has resorted to other means to continue its war for the domination of SA. That commonly agreed position reaffirms the obligation of the people of SA under the leadership of the ANC to escalate their offensive using all means, including armed action, for the overthrow of the criminal apartheid regime and the transfer of power to the masses. We remain and shall remain loyal to this perspective.

The Pretoria regime is acting in the manner that it is to try to extricate itself out of the crises that confront its racist and colonial system of apartheid. It hopes that after it has pacified our neighbours and driven the ANC out of our region, it will then have a free hand to suppress the mass democratic movement of our country and thus create the conditions for it to spin out its intricate web and measures for the refinement and entrenchment of the apartheid system.

Our principal task at this moment, therefore, is and must be, to intensify our political and military offensives inside SA. This is the urgent call that we make to the masses of our people, to all democratic formations and to all members and units of the ANC and *Umkhonto we Sizwe*. Relying on our own friends, through action, we will frustrate the schemes of the enemy of the peoples of Africa and continue our forward march for the destruction of the system of White minority colonial domination in our country.

The central and immediate question of SA politics is the overthrow of the White minority regime, the seizure of power by the people and the uprooting by these victorious masses of the entire apartheid system of colonial and racist domination, fascist tyranny, the super exploitation of the Black majority and imperialist aggression and expansionism. This question will be and is being settled in struggle within the borders of our country and nowhere else. We are entitled to expect that all those anywhere in the world who count themselves among the anti-colonial and anti-racist forces will join hands with us to bring about this noble outcome.

The peoples of Southern Africa know from their own experience that there can be no peaceful coexistence between freedom and independence on the one hand, and colonialism and racism on the other. We are confident that these masses, their parties and governments, which have over the years demonstrated their commitment to the cause of the total liberation of Africa, will themselves remain loyal to this cause and firm in their resolve to stand with our people until victory is won. We are equally certain that the rest of Africa and the world's progressive community will continue to deny the Botha regime the legitimacy it craves so desperately and to adopt new measures to isolate it and increase their political, diplomatic, moral and material support to the ANC.

The struggle for the liberation of SA under the leadership of the ANC will continue and grow in scope and effectiveness until we have won our victory. Forward to a people's government.

Compatriots, the PRM (People's Republic of Mozambique) and racist SA have met and signed what they called the non-aggression pact. This pact had been preceded by an unending campaign of destabilization and terrorism launched by the apartheid regime against its neighbours and now it is being fed by the imperialist media and the facist information media on the expected results of the signing.

Among other things it has been claimed that the pact will lessen the effectiveness of the people's army. *Umkhonto We Sizwe,* which these media claim is operating from the territory of Mozambique. But, on the other hand, the ANC has stated this categorically that the so-called Nkomati accord will have no effect whatsoever on the activities of our army. The armed liberation struggle will continue unabated.

The two daring operations that took place at the weekend, the blowing up of oil tanks in Ermelo and the armed skirmish that took place in Everton prove that *Umkhonto We Sizwe* is not affected by the so-called non-aggression pact. These daring operations prove beyond any doubt that our combatants are based right inside our country and that nothing short of the total transfer of power into the hands of the majority will ever bring peace in our region. As long as our people continue to be treated as third-class citizens, as long as we are still being forced to live in the Bantustans and as long as we are denied the internationally recognized rights of determining our own destiny, our brave people will continue the armed liberation struggle whether the Pretoria regime can enter into thousands of non-aggression pacts—this will never stop our fight for freedom.

On the other hand, there is no doubt that international imperialism is squarely behind the signing of this pact. They naively thought that such signing might lessen the intensity of the liberation struggle in our country. Their main objective is to preserve our country, SA, as the main bastion of exploitation and imperialist expansion in the region.[50]

Although the ANC was at pains in this statement to avoid any direct criticism of Mozambique, it did give serious offence to Machel, especially by its statement that 'international imperialism is squarely behind the signing of this pact'—a statement which not only ignored the fact that virtually all the African Governments backed the pact, but also suggested that Machel had acted in a way that was pleasing to the 'imperialists'—and, by further inference, that he had upset the world's 'progressive' movement, i.e. the Soviet bloc.

Reacting to this kind of criticism, Mozambique responded indignantly in a broadcast statement:

And now Mozambique is being attacked from the Left—at least by those who think they are on the Left. The Nkomati accord with SA has stirred the emotions of the armchair Marxists, who don't know one end of Kalashnikov from the other. We have sold out. We have betrayed the cause of SA freedom. The SA Black majority will suffer now, they say, because Mozambique has doublecrossed the ANC. Who is peddling this kind of nonsense and why? What can be the objectives, the aims of those who insist that the Nkomati Accord is a defeat for the freedom struggle in Southern Africa, those who say that Mozambique went to Nkomati to surrender? And they are saying it—there is no doubt about that—but why?

The easiest answer would be that such people are enemy agents infiltrated into the ranks of the revolutionary forces, because subjectively what they are doing is discouraging the Black majority in SA. By constantly presenting the Nkomati Accord as a defeat for the freedom struggle, the so-called Leftists are demobilizing the Black people of SA. There is no doubt that some of these apparent Leftists are infiltrated agents. But not all are. Some people, especially some students in Southern Africa, genuinely cannot understand why Mozambique has taken this stance. We would say to them: be careful. If you want to condemn Mozambique, think what you are doing. By attacking Mozambique you are helping the imperialist cause, which is to demoralize the Black people of SA.

At this moment in history the objective conditions for the freedom struggle in SA and Namibia are good. The economy is weaker than it has ever been and the White community is more divided than it has ever been before on the issue of apartheid. The subjective conditions are also good. The ANC is today the sole, undisputed leader of the SA people. Ten years ago, you may remember, many people considered there were two liberation movements in SA.

We do not want to address our enemies—the imperialist agents—and ask for their understanding. We address our friends and these include the misguided masses today. We say to them: Every time you accuse Mozambique of capitulation, you are setting back the freedom struggle of SA. You are weakening the resolve of the people of Soweto, of the townships around Cape Town and Durban, the people of the so-called Homelands. Is that what you want? We think not. If it is, then you are making common cause with imperialism.

Mozambique is the first socialist state in Southern Africa. We were able to create that State because we always fought to win. We never thought we might lose. We still don't even consider such a possibility, either for us or for the people who still live under racist oppression in Africa.[51]

The ANC seemed unsure, at first, how seriously the agreement with Pretoria would affect them; but over the next fortnight they found their offices and the homes of their members subject to raids by the Mozambique police, searching for arms but also encouraging them to move to their new quarters in the north. These pressures were kept up until July, when the last 16 ANC officials, including Joe Slovo, were told to leave Mozambique. Oliver Tambo admitted in June 1984 that the provisions of the Nkomati Accord were obviously 'a setback to our fighting cadres; it must be. But in so far as that setback affects our overall struggle, it will only be a temporary one, and we shall make up for it.'[52] He explained that the ANC never had any bases in Mozambique or other border countries: 'At most, the ANC's cadres have gone through those countries, stopping there for some time of course. But there has been no launching of attacks from any of those countries. We did not think it would be realistic to ask for any bases in the border countries.'

Other African Leaders
By far the sharpest criticisms of the Nkomati Accord came from Black anti-apartheid leaders in SA itself. Men like the Soweto leader, Dr Nthato Motlana—who had looked to Mozambique as a lodestar of liberation—felt suddenly betrayed and reacted angrily. All the Frontline leaders gave their support to Machel—at least publicly. President dos Santos assured him of Angola's 'total solidarity'. Zimbabwe's Prime Minister expressed 'total support for the efforts to

find peace in the region', adding: 'If SA honours the spirit and letter of the agreement, then Zimbabwe will (also) benefit immensely.' Zambia's President Kauda sent a special envoy with a message conveying his 'entire confidence' in the Mozambique leadership and people. 'Total solidarity' was promised by Botswana's President Quett Masire. President Nyere, while on a visit to Maputo, expressed Tanzania's support for Mozambique's peace initiative. The Prime Minister of Lesotho, Leabua Jonathan, expressed 'solidarity and understanding for Mozambique's position'.[53]

Further afield, the Ivory Coast's Foreign Minister said, predictably, that 'if Angola and Mozambique have come so far as negotiating and entering into a dialogue with SA it is the realities of the area which have imposed themselves.'[54] The President of Guinea-Bissau, expressing total support, said the Mozambicans were making a valuable contribution to the search for a peaceful solution to the problems of Southern Africa. The Prime Minister of Swaziland described the agreement as 'a triumph for peace . . . a dream come true.'[55]

However, Mugabe (like the Botswana and Lesotho leaders) said he did not feel the need for signing a similar agreement with Pretoria.[56] Referring to the dismay felt by the ANC, he insisted that the Frontline States were 'too weak and vulnerable to withstand incursions by SA.'

Malawi's Transport Minister looked forward to his country 'reaping benefits' from the accord since the country's trade routes to Beira had been disrupted by the MNR.[57]

The only countries to take a critical view of the Accord were Ethiopia, Ghana and, more surprisingly, Egypt. Radio Accra (21 May 1984) suggested that Mozambique should cast its mind back to the time when it was fighting for its own liberation. 'Is the instinct for self-preservation so great that it has to send away comrades (ANC) who have no home to go to?' It described the Accord as 'tantamount to Mozambique's surrendering its freedom.'

Reactions from other countries

The West European Governments all sent messages of support to Machel. Portugal's President, Gen Eanes, and Prime Minister Soares both praised Machel for his 'courageous attitude, worthy of a great statesman.' Britain's Prime Minister said the agreement was 'a step of great importance for the security, not only of Mozambique and SA, but for the whole region.'

The only reported message from Eastern Europe came from Romania's President Ceausescu, who described the Accord as a 'positive factor' that would help Mozambique to consolidate its 'revolutionary gains'. He added: 'What is imperative now is that SA should be compelled to respect this agreement', and that all anti-imperialist and progressive forces should give increasingly strong support to Mozambique.[58]

POST-NKOMATI DEVELOPMENTS (MARCH TO JUNE 1984)

In the week immediately before the signing of the Accord, an estimated 800 MNR recruits were reported to have crossed from SA into Mozambique; it was assumed that this move was part of SA's effort to disengage itself from the MNR. It was not known how many, if any, MNR supporters still remained at their camp in the Northern Transvaal. The MNR's Voice of the Mozambique National Resistance announced on 15 March that it was suspending its broadcasts, but it continued broadcasting for a few more days before finally closing down. It had begun its broadcasts from a station in Gwelo (Gweru) in the days of Rhodesia in 1976, but had transferred its activities to SA in June 1980. However, the MNR kept up its offensive inside Mozambique and appeared to be making a special effort in the weeks after Nkomati to show that it was still in business. Two days after the signing of the Accord, MNR cadres ambushed a convoy of commercial vehicles, including a SA truck loaded with tobacco, while it was passing through Tete province. In the following months there was no significant reduction in MNR activities. Jacinto Veloso, who was a key figure in the negotiations with SA, said in June 1984: 'The SA Government is, in my opinion, committed to both the spirit and letter of the Nkomati Accord. At the same time there can be no doubt that fresh support has come in for the *bandidos*.'[59]

In interviews conducted with Mozambican leaders in Maputo, Benjamin Pogrund, assistant editor of the *Rand Daily Mail,* was told that while they remain convinced that the SA Government was committed to the Accord, they were equally convinced that there was a split in the SA ranks and that 'certain elements' in the SADF were continuing to help the MNR.[60] According to Pogrund, one senior official who requested anonymity said of the SA leaders: 'We disagree on many things but I have formed the opinion that they are men of honour. They are not dishonest men. When they give their word they respect it.'

The Joint Security Commission (JSC) met for the first time in Maputo on 26 January. There were further meetings in April and May. After the third meeting in Cape Town, on 16 May, the delegations noted while there had been some 'positive developments', some problems (not defined) still remained.

Seventeen SA businessmen paid a three-day visit to Maputo in May to discuss the reopening of the tourist trade and other possible commercial activities. The president of the Mozambican Chamber of Commerce, Americo Mahaio, praised the visit as a sign of willingness to establish 'correct economic relations.'

A trilateral agreement on Cahora Bassa was signed between Mozambique, SA and Portugal in Cape Town on 2 May. It provided for a 50% increase in the price of electricity to be paid by the SA Electricity Supply Commission (ESCOM) to Hidroelectrica de Cahora Bassa (HCB), which operates the project. The new price was 0.75 rands per kilowatt/hour. The agreement also established a premium of 0.35 rands per kilowatt/hour to be paid in the case of 'continuous and good quality supply of Cahora Bassa power to SA.' Mozambique would receive 10% of payments received by HCB if continuous supply of electricity is maintained. SA's annual consumption of Cahora Bassa power is set at 1,450 megawatts, or 8% of its total needs. In turn, Mozambique would buy 200 megawatts of Cahora Bassa power for domestic use, payable to HCB in local currency. However, 90 megawatts would be supplied via ESCOM for the capital Maputo, and Mozambique would pay a rental fee to ESCOM for the use of the transmission lines. (Electricity for Maputo had previously been bought from ESCOM directly, resulting in foreign currency expenditure for Mozambique.) In terms of the agreement, security for maintenance workers on the transmission lines from the dam on the Zambezi river to the SA grid, and for the lines themselves, will be a joint responsibility handled by the JSC.

In June a 1m rand contract was signed between the Mozambican State airline, LAM, and SA Airways for the maintenance of aircraft turbines. It was also agreed to review flight timetables between Maputo and Johannesburg. This agreement renewed a similar one first signed ten years earlier.

THE NORTHERN FRONT
ZIMBABWE, SWAZILAND AND BOTSWANA
The Limpopo river border between SA and Zimbabwe threatened in 1983 to become an area of military confrontation as acute as the other borders with

Angola and Mozambique. The Mugabe Government remained suspiciously fearful that the Pretoria regime would exploit the troubles in Matabeleland to replicate the rebel forces of Unita and the MNR;[61] while the Botha Government was suspicious that the Zimbabweans would allow the ANC to establish themselves in Harare and to develop transit routes paralleling those through Mozambique, which would seriously extend SA's defence lines.

In June 1983, and on a number of subsequent occasions, Pretoria sought assurances from Harare that it would not harbour ANC insurgents.[62] The alarm bells had been set ringing when two suspected ANC guerrillas were detained near Messina, the border town on the Limpopo. Earlier, in April, the Zimbabwe authorities claimed that Zapu dissidents (who became known as Super-Zapu) had set up a High Command in the Dukwe refugee camp in Botswana and that they were planning to send their men for training to SA.[63] Suspicions about this developing collaboration were a constant source of trouble between Harare and Pretoria, but also between the Governments of Zimbabwe and Botswana.[64] In July, Sydney Sekeremayi, Zimbabwe's Minister of State for Defence, described SA as Zimbabwe's 'greatest external threat.'[65] He said that following Botswana's actions to stop refugees from using its territory to make attacks into Matabeleland, the dissidents were moving into SA; because of this new development it had become necessary to 'organize the army, police force and the paramilitary forces in such a way that the Pretoria regime will not be able to send its forces to operate in any part of Zimbabwe.' Mugabe and other Ministers repeated on many occasions that the SA regime was actively assisting the Super-Zapu dissident forces in Matabeleland. As positive evidence of this allegation it was able, *inter alia,* to point to the existence of 'The Voice of Radio Zimbabwe', a clandestine radio station operating on a wavelength traced to SA soil, similar to the one used by the MNR. However, both Pretoria and Harare were constrained by a number of factors from supporting each other's armed opponents. As Mugabe explained (see above), the Frontline States were too vulnerable to allow the SA liberation movements to operate from bases on their soil; besides, Zimbabwe's trade and communications across its territory with SA was crucial to its economy, more especially in view of the country's economic difficulties and the serious disruption of traffic through Mozambique. SA was also concerned with trade as well as with the risks that escalating violence held for the White community in Zimbabwe. It was also sensitive to the concerns expressed by the US and Britain about SA's possible military involvement in Zimbabwe. Despite the openly hostile attitudes of Harare and Pretoria, they in fact established an informal relationship whereby security officials held *ad hoc* meetings in secret to deal with each other's complaints.

Botswana has always been extremely careful to avoid giving SA any pretext for intervening in its affairs by keeping an extremely tight control over SA refugees and by acting toughly to prevent liberation fighters from using Botswana as a corridor to SA. However, this did not stop the SA security forces from operating clandestinely in Botswana, which remained a constant source of friction between the two governments.

Pretoria was strongly wedded to the idea of extending the mutual security accord with Mozambique to all its neighbours—a move strongly resisted by Botswana as well as by Zimbabwe and Lesotho. During his visit to Washington in May 1984, President Masire said that his country was not prepared to sign such an accord 'at any price'. He explained that 'it's a question of principle'; his country would not 'trade principles for expediency.'[66] Responding to a statement by SA's Foreign Minister that a security arrangement would soon be signed with Botswana, Masire replied: 'Well, that may be what is in the mind of the SA Foreign

Minister.' Botswana's Foreign Minister, A. M. Mogwe, added: 'It's not in the mind of the Botswana Foreign Minister.' Masire told an American audience that:

> Botswana is feeling pressure from SA to sign. The Pretoria Government is desirous that we should, and we are resisting that. We have discussed it, and we have come out of our discussions feeling that they would apply pressure, but they have not yet done so.

Asked what kinds of pressures could be expected, he said:

> Economic pressures of different kinds. Our reaction was that there was no need because we have an impeccable record of keeping our word. If we have said we are not going to allow freedom fighters to operate from Botswana to launch attacks against any of our neighbours, we have kept that word. And therefore, our credibility should be able to assure them.

Asked to comment on the accord between SA and Mozambique, he said the two countries could have ended their long history of conflict without it. 'I don't think it was necessary, but it's a bilateral matter.' However, Masire also told a press conference in New York[67] that it was unfair to criticize Angola and Mozambique for their agreements with SA. Using Lebanon as an analogy, he said:

> It is easy for someone in Egypt or Ghana to wonder why any one of the neighbouring States could not fly their flag and say 'here we are and we are going to offer our country for use as a launching pad.' The story of Lebanon is fresh in our minds. We are in that position, Botswana in particular, but perhaps other countries in varying degrees. It is very difficult to stick out and say, 'we are going to help the African National Congress and Panafricanist congress multilaterally, to go into SA. Then the South Africans are going to make a pre-emptive strike by neutralizing the people next door and, perhaps, marching in to guard their interests.

Swaziland's attitude to SA was totally different from Botswana's. On 31 March 1984, the Governments of SA and Swaziland made public the fact that they had signed a security agreement in secret more than two years earlier. Nothing about it had leaked out before. SA's Foreign Minister revealed that the agreement was similar to the Nkomati Accord, but differed in two respects: they decided to 'come to each other's aid in the fight against terrorism'; and they agreed not 'to allow foreign troops or military bases in their respective countries without due notification to the other.'[68]

This secret agreement had, in fact, been concluded at the time of another agreement about 'border adjustments' whereby two areas in KwaZulu and Kangwane were to be transferred to Swaziland.[69] The secret security agreement coincided with the beginning of a joint SA-Swazi campaign to eliminate the ANC cadres in the Kingdom. (The PAC had been eliminated earlier.) This finally culminated in open clashes between ANC fighters and Swazi security forces in early 1984.[70]

In May 1984, Prime Minister Botha publicly thanked the Swazi Prime Minister, Prince Bhekimpi Dlamini, for his country's role in 'achieving regional peace in Southern Africa. He added:

> The signing of the Accord is an event of significance which demonstrates to the international community that there is a serious drive for co-operation among the peoples of Southern Africa and shows that Africa can solve its problems without outside interference.

Prince Bhekimpi said in reply: 'We in Swaziland believe that whether White, Black, Yellow or Red, we must have cordial relations with our neighbours.'

THE BORDER WITH LESOTHO

Of all SA's neighbours, the most resolutely and openly defiant in 1983-84 was also the most vulnerable: Lesotho, whose 1.3m people occupy c.11,600 sq miles of mountainous terrain surrounded by the Orange Free State, Natal, Cape Province and Transkei. It is almost wholly dependent for its economic survival and external communications on SA, where over 100,000 of its able-bodied citizens live and work. Lesotho remained in 1984 the last of SA's neighbours which, in Pretoria's view, refused to take effective measures to control the ANC, PAC and other opponents of apartheid, despite the supposedly salutary lesson that was taught the regime of Chief Leabua Jonathan by the commando attack on his capital in 1981. Not only did Jonathan refuse to emulate the examples of Mozambique (his close ally), Swaziland and Angola; but he was reluctantly sparing in his support for the Nkomati Accord.

Chief Jonathan's bland attitude was to argue that there was no point in Lesotho signing a non-aggression pact with SA since his country had neither the capacity nor the intention to attack his neighbour; nevertheless, he added, he would be willing to consider some form of agreement on mutual security.[71] This would presumably require SA to stop its overt aid for the Lesotho Liberation Army of Ntsu Mokhehle. However, high-level talks between the two countries in December 1983 and June 1984 appear not to have brought the David and Goliath neighbours any closer to an accord.

Jonathan's other major sin in Pretoria's book was that, in May 1983, he had visited China, North Korea, Bulgaria, Romania and Yugoslavia—all of whom were invited to open their embassies in Maseru. (The USSR had already done so.) To woo the North Koreans, Jonathan broke his relations with Taiwan, a close ally of Pretoria.

This double defiance of Pretoria— allegedly allowing ANC cadres to operate from Lesotho soil, and inviting the Communist nations to establish their embassies at the heart of SA—led to the Botha regime imposing limited economic sanctions against Lesotho during 1983 and 1984 and, finally, to supporting a new opposition party to fight Jonathan's ruling party in promised forthcoming elections.[72]

According to Michael Hornsby of the London *Times* (23 April 1984):

> South Africa has toyed with the weapon of economic blockage, as well as military threats, in its efforts to bring Chief Jonathan to heel. Pretoria has also given support to the shadowy Lesotho Liberation Army of Ntsu Mokhehle, an exiled politician who was cheated of power in 1970 when Chief Jonathan declared martial law in the middle of an election which he was losing.
>
> Now, however, Pretoria appears to have dumped Mokhehle, an old Left-wing radical, who was always an improbable ally, in favour of a group of dissident politicians inside Lesotho who have formed a new party, the Basotho Democratic Alliance, to contest elections which the Government is talking of holding towards the end of this year or early next. They have promised to close down the Communist embassies if elected.
>
> The Alliance was actually formed over lunch at a government guesthouse in Pretoria on 6 January this year. Those present included the six Lesotho politicians concerned, Pik Botha, the SA Foreign Minister, and the chief of the South African security police. Botha offered financial support and, according to one participant, even discussed the possibility of direct SA intervention if Chief Jonathan managed to hang on to power.

THE ROLE OF THE LOCAL ACTORS IN THE CRISIS
South Africa, the Regional Power

The long-cherished ambition of successive Pretoria regimes has been that SA should be felt, seen and, above all, to be acknowledged as a regional power; this came close to fulfillment in 1984. Pretoria's increasingly assertive use of its military power and the crippling success of its destabilization policies since its first external military intervention on Unita's side in Angola in 1974/75 were instrumental in forcing its vulnerable neighbours—further weakened by drought and by the adverse economic winds from abroad, as well as by the inadequate support they received from the Soviet bloc—to enter into security agreements with Pretoria in order to enable them to weather their economic tribulations and to keep South Africa's army and the Pretoria-supported rebels from wreaking havoc on their still insecure and poorly-defended populations. The fact that Pretoria was able to force regimes deeply hostile to its policies to come to the negotiating table under *force majeure* gave some substance to its claims to be recognized as a regional power.

However, like all regional powers (the US in Central America, the USSR in Eastern Europe and Israel in the Middle East) there are strict limits to the way in which such power can be deployed. It can be wielded successfully only if it doesn't over-extend itself, or push governments and peoples into resistance other than by relying on traditionally organized military force, or to invoke the aid of an external strategic ally. For all the success it has had in demonstrating its strength as a regional power, the SA regime still lacks the ability to convert both its military and economic power into the kind of authority and influence which lessens hostility to its policies or reduces organized resistance to the *status quo* at home. The Achilles Heel of SA's power is the increasingly stronger internal resistance. While its opponents felt betrayed by the agreements made by the neighbour-states, they themselves showed no lessening in their resolve to carry on their struggle against apartheid. Further, the niggling fear in Pretoria is that, one day, the Communist Powers might become more of an actual threat than has so far been the case.

It was to capitalize on its Hour of Victory after signing the ceasefire agreement with Angola and the accords with Mozambique and Swaziland that Prime Minister Botha decided in June 1984 to embark on his first ever European visit in order to further his aim of winning international recognition of, and respectability for, SA's status as a regional power. The thinking in the Pretoria Establishment about its role as a regional power was well described in an officially-inspired commentary broadcast on the SABC on 15 June 1984:

> Conspicuous in the post-mortems on the European tour of Prime Minister P.W. Botha is the wide consensus over what it reflects of S.A.'s diplomatic situation in the world. The tour marked a significant shift in government attitudes on isolating this country, so much so, that European leaders were speaking of their need to maintain a dialogue with it on issues of common concern. That is, of course, partly accounted for by its emergence as a regional power capable of fundamentally influencing the course of events in Southern Africa. But it is also a consequence of the changed priorities in SA's own foreign policy, and of the events to which the change has given rise.
>
> This country today is a regional power, not only in a military and economic sense, but especially also in its international orientation. A top priority now is to build close and cooperative relations with other African countries, and, especially, with those countries in its sphere of influence in Southern Africa. It is no longer a question of the road to the West running through Africa, so much as the contribution the West can make to the first goal, which is the establishment of a stable and cooperative dispensation in Southern Africa. Such a regional dispensation is more important to SA security than being a paid-up member of a loose-knit Western alliance. But, of course,

if Western ties are improved as a result of rapprochement in the sub-continent, then it is a valuable bonus.

The policies of the Westtern nations towards SA are essentially opportunistic. The policies are not primarily the function of the country's internal political and social arrangements. Had they been, as claimed, centrally concerned with those arrangements, the substantial reforms of the past few years would have made far more impact than they did. By and large, Western policies towards SA are formed by the desire to maintain reasonably friendly relations with African governments. That is based on economic prestige and security considerations and, not least, on Africa's large voting bloc at the UN and in other forums.

Having come to accept that, SA's present rulers have reacted accordingly. Recognizing that the continental campaign against the country has more or less acquired a momentum of its own-sustained largely by an active radical group in the OAU-they have set out to expand the areas through which interstate relations are ultimately determined, mainly economic, technological and security co-operation. The obvious place to start was Southern Africa. As the regional Super Power, SA is best placed there to provide the means for stability and the kind of assistance on which a cooperative association may be based. On that course a few breakthroughs have been made and, predictably, Western governments are resuming a dialogue with SA. That is good for both sides, but the dialogue is being pursued on a new basis. Those governments are now dealing with a State that is concerned, first and foremost, with the welfare and security of its own region. International considerations come some way behind that priority.

Therefore, what Botha sought during his European trip was to re-establish the pre-1948 Smuts policy of gaining acceptance of SA as an indispensable and reliable ally of the West. By ending its isolation in Southern Africa and showing that it is possible, and desirable, for African leaders (even Marxists) to sit down at the same table with SA, it should be possible for Western leaders to do the same, and to acknowledge SA's valuable contribution to heading off anti-Western forces in the continent. What was now required was for the West to strengthen SA's initiatives and to provide the financial support needed to sustain the new momentum. As Pretoria sees it:

> The West's interest in the Southern African initiatives is a reflection of its own needs in the region. For economic and more especially strategic reasons, it would like to see the emergence of a moderate bloc of nations enjoying the stability and security that are necessary for economic development and freedom from Soviet adventurism. Western interests are best served in such a climate, Dr Chester Crocker pointed out again only last week. Creating such a climate is what the peace initiatives have been all about. In the past few months, the groundwork has been done through regional agreements in which governments have committed themselves to the essential requirements for a stable and cooperative dispensation. Legitimate security demands have been acknowledged and machinery has been created for joint action against subversive threats to the participating states.
>
> Similarly, joint action is underway to exploit economic interdependence in the region for the benefit of all the participants. The foundation is being well-laid. It is in the building of a durable structure upon it that the West is now being called on to deliver on the vague promises of the past. Southern Africa is in economically desperate straits, made all the worse by a severe drought and the prolonged international recession. The massive aid that is needed to rescue it from that plight is available only from the industrialized West.
>
> SA can and does offer a security umbrella, technical expertise based on knowledge of conditions, a source of tourist income, favourable economic arrangements, and a market for goods and labour. Portugal is prepared to offer manpower with appropriate skills and experience. But the vast sums that will be needed virtually to rebuild some

economic sectors can only come from the wealthy nations of Western Europe and North America.

What is needed is not an indiscriminate flood of handouts, Mr Pik Botha has pointed out. It is sensibly directed project aid. That is the challenge with which the West is faced. Its governments' spokesmen have welcomed the peace initiatives, as well they might considering the benefits to the West. The question now is whether those countries are going to meet their own obligations and are going to do their share to secure the future that all are looking forward to.[73]

Prime Minister Botha had become increasingly preoccupied with the cost to SA of the war in Namibia and the cost of keeping its economy afloat. Since late 1983 he has developed the habit of lecturing Western diplomats about the size of the burden SA was expected to carry 'to save Namibia from falling into the hands of the communists.' His offer, while in West Germany, that the Western Powers should take SA's place in Namibia and pay for its administration during the interim to independence was never seriously intended; it was a semi-jocular ploy thrown out to Bonn journalists over a breakfast conversation. Nevertheless, the concern about the cost of Namibia is very real. It has officially been stated to be in the region of R600m, 'apart from the hundreds of millions spent on maintaining law and order.' Indirect aid—such as the R90m written off annually by the SA Transport Services—comes on top of these figures. The territory's outstanding debt, amounting to 130% of its current income, is underwritten by Pretoria.[74] Prime Minister Botha complained to his Parliament:

> We have to curtail important development programmes, the construction of infra-structure, and even hold back salary increases in the Republic owing, among other things, to this financial assistance. Naturally, an independent South West Africa could expect to look forward to a continuation of SA's development orientation towards it. That would be in accordance with the policy of offering aid and cooperation through-out Southern Africa to promote regional stability. But the bulk of the shortfall will have to be recovered in other ways.

A central theme in SA policy statements about the situation in Angola and Mozambique has been that their governments, as well as Swapo and the ANC, are not free agents capable of acting independently of the USSR. As late as November and December 1983—on the eve of the beginning of the ceasefire agreements with the MPLA—the officially stated SA view was that 'the MPLA is little more than a puppet of the Soviets. It is they who will decide that issue (of a ceasefire).'[75] Pik Botha commented in December that 'Swapo and the MPLA were not free agents; it is the Soviet Union that is pulling the strings in Angola.'[76] Similar statements were made about President Machel's regime. The only logical conclusion, if the SA Government really believes what it says, is that it was Moscow who gave the orders to its 'puppets' to enter into agreements with SA. But this has never been suggested by Pretoria; it has not attempted to square the illogicality of its strong belief (which one must accept is the case) about the Angolans and Mozambicans being the puppets of Moscow with the independence they displayed in agreeing to sit down with SA, as well is by Swapo's offer to sign a ceasefire of its own.

Another aspect of this issue is SA's frequently expressed view (and fears) that the Soviet bloc was pouring huge quantities of arms into Southern Africa. According to the Defence Minister, Gen Malan:

> The Soviet Union had spent c.$64m in the past five years on direct support for terrorist organizations acting against SA. Training of terrorists of these organizations cost the Soviet Union c.$36m. In the same period the Soviet Union had spent c.$11m

in arms for Angola, Zimbabwe, Mozambique and Tanzania. In addition, the Soviet Union had spent c.$400m in the same period to keep its military personnel in Angola and the other so-called Frontline states. The Soviet expenditure amounted to almost $15,500m.[77]

Other figures provided by Gen Malan are that:

A total of 340 cargo ships and 224 cargo aircraft have been used by Angola and Mozambique to transport arms or supply Communist back-up. Detailed studies show that:

- During the past five years £5,800m has been spent on arms and ammunition in Angola alone. This does not include general defence expenditure. The figure for Mozambique is £212m, for Zimbabwe £24m, for Tanzania £484m, for Zambia £121m, and for Botswana £7.8m.
- It cost Marxists £2,060m during the past five years to keep military personnel in Angola. The figure for the other Frontline States is £436m. The logistic costs of the Frontline States amounted to £1,455m during the past five years.
- Since 1977 the ground forces of SA neighbouring states had increased more than 300% to 300,000 men.
- Tanks in neighbouring states during this time increased to 1,143, an increase of 200%.
- The number of aircraft increased during the same time to 600. A fifth of these are MiG fighters of the 17, 19 and 21 type. Some can be compared with the SA Mirage III.
- Apart from the arms build-up, 'tens of millions' of weapons were directly delivered to Swapo and the ANC. The cost of terrorist training for Swapo and the ANC in Africa is estimated to have cost Russia £63m during the past five years.
- The communist weapons include the latest ground-to-air missile, the so-called SAM-8, aircraft, ships, tanks, armoured troop-carriers, explosives, landmines, artillery, and infantry weapons are streaming into the countries.

Gen Malan said that SA would obviously have to spend more money on defence and safety to restore the balance of power. The country's arms would be modernized even more. He added that the advanced SAM-8 missiles being used in Angola and Mozambique, had caused SA to watch the situation very carefully. The missile creates an umbrella for Swapo and the ANC under which to operate in safety.

Assuming the accuracy of these intelligence-derived figures, and allowing for the fact that they are carefully selected and tailored for propaganda purposes and to justify the SADF's demands for ever-greater defence spending, the two interesting questions to which Gen Malan had not addressed himself were: first, why such a great input of Soviet military effort (not to mention the tens of thousands of Cuban combat troops) should have done so little to change the military equation in the region and, until recently, at least has offered no serious deterrent to the SADF striking at will against any targets in neighbouring countries; and second, why if the USSR is such a threat it has so tamely acquiesced in Angola and Mozambique negotiating their agreements with Pretoria?

It is difficult to know with Pretoria (as indeed with Moscow) how much they really believe in their own propaganda. However, about Gen Malan's obsessive concern about 'the threat of Soviet penetration' there can be no doubt.

Pretoria's stand over the withdrawal of the Cuban combat troops remained as firm as Reagan's. The UN Secretary-General said after his visit to Pretoria in September 1983 that the Cuban issue was the only remaining obstacle to implementing Resolution 435—perhaps an over-optimistic view, but one that nevertheless does reflect the priority that Pretoria has continued to give to this issue.[78]

Prime Minister Botha said in March 1984 that if the Cubans were not withdrawn SA might have to seek an alternative to a UN settlement.[79]

SA's formerly uncompromisingly hostile attitude towards Swapo was considerably modified in late 1983 and 1984; but this did not mean any lessening in its determination to curb the Organization in every way possible, militarily and politically. Although the Bothas continued to speak of Swapo as 'a pawn of Moscow', they came round to accepting Sam Nujoma as a negotiating partner without making their former preconditions that he should first renounce violence; this readiness to sit down with the Swapo leadership made possible the Namibian talks in Lusaka in May 1984. In private conversations with diplomats, the SA leaders were ready to indicate their willingness to see Swapo in government in Namibia after independence; they also floated the idea of negotiating an agreement whereby Swapo would join a coalition government with the internal parties to form a transition administration leading up to independence—an idea firmly rejected by Nujoma. (Also see Swapo's role below.)

Although the Pretoria regime continued to champion Unita's cause, it was ready because of its own interests, to damage it militarily, though not politically, by signing the ceasefire agreement with Luanda whereby they undertook to prevent arms supplies from reaching Savimbi's forces—while, nevertheless, still sticking to their denials that they ever gave military support to Unita. The SADF withdrawal from Southern Angola also freed the Angolan forces to concentrate their campaign against Unita—though, admittedly, not with any conspicuous initial success. Another aspect of SA's willingness to adjust its policies to the disadvantage of its ally was its abandonment of its earlier insistence that Unita should be given a role in any ceasefire agreement made with Luanda on the ground that it was not feasible to end the fighting in the south of Angola unless Unita were involved. However, SA did continue, after signing the ceasefire agreement, to promote the idea of involving Unita in negotiations over Namibia and for an extended ceasefire. In the run-up to the Lusaka talks on Namibia Pretoria had originally put forward the case for Unita to be present; but it later dropped this idea. It also tirelessly pressed on the MPLA the need to enter into talks with Unita to form a coalition government. (See the Course of Events, above.) The substantial change in Pretoria's view of Unita as an instrument for altering the character of the Angolan regime and of securing the removal of the Soviet bloc and Cuban presence was due to the realization that, however strong Unita was politically and militarily, it was not capable (even with SADF help) to capture Luanda. (See the Course of Events, above.)

THE ROLE OF THE FRONTLINE STATES
Although the leaders of the six Frontline States (FLS) (Tanzania, Angola, Botswana, Mozambique, Zambia and Zimbabwe) continued in 1983 and 1984 to meet regularly and to maintain a collective stand on current issues, there was also some evidence of differences of approach as well as a greater tendency by President Kenneth Kaunda to pursue independent initiatives. While the Zambian leader had the full support of his presidential colleagues for his initiative in bringing together the Angolans and South Africans which resulted in the Lusaka Agreement on a Ceasefire in February 1984, he did not have their backing—other than that of President dos Santos—for his initiative in convening the Lusaka talks on Namibia in May 1984.

One clear example of 'an agreement to disagree' among the FLS leaders was over President Samora Machel's decision to stage a show for the signing of the Nkomati Accord for, although all his colleagues supported his decision to enter into such an agreement, none of them accepted his invitation to be present on the occasion because they did not themselves wish to be seen consorting with Prime Minister Botha.

Lesotho was included for the first time as an *ad hoc* member in a FLS meeting of Defence and Security Ministers held at Inyanga (Zimbabwe) on 14/15 July 1983. Their final communiqué expressed 'great concern over the escalation of military attacks and the support for dissidents and bandits by the SA racist and fascist minority regime aimed at destabilizing the countries of the region.'[80] They agreed about the need 'to increase and strengthen cooperation and solidarity in defence and security among Southern African countries.'

Lesotho was also present at a security meeting of Defence and Security Ministers held in Maputo on 18 February 1984 where the previous decision 'to increase and strengthen defence and security cooperation' was repeated.[81] (Two days after this meeting, a Pretoria delegation arrived in Maputo to continue the negotiations that resulted in the Nkomati Accord; see Course of Events, above.)

Nigeria, which had previously been invited to attend FLS meetings on an *ad hoc* basis, was also closely involved in the tripartite talks between Luanda, Lagos and Lusaka over the ceasefire; this was disclosed by Nigeria's ambassador to Luanda, G. O. George, in February 1984.[82] There were no other reported instances of Nigerian involvement in FLS meetings.

Since mid-1983, the FLS leaders were following a two-track policy—searching for ways of improving their collective security arrangements while at the same time, encouraging a process of negotiations for stand-off agreements between Angola and Mozambique with Pretoria. The growing awareness among FLS leaders about the need for negotiations was articulated by the Tanzanian director of the OAU Bureau for African refugees, I. C. Mponzi, when he was reported to have said at Mbabane in November 1983 that 'SA is a military power to be reckoned with, and neighbouring states should not delude themselves that they could stand up to it.'[83]

Following the conclusion of the Luanda/Pretoria Ceasefire Agreement, Robert Mugabe told his Parliament that he welcomed the current dialogue between SA and its neighbours which, he said, was aimed 'at achieving peace in Southern Africa from which Zimbabwe could also benefit.'[84] He dismissed any idea of the current negotiations undermining the aims and efforts of SADCC.

President Kaunda was in an euphoric mood after the success of the Lusaka talks on the ceasefire in Angola, saying that independent Africa was looking forward to welcoming SA into the OAU, SADCC and the Preferential Trade Area (PTA), once Pretoria 'has proved that it is genuine by removing troops from Angola and granting independence to Namibia.'[85] (Normally the condition for such entry has been made subject to fundamental changes occurring inside SA). The euphoria radiated by Lusaka was reflected in a commentary broadcast from Johannesburg by the SABC on 23 February 1984:

Today in the Southern African region, a momentum for peace and stability has been created through cooperation and dialogue which hold the possibility for development and progress which was unthinkable only a few short months ago. The record reads like a peacemaker's textbook and credit must go to all the countries of Southern Africa. What is happening is that they are opting for realistic policies based on the essential interdependence of the region instead of the political rhetoric that through the years have heightened tensions, increased instability and promoted confrontation.

In a nutshell, this is the picture. SA and Angola, and SA and Mozambique, are involved in frequent face-to-face negotiations on ending the war in Angola and on normalizing relations. President Kaunda of Zambia is playing an important role in bringing SA and Angola together. Tanzania has described the SA/Mozambican talks as hopeful. SADCC, consisting of nine nations in Southern Africa, has done nothing to upset these developments and, in fact, by not inviting the ANC and Swapo—which the ANC condemned as conciliatory—SADCC promoted the cause of dialogue and peaceful process.

At the same time, the major Western powers and particularly the US, are not only actively trying to bring about reconciliation in Southern Africa but are thrilled over what has been achieved so far. The Americans have expressed pleasure and optimism while the British have hailed the peace pact between SA and Mozambique as a major diplomatic breakthrough. The British Foreign Office issued a statement declaring: 'We have long believed that only through negotiations can enduring solutions to the problems of Southern Africa be achieved.' Then there was the Portuguese Foreign Minister, Jaime Gama, who said that the normalization of relations between Mozambique and Pretoria was a great step towards world peace.

What is happening in Southern Africa, today, is that the States of the sub-continent have taken a good hard look at their security and economic realities. The point to stress is that with the Frontline States and SA, any action against one becomes an action against all, and all will resist with the considerable force and influence they have at their disposal.

The sub-continent of Southern Africa could be heading into an era of prosperity and good-will unprecedented in its history. The momentum has been created and all signs are that it is being maintained.

Further encouragement for this increasingly optimistic view was given by President Kaunda in an interview in April 1984 in which he said that the time had come for a summit meeting between the six FLS leaders and the SA Prime Minister, P. W. Botha.[86] He felt that such a meeting would 'cut across the problems of suspicions when discussing apartheid.' At the same time, he urged the need for Botha to meet with Nelson Mandela, Walter Sisulu, and Oliver Tambo. While he sympathized with SA, he warned South Africans not to allow the situation to explode since it would affect everybody in the region.

At their meeting held in Arusha after the conclusion of the Nkomati accord, the FLS leaders said they hope SA would honour its ceasefire agreement with Angola; they expressed their 'appreciation for Mozambique's commitment to continued moral, political and diplomatic support for the ANC against apartheid and for majority rule in SA'; supported Swapo as 'the sole and authentic representative of the Namibian people'; and warned that 'the alternative to free negotiations within SA' would inevitably be 'continued struggle by other means, including armed struggle. This struggle is being and will be conducted and led by the people of SA themselves, on their own initiative and within their own country'. The communiqué ended with the pledge that even though the struggle is long and hard, 'it will be carried on until final victory'. (For the full text of the Arusha Statement, see Appendix 3.)

Following the Arusha meeting, Mozambique emulated Zambia's tone of hopefulness by declaring in a commentary carried by its official news agency[87] that 'peace—always the Frontline's strategic objective—has now been accepted by SA', adding that:

> Once again the Frontline is witnessing the start of a new process. As in the past, the Frontline's first action will be to a common platform for effective action. It will define the strategy for the new process. This will certainly include demands that SA respect international law and rigorously respect the Accord it has signed. It will also include independence for Namibia. The Frontline will also act as a group in relation to apartheid in SA in this new phase in which Pretoria has said it will not resort to the use of aggression and threats of aggression.

While the failure of the Lusaka talks on Namibia in May 1984 temporarily checked this tide of euphoria, it did not dispel it altogether. Kaunda insisted on treating the failure as a setback rather than as a final defeat for the negotiating process—a view that found some echo also in Luanda. After talks with Kaunda in the Angolan capital in June, dos Santos said he regretted that the important meetings held in Lusaka had produced such poor results 'despite the devotion and dedication by Comrade President Kaunda':

> Nevertheless, Angola encourages him to pursue his diplomatic initiative in order to find a peaceful solution for the problems of Southern Africa based on the general principles of self-determination and independence of the colonized peoples, and respect for the independence and sovereignty of the countries in the region.[88]

While dos Santos continued to express his interest in seeking to resolve problems peacefully with SA, he also revealed growing anxieties about the stalemate in the negotiations in a speech he made on 15 June:

> In order to avoid implementing Security Council resolution 435, SA is inventing various pretexts, various excuses, because the whole world condemns SA's illegal presence in Namibia. Everyone is demanding that it withdraw from Namibia and hand over power to the people of Namibia. SA is resorting to these pretexts, and one of the excuses it uses is the presence of Cuban internationalists in the People's Republic of Angola. They say they cannot start to implement resolution 435 unless the Cuban internationalists leave Angola first. This is obviously nothing but an excuse; and why do they put forward this excuse? Because they want to continue to give arms to Unita; they want to continue to train the Unita bandits because they believe that Unita is going to destroy the Angolan revolution, destroy our government, and establish, here, a government of friends of SA. This is the reason for their manoeuvres. However, using this excuse merely serves to delay Namibia's independence and to try to strengthen Unita to destroy our revolution. We have no alternative but to liquidate Unita. And this is the task of all honest Angolans, of all true patriots in Angola.[89]

THE ROLE OF THE LIBERATION MOVEMENTS

Swapo and ANC were understandably upset by the negotiations between the FLS and Pretoria; while they accepted the State interests of the governments involved in the negotiations, they feared that these would take priority over their commitments to the liberation struggle. But they were trapped between their own interests and those of the governments on whom they remain so largely dependent.

Swapo's concern was that the ceasefire agreement with SA would blunt their military challenge, thereby reducing the pressures against Pretoria and so contribute to further delay in implementing Resolution 435. They were also concerned about the effects on the morale of their guerrilla forces by enforced inaction and by leaving those of their cadres already in Namibia at the total mercy of the SADF after the signing of the ceasefire. Like the FLS leaders, Swapo also chose to follow a two-track policy: on the one hand, they offered to talk directly to Pretoria to achieve a ceasefire paralleling that of Angola's (this was the central theme in Sam Nujoma's speech at the Lusaka talks) in order to help facilitate the implementation of Resolution 435; on the other hand, they fiercely insisted that, despite any obstacles put in their way, they would continue to keep up their armed struggle. Just how this second objective could be pursued so long as the Luanda–Pretoria ceasefire held up, was not explained. Clearly, though, Swapo believed (probably hoped) that the ceasefire would break down or, if it did not, that the next inevitable step would be for Pretoria to agree to sign a separate ceasefire agreement with them: this was the minimum they hoped would be achieved through their reluctant agreement to accept SA's terms to attend the Lusaka talks. Pretoria, however, was opposed to signing a ceasefire agreement with Swapo for two reasons: because it would give them official recognition as an armed movement, as distinct from recognizing its political role; and because it would relieve the pressures on Swapo's guerrillas inside Namibia. What Pretoria sought from Swapo was a formal repudiation of its campaign of violence, and its acceptance of recognized political opposition methods. These two conflicting interests remained irreconcilable. However, so long as Angola remained a party to the ceasefire agreement, Swapo was left with no real alternative other than to continue its diplomatic and political offensive and to accept, though not to admit, its seriously reduced capacity to continue its armed struggle.

The ANC's position was even more desperate than Swapo's. The blocking of transit rights for its armed cadres through Mozambique virtually shut off all their access routes to SA's borders. Zimbabwe and Botswana were already committed to denying the ANC transit facilities; Swaziland had become actively hostile since its secret agreement with Pretoria in 1982; Lesotho could not be used as a point of transit since, unless ANC cadres were airlifted to Maseru, they had no way of reaching it; besides, Lesotho was, in fact, unwilling to allow ANC guerrillas to operate from its territory.

What this meant for the ANC was that the high priority given to its armed struggle had to be altered and much greater emphasis placed on clandestine political organization within SA, as well as to try and train cadres inside the Republic for armed attacks against strategic objectives, relying on weapons already in the country and on others that might still be smuggled in. Even before this setback to their position in Mozambique, the ANC had in fact begun to make a much greater effort in organizing its supporters inside the country, working through sympathetic, unbanned political groups and the burgeoning trade union movement. It could even be argued that this shift of priority by the ANC in recruiting and training its cadres inside SA might produce a more promising method of struggle than by encouraging an increasing number of youths to go abroad to join the guerrilla forces.

THE ROLE OF UNITA AND MNR

Jonas Savimbi claimed in his 1984 New Year Message that 1983 was 'a year of great victories'.[90] Politically, he claimed, Unita was able to overcome ethnic difficulties, having established itself in 'non-traditional' support areas, i.e. in areas other than those of the Ovimbundu. Diplomatically, Unita claimed to have increased its support among African and Middle East governments. No names were given, but among those most frequently mentioned are Senegal, Morocco, Zaire, Saudi Arabia and Ivory Coast.[91] Savimbi has denied receiving aid from Israel and has insisted that Unita's ties of solidarity with Arab countries are well known. He claimed that Unita had succeeded in extending its lines more widely across the country. He pointed to the MPLA's failure to crush it after seven years of fighting despite the support it received from the Soviet bloc countries and the Cubans. The aims he set for Unita in 1984 were not only to gain more territory, but to administer the liberated areas and to mobilize public support against 'the Cuban presence and foreign domination.' However, Savimbi also followed a two-track policy by his continued offer to negotiate for the setting up of a coalition government with MPLA. This was a *leitmotiv* in all his major statements.

It is not really possible to evaluate with any degree of confidence the conflicting claims of Unita and the MPLA; all that can be said with certainty is that Unita remains in the field fighting and that it has succeeded in extending its operations; but to what extent this is due to the help received from the SADF remains difficult to determine: the proof would come only if the SA-Angola ceasefire holds up for a long enough period and if the monitoring team fails to establish continued SA help for Savimbi.

That the Pretoria regime has helped Unita is beyond reasonable doubt; even Willem Steenkamp, the *Cape Times* defence reporter, confirms this. (His standing with the SADF is shown by the fact that he was chosen by them as the first secretary to record the discussions of the Joint Monitoring Team.) He confirmed that 'there is no longer any doubt that SA supports Unita in one way or the other, though Pretoria flatly refuses to make any comment about the matter.'[92] In his view:

> There can be little doubt that Unita would be able to keep functioning without South African help. But there can be just as little doubt that without South African help it would not be as effective in harassing its opponents as is the case.

Steenkamp, who is also a reserve officer in the SADF and who has extensive knowledge of the terrain in south Angola, records these impressions:

> The latest available figures indicate Unita now has about 35,000 fighting men, and is said to be recruiting troops at a rate of more than 2,000 a year.
> It has a secure base in the Cuando-Cubango province in south-eastern Angola, a 'liberated zone', where the insurgents are in absolute control and are able to put down roots...
> After eight years of warfare, the MPLA has just two clear choices: It can continue to fight, and risk being reduced to a rump government stubbornly clinging to the area around Luanda (particularly if there was a Cuban withdrawal); or it can negotiate a settlement with Unita.
> Undue delay could be fatal to the MPLA. Dr Savimbi's overtures have been rejected time and again by Luanda, and military observers believe he is coming to the conclusion that he might as well go for the main objective, namely control of Angola and not just the southern region. He is not ready for a 'big push' yet, however. At the same time the MPLA cannot wipe him out either; so for the time being the two sides can only fight one another to a standstill, barring a sudden internal collapse or an unexpected reinforcement from outside.
> So the war's steady escalation is likely to continue for the time being (it is not generally known that so far this year Angola has had a higher incidence of armed clashes than any other country in Southern Africa). There is no doubt that from the South African point of view several benefits can be perceived if the conflict continues.
> • Dr Savimbi's movement is not hooked up to a life-support system. Therefore it does not cost much, and because it forces Luanda's troops to spread themselves thinly it makes SWA-based follow-up operations against Swapo insurgents so much easier.
> • It substantially hampers the Swapo operations in SWA. Recent figures indicate that a full 50% of the trained Swapo fighters resident in Angola are fighting with Fapla against Unita, while Swapo insurgents moving southwards must contend not only with security force raiders but also with Unita troops and informants.

Savimbi admitted that while Unita receives support from 'various countries ...the only door we have to get that support into Angola is through Namibia.'[93] Thus, Namibia's independence, or an effective ceasefire along the borders involving also the monitoring of the supply of external arms, would have a direct impact on Unita's struggle. Savimbi's response to the Pretoria-Luanda negotiations for a ceasefire was to remind those involved in the talks that:

They are (a) dealing with a weak government which, despite the backing of 45,000 Cubans, is losing more ground to Unita with every passing day; (b) dealing with a government which is isolated from the people, including even the people of northern Angola, who the MPLA claims to be its unflinching supporters; (c) dealing with a government which is incapable of reaching a decision on either war or peace and effectively honouring any agreement that might be signed; (d) they are forgetting, because of the current expedient need, that any ceasefire in any part of Angola— particularly in southern Angola—will never work without Unita participation. Unita regards the MPLA, and nobody else, as the only party it can deal with in the civil war which is setting the country ablaze. The coming weeks will prove whether Unita has a commitment and can honour that commitment it made to the Angolan people and international opinion.[94]

In Mozambique, the MNR's reliance on SA is much greater than Unita's. It has no known external supporters other than SA which supplies them with arms, logistical support and training facilities. While the MNR units already inside the country might be able to continue to maintain their operations for some time, yet, they faced inevitable defeat if their lifeline with SA were effectively cut, and if the Frelimo regime succeeds in both strengthening its army's effective strength and in removing the causes of discontent in the rural areas, which Machel has identified and which he has committed his regime to seek to remedy. The MNR is therefore likely to continue for some time to be capable of harassing Frelimo and to serve as a focus for mobilizing discontent; but it does not enjoy either the strong popular base or the military organization possessed by Unita.

THE ROLE OF THE EXTERNAL POWERS
THE CONTACT GROUP

The role of the Contact Group of the five Western members of the Security Council (the US, Britain, France, Canada and West Germany) changed considerably in 1983 when the latter four governments continued to disassociate themselves from Washington's insistence on linking Cuban withdrawals to the issue of Namibia's independence. The initiative for keeping alive the Western initiative was left largely in the hands of the Americans, who also assumed responsibility for convening *ad hoc* meetings to discuss the various stages reached in the course of its initiatives.

The French Government gained considerable kudos in Africa when its Foreign Minister, Claude Cheysson, announced on 7 December 1983 that his country was quitting the Group, saying that for the present it should 'be left dormant in the absence of any ability to exercise honestly the mandate confided to it.' However, on the day after Cheysson had made his announcement, a State Department official reported that Washington had received assurances from Paris 'that it is neither withdrawing from the Contact Group nor calling for its break-up.'[95] While the French said they felt no need for meetings of the Group at present, they said they 'looked forward to future collaboration' with their partners. The French, in fact, attended the very few *ad hoc* meetings of the Group that were arranged after their December statement.

Although Swapo called for the Contact Group to be disbanded since it was no longer serving any useful purpose, this was not the view taken by the FLS leaders.[96] Both at the Commonwealth leaders' meeting in New Delhi in November 1983, and in the following month at a meeting in New York, the six FLS members urged the Western Powers to keep their initiative alive, and urged its members to use their influence on President Reagan to drop his insistence on Cuban withdrawal as an essential condition for implementing Resolution 435.

The British Minister of State responsible for Africa at the Foreign Office,

Malcolm Rifkind, said while on a visit to Johannesburg in late 1983 that his Government did not believe the issue of Cuban withdrawal should be a precondition for Namibia's independence.[97] He also said he doubted whether the Cubans, if they remained in Angola, would move into Namibia after its independence; but if this were to happen it would be regarded as a very serious move by the Western Powers.

Both Britain and West Germany issued statements strongly criticizing SA for its renewed offensive into Angola in November 1983. The British Foreign Secretary, Sir Geoffrey Howe, described SA's policy of destabilizing its neighbours by cross-border raids as likely to precipitate the situation Pretoria feared most since it would make the Soviets and Cubans a more powerful factor in the region.[98] 'Punitive raids may buy a little time and provide a breathing-space,' he said, 'but the long-term costs are those of fear, bitterness and hatred.'

PORTUGAL'S ROLE

Lisbon played an increasingly more active role as a go-between in the negotiations between Angola and Mozambique with SA, as well as by increasing its own role as a trade and aid partner with its former colonies.[99] An unusually interesting aspect of this developing relationship was the recruitment by the retired Admiral Coutinho—known as the 'Red Admiral'—of a dozen former Portuguese army commandos who had fought in Angola to serve as trainers for Fapla. Because of their knowledge of the terrain and their command of Portuguese, this small group was seen as perhaps offering a new element in strengthening Fapla's own anti-guerrilla operations.

Lt-Col Melo Antunes, a member of Portugal's State Council, held talks with President dos Santos in Luanda in September 1983. He strongly condemned SA's 'aggression against Angola' and called on the international community to condemn, even more strongly, Pretoria's policies and its failure to implement international decisions.[100] He also condemned those who supported groups whose aim it was to destabilize Angola and Mozambique. 'Our position remains very firm in this regard,' he commented. 'It is one of strong brotherhood and solidarity with the Angolan people and their regimes.'

Although the Portuguese Foreign Minister, Jaime Gama, denied a Johannesburg report on 7 December that his country was playing a mediating role in arranging a meeting between Mozambique and SA, on the very next day the SA Foreign Minister said that he was due in Lisbon to 'discuss preparations for an early meeting between Mozambique's President and South Africa's Prime Minister.'[101] Botha claimed that Portugal had 'put forward an initiative aimed at solving the problem of Namibia'.[102] But no details were produced, either then or later. Botha's visit to Lisbon coincided with a visit there by the US Secretary of State. There seems little doubt that these talks provided an important link in the subsequent negotiations that led to the Nkomati Accord.

THE ROLE OF THE UNITED STATES

Spokesmen of the Reagan Administration describe its role in Southern Africa as that of a facilitator to promote 'the quest for regional peace and stability.'[103] The US Assistant Secretary of State for Africa, Chester Crocker, described this role as that of 'an honest broker in a region that includes many different kinds of political regimes.'[104] He added: 'It is very striking to us that everybody in that region is asking us to continue doing what we are doing. We're not being told to pack our bags and go home. We're being told to complete what we have started, and that is what we intend to do.'

Washington's view of its role as a broker or peace facilitator is that this requires of it to remain on good terms with all the parties in the conflict—the Frontline States, and SA, as well as the ANC and other opponents of apartheid; the internal parties in Namibia as well as Swapo and Unita. On the relationship with Unita, Crocker's deputy, Frank Wisner, explained:

> The present administration feels that there is a serious political problem to be solved in Angola and that Unita is one of the parties which can help reach an agreement. We believe this to be a real fact, not an assumption; it's the reality. There will not be peace in Angola without a political agreement among the interested parties. We want peace in Angola. In this context, peace in Angola means also a settlement for Namibia. Such a settlement will entail the establishment of an agreement with SA which is also acceptable to the Luanda Government, and which would allow the UN to guarantee security on the Angolan/Namibian border. In this overall context Unita is an important factor. Denying this would be pure blindness and it is important to bear this fact in mind. But at the same time, we must be aware that this is a long and hard process and that important negotiations with the Luanda Government are taking place.[105]

In what was presented as a major US policy statement, the Under-Secretary of State, Lawrence Eagleberger, told the National Conference of Editorial Writers on 23 June 1983 that:

> The US. . . . proceeds from the conviction that our national interest and the interests of the West demand an engagement—constructive and peaceful—in the affairs of Southern Africa. The US is, I believe, uniquely situated to speak to all sides in the conflict. . . . One way or another the States of Southern Africa have to evolve explicit or tacit ground rules for cooperation and coexistence, for the alternatives are all too obvious . . . Unless there is peace and stability in Southern Africa, it will prove impossible to encourage essential change in South Africa—and by change I mean a basic shift away from apartheid. . . .
> We recognize that it is not realistic to speak of regional security without reference to the domestic political dimension of coexistence between states. The dilemma we face is that peaceful domestic change in Southern Africa and regional security are both urgently needed if the risks of growing international strife are to be avoided.
> In SA the imperative of peaceful change is domestic: SA has enjoyed sovereign statehood for over 70 years. Yet, a structure of regional stability in Southern Africa is unlikely to take root in the absence of basic movement away from a system of legally entrenched rule by the White minority in SA. By the same token, peaceful change toward social justice and equality for all South Africans is unlikely to happen in a regional climate of escalating strife and polarization. . . .

While current constitutional and other reforms in SA were described as 'constructive in terms of changes in their (Pretoria's) approaches', the Secretary of State, George Shultz, told the Conservative Political Action Conference in Washington in March 1984 that the changes do not go 'nearly far enough. I don't think we can reiterate often enough the repugnant nature of the apartheid system.'[106]

The US policy towards Pretoria continues to be that defined as 'constructive engagement'—a policy which requires the retention of friendly relations with the Pretoria regime in order best to influence it to change the unacceptable features of its political system. Frank Wisner offered this closer definition of the US approach:

> Any analysis of the region must pay appropriate attention to the reality of SA. The reality of its predominance as the region's economic and military power cannot be

diminished or circumvented in dealing with questions of stability and economic development in Southern Africa. On the other hand, SA is a deeply divided nation facing an uncertain future, and the resulting acute paranoia of White SA colours its view of the region. Too few South Africans believe they can live in peace and protect their way of life except through the exercise of force; they will not—merely to make (their) critics in the West feel more comfortable—blindly surrender (their) political advantages.

A SA beset by real or imagined enemies and out of touch with the West can do grave damage to our interests in the region. The aim of the Reagan Administration's 'constructive engagement' policy is to influence in as careful and effective a manner as possible SA's bitter internal debate about how the country will face its future. The US is convinced that a SA under less of a threat from neighbouring states is a SA in a stronger position to pursue internal reform. One of the pillars of US Southern African policy, the quest for regional peace and stability, proceeds from that conviction.

The apartheid system of racial separation in SA is morally wrong and unacceptable to the US Government and the American people; that said, however, the Administration feels that SA's racial dilemma can be resolved more effectively when approached not as a 'moral issue' but as a 'political problem' of Black participation. Moral problems, are often intractable, and moralistic interpretations of political conflicts lead to all or nothing confrontations, rather than to solutions . . . We are for change—a progressive and rapid movement to a system based on the consent of the governed. In this time of flux and change, the SA Government needs a developing relationship with the West. But the relationship between Washington and SA, in particular, and the West and SA in general, must be reciprocal. The point has been made clear to Pretoria: that a constructive relationship with the West is not a one-way street; SA must respect Western interests in the region. Pretoria cannot have it both ways. SA claims to be part of the West; we accept that as an historical fact; but if that is the case, Pretoria must respect Western norms and sensibilities to a much greater extent, both in the management of its internal affairs and in the way it deals with its neighbours. SA cannot pose as a Western bastion if it offends Western values and if its behaviour serves the interests of the Kremlin.

SA attempts to persuade the US to agree to sponsor changes of Resolution 435 were firmly resisted; the State Department consistently took the view that it was an agreed package that could not be undone;[107] The Reagan Administration, however, remained wedded to the Cuban troops withdrawal from Angola as being essential to progress towards stability in the region, but continued to insist that this issue should not be directly linked to the implementation of Resolution 435, but to regional security arrangements. On this issue, the US was completely isolated in the world community, except for SA. The other members of the Contact Group publicly disassociated themselves from this stand, which was criticized by the Commonwealth leaders at their summit in New Delhi;[108] as well as by the FLS. President Kaunda cited it as one of the reasons for the failure of the Lusaka talks on Namibia.[109] Having originated the demand for Cuban withdrawal, the American view, as reiterated by Crocker, was that Pretoria could not be ignored on this issue.[110] He insisted: 'With all the goodwill in the world, UN Resolution 435 is not going to implement itself. Its implementation will require a political decision by SA which controls Namibia, albeit illegally.' He added he was convinced that 'once there was an agreement on the Cuban issue, Namibia's independence would follow.'

Instead of seeing the Cuban issue linked to Namibia, he preferred to see negotiations for the Cuban withdrawal as being 'parallel' to the talks over Namibia, related to achieving peaceful conditions within Angola itself.[111]

Critics of American policies in Southern Africa focussed on two principal aspects: the introduction of the Cuban issue, which was seen as introducing East–

West conflicts into the region; and the 'constructive engagement' approach which was seen as giving positive support to the Pretoria regime. The introduction of the Cuban issue not only complicated the negotiations over a Namibian settlement, but ended up as the last obstacle to embarking on Namibia's independence. Washington's answer to the criticism over its Cuban stand is that if Reagan had not raised the issue himself, Pretoria would have done so anyway. Even if this were so, there can't be any serious doubt that the tough American stand on this issue both encouraged and strengthened Pretoria's stand: if the US had chosen to side with the rest of the Contact Group, Pretoria could not so easily have held out against collective Western pressures.

The argument over whether the Americans are responsible for introducing the East–West conflict into the region is a circular one: the US insists that it was Soviet involvement on the MPLA's side in the Angolan civil war and the introduction of Cuban combat troops which internalized the conflict; to which the Communists' reply is that their involvement was due to Western intervention on the side of Portuguese colonialism. Both statements are true. Perhaps more interesting than pursuing this profitless argument, is the position adopted by the US in seeking to play down the idea of the Soviets being a serious threat in Southern Africa; the Washington stand on this issue is diametrically opposed to Reagan's general stance as well as to Pretoria's. In a talk he delivered in Munich in November 1983, Frank Wisner declared that even though there is 'a substantial Soviet presence' in Southern Africa, the region lies well outside the Soviet Union's zone of primary or even secondary interests.[112] He added:

> We believe that Moscow is aware of that fact and, in reality, spends little time thinking about the area. That analysis disconcerts our South African friends— perhaps disappoints those who seek an easy explanation for SA problems—as they see themselves the target of a 'national onslaught' by the Soviets. We do not believe they are.

Whatever the validity in the criticisms of US policy, what is undeniably true is Chester Crocker's claim that everybody in the region—whatever their disagreements with aspects of Washington's policies—accepts and encourages the American role as a catalyst/facilitator/honest broker in the region. However, some critics—usually themselves Americans—claim that the negotiating process in Southern Africa would have proceeded irrespective of the US role and may, in fact, have made even more progress without US involvement.[113]

As against this view, a strong case can be made out to show that on several occasions American initiatives have been directly responsible for getting the stalled talks moving again. But the facilitating role has not been left exclusively to the Americans or the Contact Group; nor did they seek to do so.

The Portuguese played a key role in arranging the meetings between the Mozambicans and South Africans which led finally to the Nkomati Accord, while President Kaunda's two initiatives—the one successful, in hosting the conference that led to the signing of the ceasefire agreement between Pretoria and Luanda, and the other unsuccessful, in convening the Namibian talks in Lusaka— contributed importantly to keeping up the momentum of the negotiating process. The US was, in fact, involved in the Portuguese initiative and in Kaunda's first, but not his second, initiative.

THE ROLE OF THE SOVIET BLOC

Contrary to what is believed by some—especially by the Pretoria regime—the Soviet leadership has been careful to limit its military commitments in Southern

Africa. It has its hands full in Afghanistan, Syria and Iraq, and is anxiously preparing for the *denouement* in Iran after the passing of the Khomeini regime; it is heavily committed, militarily, in Ethiopia, and economically in Cuba and Vietnam. Even Super-powers have limited resources and, of course, have their own priorities. For the present, at least, a military confrontation with the SADF is not one of Moscow's priorities. Its commitments in Southern Africa are limited to providing military and diplomatic support for Angola and, less so, for Mozambique; but even in Angola's case it is not on a scale matching, for example, that of Ethiopia, let alone Syria. It is also committed to providing arms and diplomatic support for the ANC and Swapo. As for economic aid, Moscow has made it clear to Presidents dos Santos and Samora Machel (and also to Chairman Mengistu of Ethiopia) that they should seek to attract whatever economic aid they can manage to extract from the West since the Comecon members are themselves under severe economic constraints.

These Soviet positions were explicitly stated to the Angolan and Mozambican leaders. It can be stated for a fact that Samora Machel was counselled on at least three different occasions by Soviet leaders to do everything possible to avoid an open military confrontation with South Africa—the first was by Brezhnev; the second by the then President Podgorny, when he paid a State visit to Maputo; and the third was by Andropov when Machel visited Moscow in 1983.

The Soviet bloc countries—while providing a fair amount of technical assistance and making an attempt to improve their trade with Angola, Mozambique and other Frontline States—have largely filled the role of armourers and military trainers in the region as well as giving important diplomatic support to the cause of the liberation struggle. The Soviet bloc's supply of weapons to Angola was substantial (see SA figures cited above) and increasingly sophisticated; but despite the considerable help in military training given by Soviet and East German teams, the Angolan army (Fapla) did not have a chance to develop into an effective fighting force. As in their earlier experience in the Middle East, Moscow was keenly frustrated by the failure of their military efforts, buttressed by the Cubans, to act as a deterrent to the SADF, which also made off with considerable quantities of captured Soviet-supplied weapons. The Soviet military effort in Mozambique was on a much smaller scale than in Angola, and even less effective there. Soviet supplies of weapons to other Frontline States (mainly Zambia and Botswana) was not on a significant scale.

Developments in 1983 and, especially, in 1984 showed up the Soviet role of strategic ally as being so weak as to be almost derisory. This was especially disappointing to the Angolans and Mozambicans whose Treaties of Friendship with Moscow had led them to believe that, whatever the limitations to the relationship by Moscow, they were acquiring a powerful strategic ally. The least that might be expected from such an ally—especially when it also happens to be a Super-power—is that it will, at least, serve as a credible deterrent to an aggressor, particularly when the aggressor is itself, at best, a middle-class power. But Pretoria was entirely undeterred. Even when, in January 1984, Moscow delivered a warning message to Pretoria (sent through the SA ambassador at the UN) it was careful to explain that its message should be regarded not as 'a threat' but as a warning to Pretoria of the 'logical and reasonable consequences of its conduct'.[114] However, the consequences were not spelt out.

A week after this Soviet Note was delivered, military delegations from Angola and Cuba met with the Soviets in Moscow in a well-publicized meeting (unusual for such events) to examine ways of meeting the offensive launched against Angola by SA six weeks earlier.[115] *Tass* reported that the talks had stressed 'solidarity with the Angolan people's struggle in defence of their revolutionary gains', and that an accord (Russian: *dogovorennost*) had been reached to provide additional aid to help strengthen Angola's defence capacity, independence and territorial integrity.[116]

Just one month earlier, Angola's Minister of State Security, Juliao Mateus Paulo Dino Matross, had declared at a ceremony marking the 27th anniversary of the founding of the MPLA that:

> Naturally, our allies are the socialist countries which render all-round and funda-
> mental assistance to our country in the defence of the fatherland and in various other
> fields of national reconstruction. Standing at our side, cooperating with us in the
> building of a socialist society, are the USSR and the Federal Republic of Cuba. At the
> same time, they are helping us wage a continuing struggle to guarantee the protection
> of the legitimate interests of our people.[117]

However, also at that precise time, the Angolans were entering upon negotiations with the US and SA about arrangements for a ceasefire because of the failure of Fapla and its allies to halt the SADF invasion of Angolan territory.

In the case of Mozambique, the USSR's military posture against Pretoria was confined to its navy 'showing the flag' by making periodic visits to the area. In late November 1983, a Soviet naval force rounded the Cape on its way from Luanda to Maputo.[118] In June 1984 two Soviet warships, the frigate *Rezky* and the landing ship *Aleksandr Tortsev,* paid a brief visit to Maputo.[119] However, the Soviet navy did not deter SA submarines from landing MNR rebels on the coastline of Inhamba province. (It is apparently almost impossible even for modern navies to detect small submarines in the turbulent coastal waters as are encountered in the Mozambique Channel.)

Diplomatically, it was humiliating for the USSR to stand passively by while two of its allies, bound by Friendship Treaties, were being ravaged by SA, forced to turn for economic and diplomatic assistance to the US and other Western nations and, finally, compelled to enter into agreements with Pretoria. It was a salutary lesson of the present limits of Soviet military commitments in Southern Africa.

THE ROLE OF CUBA

Despite an increasing number of casualties and of prisoners taken in Angola, Cuba showed no eagerness to withdraw its 10,000 to 15,000 combat troops from Angola except under conditions agreed between President Dos Santos and Castro in Havana in 1983.[120] The Angolan leaders insisted that they would not ask the Cuban combatants to leave until Namibia's independence had been obtained. Cuba's Vice-President, Carlos Rafael Rodriquez, declared in an interview in March 1984: 'We have never envisaged an over-long presence of our forces. We are prepared for the moment when it is necessary and appropriate to begin the process of withdrawal.'[121]

On 19 March 1984, after a three-day visit to Havana, President dos Santos signed a joint communiqué with Fidel Castro which demanded as 'an indispensable condition' for the withdrawal of Cuban troops that SA and the US, as well as their allies, should end all aid to Unita and other rebel groups in Angola.[122] The communiqué stated that Unita is 'funded, armed and led by SA and its allies.'

Castro also reaffirmed his support for Swapo when Sam Nujoma visited Havana in June 1984.

NOTES

1. See Colin Legum: *The Crisis in Southern Africa; Africa Contemporary Record (ACR)* 1982–83. All references to country surveys and essays are to *ACR* 1984–85.
2. For the history of the MNR, see *ACR* 1982-83, ppA12-19.
3. Interview with *Seminario*, Lisbon, 17 December 1983.
4. SA Broadcasting Corporation (SABC), Johannesburg, 10 January 1984.
5. *The Star*, Johannesburg, 24 October 1983.
6. SABC, 29 October 1983.
7. *Rand Daily Mail* (RDM), 16 June 1983.
8. SABC, 9 January 1984.
9. *Africa Wireless File (AF)*, US Embassy, Paris, 1 December 1983.
10. SABC, 9 January 1984.
11. SABC, 31 January 1984.
12. Radio Luanda, 17 February 1984.
13. SABC, 17 February 1984.
14. *AF*, 24 February 1984.
15. SABC, 26 February 1984.
16. Radio Luanda, 2 March 1984.
17. *SABC*, 12 March 1984.
18. *Daily Telegraph (DT)*, 21 March 1984.
19. *The Times (TLT)*, 24 March 1984. 1984.
20. *Ibid*, 26 April 1984; SABC, 26 April 1984.
21. See *ACR* 1980-81, ppA6-10.
22. SABC, 22 May 1984.
23. *The Guardian (GDN)*, Manchester, 28 May 1984.
24. *TLT*, 1 June 1984.
25. *DT*, 14 June 1984.
26. *Ibid*.
27. *ANGOP*, 24 June 1984.
28. *Ibid*, 4 July 1984.
29. SABC, 19 October 1983.
30. Radio Maputo (RM), 3 February 1984.
31. *Ibid*, 27 December 1983.
32. See *ACR* 1982-83, ppA12-19.
33. *RDM*, 7 October 1983.
34. *International Herald Tribune (IHT)*, Paris, 10 October 1983.
35. *RDM*, 8 June 1983.
36. SABC, 9 December 1983. Also see essay on Portugal and Africa.
37. Radio Lisbon, 20 December 1983.
38. *GDN*, 21 December 1983.
39. SABC, 21 December 1983.
40. *Ibid*, 17 January 1984.
41. For text of the treaty see *ACR* 1977-78, ppC17-19.
42. *GDN*, 21 February 1984.
43. *RM*, 3 March 1984.
44. *RM*, 6 March 1984.
45. *GDN*, 22 May 1984.
46. *RM*, 7 March 1984.
47. *Mozambique Information Agency (AIM)*, 26 June 1984.
48. *RM*, 28 May 1984.
49. *Financial Times (FT)*, London, 21 March 1983.
50. *Radio Freedom, Addis Ababa (RFAA)*, 16 March 1984.
51. *RM*, 11 April 1984.
52. *RFAA*, 4 July 1984.
53. *RDM*, 22 March 1984.
54. *AIM*, 15 March 1984.
55. Lisbon Radio, 18 March 1984.
56. *Ibid*.
57. SABC, 17 March 1984.
58. *AIM*, 16 March 1983.
59. *IHT*, 12 June 1984.
60. *RDM*, 22/23 May 1984.
61. For details, see chapter on Zimbabwe.
62. *Star*, 20 June 1983.
63. Radio Harare (RH), 4 April 1983.
64. See chapters on Botswana and Zimbabwe.
65. *RH*, 25 July 1983.
66. *AF*, 10 May 1984.
67. *AF*, 11 May 1984.
68. *SABC, 31 March 1984*.
69. *See ACR* 1982-83; also see chapters on Swaziland and SA.
70. For details see chapter on Swaziland and SA chapter under 'Black Politics'.
71. For details, see chapter on Lesotho; also see Michael Hornsby, *TLT*, 25 July 1983; and Mike Pitso, *RDM*, 2 December 1983.
72. Radio Maseru, 27 May 1984.
73. SABC Commentary, 5 June 1984.
74. SABC, 6 June 1984.
75. SABC, 9 November 1983.
76. SABC, 28 December 1983.
77. Interview with *Rapport*, Johannesburg; quoted by *South African Newsletter*, SA Embassy, London, September 1983.
78. *TLT*, 1 September 1983.
79. *IHT*, 24, 25 March 1984.
80. Radio Luanda, 17 July 1983.
81. Radio Maputo, 18 February 1984.
82. Radio Lagos.
83. *RDM*, 8 November 1983.
84. *RH*, 23 February 1984.
85. *Zambia Mail*, Lusaka, 22 February 1984.
86. *Leadership SA*, Johannesburg, April 1984.

87. *AIM* 30 April 1984.
88. Radio Launda, 7 June 1984.
89. *Angola Information Bulletin,* London, 5 July 1984.
90. Voice of the Resistance of the Black Cockerel (VRBC), 7 January 1984.
91. *Ibid,* 19 February 1984.
92. Quoted in *RDM,* 23 September 1983.
93. Quoted in *SA Digest,* London, 15 July 1984.
94. VRBC, 19 February 1984.
95. *AF,* 8 December 1983.
96. *New African,* London, February 1984.
97. SABC, 9 November 1983.
98. *DT,* 15 November 1983.
99. See essay on Portugal and Africa.
100. Radio Luanda, 7 September 1983.
101. Radio Lisbon, 7 and 8 December 1983.
102. *Ibid,* 12 December 1983.
103. Frank Wisner, US Deputy Secretary of State for African Affairs, *AF,* 25 November 1983.
104. Chester Crocker's TV interview, Washington, *AF* 24 May 1984.
105. *AF,* 23 December 1983.
106. *AF,* 5 March 1984.
107. See, for example, the statement by Daniel H. Simpson, Director of the State Department's Office of Southern African Affairs; *AF* 26 March 1984; and a statement by Alan Romberg, State Department Deputy Spokesman, *AF* 6 June 1984.
108. See text of resolution in Documents Section.
109. See President Kaunda's speech, Appendix 2.
110. Crocker in USIA-TV interview, *AF,* 30 August 1983.
111. *AF,* 12 January 1983.
112. *AF,* 25 November 1983.
113. See Ed Brown; *op cit.*
114. *GDN,* 3 January 1984; SABC, 4 January 1984.
115. *TLT,* 6 January 1984.
116. *Tass,* 12 January 1984; 6 January 1984; *Pravda,* 13 January 1984.
117. Radio Luanda, 11 December 1983.
118. SABC, 29 November 1983.
119. Radio Maputo, 5 June 1984.
120. See *ACR* 1982-83, pA39.
121. *IHT,* 14 March 1983.
122. *ANGOP,* 27 June 1983.

Appendix 1.

The Nkomati Accord

Agreement on non-aggression and good neighbourliness between the Government of the People's Republic of Mozambique and the Government of the Republic of South Africa

The Government of the People's Republic of Mozambique and the Government of the Republic of South Africa, hereinafter referred to as the High Contracting Parties; RECOGNISING the principles of strict respect for sovereignty and territorial integrity, sovereign equality, political independence and the inviolability of the borders of all states; REAFFIRMING the principle of non-interference in the internal affairs of other states; CONSIDERING the internationally recognized principle of the right of peoples to self-determination and independence and the principle of equal rights of all peoples; CONSIDERING the obligation of all states to refrain, in their international relations, from the threat or use of force against the territorial integrity or political independence of any state; CONSIDERING the obligation of states to settle conflicts by peaceful means, and thus safeguard international peace and security and justice; RECOGNIZING the responsibility of states not to allow their territory to be used for acts of war, aggression or violence against other states; CONSCIOUS of the need to promote relations of good neighbourliness based on the principles of equality of rights and mutual advantage; CONVINCED that relations of good neighbourliness between the High Contracting Parties will contribute to peace, security, stability and progress in Southern Africa, the Continent and the World; Have solemnly agreed to the following:

Article One

The High Contracting Parties undertake to respect each other's sovereignty and independence and, in fulfilment of this fundamental obligation, to refrain from interfering in the internal affairs of the other.

Article Two

1. The High Contracting Parties shall resolve differences and disputes that may arise be-

tween them and that may or are likely to endanger mutual peace and security or peace and security in the region, by means of negotiation, enquiry, mediation, conciliation, arbitration or other peacful means, and undertake not to resort, individually or collectively, to the threat or use of force against each other's sovereignty, territorial integrity or political independence.

2. For the purposes of this article, the use of force shall include *inter alia-*

(a) attacks by land, air or sea forces;

(b) sabotage;

(c) unwarranted concentration of such forces at or near the international boundaries of the High Contracting Parties;

(d) violation of the international land, air or sea boundaries of either of the High Contracting Parties.

3. The High Contracting Parties shall not in any way assist the armed forces of any state or group of states deployed against the territorial sovereignty or political independence of the other.

Article Three

1. The High Contracting Parties shall not allow their respective territories, territorial waters or air space to be used as a base, thoroughfare, or in any other way by another state, government, foreign military forces, organisations or individuals which plan or prepare to commit acts of violence, terrorism or aggression against the territorial integrity or political independence of the other or may threaten the security of its inhabitants.

2. The High Contracting Parties, in order to prevent or eliminate the acts or the preparation of acts mentioned in paragraph (1) of this article, undertake in particular to—

(a) forbid and prevent in their respective territories the organisation of irregular forces or armed bands, including mercenaries, whose objective is to carry out the acts contemplated in paragraph (1) of this article;

(b) eliminate from their respective territories bases, training centres, places of shelter, accommodation and transit for elements who intend to carry out the acts contemplated in paragraph (1) of this article;

(c) eliminate from their respective territories centres or depots containing armaments of whatever nature, destined to be used by the elements contemplated in paragraph (1) of this article;

(d) eliminate from their respective territories command posts or other places for the command, direction and co-ordination of the elements contemplated in paragraph (1) of this article;

(e) eliminate from their respective territories communication and telecommunication facilities between the command and the elements contemplated in paragraph (1) of this article;

(f) eliminate and prohibit the installation in their respective territories of radio broadcasting stations, including unofficial or clandestine broadcasts, for the elements that carry out the acts contemplated in paragraph (1) of this article;

(g) exercise strict control, in their respective territories, over elements which intend to carry out or plan the acts contemplated in paragraph (1) of this article;

(h) prevent the transit of elements who intend or plan to commit the acts contemplated in paragraph (1) of this article, from a place in the territory of either to a place in the territory of the other or to a place in the territory of any third state which has a common boundary with the High Contracting Party against which such elements intend or plan to commit the said acts;

(i) take appropriate steps in their respective territories to prevent the recruitment of elements of whatever nationality for the purpose of carrying out the acts contemplated in paragraph (1) of this article;

(j) prevent the elements contemplated in paragraph (1) of this article from carrying out from their respective territories by any means acts of abduction or other acts, aimed at taking citizens of any nationality hostage in the territory of the other High Contracting Party; and

(k) prohibit the provision on their respective territories of any logistic facilities for carryin' out the acts contemplated in paragraph (1) of this article.

3. The High Contracting Parties will not use the territory of third states to carry out or support the acts contemplated in paragraphs (1) and (2) of this article.

Article Four
The High Contracting Parties shall take steps, individually and collectively, to ensure that the international boundary between their respective territories is effectively patrolled and that the border posts are efficiently administered to prevent illegal crossings from the territory of a High Contracting Party to the territory of the other, and in particular, by elements contemplated in Article Three of this Agreement.

Article Five
The High Contracting Parties shall prohibit within their territory acts of propaganda that incite a war of aggression against the other High Contracting Party and shall also prohibit acts of propaganda aimed at inciting acts of terrorism and civil war in the territory of the other High Contracting Party.

Article Six
The High Contracting Parties declare that there is no conflict between their commitments in treaties and international obligations and the commitments undertaken in this Agreement.

Article Seven
The High Contracting Parties are committed to interpreting this Agreement in good faith and will maintain periodic contact to ensure the effective application of what has been agreed.

Article Eight
Nothing in this Agreement shall be construed as detracting from the High Contracting Parties' right of self-defence in the event of armed attacks, as provided for in the Charter of the United Nations.

Article Nine
1. Each of the High Contracting Parties shall appoint high-ranking representatives to serve on a Joint Security Commission with the aim of supervising and monitoring the application of this Agreement.
2. The Commission shall determine its own working procedure.
3. The Commission shall meet on a regular basis and may be specially convened whenever circumstances so require.
4. The Commission shall—
(a) Consider all allegations of infringements of the provisions of this Agreement;
(b) advise the High Contracting Parties of its conclusions; and
(c) make recommendations to the High Contracting Parties concerning measures for the effective application of this Agreement and the settlement of disputes over infringements or alleged infringements.
5. The High Contracting Parties shall determine the mandate of their respective representatives in order to enable interim measures to be taken in cases of duly recognised emergency.
6. The High Contracting Parties shall make available all the facilities necessary for the effective functioning of the Commission and will jointly consider its conclusions and recommendations.

Article Ten
This Agreement will also be known as "The Accord of Nkomati".

Article Eleven
1. This Agreement shall enter into force on the date of the signature thereof.
2. Any amendment to this Agreement agreed to by the High Contracting Parties shall be effected by the Exchange of Notes between them.
IN WITNESS WHEREOF, the signatories, in the name of their respective governments, have signed and sealed this Agreement, in quadruplicate in the Portuguese and English languages, both texts being equally authentic.

THUS DONE AND SIGNED at the common border on the banks of the Nkomati River, on this the sixteenth day of March 1984.

Samora Moises Machel, Marshal of the Republic, President of the People's Republic of Mozambique President of the Council of Ministers

Pieter Willem Botha, Prime Minister of the Republic of South Africa

For the Government of the People's Republic of Mozambique

For the Government of the Republic of South Africa

Appendix 2.
Machel's Speech
Speech by His Excellency the President of the People's Republic of Mozambique, Marshal Samora Moises Machel, on the occasion of the signing of the Accord of Nkomati, 16 March 1984.

Mister Prime Minister of the Republic of South Africa, Mrs Botha, Ministers, Dear Guests, Ladies and Gentlemen.

The signing of the agreement of non-aggression and good neighbourliness is a high point in the history of relations between our two States and a high point in the history of our region. The principles we have enshrined in the Accord of Nkomati are universally valid ones that govern relations between sovereign states regardless of their political, economic and social systems. They are principles that open new perspectives for the relationship between our States, in so far as they guarantee a solid and lasting peace between the two neighbouring countries. They are principles that establish a new situation in our region, a situation of peace and good neighbourliness.

The Accord of Nkomati is a unique document among the states of our region. The need for it arose not so much from the differences between us, but above all from the process of confrontation that developed and created the awareness that this was not the road that would be in the best interests of our two countries. By undertaking here a solemn commitment not to launch aggressive actions of any sort against one another, we have created conditions for the establishment, with honour and dignity, of a new phase of stability and security on our common borders.

We do not want southern Africa, and our two countries in particular, to be the theatre for a generalised conflict. That is why we have enshrined in the Accord of Nkomati the principle that our states will not be used by any other state or group of states to jeopardize the sovereignty, territorial integrity or independence of our countries.

We are thus laying the foundation for a definitive break of the cycle of violence that had been established in this region of the continent. A violence that was above all the result of the burdensome legacies we carry with us. A violence that began some centuries ago, when the dignity and personality of African peoples were trampled on by the aggression, domination and exploitation of European colonialism. Africa was ravaged by the brutality of slave wars and colonial conquest, which brought division, humiliation, poverty and destruction to the peoples of the continent.

We are a continent of survivors. We survived slavery, we survived wars of conquest and we survived the brutality of repression when we decided to become masters of our own destinies. For that reason we are fully cognisant of the value of peace and of the need to reject the legacies that divide us. We thus assume, before the world and before history, responsibility for guaranteeing the perpetuity of this agreement and eliminating the root causes of violence, war and confrontation.

Mr Prime Minister, the differences between our political, economic and social concepts are great and even opposed to one another. We recognised these differences honourably on the difficult road of frank and open talks that led to this agreement. We shall continue to be aware of the remaining contradictions but we are able to recognise that we are indissolubly linked by geography and by proximity.

Peaceful coexistence, mutual respect, and relations of good neighbourliness are the only rational alternative for our future to be free of the spectre of violence and destruction. The People's Republic of Mozambique cherishes peace as the most precious possession of mankind, the deepest aspiration of all peoples. Peace and coexistence are written into our constitution. Based on our socialist policy of peace we have proposed, since the first meeting between our Governments on 17 December 1982, that we should agree, formally or informally, to let peace and coexistence prevail between our States.

There is peace when there is respect between states for sovereignty, independence and territorial integrity. Peace is when there is harmony, and physical, material, spiritual and social tranquility. There is peace when the life, liberty, equality and dignity of man is respected without any discrimination. Peace generates conditions for progress, economic development and social well-being.

After a long period of armed conflicts, hopes of peace are emerging. They must be converted into reality. They must grow and become progressively more fertile and enriched. The prospect of peace opens possibilities for developing the vast resources in which our region abounds. These resources must as a matter of priority be exploited for the benefit of the people, while always safeguarding the national interests of each state.

Economic relations between our States must develop in a healthy and correct manner. We neither can nor should ignore the fact that our relations have a historic tradition, which enhanced the geographical contiguity of the two countries. But we must also recognise that relations of economic dependence are not conducive to stability and harmonious progress. For this reason our State rejects any type of relationship that might in any way limit its independence or make it economically dependent on another country.

In the economic sphere, let us find ways of developing resources, infrastructures and circumstances which, being part of the experience of our relations, are likely to bring reciprocal advantages and benefits on the basis of equality. It is within this context that the agreement of non-aggression and good neighbourliness has an important role to play, as there can be no development without peace and tranquility.

We have established relations of cooperation with the States of Southern Africa in the framework of SADCC. As we have already had occasion to state, the SADCC was not created against South Africa. Its central objective is to eliminate hunger, wretchedness and illiteracy and to improve the standard of living of the peoples of the region. Its member-states refuse economic dependence on South Africa as on any other country. These objectives are solemnly proclaimed in the Lusaka Declaration which created the SADCC, and we would like to reaffirm here our total adherence to these principles.

Mr Prime Minister, our States have been able to map out the path of coexistence. They have been able to discuss these matters between themselves. Between themselves they have been able to define their interests and objectives. Many have been surprised at the speed with which we found the answers, and by our ability to do so without external interference.

None of us, Mozambicans or South Africans, have another country. We are not foreigners to our continent or our countries. We have to live together on a basis of mutual respect, freedom, equality and justice. These are fundamental principles of our State, principles that are the very essence of our concept of a free and democratic society. They are principles with which we remain consistent and to which we are intransigently loyal.

Our objective is that our region should assert itself as a model of peace. We do not want Southern Africa or our continent to be the base for any armed conflicts. In particular, we do not want to be the ones to trigger off a confrontation on a worldwide scale. The liberation struggle of the African peoples was a struggle to achieve peace. The whole of Africa is continuing the struggle to become a Zone of Peace, and for her oceans to be thoroughfares of peace, unity, friendship and cooperation between peoples. The whole of Africa is fighting to avert the horrors of a nuclear holocaust from the continent. The peoples of Africa have always struggled to eliminate the motive causes of conflicts, tension and wars. They have always struggled to eradicate foreign domination and exploitation, and to build progress, prosperity and happiness in peace.

In this struggle to affirm the dignity and personality of African man, the Organisation of African Unity was and continues to be an important instrument for materializing the legitimate aspirations of the peoples of our continent. We cannot lose this opportunity to pay our tribute to those who founded and inspired the OAU. More than twenty years ago a galaxy of illustrious African leaders had the lucidity, the historical vision and the courage to give form to the aspiration of unity so that the struggle of the African people for the liberation of our continent could continue. In this great epic, the liberation of Africa, many were the heroes who sacrificed their lives for the noble cause. It is with deep emotion that at this moment we evoke their memories which will remain immortalised with affection and respect and in the history of Africa.

We would like to emphasize the decisive role of the leaders of the Frontline States with which we have been united for a long time in the cause of the liberation of our continent and in the search for peace and progress, for justice and equality in this region of Africa. We salute Mwalimu Julius Kambarage Nyerere and Doctor Kenneth David Kaunda, those distinguished figures who transformed their peoples into firm and unwavering allies in the liberation of the Mozambican people. This respectful tribute to the peoples of Tanzania and Zambia is extensive to all peoples who made our struggle for peace and freedom their own.

The agreement we have concluded is a significant contribution towards these noble objectives. Furthermore, it enables the region to concentrate its efforts on the prime struggle of the continent and humanity—the struggle against hunger, disease, ignorance, poverty and underdevelopment. Let Africa emerge as a region of progress where reason prevails over hate and prejudice and where the efforts of man are concentrated on the struggle for development and well-being.

Peace, security, stability and progress have always been objectives of the Mozambican people's struggle. In 1964 our people launched the armed struggle against Portuguese colonialism to win national independence and eliminate one of the factors that disturbed peace in our region. In 1974, ten years later, that objective was attained. Another ten years have elapsed, and we are here to establish the basis for a climate of good neighbourliness and peace to prevail between two states of the Southern region of our continent.

Mr Prime Minister, the effort to achieve peace required determination, a correct historical perspective and steadfastness. The moment has arrived when for us, what counts for more than legal texts and formulations is the given word, the sense of commitment and good faith. The Government of the People's Republic of Mozambique will keep its word, both in letter and in spirit.

Mr Prime Minister, dear guests, we have always fought for peace, equality and progress, proclaiming Frelimo's watchword, 'The Struggle Continues'. Today the struggle continues for equality, for democracy, for justice so that on our continent we should all be equal. Today, for peace, stability, good neighbourliness and progress, '*a luta continua*'.

Appendix 3
Botha's Speech
Speech by the Hon P. W. Botha, Prime Minister of the Republic of South Africa, on the occasion of the signing of the Accord of Nkomati, 16 March 1984.

Our action today in signing this treaty, the Accord of Nkomati, sets a new course in the history of Southern Africa. We have signalled to the world our belief that states with different socio-economic and political systems can live together in peace and harmony, and work together in the pursuit of common interests. Our meeting today on the border between our two countries indicates our willingness, and our ability, to reach peaceful accords which enshrine our commitment to the principles of good neighbourliness.

Another principle that underlines the agreement we have signed today is that each country has the right to order its affairs as it sees fit, and that inter-state relations, particularly between neighbours, should not be disturbed by differences in internal policies. This is sensible and practical, as it recognises that each country has its own set of conditions for which it must seek its own solution in the interest of its citizens.

South Africa was one of the first countries of Africa to confront colonial occupation and foreign exploitation. The people I belong to know the feeling of powerlessness in the face of and external force far greater than ours. Our independence did not come easily. Countless numbers of our women and children died in concentration camps while their husbands, fathers and brothers fought the might of a great empire. Their sacrifice has kept the flame of freedom burning in the hearts of South Africans ever since.

Neither South Africa nor Mozambique had a hand in drawing the political map as we know it today. Our borders were arbitrarily drawn by others, by people who served the interests of colonial powers and who spared little thought, if any, for the inhabitants of the region. Having gained our political independence, we have the duty to use it to free our peoples from the chains of poverty, ignorance and disease. The means we have chosen may point in opposite directions: they often conflict, but we cannot allow our divergent outlooks on life to distract us from the urgent need to create better opportunities for our peoples, to enable them to break out of the debilitating cycle of poverty, and to work for a future which offers realistic prospects for peace and a better standard of living.

This is the logic and purpose of the accord of Nkomati. It is an act of faith on the part of our two governments—faith in the promise that given a climate of stability and mutual coexistence we will be able to focus our energies on the problems which really matter in our region, and get to work on the fundamental requirements of our peoples. We face extremely complex social, political and economic problems in Southern Africa: so complex that they can result in conflict and it is often difficult to avoid being drawn into the resultant spiral of confrontation and conflict. In these circumstances the real issues are avoided—uncomfortable facts and harsh realities are dusted under the carpet while nations wage an ideological war of words and act with hostility toward each other. But fact and realities are remarkably resilient companions of mankind. They will not simply disappear because we banish them from our sight. Indeed, unless we attend to them honestly and frankly the problems which they present will merely be compounded.

The republic of South Africa, in voicing its concern several years ago at the increasing signs of confrontation and conflict in our region, came to the conclusion that the leaders of our sub-continent would have to face these realities and rearrange their priorities accordingly. As governments we have a duty to view the welfare and prosperity of our peoples as our first priority. South Africa recognized that it had the stability, the economic strength and the productive capacity to assist its neighbours in achieving the regional goal of progress and development, provided the countries concerned were prepared to seek healthier mutual relations. My country offered to sign non-aggression pacts with all its neighbours in pursuit of that objective, and today with the People's Republic of Mozambique we are taking an important step in that direction.

In signing this agreement today we have opted for the road of peace. I know that it is a difficult road, not without risks for either of us: nor can we escape the fact that peace, too, has its price. We start off with a burden of mutual suspicion and bitter memories which, as we progress, must be shed by the wayside. There can be no question of this agreement being a temporary expedient from which one side or the other might desire to derive unilateral advantage. This is so because the factors which have brought us together are themselves immutable. It is the economic and geographic realities of our region which have brought us together and which will be the best guarantee of the success and permanence of this agreement.

We can explore numerous possibilities for expanding our relations for mutual benefit in the atmosphere of peace and trust that we are now creating. Such an atmosphere will lead to confidence and will encourage the private sectors of the South African economy and of other countries to play a constructive role if they can be assured that their investments will be secure and of mutual benefit to producers and consumers alike.

We are both African countries, inhabited by African peoples whose past and whose future are firmly entrenched in the southern part of the African Continent. We are of Africa. We share a common future in this part of the world, and a common responsibility to ensure that the generations which follow us will inherit a better world than we did. This agreement can contribute significantly towards such a better world. We have signed it before an assembled group of dignitaries and guests, civilians from many walks of life, as well as before representatives of our armed forces on whom we rely to defend our countries with their lives. By ensuring the successful implementation of this agreement we will creat a situation in which, if our armed forces are called upon to do battle, it will not be between our respective countries.

By agreeing to the spirit and letter of this accord, my government looks forward to a new era of cooperation and peaceful coexistence between South Africa and Mozambique in the search for a better life for our peoples. I see a sub-continent in which countries work together to rationalize and increase food production, develop regional trade, establish housing programmes, education and training schemes, health services, employment opportunities, and many other mutually beneficial activities. We can exchange information on programmes to overcome the consequences of droughts, floods and other natural disasters. Together we can form an economic alliance to negotiate better prices on world markets for our minerals and raw materials.

Given the necessary stability and good neighbourliness, we have a vision of nations of Southern Africa cooperating with each other in every field of human endeavour: a veritable constellation of states working together for the benefit of all on the basis of mutual respect. It is most appropriate that leaders and representatives of states in Southern Africa, as well as representatives of other states, are in attendance on this historic occasion. I wish to thank them for their presence. Some I have met before: others I am meeting for the first time. All have, in one way or another, contributed to the process of communication and negotiation which has culminated in our proceedings today.

When, later this afternoon, we have to part, the structures which have been erected here, will be taken down and removed, and this beautiful valley will again be the domain of the hippopotamus and many other creatures of the animal kingdom. I would like us, together to build a memorial on this spot where the accord of Nkomati was signed, so that long after we have gone, future generations will know that we met here today to charter a new and promising course in the history of our two countries.

Our task now is to return to work, to put our agreement into operation, and do all we can to ensure that historians of the future will mark today as a major turning point in the destiny of our sub-continent. Once again something new has emerged from Africa. We believe that this agreement between our two countries can serve as a model for relationships throughout our region, and, indeed, throughout the world. We cannot allow Southern Africa to wither away and die. Our responsibility as Africans is to give our sub-continent a chance to live. To grow, to develop, and to show that we can succeed without the interference of outsiders. As Africans we take pride in our identity and in our traditions in this part of the world. Instead of dividing our energies and resources let us pool them, for it is in our combined economic strength that the promise of a more prosperous region will best be realised.

By our meeting here today we are sending a message to the world that Southern Africa will survive and her children will prosper. May God grant us the courage and strength to fulfil our mission.

Appendix 4

Arusha Statement
The full text of the final communiqué issued after a one-day summit meeting of six African Frontline leaders at Arusha, northern Tanzania:

The heads of state and government present were: President Jose Eduardo dos Santos of the People's Republic of Angola, President Quett Masire of the Republic of Botswana, President Samora Machel of the People's Republic of Mozambique, President Julius K Nyerere of the United Republic of Tanzania, President Kenneth Kaunda of the Republic of Zambia and Prime Minister Robert Mugabe of the Republic of Zimbabwe.

Also in attendance were: Comrade Oliver Tambo, President of ANC, and Comrade Sam Nujoma, President of Swapo of Namibia.

The leaders stood for one minute of silence in tribute to the late Edward Moringe Sokoine, whose very valuable and practical contributions to the liberation struggle of southern Africa will be greatly missed by the Frontline States and the liberation movements.

The heads of state and government and the leaders of liberation movements reaffirmed their total and qualified commitment to the liberation struggles of the people of Namibia against colonialism and of the people of South Africa against apartheid.

They reasserted their conviction and that of the Organisation of African Unity, that the total liberation of Africa from colonialism and racism is essential for the security of all the independent states of the continent and in particular of the Frontline States.

Further, they reiterated that the root cause of the problems in South Africa is apartheid itself. Apartheid is the cause of Africa's hostility to the South African racist regime and of the existence of South African and Namibian refugees. None of these things is caused by the Frontline or other states neighbouring South Africa.

Apartheid has been condemned in categorical terms by the United Nations and by the leaders of Europe, America, Australasia and Asia as well as by Africa. It cannot be made acceptable by the use of South Africa's military power and economic strength, nor by the use of mercenaries and traitors.

The heads of state and government and the leaders of the liberation movements discussed the understanding reached by the People's Republic of Angola and the Pretoria regime, and they hoped that South Africa will honour its commitment to withdraw its troops from Angola.

This withdrawal will constitute an opportunity for the immediate and unconditional implementation of Security Council Resolution 435 of 1978. They welcomed Angola's reaffirmation of its continued commitment to the struggle of the Namibian people under the leadership of Swapo.

The heads of state and government expressed their support for the Angolan actions against the externally supported armed bandits who are causing death and misery to the Angolan people and destruction of the economic infrastructure of the state.

They expressed the hope that the South African Government will live up to the commitment to cease its acts aimed at the destabilisation of Mozambique through the use of armed bandits and gave their support to the Mozambican actions aimed at the total elimination of these vicious bandits.

They expressed appreciation of Mozambique's commitment to continued moral, political and diplomatic support for the ANC in the struggle against apartheid and for majority rule in South Africa.

The heads of state and government and the leaders of the liberation movements declared that the immediate objective for Namibia is and must be the rapid implementation of the UN Security Council resolution 435 of 1978, in order that Namibia may attain full and internationally recognised independence on the basis of self-determination by all people of that country.

For South Africa, the objective of the Frontline states and liberation movements is the abolition of apartheid by whatever means are necessary. The leaders present again reiterated their strong preference for apartheid to be brought to an end by peaceful means.

This can be achieved only through a process agreed upon in free discussions between the present South African regime and genuine representatives of the people of South Africa who are unrepresented in the present Government structure of that country.

Difficult as this step may be in the eyes of the present South African Government, there is no way to peace in Southern Africa except through discussions between the South African Government and the African people of South Africa.

The alternative to free negotiations within South Africa aimed at the ending of apartheid will inevitably be continued struggle against that system by other means, including armed struggle.

This struggle is being (led) and will be conducted and led by the people of South Africa themselves, on their own initiative and within their own country. However, their struggle is, and is seen by Africa to be, a struggle for the freedom and security of all the peoples of this continent and for the human dignity of all men and women regardless of colour.

It therefore receives and will continue to receive, the full support of the peoples and the nations represented by the heads of state and government of the Frontline States.

Involved in this struggle for the total liberation of Africa from colonialism and racism is the consolidation of the freedom and the security of the states which have already achieved independence. To that end and in the light of the difficult circumstances which do from time to time confront such states, the leaders of the Frontline states and the liberation movements reaffirmed their understanding of steps which are taken for this purpose by states which are fully committed to the liberation struggles.

The heads of state and government of the Frontline states and the leaders of the liberation movements condemned without reservation the open and the covert aggressive actions of South Africa directed at the de-stabilisation of African states and those aimed against refugees from Namibia and apartheid South Africa.

They also repeated their rejection of the attempt to link the freedom of Namibia with any Angolan Government decisions relating to its security requirements and its internal political structures. The political and the armed struggles being waged by the peoples of Namibia and South Africa led by Swapo and ANC respectively are taking place inside those two countries.

331

The struggle is between the people of Namibia and the occupying power, and between the people of South Africa and the apartheid regime. Therefore, the strategy of the liberation movements is that of internal struggle, firmly based on the people's will and determination.

As the denial of human rights, and the ruthlessness of the oppressor, has made it impossible for many active leaders of the liberation movements to live and work inside their own countries, it has been necessary for both Swapo and ANC to have an external wing.

The international implications of the problems with which the liberation movements are contending also require international diplomatic and political activity, together with offices and representatives in other countries.

The Frontline States reaffirm their recognition of these external operations of the movements and reassert their intention to give shelter to them. They appeal to the international community for diplomatic and economic support and protection as they carry out these international responsibilities.

The heads of state and government of the Frontline States and the leaders of the liberation movements represented at the Arusha meeting, in reasserting their commitment to the struggle for freedom in Namibia and South Africa, also draw attention to the burden they are carrying on behalf of the world conscience and the international condemnation of colonialism and apartheid.

They therefore appeal for active participation in the struggle by all other nations, other organisations and institutions and all people who accept the principles of human dignity and equality.

In particular, they appeal for political, moral, material and diplomatic support to be given to the liberation movements. They appeal also for concrete support to be given to the efforts of the Frontline States aimed at the consolidation of their independence and their fragile economies, as they are of direct relevance to their ability to play a constructive role in the search for peace and freedom in Southern Africa.

For the heads of state and government of the Frontline States and the leaders of the liberation movements repeat a truism. Peace is incompatible with racism and with colonialism. Neither military might nor devious political machinations, whether directed against the peoples inside Namibia and South Africa or against the free states of Africa, can defeat the idea of freedom and racial equality.

The struggle will be long and hard. It will be carried on until final victory—'A luta continua'.

1984–1985
SHIFT FROM THE PERIPHERY TO THE VORTEX
OF THE VIOLENT CONFRONTATION

South Africa's euphoric expectations of attracting more adherents to its *Pax Praetoriana* receded rapidly when Botswana, Lesotho and Zimbabwe resisted all entreaties and pressures to emulate Mozambique's example in signing the Nkomati Accord (March 1984), Angola's in endorsing the Lusaka Agreement on ceasefire arrangements (February 1984), and Swaziland's in entering secretly into a mutual security treaty (1982).[1] The idea of a peace order in the sub-continent under the military and economic umbrella of Pretoria faltered for the most obvious of reasons: mistrust of the peace guarantor.

If the promise of Nkomati had been fulfilled and the SA Defence Forces (SADF) were withdrawn from Angola, closer to the agreed time,[2] at least the minimal conditions for confidence would have been established and so provided the missing prerequisite for an agreement based, not on equality or friendship, but on mutual interests: pragmatic, suspicious association was the most that White-ruled SA could expect in its political environment. As Dr Erich Leistner, Director of the Africa Institute, pointed out—a genuine change in attitude towards SA by its neighbours depends on their seeing 'credible Black South Africans' speaking on behalf of their country.[3] But in 1985 those credible leaders were speaking against their country's regime and had succeeded in rocking the system of apartheid to the point where Pretoria was no longer able to dictate the pace of change.[4] Although the security problems along SA's borders still remained serious, they were over-shadowed by the violence inside SA itself, and the focus of international concern shifted from the periphery to the vortex of the conflict. As President Samora Machel pointed out: 'SA's apartheid system is the main cause of instability and tension in the southern zone of our continent.'[5] Elaborating on this statement, an official Mozambican source[6] described it as paradoxical that:

> Pretoria says attacks against it come from outside; therefore cross-boundary actions against the neighbouring States are the answer. However, inside SA the State has deployed thousands of soldiers and policemen against civilians in the Black town-ships. The sustained resistance in the townships since the middle of last year reveals who is really threatening the apartheid system.

In early 1984, a supremely confident President Botha had carried the message of SA's success as a regional power to the capitals of Western Europe; a year later he was reeling against the ropes as the campaign in the US for disinvestment from SA gathered such momentum that, by September 1985, President Reagan found it expedient to reverse his stand on selective sanctions rather than accept a political defeat in Congress and the imposition of an even larger dose of sanctions against SA. France, Sweden, Norway, Holland, Australia and Canada all either increased their own level of sanctions or adopted new measures. These developments in-creased pressure for collective action by the European Community. Only Britain stood out against the demand by the other eight members of the EEC to take action, short of sanctions, against SA.

Lessening confidence in the stability of the apartheid system spread rapidly from the political to the financial institutions of the West and to the SA business community itself. Only a matter of days after Reagan had signed his executive order in September 1985, SA's economy was plunged into its worst crisis for decades and, for the first time ever, the doors of the major banks in Western Europe and North America were shut against their formerly gilt-edged client. Scenting the approaching change in the balance of power inside SA, its leading businessmen led the way to Lusaka to hold talks with the ANC who, only a year earlier, had been written off as a spent force after the approaches to SA's borders had been closed against them by Mozambique and Swaziland. No longer was P. W. Botha seen to be alone in holding the key to SA's future. The feeling grew stronger that Nelson Mandela was indispensable as a negotiating partner if the country was not to be overwhelmed by violent forces.

Meanwhile, the American initiative on Namibia ended up in yet another *cul de sac*. The Angolans' surprising offer to phase out the Cuban troops' presence in exchange for the withdrawal of SA troops from their territory—a neat side-stepping of the unpopular linkage proposal—did not produce the kind of response from Pretoria that Washington had hoped for. Nor had Nkomati brought the slightest respite to the Frelimo Government; a year after signing the Accord, it was no nearer to overcoming the banditry of the Mozambique National Resistance and, to make matters worse, Pretoria was compelled on two different occasions to admit that it had defaulted in its undertakings. Finally, too, in September 1985, Pretoria dropped its pretence that it was not backing Jonas Savimbi and vowed that it would not abandon Unita to defeat.

By the third quarter of 1985 the security situation inside and around SA was more acute than at any time in the previous decade, and the international community was more deeply involved in the region's affairs than ever before.

THE COURSE OF EVENTS JULY-DECEMBER 1984

Continuing Search for Namibian Independence

Following the abortive meeting between Swapo, the SA Administration and the internal political parties of Namibia held under the chairmanship of Zambia's President Kenneth Kaunda in May 1984,[7] another attempt was made to get agreement on a ceasefire at a meeting held in Cape Verde over 25-26 July between a Swapo delegation led by Sam Nujoma and the Administrator-General of Namibia, Willie van Niekerk. At that point Pretoria had not yet fulfilled its ceasefire agreement of 16 February 1984 to withdraw all its forces from Angolan territory.[8] SADF units were still entrenched at Ondjiva, 20 miles from the Namibian border.

The Cape Verde talks followed a communication from SA's Foreign Minister, Pik Botha, to his Angolan counterpart on 7 July apropos talks with Swapo to end the hostilities in Namibia.[9] Although the US Deputy Assistant Secretary for African Affairs, Frank Wisner, was in Cape Verde at the time of the meeting he did not participate directly in the negotiations. When the talks ended in failure, Swapo blamed it on SA intransigence and insisted that it was 'not prepared to deviate from its considered opinion that a ceasefire could be declared only after the implementation of Resolution 435 under UN supervision.'[10] In a further statement it rejected any idea of a ceasefire linked to Cuban troop withdrawals.[11] Van Niekerk blamed the breakdown on Swapo which was 'not prepared to deviate from its considered opinion that a ceasefire could be declared only after the implementation of Resolution 435 under UN supervision'—thus confirming the reason given by Swapo for its rejection of the SA offer.[12] He added that Swapo's stand would retard 'the southward shift' of SADF troops.

According to the Lusaka ceasefire agreement[13] all SADF troops had to be out of Angola by 31 March 1984. Although President dos Santos was naturally keen to see the end of SA troops on Angolan territory, he was not prepared to exert pressure on Swapo's leaders to compromise on their terms to meet Angola's wishes. On its side, Pretoria was pressing Angola to meet its obligations by preventing Swapo activities in the areas vacated by the SADF. These differences were thrashed out at a meeting in Lusaka on 25 July between the SA Foreign and Defence Ministers and the Administrator-General of Namibia and Angola's Interior Minister, Alexandre Rodrigues Kito.[14] Pik Botha described the talks as useful but confirmed that the remaining SADF units would not be withdrawn before all Swapo fighters had been cleared out of the 25 mile corridor between the present line held by the SADF and the Namibian border. Another issue discussed at the Lusaka meeting was the role of the Joint Monitoring Commission (JMC) which had been set up to supervise the ceasefire. Angola agreed to extend its mandate provided SA guaranteed that its troops would not again violate Angolan territory.[15] Meanwhile, at home, Pik Botha continued to link SA's final withdrawal not only to Swapo operations, but also to the withdrawal of Cuba's combat troops from Angola—a proposition dos Santos was not willing to consider. This issue was mentioned by Lucio Lara, secretary-general of the MPLA-Workers' Party Central Committee, on 30 July when he accused 'international imperialism' of 'using blackmail' in attempting to link Cuban withdrawals to Namibian independence.[16] In the same speech he accused SA of not respecting the compromises reached at Lusaka.

A change in Angola's previously stated positions about the phasing out of Cuban troops was signalled at a press conference held in early August by Venancio de Moura, Deputy Minister of External Relations.[17] He began by affirming that Angola remained open for 'all discussions' with SA, the US and other interested Governments to find lasting solutions for Southern Africa, and went on to recall previous statements by MPLA on the principle of the gradual withdrawal of Cuban troops. Then, for the first time, he linked withdrawal not to Namibian independence but to 'a complete unilateral withdrawal of SA troops from Angola, without extraneous elements, and the cessation of all SA logistical and military support to Unita.' He added: 'The solution of these two problems would enable the Governments of Angola and Cuba, within reasonable conditions, to honour the compromises stated in the declarations of 4 February 1982 and 19 March 1984.'[18]

Another new element in the diplomacy of the region crystallized in August when Portugal came to be accepted by Angola as a negotiating partner. After a meeting in Lisbon on 12 August between Angola's Foreign Minister, Paulo Teixeira Jorge, and Portugal's Foreign Minister, Jaime Gama, the official Angolan news agency reported that 'a new channel of dialogue has been opened up between the two Governments.'[19] On the last day of August, Chester Crocker, the US Assistant Secretary of State for African Affairs, left for Cape Verde to start yet another round of negotiations on Namibia and to break the deadlock over the Cuban troops' question. Preparatory to commencing his latest effort to restore the momentum of the negotiating process, Crocker and his team of advisors had drawn up a package deal for consideration by all the major parties involved in the Southern African conflict. Its essential elements were:

1. A ceasefire inside Namibia to complement the ceasefire agreement between SA and Angola on the border. Both SA and Swapo had previously tentatively agreed to such an agreement. What was expected of them now was that they would separately inform the UN Secretary-General of their readiness to observe a ceasefire at an appropriate moment.

2. An agreement to complete the withdrawal of SA troops from the whole of Angola.

3. The ceasefire inside Namibia and the withdrawal of SA troops were to be accepted as necessary complements to further progress.

4. Progress towards producing a formula about the timing and rate of withdrawal of Cuban troops from Angola, acceptable to all the parties in the conflict.

While Crocker accepted that the Cuban withdrawal still remained the most difficult to resolve, he felt there were sufficiently good reasons to suppose that it would not prove to be insuperable once formally and convincingly demonstrated that with agreement on the first three parts of this package, it would be ready to begin implementing Resolution 435.

On the face of it, SA's failure to honour its agreement to withdraw all its troops from Angola by the end of March should have ruptured the negotiating process: that this had not happened was because it did not suit the interests of either the South Africans or the Angolans to see the collapse of the ceasefire.

Pretoria insisted that they must retain some forces on the Angolan side of the border because of Swapo's continued trans-border activities which, though small, gave some cause for concern. The Angolans, while wanting ther SADF out, did not yet feel themselves militarily ready to take over the security of their border with Namibia and to defend their position against Unita. So, although hostile noises continued to come periodically from both Pretoria and Luanda, neither side was ready to scrap the ceasefire agreement.

Uncharacteristically, optimistic reports emanated from official SA sources about the possibilities of making progress during Crocker's visit. Pretoria's view at that stage was summed up in a commentary broadcast from Johannesburg:[20]

> At one time the South West African independence issue could rightly be described as insoluble. So far apart were the premises on which the various approaches to the question were being advanced that a peaceful resolution was out of the question. Breaking the deadlock required, before anything else, that the parties should re-examine their premises and, especially, that they should begin to acknowledge the realities of international and regional power interests.
>
> Achieving that—in effect, redefining the context in which the issue had to be resolved—was bound to be a slow and laborious process. Yet, to a surprising degree and surprisingly little noticed, the redefinition is being achieved. The long succession of diplomatic sorties over SWA—of which Dr Chester Crocker's Southern African visit is the latest—is easily dismissed as an endless replay of the same arguments and accusations leading nowhere. Such a view ignores the extent to which the seemingly interminable rounds of talks have in fact changed the context, and thereby at least made feasible the attempt to reach a settlement.
>
> Most important, the regional and international dimensions of the issue are now widely recognized. That the Cuban presence in Angola is a function of Soviet involvement within the framework of the Kremlin's global strategies is at least implicitly accepted in most Western capitals. So is the corollary—that the Cuban presence undermines efforts to implement a democratic settlement for SWA, and represents a threat to the security interests of SA. Not least, there is an awareness that SA, as a regional power, insists on an accommodation of its regional interests in any initiative in the region. Prime Minister P. W. Botha warned . . . that outside Powers could not

ignore this factor. In such an event, SA would safeguard and advance its essential and legitimate interests with all the means at its disposal.

Yet shifts are discernible. The Luanda Government has had to undertake to keep southern Angola free of Cuban and Swapo forces in return for a SA withdrawal. Swapo was brought into a meeting with the Multi-Party Conference by President Kaunda, and it remains under pressure to change its strategy and join the political process inside SWA. Individually, the changes have not been dramatic, but certainly their potential effects are. By clarifying the ground rules on which a settlement for SWA must be achieved, they are slowly turning an insoluble confrontation into a manageable diplomatic challenge.

However, displaying another side to SA's ambiguous Namibian policy, its Foreign Minister announced that they would not stand in the way of a plan for Namibian independence that by-passed Resolution 435. He pointed to the costly nature of the proposed UN peacekeeping force (which he put at $600m), and added that Unita would have to be involved in any final deal otherwise the UN force would be vulnerable to attacks by Savimbi's forces.[21]

During talks between Crocker and Angola's Interior Minister, Rodrigues Kito, in Lusaka from 6-7 September, the Angolans put forward their five-point package deal for the agreement:

(1) Completion of SADF's withdrawal from Angola.

(2) A public commitment by SA to honour and contribute to the implementation of Resolution 435.

(3) A ceasefire between Swapo and SA.

(4) Angola's confirmation that it would commence the withdrawal of Cuban troops after Resolution 435 was under way.

(5) A quadripartite international agreement between Angola, SA, Cuba and Swapo, defining each party's undertakings with a view to achieving Namibia's independence and guaranteeing the security of Angola and lasting regional peace.[22]

This plan implicitly accepted a form of linkage in so far as a Cuban troop withdrawal programme was to be built in as a competent element of a four-party international agreement on Namibian independence and regional security. However, it was not the 'parallelist' form of linkage sought by SA and the US. The phased withdrawal of Cuban troops would begin only once the SADF in Namibia had been reduced to 1,500 men, in accordance with Resolution 435. As a 'gesture of goodwill', 5,000 Cuban troops would then be repatriated from southern Angola at once, and orders would be given to the remaining Cuban troops to stay north of the 16th parallel (160 km north of the Namibian border). These remaining forces in southern Angola would be withdrawn gradually over three years. The withdrawal of Cuban forced in the north of the country, including Cabinda and the capital, would not be covered by the agreement, but would be a matter for Angola and Cuba alone to determine. Finally, a condition of the agreement was that SA would 'undertake from the very start to cease all support for the Unita bands' and accept UN verification of the dismantling of Unita bases on Namibian territory.

After the Lusaka talks, a US spokesman detected 'a dynamic at work in favour of an overall regional settlement leading to Namibian independence through the implementation of Resolution 435.' He added that 'the mood in Angola is one of 'let's try to settle the problem.'[23]

Frank Wisner continued the negotiations in Luanda. On 9 October, he was handed a supplementary set of proposals, spelling out in detail a programme for the withdrawal of the 20,000 Cuban troops in southern Angola. It proposed that 16 weeks after the arrival of UN troops in Namibia, under Resolution 435, Angola would start a four month withdrawal programme for 5,000 Cuban troops. Another 5,000 troops would be repatriated between the 12th and 16th months (after the arrival of UN troops in Namibia), and a further 5,000 would go between the 20th and 24th months. Throughout this two-year period, no Cuban troops would be allowed further south than the 16th parallel. This limit would be moved north to the 13th parallel (500 km from Namibia) from the beginning of the third year; and the final 5,000 Cuban troops would be pulled out between the 32nd and 36th months. The 9 October document[24] confirmed that the Cuban troop contingents in the north, which have 'no relationship to Namibia or South Africa', would be withdrawn from Angola under an independent timetable to be agreed upon by Angola and Cuba 'when the time comes'. Cuban troops would thus remain stationed in Cabinda, Luanda, Bengo, Kwanza Norte and other 'strategic points north of the 13th parallel'. The document was frank about why the Angolan Government could not afford to commit itself to the repatriation of these troops too:

> The People's Republic of Angola does not have the organized manpower resources with the required educational level, or the available material and financial resources to wage a war against the Unita bands and other puppet organizations, and simultaneously to replace the Cuban troops and armaments at strategic points in the south, centre and north of the country. Angola has to give priority to fighting the bandits who, supported, trained and equipped from abroad, have caused and are continuing to cause the country substantial human and economic losses. [It would take] time, substantial resources and a tremendous effort in the training of skilled and technical personnel [to take on the tasks performed by the remaining Cuban troops]. To demand more of our young State would reflect a lack of realism.[25]

Wisner returned to Luanda for a further round of talks over 15-16 October, and a few days later, on 21 October, Angola's veteran Foreign Minister, Paulo Jorge, was dismissed. President dos Santos assumed personal responsibility for foreign affairs until the Central Committee member, Alfonso Van-Dunehm, was appointed in March 1985. Media speculation suggested that Jorge's dismissal implied a softening of Angola's foreign policy stance, given his supposed 'hard line' allegiance to Moscow. In fact, his dismissal seemed to have more to do with internal problems within his Ministry and the Angolan diplomatic corps (who had been brought back to Luanda for a verbal rap over the knuckles by the President on 20 September) than with the negotiations with the US and SA, from which Jorge had in any case virtually been excluded since the talks with SA in Cape Verde in December 1982.[26] Since the end of the Neto presidency, Lt-Col Rodrigues, a politburo member (unlike Jorge), had been the chief negotiator in the decisive and delicate sphere of regional diplomacy.

Luanda's 9 October document was passed on to the South Africans when Crocker met the Foreign and Defence Ministers and Namibia's Administrator-General in Nambia on 31 October and 1 November. Pik Botha said his Government welcomed the Angolan proposal, promised an early reply and added: 'Progress has been made in respect of broad consensus on a number of important principles.'[27] Crocker described the recent developments as positive: 'We view the door to an overall regional settlement to be opened.' Nevertheless, Crocker was not very surprised when he returned to Johannesburg on 15 November to be confronted with a new set of SA counter-proposals which were later made public.[28] These proposals required not only that all the Cuban troops be withdrawn from Angola, but that this should be accomplished within a mere 12 weeks, parallel to the reduction in SA troop numbers in Namibia to 1,500. Furthermore, a joint peace commission would have to be set up to supervise the Cuban withdrawal from Angola and to monitor that it proceeded in tandem with the SA withdrawal from Namibia.

In private talks with Crocker, Pik Botha also stipulated the phasing out of all foreign troops (including Soviet and East German) who would remain in Angola at the time of the proposed referendum over Namibian independence. He mentioned a total of 3,000-4,000,.[29] Botha also sought to include a further condition: the need to involve Unita in the settlement. On this latter point the American position was emphatic: while it recognized the importance of an agreement with Unita for Angola's future political stability, this was considered a purely domestic issue which lay outside the parameters of the Namibian negotiations. When Frank Wisner returned to Luanda to present SA's counter-proposals he was pleasantly surprised to find that the Angolans were not about to slam the door. For the first time his negotiations included talks with President dos Santos as well as with his military and foreign policy advisors.

The patience of the Frontline Presidents over the Namibian negotiations had worn very thin by the time they met in Arusha in December 1984. They adopted a harshly critical view of the failure of American diplomacy. The sharpest critic was Prime Minister Robert Mugabe, who said that the Contact Group had concluded that SA and the Americans were acting 'fraudulently' and suggested that the Namibian issue should be returned to the Security Council.[30] After 37 years, yet another year passed without Namibia achieving its independence. Despite the setbacks of 1984, the Crocker–Wisner team was back on the diplomatic safari trail in the New Year. Wisner's first call in January 1985 was on President Kaunda in Lusaka. The Zambian leader told him that while he thanked President Reagan for his efforts, he should know that time was running out to avoid a tragic explosion in Southern Africa, and that 1985 might prove to be a watershed. Wisner assured Kaunda that Southern Africa was among the issues at the top of Reagan's agenda, and agreed that time was running out for peaceful solutions in the region.[31] Neither man could have known at the time how close their predictions and fears were to fulfilment.

During a visit to Africa in January 1985, the British Foreign Secretary, Sir Geoffrey Howe, reiterated his Government's refusal to accept the SA or US attempts to link Cuba with Namibian independence[32]—a position that had been taken up in1984 by all the other Contact Group members as well, i.e. France, West Germany and Canada. However, Howe made it clear that Britain supported the continuing American initiative, and reminded African leaders that whatever view was taken of linkage, sight should not be lost of the hard realities of the situation produced by the presence of a large number of Cuban troops in Namibia.[33]

Swapo's leader, Sam Nujoma, struck a gloomy note in his New Year speech in which he called on Namibians for more sacrifices and for a further tightening of belts. 'We will have to fight our way out to victory,' he said, 'there is no other way.'

Early in February Nujoma warned of another attempt to sidetrack the Namibian negotiations by a SA plan to create an Interim Central Government in Windhoek as an instrument to take the territory into independence outside the framework of Resolution 435.[34] February also saw a return to the earlier hostility between Pretoria and Luanda, with the former accusing the MPLA Government of working for the overthrow of the Botha Government by hosting thousands of guerrilla armed men on its soil;[35] and with the latter accusing Pretoria of working for the overthrow of the MPLA Government.[36] Although Pretoria once again claimed that the Cuban issue was the 'last fundamental obstacle' that stood in the way of Namibia's independence, Fidel Castro told the Washington Post (7 February) that he endorsed the American mediation effort in the region as having the potential to 'exercise a positive influence in the international sphere'; but he warned that his military units would remain in Angola if the regional peace settlement sought by the US was not achieved.

Crocker returned to Cape Verde for talks with the Angolans on 7 February to try and find a way of bridging the gap between its proposals for ending the impasse over the Cubans and the SA counter-proposals. He then spent five days in SA trying to persuade the Bothas to come closer to meeting Dos Santos' terms—but beyond getting an undertaking that the SADF would soon be withdrawn from Angola under the terms of the ceasefire, he appears to have made no further progress. With the prospect of the SADF troop withdrawals, the US decided to shut down its Liaison Office in Windhoek on 12 February. Crocker's visit to Cape Town coincided with a visit being paid to the Bothas by Savimbi; Crocker did not deny reports that he had talks with the Unita leader.

The OAU Council of Ministers, which met from 25 February to 4 March, called for an emergency meeting of the Security Council to consider the question of Namibia; but no such decision appeared to have been taken at a full meeting of the six African Frontline Presidents in Lusaka on 8 and 9 March. Crocker returned to Cape Verde for talks with the Angolans, and to Cape Town for talks with SA over a new compromise devised by the Americans to bring the two sides closer over the timing and scope of Cuban withdrawals. The Angolans responded by agreeing to send home 20,000 Cubans, retaining 10,000 for training and mounting security over the Cabinda oil installations; but SA stood by its demand that all the Cubans should quit Angola.

Meanwhile, the secret plan about which Nujoma had earlier warned was unfolding in Windhoek: the establishment of an Interim Central Government which, it was announced, would be installed in June. Nujoma commented:

> After failing in its attempts to destroy the Swapo struggle on all fronts, the apartheid regime is now back to the old idea of creating an interim regime with the sole intent of perpetuating the illegal occupation of our country.

The plan to install an Interim Government in Windhoek had crystallized by April. Leaders of the political parties grouped together in the Multi-Party Conference (MPC) announced their intention to rule until the Cubans withdrew from Angola and Resolution 435 was implemented. In the meantime, they invited Swapo to join the Interim Government—an invitation that was scorned. According to some sources the new move by Pretoria was dictated by two considerations: the need to defuse the growing discontent among the non-Swapo political parties because they were deprived of any form of political participation since the Administrator-General had 'the powers of a dictator'; and to give the MPC an opportunity to develop a popular political base capable of challenging Swapo, which the Turnhalle Alliance had failed to do.

While the SA authorities were giving private assurances that the move to establish the Interim Government was not an attempt to by-pass negotiations to reach agreement on implementing Resolution 435, Pik Botha was following SA's familiar two-track policy by questioning some of the basic principles of Resolution 435 which SA, like Swapo, had long since endorsed. One of the most important aspects of Resolution 435 was that there should be free and fair elections after a seven-month transition period during which time SA's troops had to be scaled down to 1,500 while the UN peacekeeping force took responsibility for supervising the maintenance of law and order. It was this aspect that Botha challenged: 'I want to ask you,' he asked the Namibian House of Representatives on 26 April, 'could there be free and fair elections under these circumstances while 30,000 Cuban troops remain north of the border? Definitely not.'[37] At the same meeting he said that the burden on SA of Namibia for 1982-84 was R1,031m, of which R450m was for defence; but, he added, even if all SA troops were withdrawn defence budget expenditure would not be saved. He also revealed another reason for delaying Namibia's independence if it meant that Swapo would win the elections:

> If we allow Swapo to get away with achieving its aims by the barrel of the gun, we in SA will be in for a long struggle. . . . It will increase the appetite of those in the Republic who think they can reach their goals through violence and spur them to greater efforts.

He said there were 'large numbers of ANC cadres in Angola.' However, he went on, if a settlement could be reached which included Swapo in the Government, his Government would accept it.

SA finally withdrew the last of its 450 troops from Angola on 17 April 1985. The Chief of the SADF, Gen Constand Viljoen, explained that the 'intention of the unilateral withdrawal of SA troops is to help bring peace to the area.' The Angola Government, however, derided the claim of a unilateral withdrawal, saying that this was a propaganda gimmick; the withdrawal was just a very belated fulfillment of the ceasefire agreement.[38] The Chief of the Army Staff, Gen Jannie Geldenhuys, said that the pullback conformed with Government policy to seek a solution by various means, including military, political and diplomatic; however, he added that the Government had not withdrawn from its position that it would seek out and destroy 'terrorist bases' wherever they existed.[39] Asked whether Prof Reg Green's figure[40] of 2,500 soldiers having died was accurate, the General replied that while he could not quote accurate figures for every year, 'Green's figures are totally incorrect.' He added:

> You know that in places such as Algeria, Malaya and so on, seven soldiers were used for every terrorist and in some instances, 14 soldiers for every terrorist. We used the ratio of only 1.6 soldiers for every terrorist, and our casualty figure for both the enemy and ourselves are the best that I have ever come across.

The SA claim that it had, in fact, withdrawn all its troops was challenged by Luanda, which claimed that a company of the SADF was still based inside Angola and that SAAF planes were continuing to violate Angola's air space.[41] Angolan allegations about the SADF not having withdrawn entirely from their territory and that they were actively collaborating with Unita were soon confirmed. On 21 May, the Angolan army (Fapla) surprised a SA commando group of nine men who were attempting to sabotage the Cabinda Gulf oil complex in Malongo with the intention of leaving behind them material to suggest that this was part of the success of Unita's outreach to the enclave. Two SA soldiers were killed and the commanding officer, Capt Wynand Petrus du Toit, was captured. He confirmed that the operation was aimed at sabotaging the oil installations and that the intention was to give the credit to Unita.[42] The American director-general of Cabinda Gulf, Richard L. Ambrose, said he would have been 'very indignant' if the SA commandos had succeeded in sabotaging the Malongo oil installations, adding that some years ago his company had told the US Congress that Angola was a good place in which to invest. Cabinda Gulf has a production sharing agreement with the state oil company, Sonangol, whereby the former has a 49% share and the latter 51%. The SA defence of the operation offered by Pik Botha was that 'northern Angola was now the main base area for the training of ANC terrorists.'[43] If this was indeed so why not attack the ANC base rather than the oil installations? Foreign embassies in Luanda corroborated Angolan Government statements that there were no ANC training camps in the Cabinda enclave. The Reagan Administration issued a statement which spoke of its 'deep displeasure' at the SA action and demanded an explanation from Pretoria.[44]

The Joint Monitoring Commission was disbanded on 16 May, but it was agreed that SA and Angola would maintain contact through military channels on the border.

Fidel Castro, when on a visit to a Namibian military and ideological training camp 100 miles from Havana, promised he would keep every single Cuban soldier in Angola until Resolution 435 was implemented. In another reversal of his position, he accused the Americans of not acting as independent and honest brokers in the negotiations, and added: 'What can you expect from racists? What can you expect from repressors?'[45] Speaking in a Security Council debate on Namibia on 12 June, the Cuban Foreign Minister, Senor Isidora Malmierca, repeated that not a single Cuban would leave Angola before Namibia's independence and all SA troops had effectively left Angola. He added another condition: that SA must first stop all its support for Unita.[46]

The momentum to keep up the negotiating process began to run out of steam after Crocker's last shuttle in April and began to go into reverse in June as a result of a number of developments seen to be negative by all three local actors—Swapo, SA and Angola. The formal opening of the Internal Government in Namibia by President Botha on 17 June[47] was seen by Swapo and the Frontline States as evidence of Pretoria's double-dealing and a serious indication that it had no intention of ever allowing free elections in the territory as required by Resolution 435.[48] All the Contact Group nations at once announced that the Interim Government had no legal status in the eyes of the international community. However, it was a new factor in the situation and a new instrument to be used against Swapo.

SA seized on the Angola suggestion that it might end the negotiating process as a result of the Cabinda raid to say that if this were to happen, it might consider pressing ahead with a unilateral independence settlement for Namibia. Pik Botha suggested that Angola was simply using the Cabinda affair as a pretext to break off the negotiations. He added that SA was 'no longer sure' to what extent the goal of getting Cuban withdrawal was attainable. However, if agreement on this issue could be reached, SA would be prepared to abide by Resolution 435.[49]

Angola's increasing displeasure at American policies was triggered by two developments. The first was over the US Senate's substantial 63-34 vote on 13 June to repeal the Clark amendment. (It had been adopted in 1976 for the purpose of prohibiting its supply of US military assistance to Unita.) The Senate's decision was still subject to approval by the House of Representatives which had defeated a similar attempt made in 1981. But Angola's response was immediate and angry:

> How can one reconcile the peace initiatives of the Reagan Administration envoys who on several occasions met with high-ranking officials of the Angolan Government either in Angola or abroad as well as the American Government's condemnation of the aborted sabotage attempt on the Malongo petroleum complex—where important American interests are at stake—with the announced repeal of the Clark amendment and the CIA-sponsored meeting between the Unita puppets and the other counter-revolutionaries? The Government of the PRA left with no alternative other than to denounce before international public opinion the dubious attitude of the American Government as well as its tacit solidarity with the Pretoria regime and its puppet armed gangs who sow death and destruction in all countries in this sub-region of our

continent, thus becoming the main factor of insecurity and threat to peace. Accordingly, the government of the PRA vehemently condemns this further flagrant interference in its domestic affairs. It alerts the international community that should this fact materialize, it will undoubtedly compromise the efforts that have already been made in search of solutions that safeguard peace and respect for self-determination, independence, and sovereignty of the peoples in the region.

Angolan misgivings were further fuelled when a Right-wing American group, Citizens for America, organized a conference at Jamba, the seat of Savimbi, in June 1985 to found an anti-Soviet movement of guerrilla organizations, named Democratic International. There were reports[50] that Reagan had given his personal blessing to the new International. Apart from the Citizens for America, others who participated in the Jamba conference were Adolfo Calero of the Nicaraguan Democratic Front; Pa Kao Her of the Ethnic Liberation Organization of Laos; Col Gholam Wardak of the Islamic Unity of Afghanistan Mujahidin, as well as the National Student Federation of SA. Savimbi praised Ronald Reagan for his stance towards the USSR, but said he believed the State Department was trying to undermine the White House with its policies toward Southern Africa.

Angola was further concerned over what it claimed as evidence of continued SADF activities in its territory. On 11 June the Defence Ministry reported 22 violations of Angola's airspace and feared that this was the beginning of a new trans-border attack; however, this did not eventuate. On 30 June 45 Swapo guerrillas were reported by the SADF Commander, to have died in a hot pursuit raid operation—the first incident of this kind since the formal withdrawal of the SADF troops.

A second hot pursuit operation was carried out at the end of June when the SADF claimed to have killed 57 Swapo cadres. The attack penetrated to a depth of 40km inside Angola.

President Kaunda paid an official visit to Luanda on 7 and 8 June to discuss further steps to strengthen cooperation between the two countries. A joint communiqué called on the international community to find the best means of forcing the Pretoria regime to respect the independence and sovereignty of Angola.

PROGRESS OF THE WAR IN NAMIBIA: CASUALTIES AND COST

Despite the ceasefire agreement, which included an Angolan undertaking to help prevent Swapo cadres occupying the areas from which the SADF had withdrawn, there was no reduction in the level of guerrilla operations, either along the border or inside Namibia itself.[51] This evaluation was confirmed by a senior staff officer of the South West African Territory Force (Swatf), Col Kleynhans, in January 1985.[52] He said that Swapo was 'logistically stronger than before', and that it had been able to move its territorial headquarters in Angola back to where it had been two years before. Swapo guerrillas were still moving freely around southern Angola. According to Kleynhans and other SADF spokesmen, Luanda had admitted that its army, was unable to control Swapo's movements. Swapo's fighting strength was estimated by SA military intelligence at between 8,000-8,500, and claimed that half of these men were engaged with Fapla in helping to maintain internal security in Angola. An estimated 220 guerrillas were reckoned to be inside Namibia.

The International Institute for Strategic Studies. London, also calculated the strength of Swapo's force—the People's Liberation Army (PLAN)—at c. 8,000, and reported that its equipment included Soviet T-34 and T-54 tanks which were not deployed inside Namibia but were used mainly to protect Swapo's bases inside Angola.[53] The same source claimed that the major onslaught by Swapo, which usually coincides with the rainy season, had not taken place by January 1985 which was ascribed to the fact that conditions in the north were still very dry.

The build-up of Swatf continued in 1984. Its numbers were officially stated to have reached 21,000 by mid-1985 making up 6% of the 40,000 security forces in the operational area.[54] About 40% are made up of SADF units. Recruitment figures for 1984 were stated to have been 3,000. The OC of Swatf, Maj-Gen George Meiring, claimed that his force could be doubled at a day's notice.[55] Just over 60% of Swatf were said to be Black.

Swapo's sabotage activities—described as 'terrorist acts' by the Namibian authorities—doubled in 1984 to 94, and resulted in the death of 159 civilians.[56] Swapo insisted that the majority of victims were either military personnel or officials connected with the administration.

The Namibian Finance Secretary, Dr Johan Jones, said the cost of the war was between £170m-£175m annually. He apportioned the cost as £140m to SA and up to £35m to Namibia. According to the UN economic consultant, Prof R. Herboldt Green, the cost is much higher if all the costs to SA of maintaining its control of the territory were taken into account.[57] A rough estimate of the cost to SA is generally thought to be in excess of £1m a day.[58]

Estimates of casualty figures claimed by Swapo and Swatf/SADF differed greatly. The figures claimed by Swatf were 566 Swapo casualties for 1984 as against 26 of its own men, and 329 Swapo casualties in the first five months of 1985. Gen Meiring claimed that 21 Swapo guerrillas were killed in the operational areas in 1984 for every one Swatf fatal casualty.

With the negotiations temporarily stalled, the Angolans decided to capitalize on the diplomatic initiative they had captured by their concilatory offer over the Cuban issue. They lodged a copy of their proposals with the UN Secretary-General and published full page advertisements in newspapers like the London *Times*. This tactic nettled Pik Botha who accused the Angolans of a breach of faith by making a public disclosure of their secret offer, and so placing 'a question over the Luanda Government's ability to conduct serious negotiations.' Few, however, took Botha's strictures seriously, seeing it as anger at his being tactically outmanouevered by Luanda.

Although progress was blocked for the time being, neither side showed any wish to break off the negotiations or to depart from its declared policy of conciliation. Speaking at a press conference in Kinhasa, President dos Santos said it was too early to say that a solution was imminent, adding:

> Angola is playing a very important role and has presented some concrete proposals. We are waiting for the other interested parties to adopt a positive attitude so that the implementation of Resolution 435 may finally be accelerated.
> [Referring to relations with Unita, he said:] We believe that a military solution is not the only possible one.

A similarly conciliatory attitude is reflected in other Angolan official statements at that time. The Angolans, though, were upset because of attempts to interpret their conciliatory offer over Cuban troops as implying acceptance of linkage with Namibian independence, whereas their offer was linked only to the withdrawal of SADF troops from their own territory. Replying to those questioning their motives, Angop wrote on 3 December 1984:

> What motivates us is our frank and open contribution to settling current problems; surely, they must know who is trying to frustrate the intentions of those who have already worked for peace and security in Southern Africa.

The Angolan leadership seemed not to have shared the critical attitude adopted by other Frontline Presidents over the Nkomati Accord. A joint communiqué issued at the end of a visit by dos Santos to Maputo in December 1984 declared that Angola's President

> . . . expressed his solidarity with the efforts of Mozambique towards ensuring the full implementation of the Nkomati Accord by SA, and with the tenacious struggle of the Mozambican people to eliminate the armed bandits, lackeys of imperialism.

Meanwhile, SA had begun to step up its campaign calling for Angola to come to terms with Unita, and was keen to publicize Savimbi's growing challenge as expressed in an SABC report on 20 December 1984:

> The war in Angola between the Unita forces of Dr Jonas Savimbi and the Fapla (People's Armed Forces for the Liberation of Angola) and Cuban forces fighting for the MPLA Labour Government appears to be increasing in intensity. For the first time Unita has sabotaged Luanda's power supplies and Unita claims that its forces are now beginning to close around Luanda.

Savimbi attacked Angola's proposals to 'phase out' the presence of Cuban troops. In a statement on 10 December he demanded the expulsion of all Cubans and described the proposals as 'an exercise in propaganda and misinformation.'

PROGRESS OF THE WAR AGAINST UNITA

The ceasefire agreement with SA in February 1984 and the formal withdrawal of SADF units in April 1985 had considerably lessened the external military pressures on Fapla, but there was no let-up on the battlefront with Unita. By August 1984, Savimbi's forces had extended their operations to a considerable distance beyond their stronghold in Ovimbundu country and had succeeded in infiltrating saboteurs into the capital itself, as well as in mining two ships in Luanda harbour. However the boast that Unita was in a position to sabotage the oil operations in Cabinda proved an idle one. There were reports that in his anxiety to demonstrate Unita's fighting strength in order to undermine the American effort at negotiating an agreement over the withdrawal of Cuban troops, Savimbi had over-extended his lines.

Three serious efforts were made in 1984 to break Unita's resistance. A six-month offensive from February to July in the Cazombo area ended in failure. From September to October two separate offences were mounted—one from Munhango on the Benguela railway in a southern arc, and the other from Cuti Cuanavale against Unita's two strongpoints, Mavinga and Jamba, in the east. Neither proved successful.

According to SA military intelligence Unita had 35,000 troops and was 'in full control of about one-third of the country.' The International Institute for Strategic Studies confirmed this figure, but reported that only 15,000 were regulars.[59] Other reports suggested that Unita's regular army was 10,000 strong with 15,000 semi-regulars and 1,500 special commandos trained for urban raids.[60] Savimbi announced plans to build up his total strength to 40,000 during 1985. Fapla was said to be in full control of only three of the ten military regions—the First (Uige and Zaire), the Fifth (Cunene) and the Eighth (Luanda). However, Unita was still unable to establish itself in any of the major towns outside of Ovimbundu territory. 'The outcome of the battle of the towns' still remained to be decided.

The structure of Unita's army is: *Sentinela* at the base, comprising recently-recruited cadres who provide a militia and guards, with rudimentary weapons;

their main task is to maintain Unita's influence in recently-captured villages; two operational levels of guerrillas—one comprising small groups of c.20 men, and the other of c.100 men; locally recruited and trained in their home areas, where they remain for up to two years (estimated at between 16,000-20,000 men); semi-regulars who have received three months training in special Unita training camps before being sent into the field in groups of between 350-450; the regulars who have undergone a further 6-9 months training in the use of more sophisticated weapons, 25% of whom are believed to have had special training in artillery and communications in camps run by the SADF in Namibia.[61]

(For further details of Unita's political role and foreign supporters see the Role of the Local Actors, below.)

THE ROLE OF THE LOCAL ACTORS IN THE CRISIS

South Africa, the Regional Power

The Pretoria regime had hoped that the Nkomati Accord, its 1982 secret treaty with Swaziland and the ceasefire agreement with Angola would create a momentum for mutual security and non-aggression treaties with more of its neighbours, thus contributing to greater stability around its borders and stimulating a greater interest in the sub-continent in closer economic cooperation with SA as the lodestar. None of these expectations, which seemed feasible in mid-1984, was fulfilled. The ANC, though more harassed than earlier and finding it harder to infiltrate their cadres across the border, developed new tactics to make themselves even more effective than before.[62] Nor did Mozambique and other African States give up their political and moral support, for the ANC or the PAC which, though inactive in the armed struggle, nevertheless remained a focus for the militant Black Consciousness youth in SA. Botswana, Lesotho and Zimbabwe all refused to look at any agreement smacking of the Nkomati approach. By mid-1985 the Nkomati Accord itself looked frayed and less promising than it did a year earlier. Namibia was no closer to solution and remained, *inter alia,* a constant source of friction between Pretoria and the Western community. SA found that it needed, no less than before, to rely on its army and on cross-border raids to try and safeguard its own internal security. While SA had not yet fully abandoned its destabilization policies—so long denied but finally admitted by the Foreign Minister in Parliament in 1985 (see above)—it was harder to pursue this strategy while at the same time holding out the promise of acting as a regional peacemaker. It also found the US and Britain taking more sharply critical positions than in earlier years towards attempts to undermine the authority and security of the border states.

SA's failure to fulfill its potential as a regional power was due to three major factors, according to Dr Erich Leistner, the Director of the influential Pretoria-based Africa Institute: the magnitude of the continent's problems; a lack of factual knowledge and understanding in SA about African realities; and the rejection by Africa's leaders of SA's present socio–political order. In one of his lectures he emphasized:

> We must harbour no illusions about the neighbouring States' views of SA's internal policies. Further, there is no doubt whatsoever that, in the long run, common interests between States are a better guarantee for harmonious relations than force and threats. SA's dominant economic position in the region furnishes many opportunities to work in this direction.

Like other militarily powerful states (Israel in the Middle East, the US in Southern America and the Caribbean basin, the Soviet Union in its relations with its East European neighbors), South Africans learned from experience that strong armies are not all that are needed to build neighbourly relations or expand their influence. Contrary to a widely-held belief, the Pretoria regime has no master plan for Southern Africa and, as pointed out by two percipient writers on SA affairs, Heribert Adam and Stanley Uys,[63] Pretoria's regional policymaking apparatus is not monolithic. In their view:

> Interbureaucratic rivalries and personality idiosyncrasies influence decisions, as do career and status considerations of the few dozen persons involved. Only a few senior military officers support the efforts of a Department of Foreign Affairs sensitive to international opinion to reach a neocolonial disengagement in Angola and Mozambique and an internationally acceptable settlement in Namibia. The Department of Military Intelligence (DMI), unlike the less influential National Intelligence Service (NIS), views the present version of detente as premature. The police leadership, on the other hand, supports the Nkomati Accord because of its impact on the ANC.
>
> All this is in marked contrast to the usual Western perception of the upper military echelons as enlightened technocrats and the police as heavy-handed traditionalists. While the role of the SA military in the administrative disunity of the Government is similar to that of its counterparts elsewhere, there is one significant difference: the virtual veto power inherent in the informal influence of a half-dozen senior officers who cling to the belief that SA's 'enemies' can more reliably be subdued by covert and open force than by political incorporation.

The view SA takes of its role as a regional power is clearly stated in such statements as the following broadcast by the SABC (21 December 1984):

> Commentators today describe SA as a regional power, that is, in Southern Africa its relationship with the countries around it is analogous to that of the Super-powers in the international context. It is a position that implies certain rights, responsibilities, powers and interests. SA is the economic giant of the region. With a third of its population, the country has three-quarters of its gross regional product, 90% of its energy consumption, and the lion's share of the other countries' trade, transport, communications and other activities involving the outside world. With that kind of stake, SA has an absorbing interest in maintaining stability in Southern Africa. The other side of the coin is its interests in the development of its neighbours . . . Economic progress is one of the most potent forces for stability and peaceful coexistence with its neighbours.
>
> The regional strategic interests stem from that situation, coupled with the deep-rooted antipathy to the dehumanizing doctrine of communism. It accepts as an obligation, not only to itself but to its moderate neighbours, the need to counter a radical shift of power—as a result of intervention by force—of expansionist, influence-seeking outsiders. In particular, it has a commitment to continuing and, in cooperation with African and Western moderates, reversing the encroachment of the Soviet Union and its proxies in the region. Within that context, SA has asserted certain rights with respect to the neighbours themselves. It demands that they refrain from taking any action that might jeopardize its security, and it maintains its right to take appropriate protective measures. It upholds not only its right, but its duty, to enable territory under its protection—specifically South West Africa—to develop peacefully and democratically to a constitutional dispensation of their own choosing, free of outside intimidation.

The Pretoria regime's concerns have remained what they have been for the last decade, with only one major change in 1985: a more serious fear about the

347

possibility of the Western powers abandoning SA unless the apartheid system is progressively scrapped. In 1985 an increasing number of European countries began to distance themselves from SA, and some finally succumbed to pressures either to support disinvestment or even to impose selective sanctions. The biggest blow to SA was President Reagan's decision to take measures which, however disguised, can be described only as punitive.[64] Pretoria's other perennial concerns were over the threat to security posed by the ANC's armed struggle, especially with the rise of a violent mood among Black South Africans who had become much better organized and more militant in the past few years; the perceived threat posed by the Soviet bloc and Cubans whose diplomatic, military and political presence close to SA's frontiers was felt to make their role in the region more menacing; and the need to develop SA's economic links in the continent for three reasons: to increase SA's trading area at a time when it needs greater exports and finds its traditional markets in Europe less open and more competitive; to influence the policies of its neighbours who, if economic relations were expanded, would expect to become more sensitive to SA's needs and more dependent on its goodwill; and to contribute towards stability among its neighbours as a means of promoting and strengthening a *Pax Praetoriana*.

However, so far from expanding its trade (let alone its banking and other financial links), SA's exports to the rest of the continent had declined in 1984 by R200,000 from R1bn in 1982. Ron Mitchell, the vice-president of Citibank in Johannesburg, pointed out that if one strips away SA's commodity trade with the world, Africa remains one of the major markets for SA goods. SA businessmen have begun to urge a new economic strategy for SA by emulating East European countries and others, like Brazil, in developing counter-trade, whereby one country imports goods from another and is assisted in finding a buyer for its own exports in order to finance the original import/export deal. Barry Mason, deputy-managing director of Hill Samuel in SA, described banks as the lynchpin of counter-trade offensive which he frankly admitted 'could also play a vital role in helping neighbouring states . . . to enhance our economic and political relationships with these countries.'[65] SA, he added, was extremely well-placed for such a role, especially because of its transport and logistical advantages. This strategy is of course diametrically opposed to that of SA's neighbours engaged in developing the Southern African Development Cooperation Conference.[66]

Not much has been heard since early 1984 of P. W. Botha's previously much-boasted idea of a Constellation of Southern African States, with SA at its centre. Deon Geldenhuys, a lecturer in Political Science at the Rand Afrikaans University, wrote:

> SA . . . was compelled to scale down its plans for regional cooperation; it was a case of reconciling the desirable with the possible. This has resulted in a much more modest and indeed more realistic conception of a favourable regional environment. The grandiose scheme for a regional constellation of states has given way to an overriding concern with security.[67]

President Kaunda readily admitted in an interview with the SA journalist, Barry Streek, that SA was a regional economic power, but said that Zambia would never support its participation in SADCC as long as apartheid existed. He added:

> Yes, humble Swaziland agrees, humble Mozambique accepts, humble Zambia hosts meetings of unequal neighbours like SA and Angola. What else can we do? But we are not doing it with happy hearts. We do it out of fear, but that fear will end one day. It is bound to.[68]

THE ROLE OF SWAPO
Fears that Swapo would emerge as the victorious party from internationally-supervised elections remained the principal reason for SA's unwillingness to implement Resolution 435. Swapo has remained the dominant political force in Namibia despite the Pretoria regime's belief that its military strength would be weakened and demoralization set in once the ceasefire agreement with Angola sealed the border to infiltrations by the guerrillas. While there was a significant decrease in 1984-85 in Swapo's annual rainy season operations, its activities inside the territory increased, (see Progress of the War in Namibia, above). With the installation of an Interim Government for Namibia in June 1984, Pretoria hoped that the Multi-Party Conference would have more success than the Turnhalle Alliance in building up local support against Swapo; but there seemed little hard evidence to suggest that this was likely to happen.

SA's rigorous refusal to release Nelson Mandela unless he first repudiate violence, did not apply in its policy towards Sam Nujoma. Not only did SA representatives sit down with him at the Lusaka conference in May 1984 but direct talks were held at Cape Verde in July 1984. Nujoma insisted that Swapo's wish was to achieve 'an orderly political process' in Namibia's transition to independence.

THE ROLE OF THE AFRICAN NATIONAL CONGRESS
The ANC survived the blow struck at its military capacity by the Nkomati Accord to emerge as a much stronger factor in the politics of the region than before. The upsurge of militancy and of violence in SA during 1984-1985 boosted the fortunes of the ANC; this was due in large measure to the support commanded by the almost legendary Nelson Mandela. By mid-1985 the ANC had come to be widely regarded as holding the key to the direction of political events in the country. Its leadership role was seen as crucial not only by a substantial section of the Black community but also by influential White groups, such as the opposition Progressive Federal Party and by the business community. The dramatic change in the way in which the ANC was perceived was best illustrated by the decision of a group of leading SA businessmen to go to Lusaka in September 1985 for talks with the ANC president, Oliver Tambo, and his colleagues. Their example was followed by a number of other delegations, including Afrikaner groups, a Black businessmen's organization, and a HOMELAND leader.

Although the ANC made little effort to disguise its feeling of having been let down, if not betrayed, by the Frelimo Government, the two sides made every effort to remain on good terms. Frelimo's Central Committee sent a message of 'solidarity and friendship' to the ANC's National Consultative Conference held in Lusaka on 18 June 1985. Earlier, on 17 December 1984, the ANC celebrated South African Heroes Day in Maputo, marking the anniversary of the first actions of *Umkhonto we Sizwe*. Tombstones were unveiled of SA refugees killed by commando and parcel bomb attacks. Speaking for the ANC, Robert Mancu declared that the prestige enjoyed by the ANC was 'in no small measure due to the unselfish and principled support we have received from the people of Mozambique and their leaders over the years.'

President Machel went out of his way on a number of occasions to praise the ANC and to reiterate his view that 'SA's apartheid system is the main cause of instability and tensions in the southern zone of our continent.'

ZIMBABWE'S ROLE
Zimbabwe–South African relations are characterized by a mutual desire to defuse tensions and by mutual suspicions. The Mugabe Government's public stand is one

of extreme hostility towards the Pretoria regime; but privately the two regimes have maintained regular and close contacts over security affairs. In a rare interview in October 1984 with Michael Hartnack of the *Rand Daily Mail*, Zimbabwe's Minister of State for Security, Emmerson Munangagwa, frankly discussed the contacts he maintained with SA security officials. He confirmed a report in the London *Times* (11 September 1984) that at least one SA military convoy was allowed passage through Zimbabwe carrying tents and logistical supplies, but not arms, for the Mozambican army. The convoy crossed Beit Bridge and handed over its consignment to the Mozambicans at the Forbes border post close to Mutare. Munangagwa also confirmed that high-level talks took place in May 1984 when the head of SA Military Intelligence, Lt-Gen P. W. van der Westhuysen, visited Harare in plain clothes for talks with his opposite number, Maj-Gen Sheba Gava. At this meeting Zimbabwe presented a list of allegations relating to SA-sponsored destabilization activities. Munangagwa said there was evidence to show that 40 'Super-Zapu' dissidents had crossed the border from SA in July 1984. Their political orders came from a former district administrator, Muthukuki, who was said to be based in Pretoria.

Mugabe told his Parliament on 16 August 1984 that while he would not allow meetings with SA at Ministerial level to discuss political questions, permission was given to army and police commanders to meet their counterparts at the border on security matters; they could even travel to Johannesburg if the issue to be discussed was sufficiently important.[69]

The Mugabe Government also maintained its policy of refusing to allow the ANC or PAC (both of which maintain offices in Harare) to launch attacks against SA from Zimbabwe's soil. However, he foresaw circumstances under which this policy might change. He said Zimbabwe could not offer its territory single-handedly as a base because it could not withstand incursions from SA,

> but if the situation were such that Africa was united behind the Frontline States and all of us were asked by the whole of Africa to offer our countries as bases; provided there was military assistance in the form of weaponry and funds, in the form of a military presence here, with forces from Africa, I am sure the Frontline States would consider the matter in a different light and, of course, we would need the backing of progressive countries.[70]

In mid-August 1984, the Prime Minister said there had been a 'lull in bandit infiltration from racist South Africa.' Two weeks later Munangagwa, voiced suspicions that Pretoria was again allowing 'Super-Zapu' elements to infiltrate from across the border.[71] Towards the end of September the Information Minister, Nathan Shamuyarira, revealed that SA had on a number of occasions intercepted messages transmitted by Zimbabwe's communications system, especially those of a political and security nature.[72]

Six Zimbabweans (all Black) were put on trial charged with spying for SA; one of the men, Joseph Mandebvu, was also charged with recruiting spies and was said to be an enlisted member of the SADF. Two others were identified as a policeman and a soldier. Mandebvu and one other accused all gave their addresses as Messina, the border town in North Transvaal. Two members of an alleged SA spy ring, arrested in 1981, appealed to the High Court in November 1984 against their continued detention despite their acquittal at their trial on charges of having spied for SA. Colin Evans and Philip Hartlebury were both members of Zimbabwe's Central Intelligence Organization (CIO) at the time of their arrest. Mugabe revealed that he had received pleas from SA to release the two men although neither was a SA citizen—the one being British and the other holding joint British–Zimbabwean citizenship.[73]

The Prime Minister made more serious charges against Pretoria in December 1984 when he accused the Botha regime not only of continuing to recruit and train Zimbabwean dissidents, but also of sabotaging Zimbabwe's outlets to the sea in order to force it to export all its goods through SA ports.[74] He blamed Pretoria for having sabotaged the crucial Beira oil pipeline which was put out of commission in December. At the beginning of January 1986 Munangagwa accused 'Pretoria-sponsored dissidents' of holding meetings in Matabeleland and threatening to kill those who voted for the ruling party.[75]

BOTSWANA'S ROLE

President Quett Masire's Government maintained its firm policy of refusing to enter into a mutual security pact along the lines of the Nkomati Accord.[76] However, it agreed to hold talks to establish a working agreement affecting Botswana's security relations with SA. According to the Vice President, Peter Mmusi, the basis for such an agreement was:[77]

—Refusal to allow Botswana to be used as a launching pad for attacks on SA by the ANC;
—Acceptance of genuine refugees from SA provided they do not abuse Botswana's hospitality by organizing attacks on SA;
—Maintenance of a functional relationship with SA appropriate to the proximity of the two countries (they share a long border) and their economic ties (both are members of the South African Customs Union).

Peter Mmusi explained:

We will not allow the ANC to come through Botswana to attack SA. If they try to do so, we will deal with them. . . . We have a good working and talking relationship with SA. We don't think we want any more than that.

But he conceded that Botswana might be unable to prevent covert movement through its territory and across its borders. 'If the ANC can infiltrate through SA's defences, why should they not be able to infiltrate through Botswana?'

Botswana protested strongly against Pretoria misrepresenting its attitude over the talks to regulate their security relations. A statement from the President's Office insisted that the talks had nothing to do with 'a non-aggression pact,' and explained that the Government had a long-standing and well-known policy of not permitting its territory to be used for launching attacks against SA or any of its other neighbours (a reference to Zimbabwe), and that it needed no prompting from SA to arrest and put on trial anybody caught violating that policy.[78]

SA, however, continued to claim that the ANC was using Botswana as a corridor to infiltrate its cadres across the border. In August 1984 it alleged that three ANC gunmen had escaped back into Botswana after a gunfight. The ANC office in Lusaka issued a statement denying that its armed wing was using Botswana as a base for its military operations.[79] Pretoria, however, insisted that the ANC was using Botswana as an infiltration route. According to the Commissioner of SA Police, the route through Botswana had become more important for the ANC after the closing of its route through Mozambique.[80]

Pretoria stepped up its pressures on Botswana early in 1982. When Ms Gaositwe Chiepe was made Foreign Minister in place of Archie Mogwe (who had lost his seat in the elections at the end of 1984), the SA Foreign Minister sent her a note calling for 'some effective and practical arrangement between the security forces of our two countries to ensure that the territory of neither is used for the planning or execution of acts of sabotage or terrorism against the other.'[81] On 5 February, Pretoria formally accused Botswana of harbouring ANC guerrillas and allowing them to infiltrate through the border homeland of Bophutatswana, and warned that the 'situation cannot continue as at present.'[82] Both SA and Bophutatswana threatened to undertake 'hot pursuits' of guerrillas into Botswana. Masire expressed alarm at a threatened attack by the SADF to the British Minister of State for Africa, Malcolm Rifkind, when he visited Gaborone in February.[83] Rifkind warned SA that Britain and other Western countries would not take a lenient view of an attack on Botswana, adding that he was satisfied that its Government was not allowing ANC guerrillas to use its territory as a springboard for attacks on SA.[84] Masire saw the latest threats as adding a new dimension to Pretoria's pressures for it to sign an Nkomati type agreement.[85] He insisted that his country would continue to receive genuine refugees, but since they were not branded as such, it was conceivable that some were not genuine refugees.

SA and Botswana held what both sides described as 'conciliatory talks' in Pretoria on 22 February 1985. Pik Botha helped ease the tensions by announcing that he would no longer insist on a formal security agreement with Botswana in view of its assurances that it would not allow subversive elements to operate from their territory against SA.[86] Botswana's Secretary for External Affairs, Geoffrey Garebamono, confirmed that Botswana had twice refused SA demands in 1984 to sign a non-aggression pact; it therefore came as a relief that this demand was not renewed.[87] However, this spirit of goodwill was shortlived.

Early in March 1985, SA demanded that Botswana should hand over a list of ANC members whom they asked should be expelled from Botswana, and later in the month Masire repeated his earlier statements about fears of invasion by SA, 'against which his country was helpless.[88] In April Dr Chiepe said Botswana would be willing to consider hosting a meeting between the ANC leader, Oliver Tambo, and President Botha; Tambo said he would be willing to attend if the purpose was to discuss a new constitution for SA.[89]

SA's iron fist policy hit Botswana on 15 June 1985 when the SADF made a commando attack into the capital, Gaborone, and Tlokweng, 5km distant from the capital. Between 12-15 people were killed. Gen Constand Viljoen, the Chief of the SADF, said the attack was against 'the ANC nerve centre' in Botswana; it was not an attack on the Botswana Government. 'The decision to destroy the ANC targets had been taken with the greatest sense of responsibility.'[90] SA's Foreign Minister claimed that the ANC had launched 36 attacks from Botswana since August 1984.[91] He alleged that the Palestine Liberation Organization 'had played an important role in training ANC terrorists for some time.' A commentary on SABC linked ANC activities in Botswana to the Soviet ambassador in Gaborone, Mikhail Petrov,[92] (see Soviet Role, below). Masire condemned the attack as 'a blood-curdling act of murder of defenceless citizens.'[93] He added that Pretoria 'never meant a word of what it said when it accepted our assurances' at the Pretoria talks in February 1985. The commando attack, he added, was preceded by two other bomb attacks: in February a bomb blast had demolished a house and car; and in May, a second bomb blast had killed a SA refugee and caused extensive damage to property. He added that no evidence had been produced to show that the victims were 'ANC freedom fighters'.

International reaction was sharply critical of SA. The Frontline States and other OAU members condemned SA's action. It was called 'unprovoked and unwarranted' (Zimbabwe's Foreign Minister); 'dastardly and barbarous'

(Lesotho's Prime Minister); 'an aggravation of the tensions in Southern Africa' (Mozambique's Foreign Minister). The British Foreign Secretary summoned the SA ambassador in London to protest against the raid 'as a blatant violation of the sovereignty of a fellow-Commonwealth country.' The Dutch and French were prominent among other European Governments to condemn the raid. However, the strongest reaction in the West came from the US. Its ambassador in SA was recalled for consultations and the US embassy in Pretoria was told to have no further contacts, for the present, with the SA Government.[94] The State Department said the raid 'calls into question SA's sincerity and seriousness in dealing constructively with issues of regional peace.' Its spokesman, Bernard Kalb added:[95]

> This latest SA action comes against a background that raises the most serious questions about that Government's recent conduct and policy. Such cross-border violence only complicates efforts to bring peace.

LESOTHO'S ROLE

Like Botswana, Lesotho refused to enter into an Nkomati Accord type of agreement; but it sought to defuse the conflict with SA in mid-1984 after a year of mounting crisis.[96]

At a Ministerial meeting in June it was agreed that existing arrangements between the two countries had well served the security interests of both, and that these should be maintained to express, by concrete action; mutual recognition that neither country should permit its territory to be used as a base for attacks on either, or on any other neighbouring State.[97]

In June, the UN Secretary-General warned that some elements of the drafts seen in New York would place Lesotho in violation of its treaty obligations in respect of the status of refugees. However, the moves towards *détente* were again halted in mid-1985 when the Lesotho Government sent a Note to Pretoria protesting against the activities of the exile leader of the Lesotho Liberation Army, Ntsu Mokhehle, on SA territory. It claimed that there was substantial evidence to show that Mokhehle was not only resident in SA, but had planned and executed acts of subversion against Lesotho from QwaQwa, one of the homelands adjacent to the Kingdom.[98]

While SA continued to deny Mokhehle's presence on its soil, a police spokesman claimed that information obtained from the Botswana raid had shown that ANC 'suicide squads', which had penetrated the Transvaal and Cape Provinces, were controlled from an office in Maseru. These cross-accusations reheated the political climate, but Maseru showed no inclination to revert to its earlier hostile relations with its neighbour. Referring to the pressures building up inside the apartheid state, a commentary on Radio Maseru urged:

> The pressures are building. The international anger over events in SA is deepening. The demands for action designed to create changes in SA are becoming more stringent and so are the predictable responses of SA. These are times for statesmanship and wisdom. Prudence dictates the premise on which change can be effected. Foresight, reason, and enlightenment call for attitudes of mind that seek accommodation rather than confrontation.

SWAZILAND'S ROLE

Swaziland continued to play the role its Government had assumed for it under the secret treaty with Pretoria in 1982[99] as SA's policeman along the Mozambique border. The Swazi security police collaborated closely with their SA counterparts in harassing ANC supporters out of the Kingdom and in stopping any movement of men or arms across Swazi soil. Many ANC supporters were imprisoned, and some were handed over to SA. By 1985 Swaziland had become *verboten* territory for the ANC. Faced with its own internal political and security problems, the post-Sobhusa regime was in no mood to give any quarter to armed SA cadres whom they suspected of being in contact with the Swazi opposition. Swaziland's insecurely perched regime showed every sign in 1985 of moving closer to its SA ally and further from its African neighbours.[100]

MOZAMBIQUE'S ROLE

Over-optimistic expectations that the Nkomati Accord, signed on 16 March 1984, would produce quick results for Mozambique's security and economy were quickly snuffed out.[101] In July, four months after the signing of the agreement, Mozambique was still bleeding from the injuries inflicted by the Mozambique National Resistance (MNR or Renamo). There were almost daily attacks on villages, roads and rail traffic in nine out of the ten provinces. The attacks were of the nature of bush banditry, which added to the country's sad economic conditions, now heightened by the worst drought in living memory.[102] President Machel's Frontline allies privately expressed the view that SA could not be expected to honour its side of the agreement, while publicly continuing to defend Mozambique's decision against criticisms from other OAU member-states.

Speaking to a SADCC summit meeting in Gaborone on 6 July, Nyerere denounced Pretoria's efforts to force SADCC members into new or expanded forms of economic cooperation with it which, he warned, 'could weaken the anti-apartheid struggle as well as the real independence of our sovereign states.' Pretoria, he added, was trying by threats and promises to pursue the 'mirage of economic prosperity' by cooperating with it and although there were short-term economic advantages such cooperation would make SADCC members into accomplices or victims of apartheid.[103]

The Frelimo Government also adopted two different policies: officially it insisted that the Accord was bringing benefits, but through calculated leaks it voiced its suspicions about SA policies choosing, however, to blame 'certain elements' in SA rather than the Botha regime. This duality in its policy was shown in several statements in July 1984. After the fifth meeting of the Mozambique–SA Joint Security Commission (JSC) on 18 July, a joint communiqué was issued which 'took note of the effective steps that have been taken by both countries to realize the objectives of the Accord.[104] It added that 'while in general a satisfactory situation had been achieved further progress has still to be made'. Only two days earlier, the official Mozambique news agency (AIM) had commented:

> When on 16 March SA's Prime Minister, P. W. Botha, pledged before the international community to stop support from SA to the armed bandits in Mozambique, some sectors in SA reacted negatively. It is possible that they have maintained links with the bandits and are fomenting actions like the latest ones against SA citizens. This could be a way of pressurizing Botha's Government to return to its strategy of military destabilization of Mozambique.'[105]

The report also linked the role of 'certain elements' in SA with groups in Portugal 'who are looking for a way to create the right conditions for a frontal attack on P. W. Botha and his Foreign Minister Roelof Botha.' Mozambican authorities told AIM of their 'growing concern over the continued propaganda for banditry in Portugal.' However, the authorities insisted that this 'banditry' would not be allowed to cause discord between Mozambique and Portugal since Frelimo's aim was to have 'fruitful cooperation with the new Portugal.'

Over the next nine months these concerns over the activities of pro-MNR groups in SA and Portugal became a recurrent theme in Maputo's relations with Pretoria and Lisbon. The Portuguese Government at first justified its refusal to act against Portuguese citizens, like one of the MNR leaders, Jorge Correia, on the grounds that in a democracy it was not possible to curb activities that did not breach any Portuguese law.[106] Months later, after relations had worsened with Maputo, Correia and his group did run foul of Portuguese law and he went into exile in Spain and France.

Pretoria reacted angrily to suggestions that it was not living up to its side of the Nkomati Accord. When the *Rand Daily Mail* published an editorial which quoted a report attributed to Mozambique Government sources, the SA Defence Minister, Gen Magnus Malan, wrote to the paper taking 'the strongest exception' to the report. Insisting that he and his colleagues 'have stated categorically that the agreement would be followed to the letter,' Gen Malan went on to repudiate any suggestions of a 'split in the ranks of the SADF', adding:[107]

> I would like to point out that any rational, objective person could not conceive of a situation where members of the Defence Force, who have much to lose, would not strive as actively for peace as anyone else.

Within a short time the General was to be proved wrong. In the meantime, SA started at the end of July 1984 to provide logistical support for Mozambique to protect the power lines carrying electricity from the Cahora Bassa hydroelectric station to SA.[108]

Machel continued to extol the Nkomati Accord as a victory against SA. He explained this in a speech to Zanu's conference in Harare in August:[109]

> Our military victories and the success of the diplomatic offensive which brought about the international isolation of the apartheid regime, by modifying the correlations of forces in Southern Africa, caused imperialism's option in favour of military destabilization to fail. . . . The Nkomati Accord is 'an expression of the new situation created in the region, but it does not mark the end of schemes of imperialist domination.

Mozambique's Foreign Minister, Joaquim Chissano, was still confidently asserting in August 1984 that the Accord was being progressively implemented, and that his Government had 'no reason to complain against the SA Government'; however, not all sectors of SA society favoured the Accord and some continued their support of MNR despite Pretoria's stand. Difficulties, he added, were being sorted out with the SA authorities.[110] At a meeting of senior Ministerial and top army held in Maputo on 20 August, Frelimo presented detailed evidence of violations of the Accord, including the names of SA military and intelligence officers who, they claimed, were continuing to support MNR. Pik Botha asked for a week to clear up the complaints 'once and for all'.[111] Another of Maputo's allegations was that there were still 18,000 MNR cadres in SA military camps, which they wished to see shut down. SA's private answer to this charge was that they preferred to keep some of the dissidents under control rather than to let them back to join up with MNR.

Frelimo's concern in August was over the spread of dissident activities in the north where it was said to be taking root among the Makonde peasantry, who had once formed the backbone of Frelimo's liberation struggle.[112]

On the positive side, SA signed an agreement to redevelop Maputo harbour on 14 August 1984. There was an eager response from SA farmers to a tentative Mozambican offer to lease out 8,000 ha farms, according to Colin Patterson, head of the SA trade mission in Maputo. Immediate priorities, though, were tourism, medical assistance and the use of Maputo harbour. Following a Mozambican delegation visit to the Lowveld region, which lies along the Transvaal–Mozambique border, a committee was formed to promote trade, tourism and other links. Pik Botha, though, expressed his opinion that economic and commercial cooperation would have to wait until there was 'security and stability in Mozambique.'[113]

SA also appeared to be concerned over the failure to end the MNR resistance which they saw threatening the Nkomati spirit, if not yet the Accord itself. On 16 August, at SA's invitation, an MNR delegation arrived in Pretoria to discuss terms for ending their resistance. Two senior Mozambican Ministers, Jacinto Veloso and Sergio Vieira, were in Pretoria at the same time. Portuguese sources insisted that the Ministers had held talks with the MNR delegation, which was strongly denied by them.[114] There was no immediate clarification of the results of the talks between SA and MNR.

Meanwhile, the security situation both inside Mozambique and SA continued to deteriorate. While the situation on the Mozambican side had improved somewhat in Sofala province in September 1984, with the reopening of the Beira–Moatize railway line, it had worsened in the Quelimane district of Sofala province in the south. The MNR was reported to be operating from a base in Swaziland. Pretoria was especially concerned about this development because of its threat to its rail and road traffic to Maputo.[115]

The expected improvements for security in SA, following the expulsion of the ANC from Mozambique, also remained unfulfilled. Twenty actual or attempted sabotage attacks were reported between the signing of the Nkomati Accord and the attack on the offices of the Department of Internal Affairs in Johannesburg on 4 September, compared with 15 attacks over the same period in 1983. According to the Pretoria-based Institute of Strategic Studies, the number of sabotage attacks (including five by a White extremist group, the SA Suicide Squad) for the first nine months of 1984 was 27, cf. 29 for the same period in 1983. The Institute added that while the number of sabotage attacks was not decreasing, it was now more difficult for ANC cadres to avoid arrest since, instead of relying on the shorter route across the Mozambican borders, they were now forced to attempt the much longer route via Zimbabwe and Botswana.[116]

Portugal's Prime Minister Mario Soares led a delegation of 80 officials and businessmen to Maputo in mid-September. He promised that inflammatory statements made by MNR representatives in Lisbon would result in their being brought to trial; but at the same time he denied that the MNR was operating from Portugal. He added that if the Portuguese authorities became aware of the MNR operating as an organization in Portugal, 'we will not allow it to continue'. He explained that 'since we have an open system of total freedom of the Press, frequently the Government are the last to know such things.'[117] This seemingly contradictory statement clearly did not satisfy Machel.

A second round of talks with MNR was held in late September; this time the negotiations took the form of proximity talks, with SA representatives talking separately to the Frelimo delegation (led by the Minister of Security, Maj-Gen Sergio Viera, and the Chief of the Air Force, Maj-Gen Hama Thai) and to the MNR delegation (headed by its leader, A. Dhlakama, and which included its secretary-general, E. Fernandes; its secretary, J. Vaz; and two commanders, M. Ngonhamo and J. Horacio). Dhlakama said the purpose of the talks was to see if he could negotiate peace with the Frelimo Government.[118]

The Pretoria talks seemed to have reached the point of collapse on 2 October when the Mozambican delegation announced that if the problem of MNR attacks was not solved rapidly it would return home.[119] However, on the next day the SA Foreign Minister announced that the MNR had accepted a four-point Declaration 'as a basis for peace in Mozambique':[120]

> 1. Recognition of the authority of the Mozambican State, and acknowledgement of Samora Moises Machel as the acknowledged President.
> 2. Armed activity or conflict within Mozambique, from whatever quarter or source must stop.
> 3. The SA Government is requested to consider playing a role in the implementation of this Declaration.
> 4. A commission to be established immediately to work towards an early implementation of this Declaration.

Speaking at a press conference after the announcement of the Declaration, Jaconto Veloso said it had given 'the kiss of life' to the Nkomati Accord; but he added that the Declaration would not of itself be the main factor in overcoming violence and banditry, which could be ended only through the effective actions of the army. Asked about Botha's reported offer to send SA troops to Mozambique to help implement the terms of the Declaration, Veloso replied:

> This was not discussed, and therefore the only comment I can make is that if Mr Botha said that, then he is prepared for such an eventuality—but we did not discuss the matter.[121]

However, before the ink was allowed to dry on the declaration, the MNR spokesman, Evo Fernandes, announced: 'The war continues and we may have to escalate our actions. There is only speculation about peace or a ceasefire, but there is still no reality to it.'[122] The MNR insisted that it wanted agreement on a 'government of reconciliation' and a change in the political system. Pretoria insisted that despite these statements by the MNR the commission proposed to implement the Declaration would go ahead. On 8 October the Mozambican delegation under Veloso returned to Pretoria to participate in the work of the Implementation Commission, but insisted that there was no question of negotiating terms with 'the bandits'. Veloso said there was evidence that certain elements in MNR were opposed to implementating the Declaration. Despite its negative statements, the MNR at first continued to participate in the implementation talks, but withdrew on 18 October. Nonetheless, Pretoria continued to insist that 'peace efforts between the Mozambican Government and Renamo are continuing.'[123] The talks, in fact, went on until the end of the month; but Veloso warned that 'the Portuguese faction of the armed banditry is trying to sabotage the implementation of Nkomati and the Pretoria Declaration.'[124] Alves Gomes, a prominent Mozambican journalist, claimed that 'a top leader of the Portuguese Social Democratic Party (PSD) contacted one of the bandit leaders (in Pretoria). This story was confirmed by Pik Botha in February 1985.[125] Gomes did not identify the PSD politician, but named a prominent Portuguese businessman and former owner of the Maputo oil refinery, Manuel Bulhosa, as one of the central figures behind the MNR. Bulhosa now lives in Brazil; two of the MNR leaders, Fernandes and Correia, had worked for him in Mozambique.[126] He also claimed that certain serving Portuguese officers were maintaining contact with MNR and the SADF, and that a Lt-Col had been dropped in Mozambique to visit an MNR base at Tome in Inhambane province. Other sources claimed that it was Portugal's Deputy Prime Minister, Moto Pinto, whose party was in Soares' coalition Government, who had made the telephone call.[127]

A few days after Alves Gomes' article appeared, Mozambique's Foreign Minister summoned the Portuguese ambassador in Maputo to protest against the involvement of Portuguese citizens. He said that the 'Portuguese component in the global action of armed banditry constitutes one of the principal obstacles to a cessation of violence in Mozambique.'[128] The SA Foreign Minister followed up this statement by one of his own in which he warned that the 'delicate negotiations' to end the fighting in Mozambique 'are being threatened by foreign interests'. He did not identify them.[129] Botha's statement was made after Jorge Correia had accused Botha of 'bias in favour of Mozambique's 'communist regime', and announced the MNR's intention of withdrawing from the peace talks. At this point, in early November, it appeared that a serious split had opened up within the MNR which had stopped the talks and effectively ended the negotiations. At that point, according to Lisbon sources,[130] Frelimo and the MNR were on the point of signing an extendable three-month ceasefire agreement with a promise of continued negotiations through a tripartite commission.

On 23 October 1984 President Machel made his first official visit to Malawi, the immediate purpose of which was to secure Banda's support for the elimination of MNR groups who were reported to be operating across this border. Banda has always denied the truth of these allegations. Cooperation agreements signed during Machel's visit did not mention security, but contained a paragraph promising that neither would 'allow their territories to be used as bases, or give support to any organization or group of people which intends or prepares itself to launch violent acts, terrorism or aggression against the other.' The final communiqué also affirmed their commitment to 'eliminate the current armed banditry.'[131]

FAILURE TO IMPLEMENT PRETORIA DECLARATION BRINGS NKOMATI ACCORD TO VERGE OF COLLAPSE

In the last two months of 1984, the Mozambican authorities published a series of detailed allegations about continued SA support for the MNR and of other foreign interests engaged in keeping the bandits supplied with arms. The parlous state into which the Nkomati Accord had lapsed was emphasized in an article written by Carlos Cardoso, the Director of the Mozambique Information Agency.[132] He wrote that, whatever the source of the foreign military assistance received by the MNR, it was Pretoria which possessed the most important means for ending the banditry, and suggested that the reason SA had been so slow in taking effective action was because some military sectors in the SADF believed that Machel had signed the Accord as a tactical move and intended to repudiate it once his aim had been met. He cited the views of 'many SA commentators' who saw the Accord as a compromise between the two Bothas and the 'military men', and who suggested that Pretoria's real aim was to promote its economic hegemony instead of simply relying on its military hegemony. Cardoso added:

> If the SA Government sees the Accord as a way of dominating Mozambique economically, then it had better rethink the Accord because Mozambique did not sign it in order to become economically dependent on SA.

In November the Mozambican authorities published the testimony of a 16-year-old youth, Simeao Fernando, who claimed to have been captured by the MNR and taken to one of their camps in Inhambane province. He claimed that in September he witnessed an airdrop of military supplies. The provincial military commander confirmed that such an air drop had taken place that month, following an earlier one in June.[133]

Detailed information about SA's alleged role in keeping the MNR supplied for months after the signing of the Nkomati Accord was given by a defector, Constantino Reis, a former student dissident leader at Maputo University and a member of Mozambique's team at the Moscow Olympic Games.[134] He claimed that SA supplies had continued to reach the MNR until at least 10 July, the date of his defection. In the week after the Accord was signed, he said that two SA ships had unloaded armes for the MNR on the coast of Sofala, north of Beira. Military radio communications were still being maintained with the MNR rear base near Pietersberg in the Transvaal. He identified a number of SADF officers who had been in contact with the MNR.

Despite these reports, Maj Veloso said he remained convinced that the SA Government was implementing the Accord and that its top leaders desired to play an active role in the cessaton of violence.[135] He added that the crucial aspect in fulfilment of the Accord remained security. 'There are signs that individuals and organizations inside SA are compromising and, perhaps, even violating the Accord and continue to support armed banditry.' These reports, he said, were being investigated. While some people had doubts about the value of the Accord because of the difficulties encountered in fully implementing (especially) its security aspects, Veloso was confident that:

> Perhaps only in a few years from now shall we be able to measure with some objectivity the strategic importance of the Nkomati Accord. Perhaps in a few years those who study this situation will conclude that the Accord was perhaps the most important political event of 1984, not only regionally but also internationally. The spirit of the Accord will surely spread to the whole of Southern Africa. It is not only limited to two neighbours with many differences—Mozambique and SA—but the Accord points to ways of solving extremely serious problems between all neighbours, between countries with fundamental differences, sometimes antagonistic or even characterized by confrontation, who want a platform for living in good-neighbourliness.
>
> However, nothing is achieved quickly or immediately. In the field of security we have not seen tangible results. There is some mistrust, and the Accord is being viewed with mistrust and suspicion, thus immediately affecting its validity. I believe the causes of this mistrust are obstacles to implementing the Accord, but I believe that they will be overcome. However, it is true that there is a probability and some risk of progressive non-implementation of the Accord, and even failure. This can happen due to the manner in which it is implemented, or the long-drawn continuation of this situation.
>
> However, if the current obstacles are removed before the Accord is frozen, it will of course develop, flourish and bear fruit. It will come into fruition. It is therefore the duty of the institutions, organizations and individuals who understand the strategic nature of the Accord to act with good faith and good intentions. I think they will work and make all efforts to prevent the slow death or freezing of the Nkomati Accord.

President Machel appeared at times to put most of the blame for the continued banditry on SA and, at other times, on other sources of support. Speaking at a rally in late December 1984 he said:

> We are not fooled. The key to the problem of terrorism lies with SA. That is why we signed the Nkomati Accord with them. . . . [However, the SA Government] has continued to sustain, develop, equip, infiltrate and supply the bandits.

A few days later, in his New Year Message, Machel said that 'the real architects of the conspiracy against Mozambique are based in certain Western European capitals'; but that they benefit from 'the complicity of individuals and organizations in neighbouring countries from whom they receive the necessary logistic support and who infiltrate terrorists, saboteurs and merecenaries.[136]

SA spokesmen continued to deny all allegations about their clandestine support for the MNR, but Pik Botha promised to investigate specific charges through the Joint Security Commission.[137] The Chief of the SADF denied 'unequivocally' any suggestion that the army in all its branches did not fully support the Nkomati Accord, and asserted that 'no member of the SADF' supported the MNR.[138]

A significant commentary on the State-controlled SABC (30 December 1984) made these points:

> Whatever the case, it would be surprising indeed if the SA Government today numbered among Renamo supporters. The diplomatic advantages accruing to SA through the Nkomati Accord are just too numerous for this country to want to jeopardize the agreement. On the other hand, support from these other sources is a strong possibility. Where this support emanates from SA territory, it is high time the Government ensured that its foreign policy is not thwarted in this way.
>
> For SA the crumbling of Nkomati would undoubtedly constitute a diplomatic loss. It would lead to renewed ANC terror strikes across the border, and it would result in some minor economic losses. For Mozambique, the consequences would be more far-reaching. Let us assume, for argument's sake, that SA was, indeed, supporting Renamo prior to Nkomati. In the event of Nkomati crumbling, it could well be that such support is resumed, and even increased, with incalculable consequences for Mozambique.
>
> Should Mozambique summon the assistance of some Soviet surrogate power, such as the Cubans, the situation might be contained, but it certainly will not be resolved; 35,000 Cubans in Angola plus East Germans and Russians have kept the MPLA Government in power, but its influence and the area it controls are being reduced daily.

Aside from suspecting certain unnamed elements in SA of helping the MNR, Maputo's main suspicions centred on sources of support in Portugal, other West European capitals and certain Arab States. The role of Portugal's Deputy Prime Minister, Moto Pinto, and of other political and business interests is discussed above. Maputo also privately named the Bavarian leader of the Christian Social Union, Franz-Joseph Strauss, as a source of funds for MNR, which were said to be channeled through SA.[139] Mozambican intelligence sources suspected that the MNR had opened up a new source of funds among some conservative Arab Governments who appear to have believed statements alleging persecution of Muslims in Mozambique. (The Macuas, who include many Muslims, came under attack as MNR operations extended to the Makondi area in 1984. It would therefore not be too difficult to persuade Muslim leaders with little knowledge of the situation that 'a communist regime' was engaged in persecuting Muslims.) According to Maputo sources, military aid was being flown from Saudi Arabia and Oman, via Somalia and the Comoro Republic (both members of the Arab League), and dropped by air into Mozambique or, possibly, diverted through Malawi.[140] Velosa said some Islamic countries had become a major source of finance for the MNR. He suggested that the Islamic connection arose from the harassment of Muslim religious leaders by Frelimo and the desertion of some Muslim places of worship.[141]

SA's Foreign Minister was reported to have visited both the Comoros and Somalia in late 1984 in connection with the opening up of new air links to the

Middle East and, while there, he is said to have sought assurances that no planes carrying arms for MNR were using their airports.[142]

The New Year brought a number of new initiatives. Early in January 1985 the MNR's secretary-general, Evo Fernandes, returned to Pretoria at SA's insistence in order to try and resume the tripartite negotiations. The US Deputy Assistant Secretary of State for African Affairs, Frank Wisner, visited Mozambique to complete an aid agreement which included reputed $1m worth of military aid, a new departure in US–Mozambican relations. In Lisbon, Prime Minister Soares announced on 24 January that he had instructed his Ministers to examine actions against the activities of the MNR in Portugal. Now, too, Pretoria admitted for the first time that aid for the MNR may have come from SA, but not from the Government or with its knowledge. Pretoria was embarrassed when, after two British tourists were stabbed to death by bandits, the MNR band was seen to cross the SA border to safety. This open infringement of the Accord could not be glossed over. Machel summoned the ambassadors in Maputo representing the five Western members of the Contact Group to a meeting on 7 January to review progress of the Nkomati Accord. Afterwards, Machel said:

> Everyone agreed that the Accord is not being fully implemented in letter or in spirit. However, we also agreed that Mozambique has carried out the Accord fully.

The new attempt to get the MNR's agreement to implementing the Pretoria Declaration was quickly abandoned. Pik Botha announced that the demands made by Fernandes were so preposterous that he had not even passed them on to Machel because he would 'think I was crazy even to imagine that they could be acceptable.'[143] When the Joint Security Commission met in Pretoria in early February, Mozambique's Internal Security Minister, Sergio Vieira, submitted evidence of SA elements involved in supporting the MNR. Botha admitted that while the SA Government had 'gone out of its way to ensure that elements from SA do not transgress' the Nkomati Accord, 'I cannot say it has not happened. I believe there are elements in this country that are supplying Renamo with assistance in some form or another, but not a bit of evidence has been produced to indicate that this was done by the SA Government or by a department of this country.'[144] So, many months after Maputo had first produced its evidence and after repeated denials, Pretoria at last acknowledged involvement in the MNR from elements in SA. For a country that has one of the best intelligence systems in the world, it is remarkable that clandestine activities could have occurred on SA territory without the authorities getting to know about them.

On 16 March Pik Botha announced the discovery of a Mafia-like criminal and political syndicate, involving financiers on three continents, who provided funds for the MNR and who used 'sympathizers' in the SADF to collaborate with the bandits. They used millions of counterfeit US dollars and 50-Rand notes to buy arms for the MNR. The two leading counterfeiters had managed to escape to an unidentified European country. Action was promised against the guilty soldiers. (In May 1985 Gen Malan announced the dismissal of five soldiers because of proven sympathy for the MNR in one case, and suspected sympathy on the part of the other four.) Botha added that the MNR was also being supported by bankers, financiers and businessmen 'with large political interest in Africa, Latin America and Europe.' He went on:

> I have no illusions about their motives. They are apparently determined to attempt to turn Mozambique into their private economic preserve. It was up to other Governments to do what SA had done in uncovering the plot.

Botha's revelations came on the first anniversary of the Nkomati Accord, 1(March 1985. Two days earlier, Pik Botha and Gen Malan had flown to Maputo t(salvage the Accord and to report on their efforts to apprehend the backers of the MNR. A joint statement was issued in Maputo reaffirming belief in the need t(implement the Accord fully 'for the benefit of development in the whole o Southern Africa.'

On 20 March, after Machel had returned from Moscow where he had gone t(attend Chernenko's funeral, he had 'some harsh words for Botha', according t(Radio Maputo. He said the Accord had failed to attain its objectives because the SA authorities had failed to take strong measures to put an end to the banditry—a clear failure to comply with the requirements of the Accord. Radio Maputo sai(that if the activities to assist the MNR on SA soil had been happening for a few weeks after the Accord was signed it would still have been understandable;—'bu' did it really have to take a full year for the SA authorities to take action agains' certain unidentified individuals operating against Mozambique?'

Maputo's response to SA's admissions was to call on the Western countries because of their deep economic involvement in SA, to take action against Pretoria to make it honour the Nkomati Accord. The appeal was directed especially to the US as one of the countries which had praised the signing of the Accord.[145] In ar angry statement, Maputo declared that Nkomati was not a gentleman's agreemen' but a pact of non-aggression and good-neighbourliness. 'The Accord says: "The territory of one State must not be used as a springboard for attacks against the other." The agreement is categorical and says the attacks must stop. They have no' stopped.'[146]

Machel said the reason the war was continuing was because 'SA is no' fulfilling its agreement. I don't know whether it is unable or unwilling to.'[14'] Jacinto Veloso spoke of the possibility of taking the breach to the Security Counci] and added:

> Destabilization does not come only from SA, but also by other routes, from othe' countries and other forces. . . . It is a complex of forces that is now acting against us, and its against this complex that we must act.[148]

Early in February 1985 President Kaunda flew to Maputo for talks on security with Machel. Their communiqué said that 'the persistence of attacks against Mozambique from SA was aimed against the SADCC.'[149] A Mozambican delega- tion also visited Harare for talks with Zimbabwe to review cooperation in defence and security, and 'the current bilateral and regional security of the two coun- tries.'[150]

At their Frontline Summit held in Lusaka on 7 March, the six Heads of States devoted their time to discussing the security situation in Mozanbique and the Nkomati Accord. They condemned SA's failure to respect the Accord and re- solved to give 'all necessary support to Mozambique.' A month earlier, the five leaders of Lusophone Africa had met in São Tomé where they attacked SA for not honouring either the Nkomati Accord or the ceasefire agreement with Lusaka. The São Tomé Declaration (15 February 1985)[151] said these two agreements were part of 'a consistent policy aimed at achieving peace in the region.' It 'vehemently condemned the complicity of certain Portuguese political, financial and military circles in aggression against Mozambique and Angola', which had resulted in 'a deterioration of the relations between those countries and Portugal.' It also re- affirmed support for Swapo and the ANC.

The general verdict on the first anniversary of the Nkomati Accord was that there was little to celebrate.' Mozambique's security was worse even than a year earlier; its economy continued to decline, partly because of the drought; although a little more Western aid had begun to trickle in and membership of the IMF and EEC held out the promise of foreign loans; there was, in fact, little economic support from SA other than technical help for the ports and railways. (For details of SA's economic cooperation, see chapter on Mozambique.)

Botswana's leaders put the blame for the escalation of banditry squarely on SA.[152] 'They are convinced that, one way or another, SA is cheating. . . . In agreeing to sign the Accord, Mozambique sacrificed some of its dearest principles. It has earned the wrath not only of the ANC but of other forces within Africa, including some of its friends in the OAU. Some have actually accused it of capitulation.' Radio Maseru (14 March 1985) commented that the first anniversary was not accompanied by the fanfare that accompanied the attachment of the signatures:

> An agreement that was enthusiastically heralded as ushering in a new era of peace in South Africa by the White spokesmen of SA . . . The Lesotho Government has always declared . . . that it did not consider it within its competence to pass judgment on bilateral matters affecting Mozambique and SA; and in any event sincerely hoped that the sister state would derive benefits from the interests that motivated it to sign the agreement.

As the Accord entered its second year, SA agreed to a number of measures required of them by Maputo:
The Eastern Transvaal border was declared a restricted air area as part of the effort to prevent arms being flown in clandestinely to MNR, and to curb smuggling.
—Radar was to be installed along the border to detect illegal flights and track aircraft.
—All Mozambicans with the SADF, including those engaged as labourers, were to be transferred from the border, or completely removed; there would be no further recruitment of Mozambicans in the SADF.
—A corps of private security guards, likely to number several hundreds, would be established to guard key installations in Mozambique.

Pretoria decided at the end of March to abandon the attempt to mediate between Maputo and the MNR. The Deputy Foreign Minister, Louis Nel, said the two sides had hardened since SA first brought them together for negotiations; the MNR was determined to press for a military solution, while Frelimo was seeking international cooperation to cut off supplies to the rebels. 'Our priority now is to get rid of Renamo,' Nel concluded.[153]

April brought the first public admission by SA that it had actively supported the MNR until the Nkomati Accord was signed. The admission was made by the Foreign Minister in the SA Parliament on 25 April when the Government was attacked by the *verkrampte* Conservative Party of having cynically betrayed the MNR. Pik Botha added an important footnote to SA's history of destabilization policies and provided an interesting insight into his Government's approach to national interests in his reply to his Right-wing critics:

We have nothing to hide. Naturally there was a time when we helped train and support Renamo. There was such a time. Why? The honourable members are not so ignorant. SA's aid to Renamo had achieved its aim, as the Maputo Government realised what the result could be and had signed the Accord. We did not found Renamo; it was there. When SA's aim in helping Renamo had been achieved, help for the movement ceased. It's as simple as that. Some members would say it was wrong and reprehensible: 'But I have never considered reprehensible to place my country's interests first. Now it does not serve my purpose for Renamo to blow up a powerline in which I have a direct interest.'

Botha said there was a difference between the situations in Mozambique and Angola. The Frelimo Government had been installed as the official Government when the Portuguese left, whereas the MPLA in Angola were never a legitimate Government.

Pik Botha told Parliament on 24 April that Pretoria and Maputo were to establish a Joint Operational Centre to give full effect to the Nkomati Accord. For the time being, the Centre would use the facilities at the Lebombo–Ressano Garcia border post, but it would later acquire its own facilities. Botha denied that SA was planning to send its troops into Mozambique to help fight the MNR after the damage in April to the pylons bringing power from Cahora Bassa and the blowing up of a strategic bridge on the road used by SA traffic to Maputo.

Cooperation between Mozambique and Portugal was halted in April because Maputo claimed that the necessary structures to implement agreements on cooperation had not been established, or even defined. Portugal's exports to Mozambique had continued to decline over the last decade.[154]Portugal's President Eanes visited Maputo in May on a fence-mending mission. He spoke of his dismay at the gravity of the problems standing in the way of normalization. He explained the difficulties in curbing the activities of Portuguese citizens connected with the MNR, but though the new legislation would curb their activities, which were already lessening.[155] Although there had been talk about and sympathy for military cooperation, nothing positive had yet been done to achieve it.

A top-level meeting of SA and Mozambique's Foreign and Defence Ministers was held in Maputo on 9 May to discuss security issues, particularly those connected with the protection of road, rail and power links. The meeting reported that progress had been made, but no details were forthcoming.

President Nyerere's unchanging suspicions of the real intentions of Pretoria in promoting the Nkomati Accord grew in May when he warned that sufficient aid must be given to Machel to prevent his Government from being toppled. He said it was 'shameful for Africa to fail to assist Mozambique at a time when it was engaged in a struggle against SA aggression. His statement caused surprise and some dismay in Maputo over his suggestion that if the SA Government were to try and overthrow Machel 'we shall ask Frelimo to come back to their camps in Tanzania for training to relaunch the armed struggle.' However, he also expressed the opinion that SA's strategy to use MNR bandits, 'who are mainly Portuguese', would not succeed.

Pretoria, however, insisted that so far as it was concerned all aid for the MNR coming from SA territory had been completely shut off. Affirming that SA was not giving direct or indirect aid to the rebels, the Deputy Foreign Minister, Louis Nel (who also acts as his country's chairman of the JSC) pointed out that at the latest monthly meeting in June no charges were made about violations of the Accord.[156]

Mozambique's Information Minister, José Cabaco, reflected Machel's continued belief in the importance of the Accord with SA. 'If the Accord fails,' Cabaco said, it will be a major tragedy for the entire Southern African region. SA and Mozambique would be back at the point which they had done everything to avoid, particularly the internationalization of the conflict. Speaking in the same radio programme with Cabaco, the US ambassador in Maputo said the Accord had captured the imagination of the world. The US regarded it as a way of easing tensions in Southern Africa. The fact that there was still insurgency in Mozambique was not of itself evidence of the Accord's failure.

In October Mozambique captured the documentary evidence that Pretoria's hands were far from clean and had engaged in many clandestine activities throughout the period of the Accord. Pretoria's reply was that it was accused only of 'technicalities'.

UNITA'S ROLE

Dr Jonas Savimbi's principal concern since 1984 was his fear of being abandoned by the US and possibly also by SA if the mediation efforts over Namibia were successful. His apprehensions grew with the growing rapprochement between the Reagan Administration and the MPLA regime, and over the ease with which Pretoria abandoned its erstwhile ally, the MNR, as its price for the Nkomati Accord. He was also angered by the American policy of not insisting on giving Unita a role in the negotiating process over the implementation of Resolution 435, and threatened not to respect the proposed UN Peacekeeping Force unless Unita were made a party to any final agreement. The American position was that, while recognizing the necessity for an MPLA–Unita agreement if Angola were to achieve political stability, such negotiations were a domestic issue and lay outside the agreed parameters of the international negotiations over Namibia. Pretoria, however, continued to take a different view: At every new turn in the negotiations it insisted that Unita should be involved. The only encouragement Savimbi got from official Washington was the Senate's vote to repeal the Clark amendment (see above), and from unofficial Washington the decision to hold a conference launching an anti-communist International in Jamba.

Acting on his American concerns, Savimbi sought to galvanize his US supporters to urge Reagan back to his former position of open support for Unita, and to strengthen his friendship with the SA regime.[157] He also abandoned any show of discretion about appearing on SA platforms, and even went so far as to attend the inauguration of P. W. Botha as an executive President in September 1984. He visited Cape Town on several other occasions. He is in the habit of speaking of Botha as 'my friend' but acknowledges that Pretoria has its own interest to protect and that he cannot therefore rely on SA indefinitely.[158]

Savimbi welcomed Reagan's re-election in November 1984, but repeated his concern about State Department policy. He accused Chester Crocker and the State Department of undermining the White House,[159] and encouraged his supporters in Congress to work for Crocker's dismissal.

Savimbi, who appeared to be well-supplied with funds, was also conspicuously successful in arranging special occasions for overseas journalists in his capital of Jamba. In March 1984 he flew in a large party of SA editors and journalists for a press conference.[160] After visiting Jamba in June 1984, *The Times* correspondent, Richard Dowden, wrote:

> Savimbi regards the Western Press as an essential part of his struggle and flies in journalists to his camp to explain his cause and boost his credibility. Unita's propaganda must be among the best in the world, and the MPLA Government's in Luanda among the worst.[161]

Savimbi did not oppose negotiations to bring Namibia to its independence under UN supervision, but objected only to his exclusion from the negotiating process. He came out strongly against Luanda's offer of a phased withdrawal of Cuban combat troops, claiming that the offer was bogus and would never be implemented. He insisted on a total withdrawal of all Cubans, as well as of all Soviet and East German military personnel.

Unita's consistent policy has been to call for negotiations to establish a government of national unity. 'We would like peace to return to Angola tomorrow,' he told a group of Czech prisoners before their release in mid-1984.[162]

> We would like our compatriots in the MPLA to make the decision to hold talks with us tomorrow, and tomorrow there would be peace because we are ready. When we consider the suffering experienced by our people up to now, when we consider the precarious nature of African institutions and the chaotic situation of Africa's economy, we must realise that we are squandering the wealth of our people; we are squandering the Angolan soul, the soul which does not perish, that is our greatest wealth. If we are forced to go on fighting, I would like to pledge to you . . . we will be fighting in the streets of Luanda before the year is out.

Savimbi was confident that the MPLA could not hope ever to destroy Unita. We are not concerned about a military victory either. What is happening in Angola is not a West–East or ideological struggle, but purely a civil war.' The only thing Savimbi insisted he could not accept was the partition of Angola.[163]

Unita received its support from diverse sources, of which the most important clearly was SA—although Pretoria still kept up the pretence that it did not provide arms, training or logistical support to Savimbi. The SA commando raid in Cabinda, which was intended to reflect credit on Unita, was one clear example of this collaboration. There is also evidence from SA sources about Unita training camps in Namibia.[164] A month before the Cabinda raid, Luanda claimed that 40 tons of war materiel intended for Unita was dropped by four SAAF aircraft in Malanje province.[165] The MPLA regarded Unita as simply 'an extension of the SA army.'[166]

There was no evidence of any clandestine official aid to Unita from the US; but there was a strong pro-Savimbi lobby in Washington. In Britain, Savimbi's principal supporter is 'Tiny' Rowland, the tycoon who runs Lonrho. Journalists wishing to meet Savimbi find it useful to do so through Lonrho's office in Cheapside.[167] Savimbi's West European supporters include Franz-Joseph Strauss, the Bavarian leader; Right-wing groups in France, Switzerland and Portugal. In Africa, Savimbi had in the past looked for support to President Mobutu of Zaire, Togo, Tunisia, Egypt, Morocco and Senegal (at least during Senghor's time). Savimbi was said to spend a fair amount of time in Rabat.[168] Among the conservative Arab regimes reported to provide funds for Unita were Saudi Arabia and Oman.

Although Unita still draws heavily on the Ovimbundu for its mass support, it has in recent years expanded beyond its tribal base—a development also reflected in its leadership. Unita's radio station, the Voice of the Black Cockerel, broadcasts in Ovimbundu, Kimbundu, Kikongo, Chokwe, Cuanhama and Portuguese. Unita's Executive Committee comprises Jonas Savimbi (president and commander of the Unita forces, Fala); Miguel Nzau Puna, a hereditary chief of the principal Cabindian tribe (secretary-general); Ernesto Mulato, who is Kigongo (administration coordination secretary); Jeremias Chitunda (secretary of foreign affairs); Brig Joaquim Vinama Chendovava (who was made Fala's chief-of-staff in January 1985); Demosthenese Chilungutila, (chief of operations); Geraldo Nunda (commander of logistics); Antonio Dembo, a Kimbundu (secretary of military mobilization); Carlos Kandanda, a Ganguela (deputy foreign affairs secretary); Samuel Epalanga (chief of personnel). Acting members of the Executive are Armindo Gato (Unita representative in Paris); Martires Victor, a Kimbundu (Political Commissar, Northern Front); Wilson dos Santos (Unita's representative in Lisbon); Isaias Samakuva; and Alberto Miguel Kanhali Vatuva, who is a Chokwe.

THE ROLE OF THE FRONTLINE STATES
The Nkomati Accord brought divisions among the six FLS member-states (Angola, Botswana, Mozambique, Tanzania, Zambia and Zimbabwe).[169] But these differences of opinion did not significantly affect the internal cohesion of the grouping. Tanzania, Zimbabwe, Botswana and Zambia all saw Mozambique's treaty with Pretoria as a defeat for the liberation movement; only Angola publicly supported Machel's stand. President Nyerere said on a number of occasions: 'There is nothing to be gained by pretending that a defeat was in fact a victory.' While critical of Machel's claims for Nkomati, all the Frontline Presidents took the view that, under Mozambique's difficult circumstances, they could understand why it felt it necessary to come to terms with Pretoria; but they shared the strongly-held suspicion that SA had no intention of upholding its side of the agreement. Their concern, therefore, was to encourage international pressures (especially from the US and Britain) on Pretoria to ensure that it should fulfill its obligations.

The FLS Presidents also differed in their responses to the American role as a mediator between SA, Angola and Swapo over Namibia's independence. While all were critical of Washington's refusal to exert adequate pressure on Pretoria, and while all repudiated Reagan's policy of 'constructive engagement',[170] only Prime Minister Mugabe refused to meet Chester Crocker during his shuttles around the continent and expressed himself as being totally opposed to continuing in the negotiating process under America's leadership. All the other FLS leaders continued to receive American envoys and took the view that nothing was to be gained by asking the US to abandon its effort. However, Nyerere said at a meeting of the Socialist International in Arusha on 5 September 1984 that the Western Contact Group was now useless in the negotiations for Namibia's independence.

President Kaunda, who had taken the leading role in encouraging talks between Swapo, Angola and SA in 1984, adopted a different line in 1985. In one of his talks with Crocker in September 1984, he said he had previously acclaimed President Botha as 'a sincere man', but he had come to doubt this as his words 'do not match his actions.'[171] However, a few months later he said in reply to an interviewer's question as to whether he still regarded Botha as being sincere:

> Without hesitation. I still believe Mr Botha is a very sincere man. What I do not know is whether this sincerity can be matched up with sufficient courage to see through this heavy load that he carries on his shoulders today. These are two different things.[172]

Kaunda constantly repeated his warning that SA was heading for a bloodbath if apartheid were not dismantled. In 1985 he began to put a time limit of three years in which to abolish apartheid if a catastrophe were to be avoided.[173] In August he said that only 2½ years still remained for the necessary action to be taken to prevent 'a racial catastrophe that would engulf the whole sub-African region.'

The FLS leaders continued their practice of meeting at regular intervals to deal with urgent issues as they arose. President Nyerere, who has acted as chairman of the group since its inception, resigned in September and President Kaunda was elected in his place.

THE ROLE OF THE EXTERNAL POWERS

THE CONTACT GROUP
The Contact Group (US, Britain, France, Canada and West Germany) had not met

formally since early 1984, following the December 1983 French proposal that the Group should become 'dormant' because it was no longer able to fulfill its mandate. The group had, in fact, fulfilled its mandate once SA and Swapo both accepted the detailed plan for implementing Resolution 435; what was then left were negotiations over SA's conditions for going ahead with implementation. Although its prerequisites changed from time to time, the principal requirement was that the Cuban combat troops in Angola should leave before Namibia's independence. This linkage between the Cubans and Namibian independence had originally been introduced by President Reagan, and later taken up by Pretoria. None of the Contact Group members, other than the US, was willing to support the idea of linking the two issues; it was therefore left to the Americans to get some agreement between SA and Angola.[174] But while the US was left to continue on its own, its principal negotiator, Chester Crocker, maintained close contact with the other four, as well as with the FLS.

A proposal by Nyerere for a joint meeting between the EEC and the FLS was agreed in principle but, never, in fact followed up. However, the Socialist International (which includes all the West European democratic socialist parties and the socialist group of the European Parliament) held a two-day meeting with the FLS leaders in Arusha in September 1984. One of their decisions was to call for sanctions and disinvestment.

THE ROLE OF THE UNITED STATES

The US Secretary of State, George Shultz, described the American role in Southern Africa in this way:

> Of course there are limits to what we can do directly. Our influence over issues and players is not the determining factor in their actions. Nevertheless, we are not without potential to affect events. While the Soviets can fan conflicts and supply the implements of war to pursue them, they cannot produce solutions. That peacemaking role can be played only by a Power that has a working relationship and influence with all the parties including, of course, SA.[175]

Schultz insisted that 'constructive engagement' was the right policy and claimed some useful results from it. He insisted that Resolution 435 was the only basis for Namibian independence. 'Any regime other than one that flows from the implementation of the UN resolution simply has no standing.' He supported the concept of one man, one vote for SA, adding: 'It has a great variety of combinations and permutations as a glance at our own Constitutional history shows.'

Up until September 1985, when Reagan issued his executive order on selective sanctions against SA,[176] the US Administration firmly rejected any idea of economic pressures. Just six months earlier, in his major speech on SA to the National Press Club in April 1985, Shultz declared: 'No threat is worth brandishing if, in fact, it isn't effective.' In his view the pressures that would produce change were the forces that operate within the region and inside SA itself.

US relations with SA had deteriorated steadily since 1984, beginning with the recall for consultations of its ambassador in Pretoria over the commando attack on Botswana in June 1984 and culminating 14 months later in President Reagan's acceptance of selective sanctions. At the same time, its relations improved remarkably with Mozambique, but more slowly with Angola. Asked why the Administration was aiding the Marxist Government of Mozambique while opposing the Marxist Government of Nicaragua, a White House spokesman, Larry Speakes, said Washington had been working closely with 'friends and allies in Southern

Africa and others to develop a programme that leads toward democracy.'[177] He added that Washington 'has worked carefully with the Mozambique Government, despite the fact that they had previously had close ties with the Soviet Union. We think that there has been progress made in our relations with the Government of Mozambique.'

Chester Crocker, the architect of the policy of 'constructive engagement', remained strongly committed to this policy as the only way of sensibly addressing the problems of Southern Africa. He explained its aims as being:

> To advance the peace process in Southern Africa, to reduce cross-border violence, to get Namibia's independence, to get foreign forces out of countries they shouldn't be in, whether they be Cuban or South African, and to get neighbours to coexist. And then, secondly, to push the process of change inside South Africa, using the limited influence at our disposal.
> [He said the Administration feels that these objectives are being achieved.] I think on both fronts there is a clear record. There is today less violence across borders in Southern Africa than there has been at any time since the Portuguese Revolution in the mid-1970s. We can't take exclusive credit for that, but it is a fact.[178]

CUBA'S ROLE

Havana's relations with both Angola and Mozambique remained close and cordial. When the Mozambican Foreign Minister, Joaquim Chissano, visited Cuba in December 1984, he characterized relations as 'dynamic'.[179] Several new accords and protocols to existing aid agreements were signed during his visit.

Cuba reiterated its pledge to Angola to keep its estimated 14,000 combat troops in the country for as long as the MPLA Government needed them for its security. At the same time, Fidel Castro was at pains to make it clear that his troops would be withdrawn in terms of previous agreements with Luanda once the country was no longer threatened by SA and Namibia achieved its independence. President dos Santos' offer to phase out Cuban troops as part of an agreement for the withdrawal of SADF units from Angola received Havana's support.

Castro, though, took two diametrically opposite attitudes towards the US mediation effort. In one interview (with the *Washington Post* in February 1985) he said he was willing to cooperate with an American peace effort to get all Cuban and SA troops out of Angola; and, only a few months later, he attacked Washington's imperialist designs in Southern Africa (see Course of Events, above).

THE ROLE OF CHINA AND NORTH KOREA

China gave its open support to Mozambique over the Nkomati Accord. When President Machel visited Beijing in July 1984, President Li Xiannian assured him of China's backing for the action he had taken to safeguard the country's independence and security 'in the light of the country's situation.[180]

A commentary by the New China News Agency from Maputo said the Nkomati Accord was the result of 'the thirst for peace' of many African States after years of turmoil, and added: 'Therefore the peaceful action of the Mozambique Government has won understanding and support from more and more African countries.' China agreed to renew its modest aid programme to Mozambique during Machel's visit, but no details were supplied.

Although Peking and Luanda again enjoy friendly diplomatic relations, the Chinese appear to have maintained a low profile in Angola.

SA reports in September 1984 that North Korean troops had arrived in Angola to assist in fighting Unita were denied by Luanda.[181] These reports originated from Unita sources; after an initial flurry of excitement, nothing further was said about the alleged DPRK involvement in Angola. President Kim Il-Sun promised Machel full support when he visited Pyongyang after China. The North Korean Central News Agency reported Kil Il-Sung as saying:

> The struggle against enemies can take different forms. . . . We consider the series of measures to consolidate national independence and stability, and to create the peaceful environment needed for the building of an independent new society, suit the present internal and external conditions, and we support them.[182]

THE SOVIET ROLE

Despite Super-Power rivalry in many areas, both accepted that Southern Africa should not be regarded as an area of confrontation between them. This shared view emerged in a series of talks which began in Paris on 29 May 1985. The Soviet representative insisted that the conflict situation in the region was essentially the result of SA's policy of destabilizing regimes in the countries on its borders. He argued that SA had violated its agreements with Mozambique and Angola and had obstructed the implementation of Resolution 435, and emphasized the USSR's determination to back the Angolans and Mozambicans in their stand.[183]

Africa in general ranks low in Moscow's international priorities, according to Helen Kitchen, Director of African Studies at Georgetown University's Centre for Strategic Studies. She had formed this conclusion after attending a seminar with Soviet Africanists in Moscow.[184] According to her:

> It was felt in Moscow that there was a better than even chance that SA would become too arrogant over its accomplishments and overplay its hand. The regional edifice built by Pretoria would then self-destruct. Pretoria would be unable to maintain its role as a regional power. . . .

Despite the ripening detente between Angola, Mozambique and the US, neither Machel nor dos Santos showed any inclination to lessen their ties with Moscow; nor did the USSR appear to wish to reduce its commitments to either. Soviet bloc military assistance to Mozambique was nowhere as large as that provided for Angola. The Soviet bloc continued in 1985 to be the principal supplier of arms to the MPLA Government, as well as to Swapo and the ANC. A new shipment of MiG 23 and Sukhoi fighter aircraft arrived in Luanda early in 1985. The SA Defence Minister said in October 1984 that in the first half of the year, the USSR had supplied 74 MiG strike aircraft, 130 tanks, 40 armoured cars, 40 anti-aircraft vehicles, 200 heavy anti-aircraft guns and 40 artillery pieces, 11 sophisticated radar systems, 400 military vehicles and 160,000t of guns and ammunition. However, Angola has begun to diversify its source of military supplies, having bought 25 Gazelle helicopters and an unspecified number of Dauphin patrol helicopters from France in 1984 and 12 Aviocar-212 military aircraft from Spain, as well as 900 four-wheel military trucks.

The Soviet ambassador in Gaborone, Mikhail Petrov, promised military aid to Botswana if the country were attacked by SA. He stressed that the Soviet Union's opposition to apartheid did not imply any hatred for SA and recalled that Moscow had diplomatic relations with Pretoria until 1948.

A French intelligence report that Gaborone had become a major spy network centre for Soviet intelligence was repudiated by the Botswana Government. According to French Press leaks, the French intelligence reports mentioned a figure of 250 specialists employed by the Soviet embassy at a giant monitoring station in Gaborone. Immediate doubt was cast on the accuracy of this report since the Soviets have nothing like so many personnel in the country.

NOTES

1. All references to essays and country chapters unless otherwise stated are to *African Contemporary Record (ACR)* 1984–85.
2. Pretoria's reason for not making the decision for the withdrawal of its forces was that the Angolan army had failed to live up to its side of the agreement which was to curb Swapo infiltration of the area evacuated by the SADF. However, this situation had not changed by the time the SADF was finally withdrawn.
3. *Leistner: Africa Insight,* Pretoria, December 1984.
4. For an analysis of the erosion of the structures of apartheid, see the chapters on SA in *ACR* 1981-82, 1982-83, 1983-84.
5. Radio Maputo (RM), 27 June 1985.
6. *Ibid.*
6. See *ACR* 1983-84, pp. A12ff.
8. *Ibid.,* ppA9-11.
9. SABC, 27 July 1984; *Guardian (Gdn),* Manchester, 27 July 1984.
10. SABC, 27 July 1984.
11. Radio Luanda (RL), 30 July 1984.
12. SABC, 27 July 1984.
13. See *ACR* 1983-84, pA10.
14. *Gdn,* 3 July 1984; Radio Lusaka, 2 July 1984.
15. Angola Press Agency (ANGOP), 4 July 1984.
16. RL, 30 July 1984.
17. RL, 6 August, 1984.
18. For the joint Angola–Cuban statements, see *ACR* 1982-83, and 1983-84.
19. ANGOP, 10 August 1984.
20. SABC, 3 September 1984.
21. SABC, 16 September 1984.
22. Message from the Angolan Head of State to the UN Secretary-General on the Problems of Southern Africa, 20 November 1984, published in *Angola Information* No 97, 26 November 1984.
23. US Information Agency, *Africa Wireless File (AF),* Paris, 12 September 1984; *International Herald Tribune (IHT),* Paris, 20 September 1984.
24. For text see Angolan government full page advertisement in the *Times,* London, 24 November 1984.
25. Angola Information, 26 November 1984.
26. See *West Africa (WA).* London, 25 February 1985, for a particularly perceptive analysis of this affair.
27. *The Times,* London, 2 November 1984.
28. SABC, 25 November 1984.
29. *Gdn,* 16 November 1984.
30. Radio Kinshasa, 6 December 1984.
31. Radio Lusaka (RL), 29, January 1985.
32. *Daily Telegraph (DT),* London, 9 January 1985.
33. See essay on Britain's year in Africa.
34. Voice of Namibia (VON), 1 January 1985.
35. SABC, 5 February 1985.
36. RL, 22 February 1985.
37. SA Press Association (SAPA), 26 April 1985.
38. ANGOP, 22 April 1985.
39. Interview on Johannesburg TV, 25 April 1985.
40. See *ACR* 1983-84, chapter on Namibia.
41. RL, 1 May 1985.
42. For details see ANGOP, 30 May 1985 and ANGOP document No. 2, 14 June 1985.
43. *Financial Times (FT),* London, 25 May 1985.
44. *IHT,* 27 May 1985.
45. *DT,* 31 May 1985.
46. *The Times,* 13 June 1985.
47. See chapter on Namibia.
48. RL, 15 June 1985.
49. Johannesburg TV, 6 June 1985.
50. *IHT,* 8-9 June 1985.
51. For more details on the progress of the war, see chapter on Namibia.
52. SABC, 18 January 1985.
53. International Institute for Strategic Studies, *The Military Balance 1984-85,* London, 1985.
54. *Gdn,* 19 June 1985.
55. SABC, 20 December 1984.
56. *Ibid.*
57. See *ACR* 1983-84, pp701ff.
58. See Peter Wise, *IHT,* 26-27 January 1985.
59. Quoted by SABC, 27 December 1984.
60. Confidential Telex (CT), Paris, 23 July 1984.
61. *Ibid.*
62. For the ANC role, see chapter on South Africa.
63. Adam and Uys, 'Eight New Realities in Southern Africa', CSIS Africa Notes No 39, 28 February 1985.
64. See chapter on South Africa.
65. *Financial Mail (FM),* 26 October 1984.
66. See essay by R. Herbold Green on SADCC.
67. *FM* 19 October 1984.

68. Quoted on RL, 5 February 1985.
69. Radio Harare (RH), 15 and 16 August 1984.
70. Interview with the *Observer*, London, 27 May 1984.
71. RH, 15 and 16 August 1984.
72. RH, 27 September 1984.
73. *Rand Daily Mail (RDM)*, 7 November 1984.
74. RH, 31 December 1984.
75. RH, 2 January 1985.
76. See *ACR* 1983-84, ppA29-32.
77. *RDM*, 11 September 1984.
78. Radio Gaborone (RG), 13 September 1984.
79. RL, 13 September 1984.
80. SABC, 5 November 1984.
81. *Times*, 6 February 1985.
82. *Ibid.*
83. *Ibid.*
84. See essay on Britain's year in Africa.
85. Interview with Allister Sparks, quoted on RG, 18 February 1985.
86. SABC, 28 February 1985.
87. RG, 28 February 1985.
88. Interview with *Le Monde*, quoted by RG, 20 March 1985.
89. RG, 30 April 1985.
90. SABC and SA Press Association (SAPA), 14 June 1985.
91. *Ibid.*
92. SABC, 18 June 1985.
93. RG, 15 June 1985.
94. SABC, 17 June 1985.
95. AFR, 502, 14 June 1985.
96. See *ACR* 1983-84, ppA32-33. Also see chapter on Lesotho.
97. RM, 24 and 25 June 1985.
98. Radio Maseru (RM), 25 June 1985.
99. See *ACR* 1983-84, pA-31.
100. For details see chapter on Swaziland.
101. For Nkomati Accord see *ACR* 1983-84 pp12.
102. *Star*, 30 July 1984.
103. *Times*, 7 July 1984.
104. Mozambican Information Office (AIM), 25 July 1984.
105. *Ibid.*
106. Also see essay on Portugal's year in Africa.
107. *RDM*, Johannesburg, 24 May 1984.
108. Radio Lisbon, 29 July 1984.
109. *Noticias*, Maputo, 9 August 1984.
110. *Ibid.*, 4 August 1984.
111. *Gdn*, 20 May 1984.
112. *Ibid.*
113. SABC, 9 and 15 August 1984; *Times*, 6 August 1984.
114. Radio Lisbon, Commercial Service, 17 and 18 August 1984.
115. *Gdn.*, 4 September 1984.
116. *Gdn*, 5 September 1984; SABC, 5 September 1984.
117. AIM, 20 September 1984.
118. *RDM*, 29 September 1984.
119. AIM, 3 October 1984.
120. *Ibid.*
121. *Ibid.*
122. *RDM*, 4 and 5 October 1984.
123. SABC, 18 October 1984.
124. RM, 30 October 1984.
125. Capital Radio, Umtata, 1 February 1985.
126. *Tempo*, Maputo, 26 October 1984.
127. *Star*, March 1985.
128. AIM, 2 November 1984.
129. *RDM*, 5 November 1984.
130. UPI Report from Lisbon.
131. AIM, 19-25 October 1984.
132. *Noticias*, Maputo, 6 November 1984.
133. RM, 5 November 1984.
134. AIM, 14 December 1984; *Star*, 17 December 1984.
135. RM, 13 and 14 December 1984.
136. AIM, 29 December 1984.
137. SABC, 28 December 1984.
138. SABC, 30 January 1985.
139. *FM*, 30 November 1984.
140. *Ibid.*
141. *DT*, 22 January 1985; *Star*, 28 January 1985; SABC, 17 January 1985.
142. Radio Truth, 18 March 1985.
143. *Times*, 1 February 1985.
144. *Ibid.*, 11 February 1985.
145. RM, 27 February 1985.
146. For similar reactions, see *Noticias*, 6 February 1985; *Tempo*, February 1985.
147. AIM, 6 February 1985.
148. AIM, 6 February 1985.
149. *Ibid.*
150. For text see *AIM*, 7, 8 and 16 February 1985.
151. RG, 15 March 1985.
152. *DT*, 30 March 1985.
153. RM, 9 April 1985.
154. AIM, 29 April & 1 May 1985.
155. *Daily Mail*, Dar-es-Salaam, 23 May 1984.
156. SABC, 25 June 1984.
157. Savimbi was strongly supported in the US by *The Washington Times (TWT)*, which kept up a campaign to discredit Chester Crocker personally, and State Department policy generally.
158. *The Times*, 12 November 1984.
159. *TWT*, 12 and 13 November 1984.

160. See Rex Gibson, 'Dr Savimbi Carrot at the End of the World,' *RDM*, Johannesburg, 3 April 1984.
161. *Times*, 3 July 1984.
162. Voice of Resistance of the Black Cockerel (VRBC), 1 July 1984.
163. *Times*, 3 July 1984.
164. For SA sources, see *ACR* 1983-84.
165. RL, 6 June 1984.
167. *WA*, 15 October 1984.
168. *Ibid*.
169. For details about Swapo's activities, see chapter on Namibia.
170. See *ACR* 1983-84, ppA12-17.
171. SABC, 7 September 1984.
172. PANA, 17 December 1984.
173. RM, 27 June 1984.
174. For the UK position, see essay on Britain's year in Africa; for Canada's position, see *ACR* 1983-84, ppA184-5. For France's position see *ACR* 1983-84, ppA214-6. For West Germany's position see *ACR* 1983-84 ppA234-6.
175. Speech to National Press Club, 16 April 1985; AFR 202, 16 April 1985.
176. For US Policy on Sanctions see chapter on SA.
177. AFR.503, 22 February 1985.
178. CT, June 1985.
179. *Pensa Latina*, Havana, 1 December 1984.
180. New China News Agency quoted in *RDM*, 19 July 1984.
181. Radio Luanda, 22 September 1984; SABC, 13 September 1984.
182. Quoted in *RDM*, 24 July 1984.
183. See essay on the USSR's year in Africa.
184. *Star*, 30 July 1984.

1985–1986

AN EMBATTLED SOUTH AFRICA FACES A FUTURE OF INCREASING ISOLATION

OVERVIEW OF THE SITUATION IN 1985-86

The conflicts in Southern Africa finally moved to near the top of the international agenda in 1985-86—37 years after the introduction of apartheid in South Africa (SA), and 40 years after the question of Namibia's future (then still known as South West Africa) was inscribed on the agenda of the United Nations (UN). For much of the intervening two score or so years, the Western nations had not felt their interests in the region to be seriously jeopardized, even if the public conscience was troubled by the injustices of apartheid. Western complacency received its first jolt in 1974 when the collapse of Portuguese colonialism created conditions that brought the Soviet bloc and Cuba into the Southern African region—an event that marked the beginning of the end of total Western hegemony in the sub-continent, and which raised a serious possibility of its conflicts becoming internationalized. But the weak showing of the Soviet bloc in fulfilling its role under the Treaties of Friendship with Angola and Mozambique led Western Europe to relapse into its former attitude of wishing to avoid becoming too deeply involved in the region's conflicts—a view not fully shared by the US since the presence of Cuban combat troops in Angola was a major domestic issue, which was enhanced by Reagan's personal support for conservative groups committed to a militant policy of anti-Castroism.

Differences over the Cuban linkage issue led to Britain, France, West Germany and Canada ceasing to take an active part in the work of the Contact Group—whose role was to mediate between, SA, Angola and the South West African People's Organization of Namibia (Swapo) over implementation of the Security Council's Resolution 435 (SCR 435)—after agreement had been reached on all its terms of a settlement, leaving only one obstacle—the Cuban issue. The idea of linking Cuban troop withdrawal to Namibian independence was originally introduced by the Reagan Administration and only later taken up by Pretoria; the other Western nations never accepted the idea of linking the two issues. With the Contact Group fallen into desuetude, the UN was left to play a lone hand as mediator since 1985. But it virtually destroyed its hand in early 1986 by becoming involved in Angola's internal struggle.

This policy further widened the differences between American and West European policies since none of the EEC members supports the idea of intervening actively on the side of Unita. The new American line further alienates most African countries, which made it more difficult to continue engaging the Frontline States (FLS) in the negotiations over Namibia; and it spurred the USSR and Cuba to increase their support for the MPLA Government. Thus the US decision to arm Namibia contributed directly to further internationalizing the region's conflicts. Washington, however, argued that Moscow was responsible for this unfortunate development by breaching a 1975 secret understanding between the Super-powers that neither would seek to expand their role in Angola. The Americans charged that the Soviets, by substantially increasing their military aid in an effort to help the Angolan army (Fapla) destroy Unita in August 1985, had sought to change Angola's internal balance of power in their favour. In fact, it was only the timely intervention of the SA Defence Force (SADF) that saved Unita from defeat in the August offensive. Reagan promised that the US would not allow Unita to be destroyed; but his Administration continued to favour a negotiated agreement between MPLA and Unita. The decision to give military aid to Unita was dictated not only by Washington's international concerns, but was perhaps even more the result of domestic pressures by a well-organized Right-wing lobby on Reagan personally and on Congress.

American arms aid to Unita through clandestine channels (whether through Zaire or SA remains unclear) began soon after Savimbi's January 1986 visit to Washington. By May, the supply of Stinger and other anti-aircraft missiles enabled Unita to prevent the renewed Soviet-backed offensive which had been promised for mid-1986, Washington claimed that the success in blocking this offensive was due to its decision to provide Unita with the weapons it needed to keep up its resistance.

THE WEST CHANGES COURSE ON SOUTH AFRICA

The Western nations began to reshape their policies towards SA in 1985 once it became clear that their interests were likely to be jeopardized by developments in SA, and when it was felt that President Botha's reform policies could not be relied on to create opportunities to reach a negotiated settlement with representative Black leaders. Firm promises made by the SA Foreign Minister, Pik Botha, to the US Assistant Secretary for African Affairs, Chester Crocker, and to other Western leaders that President Botha would announce major reforms in August 1985 remained unfulfilled, although he did speak cryptically about 'the Rubicon having been crossed'—implying that power-sharing between Whites and Blacks was accepted as both necessary and inevitable. Western government and public opinion shifted significantly when Botha declared a state of national emergency in September 1985, followed by a policy of massive police and army repression.

The decision to declare a national emergency reflected the Pretoria Government's increasing loss of power in being able to contain the challenge coming from the Black opposition—not just from militant groups like the African National Congress (ANC), the Pan-Africanist Congress (PAC) and its affiliates in the Black Consciousness Movement (BCM), the Black trade union movement and the United Democratic Front (UDF); but also from leaders like Chief Gatsha Buthelezi, the Kwazulu leader of the Inkhata Movement, Archbishop Tutu and the Rev. Alan Boesak.[1] There were two immediate reasons for the declaration of the state of national emergency. The first was the growing evidence of support for the ANC policy of making the Black townships ungovernable—a significant development that had less to do with the ANC's armed struggle than with the rapid growth of a network of civic groups in hundreds of Black townships across the length and breadth of the country, covering both urban and rural areas.

The second contributory cause was the failure to stop incursions by ANC armed cadres from across SA's borders. Pretoria had hoped that the signing in 1984 of the Nkomati Accord with Mozambique and the Lusaka Agreement with Angola, and the conclusion of an earlier secret agreement with Swaziland, would result in substantially curbing ANC and Swapo guerrilla activities. These hopes proved illusory. Both the Nkomati Accord and the Lusaka Agreement had become rapidly eroded and the other border states continued to resist all efforts to make them sign similar security agreements. However, pressures on Chief Jonathan's

Government in Lesotho were successful in contributing to his overthrow and to the emergence of a more compliant government in Maseru. The failure to stem the guerrilla attacks and increasing militancy of the Frontline States—especially Zimbabwe and Zambia in their campaign to isolate SA—led Pretoria to extend its policy of military trans-border attacks to these countries as well as continuing its more routine attacks on Botswana and Angola. The purpose of these attacks was not just to hit at ANC targets, but to pressurize neighbouring governments into ceasing all cooperation with the ANC. This policy was spelt out clearly by SA's Defence Minister, Gen. Magnus Malan;[2]

> When the ANC commits terror against SA from neighbouring countries, the leaders of those countries are co-responsible. A leader like Dr Kaunda must realize that he cannot play host to the ANC and the Communist Party and be known as a man who seeks peace. Our fighter planes over Lusaka in June (1986) were a direct message to him to decide between peace and confrontation.

The trans-border attacks were regularly criticized by the US, Britain and other Western Governments, who saw them as escalating violence in the region and encouraging the FLS to seek increased support from the Soviet bloc.

Apart from the evidence that the Pretoria Government was beginning to lose control of the situation at home, three other significant developments in 1985-86 indicated a historic change in the internal balance of power. Although the Government had not yet lost its power to rule by force, it had lost the ability to control political developments and to compel its Black challengers to accept its own terms for beginning meaningful negotiations about a post-apartheid constitution. It became abundantly clear that no meaningful negotiations could begin unless the imprisoned ANC leader, Nelson Mandela, and other political prisoners were released; and the ANC, PAC and other Black parties were unbanned. Mandela's key role and, so, the ANC's came to be widely recognized both inside SA and in Western capitals. Prominent SA businessmen, scenting the change in power relations, undertook their significant mission to open discussions with the ANC in Zambia—an example followed by other prominent SA groups and individuals. The demand for Mandela's release found support even inside the ranks of the ruling National Party. The US, Britain and other members of the European Economic Community (EEC) launched a coordinated campaign to persuade Botha to agree to release Mandela and his colleagues and to unban the Black political parties. They came to see in Mandela the one commanding figure who could prevent a slide into greater violence and chaos in the country; and they feared that unless he were released while his authority was still so dominant—and before he died in prison—the one reasonable hope of achieving a negotiated settlement might be lost forever. Botha's failure to respond to these demands for Mandela's release alarmed Western leaders; but their failure to persuade him showed the limited power the West has to influence Pretoria through more or less friendly overtures. Recognition of this reality sharpened the challenge in the US Congress to Reagan's policy of constructive engagement; it also sharpened the demand for international sanctions as a possible means of exerting greater influence on Pretoria.

The Botha Government's response to these growing Western pressures and increasing hostility was ambivalent. On the one hand, it angrily rejected 'external meddling' in the country's internal affairs; on the other hand, it was willing to go through the motions of cooperating with Western initiatives in order not to alienate the West completely.

SA's greatest fear has always been that, one day, the West would finally yield to

African pressures and join in a campaign to isolate the Republic in the world community—a nightmare fear that came closer to becoming reality in 1986, thanks largely to the initiative taken by the Commonwealth of Nations and to a swelling tide of American public opinion.

IMPACT OF AFRICAN POLICIES ON THE WEST

Although the British Prime Minister and the West German Chancellor fought demands for the imposition of sanctions against SA, President Reagan (regarded by Pretoria as its most reliable Western ally) was forced by Congressional pressure to join in the economic war against the Pretoria regime. Despite British and German reluctance to join in isolating SA, even their Governments were unable to avoid accepting a limited number of damaging measures. What was especially harmful to Pretoria's interest was that all the Western countries, without exception, rejected as inadequate and too tardy the reforms introduced by President Botha, and had joined in the universal demand for Mandela's release and for the unbanning of all the Black political parties, including the ANC which is seen by Pretoria as 'a Moscow puppet'. The increase in Western antagonism hit the SA rulers particularly hard since it came at a time when it was struggling to try and re-establish a degree of internal security, and because it showed no appreciation of the efforts that had been made to phase out apartheid. What Pretoria's rulers had hoped for at a time when the SA ship of state was on the rocks, were lifelines thrown out by the West to save it from becoming completely shipwrecked; what they got, instead, were more missiles fired at the imperilled ship.

President Botha complained that the West was yielding to 'the blackmail of Africa'. He warned that those who stood to gain most from this Western 'surrender' were the forces of world communism, whose military build-up in the Southern African region had become a source of major concern to the SA military. If one substitutes the words 'influence and pressures' for 'blackmail', Botha was perfectly right in attributing the changes in Western government policies as being due, at least in part, to the role of the African nations. A large part of their success in maximizing their influence on Western governments was due to their decision to use the Commonwealth as the cutting-edge against Britain—a strategy that had the strong backing of influential countries like India, but even more significantly, which succeeded in winning over the old White dominions—not just Labour-governed Australia and New Zealand, but also Conservative-ruled Canada.

However, it is unlikely that these external African pressures would have succeeded by themselves; it was the recognition by Western leaders that the stage was being reached in the struggle inside SA where it had become necessary for their own future interests to begin to disengage themselves from the crumbling apartheid system and to put themselves on the side of forces likely to play a dominant role in a post-apartheid society. Western attitudes were also affected by the ruthlessness with which the Pretoria regime was trying to put down Black dissent, and by President Botha's own unfortunate manner of presenting his case to the world.

IMPACT OF EXTERNAL PRESSURES ON SOUTH AFRICA

The belief of many African and other Third World leaders, as well as of many opinion-makers in the West, that the Botha regime can be pressurized by the US and Britain to adopt a different political course from that determined by its own perceptions of how far and how fast reform policies could be introduced without losing control is as fallacious as the belief that it is only the underpinning of the SA economy by the major Western trading nations that makes it possible for the apartheid system to survive. Such views fail to take into proper account the genuine fears among White South Africans, not just Afrikaners, about their future in a country under Black rule. Their determination to remain in control of events during the dangerous and difficult transition policy away from apartheid cannot be broken by external pressures. The acceptance of the need to abandon apartheid was due entirely to the dramatic increase in internal pressures. Nevertheless, a close relationship exists between external pressures and internal pressures; each feeds on the other in building up a greater momentum towards meaningful change.

THE SITUATION IN SOUTHERN AFRICA AT THE END OF 1986

At the approaching end of 1986 all the signs were that the conflicts in Southern Africa would grow more rather than less; nor indeed is there any reasonable prospect of de-escalating the violence or of producing stability until the conflict is resolved inside SA, the core area of the region. Apartheid was the direct cause of turning a peaceful Black population into one that has increasingly come to embrace the need for a militant and violent struggle against their White-ruled society, and which has turned the rest of the African continent into being the enemies of Pretoria. Although it was the failure of Western policies in siding with Portuguese colonialism that was primarily responsible for creating the opportunity for the Soviet bloc and Cuba to establish a foothold in the region, SA's policies have subsequently been directly responsible for Angola, especially, increasing its dependence on the Soviet bloc. It was the banning of the Congress movements in 1960 that drove the ANC and PAC into exile, and which led the former to break with its own tradition of non-cooperation with the SA Communist Party and to resolve on a policy of armed struggle. Similarly, it was the refusal of SA to yield to the demand for Namibian independence that led Swapo into launching its armed struggle. Because such a struggle found no favour in the West, the ANC and Swapo were left with no alternative other than to turn to the communist world for military aid.

The civil war which has raged in Angola since its independence in 1985 has become increasingly internationalized with the USSR supporting the MPLA Government and the US supporting Unita. It is generally accepted that neither side can win the war, which has brought the country to the brink of economic collapse. The failure of the Nkomati Accord—due almost entirely to Pretoria's failure to implement it faithfully—has turned what began as an internal rebellion by the MNR, supported first by Smith's regime in Rhodesia and then by SA—into something approaching a civil war, which has shaken the country's economy and put its Frelimo Government in grave jeopardy.

SA and all the border states have been forced by internal threats to their security and by external threats to engage in a disastrous arms race within the region, which can be afforded least of all by the border states' fragile economies. If, as seems likely, Zimbabwe and Zambia implement their threat to impose sanctions against SA, the short-term impact on their economies will be much more severe on them than on SA, and are likely to result in even greater instability throughout the region.

The gravity of the situation in Mozambique increased dramatically with the death of President Samora Machel on 19 October 1986 in an air crash on SA soil. The fateful blow fell at a time when the Frontline leaders were already seriously engaged in exploring the possibility of raising an external military force to come to Mozambique's assistance. The possible collapse of Mozambique into chaos, or the establishment of a regime in Maputo compliant to the wishes of Pretoria, would critically affect the ability of the FLS to lessen their dependence on SA and, so, make it even more difficult to join in sanctions against SA. Machel's death loosened the coping stone in the political and economic structure of the FLS with the results of possible far-reaching consequences for the future.

While the Soviet Union is still only marginally involved in the region as a major arms supplier, the Western nations are inextricably involved in its conflicts and, particularly, in SA. The prospects for the immediate future are that the conflicts in the region will become increasingly internationalized. It is a dismal outlook.

THE INTERNATIONAL CAMPAIGN FOR SANCTIONS AGAINST SOUTH AFRICA

It took 25 years after the international campaign for sanctions against SA was first launched for it to become a serious threat—and then only after the repeated warnings of the dangers of racial conflict engendered by apartheid turning increasingly violent and spreading beyond SA's border were seen to have been justified. The first serious attempt to focus international attention on sanctions came as a sequel to the Sharpeville shootings and the banning of the Congress movements in 1960 when a UN committee chaired by Lord Caradon of Britain and Alva Myrdal of Sweden, investigated the implications of international pressures on SA. The first serious study of the subject, published in 1964[3] concluded that only comprehensive mandatory sanctions imposed under Chapter 7 of the UN Charter, and enforced by a naval blockade, was likely to be effective. These ideas were laughed to scorn at the time; but in 1986 even the idea of a naval blockade won support from such figures as Denis Healey, a former British Defence Minister, and Edward Heath, a former British Prime Minister (see Britain's Role below).

During the intervening quarter of a century a number of sanctions measures were taken by the world community in response to actions by Pretoria which troubled the world community; these included the sports boycott; an oil embargo; the arms embargo and the prohibition of military sensitive items. By 1984 disinvestment from SA—mainly by US firms—and restrictions on loans to the SA Government and parastatals began to gather momentum, either because of effective lobbying pressures or for hard-headed business reasons. But it was not until SA's internal security problems became menacing and Western governments found themselves divided against each other, and Africa began to line up against the West, that the campaign for sanctions found its place near the top of the agenda of international concerns. Even then the actions taken by the Commonwealth, the US and the European Community still fell far short of mandatory, comprehensive sanctions which, alone, it was argued, would make a decisive impact on SA.

The sanctioneers argue that the Pretoria regime only understands the language of toughness, and that the only way of avoiding a racial holocaust is by hitting the country's economy so hard and by isolating it so completely that it will be forced to submit to external *force majeure*. The opposite view is that, apart from the risk of permanently damaging the SA economy, the traditional siege mentality of the Afrikaners will lead them to behave more obdurately rather than become more flexible. While there are elements of truth in both these arguments, the way they are presented really misses the main point. It is not that external pressures will either compel the Pretoria regime to bend its knee or force it up against a defensive wall; the real impact of *external pressures* is that they will deepen *internal pressures* and sharpen *internal contradictions* which, alone, have so far produced a willingness to change.

Deepening internal pressures can have one of two predictable outcomes: they will either strengthen the resolution of President Botha and his supporters to press ahead more rapidly and more meaningfully towards achieving a negotiated settlement; or they will strengthen the Right-wing White backlash and produce a regim determined to resist real change by resorting to totalitarian, military repression Neither of these possibilities can be ruled out. But the predictable immediat effect was Pretoria's decision to adopt 'a siege economy', with the predictabl result of further slowing down SA's already sagging economic growth to 2%, whicl is not very far from its present actual level. The inevitable consequence of what is in fact, zero growth is a steady erosion of industrial capacity and an increase in th level of both Black and White unemployment. Although Black unemployment i already high, throwing workers out of their jobs is bound to increase social an political discontent and so raise the level of Black activist opposition. A substan tial increase in White unemployment (which has already become a feature of th economy) will predictably increase Right-wing pressures on the Botha regime. Th effects of sanctions will therefore be to make the country increasingly ungovern able and make it more difficult for the Botha regime to survive. The alternative t Botha's is not a more liberal regime, but a more reactionary one.

At some point in the next two years or so, those who favour reforms (howeve timidly attempted) will have to decide whether to grasp the nettle and to engage i genuine negotiations, or to try and survive by putting SA under some form o permanent military rule. This latter decision would greatly increase the chances o a revolutionary situation developing—a stage not yet reached in SA—and open u the prospect of a chaotic, violent racial struggle, and of seriously internationalizin the situation.

Any analysis of the likely long-term effects of the current package of economi measures against SA is bound to be highly speculative; what is more predictabl and of more immediate importance are the likely repercussions of 'a siege econ omy' on SA's highly industrialized society.

Among President Botha's advisers are economists who argue that the countr actually stands to gain by making itself self-reliant in manufacturing all it needs while exporting what it can under the net of sanctions. This is not the view of th Federated Chamber of Industries which speaks for most SA industrialists. It Business Charter describes a siege economy as a 'negative reaction, retreating int growing economic and political isolation and a drift into a repressive society necessitating greater government intervention and direct control over foreig exchange.' However, this is a political argument which does not address itself t the issue of whether a siege economy can be sustained.

Three leading SA economists and industrialists have given their reasons i interviews with the Johannesburg *Financial Mail* for believing that a siege econ omy spells disaster. Prof Sampie Terblanche, of Stellenbosch University, a promi nent government supporter, is convinced that the inevitable outcome of operatin a siege economy will be a 'tremendous deterioration of conditions.' His reason are these:

> We are vulnerable on our foreign account. If we take imports and exports as percentage of GNP and count them together it is 60%. That is high. In the US it is les than 10%—only among some smaller members of the European Economic Com munity is it 60%.
> Since 1976, we have been experiencing disinvestment. From 1965-1975, 10% of ou total investment was foreign investment and our growth rate was high. But in the te years since 1975, we have actually had an outflow of equity capital. A lot of short-term funds flowed in to cancel out that outflow, but there was disinvestment in real term and the growth rate was rather low.

In a sense, since 1975, we have become more independent of foreign investment, but we have bought this relative independence at the price of a lower growth rate. If there is large-scale disinvestment and boycotts, undoubtedly it will damage both the economy and job opportunities.

In 1980 we had a labour force of 10m, but only 7.5m could find jobs in the modern sector—2.5m could find jobs only in the peripheral sector, mainly in subsistence agriculture. By the year 2000, the labour force will be 18m, and with a growth rate of 3%—and I'm not certain we will attain that—there will be only about 11m jobs in the modern sector. So 7m will have to find jobs in the peripheral sector—at least 3.5m of them in the so-called informal or shanty-town sector in and around urban areas.

The poverty problem is so great that, even if we have a reasonable redistribution of income and opportunities, we will not be able to do much about it. All we can do is improve the quality of their poverty. Given this sombre picture, if we become a siege economy, conditions will deteriorate tremendously. Blacks will bear the brunt of the deterioration. This will cause more unrest and then we will have to take note of the possibility of a revolution.

Aubrey Dickman, the senior economic consultant to SA's largest multi-national company, Anglo American, does not believe that a siege economy 'has a chance of success.' It will, he says, 'stimulate the economy through monetary and fiscal means to increase spending; this will necessitate strong import controls and provide local industry with an opportunity to take up the slack.' But, he adds:

Industry already produces 90%-100% of our consumer goods, but it needs to import raw materials, intermediate goods and machinery—we cannot compete in these specialized areas. Under a siege economy, therefore, we would have a short-term boost, which would take up productive capacity; but after a time we would have to import intermediate goods and machinery.

By reducing competition through import controls, you create inflation and impair exports. Also, when you impose import controls, you are really imposing a control on investment, because imports in SA are closely related to investment.

The advocates of a siege economy are not stupid. Some have done interesting analyses. They have looked further down the road, and said: once we get into an upturn, imports will rise, and we must prepare now by putting the framework in place to control this rise in imports. Inevitably, this means investment control, because imports by definition will rise as investment rises. Their answer to the question of where goods will come from if controls are imposed, is to manufacture them in a hothouse economy. The more perceptive of the siege economists, and here I agree with them wholeheartedly, say that if we couple this with greater mobility of movement and training of labour, we can increase our domestic market base, lower our unit costs and make ourselves more competitive.

That's fine, but there's no need to go into a siege economy to do that. We should be doing it anyway. So we come back to investment control. Inevitably, imports will be rationed, and businessmen will be told who can invest, who can expand his factory and who cannot, and where he can expand it. This means more bureaucratic controls. And because demand for skilled labour will be raised, wages and prices too will go up. Then there will be a demand for wage and price controls and that will need a greater army of bureaucrats to administer the controls. There will also be black markets.

And I'm not even touching on two crucial aspects: Impairment of export competitiveness by driving up domestic costs; and the fact that the imposition of controls would be in defiance of the IMF and Gatt, and SA would risk losing its status under Gatt. For exports, this would be the most dangerous aspect of the whole siege policy.

Rhodesia lived with a hothouse economy for a while; but it was a much smaller economy, and eventually its capital stock was run down. This is exactly what would happen to us.

Len Abrahamse, the chairman of Syfret, one of SA's largest financial institutions, equates a siege economy with the laager mentality, which he calls 'a philosophy of despair'. 'The idea that SA can opt for a siege economy is absurd,' he believes, and argues that:

> A siege economy can become reality only if we conduct our affairs in such a way that we are indeed isolated from the rest of the world. SA essentially has an open economy and our welfare and future depend on being able to trade with, and have net investment from, the rest of the world.
>
> Our population is growing by just over 2.5% a year. If we take inflation into account, we have to grow at about 3.5% a year merely to stand still in terms of gross national income *per capita*. To uplift we have to grow at a much greater rate, and we cannot achieve that by pursuing the policies of a siege economy. The siege economy idea comes from people who have done their homework and perceive some immediate short-term gains, but the operative phrase is short-term. In practice, there would have to be increasing control over the rate of exchange, interest rates, the level of savings, and so on.
>
> The consequential increased government intervention would make us less and less a free enterprise economy. We would become introverted and ingrown, and incapable of generating enough net savings, either from the corporate sector and/or the individual sector, to provide the capital we need to sustain growth.
>
> A minority political view exists—to hell with the rest of the world—what does it matter if we don't win the approbation of Bonn, Whitehall, Washington, Paris or wherever? Let us retreat politically into the laager. A siege economy is the same philosophy; it's a philosophy of despair.

Conrad, Strauss, managing director of Standard Bank Investment Corporation, believes that 'glib talk of the merits of a siege economy may go down well on the hustings but the long-term effects of rigidly applied sanctions will be a severe degeneration of the economy.'

The idea that gold, with its new high price, could save the SA economy is strongly discounted by financial writers like Alexander Camargue of the Johannesburg *Weekly Mail*. For every $5 rise in the price of gold, SA's foreign exchange earnings rise slightly over R4m a week. For a country with a foreign debt of $22bn that needs servicing, let alone repaying, such windfalls that may come from a higher price of gold is useful but it cannot provide a lifeline to economic solvency, especially since capital outflow pressures are already so great that it is estimated it would need an almost unprecedented rise in the gold price to $370-390 to make any major direct impact.

IMPACT OF SANCTIONS ON SA'S NEIGHBOURS

Sanctions, however, are a two-edged sword which cut not only against SA but also against those Frontline States (Botswana, Lesotho, Swaziland, Mozambique, Zimbabwe and Zambia) that are dependent, to a greater or lesser extent, on their trade and communications links with SA. Whether or not they join in applying sanctions, their economies would inevitably sustain severe losses, which would be even greater if SA were to adopt a policy of counter-sanctions as it has threatened. The extent of the economic damage to the FLS and what might possibly be done to minimize it was studied by teams of experts set up by the Southern African Development Cooperation Conference (SADCC) in 1985.[4]

The estimated direct cost to all the SADCC countries in actual loss of revenues and of producing alternative structures for transport, security, import and export channels of trade was between $5,250m and $6,250m over a three-year period. Indirect costs were more difficult to calculate because of the unknown factors of the extent to which sanctions might be applied; the best 'realistic estimate' was below $1,000m. Thus, the total cost would be in the region of $7,000m over a three year period.[5]

High though this burden is, the FLS leaders claim they are low when compared to the cost of SA's continuing destabilization of their countries, which they estimate came to $10bn between 1980-84—well above the total foreign aid for the period. They estimate the current annual cost at c. $3bn. Some economists, like Prof R. H. Green, put the cost even 50% higher.[6] These estimates suggest that, as of 1986, the cost of SA's undeclared war on its neighbours was running at 10% or more of what their output could have been if it were not disrupted by Pretoria's policy of destabilization. This estimate of the cost of destabilization to SA's neighbours is crucial to understanding the temper of the FLS leaders and of their seemingly foolhardiness in demanding comprehensive sanctions.

The actual cost to the FLS would depend on the degree of international aid they might expect towards meeting their losses and contributing to the cost of providing alternative structures. However, there would also be some gains from applying sanctions. These have been estimated at:

Import cost savings—$200m (10% of average on imports from or through SA).

Export gains from replacing SA in overseas markets (e.g. metals, steel, coal and asbestos) -$25m. (But capitalization for the development of these exports would be limited by existing production and available transport capacity. There would also be export losses of between $25m-$50m since a number of existing exports to SA would be hard to re-destine and prices in general are likely to be lower.)

Lower transport costs—$75m-$150m. But this would depend on improving transport capacity and security.

Additional regional production to replace SA products—$50m; but this, too, would be limited by capacity.

Output from returnee workers—$300m (half in public sector wages);—$125m-$175m in increased peasant production;—$75m-$100m informal sector output; and—$50m-$75m in interprise wages, less $125m in remittance losses.

Improved Security—$200m; a by-product of security improvement for the transport sector.

The total estimated gains would be between $750m-$900m.

Economists who have worked on these figures, like Prof R. H. Green, admit that these estimates are very rough, and may be on the optimistic side; but they feel they are not totally unrealistic.

COUNTER-SANCTIONS

Pretoria has lost no time in announcing that, apart from the fact that the effects of sanctions on its own economy would inevitably also affect its neighbours, it would consider imposing sanctions of its own—as it has done in the past by, for example, disrupting traffic with Lesotho to force the capitulation of the Jonathan Government. (See Lesotho below). The Foreign Minister hinted in August that his Government might consider repatriating the 2m migrant workers but then quickly retreated from this threat. However, in October, SA announced that it would stop recruiting Mozambican workers after the contracts of present migrants had expired. In August 1986 Pretoria announced the introduction of an import licensing system for goods from Zimbabwe and Zambia, saying it was an economic measure instituted to protect SA's foreign sources of supply. A search was instituted in the same month on all goods passing across Beitbridge which led to lengthy delays;

but after three days the searches were stopped with the explanation that a 'statistical survey' had been completed.

Thus, despite the threat to impose counter-sanctions, by the end of October 1986, no measures were taken other than against Mozambique which, Pretoria claimed, was in reprisal for Maputo's allowing the ANC to operate from its territory.

THE DISINVESTMENT CAMPAIGN

Disinvestment from SA by foreign firms is itself a sanctions' measure—even though decisions to withdraw may have had more to do with purely business reasons rather than because of moral or political considerations. A remarkable feature of the disinvestment campaign is its success in the US and the relative failure to get a real momentum behind similar campaigns in Britain and other West European countries. The reasons for this must be sought in the greater sensitivity of American businesses to public concerns because of the pressures by bodies concerned with promoting ethics in business (not just over SA) and, of course, the pressures by the Black Caucas and other lobbies on State and City administrations (see US Role below).

The disinvestment campaign in the US really began to get off the ground only in 1978 when it was spearheaded by, among others, the American Committee on Africa which had on its staff Dumisane Kumalo, a Sowetan who had left SA after the youth uprising in Soweto in 1977. It was not until 1984 that American firms began to disengage from SA; in that year seven companies withdrew; the figure went up to 39 in 1985, and by mid-1986 it had reached 20. What is significant about the disinvestors in late 1985 and especially 1986 was that they included some of the largest US multinationals such as Coca Cola, General Motors, General Electric Xerox, AT&T, and IBM, as well as Citibank. About 200 US firms still retain their stake in the SA economy. The value of American investment in SA in real terms has declined by $50m since 1982.

Over the past three years c. 30 British firms have begun to disinvest, most of them by selling some of their plants or diluting their share capital holding. The main pressures felt by British companies have been on banks, two of whom—Barclays and Hill Samuel—are among those which have begun to disinvest. The giant Prudential Insurance Company gave as its reason for selling 92.5% of its SA subsidiary the 'growing shortage of skilled staff'. Donald Gordon, chairman of Liberty Life of Africa—the main beneficiary of the Prudential withdrawal—disclosed that his firm had been losing actuaries and accountants who, he said, have been emigrating 'in droves'. The increasing emigration of SA professionals is another indicator of increasing economic and political concerns felt among the country's business community.

A major new trend in British disinvestment was signalled in an announcement made in late October 1986 by John Wilson, the chief executive of Shell. He warned that unless the SA Government stepped up reforms of apartheid, his company would consider closing down its entire operation. He added that if apartheid policies were left unchanged, the result could be chaos. Shell is the biggest oil company in SA, with annual sales of £720m.

THE COURSE OF EVENTS: JULY 1985-OCTOBER 1986
NAMIBIA AND ANGOLA: THE DIPLOMATIC FRONT

Negotiations over Namibia's independence had reached a complete stalemate by early 1985, with the ending of the mediating role by The Consultative Group of the Five Western Powers (Britain, Canada, France, West Germany and the United tates) when it ceased to meet and left it to the US to initiate new moves to advance negotiations with SA and Angola over implementing the Security Council resolution 435 (SCR 435).

In June 1984 Pretoria, looking forward to a prolonged stalemate, took its own initiative by introducing a Transitional Government of National Unity (TGNU) also known as the Multi-Party Conference (MPC).

The Security Council condemned this move on 19 June in a 16-point resolution that was adopted by 13 votes to nil, with the US and UK abstaining because of their opposition to one point referring to sanctions. The resolution described the TGNU as 'illegal and null and void.'

It also condemned SA for obstructing the implementation of SCR 435, rejected linking the withdrawal of Cuban troops from Angola with Namibian independence, and demanded that SA cooperate fully with the Council and the secretary-general in implementing SCR 435. The resolution urged States that have not done so to take voluntary measures to put pressure on SA. Suggested measures included stopping new investments, re-examining maritime and aerial relations, prohibiting the sale of krugerrands and other SA coins, and restricting sports and cultural exchanges.

After the vote, the US delegate, Warren Clark, said that while the US is against any settlement outside SCR 435, it abstained because 'we cannot in good faith conscientiously join in urging others to undertake actions which we believe would slow down' Namibia's achieving independence. He added that despite these objections, the US refrained from voting against the resolution because of 'our strong feelings on the question of across-border violence.'

Speaking in the Security Council debate on 12 June, the US ambassador José Sorzano said:

> We deplore SA violations of Angolan territorial integrity. Violent actions across borders, be they military attacks, sabotage or terrorism against innocent civilians, can only serve to undermine the confidence necessary for the settlement of disputes. In this instance, they can only detract from the prospects of the early independence of Namibia.

Sorzano went on to say that 'a settlement could be within our grasp' if only the gap could be narrowed over the last obstacle in the way to implementing SCR 435, i.e. the withdrawal of Cuban troops from Angola. Reviewing progress made on this issue up to that point, Sorzano said

> By late last summer, it became clear that we had moved beyond the stage of rhetorical debate on the issues of 'linkage'. Cuban troop withdrawal is—as a practical matter, and with the support of all concerned—being discussed in the context of implementation of SCR 435. In November, the Angolan Government, for the first time, put a detailed and concrete negotiation proposal on the table. This major step forward was followed by a SA proposal. The two proposals showed agreement between SA and Angola on a number of broad principles.
>
> My Government has been involved for the past several months in intensive discussions with the two parties aimed at narrowing the remaining gap between their positions. We remain convinced that the gap can be bridged. Even in the wake of the events of the past days, it is our view that the door clearly remains open to a settlement and the implementation of SCR 435. The US for one, remains committed to pursuing the search for peace for as long as there is prospect for success. The only alternative would be to acquiesce in continued war and suffering for the people in the region.

Angola continued to show a keen interest in reviving negotiations. On 5 July President dos Santos announced he would resume contacts with the US and SA 'when we obtain practical and convincing signals of good faith from the other parties involved in the search for a global agreement on Namibian independence peace and security in Southern Angola.' Six days later, on 11 July, the US House of Representatives followed the Senate's lead of the previous month in voting for the repeal of the nine-year-old Clark Amendment which, inter alia, prohibited military aid going to Angola. On the following day, 12 July, Angola announced the suspension of talks with the US on withdrawal of Cuban troops from Angola. It noted that 'the repeal of the Clark Amendment will leave the US Administration and international imperialism free to openly and directly intervene in Angola and exercise military and political pressures on the Angolan State.' A US State Department spokesman commented: 'It is our view that the Angolan statement does not close the door to a negotiated settlement.'

On 9 August SA's Foreign Minister, Pik Botha, flew to Vienna for meetings with Dr Chester Crocker, the US Assistant Secretary of State for African Affairs, and Ewan Fergusson, a senior British diplomat. Namibia was amongst the subjects discussed.

On 5 September, addressing the preparatory meeting of the Non-Aligned Conference, President dos Santos accused the US of helping to sabotage regional peacekeeping efforts and appealed to American public opinion to oppose the repeal of the Clark Amendment; but, at the same time, he indicated his interest in restarting negotiations, and criticized SA for not giving 'practical signs' of serious intent to negotiate a regional peace settlement.

The SA Defence Force (SADF) once again crossed the Angolan border in September on the pretext of pursuing Swapo guerillas. On 20 September the Security Council, yet again, unanimously condemned SA for using Namibia as a springboard for invasion and destabilization, and appointed a Commission of Investigation (Australia, Egypt and Peru) to evaluate the damage caused. The Commission visited Angola in October and reported its findings to the Security Council on 6 November. It again condemned SA and demanded that SA should compensate Angola for the damage done.

Hopes for a renewal of negotiations were rekindled by Chester Crocker on 29 October when he reported that as a result of diplomatic pressures and the latest round of trans-border violence, signals had been received from both SA and Angola indicating a readiness to start fresh talks. Meanwhile, a fresh attempt was made at the Security Council to get agreement to mandatory sanctions against SA over Namibia. A resolution to this effect was presented on behalf of the Non-aligned movement and was debated from 13-15 November. The resolution was vetoed by the US and UK, with France abstaining. The resolution was raised again at a UN General Assembly meeting on Namibia which lasted from 18-21 November. M. Philippe of Luxembourg, speaking on behalf of the European Economic Community (EEC), called for the immediate implementation of SCR 435 without preconditions. The vote on six resolutions (including a demand for mandatory sanctions) met with abstentions from the five Contact Group members.

In November Crocker finally received a reply from Pretoria to proposals the US had put forward in March for closing the gap between SA and Angola over a timetable for phasing out the Cuban military presence. During a press briefing on 28 January 1986 he disclosed that 'the SA response accepted, in principle, a major feature of our proposals regarding a timetable for Cuban withdrawals from Angola, and the implementation of the UN plan in Namibia.'

Shortly before getting this SA response, Crocker had a meeting in Lusaka with

Angola's Interior Minister, Manuel Alexandre Rodrigues (Kito). The only positive outcome of that meeting was an announcement by Kito that a further meeting would be held in Luanda 'in the near future.'

The meeting finally took place in the first week of January 1986 when Crocker had three days of talks with Kito and the Army Commander Ndau, in Luanda, as well as a meeting with President dos Santos, who said in a public statement:

> We still cannot understand whether Savimbi's visit and the military and other aid which the US intends to give him should be considered as a form of pressure on Angola or as a declaration of war by the US.

Crocker was clearly given to understand that the American talks with Savimbi should not be allowed to jeopardize Luanda's bilateral relations with Washington.[7] Crocker detected a more coherent, tough-minded and nationalist stand by the dos Santos' regime after the recent purge of the party.[8] He sensed that the Angolan army (Fapla) did not expect to win the war against Unita, having suffered heavily in the September-October fighting in which they had lost c. 1,500 men (see below). The mood favoured a continuing dialogue to try and get SADF out of Angola through an agreement on Namibia. There was some fluidity in the Angolan position over the Cuban issue, and some new ideas emerged—but what they were remains unclear. While in Luanda, Crocker also had talks with Swapo representatives.

Crocker went from Luanda for three days of talks with Pik Botha in Pretoria carrying with him a letter from President Reagan for President Botha which dealt both with regional and internal SA issues. The gist of the letter can be gauged from Crocker's press conference on 14 January when he restated the Administration's position that the goals of internal reform in SA towards a just and equitable system, together with the goals of a negotiated settlement on Namibia and Angola are 'a seamless web—all of them are urgently needed, and you cannot have some without the others.' In pursuing these goals, he said, the US acted out of a sense of realism, dealing with the world as it is, 'not as we would like it to be.' He acknowledged that the difficulties are formidable, but noted that history is replete with examples of difficult situations being turned around into successes 'when men and governments are willing to act with courage, with sincerity, and with good sense.' The US, he stressed, had done its share of talking and had 'no regrets' for what it had said. But the time has come for the world to know 'what South Africans are prepared to do, what risks they are prepared to take for peace and progress, what courage they are prepared to muster to resist the temptations of violence and oppression.' His talks with President Botha and his senior aides, Crocker said, had given him 'a more informed sense of what was possible and what was not', and a better appreciation of the gaps that remain. However, the US hoped to see momentum on political and racial reform in SA and a breakthrough toward a just and equitable system of government. Crocker said Namibian independence was still a major US goal, stressing that the US does not recognize or support the interim government in Namibia. Washington, he said, maintains regular contacts with the internal parties in Namibia as well as with Swapo.

On the Angolan situation, Crocker said there were still 'tremendous issues of face and face-saving for both sides. . . . In addition, it should be noted that the issues involved are issues of life-and-death for the parties concerned.' It is vital for all sides to keep talking through diplomatic channels, he said, and stand back from the brink. He added that both sides recognize that the military track is risky.

Crocker and Pik Botha resumed their talks in Geneva in February 1986. They discussed Namibia and the possibility of releasing Nelson Mandela, which wa being strongly urged by Reagan. In March, Pik Botha wrote to the UN Secretary General, Dr de Cuellar, asking for his support for SA's proposal to implement SCF 435 on 1 August when the state of emergency would be lifted in Namibia an leaders of local parties would be invited to join in negotiations about a nev constitution. Botha did not disclose any preconditions for such a move, but the presumably were a demand for the withdrawal of Cuban troops from Angola. H noted that de Cuellar had accepted the idea of proportional representation for th elections preceding independence, and that Swapo had also accepted this metho of elections. Botha went on to ask for a 'wider and more balanced view' of event in the sub-continent from democratic governments, and claimed that the USSI had injected $2bn of military equipment over the past two years while, at th same time, Cuba had expanded its expeditionary force and the Soviet bloc ha increased the number of its military advisers.[8] Swapo categorically rejected the S/ offer, saying it was linked to the 'extraneous and irrelevant issue of Cuban troops i Angola.' The Administrator-General in Windhoek, Louis Pienaar, confirmed on March that SA's willingness to implement SCR 435 depended on 'realistic pros pects of a Cuban pull-out from Angola'. He added that SWA/Namibia was ne prepared to wait indefinitely for a Cuban withdrawal. 'Developments in interna tional politics may well overtake internal events', he warned, 'alternative pos sibilities for independence with international recognition will have to be examine at some stage.'[9]

Portugal's Prime Minister, Mario Soares, continued to play a helpful role i facilitating talks with the Angolans.[10] On 18 March, Crocker's deputy, Fran Wisner, had two meetings in Lisbon with the Portuguese Foreign Minister, Pires d Miranda, after which he said that Dr Soares could be an important force in helpin to find a peaceful solution in Southern Africa. Wisner went from Lisbon t Frankfurt for talks with Pik Botha, and on 21 April Pik Botha held talks with th Portuguese Foreign Minister in Luxembourg before proceeding to Geneva for sti another session with Crocker.

This latest round of talks, which had begun in Lusaka in November 1985 an ended in Geneva in April 1986, failed to make progress towards narrowing the ga between Pretoria and Luanda over the 'last obstacle'—the withdrawal of Cuba troops. This failure was acknowledged by President Botha on 22 June when he sai that '31st August is close and the opportunity is still hanging in the air.' He adde that the UN Secretary-General had informed him that Angola rejected any linkag between Namibia and Cuban troops withdrawals, and that its Government 'was n longer interested in negotiations with the US.'

THE NAMIBIAN-ANGOLAN FIGHTING FRONT

The Lusaka ceasefire agreement of February 1984[11] was short-lived. By Septembe 1985 SADF no longer made any pretence of observing it. On the 16th SADF unit crossed into Angola, with air support, in pursuit, it was claimed, of Swap insurgents who, according to an SA military spokesman, had begun to act 'mor aggressively' and were infiltrating into the area defined as a no-go zone under th Lusaka Agreement and attacking 'soft targets' inside Namibia.

SADF claimed that at least 60% of Swapo's guerrillas had been deployed i support of Fapla against Unita. Pretoria confirmed that nearly 500 SA and Nami bian troops split into 12 'reaction teams' of c. 40 men each, backed up by aircra were conducting what it called the 'follow-up operation' against the Swapo 8t Battalian consisting of between 400 and 800 men.[12]

It said that the operation follows at least three attempts by Swapo to infiltrate i large numbers, two of them since the withdrawal of SA forces from southern Angola on 18 May.

The statement added that the majority of the 200 Swapo forces involved in the first operation in January had been destroyed and that 72 had been killed in the latest operations.

Significantly, the latest SADF statement noted 'greater cooperation between Fapla and Swapo and accused the Angolan forces of providing Swapo with logistic help and also informing them of security force movements. Defence headquarters also accused Swapo of violating the February 1984 Lusaka agreement betwen SA and Angola 145 times. Under the accord SA agreed to withdraw its troops providing the Fapla did not allow Swapo to occupy the vacated areas.

But SADF was not only occupied with pre-empting a new Swapo offensive; its Air Force went into action in some strength to relieve Unita from a serious defect (see below).

Pretoria claimed that all its troops had been withdrawn by 22 September, but Luanda insisted on 7 October that they were still active deep inside Angolan territory as far as the area of Mavinga.[13] On 22 December Luanda claimed that our SADF battalions had crossed into Cunene province; Pretoria replied their presence was aimed at heading off Swapo's annual wet season attacks.

Although the People's Liberation Army of Namibia (Plan) failed to increase its momentum during 1985 and early 1986, guerrilla activities were nevertheless sufficient to tie down 50,000 SA troops on the Namibian front.[14] The majority of these Black troops are recruited in Namibia into the SWA Territorial Force (Swatf). In June 1985 an army spokesman claimed that Namibia was now within reach of being able to look after its own military commitment and that 60% of Swatf's strength was locally recruited. He added that the number of volunteers were greater than requirements and cited as a fact that 2,000 volunteers had presented themselves for 700 vacancies in one company.[15]

By May 1986 the military situation was back to where it had been in 1983 before SADF's major Operation Protea, according to the SA commander of Swatf, Maj-Gen George Meiring.[16]

It is difficult to be precise about the extent of casualties since both sides are concerned with magnifying the losses of the other side and minimizing their own. According to Gen. Meiring, Swapo had lost 45 men in the first half of 1986 and 599 in 1985.[17] Sam Nujoma claimed that Plan had killed 406 SADF and Swatf soldiers and wounded 373 in the first seven months of 1985. In May, Plan claimed to have killed more than 132 soldiers in a seven-week offensive that began in April, taking the total fatal casualties up to 400 in the first half of the year. Swatf, probably rightly, dismissed these claims as 'pure rhetoric'.[18]

ANGOLA'S INTERNAL MILITARY FRONT: FAPLA V UNITA = SOVIET BLOC/CUBA V SA/US

The above equation shows how what began as a civil war that developed in 1974 out of the struggle for power on the eve of Angola's independence has come to acquire a significant international dimension. After the political victory of the Marxist Movement for the Popular Liberation of Angola (MPLA), the US was bound by the Clark Amendment to stop its aid for Dr Jonas Savimbi's Union for the Total Independence of Angola (Unita). It was left to the Soviet bloc and Cuba to build up the strength of Angola's national army Fapla (the People's Armed Forces for the Liberation of Angola), and to SA to buttress Unita. In the decade since 1975, US policy was to pursue two interconnected aims: to promote negotiations to find a settlement of the Namibian problem which it linked to the with-

drawal of the Cuban combat troops from Angola and of the SA Defence Forces
(SADF) from Angola; and to encourage the MPLA Government to loosen its
dependence on Soviet–Cuban support by encouraging the growth of trade and
diplomatic links with the West.

This dual policy pursued by the US since Angola's independence in April 1975
was fortified by a secret agreement reached with the USSR in 1975 whereby both
sides agreed to avoid military confrontation in Angola. Such a policy remained
viable so long as the prospects of successful negotiations seemed reasonably
assured and the Soviet bloc restricted its aid for Fapla to a reasonable amount of
military aid and training, and Unita seemed unlikely to be defeated. Three developments combined to change American policy in 1985: the fading prospects of
achieving a negotiated settlement of the Namibian problem and the withdrawal of
Cuban troops; a substantial increase in the amount and sophistication of Soviet
arms supplied to Fapla; and the growing pressures of the Right-wing lobby in
Congress favouring support for Unita. The decisive turning-point in US policy
towards Angola came with the near-success of Fapla in seriously crippling, if not
entirely destroying, Unita's military position in the fighting in the Mavinga area in
August/October 1985.

In the build-up to that offensive the Soviet bloc had greatly stepped up its
military supplies, estimated by SA military intelligence and the CIA as being in the
region of $2bn. The Soviets also increased the number of their military advisers to
between 1,200-2000.[19] This enabled Fapla to mount an offensive by seven or eight
brigades, each consisting of 700 men, covered by considerable air cover including
Mig23 fighters and MI 25 air gunships. The extent to which Soviet military advisers
and Cuban pilots were actively engaged in the offensive remains controversial.
What is clear, though, is that Unita was saved from a disastrous defeat by the SA
military intervention. For the past ten years Pretoria has repeatedly insisted that it
gave Unita only 'moral material and humanitarian aid'; however in September 1985
SA's Defence Minister finally admitted that Pretoria had all along been active in its
support for Unita, and went on to make the significant statement that SA would
not allow Unita to be defeated.[20] Independent evidence shows that in the decisive
six days that turned Fapla's promise of success into a heavy defeat, the SA Air
Force (SAAF) carried out the following operations:[21]

- 28 September five SA planes raided Fapla positions;
- 29 September two SA planes flew over the Fapla lines.

A year after the Mavinga offensive, in August 1986, Savimbi told an American
reporter that he had miscalculated the real direction of Fapla'a attack.[22]

> When we understood the major thrust was at Mavinga, it was too late, So we had to
> ask the South Africans to take 2,000 troops in four days and four nights and put them
> here [outside Mavinga]. Then we said, 'Give us mortars, ammo and cannons of every
> quality', and they gave it.
> To fly in those reinforcements the SAAF put its American-made C-130 Hercules
> transports at risk. The South African pilots flew more than 1,000 miles round-trip
> through Angolan airspace to complete the airlift.

The ease with which the SAAF was able to dominate the skies and, so, to turn
the tide of the battle in Unita's favour was surprising in view of the care with which
Fapla's Soviet advisers had planned the offensive and had presumably built up an
air cover to protect it. Either the planners had not expected a full-scale SA
counter-attack from the air, or their air cover was still too weak to offer more than a
token resistance to the SAAF. However, a month after the failed offensive, Col Iko

arreira, commander of the Angolan Air Force, declared that SA had lost its vital
ir superiority and that a new radar system was being installed which would mean
ie 'defeat of Unita.' But Fapla's commanders were reported to be less sanguine
bout victory, having lost at least 1,500 of their best-trained men in the Mavinga
ghting.

Savimbi's near-defeat sent the alarm bells ringing in the White House, though
ot yet in the State Department. The Secretary of State, George P. Shultz, and
'hester Crocker still believed in the possibility of negotiations succeeding since
ie signals they were receiving from Luanda were of a more flexible attitude on the
ssue of Cuban troops. Besides, the State Department was much less responsive to
ie build-up of the Right-wing campaign on behalf of Savimbi than was the White
House.

The Savimbi lobby made an important gain in June 1985 when the Senate voted
3-34 to repeal the Clark Amendment. The vote was welcomed by a State Depart-
ient spokesman, Edward Djerejian, who said: 'This Administration has consist-
ntly opposed the Clark Amendment as a matter of principle. It is a unique and
ounter-productive constraint on the President's ability to conduct foreign policy.'
Jnita welcomed the decision as an indication that 'the external factors in our
truggle for liberation have greatly changed.' The momentum for the campaign
uilt up rapidly after the Mavinga offensive. At the end of September, two SA
fficials, Dave Stewart and Les Manley, met State Department officials in secret
alks where they pressed for US military aid to Unita.[23] But the SA factor was
tself one of the major reasons why the Administration was still hesitating in
oming to a decision since it was unwilling to be seen on the same side as the
Pretoria regime.[24]

The Savimbi lobby comprised a variety of Conservative and anti-communist
roups which included the Conservative Caucus, the American Enterprise Insti-
ute, the Heritage Foundation, the American Republic Foundation, and the Free
he Eagle National Citizens lobby. The lobby inside Republican Congress was led
y the House Minority leader, Robert H. Michel, Jack Kemp and Claude Pepper.
The latter had introduced a motion proposing that $27m—the same amount as was
oted for the Contras in Nicaragua—be allocated for 'humanitarian aid' to Sav-
mbi. The State Department worked to block this proposal. In October the Secre-
ary of State wrote confidentially to Michel arguing that such a move could
eopardize the current negotiations with Angola and SA. Refusing to comply with
Shultz's request. Michel termed the Congress proposal 'not only a geo-strategic
ut a moral necessity.'[25]

Michel disclosed that 27 Republican Congressmen had sent a letter to the
President reminding him of his own declaration of support for 'anti-communist
ebels' in Afghanistan, Laos, Nicaragua and Angola, attacking Shultz and
Crocker's 'constructive engagement policy'—as if it were not also the policy
epeatedly endorsed by Reagan himself.

By the end of October 1985 it appeared that the State Department was isolated
vithin the Administration on this issue. A White House official confirmed the
disagreements, but said no final decision had yet been reached.[26] One of the issues
n dispute was whether the Administration should support Unita through covert
id or come out openly on Savimbi's side. A secret policy paper opposed public
inancing for Unita and favoured covert aid channeled through the CIA. On 22
November, Reagan revealed his own position when he declared that covert aid
would have much more chance of success right now' than the open economic and
military aid proposed by some Congressmen.[27] Reagan revealed that Shultz was

not opposed to covert aid. Amplifying the President's statement, a State Depart‑ ment official spokesman said:

> The recent escalation in the fighting in Angola concerns us. There is widespread sympathy for Mr Savimbi's struggle against Soviet–Cuban adventurism, just as there is about South African occupation of Namibia.[28]

The growing strength of the Savimbi lobby activated groups opposed to aid for Savimbi. It attracted the support of 100 Congressmen, led by Ted Weiss, a New York Democrat, as well as of the Black Caucus, the Rev Jesse Jackson's Rainbow Coalition and Trans-Africa.

In November it became known that the Pentagon and the CIA were both urging the President to mount a large covert military operation 'to aid non-communist rebels' in Angola.[29]

However, both the CIA and the State Department Bureau of Intelligence and Research agreed in their evaluation of the Angolan situation that Savimbi 'can't win and can't force a coalition government.' The Pentagon's Defence Intelligence Agency (which was reported to have shared intelligence with Unita) took the opposite view.[30] The CIA analysts concluded that Unita did not[30] have the military strength to create a stalemate.

In December the Conservative Caucus announced its intention to make support for Unita its primary foreign policy objective in 1986.[31] Its chairman, Howard Phillips, declared

> Next year this will be the litmus test of the seriousness of the Reagan Administra‑ tion's commitment to the cause of freedom fighters.

The Conservative Caucus also spearheaded the campaign to force the Gulf-Chevron Oil Corporation to pull out of Angola. (Gulf-Chevron is the largest oil operating company in Angola.) Posters and advertisements vilified its chairman as a communist accomplice. A campaign was launched to boycott Gulf petrol sta‑ tions; but Gulf's Board refused to withdraw even though the State Department began to buckle under the Right-wing campaign and urged Gulf-Chevron to con‑ sider its wider responsibilities (see below).

By the time Jonas Savimbi arrived in the US in January 1986 it was clear that all the doors of the American Establishment would be open to him—a success ensured by a heavily financed publicity campaign managed by the Black, Manfort, Stone and Kelly firm whose principals have previously worked in the Nixon, Ford and Reagan Administrations. On his previous visit in 1980, Savimbi had failed to get an appointment with even the Assistant Secretary of State for Africa. On this occasion he was welcomed to the White House and received by the Secretary of State and the Defence Secretary. The President said at the start of his meeting with Savimbi that 'we want to be very helpful to his cause to what he is trying to do, and we're trying to arrive at the best way to do that.' The Defence Secretary told Savimbi he hoped Congress would give him 'appropriate support'.

Reagan's lengthy legislative message to Congress, 'Agenda for the Future', on 4 February 1986 dealt mainly with domestic issues but it included a special section on Southern Africa which read:

> We are moved by the efforts of freedom fighters such as Jonas Savimbi and the members of Unita. They deserve our support in their brave struggle against Soviet-

Cuban imperialism in Angola. We will work with the Congress to determine the most effective way of providing support.

In SA, we stand forthrightly on the principle that the Government must achieve freedom and justice for all its citizens. Apartheid, in our view, is doomed. We have a major stake—as elsewhere, both moral and strategic—in encouraging a peaceful transition and avoiding a terrible civil war. This is why we reject the approach of those on both sides who pursue violence and oppression. Our ability to affect the ultimate outcome is limited, but we will continue to employ our good offices—both official and private—to pursue dialogue and negotiation as the best way to change the system while protecting the future of all South Africans.

Three days earlier, on 1 February, Chester Crocker had signalled a State Department shift closer to the views of the White House on the situation in Angola. In a TV interview he said: 'We can't simply stand aside and watch' as other parties exploit the US position and seek military solutions. Citing the USSR and Cuba, he added that 'some inside the Angolan Government have lent themselves to a great deal of escalation recently in the fighting inside Angola.' Crocker added that Savimbi was seeking 'a signal' of support from the US; but he refused to be drawn on whether the 'signal' should take the form of overt or covert aid. However, a few days earlier, on 28 January, Crocker had said at a press briefing that the Administration 'would like to see effective and appropriate support' for Unita with the hope that 'it would nudge the Luanda Government towards a negotiated settlement of the Namibian independence issue and of its own civil war.' But, he added, 'the Administration does not believe that legislation mandating aid is an effective way to proceed.'

In another shift of State Department policy, Crocker said in his 28 January briefing that 'we do feel that it's important that our companies take into account what is taking place there [in Angola]. They should be thinking about US national interests as well as their own corporate interests as they make their decisions.' He defined US national interests as achieving peace in the region. On the same day, 25 civic and political groups associated with the Conservative Caucus announced their support for a campaign to force Chevron-Gulf to divest itself of its petroleum installations in Angola.

Savimbi said after his visit to the US that he had been promised 'material support'; but neither he nor Washington gave any public information as to the form it would take. On 29 April Savimbi announced that US military aid had begun to arrive eleven days earlier. He mentioned uniforms, trucks and medicines, but refused to say whether the equipment included the Stinger ground-to-air missiles. An article in the *Washington Post* reported that Stingers had in fact been sent. A few weeks after the *Post*'s report, the Defence Department announced that it had dismissed Dr Michael Pillsbury, an Assistant Under-Secretary for Policy Planning, because he had provided information about the US covert intelligence programme. It was alleged against him that he had failed to pass a lie-detector test about reports that Stinger missiles were being sent to Unita and Afghanistan.[32] The *Post* also printed a report that William Casey, the CIA director, had gone to Africa to arrange the operation to supply aid to Unita. According to one report,[33] Robert Frasure, who was in charge of the Africa desk at the US embassy in London, told the British House of Commons Foreign Affairs Committee, that Casey had visited SA in mid-March 1985 to make the necessary arrangements to supply arms to Savimbi. However, it seems more likely that the supplies went through Zaire rather than SA. President Kaunda claimed on 28 April 1986 that this was the case, and said that this development had been discussed at a recent meeting of Frontline leaders.[34] Zairean authorities denied Kaunda's allegation. In an earlier statement

on 4 April, Kaunda described the US decision to help arm Unita as 'a sa
development', and said it was puzzling that Reagan was back-pedalling from th
'realistic course' of pursuing negotiations. Angola, he added, was being 'supporte
by the Soviet Union and the socialist cousins, while the US is arming the Unit
rebels . . . the North and South Korea situation in Angola is imminent as th
Super-power rivalry is pursued in this Southern African political scenario.'[35]

Washington's decision to support Unita militarily was criticized by Presider
dos Santos in a letter to the UN Secretary-General as 'a flagrant breach' of a secre
and previously unpublicized document, the Mindelo Act. He claimed that th
agreement was signed by Frank Wisner, Crocker's deputy, at a meeting with a
Angolan delegation at a meeting held in Mindelo, Cape Verde, in January 1984
According to dos Santos, the agreement specified that the US would not provid
aid to Unita. The State Department denied the existence of the Mindelo Act an
claimed that the meeting at Mindelo was recorded in the form of a Note on th
Minutes signed by both parties. The Minutes recorded the commitment of bot
sides to pursue the negotiations for the implementation of SCR 435 and to secur
Cuban troops' withdrawal from Angola. It also recorded that the Angolan side ha
urged the US to use its influence on Pretoria to cease support for Unita. A Stat
Department official said that 'no commitment on this issue was made by the U
side.'[36]

The official US stand on Angola was set out in a Voice of America broadcast o
24 April:

> Unita has had help from several Black African nations as well as support from th
> SA Government. Savimbi affirms he is as much opposed to apartheid as any Blac
> African leader. But, as he has said to critics of his reliance on SA: 'When you fight
> war, you get support from wherever it comes.' And he believes Soviet imperialisr
> poses a greater threat to Black Africa than does SA racism. The recent America
> decision to support Unita lessens its need to rely on SA. And President Ronal
> Reagan is hoping that, by strengthening Unita, he can persuade the MPLA and thei
> patrons that there is no military solution to the Angolan civil war.
>
> Both the US and Unita favour reconciliation between the warring parties. Neithe
> seeks military victory. Jonas Savimbi has called for negotiations with President do
> Santos, followed by elections. The US believes that national reconciliation in Angol
> would be facilitated by a regional settlement which includes Namibian independenc
> from SA and the withdrawal of Cuban troops from Angola. An end to apartheid, whic
> is not only morally repugnant but a destabilizing force in Southern Africa, is als
> essential to a lasting regional peace. American good offices in promoting a settlemer
> are still available to all.

Savimbi's links with SA have been an embarrassment to him in his relation
with African countries and with the US (see above). While in the US Savimb
insisted that Americans should 'help the South Africans to find a way of securin
equal rights for all its population, and also support those who are fighting th
Russians and Cubans in Angola.'[37]

Unita's Chief of Staff (Intelligence), Brig Huambo Casito, headed a three-ma
delegation to SA in March 1986 ostensibly to address a students' meetings at th
Universities of the Witwatersrand, Natal and Cape Town. He announced that a
senior Cuban officer, Gen Ramirez, had recently arrived in Cuanda Cubang
province to command the 'Soviet-Cuban offensive' against Unita, and claimed tha
Soviet and Cuban forces were now more involved than ever before; it would not b
possible for Unita to withstand the planned offensive against them without U
military aid.[38] Angola's Deputy Chief of General Staff, Lt Col Roberto Monteir

denied that Cuban personnel took any part in 'combat operations under any circumstances', and insisted they were engaged only in logistical operations.[39]

Savimbi visited Cape Town for two days of talks with President Botha over 5-6 May 1986. He assured Botha that he stood resolutely by the demand for the withdrawal of Cuban and Soviet military personnel from Angola as a basis for a negotiated agreement. He also reported that the ANC had 'bases' in Angola which were in the Malanje and Cuanza Norte provinces. At the end of his visit he said that every time he met Botha be became more convinced of the President's 'willingness to talk to others in order to resolve SA's problems.'[40]

A month after Savimbi's talks with Botha, the SADF and Navy deployed new tactics against Angola by making land and sea attacks against its southernmost ports. In June they attacked and sank a Cuban ship, the Habana, in Namibe, and destroyed three fuel tanks on land. The Habana was busy unloading 6,000t of urgently-needed food. The attackers used frogmen and the Scorpion missile. Attacks on oil installations were also reported against Lobito, Luanda and Cabinda. Pretoria refused to comment on these exploits.

THE MOZAMBIQUE ARENA: THE WITHERING OF THE NKOMATI ACCORD

The Nkomati Accord, signed on 16 March 1984,[41] was intended to achieve three overt results: to improve Mozambique's internal security; to reduce tensions along the SA border by the removal of ANC cadres from Mozambique; and to strengthen economic cooperation between the two neighbours. SA also had a covert objective of its own: it hoped the Accord would be the precursor of similar security agreements with its other neighbours. By the end of 1985 none of these objectives had been met; to all intents the Accord was dead but it did not suit either side to renounce it formally. On the contrary, as late as August 1986, SA's Deputy Foreign Minister, Ron Miller, denied that the Accord had either failed or was 'just being maintained.'[42]

Pretoria's role in undermining the Accord remains a puzzle since, on the face of it, it represented the single most important achievement of its destabilization policies. In the light of the hard evidence now available it is questionable whether SA ever gave the Accord a chance of working. It is clear that the agreement to abandon the Mozambique National Resistance (MNR or Renamo)—which had been built up first by the Smith regime in Rhodesia and, when it collapsed, by Pretoria—was unpopular with a section of the SADF. Indeed, it now seems that army acquiescence was achieved only on condition that the MNR cadres on SA soil at the time the Accord was signed should be allowed to return with their arms and with enough military equipment to keep them going for a considerable period.[43] Even before the capture of the Gorongosa (or Vaz) Diaries in September 1985, Mozambican suspicions that SA was 'cheating' had turned to certainty. As early as February 1985, President Samora Machel—the ardent defender of the Accord—openly accused Pretoria of violating the agreement. The first anniversary of the Accord on 16 March 1985 went unmarked in Maputo and Pretoria. In that month the SA Defence Minister, Gen Magnus Malan, admitted in Parliament that 'individuals in the SADF' might be sympathetic to the MNR, and that steps had been taken to transfer them from the border with Mozambique. In June 1980, the Black Sash produced sworn affidavits by a number of detainees, who had previously fought with the MNR, saying the police had encouraged cooperation with the rebel movement up to the time of their arrest in April 1985—more than a year after the Accord was signed.[44] In August, Pretoria and Maputo exchanged allegations—with the former charging that ANC cadres were still being allowed to operate on Mozambican territory, and Maputo accusing Pretoria of supplying the MNR with additional arms to disrupt road, rail and oil pipeline links.[45]

Far from declining, the MNR operations showed signs of increasing in the period after the signing of the Accord. By mid-1985 the situation had become so serious that Machel was compelled to invite military support from Zimbabwe's army.[46] On 28 August a Zimbabwe assault force—helped by a former Rhodesian intelligence agent who had played a key role in training MNR in its early phase but now working for the Zimbabwe Central Intelligence Organization (CIO)[47]— captured the MNR's main base on the Gorongosa mountains. Among the documents discovered was a diary written by an MNR leader, Maj Vaz, meticulously recording the activities of the movement and of its meetings with SADF members and the Deputy Foreign Minister, Louis Nel. Although phonetically misspelt, the names of the army contacts were clearly identifiable, including Col Charles van Niekerk, a senior officer in SA military intelligence. At one point the diary records van Niekerk as saying that he brought a message from 'Gen Visloen' (Gen Constand Viljoen, then the army chief of the SADF), saying: 'As soon as we receive orders from my Government to go and fight in Mozambique against Renamo, all the generals, my colleagues, and I myself will resign from the armed forces.' Another entry records a visit to Gorongosa from the Deputy Foreign Minister, Louis Nel. After this visit, the first of two, Col van Niekerk is recorded as saying: 'The big problem for Louis Nel is how to handle his initiative within the SA Government itself, keeping out certain elements like Pick' (Pik Botha, the Foreign Minister). It was later admitted that Botha was not told of Nel's two visits. Gen Viljoen's reaction was to claim that the diary was a forgery based on an original diary and doctored, 'with the aid of specialists from Soviet bloc countries', in order to discredit the SADF. He said the trouble with the Accord was that it had assumed that it would lead to the collapse of MNR—a view the army did not share. They saw an agreement between MNR and Frelimo as the only hope. This was being worked for through their contacts and was done with the knowledge of the authorities in Maputo.[48] Viljoen said the SADF had complied with 'definite instructions' to stop supporting the rebels; but he admitted they had been told to carry on with 'normal support of the MNR' until the negotiations on the Accord had been completed. Viljoen's account was accepted by President Botha who described him as 'an honourable and brave soldier.' Louis Nel admitted he had made three secret visits to Gorongosa in order to try and promote an agreement between the MNR and Frelimo. Pik Botha said: 'On the face of it, the Nkomati Accord was violated, but it is important that President Machel did not allege that the SA Government had contravened it.'[49] He confirmed that radio communications had been set up with MNR; assistance had been given in the construction of an airstrip; SAAF supply drops had been made, mostly of 'humanitarian aid'; Renamo field officers had been transported—once by submarine in and out of Mozambique,' in an effort to re-establish the peace talks which had collapsed in October 1985.' Gen Viljoen disagreed with the Foreign Secretary's admission that there had been even 'a technical breach of the Accord.'[50]

Differences between Gen Viljoen and Pik Botha are made plain in one of the entries in the Vaz diary:

> General Viljoen agreed to send us humanitarian aid in air force C-130 planes. He recommended us not to accept the amnesty. The general recommended us not to be fooled by the schemes of Pik Botha, who is treacherous and even agreed with Chester Crocker's idea of Frelimo offering an amnesty to Renamo bandits. [In the diary, the words humanitarian aid appear between inverted commas.] General Viljoen went on

to say 'I agree with the joint strategy for putting Machel out. Because we want to remove the Russians from our region of Southern Africa, we have to employ a joint strategy to be able to defeat communism, in such a way as not to let the outside world, the US, perceive it because the world is convinced that Machel is changing, because he does not seem to them to be entirely communist.'

Gen Viljoen retired as army chief two months after the controversy over the captured diary; but he made it plain that his decision was entirely voluntary and had been planned for some time. But although Louis Nel promised that the allegations made by Maputo over the diary would be investigated Gen Viljoen said there would be no inquiry since the Mozambican Defence Minister, Col Sergio Vieira, had renounced the Joint Security Commission after the Gorongosa controversy. However, a key figure mentioned in the Vaz Diary, Gen 'Wessie' van der Westhuizen, the Chief of Military Intelligence, was taken out of the SADF and given a non-command post. A number of SADF members were also dismissed 'for being MNR sympathizers.'[51]

The Gorongosa affair happened on the eve of President Machel's first visit to the US (see Mozambique's Role, below). After a two-hour meeting with Reagan he was asked at a press conference where the Accord stood after the Gorongosa affair. He responded that he was 'a bit confused' by recent developments, and asked rhetorically: 'Should I break it? Should I renegotiate? Or should I let it lie?' Reagan praised Machel for signing the Accord, and said it was 'a pity that controversy again surrounds the agreement. SA has admitted that technically it infringed the Accord, but at the same time the SA Government indicated that its intentions were sound. . . .'

In October, the Mozambique News Agency, AIM, published reports saying that people in different parts of Maputo province reported sighting SA aircraft bringing in supplies for the MNR. Meanwhile, negotiations went on normally between Maputo and Pretoria over a new labour agreement. In 1984, 60,400 Mozambicans migrants were registered to work in SA, most of them in the mines and 3,100 on farms. SA agreed to legalize temporarily the position of 10,000-15,000 contract workers whose identity documents had expired.[52] (Pretoria suspended this agreement a year later, see Counter-sanctions, above). Also in October, Pretoria sanctioned the idea of the Electricity Supply Commission (Escom) recruiting, equipping, training and financing 'a mercenary force' to guard its interests at the Cahora Bassa dam which supplies power to the SA electricity grid.[53]

In November, Maputo reacted strongly against an SATV programme in which the Chief of the SAAF alleged that a big weapons' build-up was occurring in Mozambique and Angola, that represented a threat to SA. The programme claimed that the two countries had achieved 'military supremacy' over SA, and suggested that SA must defend itself against a 'Soviet threat', Maputo's Mozambique Information Ministry categorically denied that any such military build-up was occurring in Mozambique.[54]

Maputo accused the SADF on 11 December of destroying a bridge on the rail line linking SA to Maputo. The bridge is 50 miles from Maputo but only 5 miles from the SA border. The Government claimed that the attack was carried out by specialized saboteurs who were infiltrated from SA and were accompanied by MNR elements.[55]

In mid-December Machel accused SA of using the MNR to sabotage his country's economy and to frustrate the growth of SADCC. In a message to the MPLA's annual congress on 3 December, he declared that peace in the region was impossible until the apartheid regime was dismantled. He reiterated support for the ANC and Swapo in their struggle for 'freedom, equality, democracy and justice so that all people of all races and colours in SA can become citizens of a single motherland.'

By the beginning of 1986 all that remained of the intentions of the Nkomati Accord were occasional contacts to deal with specific problems such as Maputo' evidence about SA involvement in the MNR, and Pretoria's complaint that Mo zambique was again 'harbouring' ANC guerrillas. At a seminar in Norway in January 1986, Carlos Cardoso, director of the Mozambique Information Agency (AIM), spoke of SA's 'duplicity' in not observing either the Nkomati Accord or the Lusaka Agreement with Angola.

The second anniversary of the signing of the Accord in March 1986 passed unnoticed, as had the first. By April the MNR was again adopting a tougher stand towards any negotiations. Their spokesman, Jorge Coreia, announced that it no longer recognized Machel as a 'valid interlocutor', but added that it was continuing to maintain contact with the International Centre for Peace, a Catholic lay organi zation, which was engaged in trying to bring about a round-table meeting between MNR and Frelimo.[56] MNR's claim that it was negotiating with the US through Frank Wisner was described in a State Department statement on 9 April as 'a fabrication designed to give Renamo an appearance of legitimacy that it does not have.' Later, on 24 April, the US embassy in Maputo categorically denied a report that the CIA and the Pentagon favoured intervention in Mozambique similar to its support for Unita.

President Machel and President Botha met for the first time since the signing of the Accord when both attended the coronation of the new Swazi King in April 1986. After the meeting, SA's Foreign Minister, said that his Government still regarded the Accord as being of 'extreme importance', but that it needed support from both sides. He said that Machel had stated that he did not doubt the integrity of either of the Bothas or of Gen Malan, but merely stated that 'South Africa' was the source of attacks made on Mozambique. It was agreed at the meeting that a new commission would be set up to investigate specific complaints made by Machel. Immediately after the meeting in Swaziland, Machel attended a meeting of the five Portuguese-speaking African countries where he described Pretoria as 'the sole cause of violence in Southern Africa.'[57] At the end of April, Maputo blamed SA for being involved in a car bomb explosion in the centre of Maputo which injured 50 people. *Aim* claimed that the car, owned by a SA citizen, had driven across the border on the day before the explosion. At the same time the military commander of Manica province reported air space violations and reported his suspicions that planes were dropping supplies for the MNR.[58]

During the first visit of Tanzania's new President, Ali Hassan Mwinyi, Machel spoke of SA's refusal to implement 'the spirit and the letter' of the Accord. They issued a joint communiqué which condemned SA's behaviour as 'a flagrant viola- tion of the undertaking which (Mozambique) had freely given.' The Foreign Minister, Joaquim Chissano, told Mwinyi that SA traffic through the port of Maputo had declined from 5.5m t in 1970 to only 950,000t in 1985; this included coal shipments intended for Mozambique's own use.

During a debate in the SA Parliament on 7 May 1986, the leader of the PFP opposition, Colin Eglin, questioned whether SA was giving Mozambique the kind of assistance it needed to protect the Cahora Bassa power line and to stimulate its economy. Pik Botha said that although the question of helping to protect the line had been considered on a number of occasions, no decision was taken. At that time, he said, 525 electricity pylons were down inside Mozambique. He added that credit was available for private sector investment in Mozambique and consideraion was being given to upgrading Maputo's harbour and improving the railway ine. Botha said that Maputo was still regarded as one of the cheapest ports for SA exports.

Reporting on the 'costly stalemate' of the fighting in Mozambique, Patti Waldmeir, wrote that the economic benefits hoped for under the Accord had failed to materialize and that trade with SA was actually on the decline.[59] Defence spending, she wrote, was now absorbing 42% of total government expenditure. In May the first group of c. 48 Mozambican officers completed their training in Zimbabwe with the British Military Advisory Training Team (BMATT). A British military spokesman described the training programme as a success.[60]

During a visit to Zimbabwe in mid-June, Machel said Southern Africa was going through its 'darkest and most complex military situation' with SA extending its trans-border aggression. He confirmed that the main purpose of his visit was to discuss closer military, political and economic cooperation with Zimbabwe, adding that the existing military cooperation needed to be complemented by 'a more dynamic relationship in other areas.'[61] At about the same time the Mozambican railway authorities asked SA to hire them more diesel locomotives, as 70m t of goods bound for Maputo were stored at various places in SA while 14 railway wagons loaded with sugar were held up in Swaziland.

Reports in June that the MNR was setting up an Information Office in Durban caused new suspicions. But the director of the office, Pedro Buccelato, a Mozambican exile, claimed that his organization, the Mozambican National Relief Agency, was concerned only with helping Mozambican refugees in SA. The SA Foreign Ministry ordered an investigation into the Agency's activities, but nothing further was heard of the matter. Meanwhile, the continuing activities of MNR were causing a new kind of concern in Maputo. According to the well-informed journalist, Paul Fauvet:

> The spectre haunting northern Mozambique has a name—it is Rombezia, a separatist project formulated in the 1960s by the opponents of Frelimo, who wanted to carve out a separate state between the rivers Zambezi and Rovumu (the border with Tanzania). The separatists operate out of Malawi under the name of Rombezia African National Union (Unar); their adherents linked up with the MNR in 1982.[62] Malawi's role was referred to by Machel during his visit to Tokyo in early June. His Director of Information, Carlos Cardoso, explained that 'Mozambique has pointed out, especially in diplomatic circles and privately, that Malawi is being used by SA.'[63]

On 1 August SA activated an electrified fence to stop thousands of refugees crossing the border because of famine and to escape the fighting at home, as well as to seek work. The construction, in fact, involves three fences with two 2.5 metre high 'dead' fences on either side of the electrified fence to protect people from unwittingly being electrocuted.[64]

Machel expanded on his policies towards SA in his address to the Mozambican People's Assembly on 26 July:

> The Nkomati Accord placed the SA regime in a dilemma. It either had to implement the Accord and renounce the destabilization of our country through armed banditry, or violate the agreement thus demonstrating its disrespect for the norms of international law. Today, the international community is aware that Pretoria has violated the Nkomati Accord. It is aware that the SA regime does not respect its agreements. Above all, the international community is aware that the SA regime did not renounce its aim of dominating the States of the region. This fact contributes to the increasing isolation of apartheid at the international level. International cooperation is

today a fundamental component of mankind's progress. Consequently, the elimination of apartheid and the establishment of peace in Southern Africa demand the full participation of the international community. This is the context in which our diplomatic action is centred.

The Mozambican People's National Security Service (SNASP) claimed in August that support for MNR had been stepped up after the Commonwealth mini-summit in London and the growing demand for sanctions against SA. It reported that aircraft, identical to SA planes which used to supply the base at Gorongosa, were unloading men and war materiel on runways in Manica province. A government member of the Mozambique–SA Joint Commission alleged that these events were being carried out at a time of 'continued violations of the Nkomati Accord by SA.'[65] An SA Foreign Ministry statement on 26 August denied that the Accord was failing or that it was 'just being maintained.'[66] It denied that SA was supporting MNR, but said that Pretoria intended to raise the question of resumed ANC activity in Mozambique.

Relations between SA and Mozambique reached breaking-point in October when a landmine exploded close to the border wounding six men of the SADF. Pretoria claimed that the landmine had been planted by ANC cadres operating out of Mozambique. The tone of Pretoria's statement alarmed Maputo which issued a statement on 11 October claiming that the SADF was preparing 'to carry out direct aggression against Mozambique.' The SADF replied that reports of an imminent attack were 'no more than speculation and a sign of a severe attack of nerves on the part of the Mozambique Government which is obviously in deep waters because of its support for ANC terrorists.' On 15 October Gen Malan said in an interview:

> What I notice clearly is that Mozambique is hovering on the brink of collapse. What we have been warning as dangerous for many years is becoming true. Terror feeds on itself. It eventually turns on its host. President Machel is serving the path [sic] of terror and now experiences the results.

Four days later, on the night of 19 October, President Samora Machel died in an air crash while his plane was overflying SA territory.

THE AFRICAN ARENA

After years of complaints and warnings, the Frontline States adopted more resolute and militant policies in 1985-86 in response to the increasingly violent struggle inside SA and the Pretoria regime's military raids into Zimbabwe and Zambia as well as Angola, Mozambique and Botswana. Up to 1985 the positive aspects of the African response to developments in the Southern African region were mainly confined to:

• Support for Swapo, ANC and PAC given by individual countries and collectively through the OAU liberation committee.

• Coordination of policy through the organization of the Frontline States (FLS) established in 1982, comprising Angola, Botswana, Mozambique, Tanzania, Zambia and Zimbabwe. The FLS is recognized by the OAU as its instrument of policy in Southern Africa.

• Establishment of the Southern African Development Cooperation Conference (SADCC) on the initiative of Botswana and other members of the FLS in July 1979. Its members are Angola, Botswana, Lesotho, Malawi, Mozambique, Swaziland, Tanzania, Zambia and Zimbabwe. Its principal objective is to reduce the dependency of SA's neighbours on Pretoria by creating alternative communication routes, directing trade away from SA, and increasing cooperating among its members. Most Western countries pledged support for SADCC, but the Soviet bloc refused to join in its multilateral aid projects.

A major element of OAU and FLS policies was a demand for mandatory sanctions against SA and pressures on its major Western trading partners to 'stop their support of the apartheid regime.'[67] They explicitly opposed internationalizing the conflicts in Southern Africa, while accepting the right and the need of FLS States to seek and accept military aid from any of the major powers of their own choice. The campaign for mandatory sanctions and pressures on the West became a central feature of OAU–FLS policy in 1985; by 1986 the FLS committed its members to accepting the consequences for their own economies of a total cut-off of trade and communications with SA; but this policy was not fully accepted by all the members of the SADCC for varying reasons. Those reluctant to fall in line were Malawi, Lesotho, Swaziland, Mozambique and Botswana. It was left to Zimbabwe and Zambia to take the lead with strong support from Angola and Tanzania and, from further afield, Nigeria, none of whom stood to lose anything by cutting off trade and communication links with SA.

This new priority given to the campaign for mandatory sanctions was demonstrated by the militant lead taken by President Kaunda and Prime Minister Mugabe in rallying the great majority of Commonwealth members at the summit meeting in Nassau in October 1985 which led to the crisis at the London minisummit in August 1986 (see below). The pressures on Britain to isolate SA were also extended to the other members of the European Community whose Foreign Ministers had a collective meeting with their counterparts in Harare in February 1986.

By late 1986 the possibility of serious international involvement in the Southern African region came to be seen as a real threat by Julius Nyerere and other FLS leaders. Nyerere said there was a choice between economic pressure and a long struggle as the only ways to end apartheid; while Black Africans preferred the 'bloodless way', for that to succeed the US would have to lead the international community in applying tough sanctions against SA; but if the US failed to apply sanctions, then Blacks would turn to the alternative of armed struggle. He added:[68]

> One side of the struggle has arms. Our people would have to get arms to establish a balance, and if you are not prepared to help us economically, you are not likely to give us arms. So we will turn to the communist bloc for arms—and then you will condemn us.

Despite votes in favour of sanctions, Nyerere said he regarded the US as being on Pretoria's side in the struggle against apartheid.

> If the US were to establish diplomatic relations with Angola, which President dos Santos has said he wants, it could lead to peace in Southern Africa by opening the way to Namibian independence, an end to the civil war in Angola, removal of Cuban troops from that country and the isolation of SA.

Another significant development in FLS policy was the serious thought given to the need, not only for FLS cooperation, but also to mobilize African and even extra-continental military assistance to help secure the communication lines of the SADCC member-states. The first step in this direction was Zimbabwe's decision to commit a substantial part of its army in support of Mozambique in 1985.

ROLE OF THE FRONTLINE STATES (FLS)

At their summit meeting in Maputo in September 1985 the FLS leaders analyze 'the explosive situation prevailing in Southern Africa, and welcomed the 'growing international condemnation of the apartheid system, particularly in Western countries', who were urged to intensify pressures on the Pretoria regime.[69] The meeting paid homage to the outgoing chairman, Julius Nyerere, and stressed that 'all the victories and achievements of the FLS will forever be associated with the personality and relevant role' played by him. President Kaunda was elected as the new chairman.

In February 1986, the FLS Foreign Ministers met with their EEC counterpart in Harare and called for West European cooperation in meeting the challenge o SA. At its next summit meeting in Luanda in April 1986, serious concern wa expressed over the deterioration of the situation inside SA. The FLS leaders said they noted Pretoria's failure to take advantage of the various peace initiative presented to it to secure a peaceful solution to the country's racial conflict. They insisted that reforming apartheid would not solve the problem; it would simply perpetuate instability in SA, Namibia and the rest of the region. And they re affirmed their view that apartheid continued to be the main cause of the conflict in Southern Africa.[70] In May, President Machel and Prime Minister Mugabe met in Harare to discuss military cooperation to counter the MNR and new threats o trans-border attacks by the SADF. Machel's delegation included a large military delegation.[71]

In July 1986 Tanzania's Prime Minister, Joseph Warioba, opening the 46th session of the OAU Liberation Committee, called on Commonwealth members 'to continue pressurizing the apartheid regime by imposing economic sanctions ever if Britain continued to refuse to do so.[72] A two-day East and Central African summit in Nairobi from 14-15 July called upon the international community 'to enhance the war of liberation in SA and Namibia by adopting comprehensive mandatory economic sanctions.' The communiqué added that the people of Africa 'will never forget those who deliberately failed to join them at a crucial moment in the fight against apartheid.'[73]

The FLS leaders next met at two summits, in Harare in July and in Maputo in August. At both meetings they again expressed their concern at the growing deterioration of the situation inside SA 'as a result of the escalation of terrorism and murder daily perpetrated by the racist regime against opponents of apartheid.' The Luanda summit 'vehemently condemned the Pretoria regime's open threats of physically eliminating anti-apartheid militants living in neighbouring countries.' It called on the international community to give all possible support and assistance to all Frontline countries to enable them to 'withstand SA's retaliatory measures.' The meeting expressed the view that the Commonwealth mini-summit had given fresh impetus to the campaign against apartheid and in favour of sanctions; but it expressed 'displeasure and amazement over the uncooperative attitude of the British Prime Minister.' On the other hand it praised the American people for their incessant efforts in support of sanctions.[74]

After the Luanda meeting, Kaunda announced that the FLS proposed inviting President Reagan to visit Southern Africa,[75] and warned:

> The situation in Southern Africa has reached the boiling point, We are close to an explosion. History should not find us faulty that, realizing this we did not go to the one man who could have done something about it.

The SADCC summit in Luanda in August 1986 failed to reach agreement on a proposal that its members should join in imposing their own sanctions against

SA.[76] Its communiqué simply recorded agreement to 'reaffirm the SADCC position on sanctions.' It added that although its members were vulnerable to sanctions, this should not be used as an excuse for not applying them. The summit had before it a report by a special team of advisors on the consequences of applying sanctions on SADCC members, and the measures that were needed to lessen the impact on them.[77]

MILITARY INTERVENTION IN SOUTHERN AFRICA

The possibility of raising an African or even an international military force to strengthen the security of SA's border countries began to feature on the FLS agenda in 1986. In May, Ethiopia's President Haile Mengistu Mariam offered to train 10,000 Southern African freedom fighters.[78] His offer received little immediate encouragement from FLS leaders; but Samson Banda, chairman of the Zambia Association for the Liberation of Southern Africa, welcomed it provided it was intended only to strengthen the defence capabilities of the FLS. Zimbabwe's Foreign Minister, Witness Mangwende, declared in July that, if necessary the FLS have the right to invite friendly nations to repel SA aggression in the same way as the Angolans had enlisted Cuban support to bolster their military capacity.[80]

Robert Mugabe was the first Frontline leader to raise the possibility of mobilizing a multi-national army. His proposal was discussed at an Iranian Cabinet meeting on 18 June 1986 where it was decided that the Khomeini regime would be ready to join in such a plan if it came to fruition.[81] Earlier, in January Iran's President Khameneh, said during the visit of Frontline capitals that:

> With the same spirit that we fought against the Shah and brought it to its knees so, too, we are ready to put the same amount of effort into bringing down the Pretoria regime.[82]

On his return home Khameneh reported that FLS leaders had 'ardently welcomed our offer of cooperation and felt that Iran and the Islamic Revolution constitutes the ultimate strategic depth in the struggle against the racist SA regime.'

The idea of raising a Pan-African Force, with extra-continental support was informally discussed on a number of occasions, especially with India and Nigeria. This idea was also explored on the sidelines of the non-aligned nations summit meeting in Harare in September 1986.

Nigeria's Foreign Minister, Prof Bolaji Akinyemi (who is also the current chairman of the OAU Liberation Committee) declared that Africa 'must show that we are not cowards in the face of aggression by SA.'[83] He announced that Nigeria had pledged $4m as immediate assistance for the FLS in June 1986. Later he announced that Nigeria had decided to give $20m over a five year period to assist the FLS and the liberation movements.[84]

The Role of FLS Members

President dos Santos' attempt to maintain a balance in his foreign policy between seeking detente with the US and maintaining cordial relations with the Soviet bloc and Cuba became seriously unstuck when the Reagan Administration began providing military aid to Unita in early 1986 (see above). But although the MPLA angrily attacked Reagan's policy and announced in August that Luanda's doors were shut to further negotiations with Washington, it nevertheless avoided a complete break by continuing to hold talks with the American mediators.

Both the USSR and the Cubans proved the value of their alliance by steeply increasing their military aid during 1985—the former by supplying more sophisticated weapons and military aircraft, and the latter by increasing the number of their combat troops to 30,000. US and SA estimates of the value of Soviet military aid since 1985 agreed on a figure of c $2bn. But Soviet military aid did not come cheap; by early 1986 Angola owed the USSR $2.1bn, which was two-thirds of its total foreign debt.[85] Moscow responded postively to Angola's declaration that it was unable to continue servicing its foreign debt by agreeing to a two-year debt moratorium.

In October 1985, dos Santos warned Washington that if it decided to provide military aid to Unita, the conflict inside Angola would become more dangerous and would undermine American efforts to secure the withdrawal of Cuban troops as part of a regional peace settlement.[86] He said he was still prepared to negotiate a phased withdrawal of Cuban troops in terms of the offer he had made in 1984. Chester Crocker assured him in November 1985 that aid for Unita was still 'only an intention of some Congressmen and not a government decision.'[87] After this meeting, dos Santos said he would hold the US entirely responsible for escalating the war in Southern Africa if aid were in fact given to Unita.[88]

In late November Chester Crocker held talks in Lusaka with an Angolan delegation led by the Interior Minister, Manuel Alexandre Rodriques (Kito), in the presence of Zambia's President Kaunda. Crocker described the meeting as 'positive' and held out hope for further meetings in the near future.[89] But by then the new direction in Reagan's policy was already evident. On 17 October a State Department spokesman announced that the US firmly believed that peace within Angola could be restored only if there were political reconciliation between MPLA and Unita. He then characterized Unita as 'an authentic Angolan nationalist movement whose interests must be taken into account', and added that 'as a matter of principle', the US supports Unita's efforts to 'resist Soviet designs in Angola.' This position was strengthened by a further State Department briefing on 12 December.[90] Five days later, after SA's attacks on Zambia, Zimbabwe and Botswana, an Angola broadcast accused the US of colluding with Pretoria.

In January 1986, after a further meeting with Crocker, dos Santos warned that in the event of new aggressions from SA he would 'solicit more aid from the international community and, particularly, from our traditional friends in the Soviet Union, Cuba and other socialist countries.' He added he could not understand whether moves in Washington to aid 'anti-Marxist rebels' were simply 'a form of pressure on Angola or a declaration of war.'

In fact, according to a well-placed US source, the threat to aid Unita at that stage was a form of pressure.

After Savimbi's visit to Washington in January and the decision to supply him with military aid (see below), dos Santos declared that the US was no longer capable of mediating in the region's conflicts and had 'clearly shown it is an ally on the side of racist SA and apartheid.'[92] Angola's ambassador to the UN, Ekisio de Figueiredo, accused the US of 'outright interference in Angola's affairs.'[93] In a formal statement of 8 March, the MPLA Government accused the Reagan Administration of fulfilling 'its imperialist policy of *diktat*' and of having shown the 'dubious and two-faced character of its policy' by interfering in Angola's internal affairs.[94] In June, dos Santos blamed American policy for having 'stimulated the expansionist ideals of the terrorists from Pretoria.'[95]

However, it was not until June 1986 that Angola announced its decision to suspend its negotiating relations with Washington. Its Foreign Minister, Alfonso Van Dunmen,' announced that there would no longer be direct negotiations', and added: 'We will play our role, make our contribution directly through the UN Secretary General.' He also said, that the phasing out of Cuban troops was no longer a part of any negotiations.[96]

As dos Santos predicted, Angola's ties with the USSR were visibly strengthened after the US decision to aid Unita. At the same time as Savimbi was visiting Washington a tripartite meeting of Angolans, Cubans and Soviets was held in Luanda as 'a new demonstration of solidarity.' After the meeting an Angolan spokesman described Savimbi's visit as 'a declaration of war, not only against Angola but also against the whole African continent.'[97]

The Soviet presence and role in Angola had, in fact, increased significantly even before the new tilt in U.S. policy towards Unita. The number of Soviet and East German military advisers was generally thought to have increased to at least 1,200 by the time Fapla launched its failed attempt to dislodge Unita from Jamba in August–September 1985. Evelyn Le Chêne, the director of the West European Defence Association made the following estimate of the Soviet–Cuban military presence which, though coming from a source prejudiced to the USSR, nevertheless seems to accord with estimates made by more objective commentators:[98]

At any given time up to eight warships patrol from Liberia to Angola. Soviet submarines may be seen on the surface in the early hours. Tu-95 reconnaissance aircraft operating from Angolan bases assure surveillance of an important western route. [Similar surveillance is carried out from Cuba, Ethiopia, Yemen, Syria and the former US base of Cam Rahn Bay in Vietnam.] Soviet military personnel in Angola are principally in coastal towns where the arms they have supplied are protected by ground-to-air missiles.

At one stage it appeared that military hardware was brought into Angola from a hotch-potch of sources, mostly Warsaw Pact countries and some Arab States. Now a pattern is discernible in which individual nations play a particular role and provide, almost exclusively, a certain product. The Hungarians provide stick grenades and the North Koreans pangas, a weapon favoured for close combat in Black African States and without parts to go wrong for the mechanically unsophisticated user.

Yugoslavia contributes a 30mm grenade launcher which has a special sighting mechanism requiring Soviet or East German technical knowledge to set . . . making the weapon useless unless resighted back at base and therefore perhaps ruling out its use in what is, essentially, a bush war. Yugoslavia also supplies anti-personnel mines, trip-wire grenades, hollow-charged rockets and the only triple-barrelled anti-aircraft gun in the area. The degree of Yugoslav involvement and coordination with the Soviet Union and other Warsaw Pact nations is a new phenomenon not only in Angola but anywhere in the world.

The Russians themselves supply advanced radar and communications operated by Soviet personnel. Such sophisticated equipment apart, the accent is on man-oeuvrability. Hence the use of the six-wheeled Ural trucks from which 122mm rockets are fired with a range of up to 13 miles.

The North Koreans are engaged in the training of special forces for cross-border hit-and-run operations. They specialize in booby traps and utter ruthlessness; their recruits are known to prefer to blow themselves up rather than be captured. Soviet instructors and Koreans jointly form assassination squads using weapons with night-sights, silencers and subsonic ammunition.

The East Germans play a key role. Technically and mechanically efficient and disciplined, they train pilots, radar operators and artillery crews. . . .

Of the Cubans, some are advisers, engineers and pilots. Others provide a stiffening to the Angolan army fighting Savimbi and some help the East Germans to train recruits.

Angola's relations with Lisbon remain troubled despite the fact that the Portuguese have again become one of its major trading partners. The cause of friction is that Unita is allowed to maintain an office in Lisbon. The Portuguese argue that in their democratic society there are no valid or legal grounds for preventing this—an explanation that does not go down well in Luanda. The question of Unita's presence was raised again when Angola's Foreign Trade Minister, Ismael Martins, visited Lisbon in March 1986. Although the Portuguese–Angolan Joint Commission is still maintained it has not functioned very well.[99]

By late 1986 the military conflict inside Angola seemed to have reached stalemate. The long predicted 'final onslaught' against Unita predicted for mid-1986 failed to develop. In preliminary skirmishes, which were supposed to have marked the beginning of the new offensive, Unita successfully deployed Stinger and other aircraft missiles that had been supplied under the US military aid programme. It claimed to have shot down 31 fighters, bombers and helicopters. But if the Angolan army failed to make further inroads into Unita-held territory, Savimbi's men showed a similar lack of capacity to repeat the wide-sweeping attacks of 1984. Meanwhile, an increasingly impoverished Angola is forced to devote between 60%-80% of its national income to defence and security—a heavy burden at a time when the collapse of world oil prices left Angola facing a loss of export earnings estimated at $1bn in 1986.

MOZAMBIQUE

While President Samora Machel's Frontline colleagues understood the reasons that had prompted him to sign the Nkomati Accord with Pretoria in April 1984, they had warned him not to expect too much to come of it because they suspected the good intentions of the SA regime.[100] Although Machel had soon come to the same conclusion himself and had frequently criticized Pretoria's behaviour (see above), he found it expedient not to renounce the Accord unilaterally. His pride probably had something to do with this decision, but a more important reason was that although the Accord did not deliver what it had promised he feared that if he renounced it, the SA military would resume its open support for the MNR. He also feared that SA's counter-sanctions would further destabilize his country's already precarious economy.

In an address to the People's Assembly on 26 July 1986, Machel recapitulated the efforts made by SA to destabilize Mozambique in the past and declared that these were still continuing. He concluded by saying that:

> Pretoria is increasingly using blackmail and economic blockade against us. Side by side with its policy of destabilization, which has been affecting our economic development and placing difficulties in our people's daily lives, the apartheid regime has launched a campaign of ideological subversion, promoting its image as a country of abundance in contrast to a situation of shortages in Mozambique.

Pretoria was reluctant on its side to tear up the Accord because President Botha had presented it as a major breakthrough in his relations with his neighbours; nevertheless, Pretoria also came to suspect that Machel was not sticking to the agreement and that ANC cadres were again operating in Mozambique. The flashpoint of these mutual suspicions came at the beginning of October 1986 when a landmine exploded on the Mozambique–SA border wounding six SADF soldiers. The SADF pinned responsibility on the ANC and claimed to have information that the ANC was 'rebuilding its military structure in Mozambique.' It claimed that the

SA communist leader, Joe Slovo—who is also the third in command of the ANC's military wing, *Umkonto we Sizwe*—had been seen on a number of occasions in Maputo. It claimed that Slovo was the link between the ANC and the Soviet bloc and that he was known to have been in East Germany in August 1986 where a second ANC training camp had been opened at Talton, near East Berlin, to complement one that had existed for some time in East Germany which was manned by Soviet instructors.[101] Pretoria followed up these allegations by banning the future recruitment of Mozambican workers for the mines refusing to renew the permits of migrant farm workers. Nevertheless, SA's Deputy Foreign Minister, Ron Miller, insisted that this act of reprisal did not mean the end of the Nkomati Accord which, he said, provided for 'the resolution of this type of problem through diplomatic channels.'[102] He added that while the process of consultation would continue, SA had a duty to defend itself.

This sharp deterioration in SA–Mozambique relations came at a time when the MNR had succeeded in capturing a strategic bridge that links the north and the south of Mozambique and in occupying several major towns in the Mlange and Tete areas bordering on Malawi and Zambia.

In the post-Nkomati phase Machel embarked on a policy of strengthening his relations with the West, but without breaking with the Soviet bloc. In September 1985 he visited Washington for talks with Reagan, who said that although Machel was a Marxist 'there has been an indication that he has gone over to the other camp. We think it is worth a try to show him that he might be welcome in the Western world.'[103] Machel congratulated Reagan for signing his Executive Order providing for limited sanctions against SA.

Machel also visited London and Bonn in September 1985. In London he confirmed arrangements to have some of his soldiers trained by the British military advisory team in Zimbabwe. Unlike all the other FLS leaders, he gave encouragement to the British Foreign Secretary's abortive mission to Pretoria in July 1986 (See below).

At the same time as pursuing détente with the West, Machel continued to nurture his fragile relations with Moscow. Vladimir Tsvetkov, the secretary of the Soviet Committee for Solidarity with Asian and African Countries, said in January 1986 that relations with the Mozambican Association for Friendship and Solidarity with Peoples (AMASP) were increasing.[104]

(For further details see chapter on Mozambique.)

Samora Machel's death in an aircraft on a hillside not far from Nkomati on 19 October 1986 closed a historic chapter.

ZIMBABWE

Notwithstanding the close economic and communications' links between Zimbabwe and SA, Prime Minister Robert Mugabe put himself in the forefront of the campaign to isolate the Pretoria regime. In a speech in August 1986 Mugabe warned Zimbabweans to prepare for 'economic war with SA'.[105] He announced his intention to sever airlinks and to ban SA Airways from overflying his territory by the end of the year. He also called for alternative road and rail links for its neighbours who depend on transit through SA. He promised to defend this position 'to the last man': Whatever counter-sanctions proposed by Pretoria, 'we shall proceed on our own way. Zimbabwe will not die.'

Mugabe's military policies brought him into open conflict not only with SA but also seriously affected his country's relations with Britain and the US.

The SADF's attack on ANC targets in Harare in August 1985 was the culmination of several years of increasing tensions. Zimbabwe has long suspected Pretoria's role behind Super-Zapu, the Ndebele dissident movement.[106] On 2 September 1985 the Harare daily, the *Herald,* placed responsibility on Pretoria for aiding and abetting dissidents who had murdered 21 people in Mwenezi. A few weeks later, on 22 September, Mugabe also accused SA of still arming Super-Zapu as well as of supporting Unita and MNR. Fears that SA was planning to infiltrate dissidents into Zimbabwe to obstruct the unity talks between Zanu and Zapu were voiced by the Security Minister, Emmerson Munangagwe, in October.[107] A landmine explosion on the SA side of the border which claimed the lives of three White South Africans brought fears that the SADF was planning a revenge attack on Zimbabwe. Pretoria claimed the mines had been planted by ANC cadres operating out of Zimbabwe. But although there was a strong demand for reprisals by Whites on the border, the incident was dealt with through diplomatic channels. SA's Foreign Minister declared that while 'it was no secret that the two Governments did not like each other's policy directions, it was still possible 'to live with each other realistically for the sake of trade and good neighbourliness.'[108] Zimbabwe's Security Minister reiterated his Government's policy of not allowing his country to be used 'as a springboard (to launch attacks) against any neighbouring state.'[109] Although this assurance was welcomed by President Botha, his Defence Minister insisted that 'ANC terrorists are misusing Zimbabwean territory to force SA to retaliate, and it looks as if certain Zimbabwean Cabinet members would welcome such action . . . so that they can again blame us for their inability to cope with a deteriorating situation in all spheres of that country.'[110] He followed up this statement by warning Zimbabwe that unless it controlled ANC activities, 'it could lead to a situation similar to that of Swapo in Angola'.[111] Zimbabwe's Foreign Minister replied that such a policy made it necessary for the country to arm itself adequately.[112]

Mugabe proposed in June 1986 that the time had come for a Pan-African defence force to fight 'the mammoth army of SA.'[113] He went even further in a speech at a mass rally in Harare on 15 June by declaring that he intended to lobby strenuously for the formation of a Pan-African force 'to topple the SA Government and end apartheid.'[114] He claimed that a well-armed and equipped African force could not be beaten by SA. The SADF's reaction was to say that 'Mugabe's obsession with the creation of a new regime in SA causes him to lose perspective completely with the real situation in Southern Africa. As the leader of a once prosperous country he should be more worried about the situation in Zimbabwe and the other Frontline States instead of conspiring against SA.'[115] The statement went on to say that 'attacks on ANC hideouts in neighbouring states are deeds of aggression against terrorist organizations and are not aimed at the neighbouring state involved.'

When Mugabe was questioned in Parliament about his proposal for a Pan-African force he said it was still only an idea which 'we are yet to sell to Africa.'[116] He revealed that at a recent meeting of the OAU Defence Commission in Harare decisions were taken on two fundamental issues—sending peace-keeping forces to countries where a conflict has arisen between two of them; and an African force to go to the defence of any country that suffers from an act of aggression. It was on the basis of that decision that he had advanced his proposal. But, he added, Zimbabwe was only one member of the FLS whose chairman, Kenneth Kaunda, 'may have his own ideas.' He went on to warn against the danger of being over-ambitious—like the frog which tried to be as big as the cow and blew itself up to the point where it burst.

Mugabe's trenchant championship of sanctions at Commonwealth meetings strained his personal relations with Margaret Thatcher, whom he accused of being 'a racist'. He denounced the British Foreign Minister's mission to Pretoria (see below). Relations with the US deteriorated to the point where it suspended aid to Zimbabwe (see US Role, below).

Zimbabwe extended its regional military role sending a substantial part of its army to the assistance of Mozambique in mid-1985. Although it had earlier sent in a small force its aim was limited to protecting the oil pipeline from Beira and its rail link to Maputo. Its decision to send several thousand men—some reports put the number as high as 8,000–10,000—to help fight the MNR was a decision of a different magnitude. It had domestic repercussions when it was reported that 151 Zimbabwe soldiers had been killed in the attack on Gorongosa (see above).[117]

ZAMBIA

President Kenneth Kaunda has been warning about the dangers of a racial conflagration in SA for almost two decades; during the intervening period he put himself in the firing line of militants on a number of occasions by playing the role of mediator. He arranged a meeting with Prime Minister Vorster in an attempt to promote a settlement in Rhodesia, and later had a meeting with President Botha; he hosted a conference between Swapo and the SA Government to try and promote a settlement in Namibia; he helped facilitate a number of meetings between Angolans and Americans. One such meeting produced the Lusaka Agreement of 1984 between Angola and SA. Finally, in 1985, Kaunda abandoned the role of peacemaker to become one of the leading figures with Robert Mugabe in the international campaign for sanctions against SA—a campaign that gained authority because of his role as the new chairman of the FLS, and as a respected senior statesman of the OAU, the Commonwealth and the Non-Aligned Conference. In 1986 he began to speak in increasingly angrier tones and more pessimistically about the situation in SA, blaming the West for failing to use its power to help avert the looming tragedy in SA with its inevitable overspill effects on the rest of the region.

Kaunda led the attack on British policy at the Commonwealth summit in Nassau and the subsequent mini-summit in London (see below). Although he committed Zambia to accepting the serious consequences of an economic war with SA, he insisted that they could not realistically act on their own without support from SA's major trading partners without whom, he said, 'there are no sanctions at all. If Zimbabwe and Zambia tomorrow applied sanctions on their own . . . it would be suicide on our part, it would be meaningless.'[118] Although the Bank of Zambia introduced curbs on trade with SA it was essentially a measure dictated by its own foreign exchange difficulties.

Kaunda also became a sharper critic of US policy. After the SADF raid on Zambia, he said that Reagan's constructive engagement policy was a contributory factor since it gave encouragement to Pretoria's aggressive policy.[119] He was especially critical of US military aid for Unita—a decision which, he said, cast doubts on US sincerity in seeking a genuine solution for the problems of the region; but he added that he had appreciated past US efforts to help find a settlement of the problems in Namibia and SA.[120] He also criticized the US bombing of Tripoli as setting an example to be emulated by SA and others.[121]

Zambia like Zimbabwe has been highly suspicious of SA's military intentions. In August 1985, Zambia's army commander, Lt-Gen Christopher Tembo, accused SA soldiers of being involved with Unita in the abduction of 18 Zambians on the border with Angola. In August 1986 Kaunda accused SA of sending spies into Zambia and other neighbouring countries. He said that four White and one Black

South Africans, who had been detained, had confessed to being 'spies and sabo-teurs.'[122] He later warned that SA was engaged in helping to train rebels against his regime, a development he regarded as a serious potential threat to the country's stability since it had taken years to eliminate a previous group of rebels trained by SA.

BOTSWANA

Botswana continued to be the only multi-party paraliamentary democracy in Southern Africa with a Government that believed in maintaining a pluralist politi-cal system. Despite sharp internal political rivalries and living under 'the constant threat of attack by SA' (as President Quett Masire described the country's situa-tion), Botswana remained an oasis of tranquillity in the turbulent region.

The SADF invaded Botswana twice in 1985-86 to attack supposedly 'terrorist targets.'[123] Nevertheless, both Governments continued to talk to each other in an effort to defuse the areas of conflict. After each attack the Security Council unanimously voted to condemn SA. The US, Britain and others gave their un-qualified support to Masire's Government. Britain agreed in February 1986 to send c. 90 Special Air Service personnel to help train the Botswana army. The SA Defence Minister, Gen Malan, responded to this news by reiterating Pretoria's promise that it had no intention of attacking Botswana but of only hitting 'terrorist bases'; therefore, he added, the country had no need to seek to strengthen its army.[124] Instead of turning to Britain, he suggested Botswana should look to SA to build on their mutual interests in the region. Masire, however, told the diplomatic corps in Garborone that his country continued to be 'haunted by threats of aggression from SA.'[125]

Despite the chronic state of hostility between the two countries, they continued to maintain regular diplomatic contacts in an effort to defuse the causes of tension. Masire said his hope was that SA would conduct its international relations on the basis of peaceful coexistence and the inadmissibility of force as a means of solving problems among sovereign states.[126] He continued to reject SA overtures for a security agreement on the lines of the Nkomati Accord because, he said, 'the White Government does not respect dialogue, but prefers to solve its internal problems by murderous raids' on its neighbours.[127]

Botswana continued to maintain its policy of not allowing its territory to be used by guerrillas to infiltrate into SA. However, the Government admitted that it did not have the means to stop all infiltration attempts, but promised to act firmly against those who refused to respect its policy of neutrality on this issue.

Pretoria remained unconvinced by Botswana's assurances and repeatedly warned that unless more effective action was taken to curb the ANC and Swapo, it would have no alternative but to use its army to deal with 'terrorist nests'. SA's Foreign Minister disclosed that officials from the two countries had met on 11 occasions since April 1983 to discuss the presence of ANC and Swapo cadres in Botswana. In his view Botswana lacked 'the political will' to deal with the ANC.[128] SA alleged that landmines planted on its side of the border was the work of ANC agents operating from Botswana. In January 1986 it claimed that Botswana was also allowing Swapo guerrillas to locate themselves on the border with Namibia.

On the issue of sanctions, Masire said his country did not have the capacity to impose economic measures against SA, but it could not stop those able to do so from pursuing such a course.[129]

LESOTHO
Pretoria's pressures on Lesotho met with success on 20 January 1986 when the Government of Chief Leabua Jonathan was overthrown by a military coup led by Maj-Gen J Lekhanya, who immediately established a new relationship with SA.[130] While the SADF played no active role in this coup, its policies were directly responsible for bringing down Jonathan's Government since it came after two weeks of an economic blockade that had deprived Lesotho of essential imports, including oil. These pressures deepened the internal conflicts in Lesotho over Jonathan's stand against SA and other purely domestic issues. SA had imposed sanctions on its most vulnerable neighbour after months of demands on Jonathan to expel all ANC elements from Lesotho. Jonathan continued to deny that any active ANC supporters still remained in the country after his decision in 1984 to order all known ANC sympathizers to leave. He counter-charged that SA was itself responsible for harbouring 'terrorists' by allowing the armed opposition group, the Lesotho Liberation Army (LLA), led by Ntsu Mokhehle, to operate from SA territory.[131] There can be no doubt about the truth of these allegations. Before the coup, Jonathan had appealed to the US and Britain for aid to beat the blockade and had announced his readiness to pay the price demanded by SA and to sign an agreement establishing a joint security commission.[132]

Gen Lekhanya announced that his regime would establish a 'more balanced relationship' with Pretoria, and that there would be a 'more candid and constructive relationship' with other members of SADCC.[133] He claimed that 'cobwebs of mistrust' had been cleared away from Lesotho's relations with Botswana, Swaziland and Zambia.

Although the new regime ordered 100 suspected ANC sympathizers out of the country, Pretoria still insisted that this was insufficient; but it denied that it had demanded the expulsion of Soviet bloc embassies from Maseru.[134]

One immediate benefit that accrued to Lesotho from its new relationship with SA was the prospect of the long-stalled $2bn Highlands Water Project at last getting under way, with its promise of annual revenues to the Kingdom of c. $25m.[135] However, because of SA's straitened economic circumstances there were doubts about whether the project would start in the near future.

Lesotho declared itself against sanctions. Its Trade Minister declared: 'Southern Africa is like a zebra. If you damage the white parts, the black parts will also die.' He added that in the event of sanctions being applied against SA, Lesotho would look to the international community for aid to enable it to overcome the problems it would have to face. Gen Lekhanya warned Basotho migrant workers in the SA mines not to get involved in the Republic's politics through their membership of the National Union of Mineworkers, which was active in opposing the apartheid system.[136]

SWAZILAND
Of the three 'captive states' in and around SA's borders, the Kingdom of Swaziland has continued to be the most compliant. It faithfully lived up to the terms of its secret agreement with SA signed on 17 February 1981. The text of this agreement finally became known in 1986. Its terms are:

Article 1
The Contracting Parties undertake to combat terrorism, insurgency and subversion individually and collectively and shall call upon each other wherever possible for such assistance and steps as may be deemed necessary or expedient to eliminate this evil.

Article 2

In the conduct of their mutual relations the Contrasting Parties shall furthermore respect each other's independence, sovereignty and territorial integrity and shall refrain from the unlawful threat or use of force and from any other act which is inconsistent with the purposes and principles of good neighbourliness.

Article 3

The Contracting Parties shall live in peace and further develop and maintain friendly relations with each other and shall therefore not allow any activities within their respective territories directed towards the commission of any act which involves a threat or use of force against each other's territorial integrity.

Article 4

The Contracting Parties shall not allow within their respective territories the installation or maintenance of foreign military units except in accordance with their right of self-defence in the event of armed attacks as provided for in the Charter of the United Nations and only after due notification to the other.

A shake-up in the Swazi Government after the coronation of the new King in 1985, led to a major Cabinet reshuffle in which the four Ministers most prominently identified with a pro-SA attitude lost office.[137] It was not clear whether these changes would substantially affect Swazi policies. Notwithstanding its agreement with Pretoria—which went much further than the Nkomati Accord—Swazi policy has been to cooperate closely with the FLS and SADCC. The government has maintained friendly relations with Mozambique. After SA's attack on Botswana in June 1985, the Government sent Masire a message saying that 'incidents of this nature are not conducive to peaceful coexistence and good neighbourliness within the region', and added that 'respect for sovereignty and the territorial integrity of States are cardinal principles which contribute to peace and security in the world.'[138]

Despite Swazi cooperation with Pretoria, the country was not immune to intervention by the SADF. In December 1985 army and police units crossed the border into five villages. The SADF insisted that its operations were restricted to the border area itself, but Swazi villagers said that SA patrols had entered their villages and warned them not to shelter ANC guerrillas.[139] Although ANC cadres could expect no shrift from the Swazi security forces, some nevertheless seemed to have risked crossing Swazi territory.

Swaziland reacted vigorously to moves by SA businessmen when it became known that they were preparing contingency plans to circumvent the threat of sanctions by using Swazi firms and labels for their exports. The Industry Minister warned in September 1985 that the Government would not tolerate operations in what he termed 'grey areas', and added that it would not allow national interest to be jeopardized 'for the sake of a few individuals who want to make easy money.'[140]

MALAWI

Apart from Swaziland, Malawi is the only African country that maintains open diplomatic relations with Pretoria; but it also maintains close relations with SADCC. Ever since 1984, Mozambique repeatedly accused Malawi of allowing MNR rebels to operate from its soil (see above). President Machel went personally to Lilongwe to seek Dr Banda's cooperation in ending this practice. Banda always vigorously denied any knowledge of an MNR presence on his territory. Finally, in September 1986, the FLS leaders lost patience with Banda and sent a delegation consisting of the Presidents of Zambia and Mozambique and the Prime Minister of

Zimbabwe to warn Banda that unless he stopped MNR operations in Malawi he would face the possibility of the borders between his country and his neighbours being closed, thus preventing transit for his country's exports and imports. Banda again denied the allegations, but promised to investigate the charges. Soon afterwards an estimated 4,000 MNR activists and other Mozambican refugees were forced back into Mozambique. This operation backfired as the MNR immediately opened up a new offensive which succeeded in taking a number of towns in border areas and in capturing the strategic bridge across the Zambezi linking the north and south of Mozambique.

Malawi and Swaziland were the only two Commonwealth countries to speak out against sanctions at the summit in Nassau.

Malawi's rigid policy of refusing to have diplomatic relations with Soviet bloc countries was eased in September 1985 when a Romanian delegation visited the country to discuss trade.

TANZANIA
Julius Nyerere ceased to be chairman of the FLS in late 1985, but Ali Mwinyi, proved to be as militant in opposition to the SA regime as his predecessor. Both in Commonwealth and OAU meetings he played a leading role in demanding the complete isolation of SA from the rest of the international community. He insisted that even if Britain refused to join in sanctions, the rest of the Commonwealth should go ahead and impose sanctions on their own.[141] He urged African countries not to allow themselves to be used to help SA conduct clandestine operations to circumvent sanctions. 'We must satisfy ourselves that we have totally isolated the SA regime through a rigorous monitoring machinery. We must satisfy ourselves, especially here in Africa, that we have totally ceased to have anything to do with Pretoria.' Comprehensive sanctions, he added, were the only possible way of avoiding 'a bloodbath' in SA.[142]

ROLE OF OTHER AFRICAN COUNTRIES
Zaire
President Mobutu and Dr Banda were regarded by the other OAU members as the twin *enfants terrible* in their dealings with SA and in ingoring the Organization's decisions. Zaire openly maintains close trading relations with SA even though, unlike Pretoria's immediate neighbours, it does have alternative trade and communications channels. The FLS was especially concerned about Zaire's reputed role as a conduit for military supplies to Unita. Mobutu's Government denied on several occasions that it was assisting the US in allowing supplies to reach Unita, and emphatically repudiated suggestions that Stinger missiles were sent through Zairean airports.[143] Kaunda openly accused Zaire of allowing itself to be used as a conduit for military supplies to Unita—a charge heatedly repudiated by Kinshasa. It insisted that:

> Since the normalization of its relations with Angola, particularly since the signing of certain agreements—including that of defence and security which calls for the interdiction of any subversive action by either country—it remains the intention of Zaire, as in the past, to respect the letter and spirit of that accord scrupulously.[144]

In September 1986, the FLS proposed to follow up its *démarche* on Malawi by sending a high-level delegation to Zaire.

At the summit meeting of seven East and Central African countries held in Nairobi in July 1986, President Mobutu signed the communiqué calling on the international community to enhance the 'war of liberation' by adopting comprehensive sanctions against SA.[145]

Nigeria

Of all the non-Frontline States, Nigeria proved itself to be the most active supporter of the group's policies. It pledged $50m towards assisting the economies of Frontline States and as direct aid for the liberation movements (see above). Its Vice-President, Ebitu Ukiwe, proposed at the OAU summit in July 1986 that a proportion of all members' subscriptions to the Organization should be allocated to the liberation movements. Nigeria's Foreign Secretary, in his role as current chairman of the OAU Liberation Committee, pursued a vigorous policy in support of the armed struggle.

A former Nigerian Head of State, Gen Obasanjo, was the co-chairman of the Commonwealth Eminent Persons' Group, and played an influential role in framing its final report. His role helped to defuse moves in some quarters for Nigeria to leave the Commonwealth in protest against British policies.

ROLE OF THE OAU

Despite its preoccupation in 1985-86 with Africa's economic crisis, the OAU made the conflicts in Southern Africa a top priority. Its support for mandatory sanctions was a key feature in the otherwise routine resolutions adopted by the 1986 summit; more attention than normal was paid to the work of its Liberation Committee. Senegal's President Diouf, became the first OAU chairman to visit the FLS capitals, and was the first Francophone African leader to take a prominent lead in the conflicts of Southern Africa.[146]

ROLE OF SOUTH AFRICA

SA was unable to use its role as the region's military and economic power either to stop guerrilla attacks or to arrest the growth of violence inside the Republic itself. Nevertheless it was able to use its military power effectively to force Mozambique and Swaziland to sign security agreements, and its economic power to overthrow Jonathan's Government in Lesotho. It has also used these levers of power to compel Botswana and Zimbabwe to refuse to allow their territories to be used as springboards for attacks against SA. Finally, its military power has been partially effective in blunting the armed struggle by Swapo, and in keeping up pressures against Angola through its support for Unita and by making regular cross-border attacks.

But although the neighbouring States all undertook to prevent insurgency operations, the ANC succeeded in one way or another to get its cadres across the border. In December 1985 Pretoria accused all its neighbours, including Zambia and Angola, of harbouring ANC 'terrorist elements'[147] Pretoria's official stand was that while it had no wish to attack the governments on its borders, it had the right to cross into neighbouring territories for the sake of self-defence in hitting against ANC bases.

Pretoria's offer to its neighbours was that they should cooperate in establishing a Joint Southern African Security Organization which would involve the removal of foreign troops and end cross-border violence. The Defence Minister, Gen Malan, told Parliament on 4 February 1986 that if SA's neighbours continued to ignore this offer 'our security forces will have no alternative but to engage, in our own interests, in cross-border actions against the enemies of SA.'

Since the border States refused to accept such an offer, the SADF continued its policy of making cross-border attacks into Angola and Botswana, and extended these to Zimbabwe and Zambia in 1986. Pretoria also gave clandestine support to rebel movements in Angola, Lesotho Zimbabwe and—despite the Nkomati Accord—in Mozambique. Zambia suspected that it was also encouraging putative rebel activities in its territory.

The trans-border attacks and policies of destabilization had three major consequences: the build-up of arms in most of the neighbouring countries, which involved also increasing the Soviet bloc's military aid to some of them; a sharpening campaign by the FLS to pressurize the West into supporting comprehensive mandatory sanctions in an effort to isolate SA from the world community; and increasingly alienating the West from the Pretoria regime. Thus, whatever ground successes were notched up by the SADF, the overall outcome of Pretoria's use of its military and economic power was to jeopardize the country's international position.

SA AND THE WEST

The policies of apartheid and the methods used to defend it were the direct cause of internationalizing not only the conflict inside SA, but also in the region. Apartheid became not only a *cause celebre* in the world community, but also a *cassus belli* for the FLS and the rest of Africa.

Public opinion in Western countries outran the policies of their Governments. In the case of the US it became so strong as to compel the Administration to embark on sanctions against SA despite its strong antagonism to such a policy. British public opinion was able to exert strong, but not yet decisive, pressures on the Thatcher Government. In Norway and Denmark it compelled changes in government policies. In Holland and Sweden, government policy was *ad idem* with public opinion. In France, so long as the socialists were in power, the Mitterrand Government swung decisively against Pretoria, but became divided after the election of a conservative Government. In Japan, where public opinion on SA was insignificant, the Government felt compelled because of its relations with Africa, to move tentatively towards imposing sanctions. Only the West German Government stood resolutely opposed to sanctions, but yielded to pressures from the European Community to agree to a limited programme of sanctions; but it successfully resisted demands to include a ban on coal, which was asked for even by Britain. The Labour Governments in Australia and New Zealand and the Conservative Government in Canada responded strongly to the Commonwealth demand for wide-reaching sanctions.

In sum, the policies of the West began to move decisively in the direction of exerting international pressures on the Botha regime but stopped well short of supporting a policy to isolate SA. The cold chill of Western hostility to the Pretoria regime and the deleterious effects of even limited sanctions increased the sense of loneliness and abandonment felt by most White South Africans.

However, so far from weakening its resolve to pursue its policies in its own way, the Botha regime was able to rally Whites behind its determined stand to resist external pressures.

So long as there was some gain to be had from a policy of allowing foreign powers to involve themselves in SA's internal affairs and to cooperate with foreign missions—such as the Commonwealth Eminent Persons Group and the Special Committee appointed by President Reagan—Botha was ready to tolerate, 'foreign meddling'. But once the West began to move along the road of sanctions, his Government's attitude changed. In a major policy statement in May 1986 Botha declared that 'continued visits from abroad by official and non-official groups' amounted to interference in his country's domestic affairs.[148] He added that while not wishing to 'break off our foreign relations', he was not prepared to tolerate 'unsolicited interference.' Soon afterwards he announced his Government's intention to adopt 'a siege economy' to withstand international pressures.

SA'S ATTITUDES TOWARDS THE COMMUNIST WORLD.

Pretoria has never deviated from its stand that SA is the target of 'a total onslaught' by the USSR—a position it has held despite repeated efforts by Washington and other Western Governments to dissuade it from this belief. In October 1985 President Botha warned his neighbours that because of their inter-dependence they were all affected by 'Soviet expansionism in the sub-Continent'.[14] Reflecting official opinion, an SABC commentary on 17 December 1985 declared that the USSR regarded Angola 'as a springboard for the subjugation of Southern Africa', hence the need 'to give humanitarian and moral support to Unita' Another SABC commentary on 19 September 1986, asserted:

> The communist presence is pervasive throughout the entire structure of life in Angola today, with tens of thousands of East bloc personnel working with, influencing and indoctrinating the local population in areas ranging from communications and intelligence services to schools and hospitals. Angola, to put it simply, is the spearhead of the Soviet empire's expansionism in Southern Africa. It is in recognition of this fact that the Reagan Administration is providing covert aid to Unita, currently amounting to 37m rana.

In late 1985 Pretoria saw a new threat from Moscow coming from Zimbabwe aided and abetted by Zambia as reflected in this SABC commentary:[150]

> Since the takeover of Rhodesia by the Marxist Mugabe Government, it has been the main task of the KGB's chief Africa expert, V. C. Solodovnikov, to organize the takeover of SA by the alliance of the SA Communist Party (SACP) and the ANC. This is being done with the full knowledge of President Kenneth Kaunda of Zambia, where Solodovnikov was the Soviet ambassador until July 1981.

The commentary went on to suggest that the Soviet alliance had succeeded in causing a complete collapse in the economies of Mozambique and Angola, and now set its sights on doing the same in Namibia and SA. Pretoria saw further evidence of a Zimbabwe–Soviet connection when Mugabe visited Moscow in December 1985. (He had refused to visit Moscow for five years because of his quarrel with the Soviets over their support for Nkomo's Zapu during the liberation war.) Mugabe was correctly reported at the end of his visit as saying that he had discussed the possibility of Soviet military assistance with Kremlin leaders to strengthen Zimbabwe in the face of SA threats. (A British military assistance training team has been in Zimbabwe since independence, and still remains there.)

SA's concern about the Soviet 'onslaught' was constantly reiterated by reports on an arms build-up in the region. Quoting from the US Defence Department annual review, one report said that in 1985 Mozambique had received Soviet Mi-24 HIND helicopter gunships, PT-76 light tanks, Sam-3 anti-aircraft missiles, artillery and multiple-rocket launchers.[151] The report claimed there were 850 Soviet military advisers in Mozambique.

If these reports are correct it says very little for the Soviets' effectiveness in helping to defeat the MNR; nor for Machel's decision to ask for military aid from Britain and other Western countries.

Apart from the 30,000 Cuban troops in Angola, SA sources claimed there were ,000 East German and 900 Soviet military advisers in the country, as well as more han 1,000 North Koreans.[152] (Western intelligence sources supported a Luanda enial of North Korean involvement in Angola.)

SA military experts claimed that with the build-up of Soviet arms in the region, he number of missile fighter aircraft may now out-number the SAAF by as much s two-to-one.[153] SADF intelligence reports suggested that SA's northern borders vere being closely monitored by a potentially hostile radar complex that reaches vell into the Republic's territory.[154] Some of these installations located in southern Angola cover the northern half of Namibia. Others located in southern Mozambique monitor the SAAF base at Hoedspruit, and reach as far as Pretoria, and mbrace the whole of Swaziland. The majority of installations are of a mobile ature and can be easily moved about Angola or Mozambique. The interception adar systems have range capabilities of 200 to 250 km. They were widely used in Egypt and Vietnam, with devastating effect. Five different types of target acquisi-ion systems have been developed, with capabilities ranging from 180 km to 275 km t altitudes of up to 30,000 feet. The missile systems vary in ranges from the SAM-2 at 40 km to the 12 km short range SAM-8, with its self-contained radar racking and acquisition system.

Brigadier H. E. Lehman, Commanding Officer, Airspace Control Command, aid there were 810 missile launchers deployed in Angola; four of these missiles are adar-controlled, and that is very important, because these radars in actual fact letect the target and also guide missiles to the point of impact. Lt-Gen D. J. Earp, Chief of SAAF, added that this equipment is the same as the equipment which Soviet Russia has deployed against NATO, and in the Middle East. 'So what we ave in Southern Africa is essentially the same equipment, but the numbers are ess.'

Gen Malan claimed in September 1986 that over the past six years, the number f helicopters in the region had increased by 400%, fighter planes by 270% and anks by 30%. He did not say what the base figure was on which these percentages re calculated. Malan said that because of this Soviet 'penetration in Southern Africa, it was premature for SA to scale down its military power and prepared-ess.'

SA perceptions of the strategy of the Soviets in the region were contained in an analysis by Prof Mike Hough, director of the Institute for Strategic Studies at Pretoria University. He concluded that the extent of the conventional threat against SA would largely be determined by six factors:

- The country's internal stability;
- The maintenance by the country of 'a credible deterrent standing'
- Regional peace initiatives;
- The outcome of the civil war situation in Angola and Mozambique;
- The outcome of the South West Africa question;
- The East-West conflict.

A civil war situation in South Africa would provide opportunities for a conventional offensive, as would an East-West conflict which also involved the Southern African region.

The aim of the ANC was to conduct a conventional war with a 'weakened' SA Government. This was seen as a concluding phase of the revolutionary war and hinged on the formation of a 'Peoples Army' and on the possession of conventional arms.

In this sense the stock-piling of arms in neighbouring countries as perceived by SA could be relevant in suport of a conventional phase in ANC strategy.

It is instructive to compare this SA analysis of the 'Soviet threat' with that made by US Soviet analysts as reproduced in the section on the US Role, below.

SA'S POLICIES OF DESTABILIZATION: RELATIONS WITH UNITA AND MNR

Pretoria had always denied it was involved in giving military assistance to the MNR until its role was revealed during the negotiations leading to the Nkomati Accord and by subsequent disclosures (see Mozambique, above). It has similarly denied it was engaged in supporting Unita; but in September 1985 Gen Malan put on record that SA was giving Unita material, humanitarian and moral support.[155] He added that SA had 'maintained ties with Unita for a number of years', and that it proposed continuing to do so until all foreign forces had been withdrawn from Angola. Its support for Unita, he said, was to 'put a stop to Marxist infiltration and expansionism.'

Pretoria also continued to deny its support for the Lesotho Liberation Army during Jonathan's rule despite positive evidence of its collaboration with Mokhehle. It has remained silent over Zimbabwe's repeated accusations that it was helping Super-Zapu (see Zimbabwe, above).

SA's reply to allegations that its policies are responsible for destabilizing the region is that the blame for this is fixed 'squarely on the shoulders of the rulers of the countries to the north of SA.'[156]

ROLE OF THE AFRICAN NATIONAL CONGRESS

It took the ANC almost 20 years since its armed wing, *Umkonto we Sizwe*, launched its struggle to win international recognition as a key actor in SA political developments. Its pre-eminence as the leading challenger to the apartheid system owes much, perhaps most, to the recognition that the ANC's imprisoned leader and the man who launched *Umkonto*'s struggle, Nelson Mandela, has become the touchstone for Black participation in any negotiating process with the SA regime. Recognition of this reality was demonstrated in the significant visit made in 1985 by leading SA businessmen to Zambia to hold talks with the ANC exile leader, Oliver Tambo, and his colleagues. Other SA groups, including students and church leaders, sought to engage in similar talks with the ANC. Botha himself recognized Mandela's key role by offering his conditional release—the condition being that he should repudiate violence. A growing number of government supporters openly declared their belief that no meaningful negotiations could begin until Mandela was released—a position also adopted by the US, Britain and other members of the European Community.

In 1985 the US began to engage in secret talks with the ANC which led later to public talks with Oliver Tambo. Britain also established unpublicized contacts with the ANC in 1985, and finally reversed its policy of not 'talking to terrorists' when the Foreign Secretary held official talks with Tambo in London. This was followed by an invitation from the US Secretary of State to come to Washington for talks.[157]

The ANC has never denied the support it receives from the Soviet bloc countries and Cuba; but it has always insisted that it was not interested in getting aid from that side alone, and complained of the failure by Western countries to respond to its repeated appeals for aid. Only Sweden, Norway and Holland have given support in the form of non-military aid to the ANC.

The ANC's official alliance with the SA Communist Party is naturally cited by its critics as evidence of its international orientation. The SA Government repeatedly claimed that this alliance clearly showed that the ANC is a 'Soviet puppet' and an instrument for Moscow's policies in Southern Africa. But, at times, Pretoria has also indicated that it recognized a division between the nationalists within the ANC ranks and the communists.

ROLE OF THE SOUTH WEST AFRICAN PEOPLE'S ORGANIZATION OF NAMIBIA
Swapo has long been recognized by the UN as 'the sole authentic representative of the peoples of Namibia.' Its leader, Sam Nujoma, has been an active participant in all the negotiations for Namibian independence by the Western Contact Group, until it suspended its role in 1985.

Nujoma has conspicuously followed a policy of non-alignment in his relations with the major powers, and travels frequently between Western, Soviet bloc, Cuban and Chinese capitals. Apart from the support his Organization gets from the OAU's Liberation Committee, its military aid comes from the Soviets, Cuba and China. Swapo's querrillas, which are based in Angola, have had the advantage of getting Soviet military supplies through Luanda and of having Soviet, East German and Cuban military trainers in its base camps.

Although Swapo continued to make attacks against targets inside Namibia in 1985 and 1986, it failed to increase the momentum of its offensive due largely to the reluctance of the MPLA Government to breach the 1984 Lusaka Agreement despite the fact that it had become moribund. Politically, however, Swapo retains the political initiative with its insistence that SCR 435 should be upheld as the only basis for independence. Its repudiation of the Interim Government of National Unity established by Pretoria for Namibia has the unqualified support of all the UN member-states. Few doubt that Swapo would emerge as the major political force if elections were held in Namibia under the terms envisaged by SCR 435.[158]

THE INTERNATIONAL ARENA
ROLE OF THE COMMONWEALTH OF NATIONS

The Nassau Accord
Fifteen of the 49 Commonwealth members are African, and six of them lie in the Southern African region, including four of the six Frontline States. All but four (the old Commonwealth) belong to the Third World. This composition of the Commonwealth ensures that its role in the conflicts of South Africa and the wider region will be radical and intensely sensitive. There was a time when it was possible to talk about the 'White' Commonwealth, but that is no longer true when it comes to the issue of South Africa. Australia and Canada (even with Conservative leaders) and New Zealand have all moved close to the African position in their dealings with Pretoria—a development that left the 'mother of the Commonwealth', Britain, virtually isolated within the club. This isolation was made more pronounced by the determined resistance of Margaret Thatcher to any idea of imposing economic sanctions on SA—as opposed to military sanctions and a sports boycott, both of which she endorses.

At the Commonwealth meeting in Nassau, Bahamas, in October 1985 Thatcher fought with only the support of Malawi and Swaziland in resisting a tough programme of sanctions. In the end she yielded only 'a teeny-weeny bit' (in her own words) to a programme that included the following new measures: a ban on all new loans to the SA Government and its agencies; a ban on the import of Krugerrands; no government funding for trade missions to SA, or for participation in SA trade fairs; a ban on computers likely to be used by the SA army and police; a ban on new contracts for the sale and export of nuclear materials. (Other measures related to tightening up bans on previously agreed items such as arms, oil and military cooperation. It was also agreed to discourage all cultural and scientific contact except where they contribute towards the ending of apartheid or have no possibl role in promoting it.

The stalemate between Britain and the great majority of Commonwealth men bers was eased by an agreement to appoint an Eminent Persons Group from th Commonwealth (CEPG) to encourage 'through all practicable ways' the evolutio of a process of political dialogue within SA. The CEPG was given six months t fulfill its mission at the end of which, if there was no substantial progress, th Commonwealth would meet again to consider adopting further sanctions, incluc ing a possible ban on air links with SA; a ban on new investments or reinvestmer of profits earned in SA; a ban on imports of agricultural products; termination c all double taxation agreements; termination of all government assistance to inves ment in, and trade with, SA; a ban on all government procurement in SA; a ban o government contracts with majority-owned SA companies; a ban on promotin tourism.

The Commonwealth Eminent Persons Group

The CEPG was composed of distinguished leaders, appointed to reflect the mai regions in the Commonwealth. They were: Malcolm Fraser, a former Australia Prime Minister; Gen Olusegun Obasanjo, a former Nigerian Head of State; Lor Barber, a former British Chancellor of the Exchequer and now chairman of th Standard Chartered Bank; Dame Nita Barrow of Barbados, a former president c the World Council of Churches; John Malecela, a former Foreign Minister an Minister of Agriculture of Tanzania, Sardar Swaran Singh, a former Indian Foreig Minister; and the Most Rev Edward Walter Scott, Primate of the Anglican Churc of Canada.

After some hesitation, President Botha agreed to allow the Group to visit S/ for talks with his Government and representatives of all shades of opinion, includ ing visits to the imprisoned ANC leader, Nelson Mandela.

The CEPG was able to produce a unanimous report which was published unde the title of *Mission to South Africa* by Penquin Books in July 1986. Its mai findings were:

- As a contrivance of social engineering, apartheid is awesome in its cruelty; it i achieved and sustained only through force, creating human misery and deprivatio and blighting the lives of millions.
- The SA Government's actions up to this point do not justify any claim that aparthei is being dismantled.
- SA is sliding even further into a permanent state of emergency in terms of th ordinary laws of the land.
- The call for the unconditional release of Nelson Mandela and all other politic prisoners remains unheeded; it is one to which the highest importance attaches.
- No movement has been made towards the call on the SA Government to establis political freedom and specifically to lift the ban on the ANC and other politic parties.
- The CEPG was forcibly struck by the overwhelming desire in SA for a non-violer negotiated settlement.
- There is no prospect for the initiation of a process of dialogue across lines of colou politics and religion with a view to establishing a non-racial and representativ government, within the context of a suspension of violence on all sides.

At one stage in their talks the CEPG was encouraged to prepare the followin draft of what they described as a Possible Negotiating Concept:

The SA Government has declared its commitment to dismantling the system of apartheid, to ending racial discrimination and to broad-based negotiations leading to new constitutional arrangements for power-sharing by all the people of SA. In the light of preliminary and as yet incomplete discussions with representatives of various organizations and groups, within and outside SA, we believe that in the context of specific and meaningful steps being taken towards ending apartheid, the following additional action might ensure negotiations and a break in the cycle of violence.

On the part of the Government:

(a) Removal of the military from the townships, providing for freedom of assembly and discussion and suspension of detention without trial.

(b) The release of Nelson Mandela and other political prisoners and detainees.

(c) The unbanning of the ANC and PAC and the permitting of normal political activity.

On the part of the ANC and others:—Entering negotiations and suspending violence.

It is our view that simultaneous announcements incorporating these ideas might be negotiated if the Government were to be interested in pursuing this broad approach.

In the light of the Government's indication to us that it:

(i) is not in principle against the release of Nelson Mandela and similar prisoners;

(ii) is not opposed in principle to the unbanning of any organizations;

(iii) is prepared to enter into negotiations with the acknowledged leaders of the people of SA;

(iv) is committed to removal of discrimination, not only from the statute books but also from SA society as a whole;

(v) is committed to ending of White domination;

(vi) will not prescribe who may represent Black communities in negotiations on a new constitution for SA;

(vii) is prepared to negotiate on an open agenda.

The concept was transmitted to the Minister for Constitutional Development and Planning, Chris Heunis, and to the Foreign Minister, Pik Botha, under cover of letters dated 13 March which stated the CEPG's belief that it offers 'a real chance of establishing productive negotiations about the future of SA. But this proposed route to a negotiated settlement was rejected by the Government with the following explanation by the Foreign Minister:

There are four major questions which are exercising the mind of the SA Government about the possible negotiating concept presented by your Group.

1. The concept of ending or suspending violence.

It is not the choice of a particular word but the concept of terminating violence as a means of achieving political objectives which is relevant. The SA Government cannot accept the suggestion that violence should be discontinued only for as long as negotiations take place. To use violence or the threat of violence as a bargaining counter is unacceptable to the SA Government.

2. Evidence of commitment to a peaceful solution.

The use of violence for political ends cannot be equated with the responsibility of Government to maintain law and order. The SA Government has committed itself to a constitutional dispensation which guarantees

• the removal of racial discrimination;

• sharing of power up to the highest level of government;

• democratic principles including an independent judicial system and the equality of all under the law;

• private property rights;

• private initiative and effective competition;

• fundamental human rights and civil liberties;

• the protection of minority rights in a manner which would ensure that there will be no political domination by any one community of the other;

- freedom of the press and of expression in general;
- freedom of religion and worship;

and is taking substantial steps to carry out this commitment. It would, therefore, be reasonable to expect evidence that the parties presently involved in violence are in principle willing to commit themselves to a peaceful solution through negotiation and in an environment free of violence. A substantial reduction in violence would help to create the atmosphere in which the additional steps could be taken.
3. Intimidation to be abandoned.

It is not only the Government which should permit 'normal political activity' and 'freedom of assembly and discussion'. Other parties need to respect these principles in practice and commit themselves to abandon all forms of intimidation.
4. The nature of the negotiations that are envisaged.

The SA Government is prepared to negotiate with SA citizens about a new constitutional dispensation which will provide for power sharing. It is not interested in negotiation about a transfer of power. The SA Government is committed to a negotiated democratic settlement which addresses the legitimate political aspirations of all South Africans. In contrast, others are on record as wanting a diminished democracy in the form of a one-party state with restricted personal and other freedoms.

The SA Government would welcome further discussions which could accommodate the concerns addressed above.

I would like to thank you and your colleagues for the spirit in which we have been able to conduct our discussions.

However, without explanation, Pretoria's attitude to the Mission underwent a change in August 1986; instead of its Ministers continuing to cooperate in a friendly manner, their attitude became chilly. Provocatively, the regime unleashed three attacks across its borders into Botswana, Zimbabwe and Zambia on the eve of a crucial meeting arranged between the CEPG and a group of Ministers. President Botha's rejection of the proposals made by the CEPG was uncompromising.

Reporting on their experiences and the failure of the Mission, the CEPG declared:

We rejected as impractical the suggestion that the whole complex web of apartheid legislation be repealed as a prelude to negotiation; we were concerned to ensure however, that there should be a firm and unambiguous commitment by the Government to ending apartheid in order to provide integrity to the negotiating agenda and the negotiating process—as well as specific and meaningful steps taken to that end. It needs to be remembered that apartheid goes beyond institutionalized racial discrimination and economic exploitation; it is primarily a means of keeping ultimate political and economic power in the hands of the White minority. Any reservations by the Government about dismantling apartheid would inevitably and understandably be viewed by the vast majority as a ploy for perpetuating White power in a new guise, a willingness to change its form but not abandon its substance.

The Government told us categorically that it was prepared to contemplate negotiations with a completely open agenda, where everything would be on the table. However, as we have pointed out elsewhere, in some respects, the open agenda appeared to be circumscribed. Nevertheless, for the purposes of our discussions we gave the SA Government the benefit of the doubt in our minds. In the Government' thinking, there were a number of non-negotiables; for example, the concept of group rights—the very basis of the apartheid system—was sacrosanct; the 'homelands created in furtherance of that concept would not disappear, but be reinforced with the emergence of an 'independent' KwaNdebele; the principle of one-man one-vote in a unitary state was beyond the realm of possibility; the Population Registration Ac vould continue; and the present Tri-cameral Constitution Act which institutionalizes racism must be the vehicle for future constitutional reform.

From these and other recent developments, we draw the conclusion that while the Government claims to be ready to negotiate, it is in truth not yet prepared to negotiate fundamental change, nor to countenance the creation of genuine democratic structures, nor to face the prospect of the end of White domination and White power in the foreseeable future. Its programme of reform does not end apartheid, but seeks to give it a less inhuman face. Its quest is power-sharing, but without surrendering overall White control.

In regard to the modalities of negotiation, the Government's position has a considerable element of wishful thinking. The Government is willing and ready to negotiate with 'responsible' leaders; if only violence and 'intimidation' would abate, these leaders would be ready to come to the negotiating table to strike a deal. Although we were never told by the Government who these 'responsible' leaders might be—indeed, the Government assured us it would not prescribe or limit the people's choice—it could be inferred that prominent among them would be the 'homelands' leaders whom the government repeatedly urged us to see. With the exception of Chief Buthelezi, the 'homeland' leaders have no real political standing or following and would not, in our view, be credible parties in a negotiation to resolve SA's deepening crisis. It is not for us to prescribe or advise who the parties to a genuine negotiation might be; but we noted as significant the Government's allergy to our proposal that they should be the true', 'authentic' or 'acknowledged' leaders of the people.

Negotiations leading to fundamental political change and the erection of democratic structures will only be possible if the SA Government is prepared to deal with leaders of the people's choosing rather than with puppets of its own creation. President Botha's recent statements expressing his determination to 'break' the ANC bode ill for the country's future. There can be no negotiated settlement in SA without the ANC; the breadth of its support is incontestable; and this support is growing. Among the many striking figures whom we met in the course of our work, Nelson Mandela and Oliver Tambo stand out. Their reasonableness, absence of rancour and readiness to find negotiated solutions which, while creating genuine democratic structures would still give the Whites a feeling of security and participation, impressed us deeply. If the Government finds itself unable to talk with men like Mandela and Tambo, then the future of SA is bleak indeed.

The Government made it clear that it did not regard the ANC as the only other party to negotiations. We agree, but would emphasize that the ANC is a necessary party. The Government itself acknowledges this, if only by blaming the ANC for most of the violence. The open identification with the ANC through banners and songs, in funerals and in churches throughout the country, despite the risks involved, supports the widely-held belief that if an election were held today on the basis of universal franchise the ANC would win it. Whatever the truth of that assertion, we nonetheless recognize that Black political opinion is not monolothic. If, therefore, the Government is serious about negotiations, it must create conditions in which free political activity becomes possible, and political parties and leaders are able to function effectively and test the extent of their popular support. Tragically, the whole thrust of Government policy has been to thwart such legitimate leadership from emerging and destroy it where it does. Even non-violent organizations like the UDF have been subjected to harassment and persecution.

Behind these attitudes lurks a deeper truth. After more than 18 months of persistent unrest, upheaval, and killings unprecedented in the country's history, the Government believes that it can contain the situation indefinitely by use of force. We were repeatedly told by Ministers that the Government had deployed only a fraction of the power at its disposal. Although the Government's confidence may be valid in the short term, but at great human cost, it is plainly misplaced in the longer term. SA is predominantly a country of Black people. To believe that they can be indefinitely suppressed is an act of self-delusion.

By pandering to Right-wing anxieties and demands, the Government fortifies them, compounding its own problems and losing whatever initiative it may have possessed. It is also in danger of falling between two stools. Its promises of reform have created anxiety among certain sections of its supporters and contributed to growing White backlash; yet the reforms themselves have made little impact on Black attitudes or aspirations—save to confirm the Government's implacable resistance to significant change.

While Right-wing opposition cannot be ignored, it would be fatal to give it a veto. Indeed, we gained the impression that White opinion as a whole may be ahead of the Government in significant respects, ready to respond positively if given a bold lead.

We are left with the impression of a divided Government. Yet even the more enlightened Ministers whom we met seem to be out of touch with the mood in the Black townships, the rising tide of anger and impatience within them, and the extent of Black mobilization. And so, of course, are the great generality of White South Africans—only some 10% of whom, we were told, have ever seen conditions in a township.

Put in the most simple way, the Blacks have had enough of apartheid. They are no longer prepared to submit to its oppression, discrimination and exploitation. They can no longer stomach being treated as aliens in their own country. They have confidence not merely in the justice of their cause, but in the inevitability of their victory. Unlike the earlier period of unrest and Government attempts to stamp out protest, there has been during the last 18 months no outflow of Black refugees from SA. The strength of Black convictions is now matched by a readiness to die for those convictions. They will, therefore, sustain their struggle, whatever the cost.

The campaign against collaborators, and the ruthless elimination of agents of White authority, will continue. More and more Black townships will be rendered ungovernable, and the process of creating popular structures of self-government within them will gather momentum. The number of street and area committees will increase and their functions will progressively enlarge.

The writ of the Government will be increasingly circumscribed. Inter-Black rivalry and violence, partly encouraged and fomented by the Government, will grow, making the task of negotiating a settlement even more difficult. Political upheaval and social unrest will accelerate the flight of capital and professional skills and the economy's downward spiral.

Amidst all this gloom the quality of the country's Black leaders shines through. Their achievement in bringing about popular and trade union mobilization in the face of huge odds commands respect. Their idealism, their genuine sense of non-racialism and their readiness not only to forget but to forgive, compel admiration. These are precious assets which a new SA will need; they may be lost altogether if the Government continues to shrink from taking the necessary political decisions with a sense of urgency. The options are diminishing by the day.

The Government faces difficult choices. Its obduracy and intransigence wrecked the Commonwealth's initiative, but the issues themselves will not go away, nor can they be bombed out of existence. It is not sanctions which will destroy the country but the persistence of apartheid and the Government's failure to engage in fundamental political reform. . . .

Against the background in which ever-increasing violence will be a certainty, the question of further measures immediately springs to mind. . . . While we are not determining the nature or extent of any measures which might be adopted, or their effectiveness, we point to the fact that the Government of SA has itself used economic measures against its neighbours and that such measures are patently instruments of its own national policy. We are convinced that the SA Government is concerned about the adoption of effective economic measures against it. If it comes to the conclusion that it would always remain protected from such measures, the process of change in SA is unlikely to increase in momentum and the descent into violence would be accelerated. In these circumstances, the cost in lives may have to be counted in millions.

From the point of view of the Black leadership, the course now taken by the world community will have the greatest significance. That leadership has already come to the view that diplomatic persuasion has not and will not move the SA Government sufficiently. If it also comes to believe that the world community will never exercise sufficient effective pressure through other measures in support of their cause, they will have only one option remaining: that of ever-increasing violence. Once decisions involving greater violence are made on both sides, they carry an inevitability of their own and are difficult, if not impossible, to reverse, except as a result of exhaustion through prolonged conflict.

The question in front of Heads of Government is in our view clear. It is not whether such measures will compel change; it is already the case that their absence and Pretoria's belief that they need not be feared, defers change. Is the Commonwealth to stand by and allow the cycle of violence to spiral? Or will it take concerted action of an effective kind? Such action may offer the last opportunity to avert what could be the worst bloodbath since the Second World War.

We hope that this Report will assist the Commonwealth—and the wider international community—in helping all the people of SA save themselves from that awesome tragedy.

ir Geoffrey Howe's Mission to Pretoria

fter the breakdown of the CEPG's mission and in anticipation of a stormy assage at the Commonwealth mini-summit set for August 1985, Britain engaged in wo initiatives to win support for its policies. It sought to get agreement from its artners in the European Community on a concerted approach on SA (see below), nd the Foreign Secretary went on a mission to Pretoria to try and persuade resident Botha to make a positive announcement about the ending of apartheid nd to release Nelson Mandela. Before visiting Pretoria he visited a number of rontline capitals to impress on their leaders the importance of moving ahead in ne with an agreed EEC policy. His mission was controversial from the outset and vas doomed to failure both because of the determination of the Frontline leaders ） settle for nothing less than was agreed at Nassau, and because President Botha vas bound to react negatively to any overt external pressure to change his iovernment's policies. Pretoria's predictable reaction was foreshadowed in a statement made by Pik Botha on 27 June 1986 in which he declared that while Sir ïeoffrey's visit would be welcomed if he wished to ascertain the 'facts and ealities' in SA, the Government was 'not prepared to be prescribed to from verseas on how to solve the country's problems.' He issued a warning that if the ıternational community went ahead with more sanctions, SA would take counter-ıeasures including the repatriation of migrant workers from neighbouring coun-ries.[59]

The original intention was that the EEC should send a combined mission to ᵗretoria, but because of disagreements among its members over their attitude to anctions, Sir Geoffrey announced on 27 June that he would go on a solo mission. Iis announcement met with an immediately hostile reception among Opposition ʌPs. Neil Kinnock said the Foreign Secretary would be seen as a 'gloved puppet' vho had nothing positive to offer. Reactions by Frontline leaders was even more ostile. Nelson Mandela let it be known from Pollsmoor prison that he would efuse a visit from Howe; this, too, was the response of Oliver Tambo.[160] On the ve of his departure, Howe declared that 'The alternative to dialogue and negotiaion can only be increasing repression, polarization, and bloodshed.'[161]Howe's nission started badly when at his first meeting in Lusaka, President Kaunda ᵖublicly attacked the mission as 'completely unnecessary.' Mugabe also attacked he mission as 'reprehensible, futile and useless.' The only bright spot was when ᵗresident Machel described the aim of the mission to promote dialogue as being 'a

good thing'. He said that he did not propose that Mozambique should app
sanctions, but that he would not discourage others from doing so.[162] Howe beg
two days of talks with President Botha on 23 July. After his first meeting wi
Botha he said it was clear to him that 25 years after Harold Macmillan's 'wind
change' warning in 1960, the wind was shaking the continent's southern part to i
roots.[163] Before his second meeting with Botha, while on a quick visit
Botswana, he admitted:

> What I do may not in the end be enough to light the way to the top of the mountain, b
> somebody, somewhere, some time, is going to get the case for peace and dialog
> accepted.[164]

Howe' mission finally collapsed at his second meeting with Botha, who himse
confirmed that there had not been even a fractional shift towards the concessio
the Foreign Secretary had sought. At a press conference Botha declared:

> I can never commit suicide by accepting threats and prescriptions from outsi
> forces in disguise and hand SA over to the communist forces in disguise (a referen
> to the ANC).[165]

Howe wearily admitted that the responses he had received 'do not as yet enab
me to proclaim that I have made the progress I would like.' On his return hom
Howe reported to Thatcher that the time had come to agree to further measur
against SA. He reported these views to the Cabinet's Overseas and Defen
Committee on 30 July. But Thatcher made it clear that while further measur
would be considered she remained opposed to all-out sanctions.[166]

The Commonwealth Mini-Summit in London, August 1986

The failure of the CEPG Mission plunged the Commonwealth back into the crisis
had sought to avoid at Nassau by agreeing to a six months postponement while t
Eminent Pearsons sought to persuade the Pretoria regime to move ahead wi
fundamental reforms and genuine negotiations. Even before the mini-summit-
attended by President Kaunda and the Prime Ministers of Australia, Canad
Britain, the Bahamas, India, Zimbabwe—foregathered in London for their meeti
over 4–5 August, Thatcher had made it clear that she would continue resolutely
oppose further sanctions which, she said, was for her a moral issue. She stresse
two other objections: that sanctions would harm Black South Africans, and
would harden attitudes rather than make negotiations easier. In protest against h
stand the majority of African countries and many from other parts of the Thir
World withdrew their teams from the four-yearly Commonwealth Games in Edi
burgh. This boycott further contributed to heightening the sense of crisis an
provoked political controversy between those who supported the reasons for t
boycott and those who felt that politics were being allowed to interfere with spor
The Commonwealth Secretary-General tried but failed to prevent the boycott; h
pointed out the obvious fact that the Games belonged to the Commonwealth, n
to Britain; it was fortuitous that they were being held in a British city.

As so often, before, the media speculation was over whether the Commo
wealth would survive unless Thatcher accommodated British policy to the wish
of the majority; but this time there was some reason to question whether th
Commonwealth could hold together—especially since one of its most arde
supporters, President Kaunda, warned that he was ready to pull his country out
the association, and there was a strong lobby in Nigeria for doing the same. Th
risk was that once a single country left it would start an avalanche of resignation

ɱong the leaders who intervened to stop this from happening were Prime Minis-
ɾ Mugabe and Prime Minister Gandhi.[167] Both declared themselves against
ɑaunda's threat which he later withdrew because, he said, he had been impressed
ɣ the strength of British public opinion against the stand taken by their Prime
ʃinister.

The London mini-summit also produced a rare and remarkable constitutional
ɾisis over the Queen's reported disagreement with her Prime Minister over her
ɑtitude to the Commonwealth of which Elizabeth is the Crowned Head.[168] Anti-
ʰatcher remarks attributed by a Palace official to the Queen were never directly
ɯithdrawn and the actual relationship between the two foremost women in the
ɯnd was never clarified; but there seems little doubt that there was fire behind the
ɯmoke of this controversy.

As can always be expected when the Commonwealth (especially the Black
ʲommonwealth) behaves stroppily towards Britain and refuses to toe a British
ɯne, Right-wing Tories renewed their demand for dissolving the Commonwealth.
ɯut although a few influential voices spoke in favour of dissolving the Common-
ɯealth, the Conservative Party as a whole took a different view.[169]

Meanwhile, in Marlborough House, Thatcher battled for two days against her
ɯix adversaries. She explained her stand in this way:

> There is no case in history that I know of where punitive, general economic
> sanctions have been effective to bring about internal change.[170] It is quite possible
> that the imposition of strict mandatory sanctions on SA would add to the violence and
> not detract from it, and that it would end all possibility of negotiations between the
> Government and the Black people of SA. This is still our objective.
>
> If there were ever any question of going for total economic sanctions, it would
> cause more unemployment here and much unemployment in SA as well as fundamen-
> tal strategic problems, putting supplies of raw materials into the hands of the Soviet
> Union and strategic defence problems, and it would not bring about the change which
> all wish to see
>
> SA has colossal internal resources. A colossal coastline. And whatever sanctions
> were put on materials would get in and get out. There's no way you can blockade the
> whole SA coastline. No way.
>
> I must tell you I find nothing moral about people who come to me, worried about
> unemployment in this country or about people who come to us to say we must do
> more to help Africa, particularly Black Africans. I find nothing moral about them,
> sitting in comfortable circumstances with good salaries, inflation-proof pensions,
> good jobs, saying that we, as a matter of morality will put x hundred thousand Black
> people out of work, knowing that this could lead to starvation, poverty and unemploy-
> ment, and promoting more violence.

Having argued that sanctions were not moral and likely to be ineffective or even
ɾounter-productive, she nevertheless agreed to a further extension of the pro-
ɡramme of sanctions already imposed by Britain (the arms embargo and sports
ɓoycott, as well as the measures she agreed to at Nassau). She accepted that the
British Government would:

> (i) put a voluntary ban on new investment in South Africa.
> (ii) put a voluntary ban on the promotion of tourism to South Africa, and
> (iii) accept and implement any EEC decision to ban the import of coal, iron and
> steel and of gold coins from SA.

The other members of the mini-summit adopted a joint statement declaring:

(a) the adoption of further substantial economic measures against SA is a mor
and political imperative to which a positive response can no longer be deferred.

(b) we ourselves will therefore adopt the following measures and commend the
to the rest of the Commonwealth and the wider international community for urge
adoption and implementation:

(i) all the measures listed in paragraph 7 of the Nassau Accord, namely:

a) a ban on air links with SA,

b) a ban on new investments or reinvestments of profits earned in SA,

c) a ban on the import of agricultural products from SA,

d) the termination of double taxation agreements with SA,

e) the termination of all government assistance to investment in, and trade wit
SA,

f) a ban on all government procurement in SA,

g) a ban on government contracts with majority-owned SA companies, and

h) a ban on the promotion of tourism to SA and,

(ii) the following additional measures:

i) a ban on all new bank loans to SA, whether to the public or private sectors,

j) a ban on the import of uranium, coal, iron and steel from SA, and,

k) the withdrawal of all consular facilities in SA except for our own nationals an
nationals of third countries to whom we render consular services.

(c) While expressing both concern and regret that the British Government do
not join in our agreement, we note its intention to proceed with the measure
mentioned in paragraph 12 below.

(d) We feel, however, that we must do more. We look beyond the Commonweal
to the wider international community. We will, therefore, immediately embark o
intensive consultations within the international community with a view to securin
concerted international action in the coming months, our emphasis being on thos
countries that presently sustain a significant level of economic relations with SA.

Geoffrey Smith, *Times* political commentator, revealed that Thatcher had defie
not only the other six Commonwealth leaders 'but also the spirit of what her ow
Cabinet had decided last week'.[171] The Cabinet, he wrote, wished to avoid Britain'
isolation in the Commonwealth. He added that:

> The agreement Sir Geoffrey Howe secured from the Cabinet was that the Britis
> strategy would be to encourage common action on further measures by the Commor
> wealth, the EEC, the US and Japan. How this strategy was to be applied in negotia
> tions was left to the tactical judgment of Mrs Thatcher and Sir Geoffrey.

But the way in which the hand was played apparently owed everything to he
and little to her long-suffering Foreign Secretary.

At the end of the summit, India's Prime Minister declared sorrowfully tha
Britain had sullied its record on human rights by failing to agree with its si
Commonwealth colleagues. He added that 'if Britain cannot get the pulse of th
Commonwealth then Britain cannot retain its leadership.'[172] President Kaund
said that Thatcher had cut 'a very pathetic figure indeed' at the meeting. Rober
Mugabe fiercely attacked Thatcher and hinted that Zimbabwe might take actio
against British interests in his country.[173] Canada's Prime Minister, Bria
Mulroney, had announced before the mini-summit, after a meeting he had had wit
Thatcher in which she failed to win him over to her side, that his country wa
prepared to act alone in imposing sanctions.[174] New Zealand's Prime Ministe
David Lange, criticized Thatcher's stance, saying it was taken to 'protect Britis
financial interests.'[175]

Britain's Role: The Domestic Debate

The sanctions debate brought South Africa into the forefront of British foreign policy concerns. The issue was debated on a number of occasions in the House of Commons in July and August 1986. The debates showed that the three Opposition parties were unitedly opposed to the Government's policy; there were also signs of division within the Conservative Party itself, as well as in the Cabinet (see above). Conservatives were divided into three groups: The majority appeared to support Thatcher's stand; a substantial minority took the opposite view; while an anti-sanctions group of about 27 MP's-led by Right-wingers like John Carlisle, Julian Amery, Sir Patrick Wall, George Gardiner, Sir Ian Lloyd, Mr and Mrs Winterbottom—were opposed to any idea of economic pressures against SA.[176] The former Prime Minister, Edward Heath, not only favoured sanctions but said that, if necessary, they should be enforced by 'a trade blockade,'[177]—a possibility also endorsed by a former Defence Minister, Denis Healey. At the end of an angry debate in the Commons on 17 June, the Government had a majority of 125, with a handful of Conservatives abstaining.

The all-party Foreign Affairs Committee of the Commons, which is chaired by a Tory MP, Sir Anthony Kershaw, conducted a searching inquiry into the question of sanctions which lasted from October 1985 to August 1986.[178] Among the witnesses it examined were the SA ambassador in London, Dr Dennis Worrall, and the ANC leader, Oliver Tambo. It reported that 'unless the SA Government released political prisoners and began constitutional talks, Britain was likely to be 'compelled' to introduce further sanctions. It proposed that Pretoria should be offered the chance to agree to negotiations with Black political leaders, in return for 'substantial' financial and technical support from Western countries directed mainly to the Black community and designed to stimulate the economy and help resolve the consequences of apartheid. But the offer should only be pursued 'if the SA Government is prepared to accept the inevitability of rapid progress towards majority rule.'

The committee's report assessed two approaches to SA: the 'carrot' of positive measures such as assistance with Black housing and education as part of a Western-backed 'Marshall Plan' and the 'stick' of further sanctions. 'We cannot be sure that either will work' the committee declared. 'Things may have gone too far already.'

The report went on to say it is 'certain' that 'whatever the eventual outcome in SA, the British Government itself faces the probability of more immediate difficulties, particularly in its relations with the Commonwealth, if it decides to resist the weight of sentiment in favour of strong and concerted international action to try to force, rather than encourage, the SA Government to the negotiating table.

The committee also reviewed the effectiveness of sanctions, saying first that the mere expression of moral outrage is not sufficient justification. It is impossible to estimate the effect in political as well as economic terms.' The economy 'might survive in the short term for rather longer than was sometimes thought . . . (but) . . after a while the sanctions would be ·likely to bite very hard, and no SA Government would be able to ignore their effect in the framing of its policies.'

The report was cautious in its assessment of the effects of sanctions on the British economy. Estimates of job losses range from 26,000 to 120,000. The committee found it difficult to assess Black opinion on the merits of sanctions, but acknowledged that many Black South Africans are prepared to make sacrifices in order to achieve the end of apartheid.

It was three months before the British Government published its reply to the Foreign Affairs Committee report on 22 October. It agreed with only two points of substance in the report: Its warning that sanctions may not work; and that 'the onus for breaking the present deadlock rests with the SA Government.' For the rest it simply reaffirmed the tough stand taken by the Prime Minister at th Commonwealth meetings.

The Foreign Office published a confidential memorandum in August 1986 in which it reviewed the likely impact on British interests if further economic mea sures were taken against SA. It estimated that SA is the 17th largest market for UI exports, valued in 1985 at £1bn, and that the book value of UK direct investment in SA stood at c. £2bn, with an additional £6bn held in portfolio investments. But it said that the realizable value of all UK investments is much lower. The memoran dum also pointed out that given the relatively high percentage of UK exports to SA and the high level of UK investment there, Britain has more to lose than it competitors. All measures would be likely to damage the UK's extensive interest in SA and to reduce the value of its investments in that country. The banning of SA imports—largely raw materials and agricultural products could also cause consid erable problems, disrupting supplies to industry and consumers and forcing up prices. There could also be implications for employment in a wide range of industries. Retaliation by the SA Government 'could further exacerbate the effect on Britain and on the Frontline States. In any event the memorandum added th immediate impact of any measures would be likely to be reduced over time by offsetting policy measures in SA. Measures against trade in primary commodities if implemented by all SA's trading partners, would affect the Republic's produc tion, foreign exchange earnings and overwhelmingly, non-White employment. New inward investment to SA is already extremely limited.

Reviewing possible further measures the Foreign Office memorandum pointed out that a ban on air links with SA could not be enforced legally for over a year Revenue losses to British Airways, one of the major carriers could amount to ten of millions of pounds. A ban on the import of agricultural products could initially have a significant impact on the 1.25m non-White labourers and on agricultura export earnings but these could eventually be mitigated. Stopping new expor credit, however, could have a significant impact on economic growth and develop ment in SA, but important orders would be lost to the UK. A ban on steel import from SA would be evaded easily, but a halt to coal imports would represent a serious setback for the SA mining industry. Even so, the non-White workforce would bear the brunt of any resulting cutbacks

British public opinion showed an important swing in favour of tougher mea sures against SA.[179] An opinion poll in November 1985 showed that 42% of the British public thought the Government's policy on SA was 'not tough enough'. In May 1986 the poll showed that 46% were of this opinion, while in July the figure had risen to 56%. Of those polled, 65% expressed dissatisfaction with the way the Prime Minister was handling the SA issue.

ROLE OF THE EUROPEAN ECONOMIC COMMUNITY

The EEC members found themselves deeply divided over the question of sanc tions in 1985-86. The strongest supporters of sanctions were Holland, Denmark Ireland and Norway; the more cautious members were France, Luxembourg Belgium, Italy and Greece; the strongest antagonists were Britain, West Germany and Portugal.

In February 1986 the 12 EEC Foreign Ministers had a meeting in Harare with their counterparts from the six Frontline States. Their final communiqué failed to mention sanctions but affirmed that the EEC would consider further 'restrictive measures' on SA if the five demands agreed at the meeting were not met. These included a call on SA to dismantle apartheid; end the state of emergency in SA; release Nelson Mandela and other political prisoners; lift the ban on the Congress movements; and a call for Pretoria to open negotiations with the country's recognized Black leaders.

On the sidelines of the meeting, the British delegation for the first time had talks with the ANC. Sir Geoffrey Howe explained this departure from British policy as being useful to 'get across to them the case against violence and to underline the importance of the CEPG mission initiative.[180]

The European Commission made a political declaration in July 1985 in which it condemned the state of emergency in SA and expressed its 'total condemnation of the apartheid system in all its forms.'

The Commission called upon SA 'to change its attitude as quickly as possible otherwise economic sanctions, it believes, will become inevitable. The Community must, in the Commission's view prepare itself for this eventuality. . .'

In May 1986, the Commission condemned the attacks made by SA forces on Botswana, Zambia and Zimbabwe—three countries which are signatories of the EEC-ACP Lomé Convention. In the same statement, the Commission associated itself with the call for the release of Nelson Mandela and for real negotiations on the part of the Botha regime, 'with the true representatives of the SA people including those currently in prison.' The commission also expressed its deep dismay at the arrest of Father Mkhatshwa, general secretary of the SA Catholic Bishops Conference. It is very rare for the Commission—which is after all basically the manager of the Community's common trading market—to make statements about individual human rights cases, but it was felt that the situation inside SA had deteriorated so badly that silence on its part would be incomprehensible.

In September 1985, the European Council decided to implement a limited programme of positive and negative measures against SA. The negative measures—to be enacted by national governments themselves—took the form of minor sanctions, such as the recall of military attachés, an embargo on the sale of military equipment, the banning of trade in oil and nuclear materials etc. The positive measures included an aid package for 'non-violent anti-apartheid organizations' operating inside SA.' It was agreed that these funds (totalling £6m) would be distributed by the Commission and would principally benefit church groups and trade unions. The Commission undertook the distribution of these funds with Church leaders, including Father Mkhatshwa, and with representatives of Congress of South African Trade Unions (Cosatu) and the Council of Unions of South Africa (Cusa). The money will be made available for humanitarian, social welfare and education purposes.

This was the first time that any Commission had made such an unequivocal declaration about apartheid. In spite of the objections of some member Governments, the Commission continued to make statements consistent with this approach.

Of the EEC members only Holland, Ireland, Denmark and France had unilaterally imposed economic measures against SA by mid-1986.

The EEC first faced up to the question of sanctions seriously at a summit meeting in The Hague towards the end of June 1986 when the Dutch Prime Minister proposed a Community ban on the import of SA coal, iron, steel, wine, fruit and vegetables. The principal opposition to this proposal came from the British and the West Germans; Denmark, Greece, Ireland and Spain supported the principle of sanctions; Belgium, France and Italy were prepared to support limited action. Although no agreement was possible, support was promised for th proposed mission by the British Foreign Secretary to Pretoria (see above).

In August 1986 the European Commission published figures [181] which showe that Community imports of coal from SA in 1985 accounted for ECU1.271r (£875m) by value—between a fifth and a quarter of total EEC coal imports. Ital and France are SA's biggest customers for coal, followed by West Germany an Denmark. A ban on iron and steel imports, on the other hand, would be les serious from the Community's point of view. SA accounts for only ECU424m c the more than ECU10bn of imports into member-states. Germany with a ECU147r share is comfortably the biggest taker.

Krugerrands represent just over ECU142m of the total ECU404m imported b the EEC in 1985. The Germans, Belgians and Luxembourgers account for almos all the SA element, after Britain's unilateral ban. Total EEC gold imports from S were ECU1.74bn in 1985.

Total Community imports for SA (including Spain and Portugal) amounted t ECU9.1bn in 1985, with exports of ECU5.54bn.

Between 1980 and 1984 net new investment by EEC countries in SA (excludin Britain) rose from ECU337m to ECU482m. Direct investment by the UK (exclud ing oil companies) totalled ECU504m in 1983.

EEC-SOUTH AFRICA TRADE, 1985
(US$m)

	Total Imports	Imports from S.
Coal	4,226.4	969
Iron and Steel	7,687.9	324
Gold Coins	308.5	108.6

The Commonwealth mini-summit decisions faced the EEC with two options whether to support the major demand for a trade ban and a cut-off of airlinks witl SA, as agreed by the majority of Commonwealth members; or to agree with the most limited proposals of the British. The EEC Foreign Ministers faced thi challenge at their meeting in Brussels on 16 September 1986 where the Danes lee the demand for comprehensive sanctions. Agreement was finally reached on a limited package which included a ban on SA iron and steel, agricultural and frui imports. A ban on Krugerrands and the ending of new investments in SA wa delayed pending further studies. But no agreement was to be had over a ban o coal imports despite a strong demand by Britain for this action. Sir Geoffrey Howe admitted afterwards that the EEC package was not as effective as it would have been if the coal ban had been included. The Danes described the package a 'amputated'.[182]

The British Prime Minister and the West German Chancellor held bilateral talk in Bonn on the same day as the European Foreign Ministers were meeting ir Brussels. Both declared themselves opposed to sanctions. West Germany is SA' largest trading partner in the EEC. Austria, which is not a member of the EEC, announced a programme of sanctions in late September 1986 which included a ban on Krugerrands, on investment by the Government, and reduced sporting con- tacts. Another nonmember of the EEC, Sweden, has maintained trade and new investment bans for several years. Its Foreign Minister announced that Sweden would agree to comprehensive sanctions only if the decision was taken by the Security Council.

HE ROLE OF THE UNITED STATES

o single event exemplifies more clearly the extent to which SA had come to ominate the agenda of Western concerns in 1986 than the defeat of President eagan over sanctions at the hands of a Republican-dominated Senate—his first efeat on a foreign policy issue. Even two years ago few could have predicted that ae SA question would come to assume such a high profile in American politics— n issue, moreover, that united Republicans and Democrats in a rare display of ational consensus on a foreign policy issue that does not touch directly on the oviet Union or Cuba. Reagan's defeat on an issue about which he personally felt o strongly as to exercise a veto is not easily explained.

Moral outrage has seldom had a direct impact on major foreign policy deci- ions; yet a sense of moral outrage was certainly one of the factors that accounts r the stand taken by Congress against the President. But it was the canalization f this outrage into direct political action that made it an effective force. The credit r this success belongs largely to a broad network of interests loosely identified as ae Black Caucus. Yet it was not primarily the Black Caucus in Congress that took ae lead, but an array of small groups of activists such as those of Randell obinson's TransAfrica which evolved the strategy of mobilizing Black Americans ato active pressure groups. By making the Black vote count in Democratic olitics, pressures were mounted that resulted in city administrations and State egislatures adopting internal sanctions against American firms trading in SA hich became a cutting-edge against the Administration's policy of constructive ngagement.

Ethnic bloc parties is a well-established tradition in American politics. Ethnic ermans in the Midwest, the Irish in Boston and New York, the Italians and the ispanic community in Florida, but expecially the influential Jewish community ave at different times and on different issues affecting their ethnic sentiments all ucceeded in making their votes count in US domestic and foreign policies. lthough the Black American community first began to make its influence felt uring the struggle for civil rights in the 1960's, the first time it was mobilized on a reign policy issue was, not surprisingly, over the rights of Blacks in South Africa nd out of a sense of kindred spirit with the Frontline States' struggle in the region. his development was a new political phenomenon that developed with surprising peed in the course of a few years.

So long as constructive engagement—the policy originally devised by a com- aitted liberal Republican, Dr Chester Crocker,—could be presented as a credible pproach to the problems of Southern Africa, it could rely on a fair measure of upport—except from liberals who saw it as appeasement to the Right, and the far ight who saw it as appeasement of Left-wing radicals, communists and terrorists ngaged in undermining 'safe Western bastions' such as Southern Africa. What- ver its merits, and even achievements, the policy of constructive engagement lost redibility with the failure of the Western Contact Group to advance independence a Namibia, or to secure the withdrawal of Cuban troops from Angola, or to ersuade the Pretoria regime to release political prisoners like Nelson Mandela nd to open serious negotiations with representative Black leaders. Although the dministration was strongly committed to these objectives, neither the carrot nor ae stick approach of constructive engagment proved an effective instrument to ring any of these immediate objectives closer to realization. Impatience with onstructive engagement had spread from the ranks of Democrats into the ranks f Republicans themselves. Prominent Republicans like Senator Nancy Kas- ebaum, chairman of the Senate's Sub-Committee on Africa, became increasingly esty in their treatment of Chester Crocker at committee hearings.

Three other factors combined to change Congressional opinion. The first wa growing outrage at the repressive policies of the SA regime—especially over it decision to declare a state of national emergency in September 1985, detainin thousands of political opponents and imposing draconian press censorship; it refusal to release men like Nelson Mandela whose importance to any successfi process of negotiation had come to be recognized by all Western leaders, includin Reagan and Margaret Thatcher; and Botha's truculent attitude towards even sym pathetic Western leaders who had tried to persuade him to move faster toward sensible negotiations. American legislators were mostly inclined to be quiescer so long as the promise to phase out apartheid held out some hope of a peacefi transition to a different kind of society; but when the situation inside SA and in th region turned increasingly violent in 1985, they became more receptive to argt ments in favour of sanctions.

One factor that became crucial in finally persuading a majority of Republica Senators to abandon the President was the looming elections in November, wit the prospect that Black voters and liberal Republicans could tip the balance i marginal constituencies against incumbent Republican Senators with the possibl loss of the Republican majority in the Senate.

The last major factor was the successful disinvestment campaign which con plemented the boycott campaign aimed at City and State administrations. Th strategy of picking on individual firms with special interests in SA and mobilizin stockholders—especially universities and City administrations—to sell their stoc in companies that refused to disinvest from SA proved to be highly effective, bot in forcing company boards to look at the moral issues concerning their policie (not just in SA) and in politicizing public opinion.

The disinvestment campaign was greatly helped by the downturn in the S/ economy which made trading less profitable and more risky; instead of being on of the highest no-risk countries in the world, SA's risk factor came to be regarde as a high medium-term risk in 1985. These adverse economic conditions and wha businessmen came to speak of as the harassment factor produced by the disinvest ment campaign meant there was much less resistance by US firms to demands fo disinvestment.

The impact made by these various pressures on US firms with a stake in the S/ economy is shown in the increased radicalization of the policy of the Rev Leo Sullivan, author of the Fair Employment Code for American firms operating in SA In 1985 he won the support of subscribers to his Code for a programme calling o US firms to adopt a higher political profile in SA. But even such an unprecedente commitment by American businessmen to become directly and publicly involve in the politics of a foreign country (so different from the clandestine practices o some of the larger multinationals) came to be regarded as insufficient by Sullivar In May 1985 he announced that unless apartheid was brought to an end by the en of May 1988 his organization would demand a total pull-out by all US firms from SA.

Sanctions vs Constructive Engagement

A proper appreciation of the significance of the effective collapse of the policy o constructive engagement in 1986 requires a brief recounting of its history as set ou in a State Department document.

> Upon taking office in January 1981, the Reagan Administration determined to focu on the many threats to stability in Southern Africa. The Administration identified fou

major goals, all of them inter-related but centring on SA's 'morally abhorrent policy' of apartheid. We have sought to:
- Accelerate movement away from apartheid and toward a government based on consent of the governed;
- Diminish regional violence and develop an overall framework for regional security;
- Achieve independence for Namibia; and
- Reassert US influence in the region.

Our ability to play an active role in achieving these objectives depends in large measure on the ability of the US Government to work with a range of governments and movements in Southern Africa, from Marxist Angola to White-ruled SA, with liberation movements as varied as Swapo and Unita; and with the UN and our Western allies (Britain, France, West Germany, and Canada) in the Contact Group on Namibia. Only by being an interlocutor with all parties can we hope to influence the process of peace and nonviolent change. This often means eschewing public demonstrations against practices we abhor in favour of quiet, frank exchanges in diplomatic channels. It means working to create consensus on a framework for peace, stability, and respect for territorial integrity and lending support to countries and leaders willing to commit themselves to these processes. It means painstaking, often slow, and meticulous progress on detailed arrangements and interim steps toward these objectives, without the rewards of dramatic (but unrealistic) break-throughs, yet with the knowledge that only a steady, resolute course of action can achieve peaceful change.

The US is uniquely suited to play this difficult role. As leader of the free world, we are vitally concerned about peace and economic development in Southern Africa. And as a society that has worked to resolve its own racial problems with humanity and justice, the US has earned the confidence of many Black African nations.

The campaign for sanctions and disinvestment posed a direct challenge to the Administration's policy of constructive engagement; to save its policy required of Reagan that he should be able to defeat the call for sanctions since his policy required as a pre-requisite for its success that the US should retain at least its potential for influencing Pretoria—which required direct access to President Botha. By the same argument the US needed to retain direct access to Angola's President, which was seriously jeopardized by the decision to support Unita with arms. This was the view taken by the State Department which, though it went along with repeal of the Clark Amendment, fought hard to stop Congress from supporting Unita with arms. As late as September 1985, Chester Crocker was still insisting that despite the repeal of the Clark Amendment 'we have no plans in regard to assistance for Unita.'[183] The State Department lost that fight for two reasons. First, because the Conservative Caucus and its allies succeeded in linking Unita's struggle to that of the Contras in Nicaragua, the Afghanistan mujaddihin and other similar movements identified as offering resisting 'the spread of international communism'. By directly linking support for Contras (which had enjoyed a measure of support from Democrats as well as Republicans) to aid for Unita, it became possible to build up a majority in Congress for such a programme. This world view of the threat of international communism reflected precisely Reagan's own world view, as shown by his statement during Savimbi's visit when he received Savimbi in January 1986.[184]

But although the State Department failed to persuade the White House to behave consistently in implementing its policy of constructive engagement, it had a small but not really a significant success in getting Reagan to use his influence to stop Congress committing the Administration to a specific programme of aid to Unita, leaving it free to provide clandestine support. But it was a funny kind of clandestine operation that was openly admitted by the White House and enthusiastically trumpeted by Savimbi. Although President dos Santos reacted angrily to this change in American policy, he did not immediately break off further negotiations—and even when Luanda announced that its door was closed because of the regime's vulnerable position it still expressed a wish to maintain contacts with Washington. However, the former *esprit* was lost.

One curious feature of the policies of the Conservative Caucus which lobbied successfully for Unita is that it failed to interest itself seriously in supporting the opposition to the Marxist regime of Ethiopia where there is a greater threat of spreading Soviet influence than anywhere else in the African continent.

The Sanctions Campaign

A fundamental of US policy towards SA was that 'economic growth has been—and will continue to be—a principal engine of constructive change.' However, successive US Administrations accepted the need for specific, limited sanctions as a means of exerting pressure on SA. The progressive increase in the programme of sanctions since 1963 is shown in the following record:

• US arms sales to SA were embargoed in 1963, and in 1977 the US joined the UN in imposing a mandatory arms embargo on SA. US regulations are, in fact, more severe than the UN embargo, and restrict US exports to the SA military and police of items not covered in the UN embargo.

• In December 1984, the US joined with other UN Security Council members in voting for an embargo on imports of arms and ammunition manufactured in SA.

• The US Export-Import Bank (Eximbank) is essentially prohibited from financing US sales to SA.

• The US Overseas Private Investment Corporation (OPIC) does not provide guarantees on private US investments in SA.

• US trade fairs do not travel to SA.

• The US representative at the IMF is required to 'actively oppose any facility involving use of fund credit by any country which practices apartheid.'

• The Reagan Administration has followed a policy of prohibiting the sale of computers to the SA military, police, or other entities involved in enforcing apartheid laws.

• In the area of nuclear technology, the US has approved for export to SA only unclassified, non-sensitive items for use in fully safeguarded civil facilities. No US help has been given to weapons-related nuclear research in SA.

• On 9 September 1985 President Reagan signed an Executive Order providing for a range of new measures against SA in the hope of heading off a Congress demand for a much tougher programme. What is frequently overlooked is the preamble to the Order which 'declared a national emergency to deal with the threat posed by the policies and actions of the Government of SA to the foreign policy and economy of the US.' The Order prohibited the following transactions:

(1) The making or approval of bank loans to the SA Government, with certain narrow exceptions.

(2) The export of computers and related goods and technology to certain government agencies and any apartheid enforcing entity of the SA Government.

(3) Nuclear exports to SA and related transactions, with certain narrow exceptions.

(4) The import into the US of arms, ammunition, or military vehicles produced in SA.

(5) The extension of export marketing support to US firms employing at least 25 persons in SA which do not adhere to certain fair labour standards.

(6) The Secretary of State and the US Trade Representative were directed to

consult with other parties to GATT with a view toward adopting a prohibition on the import of Krugerrands.

(7) The Secretary of the Treasury was also directed to complete a study within 60 days regarding the feasibility of minting US gold coins.

(8) The Secretary of State was directed to take the steps necessary to increase the amounts provided for scholarships in SA for those disadvantaged by the system of apartheid and to increase the amounts allocated for SA to establish an Advisory Committee to provide recommendations on measures to encourage peaceful change in SA.

Reagan's Executive Order of September 1985 failed to placate Congress whose demand for tougher sanctions continued to attract increasingly wider support. In June 1986 the House of Representatives adopted a Bill calling for a trade embargo and complete disinvestment by US companies. The White House's reaction to this vote was given in a statement by the US ambassador to the UN, Gen Vernon Walters, at a press conference in Brussels on 10 July in which he promised that the Administration's policy of opposing mandatory sactions 'is not going to change.' A fortnight later, after a meeting with the British Prime Minister, Reagan declared that she was right to denounce 'the international clamour for punitive sanctions against SA as immoral and utterly repugnant.' When a leading Republican Senator, Robert Dole, asked Reagan 'what the hell does constructive engagement mean', the President replied:[185]

> It means that we're not going to turn our back on SA; we're going to stay there and talk to them. If we were to pull our ambassador out, put sanctions on them and the like, we're not a player. We have to sit at the table and deal, even though we may not like what is happening on the other side of the table.

The Administration showed its increasing concern about the challenge developing in Congress when it announced in July 1986 that it was undertaking a major review of its policy towards SA. Expectations that this would lead to substantial changes in US policy were dampened by Reagan's speech on 23 July at the conclusion of the review.[186] (For details of his speech see below.) His emphasis was on moral persuasion rather than further sanctions in order to achieve the following goals: A timetable to end apartheid; the freeing of political prisoners, including Nelson Mandela; and the start of a White–Black dialogue. Reagan declared:

> The US cannot maintain cordial relations with a Government whose power rests upon the denial of rights to a majority of its people based upon race.

SA's Foreign Minister said his Government's reaction to Reagan's speech was 'mixed'. It was encouraged by Reagan's acknowledgment that 'dramatic changes' had been brought about, and his realization that SA's problems were complex. While SA was willing to discuss the 'realization of Western ideals for the country', he warned against outside interference in its internal affairs. Nevertheless, the SA Government felt that 'fruitful discussions could be held with the US Administration and other Governments about the real situation in Southern Africa.'[187]

African leaders' reaction to Reagan's speech was harsh. The OAU Council of Ministers adopted a resolution denouncing his speech and reiterating its demand for mandatory sanctions. The ANC described the speech as 'the new characteristic and hypocritical condemnation of apartheid while at the same time giving the usual support and comfort to the apartheid regime by refusing to accede to the

demands of the oppressed people of SA for the imposition of comprehensiv
mandatory sanctions.'[188] It called on Reagan to listen to the voice of the America
people on this issue.

The campaign favouring sanctions built up to a climax in mid-1986 whe
committees of the two Houses of Congress met to reach agreement on a packag
of sanctions that was likely to win a decisive majority in the Senate; this require
diluting some of the proposals adopted by the House of Representatives. Th
presidents of 95 colleges sent a letter to Congressmen urging support for stron
sanctions which would 'convey more than anything else the breadth and depth o
national feeling against apartheid.' About 200 representatives of churches, civi
groups and trade unions held a vigil outside the Senate on 29 July to show suppo
for comprehensive sanctions against SA. The meeting was organized by th
Washington Office on Africa, a 14-year-old lobbying and research group.

Senator Richard Lugar, the Republican chairman of the Senate Foreign Rela
tions Committee—normally a firm supporter of Reagan on foreign policy issues—
stressed the importance of getting agreement on a sanctions package that woul
command the support of two-thirds of the Senate in order to override a presiden
tial veto which he anticipated was inevitable.

The aim of a two-third majority of the Senate was achieved in September: 84 ou
of 100 Senators voted in favour of a Bill which included a ban on new U
investment in SA; an end to some imports of SA steel and other products
restricting US visas to South Africans; freezing SA accounts in US banks; and
ban on landing rights by SA Airways. On 12 September the House of Representa
tives accepted the compromise Bill by a massive 308-77 votes. As expected, th
President vetoed the Bill on 28 September declaring that:

> The sweeping and punitive sanctions adopted by the Congress are targeted d
> rectly at the labour intensive industries upon which the victimized peoples of S
> depend for their very survival. Black workers—the first victims of apartheid—woul
> become the first victims of American sanctions.

The President's veto was promptly overridden by more than the two-third vot
required in the Senate. The President was therefore compelled to put his signatur
to a set of sanctions which only two months earlier he had described as 'immor
and utterly repugnant.'The new sanctions restricted US visas to South Africans
froze South African accounts in American banks; embargoed goods produced b
SA government-owned industries; and ended landing rights for SA airlines at U
airports.

American legislators did not deceive themselves into believing that their actio
would necessarily produce the changes they hoped for in SA but, as Senato
Nancy Kassebaum explained:[189]

> Nearly all of us would agree that sanctions are not going to do anything to chang
> the SA government's policies, but I think that those of us in the House of Representa
> tives and Senate who have come to support sanctions felt . . . that this was a
> expression of our frustration with the intransigence of the SA Government. Othe
> than the support that we give to strengthening the countries in the Frontline areas,
> think that is the most constructive approach we can take at this point.

US Policy Towards South Africa

The US recognizes that its influence on SA is 'at the margins, but it is there, an
we are determined to use it.' This statement by Chester Crocker sums up Wash

ington's view of its role in SA. The question that has confronted US policy-makers is what Americans can do to avoid what the Secretary of State, George Shultz, described as 'the mounting tragedy in SA', and how to stop 'the violence and destruction apartheid generates, and about the spillover effects of SA's trauma on its many neighbours.'[190] He described SA as 'a society ruled by fear. Fear on the part of the Whites that their property and their values will be destroyed if Blacks attain real political power; fear on the part of Blacks that they will be subjected to even greater violence and repression; and despair that their legitimate grievances will ever be redressed.' After the mid-1986 review of US policy towards South Africa, Reagan summed up its main conclusions:

> The primary victims of an economic boycott of SA would be the very people we seek to help. Most of the workers who would lose jobs because of sanctions would be Black workers. We do not believe the way to help the people of SA is to cripple the economy upon which they and their families depend for survival. . . .
>
> Wherever Blacks seek equal opportunity, higher wages, better working conditions, their strongest allies are the American, British, French, German, and Dutch businessmen who bring to SA ideas of social justice formed in their own countries. If disinvestment is mandated, these progressive Western forces will depart and SA proprietors will inherit, at fire sale prices, their farms and factories, plants and mines. How would this end apartheid? . . .
>
> Our own experience teaches us that racial progress comes swiftest and easiest, not during economic depression, but in times of prosperity and growth. Our own history teaches us that capitalism is the natural enemy of such feudal institutions as apartheid.
>
> Nevertheless, we share the outrage Americans have come to feel.
>
> In defending their society and people, the SA Government has a right and responsibility to maintain order in the face of terrorists. But by its tactics, the Government is only accelerating the descent into blood-letting. Moderates are being trapped between the intimidation of radical youths and counter-gangs of vigilantes. And the Government's state of emergency went beyond the law of necessity. It, too, went outside the law by sweeping up thousands of students, civic leaders, church leaders and labour leaders, thereby contributing to further radicalization. Such repressive measures will bring SA neither peace nor security. . . .
>
> SA is a complex and diverse society in a state of transition. More and more South Africans have come to recognize that change is essential for survival. The realization has come hard and late; but the realization has finally come to Pretoria that apartheid belongs to the past.
>
> In recent years, there has been dramatic change. Black workers have been permitted to unionize, bargain collectively, and build the strongest free trade union movement in all Africa. The infamous pass laws have been ended, as have many of the laws denying blacks the right to live, work, and own property in SA's cities. Citizenship, wrongly stripped away, has been restored to nearly six million blacks. Segregation in universities and public facilities is being set aside. Social apartheid laws prohibiting interracial sex and marriage had been struck down. Indeed, it is because State President Botha has presided over these reforms that extremists have denounced him as a traitor. . . .
>
> It is tragic that in the current crisis social and economic progress has been arrested. Yet, in contemporary SA—before the state of emergency—there was a broad measure of freedom of speech, of the Press, and of religion there. Indeed, it is hard to think of a single country in the Soviet bloc—or many in the United Nations—where political critics have the same freedom to be heard, as did outspoken critics of the SA Government.
>
> But, by Western standards, SA still falls short, terribly short, on the scales of economic and social justice. SA's actions to dismantle apartheid must not end now. The state of emergency must be lifted. There must be an opening of the political process. That the Black people of SA should have a voice in their own governance is

439

an idea whose time has come. There can be no turning back. In the multiracial society that is SA, no single race can monopolize the reins of political power. . . .

Many Americans, understandably, ask: Given the racial violence, the hatred, why not wash our hands and walk away from that tragic continent and bleeding country? The answer is: We cannot.

In Southern Africa, our national ideals and strategic interests come together. SA matters because we believe that all men are created equal, and are endowed by their creator with unalienable rights. SA matters because of who we are. One of eight Americans can trace his ancestry to Africa.

Strategically, this is one of the most vital regions of the world. Around the Cape of Good Hope passes the oil of the Persian Gulf—which is indispensable to the industrial economies of Western Europe. Southern Africa and SA are repositories of many of the vital minerals—vanadium, manganese, chromium, platinum—for which the West has no other secure source of supply. . . .

Apartheid threatens our vital interests in Southern Africa, because it is drawing neighbouring States into the vortex of violence. Repeatedly, within the last 18 months, SA forces have struck into neighbouring states. I repeat our condemnation of such acts.

William B. Robertson, Deputy Assistant Secretary of State for African Affairs, reiterated that SA's future 'rest with the Nelson Mandelas and those others incarcerated at the present time. They must be freed to sit at the negotiating table to hammer out a solution that will end apartheid.'[191] In July 1986 George Shultz told the Senate Foreign Relations Committee he was willing to meet the ANC president, Oliver Tambo, despite the Administration's disapproval of violence.

Throughout 1985 and 1986, the State Department made statements condemnatory of SA policies. Among a number of such statements were the following:

• In December 1985 SA's military raid into Angola was denounced, and described as a probable violation of international law.

• In July 1986 the State Department criticized measures imposed on SA's school system. It said that such 'regulations may succeed in the short run, but will not eradicate the underlying causes of the unrest. . . ."

• In August 1986 the State Department regretted SA's decision to apply economic sanctions against its neighbours.

• A dark view of SA's future was presented in August 1986 by Robert C. McFarlane, a former Assistant for National Security Affairs to the President: [192]

> It is entirely plausible that by this time next year tens of thousands of South Africans will have been killed as the current bloody impasse degenerates into a civil war. Faced with that prospect it is a telling comment on the health of the American political system that the leaders of the Left, the Centre and the Right seem devoted not to helping to solve the problem but to assuring that their moralistic positions are properly recorded for history.
>
> Even those who call for economic sanctions concede that such pressure is unlikely to have much effect on SA policy. But they say, 'at least we stood for what is right.' Meanwhile, people keep dying.
>
> At the same time, Americans of the Right go on putting forth platitudes about 'staying engaged' while refusing to acknowledge the bad faith with which the past efforts to help have been met by SA leaders. And in the face of these stonewalling tactics by Pretoria there has been no willingness to raise the stakes in a serious way against people who are clearly mean-spirited and brutal.
>
> To be fair, the fatalistic gloom that dominates American opinion derives from some stark realities. The Boers are a stubborn people and dispose of the economic and military strength to defend their position for years while inflicting staggering casualties. And the US simply does not possess credible sticks to use with the carrots of

diplomacy. If every American businessman pulled out of SA tomorrow, it would affect no more than 3% of the gross national product. Some qualified observers believe that SA could withstand a total global trade embargo for three to four years, so great is its self-sufficiency in agricultural commodities, oil reserves and so on. And SA is a net exporter of weapons producing all its needs in the way of artillery, missiles and even combat helicopters.

One thing is clear. It is time that we in the West realize that we are contributing by default to an inexorable movement toward genocide. And as SA goes down into chaos so will the six countries around it, as their trading lifelines are choked off.

We in the West, as well as the people of SA, will be the losers. We have enormous interest in SA remaining independent of Soviet influence, and the Soviets, with their strong position in Angola, are well-placed to exploit turmoil.

Finally, we do have a moral obligation to try where possible to influence change in peaceful directions.

Where does all this point? First, it would seem reasonable for the US to seek to convene a conference with those whose leverage and experience with SA are stronger—European and Commonwealth countries. Prime Minister Bob Hawke of Australia could host such a conference.

The first purpose would be to try to forge consensus on the dimensions of the West's strategic interest, the weakness of the internal leadership and the potential utility of an outside mission presenting its good offices.

The second goal would be to impanel a negotiating team, headed by a distinguished expert and backed by a mandate from the assembled countries. The team would present its good offices to the SA Government and to the Black leaders and seek to engage both sides in sustained negotiations to bridge political and economic gaps.

To be effective such a mission would need to be armed not only with good will and diplomatic skill; it would have to be in a position to use the enormous economic leverage that exists among Commonwealth countries plus West Germany, France and the Netherlands. Also, it would have to be prepared to stay for the duration—until peace was achieved, and not merely to 'find facts' for a few weeks and go home.

Whoever is sent should be armed with carrots as well as sticks.

US Role in Angola and Mozambique

Chester Crocker told the Senate Foreign Relations panel on 18 February 1986 that US policy had not changed in Angola despite the decision to provide aid to Dr Jonas Savimbi's Unita:

> I want categorically to state here that the basis of our and goals of our policy remains unchanged: we seek a negotiated solution that will bring independence to Namibia and withdrawal of Cuban forces from Angola. Such a solution opens the way for Angolans to reconcile and achieve peace.

But while the goals of US policy may not have changed, the decision to intervene directly in Angola's civil war by voting military and economic aid to one side did mark a crucial departure of policy. The means for achieving the declared objectives robbed the US of its role as an impartial mediator in the region's conflicts.

In his testimony to the Senate panel justifying aid to Unita, Crocker said the Administration wished to make it clear 'that we support those who fight for freedom and political solutions.'

This decision to support, selectively, 'freedom fighters' around the world has been described as 'the new globalism' of the Reagan Administration. Tony Lewis viewed this as the 'most important conceptual movement in American foreign policy in years.'[193] Lewis described this concept, deriving from the 'ideological Right', as meaning that:

> The US should intervene in wars in the Third World whenever there is a chance to fight Soviet or Marxist influence. It should do so all around the world, without regard to particular local conditions. Constraints on American power, too, must yield to the ideological imperative.

One aspect of this globalist concept is that, wherever it seems the Soviets are likely to remove a pro-Western ally, counter-measures must be taken to maintain the present balance. This was precisely the position taken by Crocker in his testimony to the Senate panel:

> This past year we have seen the MPLA Government, strongly backed by Moscow and Havana, pursue as escalation of the war. They sought to reverse two years of Unita gains and deal a body blow to that movement. They failed. It is important in our view that they continue to fail.

Crocker went even further in a speech he delivered to the American Legion on 24 February 1986:

> We do not intend to see Dr Savimbi and his Unita forces overrun by Soviet-backed armed aggressive elements. We will help Dr Savimbi in ways which we feel are appropriate, relevant and effective in terms of his needs.

The near-success of the MPLA in dealing a body blow to Unita in August-September 1985 was prevented only because of SA intervention, (see above). Instead of leaving it to SA to continue to defend Unita's position, the US decided to make its own contribution towards ensuring that Unita's position should remain impregnable.

As already described, this was not always the policy of the State Department since it ran counter to the policy of constructive engagement. It was forced to change its position only when a majority evolved in Congress which, having successfully moved to repeal the Clark Amendment in July 1985, favoured direct and open aid for Unita.

The Congress majority evolved in a way peculiar to American politics. It was due to an alliance between a relatively liberal Congressman like Claude Pepper and Right-wing Republicans and Democrats. Pepper, a Southern politician with a sound record on civil rights, was persuaded to adopt a pro-Unita position by the Cuban American National Foundation, which is part of an interlocking web of conservative groups who pumped a great deal of money into a lobbying effort on behalf of Unita. The Foundation's interest in supporting Unita is explained by its concern with the presence of Cuban combat troops in Angola; and Pepper's interest in the Foundation was that 40% of his Florida constituency are Cubans. This remarkable criss-crossing of interests helped to shape the shift in American foreign policy. But the strength of the lobby was naturally helped by the fact that its basic aims reflected the gut feelings of a President whose pledge to the Republicans was that 'we will stand a lonely vigil to guard the gates of freedom.' This high-flown rhetoric has translated into the 'new globalism', with the US once again returning to an earlier role as the world's policeman—a world in which the cops are the free nations and the robbers are the Marxists and communists.

However, beyond this over-simplified view of the world, there remains a sober realistic assessment of the actual power relations in Angola as seen by the State Department—the permanent enemy of the Ideological Right. Crocker told the Senate panel in his February 1986 testimony:

> It remains our analysis that neither the SA Government nor the Angola Government nor Swapo nor Unita can accomplish their goals through outright military victory. The only ones to benefit by continued warfare are the Soviets and Cubans. Hence the continuing relevance of a political framework.

On a later occasion, in his address to the American Legion on 24 February 1986, Crocker said the Administration's assessment agreed with Savimbi's own assessment 'that there can be no military victory for any party in Angola', and that the MPLA Government will be 'obliged to negotiate with him on the issue of an ultimate power-sharing in Angola. We, too, support that goal.' Crocker did not accept the view that US support for Unita damaged the political framework of negotiations with Angola. In his opinion the MPLA Government would be forced to continue to negotiate with and through Washington because it badly needs the support the US can give in trying to evolve solutions in Southern Africa.

The differences between the White House and State Department, on the one side, and Congress on the other about committing 30m for military and other aid to Unita is described above in the section on Namibia and Angola.

ROLE OF THE SOVIET BLOC

Soviet bloc's inteventionist policies in Southern Africa have been confined largely to military support for the Angolan regime and for Swapo and the ANC—policies which have, the approval of the FLS as well as of many other OAU member-states. While Pretoria continues to see the Soviets as the major threat in the region, the Western countries, including the US, are inclined to take a less serious view of the potential USSR intervention in the region (see above).

The most significant political action by Moscow in 1986 was its warning to the Pretoria regime published in *Tass* in June that its attack on a Cuban and two Soviet merchant ships in Namibia, 'cannot be left unpunished.' (See Angola; above). It declared that Pretoria faced 'far-reaching and dangerous consequences because of its actions', and concluded with an attack on the US for its 'patronage of SA.'[194] In 1985 Moscow had taken the unusual step of having a meeting with a SA diplomat to warn Pretoria of the risks of its policy in attacking Angola.

Beginning in 1985, the Soviet bloc countries sharply increased their military aid programme to the MPLA. US and SA sources agreed that by early 1986 an additional $2bn worth of Soviet material and military aircraft had been shipped to Angola. The shipments included more Mig 23s, Sukhov fighters, helicopter gunships and tanks. At least 1,000 Soviet military advisers were reported to be in Angola. Dr Savimbi claimed that Soviet and Cuban military pesonnel were involved for the first time in the major offensive launched by Fapla against Unita in September 1985 (see Angola, above). He claimed that Soviet tactical commanders as well as Cubans were involved as drivers of tanks and in support of Fapla brigades.[195] In March 1986. SA military intelligence claimed that a group of Soviet Mig 23 fighters had moved into southern Angola in preparation for the anticipated new offensive against Unita which never eventuated.

Soviet and US officials held two meetings in 1986 to discuss regional conflicts in Southern Africa. At the first meeting in Geneva on 6 March, Chester Crocker had talks with Vladilen Vasev, chief of the Third African Department of the Soviet

Foreign Ministry. The meeting was in accordance with an agreement at the November 1985 summit meeting between Reagan and Gorbachev that there should be discussions on developments in Southern Africa. At the meeting Vasev voiced Soviet concern about the American decision to aid Unita.[196] A second meeting on regional issues of mutual concern to the Super-powers was held in Washington between the Soviet Deputy Foreign Minister, Anatoly Adamischin, and the US Under-Secretary for Political Affairs, Michael Armacost. While the Soviets were said to be keen to discuss the regional problems in Southern Africa, the US was keener to talk about Afghanistan and Kampuchea.[197] These talks were said to be in preparation for the next summit between Reagan and Gorbachev. Thus, the issue of Southern Africa has come to figure more prominently on the agenda of the Super-powers.

Crocker said in July 1986 that while there was 'no question' about the USSR seeking to exploit the situation in SA, this was primarily done through 'channels of disinformation and military aid diplomacy.'[198] He added: 'I don't think that we would want to say that the troubles inside SA have been caused by external factors . . . The troubles inside SA reflect the reality of apartheid and the growing Black rejection of apartheid and the Government's effort to deal with this rejection by trying to break the back of Black movements.'

The US Information Agency's journal, *Problems of Communism,* took the view that while Soviet security interests in Southern Africa have been peripheral to Soviet global security interests, Southern Africa has been 'central to Moscow's image in the Third World.[199] It continued:

The joint Soviet–Cuban intervention in Angola in 1975-76, more than any other Soviet foreign venture, became a symbol of the USSR's willingness and capability to project power to distant shores in support of its friends. This event, coming as it did on the heels of Washington's recognition of Moscow's military parity and Super-power status during the early 1970s, transcended its African context; it marked the emergence of the Soviet Union as a global power claiming the rights and perquisites of its new status. It also reinforced Moscow's view of the region as yet another arena in the East–West competition. With the intervention in Angola, the USSR has established itself as an important actor in Southern Africa, principally by providing military assistance. The development of arms supply relationships with Angola, Mozambique, Tanzania, and Zambia (who are among the so-called Front-line States), as well as support for insurgents in Rhodesia, Namibia and SA, has underscored the growing role of the Soviet Union in the region.

In the 1980s, however, the USSR has had to deal with several setbacks and dilemmas. Its relations with Tanzania and Zambia have leveled off, and Robert Mugabe's electoral victory in 1980 over Moscow's preferred candidate, Joshua Nkomo, has limited its opportunities in independent Zimbabwe. More important, the pro-Soviet governments in Angola and Mozambique, both of which are facing deteriorating security situations, signed disengagement and non-aggression accords with SA, in February and March 1984, respectively. They have also sought closer economic and diplomatic relations with the West. . . .

To put Moscow's current involvement in Southern Africa in a proper perspective, one should briefly examine general Soviet objectives there and the resources committed to their pursuit. Soviet policy is determined by a number of goals which have remained unchanged since the late 1950s. Moscow aims to:

• supplant or undermine US, West European and Chinese influence in the region in the political, economic, and military spheres;
• promote pro-Soviet or Leftist change corresponding to the broad ideological imperatives or Marxism–Leninism; this bolsters Moscow's claim that 'the world correlation of forces' is shifting in its favour;
• reinforce its Super-power status and perceived indispensability in settling major

international disputes by having a role in the resolution of problems in Southern Africa;
- obtain air and naval access to counter US strategic forces, monitor US military activity, and transport assistance to friendly regimes in the region;
- win the African States' political support for its initiatives in international forums.

While Moscow's long-term objectives may also include the obstruction or denial to the West of access to Southern Africa's mineral resources, Soviet behavior to date does not suggest the existence of either any immediate plans to exploit possible Western vulnerability in this respect, or a long-term strategy of denial.

Moscow's pursuit of these objectives is enhanced by a number of factors. The availability of allies, in this case the Cubans and East Europeans, has enabled it to play a role in the region without necessarily committing its own personnel and resources. The Soviet Union itself has the capability to provide weaponry quickly and inexpensively, taking advantage of the Africans' security concerns. The Soviet ideological blueprint for action and organization appeals to newly-independent States whose leaderships are in the process of consolidating their power. The appeals of ties to Moscow is further strengthened by the Black Africans' perceptions of close relations between Washington and Pretoria.

ROLE OF CUBA

The Cuban combat troops, generally accepted as having been increased to 30,000 in 1985, continued to be a central issue in the negotiations over Namibian independence. The Cubans, who had not been directly involved in confronting the SADF in previous years, were alleged to have participated in the offensive against Unita in September 1985 (see Angola, above). At the conclusion of the 10th meeting of the Cuban–Angolan Commission for Cooperation in April 1986, Jorge Risquet Valdes, Cuba's Vice-President, member of the Politburo and secretary of the Communist Party, announced a decision to 'strengthen our cooperation' in response to 'Yankee imperialism's' decision to aid the counter-revolutionary forces of Unita.[200] He said this naturally included cooperation 'in the field of defence.'

The US decision to give aid to Unita was vigorously attacked in a resolution adopted by the Cuban Communist Party congress in February 1986 which declared that the US was trying to apply its 'big stick' in Southern Africa. While seeking agreement between SA and Angola, it was at the same time giving 'firm support to the Pretoria regime in an attempt to win agreement to the withdrawal of Cuban forces.'[201]

The London *Observer* reported on 24 November 1985 that a senior Havana, official had told its reporters that Cuba was seeking Soviet approval to issue a formal declaration of war against SA in order to turn the struggle against Pretoria 'into an international crusade such as that fought against Hitler.' On the following day the Cuban Foreign Ministry issued a denial, saying the report was baseless and 'sheer fantasy'. It added that the 'moribund Pretoria regime' was already on the point of defeat by the internal Black forces so that 'it is not necessary to wage a war against SA to eliminate apartheid.'[202] A similarly optimistic note was struck by Cuba's Foreign Minister at the non-aligned summit in Harare in August 1986. He said: 'I believe that the presence of Internationalist Cuban fighters in Angola will not continue for very long.'[203]

ROLE OF CHINA

China continued to maintain a relatively low profile in Southern Africa. Although it was reputed to have favoured the PAC above ANC in the past, the Chinese welcomed a visit to Peking by Oliver Tambo. In June 1986, the Chinese staged a rally of 1,000 people in Peking in support of the Namibian independence struggle.

Swapo's leader, Sam Nujoma, was the guest of honour. Among those attending the rally were Gen Biao, vice-chairman of the National People's Congress, and Zhou Peiyuan, Vice-Chairman of the National Committee of the People's Consultative Conference. Zhou promised that the Chinese would 'consistently provide many-sided support to Swapo and the Namibian people.' Nujoma thanked China for its 'concrete material assistance.'

China also routinely attacked SA's trans-border raids.

ROLE OF THE NON-ALIGNED NATIONS

Both at its summit meeting in Harare in August 1986 and at the preliminary meeting of Foreign Ministers in Luanda in September 1985, the non-aligned nations gave firm support to the liberation movements in Southern Africa, specifically mentioning the PAC as well as the ANC and Swapo. The "Luanda Declaration'[204] affirmed that it would be impossible to achieve peace and stability in Southern Africa until apartheid is completely eliminated. It called on the Security Council to impose mandatory sanctions against SA, and 'noted with satisfaction the increased armed struggle.' It condemned Washington's 'intervention in Angola's internal affairs', and demanded the immediate withdrawal of all SADF men from Angolan territory.

NOTES

1. All references to country surveys and essays are to the *Africa Contemporary Record (ACR)*, 1985–86.
2. SA Broadcasting Corporation (SABC), Johannesburg, 15 October 1986.
3. Colin and Margaret Legum, *South Africa: Crisis for the West*, Pall Mall, London, 1964.
4. For details of this study see R. H. Green's essay on SADCC.
5. Ibid.
6. For details see chapter on Namibia.
7. *Gdn*, 10 January 1986.
8. SAPA, 5 March 1986.
9. SAPA, 8 March 196.
10. See essay on Portugal's year in Africa.
11. See *ACR*, 1984-85.
12. *FT*, 19 September 1985.
13. See chapter on Angola.
14. See Michael Hornsby, *The Times*, London, 27 August 1986.
15. SABC, 6 September 1985.
16. *The Star*, Johannesburg, 30 May 1986.
17. SAPA, 5 October 1985.
18. Capital Radio, Umtata, 4 July 1986.
19. See Jonathan Friedland, *Gdn*, 2 September 1986.
20. *The Times*, 23 September 1985 and SABC, 20 September 1985.
21. See Allister Sparks, *WM*, 11 October 1985.
22. *IHT*, 2-3 August 1986.
23. *DT*, 25 September 1985.
24. *NYT*, 29 October 1985.

25. *WP*, 23 October 1985.
41. For text of Nkomati Accord, see *ACR*, 1983-84, ppA12ff.
42. *DT*, 26 August 1986.
43. See Robert Jaster, *South Africa and Its Neighbours, the Dynamics of Regional Conflict*, Adelphi Papers 209, 1986, International Institute for Strategic Studies, London.
44. *Weekly Mail, (WM)* Johannesburg; 14 June 1986.
45. *FT*, 26 August 1986.
46. For details see chapter on Zimbabwe.
47. See Johnson and Martin (eds), *Destructive Engagement: Southern Africa at War*, Zimbabwe Publishing House, Harare, 1986.
48. *The Star*, Johannesburg, 9 October 1985.
49. SA Press Association (SAPA), 18 September 1985.
50. *The Star*, 9 October 1985.
51. *Sunday Tribune*, Durban, 6 October 1985.
52. *FM*, 18 October 1985.
53. *The Star*, 8 October 1985.
54. Radio Maputo (RM), 18 October 1985
55. *Gdn*, 7 December 1985.
56. Radio Lisbon, 14 April 1986.
57. See Mozambique chapter under Foreign Affairs.
58. *RM*, 29 August 1986.
59. *FT*, 9 May 1986.

60. SAPA, 4 May 1986.
61. SAPA, 18 June 1986.
62. Gdn, 10 June 1986.
63. Capital Radio, Umtata, 4 June 1986.
64. SAPA, 25 July 1986.
65. *RM*, 15 August 1986.
66. *DT*, 26 August 1986.
67. See essay on the OAU's year in Africa.
68. *IHT*, 27 August 1986.
69. *RM*, 16 September 1985.
70. Radio Luanda (RL), 9 April 1986.
71. *The Times*, 19 June 1986.
72. Radio Dar es Salaam (RDS), 14 July 1986.
73. Radio Nairobi (RN), 15 July 1986.
74. RL, 21 August 1986.
75. *IHT*, 25 August 1986.
76. *RL*, 22 August 1986.
77. For details of the advisors report, see Reginald Green's essay on SADCC in ACR, 1985-86.
78. *RM*, 16 September 1986; RAA, 24 May 1986.
79. PANA, 27 May 1986.
80. SAPA, 4 July 1986.
81. Radio Tehran, 18 June 1986.
82. *AE*, February 1986.
83. *The Times*, 9 June 1986.
84. Radio Lagos, 16 June 1986. For details see chapter on Angola.
85. See Tony Hodges, *FT*, 4 August 1986.
86. See interview with Jim Hoagland, *WP*, 25 October 1985.
87. *The Times*, 30 November 1985.
88. Angola Press Agency (ANGOP), 25 November 1985.
89. *IHT*, 28 November 1985.
90. See State Department Press Briefing, 12 December 1985.
91. *IHT*, 10 January 1986.
92. *IHT*, 6 February 1986.
93. *Gdn*, 15 February 1986.
94. *RL*, 8 March 1986.
95. ANGOP, 16 June 1986.
96. Interview with David B. Ottaway, *WP*, 3 June 1986.
97. *RL*, 4 February 1986.
98. *The Times*, 20 September 1985.
99. See essay on Portugal's Year in Africa, in *ACR*, 1985-86.
100. See *ACR*, 1984-85 essay on Southern African crisis.
101. *SABC*, 9 October 1986.
102. *SABC*, 8 October 1986.
103. Statement at a press conference in Washington, 17 September 1985.
104. *RM*, 4 January 1986.
105. *The Times*, 9 August 1986.
106. See chapter on Zimbabwe.
107. *The Star*, 11 October 1985.
108. SABC, 28 November 1985.
109. *RH*, 30 November 1985.
110. SAPA, 1 December 1985.
111. SAPA, 16 December 1985.
112. *RH*, 10 February 1986.
113. KNA, 12 June 1986.
114. *DT*, 16 June 1986.
115. SABC, 21 June 1986.
116. *RH*, 16 July 1986.
117. See, for example, James McManus in *DT*, 5 September 1985.
118. *FT*, 6 September 1986.
119. PANA, 21 May 1986.
120. PANA, 2 April 1986.
121. Radio Lusaka, 19 May 1986.
122. *The Times*, 11 August 1986.
123. For details see chapter on Botswana.
124. SAPA, 20 February 1986.
125. Radio Gaborone, 27 January 1986.
126. *Ibid*.
127. *Ibid.*, 21 May 1986.
128. *The Star*, 24 June 1985.
129. Radio Gaborone, 24 January 1986.
130. For details see chapter on Lesotho.
131. Radio Maseru, 25 June and 30 December 1985.
132. *FT*, 15 January 1986.
133. Radio Maseru, 11 February 1986.
134. PANA, 3 June 1986.
135. For details see chapter on Lesotho.
136. Gdn, 10 July 1986.
138. Radio Gaborone, 20 June 1985.
139. *IHT*, 28-19 December 1985.
140. Capital Radio, 25 September 1986.
141. *The Times*, 16 July 1986.
142. *RAA*, 29 July 1986.
143. PANA, 2 April 1986.
144. *RL*, 8 May 1986.
145. *The Times*, 16 July 1986.
146. For OAU resolutions see Document Section, and essay on the OAU.
147. *Gdn*, 21 December 1985.
148. *Gdn*, 16 May 1986.
149. SABC, 3 October 1985.
150. SABC, 6 November 1985.
151. SATV (Network) programme, 5 November 1985.
152. *Ibid*.
153. SAPA and Reuter, 18 October 1985.
154. SATV, 5 November 1985.
155. SABC, 20 September 1986.
156. SABC, 16 September 1986.
157. For details of these talks and ANC policies, see chapter on South Africa.

158. For details see chapter on Namibia.
159. SABC, 27 June 1986.
160. *The Times*, 12 July 1986; *DT*, 9 July 1986.
161. *The Times*, 9 July 1986.
162. *DT*, 12 July 1986.
163. *DT*, 24 July 1986.
164. *Gdn*, 26 July 1986.
165. *DT*, 30 July 1986.
166. *DT*, 31 July 1986.
167. *The Times*, 17 July 1986.
168. See *ST*, 20 July 1986; 'Could the Queen Remain Silent?' *The Times*, 16 July 1986; 'Thatcher Seeks to End Rift', *DT*, 23 July 1986; 'Woman in the News Queen Elizabeth the Second', *FT*, 19 July 1986; 'Cabinet Fears Royal Clash on Sanctions', *The Times*, 16 July 1986.
169. See Enoch Powell, 'End the Fiction', *The Times*, 17 July 1986; Peregrine Worsthorne, 'Worse Perils than Collapse of the Commonwealth', *Sunday Telegraph*, 23 July 1986; Lord Chalfont, 'Prudence and Paradox in SA', *The Times*, 22 July 1986; 'Commonwealth Matters', Leading Article in *FT*, 14 July 1986. Edward Heath, 'Commonwealth Peril Warning', *DT*, 17 July 1986.
170. Interview with Hugo Young, *Gdn*, 9 July 1986, and statements in the House of Commons, 19 and 30 June 1986.
171. *The Times*, 6 August 1986.
172. *Ibid*.
173. *Gdn*. 14 July 1986.
174. *The Times*, 5 August 1986.
175. *FT*, 6 August 1986.
176. *Gdn*, 20 June 1986.

177. *The Times*, 14 July 1986.
178. Sixth Report from the Foreign Affairs Committee, South Africa, HMSO, London, £4.60.
179. *The Times*, 1 August 1986.
180. *The Times*, 6 February 1986.
181. *FT*, 6 August 1986.
182. *The Times*, 17 September 1986.
183. Chester Crocker on Worldnet, 26 September 1986.
184. *The Times*, 23 July 1986.
185. *DT*, 13 July 1986.
186. *IHT*, 24 July 1986.
187. SABC, 23 July 1986.
188. PANA, 23 July 1986.
189. Statement at a press conference in Gaborone on 28 August 1986.
190. Testimony to the Senate Foreign Relations Committee on South Africa, 23 July 1986.
191. Statement to the World Affairs Council of Northern California, 15 July 1986.
192. *IHT*, 5 August 1986.
193. *IHT*, 12 December 1986.
194. *IHT*, 14 June 1986.
195. SABC, 5 September 1985.
196. US State Department, 6 March 1986.
197. *Gdn*, 27 August 1986.
198. US State Department statement, 10 July 1986.
199. *Problems of Communism*, USIA, March-April 1985.
200. Radio Havana, 9 April 1986.
201. *Ibid*, 5 February 1986.
202. *Ibid*, 25 November 1985.
203. *Sunday Mail*, Harare, 31 August 1986.
204. *Daily Nation*, Dar es Salaam, 9 June 1986.

Subject Index

Name Index

450

NAME INDEX